781.6   Plotkin, Fred.
PLO
           Classical music 101.

$18.95

ALSO BY FRED PLOTKIN

Opera 101: A Complete Guide to Learning and Loving Opera
Italy for the Gourmet Traveler
La Terra Fortunata: The Splendid Food and Wine of Friuli-Venezia Giulia
Recipes from Paradise: Life and Food on the Italian Riviera
Italy Today: The Beautiful Cookbook (with Lorenza De' Medici)
The Authentic Pasta Book

CLASSICAL MUSIC
101

A Complete Guide to
Learning and Loving Classical Music

FRED PLOTKIN

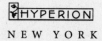

NEW YORK

For Carlo Arborio Mella

Library of Congress Cataloging-in-Publication Data

Plotkin, Fred.
    Classical music 101 : a complete guide to learning and loving classical music / Fred Plotkin.—1st ed.
      p. cm.
    Discography: p.
    Includes bibliographical references and index.
    ISBN 0-7868-8627-7
    1. Music appreciation. I. Title.
    MT90 .P53   2002
    781.6'8—dc21
                                   2002069075

FIRST EDITION

10 9 8 7 6 5 4 3 2 1

Music is that which cannot be said, but upon which it is impossible to be silent.

—Victor Hugo

CONTENTS

ACKNOWLEDGMENTS

The genesis of this book covered many years, and the assistance I received in writing it came from many sources. Above all, I am mindful that my musical education began very soon after I was born, and is due primarily to my mother, Bernice, and my father, Edward, who did everything but paint the walls of my nursery with musical notation. This early exposure was one of the greatest gifts I ever received, and one I encourage all parents to give to their infants.

I was lucky to grow up in New York City at a time when public schools offered musical education to all students, and arts organizations were accessible to any child who was eager to learn. The names of teachers who influenced me musically remain in my head decades after I studied with them: Miss Naifee, Mrs. George, Mr. Weber, Mrs. Tsaggos. Anyone you meet who loves music always remembers his or her teachers. I was also immensely fortunate in my youth and young adulthood to have regular exposure to Leonard Bernstein, not only as an audience member for his legendary Young People's Concerts with the New York Philharmonic, but also in more immediate settings. He was a splendid and natural teacher, and everyone in his orbit was enriched by him.

In bringing this book to fruition I have received help from many caring people. Mark Chait at Hyperion has been a patient and engaging editor, and I have enjoyed watching him develop his own interest in classical music. David Cashion first acquired the book and helped me structure it, and he has my special thanks. So do Rick Kot and Samantha Miller, who helped make *Opera 101* the book it is and thus blazed the path to this one. I would also like to thank the following persons at Hyperion for their important contributions: Adrian James, Katie Long, Mary Tucker, and Robin Moses. Erin Clermont and, especially, Patrick Dillon read the manuscript with care and provided valuable input.

At Black, Inc. Literary Agency I am lovingly cared for and represented by David Black, Susan Raihofer, Joy Tutela, Gary Morris, Jason Sacher, Leigh Ann Eliseo, and Carmen Rey, all of whom have my deepest thanks.

I am very grateful to all of the musicians who gave me considerable time and reflection in discussing all matters musical. Their voices and opinions are important elements of *Classical Music 101*. Claudio Abbado, Marilyn Horne, and James Levine have been important ongoing musical influences in my life, and they have my particular admiration.

Thanks to Jane Covner, Leah Morris, Carolyn Hellman, Kathleen Cuvelier, Nicole Fallat, Melissa Sanders, Maria Yatskova, and, especially, Ken Hunt and Alison Glaister, all of whom gave of their time and effort in key ways.

Peter and Kathy Henschel, devoted music lovers and dear friends, helped me evolve concepts for this book in its earliest stages.

Much gratitude to the entire staff in the classical music department of Tower Records near Lincoln Center. All of them were helpful and responsive to my numerous inquiries about recordings and repertory, and balanced their own taste and preferences with the particular needs of this book. My special thanks go to Paul Linkletter, who was as generous with his vast knowledge as he was with his time.

Eric Foinquinos provided a wonderful sounding board for my ideas throughout the writing of this book, and brought his considerable talents to bear in considering my questions.

Thanks to my friend Uwe Rau for vetting my German and discussing the fine points of text and translation. Thanks also to Joan Glatman, with whom I had valuable conversations about the piano and theory.

Fern Berman is special to me in many ways, and has my unwavering devotion.

Cara De Silva is a caring friend who makes everything more musical.

Thanks to Cheryl Taylor and Jeanie Glock of the Smithsonian Institution, who have inspired me in my work in numerous ways. And to Ann Patchett, who has struck a special chord.

My appreciation for information provided by employees of, and representatives for, the tourism authorities for many nations, especially: Sigrid Pichler and Gabriele Wolf (Austria); Liliane Opsomer and Sabine Griffel (Belgium); Sarah Widness (Brazil); Katerina Pavlitová (Czech Republic); Lillian Hess (Denmark); Marion Fourestier (France); Liz Nichols (Great Britain); Einar Gustavsson (Iceland); Antonia Imperoli and Eugenio Magnani (Italy); Brigitta Kroon-Fiorito and Els Wamsteeker (the Netherlands); Harald Hansen (Norway); Pilar Vigo and José Carlos Fernández Gancedo (Spain); and Annika Benjes (Sweden).

A special expression of gratitude to Ilkka Kalliomaa, Finnish cultural attaché in New York, and Johanna Lemola in Helsinki, each of whom helped me discover the depth and range of the classical music scene in Finland.

Great appreciation to the information and press people at the New York Philharmonic, Alice Tully Hall, Lincoln Center, Inc., the Chamber Music Society of Lincoln Center, Carnegie Hall, the 92nd Street Y, and the orchestras of Chicago, Philadelphia, Boston, Cleveland, Los Angeles, San Francisco, San Diego, Houston, Dallas, Atlanta, Washington, Pittsburgh, Baltimore, Cincinnati, Detroit, Minneapolis, St. Louis, Kansas City, and Seattle.

My gratitude to Emily Botein and Dean Olsher for their patience and inspiration. Thanks also to Rex Levang of Minnesota Public Radio.

My friend Nimet Habachy has the nation's finest classical music show on New York's WQXR-FM radio. She programs with more passion, intelligence, and insight than anyone else, and communicates what makes music a lifetime love affair as few others can. Her program, "New York at Night," has been my constant companion for more than twenty years. Her voice is music.

FIRST HEARING
Developing Your Listening Skills

Music is a higher revelation of science and philosophy.
—*Ludwig van Beethoven (1770–1827)*

L oving music is such a complete experience because, like romantic love, it has a way of getting under your skin, penetrating your thoughts, affecting your gait, and bringing a smile to your face or an unexpected tear to your eye. This tear may reflect sadness, joy, or release of one kind or another. But unlike romantic love (as distinguished from the love between parents and children or the love of friends), the love of music seldom seems to wane once the period of infatuation and intense involvement has come and gone.

In fact, the more discoveries you make about music, the deeper the connection to it becomes. This does not mean merely that listening to more works by Mozart enables you to know Mozart better. It means that you can hear his Piano Concerto no. 23 several times and get to know that piece better. It will also bring you closer to Mozart and him to you. This is how a musical life works. Developing intimacy with hundreds of pieces of music, with their creators *and* with their performers, helps to enlarge our whole, making us beings who experience many things—not only music—much more profoundly.

I know many people who complain about getting older, lamenting the passage of time and opportunities missed. But I detect in people who perform music or love music that one of the compensations of age is that more time spent with music results in more satisfaction and insights in many areas of life. Not long ago I heard James Levine, the splendid conductor of the Metropolitan Opera Orchestra and guest conductor at most of the major orchestras around the world, observe that "as you get older, and use your life experience more, everything means more than it did before. The one hundred percent is greater than it was earlier." Levine, who was fifty-seven when he said this and had been performing as pianist and conductor for more than four decades, was referring to life as a musician. But he also could have meant more generally the kind of life in music that you, as an incipient music lover, are about to embrace.

What I have just described may sound lofty, and perhaps a bit intimidating, but I will ask you to take my word on this now, knowing that sooner or later you will come to this conclusion on your own. That will occur at the moment when a particular piece of music gets under your skin, causes a tingle here and there, and makes you sit up and *listen*.

There is a huge difference between hearing and listening. If we have been blessed with good hearing, then we hear most everything. As I am writing this paragraph on a summer evening in New York City, I hear sirens from police cars, falling rain hitting my window, voices from the street, cars rolling down the avenue. I hear the screech of brakes, dogs barking, and the beeping sound emitted as a truck goes into reverse. I hear someone whistling. I hear a car door slam shut and then a motor starting. I hear the rumble of my neighbor's air conditioner. And I hear the *Romeo and Juliet* Symphony by Hector Berlioz on the radio. It cannot be said that I am listening to this music. It is there, and part of my environment—pleasantly so—but I am not listening to it as one should listen to music. In part this is because there are other sounds in the air, but the main reason is that my mind is engaged in writing, in the capturing and assembling of words into sentences and paragraphs to express the thoughts that are in my head.

My mind is in a verbal and linguistic mode, not a musical one.

The spoken and written languages that we use to communicate are marvelous things, and the foundation of our existence just as much as air and water, but they do have their limitations. They can express concepts and things that we commonly agree upon, but they are conditioned by our perceptions and experience. Verbs tend to be the words we find most concurrence on: "sleep," "eat," "go" are concepts we accept. But even these have a lot of room for interpretation. Instead of "sleep" try "rest" or "doze"; for "eat" substitute "gorge" or "nibble"; and in place of "go" put "depart," "leave," "move," or "dash." These are all different meanings. We encounter the same thing with nouns, such that "man" can signify "fellow," "guy," "gentleman," "male," or "all of humanity."

(In writing the above paragraph, I was so engaged with language and words that I did not even hear the Berlioz. I only came to this realization when I stopped writing and suddenly noticed the music again.)

Adjectives, much more than verbs and nouns, can be highly subjective, based on our values, interpretations, and preferences. If I tell you that a tomato is red, that a news event is tragic, or that a piece of music is moving, you will have a general sense of what I mean, but what is red or tragic or moving for you may differ from what these sensations are for me.

All of these discussions and speculations are *analytical*. They are based on our applying experience and knowledge to come to conclusions. We recognize what we already know and believe, and use intuition and instinct to establish connections where we do not immediately see them. This is the work of an active mind. It is also typical of the way much of Western thought is used, not only in the understanding of behavior and ideas, but also the description of how things work. I could explain to you the architecture of a piece of music—the structure, the instruments that are used, the length of notes, the impact of changes of keys or volume, and so forth—but this would only describe the science and the philosophy, and not open the door to the *pleasure* and the *mystery* of a piece of music. You see, understanding does not come only through description and analysis. Real understanding, especially in something abstract such as music, comes in allowing it to suffuse your being or, as I more plainly stated it above, letting it get under your skin.

Compare listening to music with tasting a wine. You may know the grape varieties that were used, you can learn whether the wine was aged in glass, steel, or wood (all of which would affect its fragrance and flavor), you can find out when the wine was made, its level of alcohol and acidity. All of these are facts and give you some information. But they do not enable you to enjoy the wine. You must look at it, smell it, taste it, let it spread across your tongue and palate and slide down your throat. Then notice the aftertaste (or its resonance, in musical terms). All of these acts are sensory, and all connect to pleasure. You may be able to describe the components of a wine, but you can only perceive its essence, which is to say its soul, through getting it, so to speak, under your skin. The same thing goes for music.

This book is about learning and loving music. As you proceed, you will discover more than you ever knew existed about technique, theory, history, and the nuts and bolts that music is made of. But these will come in the act of learning how to let yourself be open to the pleasure and mystery that I alluded to above. In music, the ears are the window into the soul.

Learning and loving music—in this case, "classical music"— is not about cracking a code by knowing the technicalities and structures. Rather, it is like gaining fluency in a new language. The more contact and exposure one has, the more at home one becomes and, most important, the more you feel this language is part of you.

The first thing you must accept is that *understanding*, in the plainest and most literal sense, is not what you are after. And you should discard from your vocabulary the word "appreciate," as in "music appreciation." Such a polite and tepid term has no place in approaching something so compelling as music.

The path to learning and loving music, which is to say connecting to its pleasure and mystery, is to accept that listening is about active absorption plus passive, almost unnoticeable, analysis. This may seem counterintuitive to everything we are taught about how to think and learn, but it is a central concept here. If you and I are engaged in a deep conversation in which I am describing something that is very meaningful and personal to me, you are probably listening very carefully to what I am saying, trying to absorb rather than immediately analyze. In other words, if you are analyzing while I am talking, you are not hearing everything I am saying. Yes, you may hear the words as the symbols they are, but are you hearing the inflection in my voice, whether it is cracking at any point or might be rich and full? Are you getting information beyond the words?

Think of a person you know who tends to interrupt others. This person is not a good listener: his or her mind processes what it takes in and anticipates what the person speaking might say. This behavior is about impatience, insecurity, arrogance, and a lack of caring. It is about an absence of openness in the sense of being truly receptive to what one is listening to.

Remember that listening combines the perception and recognition of the familiar—whether it be words or sounds—with an openness to countless intangibles, many of them unfamiliar. Doing this takes practice and, curiously, once it is achieved it must become second nature. You cannot actively think if you are actively listening. This applies to most things, music above all.

If you awaken to your clock radio in the morning and go about washing, dressing, and eating breakfast, you cannot actively engage in what you are hearing. So you will hear snippets of music interspersed with weather and traffic information and quick news reports. As you commute to work this process continues. Even if you switch to a music station and hear the New York Philharmonic play the opening bars of Beethoven's Fifth Symphony ("Bah-bah-bah-baaaaah, Bah-bah-bah-baaaaah") or Diana Ross and the Supremes sing "I Hear a Symphony," you will more likely *hear* this music than listen to it. In part, this is because you have surely heard it before so your mind does not focus on absorbing it, but also because there are so many visual distractions. If you are watching the road as you drive, or anticipating your stop on a train or bus, you are not able to give full attention to the music. Nor should you.

In the course of your day, music might be playing in your office, in an elevator, in the restaurant where you have lunch, and in the market where you buy your food. You can even stream a radio station from your computer while doing your work. If you call an airline or the telephone company, music of a sort will be playing as you endure the interminable wait until someone answers your call. In all of these cases, the situation is not *about* music, but the music is there. Even if you are really listening to a wonderful song while waiting on the phone and someone answers your call, this interruption disconnects you from the experience of listening. Notice, if you are truly listening rather than waiting impatiently, how your mind must snap from one kind of functioning—that of listening to an abstraction in a concentrated way—to focusing and then finding the language to discuss the topic of your phone call.

You have acquired this book, in part, because you want to become a better listener of classical music. The skills you develop can be applied to all music, and to other types of listening. So for the purposes of your education, and to best use this book, we must begin with the indispensable art of listening to music. It involves suppressing the analytical as I described above. You have already absorbed those concepts and given them consideration.

Good listening also requires the proper environment. I imagine that you have a compact disc player and a pair of speakers somewhere in your home. If you do not, these are essential. I don't believe that you need to spend a fortune to acquire these. Because I live in an apartment building, it makes no sense for me to have fancy equipment and speakers that can blast out the sound. This would disturb my neighbors and, frankly, would disturb me. There is classical music that is played loud— we will encounter some of these works in the book—but few pieces of any kind of music need to be played at the kind of decibel level that we have become accustomed to in the modern world. If your ears ring, it is too loud and should be turned down. Slightly lower volume also requires you, the listener, to pay closer attention.

I am not a fan of headphones (and, by connection, portable CD and tape players). In its original form, music was played to be heard in a space in which musician and audience shared that environment. Music resonates in this space and then dies away. If you listen to recorded music in a room, the effect is similar—it becomes part of the environment. "Personal stereo," aside from being very harmful to your ears after long-term use, also puts sounds only in your head, and not in a room where you perceive them. I assure you that as you become a devoted music listener, you will suddenly find that it is in your head—in your brain—and you do not have to pipe it in. One of the great thrills you can have is when you begin to be able to summon in your mind music that you have already heard.

In creating a listening environment in your home (or classroom, if this book is being used for a course), you want to approximate the conditions of a concert hall, which is to say a place where your sense of hearing is used to the fullest and your other senses are not engaged or distracted. If the person in front of you is wearing heavy perfume in a concert hall, your senses of smell and taste are distracted and perhaps irritated. At home, if there is a vase full of flowers near where you will be sitting, move them.

Activate the answering machine on your telephone, and turn off the volume so you do not know when you are receiving an incoming call. Turn off the phone's ringer so you will not hear it. Do the same for your cellular phone. Turn off your beeper or pager. Turn off the beeper on your watch, if there is one. If you have a ticking clock in this room, move it out of earshot.

Find the most comfortable chair in the room where your stereo equipment is. Do not stretch out on a bed or on a sofa. Set the lighting in the room so that it is just bright enough for you to see (and so that you will not be inclined to doze off) but not so bright that your tendency will be to visually focus on something in the room. Ideally, the light might be placed to one side of your chair or behind it. While listening, do not focus on a painting, poster, person, or definable object. I tend to look into the middle distance, either at a wall or a bookcase far enough away that I cannot make out the titles. In other words, no distractions. I close my blinds or curtains so that there will be no outside interference in my listening environment.

The idea of diminishing visual stimulation is crucial for listening to music. In opera and theater one tends to see and hear equally. In dance it is probable that one looks more than listens. In music one can have a totally transporting experience with eyes closed. I am not only referring to classical music here. I love all kinds of music, and at live performances of rock or jazz I have been known to shut my eyes so that I absorb the music more completely. For example, when I heard Ella Fitzgerald embark on a brilliant tear of scatting, the act of closing my eyes enabled me to follow her thoughts (and often be surprised by them) to a degree that would not happen with open eyes. Try it and you will discover what I mean. The same thing could apply to a guitar riff by Eric Clapton or Keith Richards.

When I teach, I notice that many students close their eyes when I play music. If you are not sleepy, this is a good way to listen. Otherwise, I would keep my eyes open. Whether your eyes are open or closed, it is also possible, with music, to go into a blissful, trance-like state, as you might do while practicing meditation or during a fine massage. Entering into this state, I believe, is due in part to the disappearance of the analytical component of our thought. We perceive and are affected, but do not consider what is happening or why.

But there is a fine point here that must be mentioned. This blissful state is not the goal. It is pleasant—wonderful—when it happens, but it means that we have gone into a restful, quietly ecstatic drift. This is not the same as listening to music. For comparative purposes, think about going to the theater. At a play we listen to every line, knowing that if we miss something it compromises our ability to absorb the whole. This is how we should listen to music.

Perhaps the first time you hear a piece of music, especially one that is almost forty minutes long, you will lose yourself in it. This is perfectly fine—remember, you are developing a passion, not taking an exam. In "losing yourself" in the work, you can wallow in its sensuous pleasures—beauty, pathos, joy, and so on. This is an emotional, personal response, and it is central to loving music.

But your first hearing of a piece of music is only the start of your relationship with it. This is only your first contact, your initial acquaintance. But this is not knowledge. Similarly, when you meet a likable person, she is an acquaintance—she does not immediately become your friend or, perhaps, lover.

At this point you have the necessary guidelines for listening to the first piece of music we will consider in the book, Symphony no. 7 by Ludwig van Beethoven. I will not tell you what to listen for, or give you any background about the work or the composer. I want you to approach this, and all pieces of music, with similar purity. With rare exceptions in this book, I will ask you to listen to pieces of music before reading about them.

Now create the listening environment described above. The recommended recording is:

• ⟨⟩ •

Beethoven: Symphonies 4, 5, 6, 7; Royal Concertgebouw Orchestra; Wolfgang Sawallisch, conductor; EMI Classics 7243 5 73326 2 0
(An alternate is Beethoven: Symphonies 5, 6, 7, 8; Philadelphia Orchestra, Eugene Ormandy, conductor; Sony SB2K 63266).

We will later be considering Beethoven's Fifth and Sixth symphonies, and each of these is a well-priced recording of the three works, with excellent performances.

For now, play only the Seventh Symphony. Sit down, breathe deeply, and let other thoughts and cares leave your mind. Start the recording. *Listen.*

2

MAKING MUSIC

I think that composers do not invent music.
They find music that is already there.
—*Gian Carlo Menotti*

There is a particularly felicitous term in the English language that elegantly and clearly expresses the totality of what this book is about and where you fit into it: *making music*. In other languages one can describe the act of playing an instrument, of performing, of being present while the music is emanating from the stage. But no other expression really conveys the feeling that wells up in composers, in singers, conductors, and instrumentalists, and in those of us who listen to their work.

Making music, certainly, is the act of *creating* it, but what would that music be if there were no one to play it? It is also quite true that musicians can experience transporting elation simply in the act of rehearsing and playing music by themselves, but their joy is probably limited unless they have another essential component in the music-making equation: *you*. Listening to music on recordings, but especially in a live concert with other people, means you are a participant in the act of music-making. You bring to it your senses, your feelings, your mood, your mind, and, above all, your heart. Passive hearing in the presence of music will probably not connect you to the larger experience, one for which few words are adequate.

If I were to ask you to describe what occurred during an outstanding concert, you could recount what was played and who the performers were, and then find some enthusiastic adjectives to communicate your sense of pleasure. But all sorts of things happened within you and all around you during this music-making. You were part of a one-time event that represents a few intensely lived pages in the book that is your life.

We participate in music-making, whether as composers, musicians, or listeners, because it fills us with rich, indescribable emotions that become part of the texture of who we are and become pieces of the fabric of memory. When we hear a musical work the first time, we begin to integrate it into our beings. With every new hearing, we deepen our relationship to the work, revisiting the feelings we already had, or perhaps discovering something entirely new in the music and in ourselves.

It is very common to hear musicians talk about "a life in music." This is quite different from music in our lives. A life in music is an ongoing commitment to study, think, play, practice, repose, reflect, and then revisit a vast repertory of works. While this life in music is more complete for composers and performers, there can be a similar degree of engagement for any audience member who loves music. I am often asked why I, such an ardent music lover, do not own "personal audio" equipment—a CD or tape player with headphones—so that I can listen as I go about my life. The simple answer is that if I have music on while engaged in other tasks I am not really listening. I also prefer to hear music in a space greater than headphones cupped around my ears.

But the real reason I do not use personal audio equipment is I do not need it. My life in music—as someone who grew up with it and continues to listen to it with care and joy—has given me a head full of melodies that surge forth unbidden. They resonate in my mind and in my ears and then float away, only to be replaced by others. A life in music can do this, and you can be a part of it.

You may have noticed that up to this point, I have spoken of music in general and not simply classical music, which is the subject of this book. That is because all forms of music can be gratifying if they reach you in some special place. Ignore the fact that music often tends to be separated into popular and serious, the latter term being offputting and intimidating to those who don't know of the immense satisfactions that are behind it.

As my father often told me, there are only two types of music: good and bad. By "bad" music he probably meant music that did not have the honesty, integrity, and dusting of genius that good music possesses. For me good music includes classical, opera, religious, jazz, folk, American popular song, rock, blues, gospel, country, and much of what falls under that catch-all category of "world music." This might include the folk melodies of many countries (most every state in Europe has its own tradition, for example), or the distinct styles of music that come from nations as diverse as Brazil, Argentina, Bolivia, Mali, Niger, Senegal, South Africa, Morocco, Egypt, Israel, Jordan, Iran, India, China, and Japan. All of this is wonderful music, and much of it can be classified as classical music—that is, music played on traditional instruments or sung in a particular language and style that represent the ongoing legacy of a people's understanding of themselves.

Many Asian societies have their own classical music. My favorite is the gorgeous and intricate music of India, whose traditions go back to ancient times and whose instruments (stringed ones such as the sitar, and drums such as the tabla) are as expressive as their counterparts in the West. The music of India has ancient roots and continues to this day. The best known sitarist is Ravi Shankar (born in 1920), who has recorded extensively and whose music-making is magical indeed. He has trained generations of musicians who follow in his tradition. Vocal music is as important as instrumental in the Indian tradition. Rabindranath Tagore, who was the first Asian to win the Nobel Prize (for literature, in 1913), also wrote more than two thousand songs. They form a large part of the body of Indian classical music and are as notable in their range of musical and emotional ideas as Schubert's six hundred songs.

All the "classical" musics of the world merit your investigation and are sure to give you pleasure. But they are not what this book is about.

• ⟳ •

What this book proposes to address is *Western* classical music, that extraordinary and universally affecting body of works whose foundations began in Italy, Germany, and Austria, and quickly included composers in the British Isles, France, Spain, the Netherlands, Scandinavia, Eastern Europe, and Russia. Classical music would, by the early nineteenth century, plant deep roots in the United States and Canada, and later in Argentina and elsewhere in the Americas, along with Australia and New Zealand. In the twentieth century it was embraced by Israel, Japan, and Korea, and found pockets of appreciation in most every nation. Indeed, Western classical music is as much world music as the best of the indigenous sounds of Asia, Oceania, Africa, and the Americas.

I do not intend to teach you, as some books might, "everything you need to know" about classical music. That is a preposterous notion for many reasons, but primarily because I do not wish to define music that way. If you chose to study music only to learn enough about it not to look foolish, then your approach is wrong. Similarly, I do not presume my reader to be a "dummy" or an "idiot" or a "bluffer," as other books do.

The central assumption of this book, and all of the books in the *101* series, is that you are an intelligent person who has not had the occasion to be exposed to opera, ballet, jazz, and classical music to the extent you wish. These books are meant to give you a solid foundation and, importantly, the tools to learn on your own once you have reached the last page. When you have read *Classical Music 101,* you will be able to listen to any work written over many centuries in the vast repertory of what is called "classical music" (a misnomer, since music from the Classical era of composition extends from about 1750 to about 1825) in a more perceptive and insightful way. I dare say that your listening skills will become so honed that you will be able to listen to any sort of music in this way. This book should be a launching pad for many ideas and interests in music that you can pursue on your own.

Many books can provide you with a time line of music history. The time line approach is interesting for observing forward progression, but it is not the best way to learn to love music. Would you start an art history course with cave paintings, or with a work of art that is immediately compelling and engaging? We will move about in the history of classical music, discovering and often returning to great composers as we explore numerous ways to approach classical music.

We will learn something about these composers, and about the musicians who perform their works, but the main goal here is giving you the tools you need. If you wish to learn more about individual composers, there are numerous biographies that also contain listings of their major works.

Much of this information about names and dates will come to you in the text of this book anyway. I am not interested in having you memorize a great many terms and facts, all of which is the kind of learning that does not acknowledge the *pleasure* of music. More people have turned off to classical music because their primary exposure was in the type of "music appreciation" class that values memorization more than absorbing and feeling the music.

I believe that learning to listen more completely than you ever thought you could will be central to your coming to love classical music, and will be useful to you in other areas of your life as well. The ability to listen and concentrate on taking in great amounts of information (in this case, sound) is essential to success in many fields, professionally and socially.

The subtitle of this book says what it is: *A Complete Guide to Learning and Loving Classical Music.* Because music is such a personal experience, one that relies on many factors and variables, my principal aim is to teach you how to make music a part of who you are. This involves developing listening skills and memory, and nourishing an eagerness to make connections among different composers and their works so that you understand some of what they attempted with each piece they wrote.

I aim to give you these tools through an incremental building-up of your skills and knowledge. To achieve this, I will ask you to think about different things and take varying approaches from one piece of music to the next. With each new work you listen to, you will take the knowledge and talents you have acquired and apply them. What will also happen is that, as you move further along in this book, you will be able to return to pieces you have already listened to and hear things you did not hear the first or second time.

I cannot (and would not want to) tell you what to feel or think about pieces of music or their composers and performers. My role is to help you make links to the art form. With music, we are on another, more spiritual plane than with spoken language, one where words can take you only so far and no further. To make certain connections, you need to reach within yourself, bringing forth feelings and emotions that are part of your unique formation and character.

· ✧ ·

Think of our journey as going to a vast and beautiful field dotted with huts, houses, gazebos, stately mansions, soaring cathedrals, and sky-scrapers. I want to take you there, show you the lay of the land, and teach you how to get about on your own. These edifices are the places where music resides. The small structures are no less beautiful or inviting than the larger ones. Each has an exterior that draws you close, invites you inside. Most of these have many doors within that I can point you toward, perhaps hinting at what may lie behind them. But it will be your choice as to when and whether to open those doors.

For example, the House of Mozart (let's call it) has 626 doors, each holding a piece that he wrote. But the grand central halls contain Mozart's life and ideas and experiences, all of which contributed to the music he wrote.

But every house does not necessarily represent a composer. There may be a cluster of buildings that relate to music of a particular era, or age, or music composed for a particular instrument. Think how won-derful and varied the house of songs must be. All of these houses and castles lead from one to another, as does the progression of the history of music. You cannot visit them all, nor should you hope to do so. We will go to more than a hundred of them in *Classical Music 101*, and then you are on your own. The joy of learning comes in the discovery of things, and there is enough divine classical music for you to discover— and revisit—for several lifetimes.

•   ◁▷   •

Making music, for composers, performers, and listeners, is part inspiration and part perspiration. The percentage required of each will vary from one person and one piece of music to another. Think for a moment of what can inspire the creation and performance of a piece of music: religious faith, a character from literature, a poem, personal experience, a single work of visual art or a whole exhibition, folk melodies, travel, sights and sounds of nature, laughter, chatter, and so forth. Can you think of other sources of inspiration that might be used to create music?

Some music may have been inspired by commissions from particular patrons, by performers, or by an event in a composer's life. A love affair, or the end of one, or a love that has gone unrequited, has often been the source of incredible music. You will discover works by Ludwig van Beethoven, Hector Berlioz, and César Franck, among others, that were created through the inspiration of a beloved but unattainable woman.

Often the most wonderful music has no definable source. Most music, I believe, does not have an inspiration that is documented for us. So we are called upon to make an emotional connection of our own. We find what inspires us and, perhaps, we connect to what the composer felt. But it is not essential that we do the latter to enjoy the music. Great music is at once universal and personal. We are part of a continuum that includes the composer, the performers who have played his music through the years and created a tradition, the performers we are hearing at a given moment, and everything that *we* bring to the performance (our own background and musical education, our mood on that day, our focus and preparedness). In other words, *listening to music is not a passive experience.*

• ‧◇‧ •

Where did music come from?

Can you imagine what it must have been like, tens of thousands of years ago, when some early human began to speak? There might not have been language as we know it now, with words that represent all sorts of actions, objects, and sensations. Original communication was surely more elementary, and sound—pure sound—played a role in expressing ideas. Shouting or cooing or grunting or using more or less breath changed the character of these sounds. When words and sounds combined in speech, early people probably found that by raising or lowering the tone and volume of their voices, more specific and complex ideas could be expressed. In the act of modulating the voice to hold a sound longer or spread it over a range of tones, some long-ago person created the very first bit of man-made music.

Ancient peoples lived in contact with nature and the elements to a degree most of us cannot imagine today. Their very survival depended on learning the rhythms of the seasons and about all of the earth's properties and creatures. The rustling of wind through trees was a sound in nature, as were roaring waves, babbling brooks, and drops of water from melting icicles in steady cadences.

The cry of a wolf, the croaking of a frog, the bobbing head of a camel, the continuous swish of the tail of a dog or beaver—these are just a few examples of the sounds and rhythms to be observed in nature.

And birds! If they never served another purpose, birds contributed to history by awakening man to the idea that music could exist. Each bird, with its different sounds and unique songs, turned humans into listeners of languages that had no words but were remarkably expressive and differentiated. Some birds repeat the same tune, others improvise and create variations on their original themes. A walk in the woods may let you hear one bird singing a solo, or two singing a duet. Or there might be a call and response, with a bird in one tree having a dialogue with another. Or you might be in a forest full of birds all singing at once. This may seem like cacophonous confusion or, if you listen closely, you may find that the amalgamation of all these distinct voices forms an overall music in the way that eighty instruments in an orchestra join to make a remarkable sound.

Even the woodpecker, not known for his singing skills, makes a contribution. Perched on a branch, he taps his beak rhythmically into the bark like so: *peck-peck, peck-peck, peck-peck.* Maybe another one will go *peck-peck-peck, peck-peck-peck, peck-peck-peck.* Whatever his choice, the woodpecker shows us how to set a beat, the structure in which others might make their pretty sounds.

Nature also provided man with rocks to hit, reeds to blow into, animal skins to stretch and pound on, metal or animal parts to make into strings to be plucked, and wood to carve into instruments to tap or blow. Animal horns could be blown into to make a peculiar sound. Archeologists have found whistles that are thought to be more than forty thousand years old. There are cave paintings from about 18,000 B.C. that depict musicians.

With their own voices and their rudimentary instruments, early humans could set about imitating the many sounds of nature. At some point lost in the mists of history, someone created a new collection of tones and sounds that may have been drawn from familiar ones but had never been assembled in this new way. This was a musical composition. It may have been committed to memory and played again, or it might have had but one performance before vanishing.

The most pleasing early compositions were probably songs. If it only had a repeated syllable (such as "ah" or "la"), then the beauty and interest of that song would be centered on the sound. Such a song would now be called a *vocalise* (vo-cal-eese). If there were words to the song, then the words and music would have more or less equal importance and the music might attempt to communicate the meaning of some of the words.

These songs would be sung by individuals or groups. A single voice is very compelling. If a man and woman sang together, he with a lower voice and she with a higher one, then the sound of the song to the ears of a listener would be different than if only one person were singing. If ten or twenty or fifty people sang together, the variety and impact of the song would be different from that of a person singing alone. And if one person were singing in alternation with the group, this would be another interesting variant.

All of the examples in the paragraph above exist in instrumental music. There could be a solo violin playing a tune. Or a violin and cello could play together. Or these instruments could join many others in an orchestra. Or the violin can play the type of composition called the concerto, in which a solo instrument plays in tandem with an entire orchestra, sometimes all together, sometimes only the solo instrument, and sometimes only the orchestra.

It is hard to say what most of this ancient music sounded like because none of it was written down. We can hear faint echoes of it in pastoral societies around the Mediterranean, in which shepherds in places like Crete, Sardinia, Tunisia, and Syria sing plaintive songs that have been passed down through many centuries. Their music is purer and less adulterated because it was sung in rural contexts, far from the many currents that swept through music in the past two thousand years.

· ◇ ·

It is important at this point to establish a concept that is implicit in the ideas of this book. When we refer to "classical music" we mean all of the music that was created in Europe (and subsequently elsewhere in the European style) from about the year 600 to the present. For the most part, this is not music from the folk tradition (the songs and instrumental pieces of many nations), although melodies from the folk tradition have entered into classical music, where they have been elaborated upon.

Genuine "classical" music refers to the era from about 1750 to 1825 and features the works of composers such as Haydn, Gluck, Mozart, Beethoven, and Schubert. Because their works became the point of reference for what later composers thought of as classical music, the name stuck. In the years since, some composers deliberately wrote in what they thought of as the classical style, while others incorporated what they learned from that era and then sought to move forward. In the twentieth century, composers such as Sergei Prokofiev, Igor Stravinsky, Richard Strauss, and Benjamin Britten, who were in most ways very modern, wrote a few pieces that evoked classical style.

There are many important periods before and since the Classical era, all of which will be addressed to some degree in this book. They all will be "Western" classical music, the style of music that developed in Europe and then spread to other continents. This music should not be confused with the many other types of music that deserve to be called "classical," but come from other parts of the world. For example, the courtly music of the ancient Islamic world is splendid and varied, but is played on different instruments in a style different from European music. African music and the sounds of the ancient societies of the Americas are also quite important.

The millennium of music in Europe from about the year 600 to 1600 comes under the general term of Early Music. Of course, there were many eras in this long period, and they will be addressed to some extent in these pages. Probably the most important musical event of those thousand years was the invention of musical notation in about the year 1000 by an Italian monk named Guido d'Arezzo. Because of him, a system existed in which agreed-upon symbols represented certain sounds (call them "notes"), and these universally recognized markings gave the performer instructions about how the composer intended for the music to be played.

The seventeenth century was transitional from the Renaissance to the Baroque eras of music. It is also notable for being when opera was born. Claudio Monteverdi (1567–1643), the first great opera composer, was also the first composer/conductor to divide the orchestra into sections: bowed strings and wind instruments. There has always been overlap in the topics of opera and classical music, in part because some major composers (including Monteverdi, Vivaldi, Handel, Mozart, Beethoven, Berlioz, Tchaikovsky, Dvořák, Janáček, Debussy, Strauss, Gershwin, Prokofiev, Poulenc, and Britten) were accomplished in both forms. Composers such as Beethoven, Rossini, and Wagner had great influence on the growth of the orchestra, which had an impact on all music, including opera. To learn more, read *Opera 101: A Complete Guide to Learning and Loving Opera*.

Another important innovation in the Renaissance was printing. We know that Gutenberg in Germany invented the printing press, but the first publishing houses were in Venice. There, Ottaviano Petrucci (1466–1539) developed a method for printing music, which meant that it did not have to be hand-copied. The first printed music is thought to be a collection of vocal pieces printed in Venice in 1501. Within a few decades, printed music was published in important cities throughout Europe, so that works of composers could be played in many places at once. The spread of printed music was accompanied by the growth of musical literacy, so that a work written in Madrid could be read and performed in Naples, Amsterdam, or Vienna.

The Baroque era (approximately 1675–1750) is where we find the real foundations of "classical music." Handel and, especially, Bach were such innovators that they created much of the structure—called "theory"—upon which this music is based. We will discuss the work of these men throughout this book. This was also the era when Stradivarius and other great Italian violin makers created instruments that have never been bettered. And the piano was invented in 1700, forever changing how music would be heard and played. Two other key Baroque composers were Antonio Vivaldi, who had considerable impact on the role of string instruments in music as well as the development of vocal music in Italy, and Georg Philipp Telemann, who was very popular at the time primarily because he understood the value of music publishing and made sure his scores were everywhere.

The Classical era (1750–1825) had many composers, but a few of them, all based in Vienna, dominated the scene. Franz Joseph Haydn (1732–1809) is the father of the symphony (he wrote 104), but his compositions covered most forms of music. I believe he is the most underrated of all composers. Wolfgang Amadeus Mozart (1756–1791), by contrast, is probably the most beloved of composers. He had a famously difficult life, and his biography is, by now, inextricably entwined with many of his compositions. His music seems so facile and accessible that we often fail to acknowledge its brilliance and sophistication. With Mozart, and so many composers, the more you listen to his music the more you hear. Ludwig van Beethoven (1770–1827) wrote some of the most popular of all works, many of which you will recognize as soon as you hear them. He was one of music's great revolutionaries, always struggling to say things in new ways and always seeking to improve what he had done. His was a life of pathos and heroism. Franz Schubert's tragically short life (1797–1828) and failure to achieve any meaningful success only make it seem more astonishing how much extraordinary music he was able to create. Aside from great symphonies and chamber music, he virtually invented *Lieder,* the German-language songs, based on poetry, that are central to the art of the vocal recital.

These composers were profoundly affected by the political and intellectual currents of their times, as were all Europeans and those men and women who created the United States of America.

The old order was being pushed aside, and with them some of the royal courts that supported composers. This was the era of the Declaration of Independence and the creation of the Bill of Rights in the United States. There was the French Revolution (1789), the fruit of the philosophy of the Enlightenment. Then came the realignment of Europe (in effect dividing it among Napoleon, the Austro-Hungarians, and the Danes, with England going its own way). As people were discovering a sense of national identity and striving to create new nations (such as Italy, Germany, Belgium, Poland, Bohemia, and Norway) an interest in national character, language, folk traditions, and the exaltation of nature all became important. This was known as nationalism.

An outgrowth of nationalism, and the most important artistic movement of the nineteenth century, was Romanticism. This was not about love (as in "being romantic") but was the product of the philosophical movement that embraced a return to nature and the glorification of national characteristics. While the prized trait of a man in the eighteenth century was an enlightened mind and quick and clever reasoning, in the nineteenth century one sought heroism and nobility and a fiery soul. The Romantic ideal was epitomized by writers such as Goethe and Byron, and certain composers. Schubert and Beethoven, who had deep classical traditions, picked up on the Romantic tradition and fused the two in some of their works.

Probably the first Romantic composer was Carl Maria von Weber (1786–1826), a German who used nature and a return to German traditions of language and literature to embody his Romantic ideals. The Frenchman Hector Berlioz (1803–1869) wrote music of stupendous grandeur that glorified Romantic heroes such as Byron's Childe Harold (in *Harold in Italy*) and Berlioz himself in the *Symphonie Fantastique*.

Mendelssohn, Schumann, Chopin, Auber, Meyerbeer, Bellini, Donizetti, and others took Romanticism further, all with their very distinct musical personalities. Franz Liszt was the epitome of the Romantic hero as he toured Europe playing huge and passionate compositions on the piano—he was the instrument's first superstar. Romanticism in different forms was embraced by the likes of Verdi, Wagner, Tchaikovsky, and Brahms. Late Romantic composers such as Anton Bruckner (1824–1896) and Gustav Mahler (1860–1911) took the symphony in directions that would have been unimaginable only a few years earlier.

Gradually, Romanticism began to change and wane as other movements began to blossom. Europe went through many wars and rebellions, including those of 1848, 1859, 1866, and 1871. With each conflict, nationalism hardened and went from being love of country to defiant aggression against other states. Colonialism brought European nations into increased contact with the rest of the world, and foreign flavors and melodies came to the Continent. Exoticism became a thread in music, especially in works of French composers such as Saint-Saëns and Massenet. The visual arts would influence music with movements such as Impressionism, Symbolism, and, in the twentieth century, Fauvism, Expressionism, Surrealism, Neorealism, Abstract Expressionism, Minimalism, and Deconstructionism; all made composers think in new ways. So did influential thinkers such as Schopenhauer, Nietzsche, Freud, Einstein, and, later on, Stephen Hawking.

Europe's inability to avoid war, and its increasing tendency to drag much of the rest of the world into its conflicts, profoundly affected all artists, including composers. The First World War was devastating for Maurice Ravel, Edward Elgar, and others. The period between the two wars saw many composers and musicians seek refuge in the United States. This was a great benefit for America, which welcomed many of the world's great composers and musicians to its concert halls and music conservatories and onto its orchestra podiums. Sergei Prokofiev, Arnold Schoenberg, Béla Bartók, Benjamin Britten, Kurt Weill, Sergei Rachmaninoff, Erich Korngold, Arthur Rubinstein, Vladimir Horowitz, and Jascha Heifetz are just a few of the many great artists who spent a few years or the rest of their lives enriching the American musical world.

The Second Viennese School (Schoenberg, Alban Berg, Anton Webern) sought to totally revolutionize the way music was written and played. The traditional scale (think of a piano with eight white keys and the black keys in between to understand this concept) was redesigned to twelve, with every key having equal importance. Schoenberg (1874–1951), in particular, would be among the greatest musical revolutionaries since Beethoven. It would be interesting to do a recording or a concert program that includes the violin concertos by Beethoven and Schoenberg together to compare the works of two men who pushed the boundaries of musical thought.

Critics in Beethoven's time said his music was incomprehensible and too fast. They were also quite severe about Schoenberg, which is an important lesson: you should not ever reject a piece of music (or a food or a person or so much else) on first contact just because you do not appreciate it. We change and grow and, with life experience and more knowledge, come to see things differently than we might have when we knew less. *If, on first hearing, you don't care for a piece of music, this does not mean you won't like it when you encounter it again.*

Do not think that you are the only person who may not appreciate some challenging music. "He'd be better off shoveling snow" was Richard Strauss's terse assessment of Schoenberg. The composer was unyielding about his music; when told that a soloist would need six fingers to perform his piano concerto, Schoenberg replied, "I can wait."

World War II inspired composers, especially Dmitri Shostakovich (1906–1975) and Benjamin Britten (1913–1976), to write towering music of great emotion and insight. Richard Strauss (1864–1949) spanned most of these eras from late Romanticism onward, and his music seems to embrace or reject almost all of these events and ideas. Sometimes he looked back to Mozart; at other times he seemed to point the way to new radical forms. Much the same could be said for Igor Stravinsky (1882–1971), who, like Picasso, shifted freely among many styles and ideas but always seemed truest to his own aesthetic priorities. Stravinsky is often called the twentieth century's most important composer. His music still startles us and we need to approach it with the same open minds and ears that we bring to all music.

There are fewer -isms for contemporary composers. A challenge they face is that there is now more than three hundred years of great music that is part of Western musical tradition. As the twentieth century saw the growth of many other musical forms (most notably jazz and rock and roll), classical music was no longer the prevailing musical style. So classical composers in recent years have sought to find ever newer ways of expression, one of these being a return to some of the more melodious ways of the past.

The twentieth century was also different from previous ones because recordings could document and spread music, capturing specific performances that we still look to for how this music must be played. Through recordings and radio, music became available to almost everyone in ways that were unthinkable before Edison and Marconi. It became possible to purchase a performance that could be listened to again and again—whenever it suits your fancy—which is a very different phenomenon from hearing a piece of music only once in a concert.

Attendance at live performances is another sensation entirely. This is a special event for most people, in that concertgoing requires advance planning, effort, and often considerable expense. The anticipation and expectation involved in attending a concert is elevated, but for a music lover or even someone who is new to the experience, this can prove to be a thrilling and memorable event. You will discover concert-going secrets in these pages.

Classical music is still growing, though more slowly, and creating new styles. Finland (population about five million) is, per capita, the superpower of classical music. It is a nation devoted to music, and encourages the training of instrumentalists, composers, and audiences. Helsinki, with a metropolitan area of little more than a million people, has four symphony orchestras, three important concert halls, and another one on the way. Large sections of record stores there are devoted to Finnish composers such as Joonas Kokkonen (1921–1996), Einojuhani Rautavaara (1928–   ), Aulis Sallinen (1935–   ), Leif Segerstam (1944–   ), Kaija Saariaho (1952–   ), and Magnus Lindberg (1958–   ). I could add another twenty prominent names quite easily. This small nation has also produced a crop of outstanding conductors, many of whom you will hear as you start your listening.

Though nothing can compare to Finland as a hive of musical activity, England, France, Germany, Austria, Italy, and Russia all nourish new composers, but they have to struggle for audiences because in our times new music is considered less desirable than older music. This is a change from the past, when there was often a hunger for the new.

Let us think about this significant change in the culture. Every age thinks of itself as modern, contemporary, and new, and seeks to contrast itself with everything that came before it. Bach, who was less well known in his own time than Telemann, fell into obscurity until interest him in revived in the nineteenth century thanks to Mendelssohn, Brahms, and others. In music, the past has a curious effect. Much of it is forgotten by the public at large, yet all composers stand on the shoulders of Bach, Haydn, Mozart, Weber, Beethoven, Chopin, and many others. The ideas and works of these masters are intricately and obsessively studied by aspiring and established composers and, frankly, they cast a rather intimidating shadow.

This does not mean that composers of the past hundred years do not compare favorably. Naming Strauss, Schoenberg, Berg, Bartók, Prokofiev, Stravinsky, Shostakovich, Britten, Ravel, Poulenc, Gershwin,

Copland, Lutoslawski, Messaien, Cage, and Nono only begins to hint at the riches that so-called modern music holds. This means that, in programming concerts for major symphony orchestras, music directors have about 250 years of music to choose from. Contemporary composers do not compete so much with each other for attention as with all the dead composers of the past whose reputations are established.

There are outstanding composers at work today, many of them Americans, and all merit your attention. John Adams, Thomas Adès, William Bolcom, Pierre Boulez, John Corigliano, Deborah Drattell, John Eaton, Lukas Foss, Philip Glass, Osvaldo Golijov, John Harbison, Hans Werner Henze, Aaron Jay Kernis, Libby Larsen, Steven Mackey, Thea Musgrave, Arvo Pärt, Krzysztof Penderecki, Tobias Picker, Steve Reich, Ellen Taaffe Zwilich, and innumerable Finns are only some.

Modern composers, and the musicians who admire them, have to struggle to get their music played by orchestras and, still more important, played again. Part of this issue is that musical institutions must always consider the relevance, and irrelevance, of what they do. One of the chief difficulties they face is not only financial stability and audience development, but keeping priorities as an institution. They must be not only curators of tradition, but innovators. They are fearful of presenting new works because they believe audience members only want tried and true masterpieces.

The woman who sits behind me at my New York Philharmonic subscription is the audience member they think is typical. She always refers to "my Beethoven" as a means of suggesting that she is content so long as that composer's music is on the program. She wrinkles her face as if she has to ingest cod liver oil whenever there is an unfamiliar piece on the program, even if it is from the eighteenth or nineteenth century. But many audience members are eager for new and different music to be part of the mix. Most conductors and music directors want to present repertory by new composers, or lesser-known ones from the past, but find opposition from some segments of the audience, from many members of their boards and patrons, and sometimes from critics who are not adventurous. When a new piece is introduced and is not well received, many of those people say, "See? We told you!"

It is important to bear in mind that a lot of unsuccessful music from the past is no longer played today because it fell into obscurity. In general, only the most successful music of the past is regularly heard today. The only way modern classics will be born is if we regularly give new music repeated hearings. This means that audiences must be open to the new.

Here is something to think about: What is the difference between that which is new and that which is original? In a society that worships the new in so many things, even if their only distinguishing characteristic is their newness, true originality is often overlooked, disdained, or feared. Part of your obligation as an incipient lover of classical music is to encourage the musical institutions you frequent to strive to present that which is truly original, at the same time that they continue to return to the famous and less famous classics of the past and give them carefully prepared performances.

· ◇ ·

To help you discover classical music, I consider it important that you hear not only my observations but those of people whose lives are devoted to making music. You will have the chance in this book to read extensive interviews with singer Marilyn Horne, pianist Emanuel Ax, violinist Joshua Bell, and conductor James Levine. These artists generously sat down with me to discuss specific composers, musical works, and aspects of their art. In addition, I have included comments from conversations with singer Christa Ludwig, pianist Alfred Brendel, conductor Valery Gergiev, and conductor-composer Leif Segerstam. Throughout this book there are comments and observations from musicians whose views you may or may not come to share, but whose ideas will help you come to your own conclusions about what music means to you.

• ‹◇› •

All good music has something to say to us, and has a means of giving us insight and comprehension about aspects of the human condition that seem to make no sense. This was true when Bach created structure and new forms. It was true when Mozart wrote during the era of the Enlightenment and Beethoven in times of revolution and turmoil. Countless composers since have sought to answer chaos and crisis with beauty and soul-searching.

As this book was being completed, I learned again the power of music to provide insight, solace, and healing. On September 11, 2001, I was writing the chapter about Mahler's Second Symphony (the "Resurrection") at my home in Manhattan when terrorist attacks were launched on my city and nation, destroying the World Trade Center and killing thousands of people from many countries. Of course, all television stations (except for children's channels) interrupted their programming to cover the emergency. So did every radio station. Except for one.

The management of WQXR, New York's oldest and foremost classical music station, elected to continuously play its regularly scheduled programming. This was clearly intended to provide solace and comfort and, importantly, to be an alternative to the endless barrage of sad and tragic news that would dominate the city for days and months to come. Music became a refuge when other aspects of life were intolerable. The gesture by WQXR brought to mind something Leonard Bernstein said in 1963 that greatly influenced my world view: "This will be our reply to violence: to make music more intensely, more beautifully, more devotedly than ever before."

In the days and weeks after the disaster, I made it a point to go to musical performances all over the city as frequently as possible. This was not only to find comfort for myself but to show solidarity with, and appreciation for, orchestras that traveled from Chicago, Berlin, Helsinki, and elsewhere to bring music to New York when travel was still quite perilous and fears were real. The New York City Opera and then the Metropolitan Opera bravely relit their theaters soon after the attacks, though both companies had lost many loved ones at Ground Zero. The

New York Philharmonic gave a powerfully moving performance of Brahms's German Requiem, a work of great universality. One of the most beautiful events was a concert of remembrance at Carnegie Hall that featured Yo-Yo Ma, James Levine, and, extraordinarily, Leontyne Price, who came out of retirement to lend her voice to the efforts all New Yorkers were making to heal.

It can sometimes sound trite to speak of the redemptive and healing properties of music. I have heard this assertion often and understood it only in the most general and benign way. I can assure you now that those feelings are very real, and the power of music is greater than even I, with a life in music stretching back forty-five years, could ever imagine. It was a blessing to be writing this book during that time, and it was a reaffirmation and source of great pride that music was one of the chief weapons my city used to address both barbarism and grief.

No single volume could teach you everything there is to know about music, and nor should it attempt to. Whole books can be written on a single piece of music or the life of one composer or conductor. But once you begin the journey of musical discovery, a lifetime of deeper understanding—not only of music but of the human heart—is what will await you. Let the music begin.

3

SOME THOUGHTS ON THE RECORDINGS USED IN *CLASSICAL MUSIC 101*

In 1877, Edison invented the cylinder phonograph, a crude affair which was not perfected until 1890, and which was still undergoing refinement when World War broke out in 1914. The average parlor music up to that time was provided by the harmonium, or the piano on which some musical maid practiced her scales or laboriously picked out tunes like "Hearts and Flowers." There was a monotony and a tameness to the household melody, even in the cities, and the fiddle held indisputed sway in rural districts. Then came the phonograph—at first a novelty, then a luxury, and finally a commonplace. It brought the great arias of opera into the tenements. Caruso's voice soared for flat-faced Tibetans in the hill villages near Darjeeling. Traders saw to it that the spear-carrying natives of Central Africa had a chance to hear crack orchestras from Broadway and Piccadilly grind out jazz, with a faintly reminiscent note. And, fifty years from now, the voice of Caruso and all his contemporaries will be heard by those not yet born.

Edison had a hand even in the perfection of the radio, that invention which has given the phonograph a back seat in much of the progress. In 1876 he perfected the carbon telephone transmitter, which, in turn, helped in the evolution of the microphone.

—From the New York Times *obituary for Thomas Edison, October 18, 1931*

U ntil the inventions of the phonograph and the radio, the only way music could be heard was if someone played it in a room you were in or if you were playing it yourself. By "playing" I mean "performing." The notion of recording—the capturing and pre-serving of sound for repeated hearing—was once as inconceivable as capturing images on celluloid that would then be projected on a screen.

The original records, such as those containing the voice of Caruso, could only hold a few minutes of music. They were heavy but fragile, and could scratch easily. The fidelity (the faithfulness with which an accurate representation of the performance could be achieved) was variable. Yet today these voices of a distant past—whether a tenor, a piano, or an orchestra—are precious miracles. If you listen to a recording of a seventy-five-year-old pianist recorded in 1910, you realize that this artist may have heard Chopin, Liszt, Brahms, or Grieg play, or perhaps even might have studied with one of these composers. When we think of recordings as documentation not only of performances but of styles and traditions, we realize that we think of music not so much as what is on the printed page of what we occasionally hear live, but as what we know from recordings. For most of us, this is music.

In the nineteenth century and before, it would be a rare luxury to hear a full orchestra give a live performance of, say, Beethoven's Seventh Symphony. One had to live close to where the orchestra would perform, and then have the money and luck to acquire tickets. Even in major cities where orchestras had large followings, concert halls held only a limited number of people. And audiences had to content themselves with what the orchestra chose to perform.

With the advent of recordings, everything changed. A performance, once committed to a vinyl disk, could travel to places the orchestra would never reach. Music lovers could discover unfamiliar works simply by purchasing a record and playing it. *And playing it again. And yet again.* Discovery of, and intimacy with, music changes when it can be heard repeatedly. Similarly, the relationship to that music changes. You do not merely own a recording of a work, but you own the music itself. Many people might say, having begun the learning process in this book, that they now own Beethoven's Seventh Symphony.

Records had to be handled carefully so that they would not break or scratch. They would be stored in album covers that displayed art or illustrations on the front and essays and information about the music and performers on the back. The profession of designing covers or writing the text on the back was an integral part of the business and pleasure of making recordings.

• ◇ •

The invention of radio altered the relationship again between music and listener. You could hear a recording on radio and then be motivated to purchase it to "own" that music, too. It might be that you would choose one recording of a work over another because the recording you heard on the radio pleased you. Record companies vied to get their recordings rather than those of their competition played.

The other source of excitement about radio was that it could broadcast performances *live* from the stages of concert halls. One's imagination could run wild thinking of music played by a great orchestra being beamed from a concert hall in New York, London, Rome, or Vienna. Most national radio networks in Europe created orchestras specifically to play on the air. These ensembles still exist today in most European countries. In the United States there was the NBC Symphony from the 1930s to the 1950s, but radio orchestras are now basically extinct in North America.

The original terminology for radio was actually *radiodiffusion*, or the distribution of words and music via radio waves. Some European radio programmers still think in terms of *radiodiffusion*—the sending out of sound—while many American and Canadian stations seek to create a sense of community in which radio is interactive and listeners have considerable input as to what music is played.

American radio, which is filled with advertising (except for National Public Radio and some university stations), has a radically different character from the grand old *radiodiffusion* broadcasts. American commercial radio is faster and louder, and at many hours of the day even classical stations only play short pieces so that advertisements can be sandwiched in between. European networks that broadcast classical music often have state funding, so there are no commercial interruptions.

It is highly unfortunate that classical music station owners in many major American cities claim that their audiences only want classical "lite," those little snatches of Baroque music or single movements from a sonata or a symphony. The real reason is that by playing shorter pieces of music, more advertising can be inserted in each hour. My response would be to not listen to those stations, preferring some public radio and university stations, to which I then donate money to help keep them advertising-free. If you live in a city that also has a commercial classical station that presents large works of music and sensitively inserts advertising, then you are lucky.

Until the 1980s, it was quite common for American and European classical music stations to have programs that included discussions of music and musicians. A significant part of my education came through listening to Karl Haas, Robert Sherman, and others talk about music on New York's wonderful station WQXR. I am sad that there are so few such programs today, although some stubbornly hold on at independent classical stations, college radio stations, and on National Public Radio. If you can listen to foreign stations on the Internet or shortwave radio, you will find that a few other countries still have discussions about music in addition to actual performances.

• ⌖ •

Recording technology continued to improve throughout the twentieth century. Monaural (mono) sound, in which music was recorded to produce a singular stream of sound, gave way to stereophonic (stereo) sound, which was more spacious and differentiated. This means that you could play your record on a turntable and sound would come through two speakers and you might hear, for example, an orchestra emanate more from one and a solo violin more from the other.

Long-playing records (LPs) became more common in the 1950s, and with them thirty minutes or a little more of music could be put on one side. An LP could contain a symphony or a piano concerto. Advances in the technology of recording continued at a dizzying pace through the decades and were revolutionized by two developments around 1980: the compact disc (CD) and digital recording, which broke down sound into bytes.

The CD could hold about 75 minutes of music and did not have to be turned over in the middle of a piece of music. Because of digitalization, a listener could go to almost any spot on the disc to hear a particular passage of music without having to lift and drop a needle as on a record. CDs are virtually indestructible, small, and elegant, and loved by most listeners who never held a big, round black record. CDs come in little plastic cases called jewel boxes. Cover art has been miniaturized or eliminated altogether, and notes are either printed in little booklets, or eliminated.

There is a never-ending debate among music lovers as to whether vinyl or CDs are better. Some love the tactile aspects of records and believe that the sound is warmer. Others love the convenience and durability of CDs, arguing that we would have lost ancient recordings had they not been remastered and transferred to CDs. Many listeners, especially younger ones, like the cooler, more clinical sound of modern CD recordings. In my career and in my tastes I straddle the two technologies and find merits in both. But the reality of today's recording industry is that almost nothing is issued on vinyl, so the medium of choice must be the compact disc and the CD player.

• ◌ •

In the glory years of classical music recording, from about the 1950s to the mid-1980s, thousands of sublime performances were preserved under technical conditions that ranged from acceptable to excellent. The major recording companies, including EMI-Angel, Capitol, Columbia (later CBS and Sony), Deutsche Grammophon, London/Decca, Philips, and RCA, all vied to have exclusive recording contracts with the top orchestras, conductors, and soloists.

The three titan conductors in this era were Leonard Bernstein (at Columbia), Herbert von Karajan (at EMI and DG), and Georg Solti (at London/Decca). Such was their power and sales potential that they could record just about anything that interested them. All recorded one or more complete sets of the Beethoven symphonies, for example, and also managed to do most of the symphonic works of Schubert, Schumann, Mendelssohn, Brahms, Dvořák, and Tchaikovsky, as well as many of the major symphonies of Haydn, Mozart, Mahler, and Bruckner.

In addition to these conductors, others also had major contracts. For example, Eugene Ormandy and his Philadelphia Orchestra recorded many of the same works for Columbia that Bernstein and the New York Philharmonic did for the same company. If a recording company had a famous soloist under contract—say, violinist Isaac Stern at Columbia— an attempt would be made to have that artist play with conductors and orchestras in the fold. So Stern might have recorded one violin concerto with Ormandy and the Philadelphians and another with Bernstein and the New Yorkers. He would have to get special permission to record with Solti and the Chicago Symphony or Karajan and the Berlin Philharmonic. Those orchestras would more likely work with a violinist under contract with their own record companies.

In 1975 it would have been quite easy to go to a record store and find fifteen different recordings of Mendelssohn's *Italian* or Dvořák's *New World* symphonies to choose from. There would be classic versions from a generation before that were kept in print, as well the interpretations of all the top living conductors performing with their own orchestras or as guests of another. Usually, a consensus would form and name one or two of these recordings as the best, and then positive things could be said about most of the others. Recording companies knew that most of these would sell enough to make sufficient income. In fact, big sales of standard repertory helped subsidize recordings of more esoteric works that were of artistic merit but did not have mass appeal.

Many of the more unusual pieces were championed by smaller companies in many countries, including Nonesuch, Nimbus, Erato, Hungaraton, and Melodiya (this last being the company that recorded many of the marvelous artists who performed only in the Soviet Union and Eastern Europe).

When the compact disc came on the market around 1980, most

of the great performances on record were reissued on CD. At first many of these transfers were shoddily done, so the original tapes had to later be remastered and issued on CD with more pristine sound and balance. Because record companies owned most of the rights to older performances, much of the revenue from CD sales became pure profit for these companies with no royalties going to performers. The CD represented a golden opportunity to make a lot of money without too much expense, and record companies pounced at the chance.

For example, I own at least two hundred LPs that I bought again as CDs, because the new technology is more convenient and I did not want to wear out my precious LPs. Many music lovers who were around when that transition occurred made similar outlays.

A generation of older conductors (including Bernstein, Karajan, Solti, Carlo Maria Giulini, and Karl Böhm) were around to make new recordings directly for CD. These were more expensive to produce and sell, but still benefited both recording companies and artists because of the great appeal of the people involved. The next generation of conductors (including Claudio Abbado, Daniel Barenboim, Colin Davis, Bernard Haitink, Neeme Jarvi, James Levine, Lorin Maazel, Riccardo Muti, Seiji Ozawa, and Zubin Mehta) all had major recording contracts and their musical achievements could be documented along with those of the great orchestras. They all had enough of a following that the recordings sold and companies made profits.

Instrumental soloists in the same age group (including Itzhak Perlman, Yo-Yo Ma, and several pianists) also managed to create a discography that represented the range of their abilities.

Then, by the mid-1990s, a few calamitous events happened that destroyed the golden egg. Most of the recording companies were purchased by corporations that expected every new CD to make big profits. No longer could a huge seller subsidize the costs of a smaller but artistically important recording. Fine artists who were not huge stars lost their contracts. A younger generation of conductors and soloists did not have the clout of their elders, even if they had great talent, so they were underrepresented in recordings.

Then things got worse. As the new owners of record labels dug deep into the archives for old performances for which no royalties had to be paid, these cheaper issues competed with full-priced new recordings. For example, a budget-priced 1950s recording of the Brahms Violin Concerto by Jascha Heifetz or a midpriced version with Isaac Stern from the 1960s, each with a great conductor and orchestra, could probably outsell a new recording by a rising young violinist with a stellar conductor and orchestra simply because the older recordings are considered classics and cost less. Most shoppers would not care that the older performances (which would be labeled AAD or ADD to indicate that they are not all digitally produced) usually cannot compare sonically with a newly minted all-digital (DDD) recording.

The prevailing, and unfortunate, impression is that classical music is an art form living in the past. From a performance point of view, I leave that up to music critics. But it is highly unfortunate that today's outstanding artists have fewer recording opportunities than musicians of one or two generations ago. Recordings are not merely sales tools, they are also historical documents. I encourage you, where possible, to purchase and support recordings by active artists. I also hope that you will permit yourself numerous immersions in the classic performances from the past. These have much to teach us and entertain us.

• ◌⟡◌ •

As I created the structure of this book, my first consideration was to decide which pieces of music I wanted you to study. Then I had to determine which recorded performances I would select for you to learn. This process was quite painstaking, and I realize that several disclaimers and explanations are required.

First, needless to say, no recording company or artist had any influence over my decisions. I think it is important to introduce you to a wide range of styles, interpretations, and technical components of a performance and of its recording. So you will find a vast variety of choices.

Second, it is important to state that the works of music in this adventure you are commencing are not, per se, my favorites, though I love almost all of them. Rather, they are a cross-section of pieces from several centuries by most of the major composers that will serve to open doors to you to discover more about their creators. Similarly, some of these recordings may feature performers who are my very favorites, but often they feature other artists whose work I admire and who represent different approaches or points of view.

I know that many music lovers will fume if I leave out a piece of music or a particular performance that they adore. My choices do not imply negative judgments of recordings I did not include but simply the awareness that in the vast repertory of music and recordings, I could only introduce you to at most a hundred works, and then encourage you to learn more.

As your CD library grows, I want you to own performances by a vast spectrum of performers. For example, your favorite contemporary pianist may turn out to be Martha Argerich, Emanuel Ax, or Evgeny Kissin. But I would still hope that you acquire performances by other active pianists such as Murray Perahia, András Schiff, and Mitsuko Uchida. And then I would insist that you seriously investigate most of the great pianists of the past, a list of whom you can find on page 293. If you stick with only one artist, no matter how brilliant he or she is, you are depriving yourself of one of the joys of music—listening to and comparing performances of the same music by different artists.

Third, I want every recording that I include to be widely available in stores and for purchase over the Internet. Given the huge amount of recordings that exist, not all of them find mass distribution. Occasionally, I opted for a commendable—but easily located—recording instead of a cherishable performance that is hard to find. If you absolutely cannot locate the recording I suggest, try to purchase another that contains the very same pieces, because I might refer to the other pieces later on. This is especially true for two-CD sets such as those released in the London/Decca "Double Decker" series and the Deutsche Grammophon "Panorama" series. Also, all the recordings I recommend contain nothing but wonderful pieces of music, and I would like these to be in your collection.

Fourth, I do not want you to spend more than necessary for recordings. Just as this book is moderately priced to make it accessible to those interested in classical music, I intend that most of the CDs you purchase be fairly priced. For that reason, I often suggest mid-priced 2-CD sets that cost the same as one new one. This will give you more music to listen to, and most of these sets feature outstanding performances.

Fifth, I want the list of recordings to include performances that date from the past as well as today so that you can hear some timeless interpretations but also have the chance to own recordings by artists whom you might be able to hear live in concert halls. The difficulty, as mentioned above, is twofold: Fewer contemporary artists have the opportunities to make recordings when compared to artists of twenty or forty years ago. Also, new recordings will invariably be more expensive than budget reissues, and I want to be mindful of your pocketbook. There are some performances that are so indispensable that I made sure to include them so that you would own these classics.

• ◇ •

If some readers of this book believe that I left out certain great performances or recordings, I remind them that my goals were not to create a list of bests but a learning curriculum that must take many factors into consideration. I would ask you to do me the big favor of sharing your ideas and beloved recordings with people who are only now learning to love classical music. In so doing, they will benefit from your knowledge and experience as well as mine.

I have discovered that many readers of *Opera 101* joined forces to purchase recordings and study music together. This strikes me as a good idea if money is a consideration as you approach classical music. You can all listen together (don't talk—just listen!) and then discuss the work afterward. Or a recording can be passed from one friend to the next for private listening. Another option is the library, which may have some of these pieces in its collection. Yet I would encourage you to purchase recordings of the works you really love, so that you may have them to listen to anytime the mood strikes you.

Keep your CDs in a clean, dry place at room temperature and they will give you a lifetime of pleasure, making the cost of your initial investment quite minimal.

• ∽ •

Important: Recordings crucial to your study in *Classical Music 101* will be indicated in **bold type**. Those intended as optional choices for further study or comparison will be in normal type.

THE VOICES OF THE ORCHESTRA

The oldest musical instrument known to man is the human voice. Before people ever hit an animal skin pulled tight over a wooden cylinder or plucked a string or blew into a seashell or hollowed wood, they made sounds—they made music—with their voices. Think about the people you know: family, friends, coworkers, people you routinely encounter in your daily life. Now think for a few moments about their voices, the sound, the texture, how high or low they go: are they strong or fragile, do they inspire a sense of beauty, or are they irritating? The more you think about each voice you regularly hear, the more adjectives you can apply to it.

There are voices that growl or purr or croon. They may soothe or excite or charm. I am certain you know somebody whose speaking voice is unmistakable, irresistible, whose *timbre* (the characteristic quality of sound that distinguishes one voice or musical instrument from another) particularly captivates you. In my case, one of these voices belonged to my father. Although he died in 1996, I can still clearly hear it in my head. Interestingly, the voice of the actor Marcello Mastroianni was very similar in timbre to my father's, and when I see one of his films I vividly hear my dad. You might say that I responded particularly to my father's voice because I loved him, and there is truth in that. But it is also, I believe, that two persons can be synchronized not only in terms of affection but also *frequency.*

Let us return to the idea of timbre to understand frequency better. In describing sound, there are subjective and objective assessments. We subjectively can describe how high or low something seems to us (this is based on the frequency—the higher the number, the higher the sound), what sensation we get and feel when hearing a sound, and what a particular timbre is. More objective evaluations come where we can apply measurement: *frequency,* a number of vibrations in a given period of time; *intensity,* how loud or soft a sound is, which can be measured in decibels; and *spectrum,* the totality of frequencies that make up a particular sound. Again, we have Beethoven's dictum that music is a higher revelation of philosophy (what we believe or perceive) and science (what we measure and categorize).

So the frequency of my father's voice (and Marcello Mastroianni's) was especially gratifying to my ears. The frequency and tonal quality of the cello and the clarinet appeal to me for similar reasons. In retrospect it does not surprise me that as I was discovering opera, two voices that I responded to immediately and profoundly—those of Mirella Freni and Marilyn Horne—happened to be two of my father's favorites. I am not referring here to their formidable singing skills but to the quality (the timbre) of their voices when they emitted pure sound. Thinking in terms of musical instruments, you can say that my father and I were tuned to the same key and heard sound the same way.

To understand this concept further, I present my mother for contrast. She has a very pleasing voice, considerably higher than my father's, of course, but also of a distinct timbre. She has an appealing and unmistakable ring in her voice that sits slightly above the main tone, with a result that is quite harmonious. If my father's voice was like a bow gliding slowly and smoothly across one string of a cello, my mother's is more like a bow that moves a little more quickly across the two deeper-sounding strings of a violin, creating harmony. Hers is not a highly pitched voice, so it is pleasing because it fits quite comfortably in the range we might call "easy on the ear."

With most of us, the voices of our parents are the ones we know first, longest, and best. I described my parents' voices for you to provoke ideas about listening to voices you know. But remember that there are many voices out there in the world that we all know and respond to. Think of radio announcers. Because you cannot see them, you listen more closely to them than you would to the man or woman who presents the nightly news on television. Good radio people have vocal personalities, with timbres that travel beautifully through the airwaves. By "vocal personality" I do not mean human personality, but that we perceive a character in these people based on the tone—the timbre—of their voices. They might be likable, trustworthy, humorous, naughty, sexy, or vulnerable. Your opinion may change once you hear what they have to say, and you might ask, "Why is such a nice person saying those terrible things?" Think of a suave and glib politician whose voice may grab you but who uses it to say repugnant things.

We know voices of certain actors and immediately recognize them because they are distinctive, if not necessarily beautiful. Again, I am not referring to how these actors speak but to how they sound. Katharine Hepburn and Lucille Ball had very distinctive voices that captured our ears and attention. Were they beautiful voices? Not necessarily, but they were singular and immediately identifiable.

We have been discussing speaking voices. Now let us think of singing voices, which are not the same thing. The speaking voice is like the sound of an instrument, while the singing voice is that instrument being played. In the most general terms, we can divide the female singing voice into the categories of soprano, mezzo-soprano, and contralto, and the male singing voice into tenor, baritone, and bass. There are numerous subcategories and some degree of overlapping, but the concept is clear.

The soprano is the highest female range and can reach the highest notes. The mezzo (Italian for "middle" or "in-between") is just that. She can sing some of the lower notes of a soprano and some of the higher notes of the contralto, which is the lowest female voice. In addition to being able to sing certain notes, each voice has a different texture.

The soprano may be ringing (bell-like) or honeyed, while the mezzo can be soothing or lusty and the contralto chocolaty and rich. All of these adjectives are subjective, but give you a sense of how one might describe sound.

The highest male voice (not including countertenors, who are in a separate category whose tone is not, in the strictest sense, natural) is the tenor. He can sing some of the notes in the range of those sung by sopranos and mezzos, but his timbre is different, and will sound different even if he sings the same music as his female counterpart. The middle male voice is the baritone and the lowest is the bass, which typically can go much deeper than the contralto.

What we have here—in the range from soprano to bass—is a series of vocal ranges (highest and lowest notes that can be sung) and different timbres. Think of the keyboard of a piano with the bass all the way on the left and the soprano on the extreme right.

When people sing together in small groups or in choruses, we bring together these ranges and timbres and make music. Think of these voices as different instruments in an orchestra or a chamber music ensemble. In the most basic sense, this amalgamation creates *polyphony*, (many sounds), wherein several voices or instruments simultaneously are combined *contrapuntally*, from *counterpoint*.

What is counterpoint? It is central to understanding music, and whole books can be written on this one topic. According to the *Oxford Dictionary of Music*, counterpoint is "the ability, unique to music, to say two things at once comprehensibly. The term derives from the expression *punctus contra punctus*, i.e. 'point against point' or 'note against note.' A single 'part' or 'voice' added to another is called 'a counterpoint' to that other, but the more common use of the word is that of the simultaneous parts or voices, each of significance in itself and the whole resulting in a coherent texture."

Contrapuntal music is said to have begun with vocal works in the ninth century and continued in pure form well into the seventeenth century. Certainly counterpoint has carried on in music to our day, but things changed as more and more instruments were born and brought more distinct voices to musical ensembles (which would come to be called symphony orchestras). The two most important instruments in this regard were the *violin*, which acquired the physical and tonal qualities we know today in the early 1700s and became, in effect, the first among equals as a voice in the orchestra, and the *piano*, born around 1700, which can encompass a range from very high to very low and represent the notes made by almost every voice or instrument. The piano is not a traditional instrument for most orchestral works but appears with it in piano concertos—that is, works for piano and orchestra in which the piano is something of a protagonist rather than being just one voice among many.

Let us return to individual sounds and voices. Not only do two different vocal types, say, tenor and mezzo-soprano, sound distinct when singing the same music in the same *register*—that is, range of high or low—but even two voices in the same vocal type can make the same music sound significantly different. For example, Plácido Domingo and Luciano Pavarotti are both splendid tenors whose voices can sing more or less in the same vocal range (in their primes, Domingo could probably go a little lower and Pavarotti a little higher). But if we were to ask each of these tenors to sing the same piece of music that would lie comfortably in the meatiest part of their voices, we would find that the music sounded different first and foremost because each man had a distinctive timbre. Never mind issues such as volume or pronunciation of words. If each tenor sang the same series of wordless notes, they would sound different simply because of timbre. One could attach adjectives to these timbres, but I think that would be confining in describing two great artists. If you listen to recordings of them singing Verdi and Puccini arias, you will immediately understand.

If you had a tenor and a mezzo sing the same music in the same register, the effect would again be different from having two tenors singing it because of the very distinct timbres of these two voices. The same thinking applies to musical instruments. Their sounds are distinct and palpable, and they evoke certain feelings when we hear them. If you hear an oboe and a clarinet play the same note in the same register, the note will sound different because of the distinct characteristics—or voices—of each instrument. Think, if you wish, of a tenor and a mezzo-soprano, replace them with an oboe and a clarinet, and you will get the idea.

When a composer creates a melody in his head, he then needs to decide in which orchestral "voices" it sounds best, or interesting. Think back to the first movement of Beethoven's Seventh Symphony. The first melody, or theme, is introduced by oboes and then quickly picked up by clarinets. There is some dialogue between these two instruments, which is commented upon or seconded by the strings. The second melody, which sounds somewhat pastoral, is presented by the oboe and then is swept up by strings and other wind instruments. Then it reappears, sounding somewhat changed, in the voice of the flute. For the rest of the movement, these themes are, in effect, batted around the orchestra and sound different, intriguing, exciting, as they journey.

Do not think that oboes and clarinets corner the market on introducing melody in a symphony orchestra because of the example I just gave. It could happen in the stringed instruments, in other wind instruments, or in the brass. When we study Ravel's *Boléro* later on, you will have one of the most vivid examples of how the same melody can sound very different when played by various instruments. The act of assigning different musical parts to particular instruments when a work is composed is known as *orchestration*.

What are the instruments of the orchestra that a composer has to choose from? There are two things to bear in mind. The first is that when we speak of the symphony orchestra and classical music, we are speaking of *Western* classical music and the instruments that serve it. The art form we are studying here is European in origin and has found congenial soil in North and South America and Australia and New Zealand (in other words, places where Europeans migrated). Most of the instruments used in Western classical music (hereinafter we shall call it classical music) are European in origin.

There are other forms of classical music that are wonderful, special, and important, and should not be disregarded by people with a

Eurocentric orientation. India, in particular, has a glorious musical tradition dating back to ancient times, and so does Sub-Saharan Africa. Music of ancient Egypt and Greece fed more into the European tradition. China also had its own classical music and Japan drew from that and created its own. Indonesia also has an important musical heritage, as do smaller Asian countries. There are also formidable musical traditions in the Middle East and notable ones in South America. I believe that jazz (led by Duke Ellington, 1899–1974) and American popular song (by Irving Berlin, Cole Porter, Harold Arlen, and many others) can and should be considered *American* classical music, as opposed to the vast body of music by Americans such as George Chadwick (1854–1931), Charles Ives (1874–1954), Howard Hanson (1896–1981), Aaron Copland (1900–1990), Elliott Carter (1908–) Samuel Barber (1910–1981), John Cage (1912–1992), Philip Glass (1937–), John Corigliano (1938–), William Bolcom (1938–), and John Adams (1947–), who write in the continuing classical tradition of European music but with distinctly American voices. George Gershwin (1898–1937) and Leonard Bernstein (1918–1990) stand in both the European and American classical traditions, which makes them harder to pigeonhole.

The other thing to keep in mind when you think about musical instruments is that they are not merely objects unto themselves, but extensions of the people who play them. Some of these sit before the player (the piano, the organ, drums, other forms of percussion) and the musician must adopt a physical stance that is both comfortable and practical for playing the instrument.

String instruments (violins, violas, cellos, double basses, guitars, harps, lutes) are embraced in an intimate and affectionate way. A violin and viola are held in the arms almost like a baby. It has often been remarked upon in literature and art how much the cello and the guitar seem to represent the human (particularly female) form, and their players (of either gender) tend to show an almost sensuous attachment to their instruments. The cello in particular develops a close physical connection with its player, who places the instrument between the legs and rests the scroll (the uppermost part) on the shoulder next to the ear. The double bass, which is taller than the cello, can be played by holding it close to the musician's body, with the musician standing or seated in a tall chair.

Wind and brass instruments are brought to the mouth and held in hands in one way or another. With their requirement of exhalation from the musician, these instruments can often be thought of as extensions of the human voice, wherein the vocal cords are silent but the instrumental sound comes forth on a wave of breath.

So from now on, when you think of a musical instrument, also picture in your head the musician who is attached to it.

♭ Strings ♭

Instruments in which strings, cords, or wires are stretched tautly and then plucked date back to ancient times. The most primitive come in the shape of a hunting bow (as in bow and arrow) that would be plucked. The tone would be changed by flexing the bow and thus the tautness of the string. It is thought that gourds and turtle shells were among the earliest *sound boxes*, the chamber in which the plucked sound resonates. Strings stretched above them provided the sounds. Each string was a different length or tension, which produced a different sound. The hollow insides of a modern violin or cello or guitar were their sound boxes.

In Egypt, a harp was discovered at the royal tomb at Ur, this being the favored instrument at court. Giuseppe Verdi (1813–1901) knew what he was doing when he put harps prominently in the score of his opera *Aïda*. Smaller, handheld harps were played in Egypt, along with lutes and lyres (from the latter we have the root for words such as "lyrical"). You know that Orpheus, Greek god of music, played a lyre.

Ancient Greek musicians, including Homer, played a *cithara*, whose name sounds to me like a forerunner of *guitar*. A cithara was held close to the body and strings were plucked while the musician sang or spoke poetry. Stringed instruments also existed in ancient Asia. The most famous string instrument in India is the *sitar*, whose ancestors date back many centuries. China, Japan, Korea, and Indonesia all have traditional string instruments dating back to ancient times, as does Africa. One is the *banjar* which, when transported to America and played by slaves, evolved into the banjo. The Arab world also had string instruments, one of the most notable being the *rabab*.

Eventually, almost all string instruments were made of wood because this material provided the most resonant and beautiful tone in the sound boxes. String instruments without sound boxes, such as the harp, are often made of wood, too.

Some time during the Middle Ages, if not earlier, instruments developed in which the sound boxes were placed on legs, like a table. There were strings in the box, which were plucked by musicians who either stood or sat over the box. A famous example of this is the zither, which is thought to be native to Austria. At the same time, and in the same part of the world (probably Hungary), an instrument that looked like the zither was invented, but it was played differently. The musician held light wooden hammers and struck the strings to get different sounds. This instrument was called the *zimbalom*, or *cimbalom*. The name is the forerunner of the Italian *cembalo* and describes the family of instruments that had sound boxes on legs with strings within which were struck by hammers.

By the seventeenth century, cembalo instruments were designed with keyboards. When you pressed a key, it triggered a hammer that struck a string. The Italian *clavicembalo*, or key cembalo, is what we call the harpsichord, the immediate forerunner of the piano.

Throughout history instruments developed that expressed a sound or frequency (think back to my description of my father's voice) that especially appealed to a people or a culture. For example, think of the particular shape and sound of the Irish harp. This instrument has been part of Irish music for more than a thousand years and is so central to Irish identity that it appears as an icon in many places—even an ale is named for it. The guitar, universal though it is, has found a special home in the music and affection of Spain (which also has the castanets), while the mandolin is cherished in Italy, the bouzouki in Greece, the Gypsy violin in Eastern Europe, the balalaika in Russia, the Hardanger fiddle in Norway, used since the sixteenth century, a similar fiddle in the southern part of the United States, and even the ukelele in Hawaii.

If you think about instrumental associations with particular places, you can understand how a composer creating music in a more international style, or idiom, can communicate a sense of place by featuring an instrument that immediately brings to mind a country or culture.

In our express train journey through the development of stringed musical instruments, we now reach the Renaissance and the lute. This is a beautiful instrument to behold, and it is frequently depicted in paintings of the age. Think, for example, of the famous picture by Carpaccio of the angel playing a lute that rests on his crossed legs.

The lute as known in Europe probably arrived in the late eighth century from the Maghreb (now Morocco and Algeria), where it was called the *al-'ud*, into Spain. The Arabic word meant "wood," but also meant "flexible stick." It was a sensuously pear-shaped instrument that had an artfully decorated hole cut into its sound box. Up to fifteen strings were suspended from the bottom of the lute over a carved piece of wood called the bridge, then past the hole in the sound box and up the length of its neck, where a series of knobs could individually tighten or loosen each string. This adjustment of each string is known as tuning, and is done on all stringed instruments, including the harpsichord and the piano. Another name for the neck on string instruments is the fingerboard, because when the musician presses down on a string, the tension on the string changes, and a new note can be produced. A cousin of the lute in the Renaissance was the *theorbo*, which was larger and produced a deeper tone.

Do you remember the bow? Back in ancient times it was part of the bow and arrow used for hunting and war, as it was well into the early nineteenth century. The bow was used more peacefully for stretching and flexing to pluck and make sounds. Somewhere in the mists of history—some scholars think it was the seventh or eighth century—a person figured out that if you slide a bow across the strings of an instrument you can produce an appealing sound and, most important, a sound that can be sustained longer than one that is plucked. This probably was not a European person, but more likely someone from India or central Asia. The bow reached the Arab world and then Europe.

Try this: Make one clucking sound with your tongue against the roof of your mouth. Listen how long that lasts. Now take a deep breath, close your lips and hum, holding it as long as you can. The first sound was a pluck. The second was a bow across a string. Put another way, the first sound was a short word, the second a full sentence. Can you envision the possibilities this means for music-making?

Throughout history strings and bows evolved. Strings have been made of whatever the instrument maker could procure that would resist repeated plucking. In ancient times it might have been a strong reed or grass, or a piece of animal gut (specifically, intestine) that was stretched. In fact, the use of animal gut lasted for centuries, but as metalworking became more refined, strings would be made of brass or other metals. Certain modern strings are made of plastic or other man-made materials.

Until the fifteenth century, bows were shaped like hunting bows, and then gradually took the more elongated form we know today. At the start of the eighteenth century, Arcangelo Corelli (1653–1713), who composed a lot of gorgeous music for strings, created a nonelastic bow that was easier to handle. By 1780, a French bow maker named François Tourte designed the bow that is basically still in use today. It is a nearly straight piece of wood, except that it curves inward near its top end. From the top and bottom, long hair (often from horse tail) is suspended. There is a mechanism to tighten the hair so that it will be taut.

In the Renaissance courts of Europe, bows were used to play a family of instruments called the viols, the immediate forerunners of modern violins, violas, cellos, and basses. Viols usually had five or seven strings. As a group these instruments were often called *viola da gamba*, the latter word being Italian for "leg." Most were played between the legs and supported on a chair, or placed on one knee. Interestingly, the pitch (how high or low the sound could go) was related to singing voices. The highest was the soprano viola da gamba, then the tenor viola da gamba, and the bass viola da gamba. There were other members of this family of instruments, but these were the major ones.

The modern viola did not descend from this family, but rather from the family that produced the violin. These were called the *viola da braccio* (arm viol) or *lira da braccio* (arm lyre) instruments, and they were held toward the musician, much as is done today, with fingers pressing on the fingerboard as the bow—held in the other hand—is swept across the strings.

Violin Violins as we know them began to appear around 1560 in Florence, and during the early and middle parts of the eighteenth century, violins and other string instruments were produced by master artisans in northern Italy that are still considered the finest ever made. The most famous of these was Antonio Stradivari (1644–1737), who is referred to in English as Stradivarius. He, and families such as the Guarneri and the Amati, made violins and other instruments in Cremona, near Milan. The city is a destination for all who are fascinated by the violin and, in fact, violins are still made there. Elsewhere in northern Italy, especially Bologna and Brescia, violin-making became a high art. While violins, violas, and cellos from this era command phenomenal prices and many of the great performers own one, it is important to remember that the making of wonderful string instruments is hardly a lost art. Many have been produced in the centuries since that make beautiful music.

The violin, as you surely know, is a graceful and elegant thing to behold, with its curvaceous body varnished a tawny color ranging somewhere from gold to reddish brown. Instead of the central round sound hole of the lute, this instrument has two that are *f*-shaped incised into the sound box. Four strings go from the base of the instrument over a bridge and up the length of the fingerboard before being twisted into four pegs just beneath a sensuous scroll.

Music is made by bowing over the strings, whose notes (the sounds we hear) can be changed depending where the violinist places his or her fingers on the strings. Fingering will be done with the left hand and bowing with the right. In my experience I have only seen one violinist who fingers with the right and bows with the left. The sound is produced thanks to vibrating strings and the resonating sound box. The choice of varnish also has an impact on the quality of the sound. If you have seen the film *The Red Violin* you will understand how serious the question of varnish can be. Finally, at the base of the violin is a chin rest that the musician tucks under the chin (almost always on the left side).

The violin is a remarkably versatile and expressive instrument capable of communicating all manner of emotions. It is fair to say that it is the surrogate for the human voice in a symphony orchestra, and one often hears about the violin as being capable of singing.

With only the rarest of exceptions, there are more violins in a symphony orchestra than any other instrument. There are almost always parts written for first violin and second violin. The instruments are identical, but the musical parts may be different, which gives more texture and variety to the sound. The first section can have up to twenty players, while the second violins may number up to eighteen. Many orchestral works are composed in such a way that violins take the lead on the melody, which is then answered or echoed by other instruments.

The first chair of the first section violins is occupied by the *concertmaster*, who, despite the name, may be a man or a woman. This is the person who is something of the leader of the permanent orchestra— your typical symphony orchestra may have an artistic director/principal conductor, and there will be many guest conductors, too. But the concertmaster is a fixture and is paid considerably more than the other musicians.

When an orchestra is seated on stage before the concert, the first chair will be empty. Just before the performance starts, the concertmaster enters and takes a solo bow. The orchestra will do any last bit of tuning up necessary. Then the conductor enters, shakes the concertmaster's hand, takes a bow, and starts the concert. In the past, orchestras were often led (not necessarily conducted, but guided from the first chair) by the concertmaster. Some of these went on to become conductors. If an orchestral piece has a solo violin passage, it will almost always be performed by the concertmaster. Examples include the second movement of the Symphony no. 1 by Johannes Brahms (1833–1897) and the *Capriccio Espagnol* by Nikolai Rimsky-Korsakov (1844–1908).

When an orchestra performs one of the many famous violin concertos (that is, a piece for orchestra and solo violin) in the repertory, the solo part will almost always be done by a guest violinist rather than the concertmaster. But there are rare special occasions when the concertmaster might be given the honor of performing the solo part. We shall study some of these concertos and other violin works in chapter 11.

Viola Slightly larger than a violin, though virtually identical in design, the viola's fuller tone provides a beguiling, and sometimes sad, contrast to the singing sound of the violin. It adds depth and warmth to the sound of the string section. Like its more slender sister, the viola is supposed to be a manageable size. There are special bows for violas that are slightly shorter and heavier than those for the violin, but in modern times many musicians use violin bows for either instrument.

Many viola players began as violinists and moved to their larger instruments later on. It may not surprise you to know that there are many violist jokes, all centered around their not being bright enough or talented enough to be violinists. This assumption is not accurate, but the perception has stuck. In fact, the viola is a very beautiful instrument that gives gratification to the person who plays it. There is solo viola repertory, though it is not nearly as large as that for violin. The instrument is a real star in Hector Berlioz's (1803–1869) orchestral work *Harold in Italy*. It also figures prominently in *Don Quixote* by Richard Strauss (1864–1949). There are usually ten to twelve violas in a modern symphony orchestra. We shall study some works for viola in chapter 12.

Cello The cello (its full name is violoncello) is a favorite instrument of many music lovers, who revel in its lush, romantic sound. It is about twice the length of a violin, and its sound box is much wider (from front to back) than that of its smaller relative. It is played with a bow that is shorter and thicker than the one used for violins. Because of its size, it is of course not lifted to the chin; instead, it has a metal endpin that extends from the cello to the floor. The scroll (top) of the instrument is placed on the left shoulder, the fingering is done with the left hand, and the bowing is done with the right. The cello has a large and impressive repertory of solo and concerto music that we will explore in chapter 12, but it is worth noting that there are important cello solos in Strauss's *Don Quixote* and Beethoven's Symphony no. 3, in which it plays the main theme. There are usually ten to twelve cellos in a modern symphony orchestra.

Double Bass In the sixteenth and seventeenth centuries the forerunner of this largest member of the violin family was known as the *violone,* or the "big viola." It came to resemble the violin, viola, and cello in form, only on a much bigger scale. The player stands behind the instrument or sits on a high stool. The double bass is held vertically, with the player's left arm extended upward to reach the fingerboard while the right arm reaches around the instrument to do the bowing. There are two types of bows: The French bow is held with the palm facing downward, as one does with a cello bow. It is lighter and allows the player more versatility. This bow is more popular in France, Britain, and North America. The German bow is held with the palm facing upward. It is shorter and heavier than the French bow and produces a fuller sound than the French bow. There are typically six to ten double basses in a symphony orchestra, either playing a lower (deeper) version of the cello's music or providing a deep musical underpinning to other instruments. The bass has found a second home in jazz, where it provides a steady low voice and often sets the tempo against which other instruments (trumpet, saxophone, clarinet, voice) may play. In classical music, there are notable bass passages in Beethoven's Symphony no. 5 and in the fourth movement of his Symphony no. 9, in Franz Schubert's (1797–1828) *Trout*

Quintet, and Camille Saint-Saëns's (1835–1921) *Carnival of the Animals*, which we shall soon study.

String Instruments in Ensembles We have been discussing string instruments and their use in orchestras. However, there is the whole category of *chamber music,* in which string instruments figure prominently. The term "chamber music" implies the setting where the music is played. It might once have been in a royal drawing room or later in the salon of a wealthy person's home. Long before there was radio or recorded music, the way to have music in the home was to have *musicales,* afternoons or evenings dedicated to chamber music for a small group of guests. The performance of music before small groups dates at least back to ancient Greece and Rome, although the instruments were more likely to be a lyre or harp, lute, some early wind instrument, and the human voice. Intimate performances of music for a few instruments and voice would continue through the Renaissance.

With the rise of the Baroque era in music in the seventeenth century, a different style of chamber music emerged that relied on the instruments most in favor at that time. Violins, violas, cellos, and harpsichords were prominent, and harps, mandolins, guitars, flutes, bassoons, trumpets, and a few other instruments appeared as well. A popular form was the *sonata.* This is a form we will discuss in more detail later on, but the word at its most elemental suggests music that is played (from the Italian *suonare,* "to play"), as opposed to the *cantata,* or music that is sung (from the Italian *cantare,* "to sing"). Corelli was a master of the sonata for two violins, cello, and harpsichord. He and Alessandro Stradella (1644–1682) were also leaders in the form known as *concerto grosso* (for a larger ensemble of instruments), which would later be used by Antonio Vivaldi (1678–1741), Johann Sebastian Bach (1685–1750), George Frideric Handel (1685–1759), and other composers of the early eighteenth century.

The lower voices of this music were known as the *basso continuo,* which we might think of as the bass line (not *base line*) in a musical score, or harmonies that are played in a low musical register (that is, low notes). This continuous bass might be played by cello, double bass, bassoon, organ, or, frequently, the harpsichord. In effect, it is the continuous sound of lower instruments that provided harmonic contrast to the melodies played by higher instruments, such as trumpet, flute, viola, and, most especially, the violin.

The violin gained its prominence as the leading voice—the first among equals—thanks to Giuseppe Torelli (1658–1709), a composer and violinist who wrote sonatas and concertos in which solo violin was featured or in which one violin took the leading part in the ensemble. This style of composition was embraced by Vivaldi, who institutionalized it.

Chamber music (*musica da camera*, in Italian) was distinguished from church music (*musica da chiesa*) in that it was not intended to be performed in religious settings. This distinction was applied until at least the late nineteenth century, and in some places even later, but nowadays it is not unusual to hear chamber music in acoustically rich churches while sacred music is performed in concert halls throughout the world. Similarly, a *cantata da chiesa* would be based on a religious theme while a *cantata profana* (such as Bach's wonderful "Coffee Cantata") would be performed in a nonreligious setting.

Composition of chamber music continues to this day, though composers now select from a wider range of instruments. They might create solo music, duos (frequently violin and piano), trios, quartets (the most typical being two violins, a viola, and a cello), quintets, sextets, septets, and octets. There are famous octets by Schubert, Felix Mendelssohn (1809–1847), and Igor Stravinsky (1882–1971).

Harp After the human voice, there is probably no other instrument that has had such ongoing use in musical performance as the harp. Documentation of the harp dates back to the thirteenth century B.C. Typically triangular, harps were, until a few centuries ago, handheld. They were commonly used by the Sumerians and Abyssinians, and in ancient Egypt, Greece, and Rome. From the Bible we know of the harp of David. In the Middle Ages in central Europe, the *minnesingers* were a form of touring minstrels who accompanied themselves on harps that ranged from nine to twenty-five strings. The minnesingers are central to Richard Wagner's (1813–1883) opera *Tannhäuser* (you can learn about this in great detail in chapter 12 of *Opera 101*). The harp has long been a popular instrument in the British Isles, especially in Ireland, as well as in Scandinavia. Composers from the time of Claudio Monteverdi (1567–1643) used harps in their works, with Handel finding particular application for it in his operas, oratorios, and a concerto. The harp figures prominently in the music of Pietro Paradisi (1707–1791). Its ethereal sound often found it paired with the flute in compositions, especially by Wolfgang Amadeus Mozart (1756–1791).

All through the years the harp evolved to suit the needs of composers. The modern harp now used in a symphony orchestra has 47 strings and 7 pedals (introduced in 1812) at the base of the instrument, whose purpose is to alter the pitch of the strings. It is quite large and heavy (approximately 1,000 pounds/450 kilos). The harp has the largest harmonic range (from high notes to low notes) of any instrument. The strings for the high and middle registers (ranges) are made of gut and are usually played by the right hand. The strings for lower notes are made of steel or silk coated with brass, and are usually played by the left hand. From the end of the eighteenth century onward the harp was placed on the ground between the player's knees and tilted back to rest on the right shoulder. The characteristic sound when the harpist runs her fingers up the strings is known as a *glissando*. Notable orchestral passages with harp appear in Berlioz's *Symphonie Fantastique* and *Enfance du Christ*, Saint-Saëns's Concert Piece for Harp and Orchestra, and works by Maurice Ravel (1875–1937), Paul Hindemith (1895–1937), Benjamin Britten (1913–1976), Witold Lutoslawski (1913–1994), Luciano Berio (1925–   ), Hans Werner Henze (1926–   ), and Alfred Schnittke (1934–1998). Famous harpists include Nancy Allen, Sidonie Goossens, Marisa Robles, and, of course, Harpo Marx.

Guitar The guitar is a descendant of the lute family (unlike the violin, viola, cello, and bass, which are viols). Instruments similar to the guitar we know today already existed in the thirteenth century, and it was used to accompany voice as well as for chamber music. In the sixteenth and seventeenth centuries it was a popular chamber instrument in Italy and Spain. It had a slight decline for a while but then was redesigned to have six strings (as opposed to the earlier four or five) and in the first decades of the nineteenth century the guitar had a golden age with works by the Italians Ferdinando Carulli (1770–1841) and Mauro Giuliani (1781–1829) and the Catalan Joseph Fernando Macari Sor (1778–1839). The most famous performer of classical guitar music was Andrés Segovia (1893–1987), who not only played most of the notable pieces written for the instrument but also *transcribed* (adapted music written for other instruments) works by J. S. Bach, Domenico Scarlatti (1685–1757), Frédéric Chopin (1810–1849), and Isaac Albéniz (1860–1909). He was also a master teacher, and all the guitarists who followed owe him an enormous debt. Other well-known classical guitarists include Narciso Yepes, Christopher Parkening, Julian Bream, and members of the Romero family. Needless to say, the guitar, whether electrified or not, is the iconic instrument of rock and roll and the blues, and figures in many other forms of popular music.

♪ Woodwinds ♪

This category might be better termed "wind instruments" in that it is wind, in the form of breath, that creates the sound as it passes through the instrument. The fact is that not all "woodwinds" are made of wood. It is probably better to think of instruments that are traditionally called woodwinds in two categories: those one blows air into (such as the piccolo, flute, and recorder), and those in which one blows through a reed to create sound (oboe, clarinet, English horn, saxophone, bassoon). In addition, there are the "wind" instruments we call the brass (trumpet, bugle, cornet, French horn, trombone, tuba) in which one blows into a metal mouthpiece. We will discuss the brasses as a separate section, even though their genesis relates to the development of woodwinds.

The idea of blowing into something to produce a sound probably dates to the dawn of human history. Somebody must have picked up a conch shell and blown into it to discover the sound that it could make. Reeds gathered along the Nile and other rivers of antiquity could be blown upon to make a sound that is a cross between a buzz and a hum. Ancient flutes, which were simply long hollowed pieces of wood into which holes were carved, existed in ancient Egypt and long before. Peoples thoughout the ancient world discovered that blowing into animal horns (such as antelope or ram) produced a compelling sound.

Such instruments were not confined to Africa, Asia, and Europe. Ancient peoples in Oceania and Australia produced rudimentary flutes. In the yet-to-be-named Americas there were Mayans, Aztecs, Incas, and peoples all over what are now the United States and Canada who fashioned wind instruments. In ancient times the peoples of the Amazon and the Andes made flutes of clay, bone, wood, cane, and other materials. The Americas had panpipes, which were made of a series of hollowed canes of different lengths that were bound together in a row. Most panpipes were arranged in one or two rows, ranging from large to small, although some panpipes are gathered in a bunch. A musician would create a different note—higher or lower—depending upon which one he blew into. Versions of the panpipe also existed in Africa, Asia, and Europe.

Panpipes, also called "Pipes of Pan," were so named after the Greek god of woods, fields, and flocks. Legend has it that the nymph Syrinx was turned into a reed by a river god so that she would escape Pan's wooing. Pan made a musical instrument with this reed, which is why it is known as the Pipes of Pan. In ancient Greece, and even today there, the instrument is called the syrinx.

The Greeks and Romans also blew into other instruments. Forerunners of modern clarinets and horns included the *salpinx* in Greece and the *lituus* in Rome. The ancient Scandinavians played the *lur,* which was made of bronze and had an elegant curving shape that ended with a flat disk from which sound was emitted. Notably, it had a metal mouthpiece not unlike that of the modern trombone.

One separate category of wind instruments did not make it into the classical orchestra but survives to this day in traditional music. This is the bagpipe, whose origin is probably with shepherds, made of an animal bladder that inflates when air is blown into it. At least two pipes come out of the "bag." One, the chanter, has finger holes on it, while the other, the drone, does not. The player manipulates the flow of air and does fingering to achieve certain notes. The best-known bagpipes are those of Scotland and Brittany, but they are found throughout Europe (the *zampogna* from Italy is quite popular) as well as India and the Middle East.

Once the ancients discovered all of these means of producing sounds with air, it was only a matter of time until all manner of wind instruments evolved. Many of the intermediate instruments are no longer in use, but the following are important protagonists in most classical music ensembles.

Flute Both the flute and the piccolo, which is half the size of the flute but with the same construction and keys (*piccolo* means "small" in Italian) descend from ancient pipe instruments, usually made of wood, that were designed with finger holes that would be covered or uncovered to change the note that is sounded. Older instruments in this family were often played by wrapping the lips around the top and blowing. The modern flute, known as the transverse flute, is different, although it has antecedents dating back to ancient times. This flute is cylindrical, almost always made of nickel, silver, gold, or stainless steel (though in the past wood was preferred), and is held out to the right to be played. The flautist blows into a mouth hole and then uses both hands to operate lever-connected keys that open or close different sound holes and produce different notes. The flute used today was designed by Theobald Boehm (1784–1881) in the 1840s, and he subsequently made design improvements on other instruments, including the oboe, clarinet, saxophone, and bassoon.

The flute's lower register can be quite soulful and meditative, its middle range clear, and the upper register sunny and penetrating. It often is used to evoke sounds of birds and nature and, in opera, the workings of the mind. It has been part of orchestras and chamber ensembles since the late sixteenth century and many composers have written concertos and chamber music for it. Bach, Handel, Franz Joseph Haydn (1732–1809), and Mozart all created works with flute solos (think of it as the wind equivalent of the violin for its versatility and bright, expansive sound). In more recent times, Claude Debussy (1862–1918), Ravel, Hindemith, Sergei Prokofiev (1891–1953), and Cage have all written music in which the flute is prominent. Among orchestral works, the Brahms Symphony no. 4 and the Symphony no. 9 (*New World*) by Antonin Dvořák (1841–1904) have outstanding passages for flute. The typical orchestra has two or three flutes.

The piccolo is usually played by one of the flautists in the orchestra. It has been used since the seventeenth century, but only acquired permanent status about one hundred years later. Its clear, piping sound—the highest in the orchestra—can occasionally be strident but is usually exhilarating when employed effectively. The best example of this is when the piccolo sings out over the orchestra in the Fifth, Sixth, and Ninth symphonies of Beethoven.

Notable flautists past and present include Jean-Pierre Rampal, James Galway, Paula Robison, Ransom Wilson, and Eugenia Zukerman.

Clarinet Just as the violin and flute have a particular capacity to "sing"—seeming almost like human voices set in musical instruments—so too does the clarinet. Many people consider the clarinet the most expressive voice in the orchestra. Its sound often inspires feelings of love and happiness, and composers use this sound when those sensations are being described. In opera, particularly, it can accompany arias about love. This instrument can also be sinuous and sexy, or suggest wistfulness, darkness, and many other emotions. And when played in jazz or klezmer music by the right musician, it can really swing.

The clarinet, like most wind instruments, uses a reed as part of its sound production. A reed is typically made of cane or other woods and is shaped to fit the instrument in question. The clarinet has a simple one, basically a single piece shaped like the end of a tongue depressor or a little wooden ice-cream spoon. It is inserted behind the mouthpiece and tightened with a sort of screw or clamp (called a ligature). The musician blows into the mouthpiece while placing the tongue against this single reed, whose vibrations go down the length of the clarinet while the musician adjusts keys to cover certain sound holes (there are between twenty-three and twenty-six) along the length of instrument to produce different notes.

The first clarinet was made in 1690 in Nuremberg, Germany, although the one used today dates from 1855. The modern clarinet is made of ebony or coco wood, though some modern ones are made of plastic. It opens into a flared bell from which the sound exits. There are usually two clarinets in an orchestra, though sometimes more. In addition, there might be a bass clarinet, which is larger. Unlike the regular clarinet, which is straight, the bass clarinet has a curving neck like that of a swan and, at its bottom, the bell is much larger and curls upward like on a saxophone. The bass clarinet, as you might expect, plays in a lower register than the clarinet. Another instrument, shaped like the bass clarinet, but smaller, is the basset horn. It is higher in range, and can be found in works by Mozart, Beethoven, Mendelssohn, and Richard Strauss.

There is a great deal of music in which the clarinet is featured. Franz Tausch (1762–1817) was probably the greatest clarinetist of his era, and composers wanted to write for his talents. Mozart loved the instrument and wrote a quintet and a very famous concerto. Bernhard Crusell (1775–1838), was a student of Tausch, was a great performer and also composed outstanding works for the instrument. Carl Maria von Weber (1786–1926) wrote two clarinet concertos. Other great works for clarinet were written by Karl Stamitz (1745–1801), Ludwig Spohr (1784–1859), Brahms, Ferruccio Busoni (1866–1924), Béla Bartók 1881–1945), Darius Milhaud (1892–1974), Debussy, Stravinsky, and Hindemith. Aaron Copland wrote a concerto geared to the talents of the great Benny Goodman, who was equally adept at classical, jazz, and big band music. In orchestral repertory, the clarinet figures prominently in

Schubert's Eighth Symphony, Peter Ilyich Tchaikovsky's (1840–1893) Fifth Symphony, and, most memorably, Gershwin's *Rhapsody in Blue.*

Famous clarinetists include Michael Collins, Benny Goodman, Sharon Kam, David Shifrin, Richard Stoltzman, and Frederick Thurston.

Oboe The first oboes are thought to have appeared between 1610 and 1640, and were used in chamber ensembles and early orchestras almost from the start. The origin of the instrument is thought to be in France, where it was called *hautbois* (or "high wood"). Both the oboe and the bassoon are descendants of the *shawm,* a wind instrument used since before the Middle Ages. It is a narrow wooden instrument with a very particular and penetrating sound. While the flute is clear and the clarinet mellifluous, the oboe is somewhat nasal. Its bell (at the base, where the sound comes out) is much narrower than the clarinet's. It has twenty-five sound holes, all covered with keys. Unlike the clarinet, the oboe is a double-reed instrument. Actually, it uses a single cane reed that is bent and then cut in the middle and attached to a conical brass tube that is inserted into the oboe. The vibrations of the double reed, when played, are part of the oboe's particular sound quality as they cause the air column in the instrument to vibrate.

The oboe is a prominent instrument in baroque works, especially those of J. S. Bach, Handel, and Vivaldi. Notable orchestral pieces that feature the oboe are the second Brandenburg Concerto by J. S. Bach and the Concerto for Orchestra by Bartók. The most famous oboist is Heinz Holliger; others include Evelyn Rothwell, Jean-Claude Malgoire, and Leon Goossens.

English Horn This instrument is related to the oboe in sound and design (wood construction and double reed), except that while the oboe is straight, this one curves significantly. There is some debate as to the real name of this instrument, which originally was used for hunting and probably was born in France or perhaps Germany. It is probable that it was called *cor anglé* (angled horn) because of its shape, but came to be pronounced *cor anglais* (English horn). Its sound is similar to the oboe, but deeper and somewhat dreamy. It appears in many orchestral pieces, with particular prominence in works by J. S. Bach, Haydn, Gioacchino Rossini's (1792–1868) *William Tell* Overture, Berlioz (*Roman Carnival* Overture), Giacomo Meyerbeer (1791–1864), Dvořák (Symphony no. 9), Jean Sibelius (1865–1957), and Karlheinz Stockhausen (1928–   ).

Saxophone Here is the youngest member of the woodwind family that appears regularly in classical music. You probably associate the "sax" with jazz and other popular music, but it was invented in the 1840s by a Belgian named Adolphe Sax (1814–1894) to be used either in military bands or in the orchestra. The instrument is something of a hybrid, with a mouthpiece and single reed like the clarinet, keys similar to the oboe, and made of metals such as copper, zinc, brass, or nickel, with plating in gold or silver. Most of them are bent at the bottom so the bell faces upward and out. Through the years saxophones have ranged in size from the sopranino to the sub-contrabass with the soprano, alto, tenor, baritone, bass, and contrabass in between. Nowadays, most players and composers confine themselves to the soprano, tenor, alto, and baritone. It is thought that the earliest "classical" use of the saxophone was the alto in the opera *Hamlet* (1868) by Ambroise Thomas (1811–1896) and the first symphonic use was in *L'Arlésienne* (1872) by Georges Bizet (1838–1875). Ravel used the sopranino in his *Boléro*, Ralph Vaughan Williams (1872–1958) used the alto in *Job*, and Stockhausen used the baritone in his *Carré*. Saxophones of one type or another appear in concertos by Alexander Glazunov (1865–1936), Copland, Jacques Ibert (1890–1962), as well as in Debussy's Rhapsody for Saxophone and Piano and Heitor Villa-Lobos's (1887–1959) Fantasia for Saxophone and Piano.

Bassoon This is the longest of the woodwinds and the one with the deepest sound. It descends from Renaissance instruments such as the *bombarda bassa* and the *dulcian*. The bassoon is a very long tube with a curving metal tube, called the crook, attached to it. A double bamboo reed is inserted in the crook. There are two types of bassoons: the German, made of maple and with an ivory ring at the top, and the French, made of rosewood and without the ring. The bassoon uses keys to cover the sound holes, much like its smaller relative the oboe. This instrument has a deep sound that nonetheless has singing qualities like a lower version of the violin, flute, and clarinet. It figures prominently in Prokofiev's *Peter and the Wolf*, which you shall soon listen to, in concertos by Mozart and Weber, in Tchaikovsky's Symphony no. 6, and in orchestral works by Mikhail Glinka (1804–1857), Saint-Saëns, Hindemith, Edward Elgar (1857–1934), and Francis Poulenc (1899–1963). The bassoon has a major moment in the sun at the opening of Stravinsky's *Le Sacre du printemps* (The Rite of Spring).

The contrabassoon (also called the double bassoon) is an even larger, deeper bassoon that is quite heavy and hard to manage. It is twice the length of a bassoon, and so is curved around a couple of times, a bit like the digestive track. It has an endpin like a cello's to hold it in place. Handel wrote for it, as did Haydn (in *The Seasons* and *The Creation*) and Beethoven featured it in the Fifth and Ninth symphonies.

Recorder The recorder, like the flute, dates to ancient times and can be found in different versions throughout the world. For many children it is their first contact with playing a musical instrument. It is held in both hands and inserted in the mouth, unlike the flute. In the Baroque era (ca. 1600–1750) there were recorders in many sizes, the smaller ones playing in the higher registers and the larger ones in the lower ranges. They were named like human voices: sopranino (little soprano), soprano, alto, tenor, bass, contrabass. In modern times recorders come in three sizes—tenor, alto, and soprano (this last being the one most children play).

The various recorders often appeared in solo and sonata pieces in the Baroque repertory, especially in works by Vivaldi and Georg Philipp Telemann (1681–1767), but also by Handel, Corelli, and Benedetto Marcello (1686–1739). In modern times it has been used by composers such as Hindemith, Robin Milford (1903–1959), whose *A Prophet in the Land* is one of the rare uses of recorders in the orchestra, Antony Hopkins (1921–   ), Luciano Berio, and Francis Baines, who wrote a Quartet for Recorders and a Fantasia for Six Recorders. By far the most famous recorder player is Michala Petri.

♪ Brass ♪

This family of instruments, all of which require blowing, are referred to as the brass because this is the metal with which they are made. All descend in one way or another from ancient horns that first found application in military and royal contexts, or as part of the hunt. There is a unique nobility to the sound of trumpets and horns that is part of their appeal.

The association with hunting is palpable in certain pieces written for brass instruments. For example, Sonata no. 1 for two horns by Otto Nicolai (1810–1849) has a strong hunting flavor that will probably please most ears, except perhaps those of a fox. The sounds of trumpets, horns, trombones, and the tuba are compelling and exciting, and these instruments require great skill and breath control to play well. The florid trumpet fanfares in the music of Handel are an example of the *virtuosity* (great technique and expressiveness) required of a trumpet player, as is the solo in J. S. Bach's second Brandenburg Concerto.

Some horn players I have met have likened horn playing in many works of music to the act of hunting. In other words, while the strings are sawing away and the flute, oboe, and clarinet are actively engaged, the horn player sits like a hunter in tall grass, waiting for that moment when he gets his big shot. And when the horns start playing, everyone notices. But to play brass instruments continuously throughout a long piece of music would be incredibly taxing. One common feature in most brass instruments is the water key. When a player blows steadily into his instrument, a fair amount of saliva can gather inside, and the water key is used to release the unwanted liquid.

As with strings and woodwinds, brass instruments have ancestors dating back to antiquity. For example, a trumpet-shaped instrument (long and thin, with a bell-shaped opening at the end) was found in the tomb of Tutankhamen in Egypt. Trumpets of gold or clay, dating from the fifth century, were made in Mexico, Colombia, and Peru. Ancient metal trumpets have been found in China and Mongolia.

There are also traditional European horns, including the Swiss alphorn, which are very long and need to be propped on a stand to be played. Originally made of wood, they subsequently were made of metal. The Swiss also made long, slender glass trumpets which, as you might expect, were very fragile. By the eleventh century, long thin metal trumpets, called fanfare trumpets because they were played to announce the arrival of royalty, were common throughout Europe.

Trumpet More than any other instrument in the orchestra (except perhaps when an organ is present), the trumpet really makes you sit up and listen. Its sound is penetrating and sunny, regal and soulful. Its shape is usually described as oval, though that suggests "egg-shaped," when it is really shaped more like a paper clip. At one end is the mouthpiece, and then the tube goes forward, then curves back toward the player, and then curves upward and away from the player, gradually widening to a bell-shaped opening from which the sound is emitted. The instrument is held in the left hand and in the middle of the trumpet are three valve pistons that can be depressed by the second, third, and fourth fingers of the right hand. Opening a valve allows air to pass into the tubes below, which lowers the pitch of a note.

The trumpet, like most brass instruments, comes equipped with mutes. These are variously shaped pieces of metal, wood, plastic, or papier-mâché that can be inserted into the bell to muffle the sound, which creates a more subdued, less bright sound.

Modern trumpets date from the mid–nineteenth century, and earlier versions were suited to their times. An instrument called the *clarino* had no valves, was about seven feet (two-plus meters) long, and had a thinner, less brilliant sound. Early composers who wrote music featuring the trumpet—Monteverdi, who first included it in an orchestra in

1607, Torelli, Vivaldi, Handel, Telemann, and Johann Nepomuk Hummel (1778–1837)—probably envisioned different trumpets from the ones used today. Perhaps the most popular music for trumpet, and one of the most beloved of all classical music works, is the trumpet concerto by Haydn.

Beethoven featured the instrument prominently in the overtures he composed for his opera *Fidelio* (he wrote four before declaring himself satisfied; the first three are called the *Leonore* Overtures). The trumpet is an essential part of Gustav Mahler's (1860–1911) Second and Third symphonies and in chamber music by Saint-Saëns, Hindemith, Poulenc, Shostakovich, and Henze. It is also an essential part of Copland's *Fanfare for the Common Man*.

An average orchestra will have two or three trumpets. There are many other instruments that fall under the heading of trumpet. These include the piccolo trumpet (also called Bach trumpet), which is played where a clarino was once called for. A bass trumpet is an *octave* (eight notes) lower than a standard trumpet. You can hear it in Stravinsky's *Rite of Spring*. The Aïda trumpet was built expressly for Giuseppe Verdi's opera to be played by musicians onstage during the Triumphal Scene in Act II. It looks like the long trumpets of antiquity but has a more modern sound. The alto trumpet, built specifically for Rimsky-Korsakov, sounds lower than a standard trumpet but higher than a bass trumpet. The cornet is a bit larger than a trumpet and has a more assertive sound. It is popular in marching bands, but also is used in classical music.

Needless to say, the trumpet is one of the cardinal instruments of jazz, and it is hard to think of it without seeing the faces of Louis Armstrong, Dizzy Gillespie, or Wynton Marsalis behind it. Marsalis is equally accomplished in the classical repertory. Other notable classical trumpeters include Maurice André, Adolph Herseth, Pierre-Jacques Thibaud, Edward Tarr, and Håkan Hardenberger.

French Horn This instrument, with its flamboyant curves, funnel-shaped mouthpiece, three valves, pistons, tubes, and wide flared bell, is singular and rather dramatic in design. That keen observer and great

musical comic Anna Russell believed that perhaps the best use for the
French horn is as a lady's hat.

Its origins are as a simple hunting horn without all of the attach-
ments described above. While in the ancient past horns were made of
animal horns, they evolved by the start of the sixteenth century to be
tightly coiled and made of metal. About a century later, in France, a
hunting horn was devised that was simply one large loop. In Germany
and England this horn was used in orchestras and called French horn in
English because of its origin. The French call it *cor* (horn), and it did not
enter their orchestras until the 1730s. But it was not until the nineteenth
century that valves were added to make the French horn the instrument
we know today. Instruments called a double horn have four valves,
which enable the player to achieve higher notes.

The instrument is played by blowing into the mouthpiece while
inserting the right hand or a mute into the bell to change the sound or
intonation. The pistons are manipulated with the left hand—the only
instrument in which the left hand performs this task.

Mozart, Beethoven, and Brahms all wrote chamber music for the
French horn. Mozart, Haydn, and Richard Strauss wrote concertos for
it, as did Thea Musgrave (1928–   ). Robert Schumann (1810–1856)
wrote his *Konzertstück* for four horns. The instrument also figures
prominently in Anton Bruckner's (1824–1896) Symphony no. 4 and
Brahms's Piano Concerto no. 2.

The most famous French horn player was Dennis Brain
(1921–1957), for whom Benjamin Britten wrote his Serenade for Tenor,
Horn, and Strings. Other players include Norbert Hauptmann and
Barry Tuckwell.

Trombone The trombone developed from larger members of the
trumpet family. In Italian the word for trumpet is *tromba*, so *trombone*
means "big trumpet." Earlier versions of the modern trombone first
appeared in Europe in the Middle Ages and were known as *sackbuts*.
Later versions more resemble today's trombone, which is shaped like a
compressed letter *S*, with a main tube that has a bell-shaped opening at

the end. At the first curve of the instrument is the mouthpiece. In front of this is a vertical piece with which one holds the trombone in the left hand. Below this, another tube extends away from the player and to this is attached another piece of curving metal known as the slide. The slide has seven positions, each corresponding to a different note that can be played. The trombonist, using his right hand, must be very careful where he positions the slide, or he will hit a wrong note. While the slide trombone is favored nowadays in orchestras because of its exquisitely clear and heart-touching sound, a valved trombone with three pistons (which redirect air in the instrument) is also sometimes used.

A trombone with a higher range is a tenor trombone, and most orchestras have at least two. A bass trombone is somewhat larger and produces a louder, fuller tone. Most orchestras have one. Famous orchestral passages for trombone can be found in Mozart's Requiem, Beethoven's Ninth Symphony, Bartók's Concerto for Orchestra, a trombone concerto by Rimsky-Korsakov, and the Symphony for Trombone and Orchestra by Ernest Bloch (1880–1959).

Tuba The largest and lowest-pitched member of the brass family, it has the "paper clip" form of the trumpet but is held upright and the sound comes up and out of the bell. It has a cup-shaped mouthpiece that extends from the instrument. There are four piston valves. The original term, *tuba*, was Latin and referred to the brass instrument that gave battle calls in the field, and also at funerals and outdoor games. The instrument we know today was designed in Germany in 1835 by Johann Gottfried Moritz and Wilhelm Wieprecht. It can have a boisterous, almost pompous sound, sort of a deep blast, but can also have a deep and serene tone. Tubas come in different sizes that tend to be favored in one country or another.

You will notice the tuba in Berlioz's *Symphonie Fantastique*, Modest Mussorgsky's (1839–1881) *Pictures at an Exhibition*, and Richard Strauss's *Also sprach Zarathustra*. There is a lovely concerto for tuba and orchestra by Vaughan Williams and a sonata for tuba and piano by Hindemith.

Wagner had a special tuba designed (and named for him) that is used frequently in his four-opera cycle *Der Ring des Nibelungen*. The Wagner tuba is softer in sound, combining elements of the tuba, trombone, and French horn. Aside from Wagner, it has been used in works by Bruckner, Richard Strauss, and Stravinsky (his *Jeu de Cartes*).

♭ Percussion ♭

Surely the oldest family of musical instruments, after the voice itself, come under the category of percussion. That which is percussed is struck forcibly. Stick against stick and rock against rock were certainly early forms of percussion, until someone discovered stick against rock sounded different than rock against rock. This is how composers are born!

Technically, the rhythmic clapping of hands can count as percussion and, when they accompany singing, music is being made.

The group of instruments that first comes to mind when speaking of percussion are the drums. They have been part of ritual in ancient societies throughout the world, particularly in Africa, North America, and India, where two small kettledrums are referred to as the *tabla*. Drums in these societies were made of gourds or wood and had animal skins stretched across them. The size of the cavity of the drum plus the texture and tightness of the skin determined the sound of the drum. They were usually played with bare hands.

The large kettledrums used in orchestras (often referred to as *timpani*, their Italian name) are cauldrons of different size, usually made of copper or brass. Timpani have a "membrane" stretched across the top. In the past it was made of animal skin, but now it is plastic. The membrane can be made tauter (resulting in a higher tone) or looser (giving a lower tone) according to the needs of the music and the person playing them. Nowadays this tuning is often done with a pedal, though many timpanists still use instruments with screws on them. The membranes are hit (percussed) with beaters, which are wood sticks that have round heads made of leather, wood, or rubber, each of which produces a distinct sound. The musician strikes the area about one inch (2.5 cm) from the edge for the best sound, and does not hit the center of the drum.

Until the early nineteenth century, timpani kept a rather traditional beat and did not really have their own voice in the orchestra. This changed with Beethoven, Rossini, and Berlioz, all of whom found a larger, more expressive musical vocabulary for the kettledrums. One of the key uses is to suggest rolling thunder and impending storms. The timpani can speak with great power, as in Giuseppe Verdi's *Messa da Requiem*. They come in four sizes, all of which have different ranges of high to low.

Unlike the timpani, which are percussed by a musician standing above them, the snare drum and bass drum stand on their sides and have two membranes instead of the timpani's one. The bass drum is hit with a beater held in the right hand while the left hand stops or muffles the vibration of the membrane as needed. It is also possible to use two beaters for the bass drum. This is a wide instrument that makes a deep sound. By contrast, the snare is thinner, higher pitched, and is often struck with two beaters made of hard wood that taper at the end (think of very hard asparagus). The characteristic sound of the drumroll (often used in operas and films when someone is facing the firing squad) comes from the snare drum. Also in this family, but much smaller, is the tambourine, of Arab origin, and popular in Spain and Italy.

Drums can affect a pulse in music (classical or otherwise) and, depending how they are played, can quicken or slow a pulse as well. There are many other percussion instruments that create a particular, often unmistakable sound that evokes particular sensations and emotions. Think of the crash of cymbals (originally from Turkey) or the echoing resonance of the tam-tam and the gongs, each of which probably originated in China. Bells suggest religion, the passage of time, and certain sounds of nature. They came from Asia to Europe in the sixth century. In addition to the sort of bells you are familiar with, orchestras usually have tubular bells, also known as chimes. This will be a rack of hanging metal cylinders (typically made of 75 percent copper and 25 percent tin), usually between thirteen and twenty, and of different lengths, each producing a different note up and down the scale. They are struck with wooden beaters. The chimes have been used in many works by many composers, including Rossini, Berlioz, Mussorgsky, Ravel, and, perhaps most famously, by Tchaikovsky in the *1812 Overture*. Then there are cowbells (with their dull sound) and sleighbells (with a bright sound).

The triangle, made of bent metal and hit with a metal beater, has its unique pinging sound. Castanets are two lightbulb-shaped pieces of hard wood that clap together either by being moved in the palm of the hand or by being shaken on a stick. They are a typical sound in music that evokes Spain. The clanging sound of the anvil can be heard when orchestras play music from Verdi's *Il Trovatore* and Wagner's *Das Rheingold* and *Siegfried*. The slapstick is made of two flat pieces of wood and make a slapping or clapping sound. Weather can be suggested with rain machines, wind machines, and thunder sheets.

Another category of percussion are the broad, table-like instruments that have a series of rectangular bars or keys that are struck with beaters. The xylophone has between forty-two and forty-eight bars made of very hard wood that sound up to four octaves (thirty-two notes) and have a slightly macabre sound, like the bones of a skeleton. The glockenspiel is smaller and made with metal bars. The marimba is akin to the xylophone, and was invented in the United States in 1910 based on an African folk instrument with the same name. It can be heard in Milhaud's Concerto for Marimba, Vibraphone and Orchestra. The vibraphone is made with aluminum bars, with a brighter sound than the instruments made with wooden bars.

♪ Keyboard Instruments ♪

The family of instruments that have a keyboard is really an outgrowth of percussion instruments. The oldest keyboard instruments are often wooden boxes with metal cords strung within them. When the musician presses a key, it triggers a hammer that strikes a string. Many keyboard instruments have pedals which, when depressed, can prolong or deepen sound.

Clavichord Early keyboard instruments descended from the mono-chord, a medieval sound box with strings strung across it. A bridge (a wooden bar) could be moved up and down the length of the strings to change their tunings, and thus the notes they produced when plucked or struck. This was not unlike the fingerboard of a violin. From the mono-chord came the clavichord, with the *clavi* derived from the Latin for "key." Imagine that these rectangular keys are touched by fingers—in effect, they become extensions of the fingers—and the keys would hit and remain on a particular string for as long as the finger was on the key. This is how notes that were meant to be held for a longer or shorter time would be sounded. The clavichord at first was placed on a table, then on a purpose-built stand, and finally was given legs.

Harpsichord The successor to the clavichord and forerunner of the piano (which is only about three centuries old) was the harpsichord. This instrument enjoyed great popularity from about 1500 to 1800, although the first reference dates to 1397 in Padua, where the instru-ment was called a *clavicembalo*. Each key was connected to a plectrum, originally made of quill but later of metal. The plectrum would pluck the strings, and the sound would last only until it naturally faded away. Therefore, the tone quality was little affected by the player's touch. The characteristic sound of the harpsichord is considerably thinner and more brittle than a piano, yet when played expertly it can present a huge range of emotions and musical ideas. A vast amount of music was written for solo harpsichord, or for the instrument to be played in tandem with other instruments or the human voice. It is central to Bach's Brandenburg Concertos, music by Vivaldi and many Italian composers of that era, and appears in operas by Handel, Haydn, Mozart, and Rossini, who was probably the last important composer to employ the instrument on a regular basis.

In 1722, Johann Sebastian Bach wrote one of the seminal keyboard works, *Das Wohltemperierte Clavier* (*The Well-Tempered Clavier*), whose subtitle said the work was for "young musicians desirous of instruction as well as those already acquainted with this art." It contains wonderful exercises in all of the major and minor keys that form the musical foundation for most any student who approaches a keyboard instrument. These exercises help impart ideas of theory and somehow make the fingers work in such a way that they (and the mind of the musician) come to understand the relationships of keys, chords, and sounds. To the listener, these are not mere exercises, however, but music that is addictive and beguiling. Simple though they sound, these forty-eight preludes and fugues belong on any short list of the great works of music.

A question that remains open to debate is what instrument *The Well-Tempered Clavier* was written for. *Clavier* or *Klavier* means keyboard instrument. It has been performed on the clavichord (listen to the 1963 performance by Ralph Kirkpatrick on Archiv 289 463 601-2), on harpsichord (listen to Wanda Landowska, on RCA 6217-2-RC and 7825-RC), and on piano (try Glenn Gould, Sony Classical SM2K 52600 and SM2K 52603). All are interesting and valid, although the tonal quality of each of the instruments is quite distinct. But these differences appeal to musicians because of their remarkable instructive capability. It is probable that Bach played it on the harpsichord, but he may also have had the piano, the newcomer on the instrumental block, in mind.

Another essential work by Bach was the two-part and three-part inventions originally written in 1720 as an instruction manual for his nine-year-old son, Wilhelm Friedemann Bach. The composer called this the *Clavierbüchlein* (*Little Clavier Book*). He later revised it and renamed the work The *Inventions*. They have been part of the pedagogical method for keyboard instruments ever since. Though written for clavichord or harpsichord, they are now used for the piano, too. Beethoven owned a copy, Mendelssohn performed them, and Chopin used them when he taught students.

Bach was a magnificent harpsichordist and organist, more famous in his lifetime as a performer than as a composer. Wanda Landowska (1877–1959) spearheaded a revival of the instrument and, with it, a rediscovery of much of the music composed for it. Composers in her own era, including Poulenc and de Falla, wrote music for her to perform on this instrument that had seemed so much a relic of another era. In our times, Anthony Newman is one of the foremost harpsichordists.

Piano The piano is surely the most popular of all musical instruments (with the guitar and violin being its only rivals). It is the one instrument that can really communicate the whole musical sound of an orchestra, although the organ can imitate the sounds of many instruments. But someone playing the piano, especially someone who has also conducted a whole orchestra, can use the instrument to bring out the musical characteristics of a score written for many instruments.

As a cross between a stringed instrument and a percussive one, the piano defies easy description. Unlike other major string instruments, which are bowed or plucked, the strings of a piano are struck with little hammers, which make it a member of the percussion family of instruments.

Relative to many instruments, the piano is quite young. Bartolomeo Cristofori (1655–1732) built harpsichords for Ferdinando de' Medici, Grand Prince of Tuscany. Around 1700 he invented an instrument that drew from the harpsichord in many ways, but with an important change: he devised hammers that are triggered by each key that would strike a corresponding string in the sound box. The hammers were covered in leather and, later on, with felt. With this innovation, the fingers had much more control of the *dynamics* of music—how loud or soft, how long a note might be played. Thus, there was room for much more interpretive playing on the part of the performer. It should not surprise you that the piano has attracted musicians and audiences who worship individual expression and statements in music-making.

The whole name of what we call the piano is *pianoforte*, suggesting a keyboard instrument that can be played soft (*piano*) and loud (*forte*). The German name is the *Hammerklavier*, or hammer keyboard instrument.

The first piano had forty-nine keys. Its popularity spread rapidly, and with it came innovations as piano makers in different countries added design and acoustical elements. In the 1720s it reached Vienna, ensuring that the great composers who would follow (Haydn, Mozart, Beethoven, Schubert) would inherit the piano tradition. In the 1730s it came to Lisbon, Madrid, Dresden, and Leipzig (where Bach lived, meaning that he came to know it and write for it). In the 1740s it reached two important capitals: Berlin and London. By the 1760s it was in Strasbourg, Paris, Augsburg, and Brussels. In the 1770s there were pianos in Stockholm, New York, Boston, Philadelphia, Charleston, and on many American plantations. In the 1780s, one could play a piano in Amsterdam, Bern, and Dublin, and by the 1790s they were in Calcutta.

There were two major schools of piano making in the eighteenth century. Although it is an Italian instrument by birth, it soon had an international pedigree. One school is called South German, and included Augsburg, Munich, Salzburg, and, especially, Vienna. These instruments had hammers that struck a string from below, so that hitting a key made the hammer bounce upward. In other words, the hammers moved in the opposite direction from the keys. This was popular in the eighteenth century, but is now obsolete. By the 1780s a piano made in Munich had sixty-three keys.

The English school, which flourished in the second half of the century, saw the thickening of the strings, strengthening of the sound box and frame, and, by the 1790s, an expansion of the keyboard to sixty-eight keys. On an English piano, the hammers went down on the strings, this being the same direction as the keys when pressed.

In 1783, a Scotsman named John Broadwood patented foot-operated pedals, which served to prolong, deepen, and change the sound, giving composer and performer another important vehicle for expression.

One can generalize and say that the German or Viennese piano was softer and drier in sound while the English piano was heavier and more resonant. But that does not mean that one people or another favored a particular piano. The English often played German pianos (especially those made by a Saxon named Zumpe), while Beethoven, Chopin, and Liszt often played on Broadwoods.

Many eighteenth-century composers embraced the piano, especially Domenico Scarlatti (1685–1757), who wrote abundant and beautiful solo music for keyboard instruments (including the piano), and Carl Philipp Emanuel Bach (1714–1788). Then came Haydn, Muzio Clementi (1752–1832), Mozart, and Beethoven. The principal kind of piano work in this era (and one that has continued in one form or another to this day) is the *sonata*. The word suggests a piece of music that is played or sounded (from the Italian *suonare*, "to play").

Before the sonata, many musical pieces were called *suites* and included several movements in different meters and styles, often drawn from dance steps. The sonata, in its most classical form, comes in three or four movements, and came to be admired for its structure, which would also influence the symphonic form.

A movement of a traditional sonata would have three parts: exposition, development, and recapitulation. The exposition is the statement of the main musical themes of the work. It begins in the key in which we say the work is written (for example, Sonata in A Major), and then might shift to another key to give us another view of the theme (it would take on a different sound in a different key). Then a second musical subject will be played in the new key. The development expands upon, or develops, the music of the exposition in new or interesting ways. The recapitulation is a return to the music and key of the exposition, often bringing the second subject back, but this time in the first key of the exposition. Sometimes there will be an additional passage called a *coda*. The word comes from the Italian, and means "tail." In other words, it comes at the end. After the recapitulation, a composer may wish to add a coda as a sort of rounding off. Beethoven, in particular, loved to use a coda.

This three-part structure I described is called the sonata form. It is almost invariably used in the first movement of a sonata, but might be used in all of the movements. Each movement might have new music, or will incorporate passages of music from previous movements, often in intriguing ways. In the traditional three-movement, eighteenth-century sonata, the movements would be termed allegro-andante-allegro.

The first and third (*allegro*) movements would have a happy buoyancy as a general characteristic. The second movement (*andante* comes from the Italian *andare*, meaning to go, flow, or move) moves in perhaps a slower and more introspective way as compared to the first and third. It is in the andante where you will find a lot of variety and personal expression from both composer and pianist. It transports you from the extroverted nature of the first movement to a deeper, more soulful place. Sometimes composers would choose not to have an allegro for the third movement, but would opt for different forms such as the minuet, a rollicking triple-time beat derived from an old dance step. Composers from Beethoven onward often called the third movement a *scherzo* (from the Italian for joke or jest), which would be invested with a considerable amount of musical humor in a marked rhythm, usually in 3/4 time. Mozart wrote eighteen piano sonatas, Beethoven wrote thirty-two, and many other composers subsequently have embraced the form. Among those to use it in the twentieth century were Stravinsky, Karol Szymanowski (1882–1937), Shostakovich, Poulenc, Darius Milhaud (1892–1974), Aaron Copland, Roger Sessions (1896–1985), and Pierre Boulez (1925–   ).

A piece called a piano sonata is usually a solo for that instrument. Pieces named for other instruments often assume the presence of a piano as well. A violin sonata would usually be for violin and piano.

By the year 1800 the piano had exceeded the harpsichord in popularity, and it was the perfect instrument for the nineteenth century, the age of Romanticism. Led by Beethoven, Schubert, Chopin, Liszt, Mendelssohn, Grieg, Schumann, Brahms, and Tchaikovsky (and later by Scriabin, Debussy, Ravel, Satie, Gershwin, and Rachmaninoff), the piano became a physical extension of the body and soul, as ideas and emotions extended from the brain and the heart to the fingers and the feet, and then into the piano. It is remarkable magic when a great pianist transfers his or her interior life to an instrument, which then speaks and sings in the musician's stead. Audiences clamored to witness this, because the music was beautiful and because the sensual intimacy of a great piano performance could provide an intense emotional—and often erotic—charge.

Music for the piano could come either in solo form or in collaboration. There are great long works for solo piano (sonatas and others) in which we marvel at the performer's virtuosity, memory, stamina, and concentration. Yet some of the most vivid works are miniatures—pieces of only a few minutes' duration that express one or more emotions, or call upon the pianist to play fiendishly difficult music that dazzles or gratifies us. Some of these miniatures go by names such as nocturne, waltz, impromptu, mazurka, and songs without words. Larger solo pieces include ballades, polonaises, fantasias, and scherzos.

Although the piano seldom figures in symphonies, the piano concerto is one of the most essential and popular forms of classical music. Since Mozart's time the concerto has typically been in three movements, drawing on many of the structural ideas of the sonata. In the concerto, the piano (or another instrument, such as the violin or cello) is something of a solo voice that is heard on its own and in dialogue with the orchestra.

Mozart wrote twenty-seven piano concertos, many of which are among the greatest in the repertory. Beethoven wrote five, all of them immortal and beloved. (Beethoven also created an unusual work, the Choral Fantasia, for chorus, piano, and orchestra.) Among the many other composers who made important contributions to the piano concerto are Hummel, Schumann, Chopin, Liszt, Grieg, Brahms, Tchaikovsky, Saint-Saëns, Rachmaninoff, Ravel, Scriabin, Bartók, Prokofiev, Shostakovich, Poulenc, Gershwin, Barber, and Copland.

As concert halls got bigger in the nineteenth century and composers and pianists continued to discover the peerless emotional and sonic range of a piano, the instrument itself evolved. One of the changes was in the pedals. Earlier there were two. The left one muted sound, while the right one could prolong it and then suddenly bring it to a stop. In 1879, Henry Steinway introduced a third one that could prolong some notes and eliminate others. In so doing, the brain-hands-feet coordination required of a pianist became more complex, but the performer was given greater musical possibilities.

Through the years, the keyboard of the piano grew. The white keys always represented whole notes (A-B-C-D-E-F-G), while black keys were flats and sharps (such as C-sharp or E-flat). You will learn more about this later on, but suffice it to say for now that an octave is eight whole notes (let us say, C-D-E-F-G-A-B-C) on white keys in which there are also four black keys interspersed. The early piano by Cristofori covered four octaves; Mozart played on a five-octave piano; Beethoven played on a five-and-one-half-octave piano. Chopin had a six-and-one-half-octave piano. By 1860, the piano had eighty-eight keys (seven and one-third octaves), and that is the piano we know today.

The grand piano, that elegant work of art that is the modern incarnation of this instrument at its finest, has a characteristic winged shaped that extends from the keyboard. In this sound box are all the strings, which are stretched along an iron frame. The shorter strings (in the area of the right hand) are for the higher notes and are made of steel. The longer the string, the lower the note. That is why the left side of the piano's sound box extends much farther than the right. Strings for low notes are made of copper. The largest grand pianos are more than ten feet (three meters) long, and they are capable of great power and brilliance.

As you might expect, as the piano evolved so did the music that could be composed for it. A wider keyboard meant more notes that could be composed for. A pianist with immense hands and arms long enough to give him a great wingspan, such as Sergei Rachmaninoff, could compose works requiring awesome physicality. This might present a challenge to a diminutive pianist such as Alicia de Larrocha, who probably could not negotiate some of Rachmaninoff's acrobatic requirements, but whose remarkable fingerwork, dexterity, and emotional sensitivity enabled her to become an ideal Mozart interpreter. Remember: just because Mozart had fewer notes to choose from does not make his work easier or less wonderful to hear.

The question of the grand piano raises another important issue, one that I will explore for all instruments later in this chapter: if Haydn, Mozart, Beethoven, and Chopin wrote for pianos that had a sound different from those of today, are we hearing the music as they envisioned it? Should we play the music of a composer on the instruments of his time, or can the often superior instruments of today bring things to the music that make it even more thrilling than the composer could have imagined?

In chapter 10, which is devoted to the piano, you will meet pianist Emanuel Ax, who discusses the Chopin Piano Concerto no. 1 in E Minor. In his first recording of the work (1978), he used a modern piano and played with an orchestra using mostly modern instruments. His second recording of the same piece (1998) was played on a piano built in 1851 and played with an orchestra using "period" instruments. It is fascinating to compare the sound of the two performances. A piano from the era of Mozart and Beethoven is often referred to as a fortepiano.

The piano is also an essential part of most recitals for the human voice. In the past, one would say that the piano would accompany the voice, and the pianist was called the accompanist. This somewhat servile name has now been largely discarded, because the pianist is a full musical partner with the singer.

It is used in a wide variety of chamber music, in sonata form and otherwise, and especially with stringed instruments. A trio might include piano, violin, and cello, and a quartet would see the addition of a viola. Some chamber music for piano also includes wind instruments, particularly flute, oboe, and clarinet.

The piano is not traditionally a part of symphonies by most composers, though certain works include it as one of the "voices" in the orchestra. Hector Berlioz was the first to include the piano in the orchestra in this way, and now every orchestra has a pianist as part of its roster of musicians.

Organ The organ is the great whale of the family of instruments. Compared to it, the piano is a dolphin. The name derives from the Greek *organon* and the Latin *organum*, each meaning tool or instrument. The organ is unique not only for its size, but also because it is really a conflation of instruments from two families: the keyboards and the winds. In effect, it takes mechanisms of the simple panpipe or flute, and the bagpipe, adds keys and pedals, and moves all of this to an exponentially monumental scale.

Early organs were used in the Catholic Church service as far back as the seventh century, when they were introduced by Pope Vitalius. Pope John VIII ordered one for use in Rome in the ninth century. Various changes and improvements were made through the centuries, removing parts here, adding new elements there. The instrument as we know it today began its evolution in Germany before 1500.

The quality of the sound of the organ relies not only on how this great instrument is constructed but on the room it is placed in. The sound box is, in effect, the room itself. Most organs were intended for specific churches and were custom-built for them. In addition, the highly decorative elements of an organ tended to correspond to the decor of the church.

There are three main elements to an organ: the pipes, the bellows, and the controls. The pipes come in many different shapes, sizes, lengths, and materials, and they all can produce different notes and musical colors. Some are known as flue pipes (open pipes, with stoppers, or stops); others are reed pipes—the reeds vibrate as might a clarinet's. Some pipes are made of wood; others of an alloy of tin (which brightens sound) and lead (which dulls it). Some organs have more than twelve thousand pipes.

The bellows of a modern organ includes a pneumatic system of fans (replacing the hand-operated works of the past), reservoirs, wind-trunks, and wind-chests. This is great underbelly of the organ, the sort of behind-the-scenes of the whole operation. Electricity was not introduced to running the organ until 1867, in Paris.

The controls are on the (up to) five keyboards, plus the pedals, and a panel full of knobs and handles—all of this is known collectively as the console. This is where the organist sits to operate the whole contraption—think of it as the open mouth of the whale.

The organist has to be amazingly dexterous and agile to move about among the controls, employing hand and feet in all directions to pull on levers that open and close stops (when all is open and the organ can be played at full blast, it is known as "pulling out all the stops"). All of this must be done while playing keyboards and moving up and down on gigantic pedals, as if rising up and down on the tongue of the whale while tickling all of its teeth.

Originally, most of the music composed for organ was sacred in nature, so it made sense that most organs were in churches. Bach, in works such as Toccata and Fugue in D Minor, plus many preludes and fugues (including the famous one written in G minor called "the Great G Minor") and in religious works with chorus (oratorios, passions, and masses) gave the organ prominence. Its power served to express the omnipresence of God; the amazing keyboard work created sounds of great mystery that were suitable in a religious context where so many stories are indeed mysterious. One of the most famous interpreters of the Bach organ repertoire was E. Power Biggs (1906–1977), whose recordings are still widely available.

Handel used the organ in *Messiah* and other oratorios. Haydn, Mozart, Beethoven, Berlioz, and Brahms all used it in masses and other religious music.

The organ is also found in symphonic music, most famously the Third Symphony by Saint-Saëns, but also Liszt's *A Faust Symphony* and *The Battle of the Huns*; Mahler's Second and Eighth symphonies;

Strauss's *Also sprach Zarathustra*, plus pieces by Hindemith, Dupré, Poulenc, and Charpentier.

It is a popular instrument in opera, where a smaller, movable organ is preferred. Among these are works by Gounod (*Faust, Roméo et Juliette*); Meyerbeer (*Robert le Diable, Les Huguenots, Le Prophète*); Wagner (*Rienzi, Tannhäuser, Lohengrin, Die Meistersinger von Nürnberg*); Verdi (*Il Trovatore, La Forza del Destino, Otello*); Ponchielli (*La Gioconda*); Massenet (*Manon, Werther*); Mascagni (*Cavalleria Rusticana*); and Puccini (*Tosca*).

Many smaller organs are still quite imposing. One is called the positive, which is the size of a closet with no pedal board. There are barrel organs, which rely on manually turned handles (think of the organ grinder and his monkey), and modern electric organs whose small consoles are fed into pipes in modern churches and concert halls. Movie palaces in the 1920s all had great organs, many of which, sadly, were allowed to decay. The electric organ, a much smaller version of the big old instrument, was invented in 1935. It does manage to convey many of the sounds of a traditional organ, but many listeners feel that the result is not as rich and profound and all-encompassing.

In a related family of the organ are all the electronic small keyboard instruments that vaguely approximate the sound of the organ and are used in rock and roll bands (think of Billy Preston or Sly and the Family Stone). Then there is the family of expandable keyboard instruments that use wind for sound: these include the accordion, the bandoneon, the concertina, and the melodeon. Don't forget the harmonica (also called the mouth organ), prized not only by Larry Adler, Woody Guthrie, and Bob Dylan. There are delightful works for harmonica and orchestra by Milhaud, Ralph Vaughan Williams, and Heitor Villa-Lobos.

Order of Instruments in an Orchestral Score

> Piccolo (if it is an independent part)
> Flutes 1, 2
> Flute 3/Piccolo

Oboes 1, 2
Oboe 3/Cor Anglais (English Horn)
Clarinets 1, 2
Clarinet 3/Bass Clarinet
Saxophones
Bassoons 1, 2
Bassoon/Contrabassoon

Horns 1, 2
Horns 3, 4
Trumpets 1, 2 (3)
Tenor Trombones 1, 2 (3)
Bass Trombone
Tuba

Timpani
Other Percussion

Harp

Piano/Organ

Violin 1
Violin 2
Viola
Cello
Double Bass

♪ Isn't It Authentic? ♪

I am sure you have noticed that the modern orchestral instruments I have described in this chapter are almost always descendants of older instruments from the Renaissance and Baroque eras, themselves often descendants of instruments from medieval or ancient times. Composers writing in the seventeenth, eighteenth, and early nineteenth centuries created music for the instruments they knew. Many of these have been superseded by more modern instruments that often afford more control in production of notes and sound. They also may have a fuller, more textured tone than those that are called "period instruments" or "original instruments."

In the 1950s a movement developed to play music of the Baroque (1600–1750) and Classical (1750–1825) eras on the very instruments for which they were written (or new instruments made in the same way). This concept was controversial at first, but then gradually gained many followers among musicians and audiences, who felt they were hearing authentic sound.

But what is authenticity? Does playing music on original instruments make it sound the way the composers intended, or must we also hear this music in the kind of spaces that were the settings for the original performances? And can a musician trained in modern schools and institutions (conservatories) understand the older style? Did musicians in Bach's day play faster or slower than we do today?

Modern instruments often have powerful, more penetrating sounds, while instruments that are three hundred years old do not always age well and may have a muffled sound. Is this how they sounded when new? We can't really know.

The original instruments movement is important for many reasons, in part because it has encouraged research and exploration on the part of musicians and musicologists who have unearthed wonderful pieces of music that had not been heard for centuries. It has prompted a renewed interest in old instruments and has encouraged contemporary instrument makers to make new instruments in the old style. It has attracted audiences and young musicians who might not have been interested in the big sound that modern orchestras give Bach, Vivaldi, Haydn, Mozart, and even Beethoven.

But in considering this issue I would discard the word *authentic,* which often suggests the way we *think* things were rather than how they actually were. Research can tell us an immense amount, but there are things we cannot fully know. For example, was a piece written in 1650 always performed in the same way, or were different approaches taken even then?

The period instrument movement is strongest in England, Paris, Amsterdam, Vienna, a few towns in Germany, and Boston and Berkeley in the United States. Some of the leading ensembles are the Orchestra of the Age of Enlightenment, the English Concert, the Academy of Ancient Music, Les Arts Florissants, and Musica Antiqua Köln. Among the leading conductors in this area are William Christie, Trevor Pinnock, Roger Norrington, René Jacobs, Reinhard Goebel, and John Eliot Gardiner.

One of the fathers of the movement is conductor Nikolaus Harnoncourt (1929–   ), who founded the period-instrument Vienna Concentus Musicus ensemble in 1953. Vienna is arguably the city with the longest ongoing musical tradition, where one style and sound has come on top of another for centuries, so it was quite a challenge for Harnoncourt to seek to turn back the clock. Here is a city that has heard the sounds of Haydn, Mozart, Beethoven, Schubert, Johann Strauss Senior (1804–1849) and Junior (1825–1899), Brahms, Bruckner, Mahler, Richard Strauss (no relation to the other Strauss family), Arnold Schoenberg (1874–1951), Anton Webern (1883–1945), and Berg, to name only the most famous in a continuous line. The Vienna Philharmonic is one of the world's oldest and most august orchestras, founded in 1842 (the same year as the New York Philharmonic, a remarkable fact given that Vienna and other imperial capitals had long music traditions and the American frontier was far from being closed).

Since its founding, the Wiener Philharmoniker (as the Vienna Philharmonic is known at home) has played the works not only of Vienna's past (Haydn through Schubert) but of all the newer composers when the ink on their new pieces was barely dry. The Vienna Philharmonic has never had a permanent conductor, but instead selects with whom it will perform. This means that most of the great *maestros* of the world have stood on the podium before the musicians, who have been the true guardians of traditions, arbiters of taste, and the ones who most influenced how music would sound.

With all of this history in mind, imagine how audacious and controversial it must have been for Harnoncourt to stand up in Vienna, of all places, and say that music was not being performed the way it was meant it to be. His original intention was to restore what he considered the sound of music as composers and instrumentalists might have heard it 250 or 350 years ago. The key to this effort was using instruments that the composers actually wrote for—such as J. S. Bach calling for a hunting horn instead of a mid-nineteenth-century French horn. But in the process Harnoncourt realized that there was another issue that was just as vital in rediscovering the "original" sound. This is the thorny topic of *performance practice.*

Through the decades, styles and tastes change. While an audience in 1785 may have admired a piece of music—let us say a piano concerto by Mozart—for its rational structure, listeners in the nineteenth century may have sought more romance, more *feeling*, in the work. Perhaps audiences of today might look for clarity or for a soothing sensation in that music. These changes in approach are due to many factors.

First, modern instruments often produce a robust sound. We sit back to listen rather than lean forward. Also, musicians in eras since 1785 became accustomed to performing music of their own day, and the techniques they applied, such as more aggressive attacks on piano keyboards or prolonged use of pedals, which might work for Brahms or Rachmaninoff, would find their way into performances of Mozart. Individual performers through the years might bring their own ideas and interpretations of Mozart to bear on the music, which in turn would influence audiences and the next generations of pianists. If these performances met with acclaim, and especially if they were recorded, then they became our received impression of what this music should sound like. The accretion of these changes and preferences is known as performance practice.

In response to this, the period-instrument movement has sought to turn back the clock, much like wiping decades' or centuries' worth of grime off the façade of a palace to reveal what the building looked like when it was new. What you must ask yourself is whether, after the grime is removed, the building looks as it did when it was new, or whether it is a 250-year-old building that has been cleaned. There is a difference, I believe. We can have an idea of what it might have looked like, but we cannot really know. For example, the buildings or trees that surrounded it may no longer be there, or may look different. The people who inhabit this building look different and dress differently from the ones who were there when it was new.

Another way to think of this is to ask yourself whether music or art is of its time or of all time. There is no answer to this, certainly no simple answer, so it should be part of what you think about when you listen to music. This applies not only to music from the sixteenth through nineteenth centuries. Is the work of Ravel, Alban Berg (1885–1935), Gershwin, Richard Strauss, and Prokofiev *of* the 1920s and 1930s because it might have been composed in those decades? Is the music of Henze, Berio, or Glass *of* today?

The important work of the period-instrument movement, and the conductors and scholars who have led the way, should not be undervalued. They have expanded the ways we hear and think about music. They help us ask new questions and see new things. But if they declare that theirs is the way certain music must be played to be genuine or right, then they do themselves, the music, and audiences a disservice.

As you come to learn the music of all eras as performed on recordings dating back up to one hundred years ago, or in the concert halls played by today's artists, bear in mind that everyone who ever played a particular piece brought his or her talents, point of view, and unique experience to that music. There never has been, can be, or will be a definitive way to play a piece. There is no best, though we can say that so-and-so gave the best performance we have ever heard of a particular piece. But isn't the quest for new meanings and insights more important than reassuring oneself of having heard the best, yet also having to accept that it is now behind us?

One of the joys of living a life with music is that you are part of a grand continuum. And you, my friend, are at the start of this adventure, with so much pleasure to come. So let us proceed.

• ∽ •

Children's Classics; *New York Philharmonic; Leonard Bernstein, conductor; Sony SMK 60175 (Prokofiev:* Peter and the Wolf; *Saint-Saëns:* Carnival of the Animals; *Britten:* The Young Person's Guide to the Orchestra*)*

Leonard Bernstein, in addition to being an outstanding composer, conductor, and advocate for musical and political ideas he held dear, was also one of the most wonderful and natural teachers of music, especially to children. If you were a child in New York City in the 1960s, as I was, it was very likely that you would cross paths with Bernstein in schools, on television, or in the fabulous Young People's Concerts he did with the New York Philharmonic. Since Bernstein, many conductors and musicians have made audience education—especially for children and young adults—a crucial part of their musical activities. I believe that Bernstein's natural heir in this is Michael Tilson Thomas, the excellent conductor of the San Francisco Symphony, who also has all the right gifts to communicate not only the ideas of music, but the *joy* of it.

I was lucky to have a great deal of exposure to Bernstein throughout my childhood and frequent contact with him during my adulthood. I can tell you that when he taught music, children were captivated, as if he were the Pied Piper of Hamelin. The recording you are about to listen to, which I think is unfortunately named *Children's Classics* since it actually engages people of all ages, will give you a splendid sense of Bernstein the teacher. I am going to let him pick up where I left off to fill your head with ideas about what roles and identities instruments can assume in orchestral music.

Create the same listening environment that you did for the Beethoven Seventh Symphony. This will be the ambience you will create for all recordings you will listen to from here forth. Listen only to Prokofiev's *Peter and the Wolf*, track 1 on the recording, with a running time of 26 minutes and 56 seconds (or 26' 56", as we will notate time from now on), and read my comments after you have finished.

• ◦⟩• •

Now that you have heard the piece, read the following observations and think about whether any of these things crossed your mind as you listened.

First, you probably have heard *Peter and the Wolf* in the past. How closely did you listen then and how closely did you listen now?

You heard characters in the story depicted by instruments:

3 French horns	The Hunter
1 Oboe	The Duck
1 Flute	The Bird
1 Clarinet	The Cat
Drums	The Shooting of Guns
1 Bassoon	The Grandfather
4 Stringed instruments	Peter

If you were to hear these instruments again, playing other music, would you recognize them?

The composer, Sergei Prokofiev, was incredibly versatile at using instruments for storytelling, not only in this work but in ballets such as *Romeo and Juliet* and *Cinderella*, in which individual instruments and the music itself tells us an incredible amount about what is happening in the story. You should not take from this that all music, or even all music by Prokofiev, *has* a story. That would be a mistaken assumption, but there are times when a story is told in music, or when literature influences the musical ideas of a composer. But *Peter and the Wolf* was conceived as something of a musical fable and occupies a special place in the musical repertory. Its narration makes it unusual, and you should know that it is not typical that the conductor be the narrator. There are famous recordings of this work with narrators as varied as John Gielgud, Hermione Gingold, and David Bowie.

Before you listen to *Peter and the Wolf* again, read the questions below and see how many things you detected the first time.

- When Bernstein says, "Even the pond was still as there was no wind to ruffle it," listen to the music that follows. What do you see?

- Listen to the musical argument between the duck and the bird as played by the oboe and the flute. Does it work for you?

- Notice the sound of the clarinet, flute, and delicate cymbals as the walking cat pursues the bird. The sounds of these instruments make perfect sense for the action. What do the cymbals add?

- Compare the sound of Peter's running with the Grandfather's walking. Do you hear any relation, any mathematical proportion, between the sound of one and the sound of the other?

- Did you hear the Grandfather locking the gate?

- There is menace, strength, and drama in the first music we hear for the Wolf. If you did not know what this music represented, let your mind run free and think what else this music may say to you. It does not have to have an association with something tangible, but may simply evoke a bunch of feelings or a set of adjectives.

- As the Duck moves faster as she is pursued by the Wolf, compare in your mind—based on memory—what the Duck's music sounded like slower and how it sounds now. Do you hear the pursuit of the Duck by the Wolf? Can you identify the moment he captures her, and perhaps the moment when his jaws open and he swallows her whole?

- Notice the sound of the Bird as it flies furiously above the Wolf's head. How does the use of bells change the sound of the flute?

- In the victory parade, notice how the drums intensify the strings that play Peter's theme.

After you have listened to *Peter and the Wolf* a second time, with some questions prompted by me, you may have begun to realize the questions one can ask, the things one can see and hear when listening to a piece of music. Although there are few pieces of music so overtly narrative as this one, the questions and reactions are similar. If you hear a theme in a symphony played by strings, and then it returns seconded by percussion, this is a new effect, a new way that a composer looks at an existing idea, which is what that theme is.

You may also have noticed that in some circumstances music can be visual. In Prokofiev's piece there is a story, of course, but I also asked you to see other things in place of what we were told to see. How we see what we see is part of the fundamental triumvirate of a musical experience: the composer, the musician, and the listener.

First there is the person who writes the music. That does not change, though there are circumstances in which other composers take certain pieces and create a new orchestration, using different instruments to make us hear things in new ways. Busoni, Brahms, Mahler, and others did this with Bach; Liszt did it with Beethoven and Verdi; Ravel did it with Mussorgsky; and so forth.

Then there is the performer. In some cases it is the person who wrote the music; in most cases it is not. Each person's performance of the same piece of music is somewhat different. And they may interpret it differently each time they approach it.

Finally there is you, the listener. The ideas you get when you hear three or five or ten performances of the same piece of music may differ from one hearing to the next because each one is different, but also because you will be different from one time to the next. For starters, having heard the piece before, you will recognize and be gratified by certain passages, and you will also hear things you did not the previous times. And when you hear this work in a concert hall, each experience will be unique because the audience will be different.

One of the most important thresholds to cross as a listener is to recognize that we develop an ongoing relationship with each piece of music we hear.

• ⌒ •

And now to Camille Saint-Saëns and his *Carnival of the Animals*. This amusing and beautiful collection of musical snippets is the confident work of a great artist who never intended it for public performance. It was a pleasurable exercise for him, meant to be one for music students, but it has now entered the repertory. He takes the simple device of describing animals musically, and he does so vividly.

In this rare case, read my questions and comments as you are listening unless I tell you to listen first. If you wish, you may listen to a track again after reading my comments about it so that you can form your ideas. Start the recording at track 2 and note Leonard Bernstein's remarks about the uses of music.

Track 3, Lions (listen first, then read my remarks):
- Saint-Saëns was very interested in the exotic sounds, smells, and life of the Arab world and, in fact, died in Algiers. Regarding the theme you first heard played by the cellos and basses and then on the piano—does it have an Arabic sound to you? Does it matter that an Arabic theme is applied to a Sub-Saharan animal such as the lion? Or would you have been better off without knowing of Saint-Saëns's interests and just letting your mind have lions suggested to you by the music? In other words, does some superficial information cloud your perception—your pure perception—of the music?

Track 5, Turtles:
- Note how the can-can music that you already know well sounds entirely different when played at a turtle's pace. Think how other music you know well would sound when slowed down or speeded up significantly.

Track 6, Elephants:
- Make note how a theme originally played on violins and flutes sounds on double basses. Having just thought

about how speed affects a melody, now think how a change of instrument—a change of *voice*—affects the melody.

Track 8, Aquarium (listen first, before reading):
• This music, combining piano, strings, flute, and bells, is an evocative little gem which, when we are told that it represents fish in an aquarium, makes perfect sense. But how beguiling this music is even if we don't know what it depicts. In other words, we respond to it as pure music.

Track 13, Fossils:
• Listen as Bernstein plays six melodies individually and then notice how they sound when played in various combinations. Are you able to pick out individual melodies even when they are played with others?

Track 14, Swan:
• While you listen, create choreography in your mind as to how a ballerina might move to this music.

Once the piece is finished, think how much music you can remember if someone said to you "turtles" or "cuckoo" or "fossils" or any of the other segments of this piece. If you cannot hum or sing them, go back to that track and play it again until you think you know it.

Then put this piece aside and proceed to the last work on this recording, *The Young Person's Guide to the Orchestra* by Benjamin Britten, based on a theme by Henry Purcell (1659?–1695), who along with William Byrd (1543–1623), ranked as the earliest great English composer. This piece will give you a definitive sense of how the major instruments fit into a larger entity called the orchestra.

Britten takes a theme by Purcell and has created *variations* (different musical passages always drawn from—or inspired by—the original theme). The idea of theme and variations goes back at least to ancient Greece, and since the sixteenth century this style of composition has been a major aspect of music. We will be exploring this concept more at a future time, but for now it suffices to know that the music you are listening to derives from a single source.

The performance is narrated by young Henry Chapin, son of Schuyler Chapin, a leading figure in the arts world for more than half a century. It bears repeating that this recording with narrated performances is the exception rather than the rule, but happens to be ideal at this point in your journey. From now on, no narration. In many cases, you will provide the ideas.

In *The Young Person's Guide to the Orchestra* Benjamin Britten cleverly introduces you to most of the major instruments of the orchestra and the possibilities inherent in each. You will notice, as you read along on pages 4 and 5 in the program book, that many terms in Italian are listed. These are all common terminology in music, and you will come to know them as you learn classical music. Most of them concern *tempo*, which is Italian for time. Tempo in music means the basic rate of speed of a composition. The terms indicated generally govern a movement (section) of a symphony, concerto, sonata, or other work. In shorter compositions, the suggested tempo may relate to the entire piece.

These Italian words deal with the relative speed at which particular music should be played, as well as what sort of feeling might be suitable. Time, in most things, is an absolute, something we feel we can measure. In music, time and tempo are relative, and vary greatly from one composer to another and one conductor to another. Not only is time relative, but so is each person's concept of what some of the word cues mean. In the piece you are about to learn, the theme is supposed to be played *allegro maestoso* (majestically happy) and *largamente* (broad and dignified). While each of us may have a different idea what "happy", "majestic", or "dignified" means, instrumentalists and conductors must find a consensus during the rehearsal period. This is how the piece is shaped for performance and why no two versions of a composition ever sound entirely the same.

There is a great deal of room for interpretation of the meaning of these words. For example, *andante* in one piece of music may be the equivalent of *moderato* in another. These indications are in Italian and are universally known by musicians. However, with the rise of nationalist feelings in Europe in the nineteenth century, some composers began to list indications in their own languages instead.

Consult the table for some of the most common terms connected with tempo.

COMMON MUSICAL TERMS

accelerando	accelerating, speeding up
adagio	slow, slowly (not as slow as lento)
agitato	lively, agitated
allargando	broadening of tempo or volume; making wide or expansive
allegretto	moderately fast and lively
allegro	fast, lively, merry
andante	moving at a walking pace or steady pace
andantino	moving just a little faster than andante
animando	growing more animated
appassionato	impassioned
assai	very, a lot (such as allegro assai)
a tempo	return to a normal tempo after some deviation

brillante	brilliant, sparkling, vivid
calmando	calming down
cantabile	singable, in a singing manner
con brio	in a spirited, upbeat way
doppio movimento	at double speed
grave	deep, serious, grave
istesso tempo	to maintain the same beat despite a change in meter
largamente	broadly; with dignity
largo	broad
lento	very slow, dragging, sluggish
maestoso	majestic
ma non troppo	but not too much (as in allegro, ma non troppo)
meno	less, fewer
moderato	moderate, middle speed
mosso	lively, animated
molto	much, very, a lot (as in molto grave)
pesante	weighty, ponderous
più	more
poco	a little, not very much
poco a poco	a little at a time, gradually
pomposo	pompously, somewhat grand and overwrought
presto	very fast (faster than allegro)
prestissimo	as fast as possible
rallentando	slowing

ritardando	gradually reducing speed
ritenuto	holding back, immediately reducing speed
rubato	allow some freedom in the time (rubato gives musicians more interpretive leeway than most)
sostenuto	sustained, holding, maintaining
tempo giusto	in strict time; at a fitting speed
tranquillo	tranquilly, calmly
veloce	very, very fast
vivace	lively and forceful
volante	flying; also suggests light and airy

Let us see how these terms are used by Britten with different musical instruments. We shall discuss them according to the tracks of the compact disk.

Track 16 presents us with Purcell's theme played by the full orchestra: "Allegro maestoso e largamente." *Allegro* in Italian means happy, and in a musical context suggests cheerful and fast. *Maestoso* means majestic. *Largamente* means broadly, and in music can suggest slow and dignified. So what we have at first is music that is happy and majestic all at once and then becomes slow and dignified.

Tracks 17 through 20 present the theme as it would sound when played only by certain parts of the orchestra: the woodwinds, then the brass, then the strings, and then percussion. Are you beginning to understand the concept of orchestral voices? Track 21 returns the theme to full orchestra, but briefly.

With track 22 we begin with the *variations on the theme*. I will let you sort out how each variation sounds, and the role of each instrument—each orchestral voice—in making the variations distinct. The first variation, for piccolo and flutes, has no verbal indications from Britten as to how it should be played.

Track 23, for the oboes is lento.

Track 24, for the clarinets, is moderato.

Track 25, for the bassoons, is allegro *alla marcia*. This means with a marching cadence (think of soldiers in a parade marching one-two; one-two, etc.). Pause for a moment and reflect how the bassoon works with marching and try to imagine how this might sound with flutes, oboes, or clarinets. Does it work?

Track 26, for the violins, is brillante–*alla polacca*. This means "in the Polish style" and denotes triple meter. We will explore the concept of *meter* later on, but for now see if you can hear any kind of swirling one-two-three cadence in this music. Don't worry if you can't.

Track 27, for the violas, is meno mosso.

Track 28, for the cellos, does not have an indication. Listen to it and see if you can ascribe a tempo to it.

Track 29, for the double basses, is *cominciando lento ma poco a poco accelerando*, which means starting slow but gradually accelerating.

Track 30, for the harp, is maestoso.

Track 31, for the French horns, is istesso tempo.

Track 32, for the trumpets, is vivace.

Track 33, for trombones and tubas, is allegro pomposo. Think for a moment of the concept of being pompously happy or lively. It may not make sense in life, but it does in music.

Track 34, for percussion, is moderato. Are you able to follow the sounds of the variation when percussion play it? This is a different sensation from hearing the other individual instruments.

Track 35 is the conclusion of the work, the amalgamation of the many orchestral voices. Britten calls this a *fugue*, which is a term found throughout musical composition, perhaps most famously in J. S. Bach. In simplest terms a fugue is a work for two or more voices that sound in contrasting ways, often creating a thick texture in the music. This thick texture is not a requirement, but is often an aspect—a very pleasing one—in a fugue. It is often typical in a fugue for music and orchestral voices to accrete one on top of another until this texture is achieved, making it a sort of summation of what has come before.

The fugue in Britten's *Young Person's Guide to the Orchestra* is a fitting way to conclude your introduction to instruments—the voices of the orchestra. Now we can discover how composers have used these voices in an almost infinite number of ways.

COLORS AND PICTURES
More Thoughts About Listening

This chapter, and the music you discover, is about honing your listening skills. We listen not only with our ears, but with our minds.

Approaching and coming to know classical music should be done through numerous means. Of course, there is the learning you can do about when composers lived and how they influenced one another. There is the necessary time spent getting to know musical instruments and their characteristics. And there is the important work that each of us needs to do alone: finding ourselves in the music. This means making the emotional and spiritual connections to music that will be different for each one of us. To do this, we need to work on self-understanding and honesty. And we also need to use various tools to make ourselves better listeners.

One tool for accomplishing this is to understand that each composer—indeed, each piece of music—has its own *sound world*. By this I mean those unmistakable traits (such as combinations of instruments or preferences for certain combinations of notes) that help us recognize that a piece of music might be by a particular composer. Your goal should not be to "name that composer," but to develop your hearing and sensitivity to music so that you can find pleasure and insight in recognition. But that is a only way into a piece of music, not the end of your journey.

For example, many people may recognize a typical Beethoven sound by its muscularity and heroism, or perhaps its painful introspection. Yet this is only a portion of this composer's style. His early works seem to grow out of Haydn and Mozart and often resemble pieces by those other composers, while some of his last works, such as the string quartets written in 1822, have a sound and character all their own that you would likely not equate with "typical" Beethoven.

Some composers flourished in a wide range of styles and musical genres, and their music is less readily identifiable. This does not make them less appealing; if anything, this versatility and deceptiveness is quite engaging. For me, the most difficult composer to identify is Saint-Saëns, although his music almost always pleases me. Some works by Stravinsky immediately connote the composer, such as *Le Sacre du Printemps*, while works such as *Pulcinella* may entirely fool you.

If this concept is not yet clear to you, think of the visual arts. We see in Michelangelo a human grandeur that is akin to Beethoven's. Most of his work is instantly recognizable as being only his, and it is part of what we admire about him. Similarly, the proportion, rationality, and quiet humanity of Raphael may bring to mind Mozart. The overwhelming versatility and restless genius of da Vinci might make us think of Bach. It is not important that these Renaissance artists were long dead by the time Bach, Mozart, and Beethoven set to work. You should not think that these three German-speaking composers were influenced by the Italian artists. It is better to think of these six men as titans in their fields, and that we can find corresponding identities for them in their separate art forms.

I think there is an interesting parallel between Picasso and Stravinsky. They were essentially contemporaries, lived for long periods in exile from their native lands, and worked in so many styles and phases with such superior accomplishment in most everything they touched that they cast a shadow on all the other painters and composers in their era. Each man was aware of other art forms, including literature, dance, and circus, and was influenced by them. Similarly, they addressed the events of their times, such as war and genocide and the changing role of women.

Yet it is not a given that visual artists and composers necessarily have a kinship. In the visual arts, most painters and sculptors use technique and subject matter that are uniquely theirs. Think of Rembrandt, El Greco, David, Goya, Seurat, Modigliani, Munch, Mondrian, or Pollock. We immediately recognize their work, are fascinated and challenged by their singular visions, and regard them as geniuses.

Similarly, Vivaldi, Handel, Haydn, Schubert, Chopin, Berlioz, Tchaikovsky, Mussorgsky, Debussy, Ravel, Schoenberg, Gershwin, and Glass are all composers whose style, voice, and vision—all components of their unique sound worlds—are unmistakable, yet generally regarded as brilliant.

You can think of music in pictorial terms. Often, certain sounds or passages will summon an image in your head. It may be a picture or setting you know from art or from life, or an image of your own creation. A particular minute of music may bring to mind someone you love, or someone you used to love, purely because sound has brought forth this image in your head.

It is also possible for music to put you in the more abstract world of color. Rather than seeing the moon, you might see an amalgam of shades of white and will not associate them with the moon. Instead, it is simply these colors that you see, with no cognitive or predictable story behind them. In music that suggests fire and flames to you, the picture that comes forth may not be of a candle, a torch, a blaze, or the setting sun. Instead, it could just be an abstract series of shades of red, orange, yellow, gold, and flecks of blue. The image you see of these colors is as valid, and important, as would be a literal picture.

Thinking in colors and pictures is akin to describing a mood or a state of mind. In American English, someone who is blue is downhearted, although in British English and in French, something blue is naughty or risqué. In French it also means meat that is served almost raw. White sometimes suggests purity, and black is often mysterious (though older usage of the word implies something negative). Gray is neither here nor there, as in a gray zone. It can suggest fog, or the color of pearls. Red can be sexy and hot, or can refer to indebtedness. Yellow can mean inexperienced or frightened. It also suggests sunshine, brightness, and joy. Green is the color one is said to become when one is envious, but is also the dominant color in much of nature. Something purple is often overripe, as in prose, or a bit lewd. Pink on little girls is sweet, and to be "in the pink" means to be in top condition. Something brown is muddied and unclear, but as a verb "to brown" means to cook over heat.

The colors mentioned above are the general categories under which many variations and subtleties can find room. Think for a moment how many types of red there must be. Or blue, or most any other color. Each shade is different and creates a different feeling or idea when you look at it. If you think of these many shades in musical terms, they produce different sounds and sensations.

If I were to play a piece of music for you and ask you what colors you hear, they might well change from moment to moment, depending on the sounds and moods in the music. Or it might be that you do not hear any colors, but instead pictures will come into your head. They may be realistic, like a soft green meadow, or a rolling sea with gray, green, and many blue tints in the water, with white foam. Or the picture you hear may be a total abstraction, and no less meaningful because of that.

"Colors" and "pictures" in a musical context mean not only the sounds of individual instruments but the sounds that result when more than one instrument play together. Think of how colors combine to create others and you will know what I mean. Just as combining blue and yellow can create green, combining the sounds of instrument A and instrument B can create sound C. Let us take the analogy further: if you add red to the green, you create brown. So if you add a third instrument to sound C, you might create sound D.

Does this seem too esoteric and theoretical? Think of it this way: a violin plays a melody (call its sound blue). Once it is completed, a viola plays the same melody (call this sound yellow). Then the two instruments play the melody together and the sound we hear is that of neither the violin or the viola alone, but a blend of the two voices (call this sound green). Now, while the violin and the viola are playing the melody, the cello (think red) joins in, also playing the same melody. The resulting sound, combining these three voices with their different colors, creates a sound (call it brown) that is not the violin, viola, or cello alone, but a blend of the three. Then take out the viola and the sound (the color) lightens. Now add a double bass, always playing the same melody, and it darkens significantly. Here we are only discussing strings. But what if a saxophone joined in, playing the same melody? That would produce another color altogether.

The example I have given you is somewhat too literal to apply uniformly to music. But it is a good point of departure to go to those places in your head and your ears where you can identify a *musical color*, knowing that it comes from a different palette altogether than the one a painter might use. Even if you "hear" a real color when you listen to a piece of music, you must recall that all colors have tints and shades (think: timbre) and textures (think: how much paint is applied here—a dot? a brushstroke? a van Gogh–type blob?). You will soon be encountering a work that makes this point. It would not surprise me if, while listening to Stravinsky's *Firebird*, that you hear a range of intense reds, oranges, and golds. But as you listen, you will decide if these are flecks of color, broad sweeping strokes, or intense, concentrated swirls.

Your first recording in this chapter is:

• ∾ •

Ravel: Boléro; *Debussy:* La Mer; *Mussorgsky:* Pictures at an Exhibition; *Berlin Philharmonic; Herbert von Karajan, conductor; DG 447 426-2*

Listen to this recording in the order that the music appears. Normally, I do not consider it important whether you listen to music with eyes open or shut, but for this recording I want you to close your eyes so that these sound worlds enable you to see and hear pictures in your mind.

Claude Debussy: *La Mer* Many music experts consider Debussy (1862–1918) to be among the most significant and influential of all composers (others might include Bach, Mozart, Beethoven, Wagner, Schoenberg, and Stravinsky). This is not to say Debussy was among the best (a word we should eschew in considering music), but that his work and ideas were hugely important in the development of music.

Debussy said, "I am more and more convinced that music, by its very nature, is something that cannot be cast into a traditional and fixed form. It is made up of colors and rhythms. The rest is a lot of humbug, invented by frigid imbeciles riding on the backs of the Masters—who, for the most part, wrote almost nothing but period music. Bach alone had an idea of the truth."

Indeed, Debussy did not seek to emulate any of his predecessors, but sought to write music to express his own ideals. His main interest was the quality of sound, and he cared little for traditional musical forms. He wrote no symphonies, concertos, or overtures in their traditional style, but rather created works for orchestra, chamber music, solo piano works, songs, and one opera.

The Paris of Debussy's time was one of rich artistic ferment and rebellion. In painting, Impressionism was the dominant style, and Pointillism was also in vogue. Writers such as Baudelaire, Mallarmé, Verlaine, and Maeterlinck were deeply involved in Symbolism. It is customary to say that Debussy's work is the musical equivalent of Impressionism, in which formal structures are rejected in favor of a style that emphasizes color, sensuality, exoticism, and a new means to perceive familiar things. Debussy said that he did not believe he was an Impressionist, and felt much closer to Symbolism, in which images and symbols often represented their literal selves as well as underlying ideas.

You will discover and appreciate the whole of Debussy's music when you are much further along in your listening to classical music, but the goal here is for you to listen to his work *La Mer* (The Sea), and determine for yourself what you see and hear.

KEY CONCEPT: *The pictures you see as you listen to music do not have to be realistic or relate to the title of music you are hearing. They can be whatever comes into your head at that moment that connects your life and feelings with the sound world you are in the presence of.*

Now close your eyes and listen to *La Mer*, and only afterward should you read the notes that follow.

Now that you have listened to *La Mer*, what colors and pictures did you see? Of course there is the movement of the sea, but also its power, drama, and serenity. Did you actually see water? Did you envision sea birds, perhaps sandpipers, running along the edge of the water? Were there swells and ominous weather? Did you hear only ominous waves, or also purling waters? Did you see plants, people, sand, or shore? Could you hear wind? Was it day or was it night?

Did you derive your ideas from the combinations of sounds of many instruments, or did different orchestral voices say something specific to you?

The fundamental assumption to this kind of listening is that there is little right or wrong. Whether you think of this music as Impressionistic, Symbolist, or something else entirely, Debussy has given you much more specificity than most pieces of music ever bear. Typically, a musical composition might be identified by the type of music it is (symphony, sonata, concerto, and so forth), which number it is in the works of its type, and the key the music is written in.

Titles often attach themselves to music later on, but are not necessarily descriptive of the music. For example, is one of Haydn's symphonies about London because it is named for that city? Or is Linz portrayed in the Mozart symphony of that name? Mendelssohn gave us some guidance by naming symphonies for Italy and Scotland. Don't forget that even music that claims an influence is still music—a beautiful abstraction.

I think that if you listen again to *La Mer*, as I hope you will, you will hear the sea's never-ending force and power which, in this music, is the undertow of the entire piece. It is a thematic constant in all three parts of the work, even if this music is characterized by endless mutability and fleeting images—just like the sea itself.

Remember, this is not the definitive portrait of the sea and of water. This is how Debussy pictured them and was able to express them. Oceans, seas, and water have been depicted in music by many composers, including Handel, Mozart, Weber, Wagner, Elgar, Britten, Gershwin, and others. Each one is as valid as the next, and they are interesting to compare. For another sense of the sea, this time depicted in words and music, you might wish to listen to *Sea Pictures* by Edward Elgar (*Cello Concerto; Sea Pictures:* London Symphony Orchestra; Sir John Barbirolli, conductor; Jacqueline Du Pré, cello; Dame Janet Baker, mezzo-soprano; EMI 7243 5 56219 2 4). We will be studying Elgar's Cello Concerto later on. Do not listen to it yet—save it for later when we focus on it. For now, listen to *Sea Pictures*.

> KEY CONCEPT: *It is in no way essential or required that you see and hear pictures while listening to music. But sometimes a composer asks us to (as in* La Mer, Boléro, *and* Pictures at an Exhibition*), and many times it simply happens as we listen to a piece whose name is as generic as "Violin Sonata no. 3," but which creates unmistakably powerful and vivid images in our imaginations. Colors and pictures are a useful way of thinking about some works, but do not think you are doing something wrong if no pictures come to your mind's eye.*

· ⟡ ·

Modest Mussorgsky: *Pictures at an Exhibition*

Let us proceed to the next work on this recording, *Pictures at an Exhibition*, which was written for piano by Modest Mussorgsky (1839–1881) and then orchestrated by Maurice Ravel. You can study the piano version for comparison in the future, but for now we will be listening to the orchestral version.

Mussorgsky had a great gift for creating music that was beautiful and deeply connected to the soul. Whether writing great operas such as *Boris Godunov* (much admired by Debussy), songs, or music for orchestra or solo instrument, he imbued his music with great and unmistakable character. In this ability to reach straight for the soul, I rank Mussorgsky with Bach, Mozart, Beethoven, Schubert, and few others.

Mussorgsky was an alcoholic who led a very sad life. His insights into turbulence and unhappiness are powerfully expressed in his music, whose colors and pictures are as much about moods as they are about things. The work we will study was written following the death of the artist Victor Hartmann, who was a close friend.

Imagine yourself walking through a museum or art gallery, promenading importantly and expectantly from one work to another. You have now entered a room with paintings and drawings by one artist, in this case Victor Hartmann. *Pictures at an Exhibition* is not only about what is hanging on the walls but depicts you visiting them. The ingenious thing is that we can insert ourselves into this walkabout because the music illustrates our progress. The movement from one work to the next is done with the same music—the Promenade—but played with different emphasis: allegro giusto, nel modo russico (appropriate happiness, in the Russian way); moderato e con delicatezza (moderately and with delicacy); moderato non tanto, pesante (not particularly moderate, heavily), and so forth. Think about how your pace changes as your mood and feelings are changed by the piece you have just seen. This mood informs the walk you take to the next work.

This composition's great moments come as we stand and regard different works of art. Mussorgsky specifically set about to describe these works in musical terms. If a video, DVD, or CD-ROM could be created that presents these works while we listen to the music, that might be an interesting exercise, but we would not really fulfill what the music expects of us. Look at the names of the works of art, listen to the music composed for them, and then create your own images in your mind. They may or may not correspond in any way to the actual works of art, but that is beside the point. I want you to fire your own imagination.

Remember, as you listen to this piece, that it is the marvelous 1922 orchestral transcription by Maurice Ravel. Mussorgsky's original composition was for piano, which you will encounter in the chapter devoted to that instrument.

Here is the sequence of your visit to the pictures at an exhibition:

1. *Promenade.* This opening theme recurs throughout the piece, but notice how the pace, rhythm, and texture of it changes. Remember, this is you walking.
2. *Gnomus* (The Gnome). Does the depicted character sound menacing?
3. *Promenade*
4. *Il Vecchio Castello* (The Old Castle)
5. *Promenade*
6. *Tuileries.* This is a beautiful park in central Paris. Do you hear children playing?
7. *Bydlo* (The Oxen)
8. *Promenade*
9. *Ballet des petits poussins dans leur coques* (Ballet of the Unhatched Chicks). Do you hear them?
10. *Samuel Goldenberg and Schmuyle* (This painting came to be known as *Two Polish Jews. One Rich, One Poor.*)
11. *Limoges: Le Marché* (The Market in Limoges). Can you picture a bustling market?
12. *Catacombae–Sepulchrum Romanum* (Catacombs–Roman Sepulchre). The grave sounds of this music, depicting Roman catacombs in Paris, connect directly to the next piece.
13. *Cum mortuis in lingua mortua* (With the Dead in a Dead Language)
14. *La cabane de Baba Yaga sur des pattes de poule* (Baba-Yaga's Hut on Fowl's Legs). This recounts the story of a famous witch from Russian folktales who rides through the sky.
15. *La grande porte de Kiev* (The Great Gate of Kiev). We have reached the final work, the artist's architectural rendering of his grand design for a huge gate that would ultimately not be built. You can hear all of Russia in Mussorgsky's music and, especially, Ravel's brilliant expansion of it.

• ❧ •

Maurice Ravel: *Boléro*

Having heard what Maurice Ravel (1875–1937) could do with Mussorgsky's music, let us now move to the French composer's most famous work of his own. Surely you have heard *Boléro* many times before, perhaps in the movie *10*. It is a work of immense popularity— so much so that it irritated Ravel when people praised it. He described this music as "an experiment" from which little should be expected in terms of achievement apart from what it actually does.

Ravel explored ideas of tempo (the speed at which a piece is played) and crescendo (slowly increasing volume) in this work as sort of an exercise. It is a good piece to study for speed and volume, but I think it is particularly important for newcomers to music to also pay attention to the composer's use of so many instruments. Having studied the voices of the orchestra, you can hear in this piece how they are splen- didly put to use—the music is basically the same, but it sounds different depending on which instruments are being played. You might be inter- ested to know that this work was originally commissioned as the music for a rather erotic ballet staged in Paris in 1928.

It is time now for you to listen to *Boléro* and see what pictures form in your mind. Also, try to identify as many musical instruments as you can in this slow and inexorable musical development. Write them down on a piece of paper. Put this book down and listen (don't read on until you have listened).

• ❧ •

Now that you have listened to *Boléro*, let's compare notes. The first time I heard this music, it created a powerful image of a sunrise on the Mediterranean Sea in my head, and this was long before I had ever seen that body of water. It is the strong Spanish-sounding flavor of the music that gave me this idea. From the first tiny reddish flecks of light to the upper rim of an orange-red ball until, gradually, the whole huge hot circle is low in the sky, casting a stunning and radiant glow over everything beneath it. I wonder what you saw.

Here are my notes for the instruments I heard played in *Boléro*. Compare them with yours and see whether we heard the same ones:

1 flute, plucked cellos
Another flute, plucked cellos, snare drum
First flute, bassoon, snare, plucked cellos
Clarinet and first flute
Plucked violins, cellos and basses, oboe, snare
First flute and muted trumpet, snare
Trumpet and saxophone, snare and pluckers
Oboe, pluckers, snare, trumpet
Organ (how lurid sounding it is!), bassoons, snare, pluckers
Trombone, snare, pluckers, flute
Flute, oboes, clarinets, bassoons, snare, pluckers, bowed violins (and
     violas?)
Bowed violins and violas, plucked cellos and basses
Bows, plucks, flute, oboe, french horn, saxophone, 2 harps, 2
     snares, kettledrum
Then all strings bowed, trumpets, trombones, winds, snares,
     harps, tubas
Add sax and French horns
Then bass drum, cymbals, gong
And then CLIMAX

• ⌥ •

Stravinsky: The Firebird; *Scriabin:* Prometheus; *Kirov Orchestra; Valery Gergiev, conductor; Alexander Toradze, piano; Philips 289 446 715-2*

It is interesting to follow *Boléro* with another ballet score, this one being Igor Stravinsky's *The Firebird*. It was completed in 1910, eighteen years before *Boléro*. Which one do you think sounds more modern?

Sergei Prokofiev, the great Russian composer who was nine years younger than Stravinsky, was one of the most versatile composers, writing brilliant symphonies, operas, ballets (especially *Romeo and Juliet* and *Cinderella*), violin concertos, and other works. When he heard the score for Stravinsky's ballet *The Firebird*, Prokofiev observed, "What vivid, almost blinding colors in the score, what inventiveness in all these grimaces and how sincere is the creation. But I could not for a moment be captivated by the music. Where is the music? Nothing but deadwood."

As you listen to this piece, I wonder if you will agree. Bear in mind that it was composed as a ballet that tells a story from Russian folklore of thirteen beautiful young girls, a magic firebird, and death. The story itself would be familiar to Russian audiences, less so in other countries. This ballet had its premiere in Paris, and it delighted Debussy. Do not read the notes in the booklet in the CD until after you hear the music—I want your mind to run free.

What I want you to do with this work is to fashion your own story and your own choreography in your head. Until now, many of the images you may have seen have been relatively static (unless you saw a violent sea in *La Mer*), but *The Firebird* insists on movement.

As always, what you see is not an issue of right or wrong, but is a means of developing your musical imagination. (Leave the Scriabin for listening to later as you study the piano in chapter 10.)

• ◌ •

Panorama: George Gershwin: Rhapsody in Blue, *etc.; various artists; DG 289 469 139-2*

Some of the ideas for *Rhapsody in Blue* came to Gershwin while on a train from New York to Boston, where one of his shows was due to open. First the whistle of the train, then the clackity-clack of the wheels against the rails. He wanted this piece to communicate the sound of what he called "metropolitan madness." The piece premiered on a program of modern American music, much of it jazz-related, that was staged by conductor Paul Whiteman at Aeolian Hall on West 43rd Street in New York. Despite terrible winter weather, there was a huge turnout which included composers Rachmaninoff and Stravinsky and the great violinist Jascha Heifetz. The piece was scheduled in the twenty-second spot on a twenty-three-piece program. As cold as it was outside, it was scaldingly hot within the hall. Much of the earlier music was not well-received, and some audience members began to leave. When Gershwin sat at the piano, more than three hours after the start of the concert, people were still leaving, yet with the first cry of the clarinet, people spun around and returned to their seats. *Rhapsody in Blue* was an instant success and propelled Gershwin into the ranks of "serious" composers. Despite his new acclaim, many critics felt that his facility with popular music undermined his seriousness—whatever that means. At issue is that some critics and audience members seek to categorize, and if certain artists elude narrow definition, they are often thought to be underachievers or lightweight. Rossini faced this problem, despite his great success, and so did Leonard Bernstein.

But Gershwin was undeniably a genius with a keen musical understanding, an unmistakable voice, a veritable fountain of melody, and a relentless innovator. He has often been called the American Mozart. He was a great admirer of Maurice Ravel, whom he considered an unmatched orchestrator. When the two composers met in Paris in the 1920s, Gershwin asked if Ravel might consider giving him lessons. The French composer correctly replied, "Do you want to be a second-rate Ravel or a first-rate Gershwin?" Later on, Ravel asked Gershwin what kind of money he earned for his compositions and, when he heard the American's response, exclaimed, "Maybe I should take lessons from you!"

• ◇ •

Handel: The Music for the Royal Fireworks, Amaryllis Suite, Suite from the Water Music; *Royal Philharmonic Orchestra; Yehudi Menuhin, conductor; RPO Records/MCA Classics MCAD 6186.*

This is an outstanding recording, but most any recording you have of the *Fireworks* and *Water Music* will do.

The Music for the Royal Fireworks was written in 1749, while the

Water Music was composed much earlier, in 1717. As you listen to these two pieces (skip the *Amaryllis Suite,* which was a twentieth-century concoction of great Handel short pieces), see whether you can think of what might suggest that one work was written by a more experienced and esteemed composer (aged sixty-four), while the other was written by a man half that age.

Whether you are listening to the recording I recommend or another one, do not read the program notes until after you have heard the music at least once. When you start to listen, picture a spring or summer day, with great pomp and the presence of royalty. Note that the first piece is called "Music *for* the Royal Fireworks," which may suggest that the music was composed to be timed to the launching of fireworks (as in Tchaikovsky's famous *1812 Overture*) or to be part of a larger occasion. You shall make your own determination on this.

As to the *Water Music,* do you think this music describes water or a body of water? Does it bring to mind anything from Debussy's *La Mer*? Or could this be a river?

What I want you to focus on, in addition to seeing colors and pictures in your head, is the sort of mood this music puts you in. Handel wrote each work on command for specific occasions of very different types, but the music has endured long after memory of the occasions faded away. So the mood it creates for you is important because of the mood and feelings it engenders in you now.

KEY CONCEPT: *All music was new once. This may sound obvious, but it is important to think about for several reasons. Some music, written for particular occasions, was not necessarily intended for repeated hearings. These include many Baroque and religious works. Other music may have been considered inferior and consigned to anonymity until it was rediscovered years later and seen in all of its virtues (such was the fate of works even by masters as great as Bach and Mozart). Nowadays, many composers have a rough time getting a second performance of their new works because audiences were baffled on the first hearing.*

Most of the works you will hear are new to you, and you should endeavor to approach each with an open mind.

• ∾ •

You may listen to any or all of the next four recordings, all of them wonderful, if you wish to deepen your feeling for a sense of depiction of places and national characteristics. Nationalism was an essential component of nineteenth-century European politics and artistic expression. Many painters and musicians—especially those from small countries dominated by a foreign power—sought to evoke the flavor and character of their own nations or peoples in their works. Writers in these countries tried to evoke place and to spearhead a revival of local languages and dialects. Each of the recordings in this group draws from a sense of national pride or dedication to traditions and sounds of home.

De Falla: Nights in the Gardens of Spain; Albéniz: Rapsodia Española; Turina: Rapsodia Sinfónica; London Philharmonic Orchestra; Rafael Frühbeck de Burgos, conductor; Alicia de Larrocha, piano; London/Decca 410 289-2

Manuel de Falla (1876–1946, pronounced: day Fai-yah), Isaac Albéniz (1860–1909), and Joaquin Turina (1882–1949) were part of a group of Spanish composers who drank deeply at the well of traditional Spanish culture and melodies. More than most countries, the music of Spain gives an instant sense of place and innumerable mental pictures, even if you have never set foot on Spanish soil. Spain has attracted many foreign composers—including Bizet, Ravel, Debussy, and Rimsky-Korsakov—who have sought to portray it in music. This recording features the music-making of two great Spanish artists: Rafael Frühbeck de Burgos and Alicia de Larrocha.

• ∾ •

Rimsky-Korsakov: Scheherazade, etc.; L'Orchestre de la Suisse Romande; Ernest Ansermet, conductor; London/Decca 443 464-2

Nikolai Rimsky-Korsakov (1844–1908) played a crucial role in the history of Russian music as the composer who carried on the nationalistic tradition begun by Mikhail Glinka (1804–1857, whom Tchaikovsky described as the acorn from which the tree of Russian music grew), and continued by Mussorgsky and Alexander Borodin (1833–1887). Rimsky-Korsakov was one of the great orchestrators of all time, and often put his hand to unfinished works by composers such as Mussorgsky. He was also a famous teacher of many great Russian musicians, most notably Stravinsky.

This moderately priced recording is full of excellent and varied examples of the composer's work. Read the program notes before listening. The most famous work is *Scheherazade*, which you may well recognize. This is the story drawn from Scheherazade in the *Arabian Nights*, the young woman who must tell a spellbinding new tale each night to save herself from being killed. She tells 1,001 stories, and is allowed to live. What Rimsky-Korsakov does here so effectively is evoke the act of storytelling. You do not have to know the story being told to be entranced. I assure you that you will create your own story spontaneously in your head, just as Scheherazade does.

Much of the music on this recording should remind you of the fact that Russia is not only a European country but an Asian one as well. Close your eyes as you listen, and you will find yourself swept away to exotic locales.

· ∾ ·

Johann Strauss: Waltzes: The Blue Danube; Wiener Philharmoniker; Willi Boskovsky, conductor; London/Decca 443 473-2.

There is also a one-disc version on London/Decca 289 467 413-2. For an enjoyable live performance, try *The 1992 New Year's Concert* with the same orchestra led by Carlos Kleiber, Sony SK 48376.

Few cities, if any, can rival Vienna in the number of brilliant composers who have lived and worked there. Vienna has had Haydn, Mozart,

Beethoven, Schubert, Brahms, Mahler, Schoenberg, and Berg, to name only the most famous. Yet for many music lovers, especially those in the Austrian capital, no other composer comes close to rivaling Johann Strauss Jr. (1826–1899) in affection. His father, a composer, wanted the son to become a banker, but Strauss chose to follow in the family tradition. His *Die Fledermaus* is surely the prototypical Viennese operetta, yet Strauss is at least as well known for his waltzes, of which he wrote more than 170.

The capital of the Hapsburg Empire, Vienna was a city of great art that was also carefree and decadent. The nationalism of this music was not about yearning to be free, but was characterized by a good deal of narcissism and self-satisfaction. All of these qualities come forth in Strauss's infectious music, which set the whole city dancing in 3/4 time (the meter for the waltz). "On the Blue Danube" (the first track on the first CD) is practically the Austrian national anthem. You will recognize it instantly.

Aside from the pleasure of listening to this music, you should give yourself a couple of tasks. The first is to create a different story in your mind for each waltz. It does not need to be a narrative but should evoke specific images. The second is to try to make musical distinctions among all of these waltzes as you listen to them. They have great similarities, starting with the meter, so it will take careful listening to make each one distinct in your memory. This is an important skill to develop—that of being able to distinguish among pieces by the same composer that may sound very similar—and this is a good place to start.

• ᦕ •

Smetana: Moldau; Má vlast; *Wiener Philharmoniker; James Levine, conductor;* DG 427 340-2

The Czech Republic, which has included Bohemia and Moravia and, for much of the twentieth century was joined with Slovakia to form Czechoslovakia, has one of the greatest musical traditions of any small European country. Although composers such as Dvořák and Janáček went on to more international acclaim, Bedrich Smetana (1824–1884) in many ways did the most to capture the flavor of the national soul. The Czechs were one of the peoples under Austrian domination, and Smetana was one of the leaders of the drive for independence. He also promoted the use of the Czech language instead of German and was very active in cultivating and documenting traditional folk melodies.

Parts of Smetana's two most famous works are on this recording. The *Moldau* (the German name for the country's leading river; the Czechs call it the Vltava) makes this waterway sound like a bloodstream. It comes from *Má vlast* (My Fatherland), an expression of Smetana's love for his nation. Compare the intensity of the depiction of this river with the lighthearted evocation of the Danube in Strauss's waltz. *The Bartered Bride* is a charming expression in operatic form of Czech pastoral life, and its overture is winning. You will picture yourself in this setting even if you have never been there and have no idea about the subject matter of the opera. Such is the power and quality of this particular music.

• ◈ •

Panorama: Richard Strauss, Also sprach Zarathustra, *etc.; various artists; DG 289 469 208-2*

Before reading any further, put this book down and then place *Also sprach Zarathustra* on your CD player, turn up the volume, shut your eyes, and listen to the entire piece, all 35 minutes of it.

Now I wonder whether you experienced the same sensation I did upon hearing this music for the first time. If you have seen the 1968 film, *2001: A Space Odyssey*, directed by Stanley Kubrick, then you doubtless made an instant association. This poses a different kind of problem: if music is so entirely connected with some image (such as a commercial or film), it becomes difficult to enjoy the music as its composer intended. How long did it take you to get *2001* out of your head?

This music is by Richard Strauss (1864–1948), one of the most important and contradictory composers of all time. He wrote gorgeous melodies, was one of the greatest orchestrators ever, and created a remarkable range of musical output. Some of his music sounds delightfully traditional, almost in the footsteps of Johann Strauss (to whom Richard was not related). His opera *Der Rosenkavalier* is a prime example of this aspect of his work, as is a ballet score called *Schlagobers* (Whipped Cream). Strauss also wrote a plethora of gorgeous songs, mostly for soprano, that are by turns cozy, romantic, sensual, mystical, and occasionally scary. Yet another category of music by this rather bourgeois composer, including the operas *Elektra* and *Salome* and several pieces of orchestral music, is positively revolutionary, and we still need to listen closely to these works to understand aspects of Strauss and his art that his more "comfortable" music does not tell us.

Also sprach Zarathustra (Thus Spake Zarathustra) is part of a category of music called the symphonic poem, or the tone poem. These are works that are often the length of a symphony, and marshal similarly large orchestral forces, yet may not adopt the traditional form of the symphony, about which you will learn more in chapter 8. The other difference between a symphonic poem and a traditional symphony is that the former is based on outside thematic (usually literary) material, while this is infrequently he case in the latter.

Early symphonies that have thematic material include Beethoven's Sixth, called the *Pastoral* (1808), a large-scale depiction of the wonders of nature. Berlioz's *Symphonie Fantastique* (1830) is based on literary and personal themes in the composer's life. The incidental music to *A Midsummer Night's Dream* (1826) by Mendelssohn also has elements of what would appear in the symphonic poems of the future.

It was probably Franz Liszt who created the genre with *Les Préludes* in 1848, and in subsequent music inspired by personages and literary figures such as Tasso, Mazeppa, Faust, and Dante. The symphonic poem became a more popular form in the latter half of the nineteenth century and into the twentieth. Famous examples include *Má vlast* (Smetana); *In the Steppes of Central Asia* (Borodin); *Romeo and Juliet, Francesca da Rimini* (Tchaikovsky); *A Night on Bald Mountain* (Mussorgsky); *Psyché, Le Chasseur Maudit* (Franck); *The Sorcerer's Apprentice* (Dukas); *Danse Macabre, La jeunesse d'Hercule* (Saint-Saëns); *Penthesilea* (Wolf); *Pelleas und Melisande* (Schoenberg), *Prometheus*

(Scriabin); *The Pines of Rome, The Fountains of Rome* (Respighi); and *Tapiola, Kullervo* (Sibelius).

Strauss's symphonic poems include *Macbeth, Don Juan, Tod und Verklärung* (Death and Transfiguration), *Till Eulenspiegels lustige Streiche* (Till Eulenspiegel's Merry Pranks), *Don Quixote, Ein Heldenleben* (A Hero's Life), *Aus Italien* (From Italy), *Symphonia Domestica*, and *Eine Alpensinfonie* (An Alpine Symphony). All of these works have brilliant and incisive scoring and orchestration. Strauss's use of instruments as voices with personality and color is one of his strongest suits. His embrace of literature, philosophy, religion, and ethics in his symphonic poems, which I consider portraits, give them remarkable texture and depth. They are not always fully comprehensible on first hearing, so you may wish to return to these works further along in your listening career.

To return to our initial responses to *Also sprach Zarathustra*: my sensation on first hearing this work was profound disappointment. After the incredibly powerful opening, the music seemed to drift off in no definable direction, and I did not know what was happening. I only revved up again when the famous melody returned. But my response was due to not knowing the fact that this music was inspired by the ideas of the philosopher Nietzsche. Strauss said, "I did not intend to write philosophical music or to try to portray in music Nietzsche's great work. I meant to convey by means of music an idea of the development of the human race from its origin, through the various phases of its development, religious and scientific, up to Nietzsche's idea of the superman."

Now does the music make sense to you?

• ∽ •

Vivaldi: The Four Seasons; I Musici; *Roberto Michelucci, violin; Philips 289 468 111-1*

This is an outstanding recording, but most any recording you have of *The Four Seasons* will do.

Antonio Vivaldi (1678–1741) led one of the most colorful lives of any composer. He was born in Venice and became an accomplished violinist as well as an ordained priest; he was called "the Red Priest" because of the color of his hair. He did not let his vows get in the way of a busy amorous life, however. He also taught music in an orphanage and was music director of a church on the Grand Canal that had an all-girl orchestra. He traveled a great deal to cities such as Prague, Amsterdam, and Vienna, often in the company of a pretty singer named Anna Giraud. He had a great skill for ingratiating himself to the right people in each city, and his Venetian charm and cheekiness made him welcome in salons and bedrooms wherever he went. The details of the end of his life—he died impoverished in Vienna—have never been fully documented.

It is unfortunate that Vivaldi's exploits have in some way reduced the seriousness with which he is taken as a composer. Much of his music seems so ingratiating and facile that he is not given credit for the seriousness and craft with which this was achieved. He wrote more than 450 concertos of different types. An *orchestral concerto* gave some special music to the first violin (which he played), but it did not have a sustained solo. In his era, an orchestra contained violins, violas, cellos, basses, and sometimes woodwinds and brass instruments. By contrast, the *solo concerto* featured one instrument that often played in dialogue with the orchestra. These solo instruments included violin, viola, cello, flute, oboe, and bassoon. The *concerto grosso* contrasted the sounds of a small group of instruments with a larger orchestra. We will soon explore an example of these with Bach's Brandenburg Concertos. In Venice, concertos were part of the weekly church service, though they survive as non-religious works.

Vivaldi also produced ninety-four operas (eighteen of which survive) and a vast amount of oratorios, masses, psalms, and secular songs. All of this vocal music would exert considerable influence on the operas and singing styles to follow. At the heart of these was an open-throated approach in which beautiful sound would be used to caress the consonants and vowels of every word that is sung. Also, singers began to engage in improvisation and embellishment to give a personal stamp to that which was being sung.

The Four Seasons is probably Vivaldi's most famous composition and is among the most famous of all works of music. The instruments are solo violin, small string orchestra, and harpsichord. Bear in mind that each season is its own concerto, and each one has three movements. A movement, in music, is a self-contained section of a large composition. For example, most sonatas and concertos are in three movements, and most symphonies are in four movements.

The first concerto is Spring, the second is Summer, the third is Autumn, and the fourth is Winter. Since each of these is divided into three movements, the total is twelve. It might be convenient or interesting to think of each movement as a month, even if Vivaldi did not indicate this. Within each movement are many shifts in mood and image, much as there might be in a month.

To give you a sense of what you might experience with the first movement of Spring, here are my notes for the first movement, which I pictured as late March/early April: "First stirrings of rebirth, birds flapping their wings, feeding their young, the budding and blossoming of trees and flowers—ENERGY. Also, slow evolution of sensual feelings after the initial outburst. A storm. Then warmth."

Put the recording on the CD player, sit back and close your eyes, and listen to The Four Seasons. You might wish to recall, and perhaps write down, the images that come to you. At the very least, write down your images for the first movement of Spring.

I think that if the idea of a symphonic poem or tone poem had existed in Vivaldi's time, The Four Seasons would be cited as the foremost example. You can hear so many images, and Vivaldi's great achievement is that he did this with many fewer instruments than Strauss deployed in his works. Yet the expression of detail is no less specific, even though there are only strings and harpsichord.

Now that you have listened to the amazingly pictorial Four Seasons, I want to mention that Vivaldi actually did map out a schema of visual images and scenes for each movement. In fact, he wrote a poem to describe each season, using these words as a creative springboard for composition.

Take my notes, and yours, on the first movement of Spring, and now read what Vivaldi listed as the images (he had five): Spring's awakening; song of the birds; gushing of springs (and taps); thunder; song of birds.

How do these notes compare? It is very important that you realize that just because you perhaps had different images as Vivaldi, you are not wrong. Frankly, even if all of your images were abstractions rather than concrete, those are no less valid. One of the great things about music, as you are coming to realize, is the degree to which it can stimulate the mind and the imagination. You have read about this in scientific studies, and now you have palpable evidence.

For your reference, here are Vivaldi's images for the rest of the work:

- Second Spring movement: The sleeping goatherd [solo violin]; the rustling of leaves and plants [violins]; the barking dog [viola]. *It is interesting how instruments are paired with sounds and pictures.*

- Third Spring movement: Country dance

- First Summer movement: Languor caused by the heat; the cuckoo; the turtle-dove; the goldfinch; gentle breezes; various winds; the north wind; the lament of the young country lad

- Second Summer movement: Flies and very large flies

- Third Summer movement: Summer storm

- First Autumn movement: Dance and song of country folk; the drunkard; the sleeping drunkard

- Second Autumn movement: The sleeping drunkards

- Third Autumn movement: The hunt; the fleeing beast; guns and hounds; the fleeing beast is slain

- First Winter movement: Frozen shivering and icy snow; horrid storm; running and foot-stamping because of the cold; winds; chattering of teeth

- Second Winter movement: Rain

- Third Winter movement: Crossing the ice; moving carefully and anxiously; falling to the ground; striding boldly forth; the sirocco [south wind]; the north wind and all other winds.

Try this idea: after the Winter concerto, immediately play Spring again and see if it logically follows, as winter inevitably leads to spring and rebirth.

• ∾ •

Holst: The Planets; Orchestre Symphonique de Montréal; Charles Dutoit, conductor; London/Decca 417 553-2 (This has been reissued on other CDs, so just be sure to get one version or another of this particular perfor-mance, recorded in 1987.)

Gustav Holst (1874–1934), a British composer of Swedish descent, was in many ways ahead of his time. He had an interest in Eastern religions, studied Sanskrit, delved into astrology, communed with nature, and believed in the collective and redemptive properties of music long before the Beatles sang, "All you need is love." He was an inspiring teacher, a genuine free spirit, and composed a great deal of orchestral and, especially, choral music that is ripe for rediscovery. It will find renewed appeal in our searching times.

The one work of Holst that is a fixture in the orchestral repertory is *The Planets* (1916), a seven-movement work with names of all the planets except two. Earth was excluded because, presumably, this is the place from which the planets were observed, and Pluto was not included because it had not yet been discovered. The movements, with Holst's descriptions, are:

1. Mars, the Bringer of War
2. Venus, the Bringer of Peace
3. Mercury, the Winged Messenger
4. Jupiter, the Bringer of Jollity
5. Saturn, the Bringer of Old Age
6. Uranus, the Magician
7. Neptune, the Mystic

Now listen to *The Planets*, preferably in a dark room or at night, and see where the music leads you. Only then should you read my comments below.

Do you think that Holst evoked the names and descriptions of the planets he depicted?

Why did he not describe the planets in order—Mercury first, then Venus, Mars . . . ?

How would you feel about this music if I were to tell you that Holst did not attempt to depict the planets in outer space, but rather the meaning of the planets in astrology? He was deeply interested in astrology and, in fact, this music is about astrology, not astronomy.

After having heard this music, tell me if you still think men are from Mars and women are from Venus.

What is the meaning of the wordless female chorus at the end of "Neptune"?

· ❧ ·

J. S. Bach: Brandenburg Concertos *nos. 1–6; Bath Festival Orchestra; Yehudi Menuhin, conductor; EMI 7243 5 68516 2 7*

This is an outstanding recording, but most any recording you have of the *Brandenburg Concertos* will do.

"Music owes as much to Bach as religion to its founder," said Robert Schumann. Richard Wagner said that Bach was "the most stupendous miracle in all music," though Beethoven thought his greatest predecessor was Handel.

So lofty and iconic are many of the works of Johann Sebastian Bach (1685–1750) that they tend to dwarf much that followed. But you could also argue that Bach's music is the rock-solid, unshakable foundation on which all subsequent classical music, and much music in general, is built. I recall that my father, a trombonist whose repertory extended from classical to big band to jazz, told me that what he loved about Bach's music is that it swings. I used to think this remark was a bit of a stretch, even though my father's musical knowledge was nearly unimpeachable. But I have come to learn that many jazz musicians embraced Bach long ago.

In 1936, Fats Waller did a recording of Bach-inspired music. A year later, in Paris, Django Reinhardt, Stéphane Grappelli, and Eddie Smith collaborated on a jazz-inflected recording of Bach music on (my father would be pleased) Swing Records, the first French jazz label. Benny Goodman and a group of musicians did a swinging performance of the composer's works on a record called *Bach Goes to Town*. A pianist named Bernie Nerow did a recording called "Scratch My Bach" before changing his name to Peter Nero. John Lewis, one of jazz's great theorists and the guiding spirit of the Modern Jazz Quartet, did a wondrous jazz version of *The Well-Tempered Clavier*. The great trumpeter Wynton Marsalis, so well known for his jazz performances, is equally at home in classical music.

Obviously, jazz musicians tend not to play most of the instruments Bach composed for, but they are drawn to certain qualities in his music. Bach was a great improvisor, and part of the wonder of his music is that it can be admired for its vibrant, improvisatory feeling at the same time it persuades the listener that every note is unfailingly, inevitably the right one in the right place. But the music also has an incredible rhythmic imperative (what my Dad called swing) that attracts many listeners, among them jazz musicians. Many of their performances are improvisations on his music, itself often derived from improvisation, and that is what makes Bach hot and cool all in the same moment.

When NASA sent the *Voyager* space probe out into the heavens in 1977, the vehicle included a performance of Bach's Brandenburg Concertos, just in case there was someone out there to hear them. Such is the iconic status of this music that, when forced to select the ultimate in "desert island discs," the American space agency deemed the Brandenburgs the best the people of Earth had to offer. I suppose I would be curious to know whether the residents of Venus or Mars believe that Holst portrayed who they are and what their planet is about, but the Brandenburg Concertos would surely be better suited to winning them over to our side.

Given how revered Bach is now, it may surprise you to know that he was more admired for his work as a harpsichordist and a choirmaster than as a composer. In the same era, Handel was more celebrated than Bach because he managed to capture the interest of audiences in large cities such as Venice, Hamburg, and, especially, London, with his highly theatrical operas and oratorios. Perhaps the most successful composer of the time, at least from a financial point of view, was Telemann, who seems to have been the first composer to become involved in music publishing, at which he made a handsome living. And because most of the works he published were his own, they were widely distributed and regularly played. Only Arcangelo Corelli could rival Telemann at that time in the degree to which his published music circulated around Europe.

Bach wrote these concertos to please Ludwig, Margrave of Brandenburg, the local ruler who could offer Bach a permanent position. As it happens, the neatly tied package Bach sent to the Margrave was never opened or played. So Bach did not get the job. The music languished unopened until 1841, one hundred and twenty years after it was composed. In 1723, Bach was offered the job of music director of St. Thomas Church in Leipzig. Thus, he finally found a secure position where he could perform and compose on a regular basis for the remaining twenty-seven years of his life. We will return to Bach later in this book.

These concertos are done in a form referred to as a *concerto grosso*, meaning a large concerto. From the time of Mozart (1756–1791) onward, a concerto was usually composed for one solo instrument, such as a piano or violin, that performed with an orchestra. A concerto grosso was a composition typical of the Baroque era (about 1600 to 1750, spanning from Monteverdi and Gabrieli to Bach and Handel). It usually features two groups of instruments (one large and one small) that would play off each other. The *concerti grossi* of Handel were all for string orchestra and harpsichord, while Bach was much more adventurous.

In the six Brandenburgs, the larger group is string orchestra, and the smaller group is different from one concerto to the next. The first contains two horns, three oboes, a bassoon, and a violin. The second has recorder, oboe, violin, and trumpet. Many music lovers consider this concerto the most sublime, though a case could be made for any one of them. The fifth is more radical musically because it has three distinct musical groupings: large orchestra, small orchestra, and harpsichord. The great variety of instruments here was probably influenced by Vivaldi, whom Bach greatly admired.

Because a whole book could be written just on the Brandenburg Concertos, or on so many other individual compositions of Bach, I want you to use this hearing to focus on colors and, especially, pictures. Without making too many suggestions, I want to encourage you to think in terms of architecture, structure, balance, and proportion. See if you can create line drawings in your imagination. If you wish, draw them on paper too. You will come to understand the rationality that is central to Bach and see that this sort of music was indeed a touchstone for most subsequent composers, especially since Felix Mendelssohn helped lead the rediscovery of Bach in the 1830s.

♭ Every Picture Tells a Story ♭

One can say that everything is, or has, a story. We can talk about a news article, the summary of a business meeting, or the recounting of a romantic encounter, and think of these as stories. In most every case, the story is different depending on who tells it and who hears it. In Latin languages, the words for *story* and *history* are often nearly interchangeable, with the result that events and feelings we experience are soon considered part of our history.

This notion that everything is, or has, a story can also apply to music. We do not always know the precise story in the composer's head that led to the music composed, but that is not important. We do not need to have a detailed understanding of a work's genesis to enjoy it. Most works do not need a road map of symbols to make themselves understood. These symbols, and the stories that attach to a piece of music, become one way to describe a work of music, but not necessarily a way to understand it. These neat analyses expect us to accept their premises, when our perception of music may be completely different.

Musicologists can take apart a work, but they will define it only in terms of music theory, which, ultimately, is technical analysis. Your goal, as a listener rather than a musicologist, is to approach these works first and foremost on an emotional level, leaving analysis for another time. On repeated hearings, if technical aspects reveal themselves to you, or if you find a story in the music, that is fine. This assumes the premise that everything has a story.

There is an entirely different, perhaps opposite, approach. That is, that there is no story or concept behind the work, whose genesis may come from a creative abstraction in the brain of the composer. He may hear a melody or a sequence of notes in his brain because that is part of his gift, but that may be pure music to which the composer does not attach significance or a story. In some cases, the melody may well reflect the mood the composer was in when he created it.

What I am addressing here applies to most classical music. There are, however, many famous pieces that have specific literary or geographic references that they seek to evoke. Works may be inspired by philosophy (Strauss's *Also sprach Zarathustra*), historic events (Beethoven's *Wellington's Victory* or Tchaikovsky's *1812 Overture*), literary characters (there are endless treatments of the story of Romeo and Juliet, for example), or people (there are many works dedicated to patrons or to musicians for whom the music is specifically written).

One of the most omnipresent influences in music is the sense of place. Spain has been portrayed by composers from all over Europe, usually featuring splashes of colorful melody and orchestrations that include castanets, guitars, and other typically Spanish instruments. To a degree, these works mirror the sounds of Spanish composers such as de Falla, Turina, Granados, and Albéniz.

To me, the exploration and depiction of Italy in music is more interesting because it is less predictable and less easily described. You may know that I have written numerous books about Italy and have had the good fortune to spend much of my life there. But this is not the source of my interest in how Italy is portrayed in music. Rather, it is that over the many centuries in which music has been composed by Italians, there is no unmistakable or easily identifiable Italian sound. Instead, Italian composers have represented the sounds and styles of their own eras and, especially, their own personal art.

This line begins with the many composers we call "Anonymous" because their works survive but their names do not. We do know Giovanni Pierluigi da Palestrina (1525–1594), Carlo Gesualdo (1561–1613), and Claudio Monteverdi (1567–1643) as among the leading composers in the Renaissance. Then came Domenico Scarlatti (1685–1757) and other Baroque composers, such as Girolamo Frescobaldi, Jean-Baptiste Lully (a Florentine who changed his name when he went into the service of the French royal family), Arcangelo Corelli, Alessandro Scarlatti, Tomaso Albinoni, and, especially, Antonio Vivaldi, whose sound has come to be equated with a certain spirited Italianness. Vivaldi was something of a bridge between high Baroque and early Italian composers in the classical style (of Haydn and Mozart). These included Francesco Geminiani (1687–1762), Giuseppe Tartini (1692–1770), the notable Giovanni Battista Pergolesi (1710–1736), Pietro Nardini (1722–1793), Luigi Boccherini (1743–1805), Domenico Cimarosa (1749–1801), Muzio Clementi (1752–1832), and Luigi Cherubini (1760–1842), who was especially admired by Beethoven.

In the Romantic era, most of the greatest Italian composers—Gioacchino Rossini, Vincenzo Bellini, Gaetano Donizetti, and Giuseppe Verdi—focused on opera, writing some of the most gorgeous and enduring masterpieces in the form. Because most of these Italians wrote little for the concert hall, the mistaken notion came about, and largely stuck, that Italian composers were not suited to large orchestral composition.

In the late nineteenth to mid-twentieth centuries, most of the leading Italian composers worked primarily in opera, including Amilcare Ponchielli (1834–1886), Arrigo Boito (1842–1918), Ruggiero Leoncavallo (1857–1919), the famous Giacomo Puccini (1858–1924), Pietro Mascagni (1863–1945), Francesco Cilèa (1866–1950), Umberto Giordano (1867–1948), Italo Montemezzi (1875–1952), and Gian Carlo Menotti (1911–   ). Others, including Ferruccio Busoni (1866–1924), Leone Sinigaglia (1868–1944), Ermanno Wolf-Ferrari (1876–1948), Ottorino Respighi (1879–1936), Ildebrando Pizzetti (1880–1968), Alfredo Casella (1883–1947), and Mario Castelnuovo-Tedesco (1895–1968), may have written works for the stage but found at least as much success in the concert hall.

There is another group of Italian composers who avidly embraced the latest and most radical tendencies in music, and wrote works that are not, per se, in the Italian style, yet they represent an important aspect of Italian cultural history that is little studied or appreciated. This group includes Gian Francesco Malipiero (1882–1973), Luigi Dallapiccola (1904–1975), Bruno Maderna (1920–1973), Luigi Nono (1924–1990), Luciano Berio (1925–   ), and Giuseppe Sinopoli (1946–2001), who was best known as a conductor.

I make mention of all of these composers for several reasons. Italy probably has the longest history of musical composition that has been written down, and it is the country that has given us many of the most important instruments. But the prevailing impression of Italian instrumental music for most people seems to end with Vivaldi, with opera then taking over as the only significant musical expression of this country. Because of the indisputable achievements of orchestral composers from other nations, especially Germany, Austria, Russia, and France, the achievements of Italians is overlooked. You should think of Italian "classical" music as you would any other: as part of a great continuum that reflects primarily the views of the composer, and then of the places and time in which he lives.

Foreign composers who have been inspired by Italy have tended to create works that evoke *their* Italy in their sound, rather than one that might include stereotypical musical snippets from Naples or the cadences of a tarantella. Think of it in food terms: until most of the world learned that Italy has an unmatched range of regional dishes and traditions, people thought of Italian food as pizza and spaghetti. Although these are marvelous foods, they are stereotypical in the way they become emblems for a whole nation whose traditions, cultures, and regional distinctions the world is still discovering today.

But composers, I believe, have captured the spirit of Italy in their music, even if there is not a uniform sound. At your convenience you can listen to Bach's Italian Concerto for harpsichord; Mendelssohn's *Italian* Symphony; Berlioz's *Roman Carnival Overture*; Tchaikovsky's *Capriccio Italien* and *Souvenir de Florence*; Wolf's *Italian Serenade* for strings; Elgar's *In the South* Overture or the Symphony no. 2; or Strauss's *Aus Italien*, and then decide what, if anything, is inherently Italian in these works that were all written in, or inspired by, Italy.

Perhaps Liszt was more overtly Italianate in a predictable way in works such as the second book of music (Italy) in his *Années de Pèlerinage* (Years of Pilgrimage), *Sonetti del Petrarca, Venezia e Napoli*, and the part of *Légendes* depicting St. Francis preaching to the birds. But does Liszt's explicitness make his music more Italian, or better music? Not necessarily. Liszt lived in Rome for five years and was greatly influenced by the city, but I believe that his music is more Lisztian than it is Roman.

For comparison, listen to the compositions by Ottorino Respighi that intentionally set out to portray Roman scenes: *The Pines of Rome, The Fountains of Rome,* and *Roman Festivals*. Respighi was born in Bologna and studied there, as well as in St. Petersburg with Rimsky-Korsakov and in Berlin with Bruch. Though Respighi would later live in

Rome and die there, he was no more Roman than Liszt. His influences were pan-European, and his orchestral colors are more akin to Rimsky-Korsakov and Strauss than to other Italians.

Here is a different example: can we say, for example, that Samuel Barber's First Symphony, which he wrote while a fellow at the American Academy in Rome in 1936, has specifically Italian or Roman references in it? I don't hear any, but perhaps there were sounds or cadences that Barber heard that entered the work. But it is probably fair to say that Rome was not a major element in this symphony even though it is the city in which it was born.

⸖ An Afterthought ⸖

You may have noticed, in studying most of the music you have listened to up to this point, that I have not told you too much about the composers before you listened to the music. The reason for this is that I want you to develop the habit to first approach the music purely for what it is: music. We have a tendency in these busy, modern, analytical times of ours to take a few random facts we have and consider them knowledge or, in this case, to assume that the details we know about a composer constitute insight into his work. I encourage you to buck this trend until you dedicate yourself to exhaustive study of a composer's life through reading biographies and, especially, letters he may have written. To start with, there is a collection of letters between Mozart and Haydn that are very illuminating.

But would you really *feel* different about the music of Bach, Handel, or Frederick Delius (1862–1934) if you knew that they all went blind? Would your *understanding* of the music of Beethoven or Bedřich Smetana (1824–1884) change if you factored in their encroaching deafness? Would the fact that Schumann went insane or that Berlioz and Brahms were known to be rather gloomy really tell us what their music *means*? If we hear moments of sadness in their music, is it sufficient to tell ourselves that there is sadness because these men were often sad? No. How, then, could we account for the entire range of emotions expressed in their music, including great exultation?

Probably the most famous example of musical psychobiography concerns Tchaikovsky, who was a homosexual. The received information we have is that he was so undone by this that he ultimately drank foul water that gave him cholera and killed him. Of course, this version came from people writing from the late nineteenth century until the early 1960s. To them, homosexuality was not a sexual preference that was part of a person's integral makeup, but rather an affliction—a disease, even—that was cause for pity or contempt. Many critics dismissed Tchaikovsky's music as sentimental, which is really a coded way of saying it was cheap emotion, which was what might be expected from a homosexual.

More recent research has shown that Tchaikovsky was probably more comfortable with his homosexuality than was originally depicted, and that he may not have committed suicide at all. Composers such as Saint-Saëns and Copland, each of whom is said to have been homosexual, seemed to have led lives that were balanced, fulfilling, and positive. Their music is varied, wonderful, and much admired, and seems to have eluded being thought of as music by homosexuals, but is seen rather as music by composers who happened to be homosexual.

Nowadays, the pendulum has begun to swing the other way, as gays are finally approaching full acceptance and equal rights in most Western societies (although there still is work to be done). Certain gay scholars in major universities who study what they term "Queer Theory" say they can hear when a composer is gay just by listening to his music. They mean this in a positive sense, which is certainly much better than the previous circumstances, but I really believe that it is confining to categorize the work of any artist based on sexual preference or physical or emotional state unless the artist has clearly indicated that his work is an outgrowth of any of these qualities. There is so much more to a person than these facts, and in our fervent drive to ascribe reasons for the things that we sense, we fail to see and hear so much more—the timelessness, the humanity, the humor, the propulsive life force—that is part even of music written by composers in the most terrible situations.

This also applies to composers with negative attributes. Is the music of Wagner, Stravinsky, Ravel, or Poulenc less splendid because all are known or thought to have been anti-Semites? Or that Mendelssohn and Mahler converted from Judaism, probably to advance their careers? Or that Rossini acquired syphilis at the age of fourteen? Or that Handel, Mozart, and Beethoven could often be boorish and incredibly anti-social? Or that Mussorgsky was an alcoholic? These facts may influence what we think of these composers as men, but we must endeavor to separate music from thumbnail biography if we hope to apprehend the many messages and gratifications the music can offer.

If you really think that knowing about composer's life helps you connect to his music, ask yourself this: *does Mozart's music really sound like the work of someone mired in poverty?!*

6

SECOND HEARING
Beethoven's Seventh Symphony

Sweet sounds, oh, beautiful music, do not cease!
Reject me not into the world again.
With you alone is excellence and peace,
Mankind made plausible, his purpose plain.
—Edna St. Vincent Millay, "On Hearing a Symphony of Beethoven"

One of the recurrent issues in the chapter you have just read about colors and pictures and, in fact, one of the central issues of all art, is the topic of inspiration. Where do original artistic ideas come from? Many ideas originate when an artist—that is, a composer, musician, actor, dancer, choreographer, writer, filmmaker, or most any kind of visual artist or designer—views or hears another work of art that triggers an inspiration. This does not necessarily suggest that the artist is stealing or appropriating ideas, but rather that the processes in a creative mind are such that exposure to works of art on a regular basis is usually essential and almost always meaningful. The more we see and hear, even when returning to things that we have already seen and heard, the more we understand.

In a conversation, James Levine observed, "I have never really understood how people can deal with art as a one-time experience. When you know the general terrain from the first time, you begin to see a whole new set of elements with each return visit."

You should think of music this way. Just because you have heard Beethoven's Seventh Symphony already does not mean you know it. When you hear a piece once, you are making your first exploration of its terrain, but even if you are a capable and experienced listener, there are all sorts of things you will not hear. We go back to great works of art because they always have new things to tell us.

Yet you will also be astonished when you listen to it again at how much of Beethoven's Seventh stuck in your head after one hearing, even though you have listened to at least fifteen substantial pieces of music since then. One of the mysteries of the human mind is its ability to retain and sort information of all kinds. You will find that certain passages embedded themselves completely, and you will recall snatches of melody from other parts of the work.

Medical research has shown that memory for language is a left-brain function, as is the facility for perfect pitch (also called absolute pitch). This is the ability to recognize and sing any note. People with absolute pitch have left temporal lobes in their brains that are slightly larger than normal. Although words and individual notes are absorbed in the left brain, the processing and storage of music is a right-brain function. In the act of listening to the pieces you have already been exposed to, you have been flexing muscles and awakening synapses that may have been long dormant. Small children naturally learn a great deal of music until some of them make an active (and unfortunate) decision to resist it. Even if you did not grow up in a musical environment, you have a lot of music stored in your brain, though you may not be aware of it.

Before we go any further, I now want you to play just the second movement of Beethoven's Seventh Symphony. Listen very closely and see how much you have already committed to memory. Some of this may still seem hazy or approximate, so continue to listen very closely, absorbing as much as possible.

KEY CONCEPT: *Just as musicians must endeavor to reconnect to that which is timeless, fascinating, or daring in standard repertory, we listeners must aim to hear these pieces afresh each time we encounter them. If we only listen to them with the intention of revisiting the familiar and being reminded of what we already know, then we miss out on a great area for potential growth and discovery. We need, in listening to music we have already heard, to take what we know and try to build upon it. This means giving fresh consideration to passages we recognize, and paying extra close attention to the music that is still unfamiliar. After all, a composer did not only write the famous parts—every note is there for a reason!*

As you listen to Beethoven's Seventh Symphony again in its entirety, I would like you to focus on various concepts.

First, try to see how much of this music you remember. Some of it may be a faint glimmer. Other parts may be stronger in your memory and, in all likelihood, the second movement will resonate the most.

Second, focus carefully on absorbing as much of this music as you can. This is pleasing music, but not necessarily that easy. By contrast, the Sixth Symphony has a couple of melodies that are more immediate and memorable, but there are parts of the Seventh that will penetrate your imagination quite readily.

Third, think of this whole work as an exercise in experiencing rhythm. You may not yet be able to describe fully what rhythm is, but here you will understand it. At the base of this work is a series of pulsing, insistent rhythms that will enter your mind as completely as any melody. This is an important lesson to consider for a moment. If your ear can detect and remember a musical pattern—which, in effect, is what rhythm is—then you are well on your way to having a sophisticated musical ear. The rhythms in this work were all carefully calibrated, even if they seem indiscriminate and haphazard.

Fourth, this music is not usually thought to have identifiable colors and pictures in the manner that other works you have heard might. So this is the beginning of a process that you can use to perceive music in a more abstract way, acknowledging that most classical music is not about specific visual images, but rather about the nature and juxtapositions of sounds and orchestral voices that appeal to a particular composer. Think of this as you listen to the Seventh Symphony. If Beethoven had images in his head that were not visual or concrete, they are no less meaningful. We know that Beethoven drew inspiration from dance music for this composition, but he probably did not need to see the dances to know what the music meant to him.

Our goal in listening to this symphony, and all music, is not to try to identify a composer's inspirations, but to allow his music to inspire us.

• ◇ •

For this symphony I will give you more descriptive notes than for most music we will later study as a means of having you consider certain concepts. This will also give you some tools and words to use on your own as you listen to other music. Read the following notes as you listen, and see if you hear what I did.

- First movement: There is an efficiently quick orchestral opening, with a thread carried by the oboe. It is contrasted with an upward sweep of violins, cellos, and basses. The introductory music to this symphony is relatively slow and deliberate until it brightens with a vigorous melody led by the flute. In the meantime, voices of oboe, clarinet, French horn, and bassoon are heard in succession, each emerging from the big introductory chords.

  Much of this music, with its abrupt starts, stops, and shifts, has the effect of creating surprise and anticipation. Also, Beethoven is teasingly playing with your memory by implanting snatches of melodic phrases here and there and then simply abandoning them, only to return to them later on when we least expect it. So much of this music can seem fragmentary and indecisive, if you think of it that way.

  Notice a particular effect Beethoven uses: certain orchestral voices here, especially the cellos and basses, have a peculiar churning sound that draws you in, making you eager to hear what is coming next. This is an abstract musical sound effect. It does not represent something, but is used to touch and involve the listener.

• Second movement: The music here is slower than the first but still not slow. Some conductors choose not to slow down this music much at all. As a sensation, it is glowing yet restrained. Depending on the choice of the conductor, it can have a fair amount of pathos and sentimentalism, or it can shimmer without any sad undercurrent. This movement was greatly loved by nineteenth-century audiences and was often played on its own. Listen to how majestically it develops. It is as if a narrow path suddenly opens onto a grand vista, but rather than conclude it this way, Beethoven closes it softly, almost silently.

• Third movement: The mood changes suddenly and dancingly. There is unmistakable exuberance. Notice the lightning-fast way the same couple of notes can course through solo instruments in the orchestra. Here and there are bursts and spasms from the oboe, the strings, the full orchestra, and then from the drums. These are practically drumrolls!

If Beethoven had envisioned this piece as a three-movement concerto or sonata, then the first movement would have been allegro (happy), the second adagio (slower, more introspective), and the third would have been a smiling conclusion. This work, in three movements, might have been popular on its own. And yet, with the fourth movement, Beethoven not only adheres to traditional symphonic form, but endeavors to give us something more, something that crowns what has proceeded it rather than bringing it to a structural conclusion.

• Fourth movement: Wagner called this movement the "Apotheosis of the Dance." It is frenzied, wild, unbridled. Some have called it savage. It unlocked instincts and excitement in listeners who, to that point, may have seen what we now call classical music as pleasant and decorous rather than something that could lift you out of your seats and make you cheer.

This music is swirling, cascading, quicksilver, and mischievous. Twice it sounds as if it is building up to something important, and then, as if in a dance, it seems to take a wrong step. Obviously, Beethoven was not making a mistake but was doing this so the listener's eager anticipation would be stymied and when, on the third attempt, the music goes as expected, one becomes delirious with satisfaction and fulfillment. And then Beethoven takes the music and really runs with it for the rest of the movement, with horns and timpani leading the charge, carrying us along to its wild and exhilarating conclusion.

Catch your breath for a few minutes and reflect on all that you have heard and taken in. Then read what follows.

• ⟨∿⟩ •

Although Beethoven enjoys almost universal acclaim today, and many people say that the Seventh may be an even more popular symphony than the Third, Fifth, or Ninth, there were many critics, especially in the nineteenth century, who were less impressed. Here is an example, from an article in The Harmonicon, published in London in July 1825: "The merits of Beethoven's Seventh Symphony we have before discussed, and we repeat, that . . . it is a composition in which the author has indulged a great deal of disagreeable eccentricity. Often as we now have heard it performed, we cannot yet discover any design in it, neither can we trace any connection in its parts. Altogether, it seems to have been intended as a kind of enigma—we had almost said a hoax."

I will give the last word to Beethoven and invite you to come to your own conclusion. When he was asked why the Seventh Symphony was much more popular than the Eighth, which was written just after, the composer replied, "Because the Eighth is so much better."

• ◇ •

Although you have very fine performances of the Seventh Symphony on both CD sets I recommended, if you have fallen in love with this music, I suggest that you also acquire the riveting and highly personal performance led by Carlos Kleiber with the Vienna Philharmonic Orchestra (Deutsche Grammophon 447 400-2). You will notice that Kleiber paces the Allegretto (second movement) more quickly than the example you heard and, for that matter, most any example you would hear. In looking at the score, one might say that this is as Beethoven would have wanted it, but most conductors now attenuate this music, trying to wring pathos from it and make it stand in starker contrast with the dance-like frenzy that will soon follow.

GOOD CONDUCT

The actions and decisions of a conductor are essential in the development of a classical music performance. He or she leads a group of musicians in the rehearsal and performance of a piece, but also shapes the music to reflect not only the ideas of the composer, but the outlook of the conductor. When you look at the cover of a recording, you will often see the conductor's name and image as large as the composer's. You might see them paired in such a way that you are asked to think that one is indispensable without the other: Karajan/Bruckner; Solti/Beethoven; Bernstein/Mahler, and so forth.

I mention Herbert von Karajan (1908–1989), Georg Solti (1912–1997), and Leonard Bernstein (1918–1990) specifically because these three conductors dominated

the last half of the twentieth century and had the freedom to record just about anything they turned their
attention to. Even after their deaths, music lovers still
speak of them as if they were alive and very much with
us. This ongoing presence is due not only to their recordings, but to the enormous shadows they cast during live
performances.

They, like most important conductors, relied on considerable charisma, formidable intelligence, phenomenal energy and musicality, and the ability to motivate
large groups of musicians to work cohesively and follow
the vision and leadership of the person on the podium.
Each conductor of any consequence seems to have a persona that is part of how he or she is identified. Some of
these personas are cultivated for effect; many of them
are natural outgrowths of the character and temperament of the conductor. In the broadest of terms, one
could generalize about some of these personas, just to
give a sense of how they are often perceived by others, if
not by themselves.

They might be Sphinx-like (Riccardo Muti); a musical
purist (Muti); a passionate educator (Bernstein); a mega-
lomaniac (Karajan and several others); a lovable autocrat
(Solti); a lovable colleague (Sir Thomas Beecham); a
mythical enigma (Carlos Kleiber); a firebrand workaholic
(Valery Gergiev); a versatile and indefatigable leader
(James Levine); and a ferocious yet beloved dictator
(Arturo Toscanini). These are only the most generic
descriptions for men who are all extraordinary artists, but
they do suggest differences in temperament and
approach that can often be heard in music-making.

At the heart of understanding the role a conductor
occupies in a musical performance, you should recall the

title that all are addressed by: *Maestro*. This Italian word means both "teacher" and "master," both of which are central to the conductor's essence.

There are many wonderful anecdotes about conductors and their behavior—some of them actually true—that give you a sense of who they are. Here are a few:

- "After I die, I shall return to earth as a gatekeeper of a bordello and I won't let any of you enter."—Arturo Toscanini to the NBC Symphony
- Someone commented to Rudolf Bing, general manager of the Metropolitan Opera, that conductor George Szell was his own worst enemy. "Not while I'm alive, he isn't!" said Bing.
- "We cannot expect you to be with us all the time, but perhaps you could be good enough to keep in touch now and again."—Sir Thomas Beecham to a musician who could not keep up with the rest of his colleagues during a rehearsal
- The great German conductor Hans von Bülow detested two members of an orchestra, who were named Schultz and Schmidt. Upon being told that Schmidt had died, von Bülow immediately asked, "Und Schultz?"

One of the more perceptive comments I have ever read about how a top conductor makes music came from cellist Yo-Yo Ma, who spoke to the *Boston Globe* in October 2001 about James Levine: "In rehearsal, Levine will say, 'I want the sound to come from the center of that section.' Or he may want it from the principals, or from the back. In short, he has an extraordinary conception of sound, and of the many ways that individuals and groups can combine to create an ensemble sound. It is constantly changing, constantly evolving, and the engine it comes from is not him, but from within the group."

In other words, a conductor cannot merely have a conception and impose it on others, but must implant it in the musicians and then help it bloom.

The more you study music, the more you will be interested in listening to recordings of conductors past and present to gain insight about how the same piece of music can be approached in so many different ways. With comparative listening you will be able to learn more about the music and composers. Some of the great performances of the past are on recordings featuring these conductors:

Ernest Ansermet, John Barbirolli, Thomas Beecham, Leonard Bernstein, Karl Böhm, Willi Boskovsky, Sergiu Celibidache, André Cluytens, Albert Coates, Sergiu Comissiona, Antal Dorati, Oskar Fried, Wilhelm Furtwängler, Carlo Maria Giulini, Nikolai Golovanov, Jascha Horenstein, Eugen Jochum, Herbert von Karajan, Rudolf Kempe, Erich Kleiber, Otto Klemperer, Hans Knappertsbusch, Serge Koussevitzky, Josef Krips, Rafael Kubelik, Erich Leinsdorf, Peter Maag, Igor Markevitch, Jean Martinon, Eduardo Mata, Willem Mengelberg, Dimitri Mitropoulos, Charles Munch, Eugene Ormandy, John Pritchard, Fritz Reiner, Kurt Sanderling, Malcolm Sargent, Thomas Schippers, Tullio Serafin, Robert Shaw, Giuseppe Sinopoli, Georg Solti, William Steinberg, Frederick Stock, Leopold Stokowski, Yevgeny Svetlanov, George Szell,

Klaus Tennstedt, Arturo Toscanini, Bruno Walter, and Felix Weingartner.

It is very often said that there are no good conductors around today, especially when compared to the titans of the past. Some of the work by the greatest conductors of the past century is available on recordings that are part of their legacy. Because they are frozen in time, we can hold them up as a sort of examplar of an older style. But you should bear in mind that, despite all the fine conductors who worked in those times, most of the men who stood on podiums then have been forgotten. Recordings are the souvenirs and valuable touchstones of performance styles and interpretations that merit our attention and admiration, but we should not assume that there are no great conductors today.

When the Philadelphia Orchestra began to look for a new music director (a post ultimately accepted by Christoph Eschenbach in 2001), there were 634 conductors on the initial list prepared by the search committee. As an exercise, I decided to see how many living, active conductors I could name at this writing (in early 2002). This was intended to prove to naysayers that classical music is far from dead, as they insist, and that there are many outstanding conductors leading the much larger number of orchestras than existed fifty years ago. While a select few of these are probably considered the greatest of this era (names such as Claudio Abbado, Daniel Barenboim, Colin Davis, Valery Gergiev, James Levine, Lorin Maazel, Riccardo Muti, and Simon Rattle would probably appear on most lists), there are many excellent conductors who lead vibrant and incisive performances around the world almost every night of the year. Here is my list of many of these:

Claudio Abbado, Roberto Abbado, Yves Abel, Yuri
Ahronovitch, Gerd Albrecht, Marc Albrecht, Rinaldo
Alessandrini, Marin Alsop, Alexander Anissimov,
Marco Armiliato, Vladimir Ashkenazy, David Ather-
ton, Philippe Auguin, Christian Badea, Matthias
Bamert, Daniel Barenboim, Bruno Bartoletti, Daniel
Beckwith, Dietfried Bernet, Gary Bertini, Herbert
Blomstedt, Ivor Bolton, Gerhard Bosse, Leon Bot-
stein, Pierre Boulez, Martyn Brabbins, Iona Brown,
Semyon Bychkov, Oleg Caetani, Daniele Callegari,
Sylvain Cambreling, Bruno Campanella, Giuliano
Carella, Gianluca Cascioli, Riccardo Chailly, Jan
Chalupecky, William Christie, Myung-Whun Chung,
James Conlon, Paul Daniel, Jonathan Darlington,
Thomas Dausgaard, Dennis Russell Davies, Andrew
Davis, Colin Davis, Andreas Delfs, James De Priest,
Edo De Waart, Christoph von Dohnanyi, Charles
Dutoit, William Eddins, Sîan Edwards, Mark Elder,
Philippe Entremont, Christoph Eschenbach, JoAnn
Falletta, Adam Fischer, Iván Fischer, Ermanno Florio,
Lukas Foss, Lawrence Foster, Paul Freeman, Heinz
Fricke, Rafael Frühbeck de Burgos, Daniele Gatti,
John Eliot Gardiner, Valery Gergiev, Michael Gielen,
Alan Gilbert, Roy Goodman, Leonid Grin, Boris
Gruzin, Marco Guidarini, Leopold Hager, Daniel
Harding, Nikolaus Harnoncourt, Eliahu Inbal, René
Jacobs, Marek Janowski, Mariss Jansons, Neeme
Järvi, Paavo Järvi, Vladimir Jurowski, Nir Kabaretti,
Jeffrey Kahane, Djansug Kakhidze, Isaac Karabt-
chevsky, Robert King, Bernhard Klee, Carlos Kleiber,
Kazimierz Kord, Janos Kovacs, Bohumil Kulísnky,
Raymond Leppard, James Levine, Andrea Licata,
Mats Liljefors, Jahja Ling, Andrew Litton, Jesús

López-Cobos, Lorin Maazel, Ann Manson, Zdenek Macal, Charles Mackerras, George Manahan, Anne Manson, Andrea Marcon, Ion Marin, Jun Märkl, Neville Marriner, Salvador Mas, Diego Masson, Kurt Masur, John Mauceri, Zubin Mehta, Steven Mercurio, Ingo Metzmacher, Marc Minkowski, Nicolae Moldoveanu, David Monroe, Carlo Montanaro, Pier Giorgio Morandi, Riccardo Muti, Kent Nagano, Daniel Nazareth, John Neschling, Anthony Newman, Roger Norrington, Gianandrea Noseda, Paolo Olmi, Sakari Oramo, Daniel Oren, Eiji Oue, Peter Oundjian, Seiji Ozawa, Marcello Panni, Antonio Pappano, Yan Pascal, Krzysztof Penderecki, Christof Perick, Zoltan Pesko, Evelino Pidó, Trevor Pinnock, Antonio Pirolli, Michel Plasson, Valery Polyansky, Georges Prêtre, André Previn, Guy Protheroe, Eve Queler, Simon Rattle, Stefano Ranzani, Stefan Anton Reck, Helmuth Rilling, Carlo Rizzi, David Robertson, Stewart Robertson, János Rolla, Mstislav Rostropovich, Gennady Rozhdestvensky, Julius Rudel, Donald Runnicles, Rico Saccani, Esa-Pekka Salonen, Jukka-Pekka Sarastre, Wolfgang Sawallisch, Yeruham Scharovsky, Gerard Schwarz, Christopher Seaman, Leif Segerstam, Alessandro Siciliani, Jeffrey Siegel, Alfredo Silipigni, Yuri Simonov, Vassily Sinaisky, Leonard Slatkin, Lawrence Leighton Smith, Marc Soustrot, Robert Spano, Vladimir Spivakov, Robin Stapleton, Pinchas Steinberg, Michael Stern, Yoav Talmi, Jeffrey Tate, Yuri Temirkanov, Christian Thielemann, Michael Tilson Thomas, Peter Tiboris, Bramwell Tovey, Osmo Vänskä, Mario Venzago, Augusto Vismara, Hans Vonk, Charles Wadsworth, Jonathan Webb, Ralf Weikert, Harold Weller, Franz Welser-Möst, Keri-

Lynn Wilson, Hugh Wolff, Simone Young, Benjamin Zander, and David Zinman.

(I am certain that I have made some glaring omission that will be caught by a sharp-eyed reader.)

Each conductor communicates in a different way, and they must develop a common gestural and visual language that will serve them in rehearsal and performance. Guest conductors, who have a couple of rehearsals and then a performance with an orchestra they may have never worked with before, face a particular challenge in this regard, because they are strangers to one another. Artistic directors of orchestras, who have relationships that can last for decades (Seiji Ozawa spent twenty-nine years with the Boston Symphony), can make the most economical movement of the hand or the flick of an eyebrow and the musicians will know exactly what is being asked of them.

A fundamental question most new music lovers have is on the use of the baton. Almost every orchestra musician I know prefers to be led by a conductor who holds a baton (in the right hand). But I have spoken with many conductors who often prefer to do without one. According to Gianandrea Noseda, music director of the BBC Symphony and artistic director of the Stresa Musical Weeks, "When I am working for the first time with an orchestra, I always use a baton. Musicians can look at the white tip of the baton to know the beat I am leading them with. However, once an orchestra and I have worked together, we have established communication skills that make a baton less essential. Many conductors prefer to do without the baton because, with five fingers, you can express more and bring out details from your players that the single point of a baton can never achieve."

During concerts, I am also fascinated by the left hand of a conductor and often sit on the left side of the auditorium so I can watch this. Whether or not he or she uses a baton in the right hand, the left one is the one that deals with dynamics (speed and volume, etc.) along with the intangible expressive elements that make each conductor's interpretation distinctive. To me, Georg Solti's use of the left hand was a thing of beauty, and one of the reasons the results of his conducting were often magnificent is that he made his ideas and wishes so clearly understood to his players. But there are many other conductors whose left hand helps create memorable music-making, and it is something to pay attention to.

When a conductor and orchestra achieve great intimacy and communicativeness, sometimes hands are barely required. I once saw James Levine step on the podium in the pit of the Metropolitan Opera House, fold his arms and give a simple cue with his eyes. The orchestra played a ten-minute overture relying purely on the cues from his eyes and face, and they played wonderfully! This was not because the music was familiar to them, but because they had rehearsed it so well that Levine felt that leadership—in palpable, visual form—would be extraneous.

Our received image of a conductor throwing his full body into an evening of conducting is probably the exception rather than the rule. Certainly, Leonard Bernstein and some other conductors were often quite energetic and seemed to move with the music, but this is not required for successful conducting. I believe that Bernstein, a highly emotional and impassioned artist, was often transported by the music and was not acting for the amusement of the audience. But most conductors you will see tend to integrate the music into their bodies, hands, gestures, and facial cues in a way that communicates with the musicians but does not make the conductor the center of attention. This is music-making, not gymnastics.

James Levine addresses many of these topics, and more, in a conversation on page 191.

Lest you think that conductors are indispensable, I call your attention to the Orpheus Chamber Orchestra. The accomplishments of this New York–based ensemble have been studied not only by musicians but in business schools seeking models for cooperation, motivation, and achievement. The Orpheus is run by a committee of musicians, as is the Vienna Philharmonic. The difference is that the Viennese select the conductors they work with, while the Orpheus musicans make music in a most organic and democratic way. It is like chamber music writ large as the musicians carefully listen to each other, and the results are impressive.

7

THEORY, AND PRACTICE

How can we measure what seems beyond measuring?
—*Hans Sachs, principal character in Wagner's* Die Meistersinger von Nürnberg

T he notion of musical theory is, in a way, different from what you might think of when you ponder the word *theory*. In music, theory is not so much about the ideas and beliefs that may constitute a musical work, but might more accurately be described as the architecture and grammar of music. It is essential that music students—especially those who wish to be composers or conductors—master musical theory in a way that it becomes second nature.

Theory consists of *notation* (the writing down of music); the classification of *intervals* (the distance in pitch, which is the vibration frequency of a sound, between the way two tones are notated); the structure of *scales* and *chords;* the importance of *harmony* and *counterpoint;* plus *melody, rhythm, form*, and *orchestration.*

Much of theory, at least as applied by a composer, is the measurement in time and aural intensity (how soft or loud) of the notes that form a piece of music. The composer must also decide what *key* (or *key note*) to set a piece of music in. This is typically the key that the work begins in and often the key it ends in, though certain composers such as Mahler did not necessarily follow this practice.

Let us say, for example, that a work is said to be in the key of C major. The most vivid way for you to understand this is to look at the keyboard of a piano. If you are unfamiliar with the keyboard, have someone find middle C for you. This is an easy scale to learn and, when you play it, it will sound pleasing and familiar. You move straight up the white keys, playing C-D-E-F-G-A-B-C. You will recognize this as the *do-re-mi-fa-sol-la-ti-do* you learned as a child. Generally it can be said that the former scale (beginning with C) is more used in North America and Britain. The latter scale (identical in sound to the former), beginning with the note called *do* (rhymes with *go* or *sew*), is used more in countries that use Italian for expressing musical notes. Be aware that where we say *ti* in English, the Italians use *sí*. In French, this scale is *ut-ré-mi-fa-sol-la-si-ut*. But in all of these languages, the sounds of the notes are identical.

A scale will consist of a series of seven ascending or descending whole notes called an *octave* (though there will actually be thirteen notes to traverse as you play this octave, because you will pass five black keys). When you look at a piano, think of each key you can press as a *tone* or *note*. A black note is sort of a halfway sound between the white keys that surround it. This black note is often called a semitone because it is in between two whole tones. If you play black keys in ascending order, they are sharp (a half-step higher than the previous white note). If you play them in descending order, then the black keys are flat (a half-step lower than the preceding white note). So the black note between C and D could be called either C-sharp or D-flat. The thirteen to choose from would be, in order from C, C; C-sharp or D-flat; D; D-sharp or E-flat; E; F; F-sharp or G-flat; G; G-sharp or A-flat; A; A-sharp or B-flat; B; and C.

All of this is not nearly as difficult as it may seem. Once committed to memory (and using the piano as a visual aid), you will be able to learn these notes easily. If you learn to read music, you can then use a piano to play octaves in all keys. Keys are either *major* and *minor*. In a major scale, the distance (interval) between each note is the same and the scale is identified by the note it begins with. It is a generalization perhaps, but a useful one, to think of major scales or keys as fuller, positive, and more predictable and inevitable in their sequence and outcome. Minor scales and keys may have a sound that is slightly askew (but not unpleasant) from what we would expect to hear, and may have an air of sadness or exoticism about them. With major keys there is often a sense of completeness and accomplishment about them as they conclude. Minor key works often go off in mysterious and emotional directions, and are imbued with real beauty.

Theory is at the center of musical language. Most composers before the twentieth century (and many after) adhered to the traditional precepts of musical theory. For a musician or scholar to understand the workings and language of the music of a particular composer, he or she must first understand theory and see how it applies to the music at hand. You may choose, as you come to know classical music, to study theory to understand the architecture and inner workings of music. What I propose to do in this chapter is to give you a series of ideas and tools to work with as you listen to music. I am less interested in your learning many new words that may have little meaning. Rather, you should read the text to discover ways to think about music.

Spoken language is, at its base, a collection of sounds and symbols. Each word has a meaning, representing something: an action, an object, or an idea. Words have weight and shape, can be beautiful or ugly. Speaking has rhythm, cadence, volume, and all sorts of dynamics. If you were to read this paragraph aloud it would sound quite different from my reading of it, or someone else's.

In simplest terms, the act of creating and speaking sentences is akin to composing. The ideas and the way we express them are ours. If these sentences are written down, or *notated*, and then read by someone else, this is, in effect, performance. The words are notation, and it falls to the speaker to take that notation and make it comprehensible and meaningful, at once attempting to honor the intent of the writer while giving an individual stamp of the reader.

So musical notes on a page are just that—notation. They represent the tones or notes that, in Western music, we have agreed are indicated on a piece of paper in a particular way. Musical theory dates at least as far back as Pythagoras, who thought of music as beautiful concordances. He described this mathematically. A perfect fifth was a sound thought to be 3:2—that is, one note vibrating three times in the same time it takes another note to vibrate twice. So time is a constant, but the length of vibrations varies from one note to another. Other sounds included a third (2:1) and a seventh (4:3). These sounds were, in the most basic sense, the tickling of the eardrum in a pleasing way.

As music evolved, it always retained its mathematical component. The interest in math in music evolved during the Renaissance, which placed a premium on the idea of proportion. If you think about fifteenth- and sixteenth-century Italy, proportion was a desirable state in science, art, and commerce as well as music. When we look back to the Renaissance today with admiration, part of what we are drawn to is the proportion. It seems so natural, so rational, and, yes, so consoling. Here is part of the key to what music does for us.

It should not surprise you that many mathematicians and scientists also demonstrate a propensity for music. Many of them are particularly drawn to Bach, whose music seems to them a series of mathematical constructs that result in gorgeous sounds. There is a perfection and rationality to most of Bach's music, and those who admire it often remark that they can see the architecture and inner workings. I would respond to them that seeing these structures is valuable, but the real importance comes in feeling the music.

Part of the reason that we have scores of Renaissance music that we can read and understand is due to the work of Guido d'Arezzo, a Benedictine monk thought to have lived from 992 to 1050. He studied music at an abbey in Pomposa, near Ferrara in Italy. There he devised a system of musical notation that was the basis for everything that followed. Guido was not the first to do musical notation (it dates back at least to the ancient Greeks), but his is the system that is the foundation for notating music as it is still done today. Among Guido's writings are *Prologus in Antiphonarium*, in which he theorized notation; *Epistola ad Michaelem de ignoto cantu*, in which he further explored notes and scales; *Regulae rhythmicae*, rules of rhythm; and, most famously, *Micrologus*, in which he elaborated his theoretical (hence, *theory*) and aesthetic ideas about music.

The series of five horizontal lines with four spaces between them that we think of for music notation is called the *staff* (plural *staves*). These are divided by vertical lines to create boxes called *measures* (in the U.K. and the rest of Europe, measures are usually called *bars*). In each measure a composer will place a series of dots, circles, and other markings that indicate which note it is (we know this according to which line or space between it is placed on). The dots and circles indicate the time that each note should be held, as you will learn later.

A *clef* and a *signature* are put at the beginning to indicate general guidelines for the music. A clef is an indication that fixes a particular note on the staff and, therefore, tells you where the other notes are in relation to it. Suffice it to say that there have been many clefs throughout musical history, but most are now confined to four: the treble, alto, tenor, and bass clefs. Think of human voices (treble is like a boy soprano) and you will have a general idea. You have often seen the symbol of the treble clef (𝄞). The bass clef looks like a backwards letter C followed by a colon (𝄢).

When you have a treble clef at the start of a staff, the notes on the lines, from bottom to top, are E-G-B-D-F. I learned to remember these as a child by the words "Every Good Boy Does Fine" (which playwright Tom Stoppard cheekily called "Every Good Boy Deserves a Favour"). If the lines, from bottom to top, are E-G-B-D-F, then the spaces in between are F-A-C-E which, on the face of it, should be easy to remember. Do you see the sequence of notes? E-F-G-A-B-C-D-E-F.

You should not think that every note that is played is within the staff (that would only be nine notes). You can look at musical scores and see notes above and below the staff, but they are only indicated when the music calls for those notes. Otherwise, a score of music will only have the staff.

There are two chief types of signature: the key signature and the time signature. The key signature is a cluster of markings indicating sharps and flats of different notes used in the prevailing key. Major keys are indicated in capital letters (A, B, C, etc.), while minor keys are indicated in lowercase letters (a, b, c, etc.). The key signature is usually placed at the start of each line (though not on the staff), or at any place in the score where the signature may change.

The time signature is used to indicate the organization of the meter (time) in which a passage of music is played (don't panic now, it gets easier!). Think of the time signature as a fraction, with a number above separated from the number below by a line. For the number below, it should be thought of as relating to a note: 1 would be a whole note; 2 would be a half note; 4 a quarter note; 8 an eighth note; and 16 a sixteenth note. The number above the line indicates how many notes comprise a measure. For example, if the time signature is 6/8, that means that there will be six eighth notes in the measure, grouped in two sets of three or three sets of two. We will get to all this in a bit, but I am presenting it now because I want you to realize an essential concept: musicians tend to be very intelligent people who can look at the markings in a score and instantly process in their minds all the variations and shifts that happen in a piece of music.

What happens in performance is something more. Just as a recipe is a guideline and suggestion for what a dish may become, notated music is the basis upon which a conductor, instrumentalist, or singer will bring to bear his or her talents, insights, emotions, breath, dexterity, and other attributes to create a performance. More astonishing to me is that a musician can commit all of this to memory and play pieces of considerable length without looking at the music.

· ᴗ ·

How does a piece of music come to be? In one way or another, the composer has ideas that he begins to sketch. The first idea might be the desire to create a work that features a particular instrument, and the composer will start experimenting with ideas that would suit that instrument. Or the composer may have one or two melodies in his head and then try to decide how to best use them.

A melody is a collection of notes that create a beguiling musical passage that seems capable of lodging in the listener's mind after one or two hearings. But the melody can sound different if you change the volume or speed at which it is played, or change the instruments you use. If you are familiar with the musical *The Music Man*, you surely know the song "76 Trombones." It is played by many instruments at once (including numerous trombones) in a loud, fast-paced way. But the very same melody is sung at another point as a sort of amorous lullaby—slowly and affectionately—by one of the characters. The melody is the same, but everything else is different.

This same effect can happen in classical music, usually in the same piece of music. Ravel's *Boléro* gave you some idea of this. When played by strings or woodwinds or brass, the sounds sounds different according to the instruments. Loud or soft, fast or slow, the music will sound distinctive according to the choices the composer makes. A composer, in writing music, must ponder some of these questions: Once the principal melody is written, would it work best with solo voice or piano? Or both? Or would a string quartet work better? How about solo violin with orchestra? Or would the melody be best served by the large and varied sounds that a symphony orchestra is capable of?

After the first melody is born, the composer may think of others that will abet or contrast with the original one. This is how sonatas and symphonies are constructed. He will also think of music that connects—or bridges—these ideas. They must all be joined and have a sense of continuity. Put simply, the work must have a beginning, a middle, and an end.

One of the distinguishing characteristics of music is its *rhythm*. This is what we might also call the beat, which can be consistent or can vary widely. The heartbeat is the most elemental—and essential—rhythm known to humans. If you place your right thumb over your left pulse, you will get a good idea of what rhythm can be. You might feel it go one-two, one-two, one-two. . . . If you have a regular heartbeat, you can begin to understand what music notation might look like with a time signature of 2/4. Each "one-two" beat is a measure. Imagine that after each of these, a vertical line is drawn to separate one measure from the next. Are these beats even, or is one stronger—think "accented"—when compared to the other? Are they ONE-two, ONE-two . . . or perhaps one-TWO, one-TWO. . . ?

If you picture the beats in measures of four notes, the time signature would be 4/4, then you might have the rhythm of the notes as follows: ONE-two-THREE-four, ONE-two-THREE-four . . . and so on.

It is often thought that drumming is a close replication of heartbeat, but the beating of drums is not necessarily constant or identical. In fact, if you hear five different drummers play together, you can detect incredible variety and intricacy.

• ◌ •

I like to think of rhythm as the measurement of movement. There is a way you can understand this that is much more tangible than feeling your own pulse. Go to a park and sit on a bench on a busy path. Watch every person walk or run past. Each moves at a different rhythm. Think of each footfall as a sound or beat.

Given that they have two legs, most people walk in a one-two, one-two fashion. But there are many differences (think of these as different rhythms). Some people who pass by pound their feet in a steady one-two way. Power-walkers take faster steps. Some people glide; others lope. An older person may also walk in a steady one-two, one-two, but with a rhythm that is slower than the power-walker or the jogger. Notice someone who walks with difficulty, perhaps using a cane. How is this rhythm different from that of someone with more consistent steps?

Now look for two people walking together. Do they move the same way, in right-left, right-left steps, walking in unison? Or is each one moving with independent steps, forming a contrasting (or perhaps jarring) combination of beats?

After doing this, then look for two people of significantly different heights walking together. Does the shorter person have to take faster or more steps to keep up with the long-legged taller one? If you look at a short piece of terrain that they walk through, you will understand certain concepts. This distance may be thought of as a musical measure (or bar). The long-legged person might cover it in two steps (one-two). By contrast, his short-legged companion might require four steps (one-two-three-four) in the same amount of time to cover the same distance. In our measure, the tall person takes two steps, which could be though of as two half-notes. The shorter person has to take four quick steps in the same amount of time to cover the same distance. These four steps can be thought of as quarter notes.

Then notice a person walking a healthy young dog. With its four legs, the dog is creating a different beat from its two-legged human friend. It is very possible, if you listen closely, that the dog is doing exactly double the amount of beats in the same amount of time. So the human's rhythm is one-two, one-two in the same number of seconds that the dog goes one-two-three-four, one-two-three-four. The time is identical, but the rhythms are different (in this case 2:1).

Note that the dog and human may also walk at entirely different rhythms, especially if the human is walking in steady, purposeful strides while the dog has its nose near the ground and walks in beats with no discernable pattern because it is more focused on sniffing than walking in time with its master. This would represent music that is less structured and proportionate, but can be very exciting. For example, the human's steady gait could be the purposeful repetition of low notes played on the piano with the left hand, while the dog's frenetic steps could be a wild improvisation with the right hand on the higher notes of the piano's keyboard.

Now observe a slower person with an old dog. The dog, with its four legs, may actually replicate the slowing gait of the person. Their rhythms may be identical: One. Two. One. Two for the human, and something similar for the dog. Thinking of it as a musical measure, the *tempo* (speed at which music is played) will be slower than the one represented by the younger human and dog.

Then, if you see a frisky dog with a slower human, the dog's rhythm may accelerate wildly: one-two-three-four-five-six-seven-eight! in the time the human takes a one-step, two-step, and perhaps a lunging, out-of-kilter third step as the dog yanks on its leash.

Now notice a squirrel bounding through grass. It might take three leaps, going 1-2-3, and then pause. And then again: 1-2-3-pause.

These pauses, or rests, are not the absence of rhythm or beat. In fact, in the time-keeping that we use to describe these rhythms, the amount of time the squirrel pauses is part of a larger, ongoing rhythm (music) that the squirrel creates. The pause is just as central to the rhythm as the steps.

All of these various rhythmic timings I have described are based on even numbers—2, 4, 8, 16—that are multiples of one another. But not all rhythm is so even and precise. If you see a couple dancing a waltz, their steady rhythm will be ONE-two-three, ONE-two-three, ONE-two-three. This is not like our squirrel, whose rhythm was based on four counts (1-2-3-rest), but is a steady rhythm in threes.

Listen to the waltz's music and you can hear the unmistakable ONE-two-three, ONE-two-three, ONE-two-three rhythm.

Now look again on the dance floor for a young, energetic couple that might be dancing double-time to this music. While the other dancers go ONE-two-three, ONE-two-three, this energetic couple—in the same amount of time—goes ONE-two-three-FOUR-five-six, ONE-two-three-FOUR-five-six, breathlessly enjoying the excitement that we, in watching and listening, can become breathlessly involved in, too. And notice how you can simultaneously hear—in fact, feel—the ONE-two-three in the music and the ONE-two-three-FOUR-five-six of the dancing, happening in the very same time frame.

When you recognize that you have this ability—along with that of detecting the many rhythms you found in the park—then you have come a long way in your journey to connect with music.

It is important to distinguish between *meter* and *rhythm*. Meter is usually a more constant time pattern. Typically it is defined as duple meter (in twos: one-two, one-two), triple meter (in patterns of three), quadruple meter (in patterns of four), and so forth. The examples I gave you of footsteps that maintain a regular pattern can thus be thought of as meter. Those with a more complicated and flowing pattern, or those in which more than one meter is at play, can be thought of as rhythmic. These would be the darting dog and the bounding squirrel.

In the twentieth century and in our own, there are many musical examples of rhythm that can vary often in the course of a piece. That is, the stresses (think of these as accents) in a metric line can change. So instead of ONE-two-three-four throughout a piece of music, you can go to ONE-two-THREE-four or ONE-two-three-FOUR or, more challengingly, ONE-two-THREE-four-five. There is an example last in Tchaikovsky's Sixth Symphony, where there is an unusual waltz in 5/4 time. This may begin to sound daunting, but the key concept to take from this is that meter is a recurring pattern of pulses while rhythm is the fluid ebb and flow of music that can change through the course of a piece as the melodies change.

Another way to think of rhythm is to think of jazz, in which multiple rhythms can be played on different instruments at the same time (as can be done in classical music, too). A jazz bassist may pluck ONE-two, ONE-two on the strings of his instrument, while the drummer may be pounding a beat of ONE-two-three-ONE-two, ONE-two-three-ONE-two, and the solo trumpet may riff in an ever-changing variety of rhythms. Our ears and imaginations, if we care about jazz, are engaged by all of this, and we listen attentively.

Somehow, though, if we were to listen to the same rhythms in a piece of contemporary "classical" or "serious" music, many of us would make a face as if we had just consumed a big gulp of curdled milk. This is because many of us expect a degree of the symmetry and rhythmic order we think we hear while listening to Bach, Vivaldi, Haydn, Mozart, or Schubert. I say we *think* we hear because these composers also used rhythmic forms more complex than we necessarily recognize.

To make this clearer, consider poetry. When we listen to most poetry from before the twentieth century, part of its appeal is the consistent meter and rhythm of the phrases, and the pleasing sense that we get when a rhyme is completed just at the moment we expect it to be. There is a sense of congruence and balance to these poems that appeals to the structured mind of writers and listeners alike.

But we can also be drawn to those who break the rules daringly or ingeniously. In poetry, it is probably Rimbaud who gave a different flow and dynamic to poetry meter in a revolutionary way. In music, several composers from the end of the nineteenth century onward experimented with new rhythms as they sought to move away from the musical conventions they inherited.

Then there were composers such as Arnold Schoenberg (1874–1951), who broke new ground in the grammar of theory. His rhythmic ideas were not unlike those of other early-twentieth-century composers, but his chief innovation is his codification of the twelve-tone technique, in which each of the twelve notes (the seven white and five black, not including the thirteenth key that would complete an octave) is given equal value as notes rather than relating to one another as major and minor. In other words, if you play the twelve keys in a row, or series, they all stand with equal importance in a composition, with black key notes no longer confined to a slightly inferior status. Some listeners complained that some of Schoenberg's music was "dissonant," suggesting that it did not reach the ears in a pleasing and congruent way. What they hoped for was music that was "consonant," which is to say "more agreeable." What we are also talking about, simply, is new versus old. Rather than thinking of some music as dissonant, it is probably better to think that the twelve-tone technique meant that many new combinations of sounds could be created, and music could be more expressive. Not all music should be soothing—it is also important for some compositions to make us think and wonder and try to sort things out. This is what we do in life.

• ◁◇▷ •

Rhythm by itself would not make music what it is. There is also melody. In simplest terms it is a succession of notes on the musical staff. But it is so much more. Melody is characterized by its beauty and its catchiness. We tend to be drawn to melodies that are what the Italians call *orecchiabile* (or "earable," meaning listenable). If we manage to memorize part of a melody on first hearing, these tend to be melodies we like. This connects to a emotional response that is crucial for our belief that there are certain pieces of music we love.

We take interest in melodies whose flow we can follow. Often, we are content when we are right about where the music is headed; at other times we are startled and pleased when the melody takes us to unexpected places. Lest you think that this only applies to modern music, one of the most consistently surprising and startling melodists is Mozart.

The more music you listen to, the more you will come to realize when you are hearing a special or beautiful melody. Certain composers had a natural affinity for beautiful melody. Among them are Palestrina, Bach, Handel, Mozart, Beethoven, Schubert, Bellini, Mendelssohn, Grieg, Tchaikovsky, Brahms, Dvořák, Johann Strauss, Richard Strauss, Debussy, Gershwin, Prokofiev, and Barber.

If you hear a single, unaccompanied melody, think of this in musical terms as *monophonic* (one sound). This might be Gregorian chant or in a sonata for solo instruments. This single stream of solo melody could be played on a violin, cello, flute, or many other instruments.

Homophonic music has a principal melodic line with chordal accompaniment. This was found in early opera (seventeenth century) wherein a voice carried the melody and the same music was played on an instrument or group of instruments that provided dramatic contrast or insight.

If you hear multiple melodies played at once, think of this as *polyphonic* (many sounds). In other words, when you listen to a symphony and the strings are playing one melody and the brass another, you have a situation in which the music being made is a combination of the two. Each melody on its own may be beautiful (or seem incomplete), but it is in combination that we find the music the composer meant for you to hear.

You should not think that all of these phonic styles belong to different eras, movements, or composers. If you go back and listen to the Allegretto (second) movement of Beethoven's Seventh Symphony, you will notice that some passages are monophonic, some are homophonic, and some are polyphonic.

• ❧ •

If we break down these melodies into smaller forms, what we are talking about is harmony. This is the relationship of two or more notes played at the same time to produce a contrasting or compelling sound. If you look at a musical staff and see two or more notes played together (such as C, E, and G), you have vertical harmony. The playing of at least three notes together produces a chord. A three-tone chord is called a triad. Play C-E-G together on a piano keyboard and you will understand. Of course, chords can contain more than three notes. Some chords are consonant (and thus, pleasing), such as if you play two C's an octave apart, separated by the notes in between. Intervals of thirds (separations of three notes) are among the most harmonious. C to E and E to G are examples of this. Also harmonious are fifths (separations of five notes) such as C to G. A smaller interval (such as C to D or F to G) will be dissonant. Remember that dissonance is not necessarily a bad thing. It is simply making a different statement.

Counterpoint (from the Latin *punctus contra punctum*) can be thought of as the juxtaposition of vertical harmonies and horizontal melodies. This happens when two or more harmonic lines are combined polyphonically to form harmonies that merge in such a way that they have both coherence and independence. This may sound complicated, but you will come to understand it when you listen to Bach. It may sound like one enormous mathematical scheme, and it is, but it is also about musical contrast and insight. You do not need to be an expert in theory to connect with this, but simply keep your mind and ears wide open.

Harmonies from the time of Monteverdi (early seventeenth century) to around 1900 are built in a way that we easily connect to them. Then composers such as Debussy, Schoenberg, and Stravinsky pointed to more dissonant directions—not necessarily unpleasant ones, as might generally be described, but different, more challenging, and more perplexing. Some of these composers were actively seeking new forms of musical expression, while others reacted to the world around them with its wars and turmoil.

• ☙ •

Another essential thing to think about in music-making is *tone*, especially regarding the sound of individual instruments or voices. You can hear a singer and, in most cases, agree that she has a beautiful voice, one with a beautiful tone. Similarly, certain instrumentalists famously achieve great tonal beauty on their instruments. On the violin, perhaps Jaime Laredo and Nathan Milstein are exponents of this. Then there are other musicians (as in the voice of Maria Callas) whose tone is singular, distinctive, throbbing, emotional, but may not fit the traditional definitions of beauty. Perhaps cellist Jacqueline Du Pré sometimes fell into this category. I have twice used the word *perhaps* in this paragraph because a listener's sense of beauty is highly personal. Beauty is something almost all of us look for in music, but if it is the only characteristic we hope to find we are missing out on a lot.

Composers and instrumentalists focus on tone as a means of expression. Not every idea is a beautiful or happy one, and music covers the vast expanse of human emotion. Even the same musical idea (think of this as a particular chord or melody) can change depending on the tone it is played with. Tonal differences are achieved by using different instruments, alone or in combination. A melody played on one instrument will sound significantly different when played on another. For example, if you were to take a melody we all know, such as "Happy Birthday to You," and play it on the cello, clarinet, or trumpet, it would have a different tone and a different feeling. It also sounds different when sung by a soprano, mezzo-soprano, tenor, baritone, or bass.

How are we affected by tonal differences? We might get a different emotional feeling based on each tonal color we hear. Of course, there cannot and should not be universal agreement on this. We are talking here about nontangible (as opposed to *intangible*) things—ideas and feelings—so tonal color in a musical phrase cannot be defined in precise terms.

You have already experienced tonal color. The purling sounds of the flute were an ideal surrogate for the bird in *Peter and the Wolf*. The careful, deliberate steps of the cat were perfectly evoked by the clarinet. And the bassoon is the logical choice for depicting the gruff disciplinarian that is the grandfather. Prokofiev knew exactly what he was doing.

> KEY CONCEPT: *Most tonal color does not depict a tangible thing. Most music is made of ideas that represent thoughts, feelings, emotions, and issues that cannot and should not be definable in narrow terms.*

The more instruments a composer has at his disposal, the more possibilities there are for tonal color. In the compositions of eighteenth-century composers—Bach, Handel, Vivaldi, Haydn, and Mozart, to name but a few—they usually worked with a smaller range of instruments than the composers of the nineteenth and twentieth centuries. So tonal color in the eighteenth century might be achieved in the contrast between two similar instruments, such as violin and viola, while a twentieth-century composer such as Béla Bartók could contrast percussion and strings. Eighteenth-century composers did have flutes, oboes, bass clarinets, horns, bassoons, and trumpets, but they used them in a more restrained way because proportion and equilibrium were attributes that were prized by the aesthetic of the time.

This is not to say that the music of Mozart and Haydn is less interesting—in fact, given that they worked with a smaller palette of colors, they still managed to express an infinite range of ideas. They just did it differently from those who followed.

• ᷇ •

Composers write in a vast array of musical forms (structures) that you will discover in this book. Some of the most famous are sonatas, concertos, and symphonies. These follow certain rules, though composers often made their own exceptions that musicians need to know about as they approach individual works. For example, when we think of the typical symphony, it has contrasting themes in the first movement. Yet this is not the case, for example, in Beethoven's Seventh.

These structures are reassuring and, when they diverge, they can be jarring or compelling. The sense of direction in the long line of a symphony often feels like an inevitable one. This is not a bad thing. Listeners are engaged and feel gratified when things they envisioned develop and play out. Surprises, when they happen, can also be pleasing. Above all, structure gives a sense of coherence.

Describing forms in theory terms often means using letters. If A is one theme and B is another, then A-B-A means that the first is played, then the second, then the first is repeated. If you see A-B-A´, that means that the first theme is played, then the second, then a variation on the first.

A variation is when a composer improvises on a theme or melody to make you think of the music in different and original ways. The composer (usually a good keyboard player) must be talented at invention, or the variations will be dull. Bach was wonderful at variations (you will learn his Goldberg Variations) and Beethoven, in his Diabelli Variations, knew how to imbue them with significant humor and fantasy.

Much music in the seventeenth and early eighteenth centuries was described in dance forms: allemande, bourrée, courante, gavotte, gigue, loure, passepied, sarabande, etc., each with its own meter. Many of these came in music that was called binary (two-part) that we can think of as A-B. There would be one theme, then another. Specialists in this form were François Couperin (1668–1733) and Domenico Scarlatti (1685–1757).

Three-part forms (A-B-A) included minuets and sonatas by Haydn and Mozart in which the B section clearly contrasts with the A. The return to A was sometimes a simple repetition, but could also be a variation. Three-part form, with some small changes, appears in many compositions, include the ballade, berceuse, capriccio, elegy, étude, impromptu, intermezzo, nocturne, polonaise, reverie, waltz, and so forth. While some of these forms are not invariably in three-part form, they are often so.

Other forms are more elaborate, and when you think of them you should think of variations and contrasts in melody and expression. A rondo (or round) may go A-B-A-C-A-D-A. We always return to the original theme after a digression. These digressions provide balance, contrast, and sometimes insight regarding the A theme. There is no required number of digressions, and the A may not be precisely what it originally was but may appear in a variation.

Another category is free sectional form. This may be any sequence that makes musical sense. One might be A-B-B, another would be A-B-C-A, or even A-B-C-B, or A-B-A-C-A-B-A.

• ⌒ •

Much of this book will be devoted to the study of three musical forms: the sonata, the symphony, and the concerto. Because they will be addressed at considerable length elsewhere, we can confine ourselves here to simple definitions.

The sonata, in its original intent, is a musical work that is played, or sounded (sonata comes from the Italian *suonata*). By contrast, a cantata is something sung (*cantare*, to sing). A church sonata usually had four movements (sections or parts) that were fast-slow-fast-slow. This was the predecessor of the sonatas of Haydn and Mozart. Sonatas were written for most instruments used in the Baroque era. In the Classical era, the sonata had three or four movements and was a medium for the exploration of musical ideas by one, two, or a few instruments. Many were written for solo piano, some for violin and piano, or cello and piano. The piano has also been paired with other instruments in sonatas, including the clarinet and French horn. You can also hear sonatas for flute and harp, and other instruments occasionally appear as well. There are also sonatas for two pianos by Mozart, Stravinsky, Bartók, and Poulenc.

A symphony is an orchestral work that is usually in four movements. Some symphonies have only three movements, and some exceptional ones have five, six, seven, or more. The classical symphony is, in effect, a sonata for orchestra. Rather than having just a few instruments, as in a sonata, in a symphony there is a grander selection of instrumental voices for the composer to work with. The opening movement is moderately fast, the second slower, the third is more variable depending on what the composer wishes to do, and the fourth typically is a brisk finale. There are, of course, many different ways the construction of a symphony can be approached, but this is the most traditional way. In the eighteenth century, the goal was a perfect balance of content and form. The chief exponents were Haydn (104 symphonies) and Mozart (41). Beethoven opened the way to more personal expression, and his symphonies were statements about issues and ideas of concern to him. Other composers (Berlioz, Liszt, Strauss) introduced literary and thematic content. Beethoven, Mahler, Stravinsky, Shostakovich, and others added singers to some of their symphonies.

A concerto is a work for full orchestra with a solo instrument. It is usually in three movements. The instrumental voice often integrates with the voices of the orchestra, and just as often stands alone. You will be learning concertos that feature solo instruments such as the piano, organ, violin, viola, cello, oboe, clarinet, French horn, bassoon, trumpet, trombone, and tuba.

This introduction to theory is just the beginning. You will learn a lot more in the course of this book, and in such a way that the musical examples will instruct you. If you become fascinated by theory, I suggest you further your study at a local college or music school.

• ⟨⟩ •

How do musicians absorb all of these ideas about theory and fashion it into performance? Study and practice. Most musicians are trained over many years and devote all of their adult lives and careers to study and thought. They read about composers' lives, read their correspondence; they talk with other musicians and try to sort out musical ideas. Above all, they study musical scores.

Every musician whose home I have visited seems to have a stack of scores in an accessible place for study and review. Even if it is music that they have played for years, such as a violinist and the Mendelssohn concerto, they still return to its score for inspiration and clarification. Above all, musicians practice. This means playing or singing music they are currently performing, will perform, or are revisiting for knowledge, inspiration, or pleasure. This is how music becomes a part of them, and it is the way they live. There is no such thing as a day off, because most musicians say they need to maintain the focus and connection to the music. Above all, though, they love it. As Vladimir Horowitz used to say about practicing, "If I miss one day, I know it; if I miss two days, my wife knows it; and if I miss three days, everybody knows it."

THE SYMPHONY

The symphony is the world! The symphony must embrace everything.
—*Gustav Mahler*

T he symphony is the most famous and popular form in classical music. It was created, in fact, in the Classical era of composition. The word *symphonia* traces its origins back to ancient Greek, where its implication was of consonance, or music having a sound that is agreeable to the ear (think of dissonance as the opposite). In medieval times, a symphony was a sort of stringed instrument that was sounded with a keyboard.

During and soon after the Renaissance in Italy, the word *sinfonia* meant an overture (an opening piece of music) to an opera, oratorio, cantata, or suite. The first known use of *sinfonia* to describe a piece of introductory music was by the composer Luca Marenzio (1553–1599), who used the term in 1589. Marenzio is largely forgotten, but he was an important composer in his time for his splendid inventiveness with harmonies and melody.

Alessandro Scarlatti (1660–1725) took things further, dividing the sinfonia into three sections: allegro-adagio-allegro, basically fast-slow-fast. Scarlatti is often called the greatest Italian opera composer between Monteverdi (1567–1643) and Rossini (1792–1868). He wrote at least sixty-five operas, and was central to the evolution of the aria, or solo song for singer. For him, the opera's overture (its sinfonia) would set the stage for the action that would follow. It was meant to put the audience in the right frame of mind to hear the opera. Thus the fast section communicated excitement and brilliance; the brief slow section might be introspective, and would surely draw the audience closer and make them listen. The return to a faster section would invigorate the audience with dance-like music, making way for the raising of the curtain and the start of the opera. A Scarlatti opera overture might last eight to ten minutes.

In the eighteenth century (and ever since) there was a considerable amount of exchange of musical ideas between German and Italian cities. The most famous German traveler to the south was Handel, while Vivaldi was probably the best known Italian to go north. Each German city-state had a court, and in some of these music was an important element of social and cultural life. One of the most brilliant of these was in Mannheim, where Elector Karl Theodor's reign (1743–1778) saw an almost unrivaled musical flowering.

Johann Stamitz (1717–1757) was a Bohemian composer who founded the School of Mannheim, a collection of composers who served Karl Theodor and gave the symphony the qualities it has today. An early sinfonia in Germany would be the introductory music to an orchestral suite. Stamitz took this three-part form and expanded it to four parts (movements) and made the symphony a musical form separate from a suite or opera. The four movements are called *allegro* (Italian for "happy," but suggesting music that moves forward at a vivacious pace); *adagio* (slower); *minuetto* (a dance in 3/4 time introduced to the court of Louis XIV of France by Lully; in a symphony it has a pleasantly jaunty motion that contrasts with the adagio that precedes it); and *finale*, a last movement that would often recall elements of the opening adagio. Another key contribution of the composers of the School of Mannheim was the adoption of the sonata form (see page 178) to use in symphonies, at least in the first movement.

The School of Mannheim also promoted the use of thematic material in symphonies, such that a theme is developed and then may return later in a symphony to make a particular musical statement. The theme may be played faster, slower, louder, softer, or on different instruments when it makes its return. These composers also gave considerable attention to how musicians should be arranged on a stage so that their sound was most balanced and agreeable. To do this, they developed a sophisticated knowledge of the intricacies and properties of each instrument, the finest of which were produced in northern Italy.

Mannheim symphonies favored counterpoint, emphasized harmonic and expressive color in sound, and the contrasts among different musical groupings within an orchestra. They were also interested in dynamics (the gradations of volume in music—how loud or soft it was played). If you take a moment to think about it, almost every piece of music you know would sound quite different depending on the volume at which it is played.

The composers of the Mannheim School were indefatigably productive. In addition to Stamitz, who composed 67 symphonies, they included his son Karl (1745–1801, composer of 89 symphonies); Frantisek Xaver Richter (1709–1789, more than 80 symphonies); Ignaz Holzbauer (1711–1783, about 70 symphonies); Antonin Filtz (1730–1760, 40 symphonies); Johann Christian Cannabich (1731–1798, also prolific); and Carl Toeschi (1731–1788, more than 80 symphonies).

Although there were other contemporaneous schools (groups of composers who shared an approach) of symphonic composition in places such as Milan, Paris, and Vienna, the works of the Mannheim composers had the most influence on the first two great masters of the form, Franz Joseph Haydn (1732–1809, 104 symphonies) and Wolfgang Amadeus Mozart (1756–1791, 41 symphonies). Needless to say, with Haydn and Mozart their output is notable not only for quantity but also for quality. They are really the foundation upon which the standard symphonic repertory rests, although I believe that the best works by the Mannheim composers are due for reappraisal.

Haydn was, in effect, the last of the Viennese School (note that this has subsequently come to be called the First Viennese School, because the Second Viennese School of the early twentieth century had composers such as Schoenberg, Webern, and Berg exploring twelve-tone scales and expressionism). Haydn and Mozart, whose work you will soon discover, represent a new world of composition, one that employs order and structure, but is not enslaved by it. If the Mannheim composers used and refined a formula, then Haydn and Mozart took that formula as a point of departure to create symphonies that are elegant, lively, intellectually probing, and reveal new insights each time you listen to them. These two men are the great composers of the Classical era, and composers since their day have looked back to them for inspiration.

In his famous London concerts in the 1790s, Haydn often conducted from the keyboard, placed so that he had his back to the audience and his instrument protruding straight into the orchestra. Immediately surrounding him were violins and violas. In the next ring away from him were cellos, bassoons, horns, oboes, and flutes. In the ring behind these musicians were the double basses, trumpets, timpani, and, when required, an organ.

Before 1800, when a composer did not conduct, musical ensembles were usually led either by the first violinist or by a keyboard player.

• ∾ •

Beethoven, who was a revolutionary and innovator, wrenched the classical symphonies from his predecessors and turned the form into something more epic. In effect, he straddled the Classical and Romantic eras in music, drawing from the structure and grace of the former and adding the more overt passions of the latter.

Having arrived in Vienna in 1792, Beethoven never met Mozart, who had died the previous year. But he did know Haydn, who sought to be a generous older composer, mentor, and teacher, though Haydn ultimately felt that he had little he could impart to the brilliant and somewhat tempestuous younger man.

Beethoven's primary contribution to the symphonic form was to expand the musical language that could be used in symphonies. In other words, the instrumental voices he deployed were more varied than previously, and he attempted to say more things with them. Music can and should express more than notes on a page. Certainly composers and musicians long before Beethoven understood this, but his particular genius and triumph was in successfully making this a central part of his musical agenda. We listen to his symphonies and hear nobility, philosophy, rage, and a desire to reach utopia in whatever form it might exist.

The Third Symphony (the *Eroica*) was longer and more musically complex than any symphony yet written. Beethoven's original inspiration for it were the exploits of Napoleon, whom the composer later disavowed. This was a portrait painted in music. The Fifth was the first symphony to use a trombone, and the prominence of instruments such as the piccolo and the contrabassoon give a greater sonic range than had been previously attempted. The expansive and lyrical Sixth (the *Pastoral*) includes thematic elements—being an unabashed depiction of nature—and pointed the way to more musical compositions that are about something tangible. The Ninth introduced the use of words, chorus, and vocal soloists to the symphonic form.

In much of Beethoven's music we find the dramatic progression from darkness to light, from the evil to the noble, from the benighted to the enlightened. The examples are almost endless, but include the opera *Fidelio*, the *Leonore* Overtures, the *Egmont* Overture, and a few of the symphonies. Listen to the Fourth Symphony, with its murky and mysterious beginning and its intentional lack of harmonic clarity which is then quickly pushed aside in favor of the very bright first movement. Notice the compressed and highly dramatic character of the Fifth Symphony, and how it brilliantly resolves at its conclusion.

With the addition or expansion of the wind, brass, and percussion instrument sections in Beethoven's orchestra, he reshaped how musicians were placed to something closer to what we see today. Typically, strings are positioned closest to the conductor, with violins normally to the left, and divided into first and second violins, which might be playing different music. Then come violas, either next to the violins or to the right of the conductor; cellos, either in front of the conductor or to the right; and double basses, to the far right.

Behind the strings that are right in front of the conductor there might be a row or two of woodwinds (flutes, oboes, clarinets, bassoons) and then a row or two of brass (trumpets, horns, trombones, tubas). The percussion might ring the last row from the back of the second violins on the left around to the last of the double basses on the right.

As was the custom, many composers up until Felix Mendelssohn (1809–1847) often conducted their own work. This also applied to Beethoven, even as his deafness became severe. While it is certainly true that many subsequent composers (including Brahms, Dvořák, Tchaikovsky, Mahler, Strauss, Rachmaninoff, Bernstein, and Boulez) were also outstanding conductors of their own music and works of other composers, the important thing to remember is that the profession of the conductor as we know it today began in the early nineteenth century, and thus the performance of music was taken from the hands of the composer and placed in the hands of someone we should think of as an *interpreter* of music.

To have a sense of how orchestras have grown through the centuries, the table on the next page may prove useful.

• ⟨⟩ •

Franz Schubert died only a year after Beethoven and, though he is ranked among the finest composers nowadays, in his own time he could not rival Beethoven. His symphonies and chamber music pieces are wonderful and his songs are among the greatest musical works of all time. Schubert, Mendelssohn, Schumann, and Brahms all wrote symphonies in the traditional form and emulated Beethoven's expansion of the orchestra. They did not attempt to use complex subject matter as underpinnings for their symphonies, although two Mendelssohn symphonies (the *Italian* and the *Scottish*) drew inspiration from the nations for which they are named.

Other composers after Beethoven followed his more radical changes. Hector Berlioz's *Symphonie Fantastique* (1830) uses a huge

	1607: Monteverdi's opera orchestra, Mantua	1728: Handel's opera orchestra, King's Theater, London	1730: Bach's ensemble for cantatas and sacred music, Leipzig	1775: Court orchestra, Mannheim	1780: Court orchestra for Mozart's early symphonies Vienna	1792: Orchestra for Haydn's late symphonies, London	1824: Orchestra for Beethoven's Ninth Symphony, Vienna	1865: Gewandhaus Orchestra (for 19th-century symphonies), Leipzig	1900: Vienna Philharmonic, for Mahler and R. Strauss	1970: New York Philharmonic, for Pierre Boulez
Violins	4	22	6	20	12	16	24	30	33	34
Violas	4	2	4	4	4	4	10	8	11	12
Cellos	2	3	2	4	3	4	6	9	10	12
Basses/ viola da gamba	2/3	2	1	4	3	4	6	5	10	9
Flutes	2	2	0	3	2	2	2	2	4	4
Oboes	0	2	3	3	2	2	2	2	4	4
Clarinets	0	0	0	3	0	0	2	2	4	5
Bassoons	0	3	2	4	2	2	2	2	4	4
Horns	0	2	0	4	2	2	2	4	8	6
Trumpets/ Cornets	4/2	0	3	2	0	2	2	2	4	4
Trombones/ Trumpets	4	0	0	0	0	0	2	3	5/1	4/1
Timpani/ Percussion	0	0	1	1	0	1	1	1	2/3	2/3
Keyboard	6	2	2	1	2	1	0	0	0	2
Harps	6	1	0	0	0	0	0	0	1	1

orchestra and expands the form to five movements. It draws upon, and explicitly depicts, certain dramatic and thematic material. This led the way to the intentionally thematic works of Franz Liszt, which led in turn to the symphonic poems of the late nineteenth century that culminated in the works in this form by Richard Strauss (see page 228).

Composers such as Dvořák and Tchaikovsky wrote some symphonies without thematic material and others that clearly drew influences from music of their native lands and, in Dvořák's case, the United States. Later on, Jean Sibelius in Finland wrote symphonies infused with considerable national character.

Later in the nineteenth century and early in the twentieth, composers such as César Franck, Alexander Borodin, Camille Saint-Saëns, and Sir Edward Elgar produced excellent symphonies in a more or less traditional style that, for the most part, are not played as often as they should be. We will explore Saint-Saëns's Third Symphony in a later chapter. Georges Bizet (1838–1875) owes his place in musical history to his opera *Carmen*. He wrote his only symphony, known as the Symphony in C, at age seventeen. It was never performed in his lifetime and did not receive its premiere until 1935. Now it is quite popular and is probably most famous as music for a ballet created by George Balanchine.

The symphony as we know it changed dramatically thanks to Anton Bruckner (1824–1896) and Gustav Mahler (1860–1911), who can be said to have turned the symphony into immense canvases onto which great expressions of passion, intellect, and faith could be painted in huge strokes with heavy doses of paint. Their symphonies can be an hour or more in length and require massive musical forces to perform them. Mahler's Eighth (1907) is called the "Symphony of a Thousand," because when performed on the scale Mahler intended, it uses more than 1,000 musicians: 146 instrumentalists, two mixed choirs of 500 voices, a children's choir of 350, eight solo vocalists, and conductor. Drawing from Goethe's *Faust*, it grapples in musical terms with issues of creativity, immortality, and redemption.

Composers since Mahler did not attempt to replicate the sheer size of his symphonies but drew from their expressive qualities. These more modern works are often about something beyond musical abstraction (though there is absolutely nothing wrong with musical abstraction). Prokofiev's First Symphony, called the *Classical* Symphony, is a wonderful revisitation of the style of Haydn and Mozart, though it is unquestionably in Prokofiev's voice. His next six symphonies are considerably more challenging to musicians and listeners, but most worthy—especially the Fifth.

Dmitri Shostakovich (1906–1975) produced fifteen symphonies that cover all sorts of musical and emotional ideas. Some of them, such as the Tenth, can be considered self-portraits. The jagged and agonizing Seventh and Eighth are direct and chilling reactions to the Second World War. The Fifth, probably his most famous, is devastating in its impact.

Many other twentieth-century composers produced important symphonies that follow or reject the traditional form. They all studied the form from Haydn through Bruckner and Mahler, and then found ways to make their own musical and personal statements. We will be discussing some of these in this chapter.

Here is a list of composers whose symphonies you may wish to explore on your own: Sergei Taneyev (1856–1915), Carl Nielsen (1865–1931); Alexander Scriabin (1872–1915, particularly Symphony no. 4); Albert Roussel (1869–1937); Alexander von Zemlinsky (1871–1942); Sergei Rachmaninoff (1873–1943); Franz Schmidt (1874–1939); Charles Ives (1874–1954); Reinhold Glière (1875–1956); Igor Stravinsky (1882–1971); Zoltán Kodály (1882–1967); Bohuslav Martinů (1890–1959); Darius Milhaud (1892–1974); Walter Piston (1894–1976); Paul Hindemith (1895–1963); Howard Hanson (1896–1981); Roger Sessions (1896–1985); Roy Harris (1898–1979); Carlos Chávez (1899–1978); Aaron Copland (1900–1990); Sir William Walton (1902–1983); Karl Amadeus Hartmann (1905–1963); Michael Tippett (1905–1998); Olivier Messiaen (1908–1992); William Schuman (1910–1992); Alan Hovhaness (1911–2000); Benjamin Britten (1913–1976); Lou Harrison (1917–   ); Leonard Bernstein (1918–1990); Hans Werner Henze (1926–   ); Peter Maxwell Davies (1934–   ); and John Harbison (1938–   ).

Needless to say, many modern composers wrote music on the

scale of symphonies that go by other terminology. As you become more open to music of the past hundred years, I encourage you to listen to the many challenging but rewarding pieces of orchestral music that have remained at the fringes of the repertoire.

Let us begin listening to some symphonies.

• ◦ •

W. A. Mozart: Symphonies 40 and 41; Wiener Philharmoniker; James Levine, conductor; DG 429 731-2

Jan Morris, one of my very favorite authors, confirmed to me a statement that had been attributed to her. She told me that when she leaves her home, a recording of Mozart is left playing so that the music will penetrate the beams and make for a happy house. Her feelings about this composer are shared by millions of people the world over, for whom Mozart is the greatest composer of all. My father used to paraphrase the words of the conductor Sir Thomas Beecham that Bach and Beethoven are at God's feet, but Mozart sits in his lap.

Certain details of the composer's life—his precocious musical talent; his unmatched facility for writing out pieces of music on notation paper without having to change a thing; the grinding poverty that mocked his genius; the jealousy he allegedly aroused in the composer Antonio Salieri; his early death and burial in a pauper's grave—only add to his legend and make us feel we know him. Yet his genius, which we acknowledge even if we cannot comprehend it, separates him from us. It is through his music that we feel a connection to Mozart. It is fresh on every hearing, yet difficult to perform well because it requires deft musicianship, immense sensitivity, and the ability to make these well-known works sound fresh.

Mozart wrote more than six hundred compositions in his short life, and most of them stand as works of great art. He composed forty-one symphonies, and most music lovers consider those from no. 29 onward to be masterpieces. You will notice that the numbering of Mozart's works is different from most composers, whose pieces are indicated with op. (opus, or work) and tend to be in chronological order. The works of Mozart were organized by Ludwig von Köchel (1800–1877), who published a catalogue in 1862 which, though updated according to new scholarship, provides the standard reference. A Mozart work will be listed as K, or KV (Köchel-Verzeichnis), so that the fortieth symphony is KV. 550 and the forty-first, thought to have been composed immediately after, is KV. 551.

We will be exploring these symphonies, especially no. 40, with help from James Levine, who conducted the performances you will be listening to.

A CONVERSATION WITH JAMES LEVINE

So renowned is James Levine as an opera conductor (he has been associated with the Metropolitan Opera since 1971, most of the time as Artistic Director) that many music lovers fail to recognize that his career as an orchestral conductor, chamber musician, and pianist has been equally impressive. Levine has been an indispensable presence at music festivals in Aspen, Ravinia (Chicago), Bayreuth (the Wagner opera festival), Salzburg, and Verbier (in Switzerland).

Among the many great orchestras he has worked with are the Cleveland Orchestra, the Chicago Symphony, the Berlin Philharmonic, the Vienna Philharmonic, and the Munich Philharmonic (as Music Director). His Metropolitan Opera Orchestra has become not only one of the great opera orchestras, but one of the most outstanding ensembles in all repertory. They have a regular season each year at Carnegie Hall for symphonic works, and tour North America, Europe, and Japan. With his assumption of the leadership of the Boston Symphony in 2004, Levine continues his lifelong exploration of working closely with great musicians and expanding the repertory that audiences can hear.

While the focus of this conversation was on Mozart's G-Minor Symphony (no. 40), which was written close together with nos. 39 and

41 in the summer of 1788, Levine covered many fascinating musical topics that will give you food for thought for months to come.

Question   Mozart's Symphonies nos. 40 and 41 were written in Vienna in the summer of 1788. You recorded them with the Vienna Philharmonic in 1989. Does this city and do those musicians have any special claims on this music, and many of the great works of Haydn, Beethoven, Schubert, Johann Strauss, Mahler, Schoenberg, and Berg?

JAMES LEVINE   *I think it would be right to say that they really do indeed. You see, the Vienna Philharmonic is a very old orchestra, relatively speaking. Because of their bringing down, across one historical phase after another, their own instruments and their own hall and their own way of self-governing, they manage to retain some of their great characteristics from generation to generation because many families [are in it]—it is such a respected thing to be a member of the Vienna Philharmonic—and you might find one of the children of the next generation working with the goal in mind to join the orchestra.*

I was fortunate because I did a lot of work with them. In seventeen Salzburg summers we did a lot of operas together. Over that seventeen years, we did a lot of work in Vienna and some touring. My sense of the Vienna Philharmonic is that it is capable of absorbing all music and capable of understanding and producing almost anything that a conductor wants. It is a question of communication in musical instincts, things that have to do with that part of music which is metaphysical, under your skin, in your way of listening. You have to realize that the Vienna Philharmonic, because it is self-governing, plays under a tremendous variety of conductors in their concerts (which are not so many) and their opera performances (which are nightly).

One of my dearest, dearest colleagues was their senior concertmaster, Gerhart Hetzel (1940–1992), who died suddenly and unexpectedly in an accident up in the hills while he was taking a walk. He fell and did not recover from the injuries. I did the majority of my Vienna Philharmonic work with him. He was an amazing musician. When I looked over at him during a performance, his eyes would come up to me, and he would look in my eyes until I looked away. This meant that he did not have to look at his part [the musical score on his music stand], and he could give full attention to what I was trying to show. Two months before he died, we played a recital of Mozart sonatas together because we had a plan to play and record the whole cycle.

He is the one who said, "Can you imagine what it is like for us, in one season, to play the same Mozart piece with you and Karajan, Harnoncourt, Böhm, and other conductors? Everyone wants different accenting, different sonority, and so forth." I said, "Yes, but your orchestra has certain things that are right where I like it: the luminosity in the sound, the personality in the sound, the fact that everything—if you encourage it—can be alive and communicative without being overbearing or a kind of expressive generality." They are wonderful in the detail.

I am very lucky. I have guest-conducted for most of my life (except for the Met and until I went to Munich) and therefore I went repeatedly to orchestras that I could develop a relationship with. This recording of the Mozart Fortieth Symphony you have selected is part of a cycle that Deutsche Grammophon wanted. They approached the Vienna Philharmonic about doing it, and Vienna was especially glad to do it with me and about the way we wanted to do it. I spent many happy hours with them in the Musikverein [the concert hall of the Vienna Philharmonic] recording live to an empty hall. Then we played these pieces in concerts too, on and off.

I think the G-Minor Symphony [the Fortieth] is a miracle. And a Mozart miracle is sometimes even more miraculous than some others. It is very difficult to describe one's immersion in a piece of music in words because it is something which one feels so profoundly and thinks through constantly.

Robert Shaw, when we were both assistants to George Szell at the Cleveland Orchestra and each had to conduct children's concerts and sometimes the programs overlapped, would often choose that piece and say to the kids, "Now, boys and girls, I have been told by some of your teachers that this piece is probably too much for you to take in. But I have argued very deeply that I think they are wrong." Shaw thought that everyone has more or less experience, but that the brain power in these students was more than sufficient. He talked to them about the piece, how it was put together, what a symphony was, and how it evolved. Then he played the entire Mozart G-minor and the kids would cheer the house down, because he had captured that ambivalence about "what is this abstraction?"

Don't forget that for the original players and the original audience, symphonic music was not an abstraction. It was played by the same people who played the operas and the chamber music. The Musikverein is a miraculous hall which sounds good with a very large orchestra, with a small orchestra, with a voice recital. These Mozart recordings were fun because we did them with a balance between unifying elements in the approach and varying elements, the same as the composer did. We played with remarkably few instruments. You have an elastic possibility with Mozart. You can play with more or with less instruments. There is a certain number of players in any orchestra which produces the maximum sense of effortless unity and real individuality, and that is what one is looking for. You want to have the composer's intentions communicated to the listener, but you want it done through as committed and lively a personality as possible. Otherwise, all it is is sawdust.

Q. The Fortieth Symphony was originally scored for flute, two oboes, two bassoons, two horns, and strings. Mozart rescored it, probably in 1791, to include two clarinets, probably to use the talents of clarinetists Anton and Johann Stadler. Concerts with this symphony were held in April of that year, conducted by Salieri. Although no music was added, much of the oboe parts were recast for clarinet. What factors affected your decision about which version to perform?

A. *This subject we have to dig into a little. For me there is a basic principle: I tend to favor second thoughts. Now, if you want to take a subject on which there is absolutely no agreement, the best example I can think of is Wagner's Tannhäuser. [Note to reader: Richard Wagner did the original version of this opera for Dresden in 1845 and created a significantly revised version for Paris in 1861. In the intervening years his musical and dramatic skills as a composer expanded radically and he brought all of this to bear on the revision. Chapter 12 of Opera 101 is devoted entirely to Tannhäuser, and you should read that if you wish to deepen your knowledge about this splendid work.] I don't think the Paris Tannhäuser is perfect, and Wagner didn't either, but it is a big step toward where he wanted the piece to go.*

As to Mozart, he clearly saw the clarinets as an improvement. And because the clarinets were developed in his time, he used the timbre because it suited the musical content of this piece. That is the way he thought of it. Everyone knows that [Mozart's operas] The Marriage of Figaro *and* Cosi fan tutte, *to a certain extent, have dominance in the clarinet parts in certain passages, but let us consider what it means to get the best things into a score.*

Imagine yourself sitting in the audience of the world premiere of Così fan tutte, *and you have got no way of having heard this music before. And in the overture, after BAAH-bom-bom, the next thing you hear is a solo oboe. What an amazing thing! It doesn't happen that you hear a solo wind instrument in the context of any other Mozart overture. Sure enough, there is just another moment in the opera when the oboe becomes prominent again. It is not alone, it is accompanied, but still very noticeable. This is the moment in which Fiordiligi gives in to Ferrando. Mozart planted the seed of the oboe as a counter to the* tutti *[all the other instruments]. When he came to the point where he wanted to use the oboe again, that is how he does it.*

The genius composers were always so careful about the unifying elements and the varying elements being in just the right proportion for whatever that piece might be. In the case of the G-Minor Symphony, it is unthinkable that there wouldn't be clarinet parts for a guy such as Mozart who was waiting with bated breath for new instruments to change and be developed.

Consider, if you will, that people are always talking about what instruments to play Bach keyboard music on. You can play it on the harpsichord, on the piano, and so on. Yet every shred of evidence we have got about Bach, his character and his musical character, points to one interesting fact: his lowest priority, unlike many composers, was the sonority of any given instrument. It was the relationship between them that interested him, and I'll tell you how we know that—because he wrote a handful of major works without specifying any instrumentation at all.

And there is a second reason. Here we have Bach, who had enough ideas in his head to write a half-dozen pieces every week for the court. And what did he spend time doing? He took fresh-off-the-press Vivaldi violin concerti and transcribed them for keyboard. Now, what could sound less like a violin than a harpsichord? But he loved this music, and there was a big clamor for arrangements of this kind that you could play at home.

I just think that when you study the classical composers, and any composers for that matter, very carefully and with a maximum view for the details, it informs interpretation a lot. Lately, I have noticed, there is a tendency on the part of some of my conductor colleagues not to solve a problem but to remove it—to find a way to move the problem instead of solving it when it is meant to be part of the tension of a piece of music.

I think the G-Minor Symphony is so personal. Large-scale works written by Mozart in a minor key are rare compared to the major keys. This simply turns out to be—if you consider the last three symphonies, which were written close together in 1788 on a certain kind of large scale—each one of those pieces tells you a great deal with their specifics.

Q. There is so much about the Fortieth Symphony that sounds unsettled—there is urgency in some passages, and considerable pathos in others. At the very start there are a couple of seconds of anxious gnawing on the violas before the violins and other instruments come in with the first melody. In the Andante movement we can hear music that sounds like sighing. The ending of the symphony is abrupt, almost explosive. All of this must have been startling to the Vienna audience of two hundred years ago. What was Mozart after here, and do you think audiences took this music as a personal statement of the composer, or as pure music?

A. *We'll never know how sophisticated they were. We'll never know whether they held on to the belief that the music had to do with the mood the guy was in. I tend not to be in that camp. I think he had developed the idea for a symphony, and whether he had been down in the dumps or elated as all get-out, once he started to take the time to do it, he would just do it. People are always hemming and hawing about whether he knew they were his last three symphonies, and I just have to say, "How could he?"*

Q. Yes, it was three years before he died. But the sound of this symphony is so particular. When I play it for people while trying to persuade them of Mozart's genius, they are unsettled by it when you compare it to so many of his other works, that are immediately pleasing and congruent, predictable in certain ways . . .

A. The last three symphonies are as highly contrasted as three works by Mozart could ever be—in content, in attitude, in specifics and thematic material. The Fortieth is a significant piece in that it is probably the largest-scale minor-key symphony written until that time. But the "Jupiter" (Symphony no. 41), like the G-minor, is a very rich, filled-out piece, and in it something really important happens: The center of gravity shifts into the last movement, so that if you get a really exciting, vigorous performance of this piece, making the repeats the way they are written. . . . We played that piece once in Carnegie Hall before the intermission, and it got such an immediate roar from the audience and they stood up. I had never seen that before, and I always thought that if the piece was really played the spots off of, with repeats and all, so that everyone can feel how much tension and effort is in the last movement, they would feel this shift. The first movement is much more vertically ritualistic—what is expected. One of the themes in it is also used in a piece he wrote for voice, which has text, which only shows again how these things are always conceived vocally by the composer. There is a lot of that. The phenomenally subtle third movement leads from the original dance form (the minuet) to Beethoven, who used scherzos, and onward until we get into the nineteenth century where there are no minuets anymore. Amazing. The whole process is amazing.

Q. Are the orchestral and chamber compositions of composers who wrote a lot for voice, such as Mozart and Schubert, Tchaikovsky, Debussy, and others, different from the compositions by those who did not often write for the voice?

A. I think that what I would rather say is that the voice is the ur-instrument. You can't see it, it is of the body, and it expresses through sound, through words, through extremes of register, breath, et cetera, all kinds of thoughts and experiences and feelings. Every human being's is different.

A lot of classical composers made it clear that they expected the instruments to endeavor to imitate vocal characteristics. I guess that if you find a conductor who really doesn't know singing or like it terribly much, usually some dimension is also missing in the instrumental approach.

Q. Do we nowadays do a disservice to Mozart, and to ourselves, by regarding him as a genius?

A. *Oh yes. Not only was he a genius, but he was one of the few composers who could write pieces that were perfect. What a conception! A piece of music being perfect, meaning everything about it is exactly as it should be. And this man was dead when he was thirty-six years old.*

Twenty years ago or so, a man named Hildesheimer wrote sort of an anti-Mozart-as-genius book in which he wanted Mozart to be de-iconized. I always come up on a different side. When I first went to Bayreuth, audiences didn't applaud after any of the acts of Parsifal, regardless of whether that had been the original intention. I was asked by many people, "Didn't you hate that? Isn't that sanctimonious?" You know what my response is: I wish that every time I reach the end of Schubert's Die Winterreise *or* Die Schöne Mullerin, *or the Verdi* Requiem, *I would like to extend the whole principle so that the knee-jerk applause reaction doesn't come to the fore.*

You see this often enough: The curtain comes up in an opera house, the swag is halfway up, and the audience starts to applaud. They don't know whether the scenery works for the act, they don't know if it has been well-blocked. This is not to put down some segments of the opera audience, but it is important to observe.

To return to talking about genius, Mozart was a genius and I don't see what is wrong with that.

Q. What I mean is, do we distance ourselves from him, and put him on a pedestal such that it doesn't make his music immediate to us in a way that perhaps we go to Brahms without automatically thinking of him as a genius, even if he was . . .

A. *We do? See, I am a bad guy to ask this of. I go to Brahms the same way as Mozart and many other composers too.*

Q. Mozart had a good press agent all through the centuries in a way that other composers didn't. We come to him thinking that we have to love him and expect that he is a genius. We turn off mechanisms to really try to understand his music that we might use for other composers.

A.   *I suppose that is a constructive point of view. You see, things are put down so meaninglessly a lot of the time, that I figure that a gratuitous putting-up once in a while might not be so bad.*

Q.   I mean more for the listener who might be intimidated.

A.   *That is a terrible reaction in any case. No intimidation.*

Q.   Can you read a score and decide if the piece is meaningful to you, or do you have to play it or hear it?

A.   *No. In fact, unless it is made up of sounds that I don't know what they would sound like in a new piece, I don't play it. Generally speaking, I do the vast majority of my learning of new pieces away from the piano. Maybe I bring the piano into it later in the game. I was taught very early on that if I started learning a piece at the piano, I would instinctively gravitate toward something about how I was playing the piece. I often went all the way up to a kind of memorization phase without ever playing the piano. It was better. It kept me here and the piece there until it was time to absorb it.*

Q.   How would you develop, with any given singer, a vocal recital in which you play the piano? In the chapter on vocal music in this book, I cite a memorable recital you did with Elisabeth Söderstrom in which you did twenty-four songs by twenty-two different composers.

A.   *It was heaven.*

Q.   What did you do to prepare for that concert and evolve it with her?

A.   *I studied the songs. I knew most of them. I rehearsed with her. It is like a table-tennis match. You bat the ball. She hears it. She bats it back.*
Another artist with whom I had a particularly good rehearsal routine was Christa Ludwig. She had a system for preparing songs for a concert that was one of the most intelligent systems I ever saw. She would come to the city where she would sing days and days in advance, to get her body ready. Then we would have a rehearsal, and she would sing each song in half of the concert. I could ask questions and ask for repetitions, and then

we would put that song away. I could do whatever I wanted to, but she wouldn't repeat it. She was desperately afraid of studied-sounding rubati [a rubato, or robbed time in Italian, is when a musician takes a slight liberty with the length of a note for dramatic or emotional effect, compensating for this change soon after so that the music will in total remain in the time frame the composer wrote it. When done well, a rubato has considerable effect; when done clumsily the feeling is quite forced].

And then she would skip a day. The following day we would rehearse the second half and put it away. Then we would skip another day. On the day of the concert, we would come in, set the lights, and go. With her, this was an ideal way to work. It wouldn't be with everybody.

For some singers, they like to rehearse on the day of the concert. For some singers to wake their voice up twice is the kiss of death. For other singers, they want that rehearsal. It frees their mind.

Q. Which leads to another question. How do you, either as a conductor, or as a pianist working with a singer, know when you have rehearsed enough? Or can you ever rehearse enough?

A. *Of course, you can rehearse too much, and you can't rehearse enough. There is more to a performance than how it is rehearsed. But you should get a certain quality of comprehension and details rehearsed before you go on. Then, with people with whom you have a rapport you have ways of rehearsing. For instance, [tenor] Jon Vickers. I used to go to his dressing room before every performance and ask, "Any place you would like to try and do differently?" He might mention something and then ask if there was something I wanted to do differently. I would say, "Here's a place that I think we don't get as well as we might" and we would go over it.*

You have to know when you would be rehearsing in a way that tears down confidence or oversings the person so that they leave it in the dressing room. You have to rehearse in a way that they can release it in a performance. A performance should not be hard work for a singer. The rehearsals are. A performance should be a real release.

Q. How do you teach conducting?

A. *You can only teach certain facets, but there are people who can teach those facets. I had one very exceptional conducting teacher, and I* was exposed to some wonderful conductors. So by watching the way great conductors rehearsed and performed, I saw them use every conceivable kind of gesture. Most of them used classical gestures. It was in the age before television came around and showed everybody what the conductor looked like. I have a big determination when I conduct to give the audience so little to see that it will make their ears more pointed and their eyes more relaxed. Whereas there are people who are acting out the music, and I just find that this is not effective for the orchestra.

The orchestra will do better with rehearsing so that they agree and know what they supposed to be trying to do and have it set up. That gives you all kinds of possibilities for bringing the ear of the listener instead of the eye. And the more you put on a calisthenics show, the more the orchestra starts to look at you as if you were a television program. They would think that they don't have to do it because you are doing it. It just doesn't work.

I have seen very few conductors who have gone outside the classical gestures and were any good. I would name three conductors who did not conduct with classical gestures and got stupendous, or at least good, results: Dimitri Mitropoulos, Wilhelm Furtwängler, and Lenny (Bernstein). They had a sincere inability to think of conducting as what it really is.

Q. What is it really?

A. Well, it has nothing at all to do with miming or acting out the piece. It has to do with rehearsing in a way in which the orchestra knows exactly what they are trying to do. And then, in the performance, they must see a person whose demeanor and expression reminds them in each spot of what they need and a technique that unifies them.

I did the Haydn Creation in Munich and in Boston. At the place where they say, "God said, let there be light, and there was light," the way that Haydn set it is that on the last mention of the word Licht [light], there is complete radiant shining in the orchestral music. I have a way of rehearsing this with orchestra in a way the audience can't see the preparation, so that the musical moment of light is a revelation because I do not indicate it.

Sometimes I dream of a wonderful invention that I know we will never have. I would love to have a screen behind me the size of the podium in a way that the orchestra can see me but the audience cannot.

It is so effective in Bayreuth [where the conductor and orchestra musicians are hidden], where you don't see but you can hear.

Q. What does your right hand do and what does your left hand do, and how do orchestra musicians read it?

A. *It doesn't quite work like that. Once you have seated the orchestra correctly—and that is an important thing to think about—and you are rehearsing, on occasions where you separate, essentially the beat is kept by this [the right] hand. But there are places where they don't need it kept and you can use it for something else. I am very loath to do gestures that they don't need. I suppose anyone who told you that expressive, non-rhythmical organization and metrical gestures come from the left hand, well, they do. But what is forgotten in all this is the rehearsals and the face. These are more important than either arm.*

Q. What does the face do?

A. *It gives them the feeling of your involvement. You do all kinds of cuing and correcting with your face. Like this [he raises both eyebrows] to say that this is your entrance. Or the face can do this [he thrusts his chin and lower lip forward] to indicate emphasis or emotion.*

The process of rehearsing a lot gives the orchestra and singers a sense of how and what they need to release during a performance. And I always say, "Don't critique your performance while it is going on. Do it, and we will critique and adjust it later." You need all your brain going in the same direction.

Q. Thank you very much.

A. *You're welcome.*

Now listen to the recording of Mozart's Symphonies nos. 40 and 41, keeping in mind what you just read.

Panorama: Franz Joseph Haydn, Symphony no. 94, etc.; various artists; DG 289 469 148-2

Haydn was in the unusual position of being in the employ of a noble and incredibly wealthy family, the Esterházys, from 1761 to 1790. His music was performed in their castle, which featured several theaters. The stability this job provided him enabled him to compose at will because he had a guaranteed income. He was remarkably industrious. In his lifetime he wrote 104 symphonies, 83 quartets for strings, 52 piano sonatas, 31 trios, oratorios, operas, cantatas, and sacred music.

His life stood in remarkable contrast to his friend Mozart, who had to struggle desperately for patronage. Although Haydn was born twenty-four years before Mozart, he had a considerably longer life than his friend. The symphonies we will listen to were written after Mozart's death.

Because Haydn lived in relative isolation, he was unaware that his music had become quite popular around Europe. In 1790, the heirs to the Esterházy fortune decided to disband the musical "staff" of the household, and Haydn was out of a job. But he soon found work in London, where his music was already popular. He spent much of the 1790s there, earning considerable fees and basking in his success. Many of the pieces he wrote for London are among his most enduring and admired.

The English had already had great success with Handel, another German-speaking composer, and welcomed Haydn warmly. He, in turn, responded to the acclaim with obvious inspiration. He wrote the last twelve of his symphonies for London audiences.

This recording contains fine performances of three symphonies from that period: no. 94 (the *Surprise*); no. 104 (*London*); and no. 100 (*Military*), all given vibrant, if somewhat formal, performances by the Berlin Philharmonic under Herbert von Karajan. Note that they range in length from 23 to 29 minutes, and bear this in mind as you see how symphonies grow in length. For example, the first two movements of Brahms's Fourth Symphony last about 25 minutes, which can be the length of one movement in symphonies by Bruckner or Mahler.

Let us start with Haydn's Symphony no. 94 (the *Surprise*). Notice the wonderful way that Haydn plays around with the lovely theme in the first movement. It is almost as if he is showing off, but the goal was to delight the audience with his cleverness—this was England, where such traits are always prized. If you were to go back to symphonies by the Mannheim composers, or even a young Haydn, you would see why the playfulness and eagerness to take convention to its limits gives this music such a liberating sound. The "surprise" in the symphony (the nickname given by a flautist in Haydn's London orchestra) comes in the second movement when the kettledrums are struck. It is often remarked upon that this was a bit of humor, intended to wake up any dozing audience members. What I find special is that after this cheekiness, Haydn returns the movement to a beautiful and deeply felt musical passage that takes us by another kind of surprise because it touches us when we least expect it. The third and fourth movements pick up the pace again, and the piece concludes exuberantly.

As to the *London* Symphony, there is nothing especially London about it. It seems that most of the others Haydn wrote in the British capital got nicknames and not one bore the name of his host city, hence the *London* Symphony. This is music that is by turns serene, energetic, and majestic, and is striking for its balance and quiet grandeur.

You might expect that a symphony called *Military* would be serious and rather martial in flavor. In hearing the slow introduction, you are not prepared for the humor and surprises that are to come. At this time in Europe, there was a taste for Turkish-sounding music. Mozart employed it in his famous "Rondo alla turca" and in the opera *The Abduction from the Seraglio*. Haydn probably thought it would please his English audiences to hear his take on the Turkish fashion, and here uses the rare instrumental combination of triangle, bass drum, and cymbals not only to give Turkish flavor but to give the piece a somewhat bemusing military feel. I think of a chocolate soldier.

Many music lovers, myself included, believe that Haydn is the most undervalued of all composers. His apparent wit and lack of pretense led some people to think of his work as lacking seriousness or craft. Much the same problem afflicted Rossini, who is never given his due. Haydn was a splendid composer, one of history's greatest, but he seldom had the occasion to demonstrate this to a wider audience until he reached London.

I find that Haydn's symphonies and his trumpet concerto are among the most instantly attractive musical works to young people. As a child, this was the music I was drawn to, but I know now it is anything but childlike. Haydn's music is humane, witty, cerebral, and, within the context of his times, deeply emotional. We will hear the trumpet concerto later on, but I encourage you to further explore other works by "Papa" Haydn on your own.

• ◇ •

Beethoven: Symphony no. 5; Royal Concertgebouw Orchestra; Wolfgang Sawallisch, conductor; or the Philadelphia Orchestra; Eugene Ormandy, alternate

Ludwig van Beethoven was an extraordinary pianist who also played violin, viola, and organ. He conducted many performances of his own music, and gave numerous performances of his solo piano compositions. He also conducted his piano concertos from the keyboard, a feat that Daniel Barenboim repeated in 2000 when he and the Staatskapelle Orchestra of Berlin performed Beethoven's five piano concertos and nine symphonies at Carnegie Hall in New York.

One of the most famous and stunning facts in music history is that Beethoven wrote most of his masterpieces when he was partially or entirely deaf. Part of the driven nature of Beethoven was the imperative he seemed to feel to take the music in his head and set it down on paper. Unlike Mozart, whose scores in his own hand show little stress or reconsideration, Beethoven went through draft after draft of a piece until he felt it was acceptable.

A famous example was the overture for his only opera, *Fidelio*, whose leading female character is named Leonore. He wrote three versions of what is now called the *Leonore* Overture and ultimately rejected them all, though they are excellent, especially the third. An interesting exercise would be for you to listen to recordings of the three and think about the evolution of this music through three phases, and then ask yourself why Beethoven finally found them to be unsuitable. Then listen to the *Fidelio* Overture, the one that now precedes the opera, and see how it compares with *Leonore* no. 3.

Beethoven had a terrible, progressively deteriorating illness and considered suicide. In a letter he wrote to his brothers, to be opened after his death, he said, in part, "It seemed to me impossible to leave the world before I had brought forth all that I was destined to bring forth. So I endured this miserable existence—miserable indeed." As we listen to Beethoven's music, it is important to recall the particularly strong imperative he felt to create his music.

Beethoven was not born deaf. We do not know what particular ailment he had that caused the gradual loss of his hearing, which began when he was about thirty years old. Therefore, Beethoven had a *memory* of sound and could use this for composing even after he had lost his hearing. He wrote the music and imagined its sound. You can parallel this with a person who is born blind and one who becomes blind later in life. The former does not have a reference for colors and images, while the latter can recall them, although sometimes memory changes and mental images become different from what we call reality.

For a composer and many conductors, part of their talent is the ability to look at a musical score and hear in their heads the sounds—the voices—of all the instruments individually and together. Beethoven, as one of the most gifted of all composers, certainly had this ability. What he lacked was the ultimate proof of the value of what issued from his pen, the proof that could only come in hearing his music performed by musicians.

So, as you listen to his Fifth Symphony, one that you surely have heard before, imagine what it must have been like for Beethoven to have perceived only the faintest vibrations when this immortal symphony was performed for the first time on December 22, 1808, in Vienna on a program that included the Fourth Piano Concerto and the *Choral Fantasia*. Reports from that event speak of the fact that the heating system broke down in the Theater an der Wien, so the chilly audience was distracted from fully appreciating all of this sublime music.

You know well the opening of the Fifth Symphony, which might be among the most famous notes in all of music. Beethoven described them, saying, "Thus Fate knocks at the door." He spends much of the first movement developing these notes in interesting ways, at varying speeds and volumes and in various orchestral voices. Listen to this movement as if you had never heard it before, and try to focus on the many approaches he takes to these fundamental notes of Fate that keep knocking and knocking. Notice too how frequently things come to a complete stop in this movement, and bear in mind that silence is not necessarily the absence of sound, but is another kind of sound. Ask yourself what the inclusion of moments of silence must have meant (if anything) to a composer who was deaf.

In the second movement, note the softness and delicacy of much of the music, and note how certain themes he starts do not necessarily have a natural (or at least predictable) conclusion. Obviously this was not because Beethoven was unable to do better, but because of conscious choices he made about how the music would evolve. Compare this with the symmetry you often hear in Mozart and Haydn.

The third movement is full of drama, with revisitations of earlier music in the symphony as well as themes that hurtle us toward the last movement. Here we find the magical appearance of the piccolo, three trombones, and the contrabassoon for the first time in symphonic literature. In effect, Beethoven opens wide the terrain on which the sonic range and force of musical expression can be heard. In expanding the number of instrumental voices, he asserts the importance of the variety of ways for us to hear things. He is telling us to be open to new ideas and to new ways of seeing and hearing things we think we already know.

And there is that famous ending, which never seems to end—it just keeps topping itself, daring us to go with it. Eschewing neatness and symmetry, Beethoven takes us on one last climb, pulling us to a thrilling summit.

• ◇ •

Panorama: Franz Schubert, Symphony no. 8, etc.; various artists; DG 289 469 196-2

It is hard to believe that none of Schubert's symphonies were performed in his short lifetime. They were not even published for fifty years after his death in 1828. How can this be explained? One answer was that Schubert was not a famous performer, as were Mozart, Beethoven, and other stars of the Viennese music world. Schubert enjoyed playing in homes, and in the company of friends, and most of what was played would be chamber music and songs. The vocal music did garner him some acclaim, as did a few other pieces. In all, only about one-eighth of the music composed was published during his lifetime.

Many people found his gorgeous melodies out of step with the more ambitious scope of Romanticism, the artistic movement of the early nineteenth century that emphasized the love of nature and the embrace of great philosophical ideas. For adherents of Romanticism (which you should not confuse with romance, or depictions of love), music represented the highest possible expression of Romantic ideals because it alone could go beyond words and images to the spiritual essence of the human condition. This concept was in opposition to the rationality favored during the Enlightenment (in the eighteenth century), when reason and balance were thought to be effective means to explain that which makes us who we are. The almost clinical and scientific certainness of the Enlightenment gave way to the mystery and ambiguity that characterize Romanticism.

Ever since, there has been a seesawing between these two poles. The rise in science in the twentieth century (and its use to explain natural and physical phenomena) can be contrasted with a return to deep religiosity and even fundamentalism in much of the world toward the end of that century.

I think it is possible to look back to late Mozart, Beethoven, and Schubert and find expressions of ideals of both Enlightenment and Romanticism. But in his time, many considered Schubert a link to the old, while Beethoven's innovations and striving for radical means of expression pointed him to the new.

You will be listening to the Eighth and Ninth symphonies of Schubert. These performances, by Karl Böhm and the Berlin Philharmonic, have a great deal to recommend them, though they sometimes are a bit too grave. You might, in the future, consider hearing performances led by George Szell or James Levine to get a sense of how these works can be played more deftly without losing any character and profundity.

The Eighth, which is known as the *Unfinished*, is perhaps Schubert's most popular symphonic work. This is curious, if you think about it. The work is 23 minutes long and has only two movements. It is not known why Schubert abandoned it, though in 1822, when he wrote it, the composer faced terrible reversals in his professional and financial state, as well as the symptoms of the syphilis that would end his life.

Because Schubert later wrote a full symphony, his Ninth, we know that it was not disease that prevented him from working on the Eighth. Rather, he probably felt that he went as far as he could artistically. I liken this to the great unfinished sculptures by Michelangelo. The parts that he sculpted are sublime; the parts that were not touched speak volumes to us about potential and how inspiration can wane or change during the period when a work of art is being created. The *Unfinished* Symphony came to light in 1865.

In listening to this music, I want you to think about the mood that music can create. Notice how the first movement starts in the dark and ruminating sound of the basses. Then we hear other strings, and suddenly the aching theme played jointly by oboe and clarinet. Then cellos come charging in with a glorious melody. So much is going on here in just the first few minutes! Pay attention, as the music proceeds, to dynamics. We hear some music played pianissimo (very softly) and other music is fortissimo (very loud). Schubert explores mystery and emotion in this music through the choice of instruments, the intriguing dovetailing of melodies, and the broad dynamic range.

As you move from the gripping—perhaps pessimistic—sound of the first movement to the sunnier, more serene sounds of the second, note how deftly Schubert orchestrates this music. With every note you hear, try to identify the instrument(s) that are being used. Ask yourself how this music might sound if it were played on other instruments. What do you feel as you listen to the passage with solo violins?

Ultimately, Schubert has laced these 23 minutes of music with many mysteries, with ideas that promise clarity and explanation, but perforce remain ambiguous and beyond definition. They reach toward the spiritual and undefinable in our perceptions, and then leave us to sort things out for ourselves. In this music, Schubert wrote—perhaps unintentionally—one of the first important works to embrace the spirit of Romanticism.

Let us now turn to the Ninth Symphony. It is now called the *Great* Symphony, yet, as was so often the case in Schubert's sad life, it was not appreciated when it was new. He wrote it for the Gesellschaft de Musikfreunde (Society of the Friends of Music), which found it too challenging to perform. The score was lost and not found until 1838 when Robert Schumann discovered it among papers in the possession of Schubert's brother Ferdinand. He sent it to Mendelssohn, who gave the symphony its first performance in 1839 in Leipzig. It did not immediately catch on, and orchestras further afield were more likely to play it than in the musical capitals of Europe. In fact, it was heard in New York and Boston before being performed in London and Paris.

At 51 minutes, this is a substantial work, twice the length of many Haydn symphonies. This symphony more fully develops many of the musical ideas that exist in embryonic forms in earlier unfinished works from 1818 and 1821. It has a remarkably conceived and detailed orchestration, and I want you to pay special attention to the use of brass instruments. Because of this symphony's length and complexity, it took many years after its premiere to gain the recognition and esteem it merits.

After you have listened to it, take out your recording of Beethoven's Seventh Symphony (1813) and play the first movement only. Then play the first movement of the Schubert Ninth (1828). Do you hear stylistic, instrumental, or emotional similarities? How do factors such as energy, speed, dynamics compare?

I am not in any way suggesting that Schubert borrowed from Beethoven, but want you to think how the evolution of the symphonic form occurred in the same city through two great composers. More to the point, I want you to decide whether you can tell Beethoven and

Schubert apart. What sounds and stylistic choices do these two composers have in common? And how do they differ?

After a day or so, pick up the Schubert Ninth and listen to it again. You will discover how much you have learned about listening as you are able to recognize and appreciate many details that you did not think you noticed the first time. This step forward is due not only to your listening of Schubert, but to your prior immersion in Haydn, Mozart, and Beethoven, and the many other composers whose pieces you have sampled. I believe that, in addition to all of the other qualities you are now able to identify and describe in music, you will find something in Schubert's Ninth Symphony that you perhaps have not yet found: *eloquence*.

I do not mean to suggest that no music you have heard until now is eloquent, but rather that it is such a palpable characteristic of this symphony that you cannot help but feel it. Eloquence, whether in speech, writing, or music, is a precious commodity that we have lost contact with, and esteem for, in our rushed and casual times. Take a few minutes to think about what this means to you.

By the way, some scholars contend that Schubert wrote only seven complete symphonies, and they call this one the Seventh. But for most people who think of Schubert's symphonies, this is the Ninth.

Because so much of Schubert's music was discovered posthumously, it fell to scholars to catalogue his works. The most famous was Otto Erich Deutsch (1883–1967), who specialized in Handel, Mozart, and Schubert. He published three volumes of documentation on Schubert, and the composer's works are given Deutsch numbers, indicated with the letter *D*. The *Unfinished* Symphony is D. 759. The *Great* Symphony is D. 944.

• ∾ •

Panorama: Felix Mendelssohn, The Hebrides *Overture, etc.; various artists; DG 289 469 157–2*

This moderately priced 2-CD set includes some of Mendelssohn's greatest hits, including the Symphony no. 4 (the *Italian*), music from *A Mid-*

summer Night's Dream (you will recognize the wedding march), the *Octet* (chamber music for eight instruments written when the composer was a teenager), and other works. We will be studying other performances of the violin concerto, but the performance here by Anne-Sophie Mutter will be valuable if you wish to do comparative listening.

The work of Felix Mendelssohn (1809–1847) divides music lovers. Many are drawn to his indisputably great works, including those on this recording, while others feel that the composer never reached his potential. He was considered the greatest child prodigy since Mozart, as a composer and pianist, and grew to be the most important conductor in Europe. At age twenty-six he led the Gewandhaus Orchestra of Leipzig, burnishing the talents of an ensemble that still ranks among the world's greatest. He spearheaded the revival of interest in the works of Bach, championed the unknown works of Schubert, and regularly performed music by Handel, Haydn, Mozart, Beethoven, and others.

Despite all of the comfort (he came from a wealthy family), acclaim, and affection he received in his lifetime, the mirth and facility of his music tend to undermine it for people who equate accomplishment with ponderous gravity. There is a sparkling quality to much of the music, but I would also commend listeners to his splendid oratorio *Elijah*, in an excellent recording starring Bryn Terfel (London/Decca 455 688-2). Only Handel's greatest oratorios exceed Mendelssohn's achievement in the form.

The *Italian* Symphony was completed in Berlin in 1833 following Mendelssohn's extensive sojourn in Italy in 1830 and 1831. You might think of this as a postcard, or a series of entries in a travel diary. With the exception of a Neapolitan melody in the last movement, there is not much that is explicitly Italian in this symphony, but Mendelssohn did make many musical sketches during his tour, so we might better call this the Italian-influenced symphony.

As I have mentioned about other music in this book, you do not have to know the background of the pieces to enjoy them. The infectiously good-natured spirit of this symphony will cause you to smile.

You will enjoy the dialogue among woodwinds in the first movement, and the response they receive from the violins. Notice throughout this movement the special roles given to the oboe and clarinet, and ask yourself why Mendelssohn selected these instruments for such a plum assignment.

Pay attention to the unusual and pleasing sequence of solo instruments in the second movement: oboe, bassoon, viola, violin, flutes. All take up a particular tune and give it a different sensation. What do you see and hear as you listen to this?

After enjoying the second and third movements, make note of a couple of distinctions in the last. The first is that it begins in a minor key, although the symphony is in A major. Does this alter your view of the work and its sound world? Then notice that the final movement is given the name of an Italian dance, the saltarello. *Saltare* in Italian means to leap, as one might in a dance. With this in mind, think about how this Neapolitan dance must have sounded to the British audience that heard the composer conduct the premiere.

• ◌ •

Panorama: Hector Berlioz, Symphonie Fantastique, etc.; various artists; DG 289 469 118-2. Another excellent and inexpensive recording of the Sym-phonie Fantastique is by the Philharmonia Orchestra conducted by André Cluytens; other pieces are played by orchestras led by Carlo Maria Giulini and John Barbirolli; Seraphim/Virgin CDE 7243 5 69020 2 2.

No matter which recording of the *Symphonie Fantastique* you opt for, you are in for a treat. This epic work and only a few other pieces of music by Berlioz (1803–1869) enjoy any widespread popularity, which makes me consider him, along with Haydn, to be the most undervalued of composers. He was deeply influenced by the currents of Romanticism but read widely, including classic texts of antiquity, especially Virgil, along with Shakespeare, the great French plays by Molière, Racine, Corneille, and contemporaries such as Byron, Goethe, and Hugo.

He was a medical student in Paris before definitively giving himself to music.

Unlike most comparable musical geniuses, he did not play violin, piano, or any other instrument proficiently, although he had shown some talent for the flute. As such, he focused less on instruments that required individual virtuosity, striving instead for grand sounds and pictures, often illustrating subject matter from his reading, or from his travels, especially in Italy.

Berlioz had a taste for large, grand artistic statements, picking up on some of the tradition of Bach and Beethoven and pointing the way to Strauss, Mahler, and others. But while these other composers were from the German-speaking world, Berlioz was French, and he imparted a certain Gallic sensibility to his works. Some of this music can be thought of as a great novel or a sweeping saga. His very long and brilliant opera, *Les Troyens*, is one of the grandest and most thrilling, but it is not empty spectacle.

When you think of the music of Berlioz, keep in mind the word *texture*. It is almost as if you can feel the depth and variety of ideas and sensibilities in his pieces, all of which add up to a large and very satisfying whole. This statement applies whether speaking of a massive work such as his Requiem (called *Grande Messe des Morts*) or the cycle of six songs known as *Les Nuits d'Été* (Summer Nights).

All of these characteristics, and more, are part of his famous and popular *Symphonie Fantastique*. Think of the title not as suggesting something really great, but rather as a feverish fantasy that is the product of intense passions and wishes. Also note that the symphony was written in 1830, only three years after the death of Beethoven, when Berlioz was twenty-seven years old. You will be able to hear the Beethoven influence, but also notice the radical directions Berlioz took. The reason I had you listen to Mendelssohn's *Italian* Symphony (1833) before the Berlioz is so that you could understand how radical Berlioz was in comparison to what other composers were doing.

While Beethoven, Mendelssohn, and others drew inspiration from ideas, literature, or locales, Berlioz was probably the first composer to depict a story with a sequence of events. It is as if he were creating a novel in symphonic form. You may say that Vivaldi attempted something like this in the depiction of the four seasons, but these were really a continuum of images that relate to the progression of the year.

On September 11, 1827, young Berlioz attended an English-language performance of *Hamlet* at the Odéon Theater in Paris. Although he barely understood the words, he fell madly in love with Harriet Smithson, the Irish actress playing Ophelia. He said that the verbal music—the sound and cadence of her voice—was part of the infatuation, as were the events of the play, which he read in French before attending. You would be right to ask whether Berlioz was taken with Smithson or Ophelia (seeing himself as Hamlet, the melancholy young hero). He wrote to Smithson, who would not meet with him. The rejection pushed him toward trying to express his feelings in music. While writing the symphony, he fell in love with a pianist, Camille Moke, who then left him for another man.

When the symphony was performed in Paris in December 1832, Harriet Smithson was in attendance. She then was introduced to Berlioz and declared her love for him. They married, but it was not successful, and they soon parted. She later was paralyzed in an accident and became an alcoholic. Berlioz supported her financially until her death in 1854, even though he was with another woman. Harriet (whom Berlioz called Henriette) was the inspiration for Berlioz's *Roméo et Juliette* Symphony and a song called "La Mort d'Ophélie" (The Death of Ophelia). Theirs is a story for the era of Romanticism!

The story recounted in the symphony is not of Berlioz's infatuation with Smithson, but rather how it evolved in his mind to a more fevered and exotic tale than the events that actually happened. He created a narrative of love, passion, and tragedy, describing its protagonist as "a young musician of morbid sensibility and ardent imagination [who] in a paroxysm of love-sick despair has poisoned himself with opium. The drug, too weak to kill, plunges him into a heavy sleep accompanied by strange visions. His sensations, feelings, and memories are translated in his sick brain into musical images and ideas. The beloved one herself becomes for him a melody, a recurrent theme that haunts him everywhere."

Thus did Berlioz create a musical device that Wagner and other opera composers would use in their compositions, and many orchestral composers employed as well. In German it is called a *Leitmotiv*, which is a recurring theme or melody that always represents the same person, event, idea, or emotion. Of course, composers before Berlioz found ways to use a recurring theme, but if they were linked to a specific and tangible image, that remained in the mind of the composer.

In a letter he wrote, Berlioz gave more details about the story of this musician: "An artist, gifted with a vivid imagination, [falls in love] with a woman embodying the ideal of beauty and fascination he has long sought. . . . He imagines there is some hope, he believes himself loved." Later on, the poet takes the opium, and the story becomes a wild, drug-induced fantasy.

As you listen, pay attention to the fascinatingly pictorial use of instruments, which is one of the composer's hallmarks. Listen to the muted violins, the plucking of violas and cellos and basses, the arrival of flutes, clarinets, horns, and harps at key moments. Also try to identify the theme of the beloved; notice how it is revisited in each movement, and make note of the instruments and orchestrations with which it is played.

Berlioz broke the boundaries of traditional form by making this a five-movement symphony. He gave each movement a name: 1. Dreams and Passions; 2. A Ball; 3. Scene in the Fields; 4. March to the Scaffold; 5. Witches' Sabbath.

The composer also wrote detailed notes to accompany the publication of the score in 1845. I would prefer to let you add your own details to the story, and will thus give you only scant summary of Berlioz's specific indications for each movement. It is better for you to actively engage and create a narrative. Then, when you attend a performance of this symphony—it is performed in most major cities at least once a year—you can read all of Berlioz's notes in the program.

1. **Dreams and Passions:** The hero is overcome by a "surge of passions" upon seeing the woman of his dreams. She will always be associated with a particular musical thought (here is

the recurring theme), a "melancholic reverie" that leads to fury, jealousy, tenderness, tears, and religious consolation.

2. **A Ball:** Listen to the swirling, dancing, dizzying music, and imagine that wherever the hero goes, he sees his beloved in one form or another.

3. **Scene in the Fields:** Two shepherds playing pipes (a gorgeous musical duet), country scenery, wind through trees. The hero is full of conflicting ideas and emotions. (Listen here for influences of Beethoven's Fifth and, if you have heard it, Sixth symphonies.)

4. **March to the Scaffold:** Feeling that his love will be unrequited, the hero takes opium and, falling asleep, has dreadful visions. One is that he has killed his beloved and is marched to the scaffold, where he will witness his own execution.

5. **Witches' Sabbath:** The hero sees himself at his own funeral, surrounded by ghosts, witches, and monsters groaning, laughing, shrieking, crying. The beloved returns, her melody having lost its noble character and become vulgar. She joins the witches' dance, and then bells toll for the dead. We hear a burlesque of the *Dies Irae* (the Judgment Day requiem hymn), then witches dance, and then the dance and the *Dies Irae* are combined.

While intimations of horror and dreadful death existed in religious music for centuries, and are powerfully evoked in Mozart's opera *Don Giovanni*, what Berlioz has achieved is of a whole other order. With this work, he slams the door shut on the Classical era and made anyone who considered his music think of the future. Richard Wagner (1813–1883) said that Berlioz was one of the three greatest composers of the Romantic era, along with Liszt and . . . Wagner himself.

Although Sigmund Freud was not born until 1856, and would publish his studies and interpretations of dreams long after Berlioz's death, I think that the composer prefigured much of Freud's work. Perhaps the inspiration was in his reading of *Hamlet* and other Shakespearean plays, with their dreams, nightmares, apparitions, witches, and, especially, the enactment of true desires in sleep that are suppressed during waking life.

I hope that you have discovered with the *Symphonie Fantastique* the potential for music to do so much more than entertain. Whether or not it has a story line (and few works have as explicit a narrative as the this one), music is *about* something. It may be something entirely abstract, but utterly essential, such as the deepest stirrings of the human heart. Which brings us to Robert Schumann.

• ◇ •

Panorama: Robert Schumann, Symphony no. 1, etc.; various artists; DG 289 469 199-2 (a good collection of Schumann's four symphonies is by the Bamberger Symphoniker, conducted by Christoph Eschenbach; Virgin Classics 7243 5 61884 2 6)

Robert Schumann (1810–1856), more than any other composer, seemed to epitomize everything that was Romanticism. His music, and what it expresses, are deeply felt, often painfully so. He was the son of an avowed humanist who published pocket editions of the world's literary classics, all of which young Robert would read at home. He was steeped in Romantic literature, having read Goethe's *Faust*, novels by Sir Walter Scott, and Byron's poems. He cultivated vast literary and musical interests and, for a while, it seemed that writing might become his profession. He studied piano and poetry simultaneously, but his talent on the keyboard and the possibility for personal expression won out.

Although many composers have had excellent language skills (including Rossini, Brahms, Saint-Saëns, Vaughan Williams, Stravinsky, Copland, and Bernstein), Schumann's intense love of language and words makes him interesting because he was equally skilled in both verbal and musical communication. One would think that he could choose how to express what he felt, and therefore it is interesting to observe what he elected to say musically. Many of his musical moments are like poems—fragmented, concise—and seem to move from one to the next like turning the pages of a thin volume of poetry.

His serene world collapsed when his father died in 1826 and then his sister committed suicide. Although he would study law in Leipzig and have a phase of sowing wild Romantic oats (including extensive travels), a turning point in his life came when he was eighteen and came under the tutelage of the formidable Friedrich Wieck, a great piano teacher in Leipzig. In the Wieck household was nine-year-old Clara, a piano prodigy.

Robert and Clara, despite their difference in ages, became close, and as she grew up, they fell in love. They wanted to marry, to the outrage of Clara's father, who defamed Schumann publicly for years. Ultimately Robert took legal action against Clara's father. They wed one day before her twenty-first birthday in 1840.

The compositional outpouring in 1840 and 1841 was remarkable. Schumann wrote two marvelous song cycles inspired by Clara: *Frauenliebe und -leben* (A Woman's Love and Life), which was composed in his emotional state after the court's ruling but before their marriage, and *Dichterliebe* (The Poet's Love).

He also wrote the Symphony no. 1 (*Spring*), which you should listen to on the recording I have suggested. The titles he gave the movements are Spring's Awakening; Evening; Merry Playmates; and Full Spring. You will hear the story of Robert's idea of their marriage at that time.

Somewhere in his life, Schumann contracted syphilis. Medical care at that time was not universally good (though Rossini received better treatment in France for the same malady), and he is thought to have taken mercury for his illness, with the result that the drug paralyzed one of his hands. His career as a pianist was over, but he still wrote deeply personal music that Clara, one of Europe's great pianists, would perform. She was, in effect, his surrogate as well as his muse.

In 1844, Schumann's health began to decline and the following year he had a nervous breakdown. He still managed to compose and, with great effort, finished his very dark Second Symphony in 1846. Despite the downward spiral of his health and mental state, he kept writing his music. He also conducted the Düsseldorf Orchestra and other groups, and wrote a great deal of musical journalism.

On November 30, 1853, Schumann received a visit from twenty-year-old Johannes Brahms, then an aspiring composer. For a brief and intense period, Schumann became Brahms's mentor and advocate. In return he received friendship and esteem at a fragile point in his life. His mental state soon declined and in 1854 he jumped into the Rhine, only to be saved by fishermen. Clara, who loved him dearly, felt that she had to commit her husband to an asylum, where he died in 1856 with Clara, Brahms, and the great violinist Joseph Joachim at his side.

· ᨒ ·

Brahms: Symphony no. 4; Wiener Philharmoniker; Carlos Kleiber, conductor; DG 289 457 706-2 (a good collection of all four Brahms symphonies is by the Berliner Philharmoniker, conducted by Herbert von Karajan, DG 289 453 097-2)

In Brahms, Schumann saw the artistic antidote to the programmatic and radical musical tendencies of Liszt and Wagner, and this was how Brahms was pictured by others. Yet Brahms himself was not particularly polemical, and was much more individualistic. For him the goal was to make music that was deeply felt and meaningful. He was a perfectionist who dedicated himself tirelessly to his scores.

Brahms nurtured a deep affection—some might call it an infatu-ation—for Clara Schumann, but she responded only with kindness and a general sense of collegial supportiveness. But the Schumanns did a great deal to nurture Brahms's talents and self-esteem.

In some ways he was a late starter, and his musical career did not really accelerate until he moved to Vienna from Germany in 1863. The city's verve as well as the intensity with which it loved music and com-posers proved stimulating to him, though he would not write his first symphony until 1876, in part because he felt that after Beethoven it would be too difficult to create a meaningful symphony.

His four symphonies indicate an interest in the form as fashioned by Haydn, Mozart, and Beethoven, but are also tinged with Romanti-cism. They rank with the finest in all the repertory and are unique because they all date from his mature years. By the time he wrote the First, he was already highly accomplished as a composer and pianist, and had a deep well of emotions and some amount of life experience to bring to bear on his composing.

The Fourth Symphony is Brahms at his best, full of melodies that sing and dance, moments of introspection and invention. He pays homage to Bach in the last movement with variations on two themes. Throughout the symphony, orchestral voices rise up, whether it is dramatic music for horn and cello, a poignant melody for violin, or a bright passage for winds. It is as if Brahms had reached a summit of inspiration, yet still found a way to adhere to the Classical symphonic form and at the same time call upon all of his resources.

We will return to Brahms later on to explore other aspects of his art, including works for piano, violin, and voice.

• ◇ •

Tchaikovsky: Piano Concerto no. 1 and Symphony no. 6; Los Angeles Philharmonic Orchestra; Erich Leinsdorf, conductor; Leonard Pennario, piano; Seraphim 7243 5 690034 2 5
An excellent recording of Tchaikovsky's Symphonies 4, 5, 6 is by the Leningrad Philharmonic Orchestra; Evgeny Mravinsky, conductor; DG 419 745-2

If you thought Schubert and Schumann had tragic lives, wait until you hear about Peter Ilyich Tchaikovsky (1840–1893). Certainly other composers had travails that equaled or exceeded those of the most famous Russian to write classical music, but Tchaikovsky suffered deeply from his personal sadnesses, and one can hear the cumulative despair that blended with grand melody and superb orchestral coloring.

He was born in a provincial town, where his parents loved to play Mozart and Rossini for him. The family later moved to St. Petersburg, where he began formal musical training, although his father made him study jurisprudence. His mother died of cholera in 1855, a loss from which he never fully recovered. His father endured many financial reversals, and the family situation was unhappy.

Around 1860, a group of composers called the Mighty Five—Mily Balakirev (1837–1910), César Cui (1835–1918), Borodin, Mussorgsky, and Rimsky-Korsakov—banded together to promote Russian characteristics in their music and subjects. It was a form of nationalism that was not about forming a nation but rather an assertion of identity. The talented Tchaikovsky had considerable contact with the Five, but was ultimately made to feel unwelcome because he did not fully embrace their doctrine.

The exclusion was ironic because Tchaikovsky drew from the Russian cultural well of literature and folk music as much as anyone else. The difference was that he was more cosmopolitan in outlook, and his grounding in Mozart and Rossini gave him a feeling for the light touch it was possible to achieve in composing. He also held up Beethoven, Mendelssohn, and Schumann as models for his work. Tchaikovsky's music has an unmistakable freshness and elegance, yet it is remarkably direct and emotionally searing. Most of his compositions are technically excellent as well, though the dominant sensation is of deep and passionate feeling.

His love life was complicated as well. He was a homosexual, and after a couple of failed attempts to establish relationships with women, he retreated into his work, which became more tender, Romantic, and tragic. He took several long sojourns abroad to Europe and America, in fact conducting at the opening night of Carnegie Hall in May 1893 on the same program as Antonin Dvořák.

His varied output includes unforgettably joyous and tender ballet music, wonderful songs, great operas (especially *Eugene Onegin* and *Queen of Spades*, in which his music and characterization rival Mozart for their psychological insights), overtures, piano music, a violin concerto, chamber music, and six outstanding symphonies.

If you purchase the Leinsdorf recording of the Sixth Symphony, then that will be your way into this composer's art. Tchaikovsky's brother gave it the name *Pathétique*, but one could ask where is the pathos? The work is so aflame with emotion that the pathos is not in the expression of the music, but rather what one might have felt for the composer. Until you hear the last movement. . . .

Notice that there is not a cheerful adagio to conclude the work, but a slow lamentation. Apparently Tchaikovsky was ecstatic over his new work, so it was stunning that he was dead only a few months later.

It is generally agreed that, like his mother, he died of cholera from drinking infected water. But there is considerable debate as to whether he was a suicide.

If you can, get the Mravinsky recording of the last three symphonies. These are classic, almost definitive, versions, which capture the Russian fire and soul of the composer. You might conclude that it takes a Russian to understand the unspoken aspects of Tchaikovsky's nature. It could be, as Valery Gergiev says below, that Tchaikovsky belongs to the world, but we may not all have the keys to understanding him to the same extent.

IN HIS OWN WORDS: VALERY GERGIEV

One of the responsibilities of a conductor is to decide how an orchestra should be placed on a stage so that the musical result will best realize the vision of the composer and, obviously, that of the conductor. A few portions of a conversation with the dynamic Russian maestro Valery Gergiev might give you some insights into how he and many conductors approach the symphonic repertoire:

"Just because I am Russian does not mean that I began my studies with Russian composers. Like any other music student, for me Mozart, Haydn, and Beethoven came first, then Berlioz, Brahms, and the other fundamentals of Western classical music, including Tchaikovsky. Only later was I taught Rachmaninoff, Stravinsky, Prokofiev, and other Russian composers from the twentieth century. Most any musician and composer starts with these foundations. It is important to remember that music doesn't belong to one nation. You don't have to be Russian to love Tchaikovsky. He belongs to the world. Debussy does not only belong to the French. You know, Debussy traveled to

St. Petersburg. He was influenced a lot by Mussorgsky, and also by Rachmaninoff."

Gergiev mentioned that conductors must reconsider the placement of musicians every time they go to a new hall. "I am now traveling with the Kirov Orchestra, and we will have done the same program in Chicago, Toronto, and New York. But in each theater I had to place the brass musicians in different places on the stage because the acoustical qualities of each hall is different. This was not so much to make the music sound as I wanted it, but because I had to arrange it so the various horn players could hear one another.

"To me, a conductor must combine finesse with power, he must bring interest to the music, and he must have a great deal of drive. He must create a balance of earth and skies."

I later asked myself what Gergiev might have meant by earth and skies, and began to think of adjectives that fit both categories and how they might apply to music. Music can have earthiness, and be tangible, energetic, and real. But it can also be ethereal, spiritual, delicate, intangible, and what I choose to call "other than real."

You might have heard some of this in his performance of Stravinsky's *The Firebird* (see page 120). His visceral interpretations of works by great Russian composers, as well as Verdi, Wagner, and many others, have made him one of the most exciting conductors of our day. If you want a challenging but thrilling recording to listen to in trying to hear Gergiev's vision of earth and skies, I suggest:

Igor Stravinsky: *The Rite of Spring*; Alexander Scriabin, *The Poem of Ecstasy* (Symphony no. 4); Kirov Orchestra; Valery Gergiev, conductor; Philips 289 468 035-2

• ‹◇› •

*Dvořák: Symphonies 7, 8, 9; Cleveland Orchestra; Christoph von Dohnányi,
conductor; London/Decca 421 082-2*

Antonin Dvořák (1841–1904) is without question the most famous
Czech composer (only Smetana and Janáček come anywhere near),
although in his lifetime his homeland was part of the Austro-Hungarian
Empire. He and his contemporaries asserted a sense of national identity
by writing songs in their own language and music that evoked the Czech
folk tradition. Yet such was Dvořák's skill that the vein of Czech character fed a larger whole, and his music gained wide international acclaim
that continues to this day. Dvořák nowadays faces the problem that a
certain small number of works seem to represent him, and when we
hear a likable piece of music that we do not recognize, we seem to be
surprised that he wrote it.

Dvořák had a remarkable facility for melody, and great skill at
orchestral shading and coloring. His religious music (including a mass,
Stabat Mater, and Requiem) draws its coloring from Romanticism as
much as the church. His most expressive music easily matches the emotionalism of Brahms. Technical perfection was important to him, but it
did not matter as much as finding the most poetic way to express a
musical or intellectual idea.

He was a fine musician, playing piano, organ, and, especially, the
violin beautifully. For many years he played violin in the orchestra of the
National Theater of Prague, giving him an up-close education on
orchestral sound. When his compositions began to receive performances, they were met with great approval wherever he went in Europe.

His output included nine symphonies, a sublime cello concerto,
superb operas (especially *Rusalka*, whose "Song to the Moon" is one of
the most gorgeous arias ever written), chamber music, and songs. He
spent the years 1892 to 1895 in the United States, teaching and performing in New York and traveling to places such as Iowa, where he heard
music that inspired him.

You have surely heard Dvořák's *New World* Symphony (no. 9), composed and premiered in America. He draws threads that combine traditional American and Czech melodies, creating a sumptuous fabric. You may think a little in Berliozian terms, imagining Dvořák as an artist in the New World, but with the Old World very much in his head and influencing his impressions of the New.

The recommended recordings are vibrant and pungent. Read the program essay before you listen to the Ninth. Work backwards to the Eighth and then the Seventh, which you will particularly enjoy. Because the Ninth is the one you know, it is better to commence with it, and then explore works that are new to you.

We will return to Dvořák later on.

• ⟨⟩ •

Bruckner: Symphony no. 6; Wagner, Wesendonck Lieder; New Philharmonia Orchestra; Otto Klemperer, conductor; Christa Ludwig, mezzo-soprano; EMI 7243 5 67037 28. For additional listening: Bruckner: Symphony no. 4 (Romantic); The Philadelphia Orchestra; Eugene Ormandy, conductor; Sony SBK 47653

Although there was a gradual distancing of many creative artists from religion as the nineteenth century moved on, certain composers remained fervently devout. One of these was Anton Bruckner (1824–1896), who grew up in a family of schoolteachers in rural Austria. He took up teaching, and part of his job required him to play the organ. As it happened, he was supremely talented, and his organ playing became his key to a larger musical career. He was rather timid by nature, a temperament that did not give him the tools to advance himself in a world of large egos and temperaments.

He composed eleven symphonies, but only numbered nine, feeling superstitious about exceeding Beethoven. What is usually called his Seventh was written in 1883, and was the first to attract praise—and he was almost sixty years old. I would like you to listen to the Sixth, preferably on this excellent old performance led by Otto Klemperer.

Notice how curiously fragmented this music can sound, and then notice how effectively Klemperer shapes it to form a cogent symphonic statement. There are many false starts in the musical language, climaxes followed by whispers, tremors that come atop serenity. There is a great deal that is unexplained and perhaps perplexing here, but I want you to listen to it to lay down the foundation for the future. You may not warm up to Bruckner yet, but when you listen to a lot more music (notably Wagner, Strauss, and Mahler), you will get a sense of where Bruckner fits in.

We are quite a distance here from Mozart and even Beethoven. Bruckner sounds like a composer who lived in the twentieth century rather than the nineteenth, yet he is not thought of as a modernist. He might be better thought of as a conservative with very unusual expressive means. (Save the Wesendonck Lieder on this recording for when you study vocal music.)

If you want to explore Bruckner further, move to the more accessible Fourth Symphony. Despite its title, you may not think it Romantic, but you will no doubt be lifted out of your seat during the thrilling third movement. This symphony is another one of Bruckner's that is unorthodox in construction, given that it does not end with dazzlement, but places it instead in the third movement and then helps us climb down from that peak.

· ◌ ·

Mahler: Symphonies 1, 2; London Philharmonic Orchestra; Klaus Tennstedt, conductor; EMI Classics 7243 5 74182 5 (Mahler, Symphony no. 7; Chicago Symphony Orchestra; Claudio Abbado, conductor; DG 445 523-2)

We will explore Mahler in great detail later on. For now, listen to the First symphony only. Do not read any notes—simply get into your comfortable listening position and let the music penetrate you without too much analysis. This is music I want you to feel more than consider. I believe you have the skills to do so by now.

If you hunger for more Mahler, find recordings of the Fourth and the Seventh symphonies, but save the Second Symphony for chapter 19.

• ᔆ •

Panorama: Richard Strauss: Don Juan, Till Eulenspiegels Lustige Streiche, Ein Heldenleben
R. Strauss: Don Juan, Vier Letzte Lieder, Tod und Verklärung; *New York Philharmonic; Kurt Masur, conductor; Deborah Voigt, soprano; Teldec 3984-25990-2*

Having studied *Also sprach Zarathustra* earlier, you have a sense of the symphonic poem (tone poem) being a large musical composition with great orchestral forces in which the composer draws inspiration from literature, philosophy, or nature. When you studied Berlioz's *Symphonie Fantastique,* you discovered the work that was the great forerunner of the many tone poems to come. One could argue that it was narration more than a product of inspiration. Berlioz took his own experience and fashioned it into a singular work of art, while Liszt, Strauss, and other composers of symphonic poems tended to reach for source material outside themselves. Just as Beethoven straddled Classicism and Romanticism, Strauss had one foot in late Romanticism and the other in many of the early radical attempts to smash many musical templates in the early twentieth century.

Listen to *Don Juan* (1889), applying your knowledge of this famous libertine from various sources (originally Tirso de Molina's *El Burlador de Sevilla*, but also from Molière's play and the opera by Mozart and Lorenzo da Ponte). This music, written by a highly talented twenty-four-year-old, used an orchestra even larger than Berlioz's, and with the assurance of a much older master. Listen to the expressiveness of every instrument, from the luxuriant strings to the incredibly lusty horns. The conclusion, depicting Don Juan's damnation, is awesome.

After listening to Karl Böhm's interpretation on the Panorama album, immediately listen to Kurt Masur's version on the other recording. Ask yourself how these performances are similar and different. Take a piece of paper, write *Böhm* on one side and *Masur* on the other. Write down comparative adjectives or other words that express the sensations you felt in one or the other performance. This is a valuable activity for the music lover, and one we shall return to in discussing the Mendelssohn Violin Concerto with Joshua Bell.

Till Eulenspiegels Lustige Streiche (Till Eulenspiegel's Merry Pranks, 1895) depicts the adventures of a Puckish rogue in the style of Robin Hood or Butch Cassidy. The character is claimed both by Belgium and Germany. While the Till of legend got through life quite unscathed, Strauss decided that his Till should be captured and put to death by hanging. You can hear it in the music, though one might ask why Strauss thought this was necessary.

Ein Heldenleben (A Hero's Life, 1898) was Strauss's autobiography at the tender age of thirty-four. No modesty here. Listen to his carping critics (the sourish wind section) and the voice (sometimes pleasing, often not) of his wife, as depicted by the principal violin. In a section called "The Hero's Works of Peace," he manages to quote about thirty of his own works, including all of the symphonic poems to date. The lovely dialogue at the end between horn and violin depicts Mr. and Mrs. Strauss.

Tod und Verklärung (Death and Transfiguration, 1889) would be a weighty topic at any age, but could Strauss at twenty-five have already been facing issues of his own mortality? As it happens, he lived until eighty-five, composing almost to the end. Do you think this depiction— of an old man dying alone in a dimly lit room, battling with Death, losing that fight but then finding deliverance—rings true? Is this a story told of experience or probably not? Do you feel that he found a way to depict this subject matter?

Save the *Vier Letzte Lieder* for later on, when we study these sublime songs in the chapter on vocal music.

• ◇ •

Panorama: Serge Prokofiev, Classical Symphony, etc.; various artists; DG 289 469 172-2

This recording contains much of the most popular music of Prokofiev, including what are arguably his two most popular symphonies. What is notable in his lifetime (1891–1953) is how it spanned important events in the history and culture of his native Russia (actually, he was born in the Ukraine). He studied in St. Petersburg until 1914, and his early works, including the first two piano concertos and the *Scythian Suite* (1915), baffled and outraged many listeners. In May 1918, with his bag full of his compositions (including the Symphony no. 1, the *Classical*, composed the year before), he traveled eastward across his vast nation and left for America by ship, stopping in Tokyo before arriving in San Francisco. His first performance in America was in New York in November 1918, where he played the Second Piano Concerto. Later, the First Symphony had a huge success in Chicago and led to a commission for his opera *The Love for Three Oranges*.

Prokofiev lived and performed abroad in America and Europe, but returned in 1926 to tour what had become the Soviet Union. It proved a great success and triggered some nostalgia in the composer for his homeland. He professed to be apolitical and felt that he could live in the USSR without having to deal with the Soviet authorities and the considerable amount of intrusion that existed in the lives of many creative artists. He returned there to live in 1933. Some observers say it was the worst move of his life—he could have stayed in the West as Rachmaninoff and Stravinsky did. But other experts point out that Prokofiev experienced an amazing creative surge in the decade following his return. In the West he was sometimes labeled a Soviet composer, but when the Second World War broke out, orchestras in the Allied nations cut back on German music and increased performances of works by Russians—the USSR was fighting heroically against the Nazis and the Japanese.

Yet by 1948, Prokofiev fell out of favor with the authorities and was purged, along with many other great musicians, including Dmitri Shostakovich. Prokofiev was already in poor health, and this demoralizing episode broke him. He went on a downward spiral and died of a brain hemorrhage on March 5, 1953. Would you believe that Stalin died but one hour later of the very same cause? This is one of history's greatest and most ironic coincidences, matched perhaps only by the deaths of Thomas Jefferson and John Adams on July 4, 1826, fifty years to the day after they signed the Declaration of Independence.

Prokofiev was one of the most versatile composers of all time, writing in just about every form except religious music. There were five operas (including *The Gambler* and *War and Peace*); some of the greatest ballet music (*Romeo and Juliet, Cinderella*), which probably only Tchaikovsky could rival; seven symphonies; chamber music; superb concertos for piano, violin, and cello; solo piano works; songs; *Peter and the Wolf*; suites; and even film music for *Lieutenant Kijé, Ivan the Terrible,* and *Alexander Nevsky.*

As you listen to the *Classical* Symphony, remember that it was written during the First World War as the old order was falling apart throughout Europe. It could simply be that this was a successful academic exercise of a young composer, but surely Prokofiev was looking back over the enormous divide that was splitting the present from the past. Listen again to a Haydn symphony, and then marvel at how Prokofiev fits his music into a balanced four-movement structure but injects his unmistakable musical voice and good humor in the flavor of the piece. And then remind yourself that this was written between 1916 and 1917.

The Fifth Symphony is something else again. It was written in 1944, as the USSR bravely battled in World War II. Leningrad had endured its siege (to experience this, once you feel more at home listening to a wide range of musical styles, seek out Shostakovich's astonishing Symphony no. 7). Prokofiev conducted the premiere of his Fifth Symphony in January 1945. Listen to it with the nation's history and his own in mind. It is in parts gloriously wrenching, but also an incredible affirmation of courage and survival.

It would be the last piece he would conduct in public. After this moment of glory, he became unwell, fainted a few days later and suffered a concussion. When he recovered he resumed composing, but his life became more circumscribed, especially after the purge of 1948.

One could debate for a long time about the personal choices Prokofiev made, and many people get in heated arguments about this composer's music—is it classical and traditional, or is it radical and modern?—but he is a composer who continues to enjoy a revival, thanks to the efforts of artists such as Valery Gergiev, pianist Martha Argerich, and violinist Maxim Vengerov.

• ◦◦◦ •

Vaughan Williams: Symphony no. 5; Three Portraits from The England of Elizabeth; *Concerto for Bass Tuba and Orchestra; London Symphony Orchestra: André Previn, conductor; John Fletcher, bass tuba; RCA Victor 60586-2-RG*

It is interesting to contrast the Fifth Symphony of Prokofiev with that of Ralph Vaughan Williams (1872–1958). Although this wonderful composer is highly esteemed in his native Britain, he gets scant attention elsewhere. Surely you would recognize his *Fantasia on a Theme by Thomas Tallis* (1910) and the *Fantasia on "Greensleeves"* (1934). But he also composed nine symphonies, suites, operas, theater music, and many other works of great quality. Perhaps because he so closely identified with English history and musical traditions, he came to be thought of as an exponent of these rather than the world-class composer he was.

The Fifth Symphony was begun in 1936 and completed in 1943. Vaughan Williams had seen action in the First World War and knew firsthand its consequences in a way that Prokofiev did not. The slow evolution of this work probably mirrored the ever-changing and worsening state of the world. Yet rather than directly address the issues of the day, Vaughan Williams made this work a fantasia of sorts on the subject of morality, summoning English folk melodies and music of the Tudor era, trying to show the British some of what is great in their heritage. Think of this as the musical equivalent to Laurence Olivier's recitation of the "St. Swithin's Day" speech from Shakespeare's *Henry V*. There is a deep strain of faith in this music; you can determine for yourself whether it is formally religious or what some people nowadays call "spiritual."

Throughout his life, Vaughan Williams had an unspecified mysticism in his music, which you can hear in the early *Five Mystical Songs*

(1911) all the way through his Seventh Symphony, the *Antarctica* (1952), and beyond. Ask yourself how you connect to this mystical component. Do you think you know what he is saying to you? Does it matter if you do? Think back to earlier works you have heard and see where there might be mysticism—*Pictures at an Exhibition*, perhaps? The Brahms Fourth Symphony? Debussy's *La Mer*? A movement of Mozart's Symphony no. 40? Music by Bach? I think it is in all of these and, without a doubt, in Schubert's Eighth Symphony. I mention this because people tend to associate things mystical primarily with sensations that specifically provoke mysticism within them.

• ·◊· •

Elgar: Symphonies 1 & 2, etc.; BBC Symphony Orchestra; Andrew Davis, conductor; Teldec 0630-18951-2

If you wish to deepen your understanding of English symphonic music in the twentieth century, take a detour back to Sir Edward Elgar (1857–1934). Although some of his work sounds unmistakably Britannic (such as the *Pomp and Circumstance* march you surely heard at graduation, or the wonderful *Sea Pictures*), Elgar was in many ways a more European composer than his colleagues, much as Tchaikovsky was the most Continental of the late-nineteenth-century Russians.

I think you will hear considerable Brahmsian influence in the First and Second symphonies. They are richly melodic, soulful, rather majestic without being pompous, and well crafted. Agreeable though they are, I do not believe they can take you to places that Vaughan Williams reached. But Elgar will surprise you with his extraordinary Cello Concerto, which we shall discover later on. It is on the short list of favorite works in all music for more than a few classical music devotees.

• ·◊· •

Panorama: Jean Sibelius, Karelia Suite, etc.; various artists; DG 289 469 202-2

Jean Sibelius (1865–1957) is a towering figure in twentieth-century music, and not only because he lived so long. In Finland he is only the most famous composer in a nation that, per capita, probably has more composers and musicians than any other. As Finland gained sovereignty about a hundred years ago after long domination by Russia and Sweden, it was Sibelius in his music who helped his people see themselves as a valid cultural entity quite apart from the two neighboring powers.

Music such as *En Saga, Kullervo, Pohjola's Daughter,* the *Karelia Suite, Rakastava, Kuolema, Tapiola, The Swan of Tuonela*, and, above all, *Finlandia* became instantly recognizable touchstones of Finnish identity. Yet Sibelius also wrote seven wonderful symphonies and an excellent violin concerto. As a symphonist, he is always listed among the foremost of the twentieth century, with names such as Mahler, Prokofiev, Shostakovich, and Vaughan Williams mentioned as well.

In his time Sibelius was the paragon of the national composer, influencing and encouraging those in smaller European nations (as well as Britain and the United States) by his example. His symphonies were not great Finnish symphonies, but great symphonies that need not be cognizant of nationhood. Yet as attitudes around the world evolved and identity took on perhaps too much importance in culture as well as politics, the opinion on Sibelius was that he was a great exponent of things Finnish.

Sibelius knew Mahler (who came to conduct in Helsinki), intensely admired the color and technique of Tchaikovsky, and was transfixed by Richard Strauss's prowess as an orchestrator. He attempted to study with Brahms in Vienna, but that composer (forgetting the generosity of Robert and Clara Schumann) turned Sibelius away.

Listen to all of the music on this 2-CD set, and then write down as many descriptive words as you can find about the Second and Fifth symphonies. These are from different phases of Sibelius's life, and you will find it an intriguing challenge to put into words what this music inspires in you.

Then listen to *Finlandia* and you will understand the power that a piece of music can exert in the right time and place. When written in

1899 it was a direct challenge to czarist Russia's occupation of Finland. The Russians banned this music, yet the Finns defiantly continued to play it. As sympathy for the Finnish cause swept Europe, *Finlandia* was heard in concert halls across the continent.

· ∽ ·

Corigliano: Symphony no. 1; Chicago Symphony Orchestra; Daniel Barenboim, conductor; Erato 2292-45601-2

John Corigliano (1938–   ) is but one example of the many fine composers at work in the United States today. He is a professor of composition at the Juilliard School, the composer of one of the most successful contemporary operas, *The Ghosts of Versailles* (1991); concertos for piano and oboe; film music (*Altered States; The Red Violin*); and this 1989 symphony, which became an immediate classic. The *New York Times* hailed it as "a major new orchestral score. . . . By turns anguished, hysterical, and deeply moving. . . . With its dazzling instrumental colors, this may be the · most brilliantly orchestrated showpiece for a virtuoso orchestra since Bartók bequeathed his Concerto for Orchestra to the Boston Symphony."

This work is often referred to as the *AIDS* Symphony, although the composer's title is simply Symphony no. 1. However, the grief, rage, and loss provoked by the ongoing epidemic were the principal sources of inspiration for Corigliano as he wrote this symphony. He has said that the work was written for his friends, one who was dying, and the many who had died. This could be thought of as a tragic symphony; both the composer and the listener go from the very specific to the universal, which is part of its genius. I believe that when that much-longed-for day arrives when the world will be rid of AIDS, this symphony will retain all of the power and meaning that it did during the era when it was composed.

The first movement, called "Of Rage and Remembrance," begins with one note on strings played twice. Corigliano said that his image in creating this passage was of a fist pushing through concrete. Much of the music in this symphony depicts tenderness alternating with rage.

Corigliano has observed that this rage is not necessarily against an infection, but is directed toward an injustice.

Notice that Corigliano has amassed a huge percussion section to create a singular sound world for this symphony: timpani, two bass drums, brake drum, snare drum, field drum, tenor drum, xylophone, vibraphone, glockenspiel, crotales, marimba, chimes, anvil, temple blocks, suspended cymbal, finger cymbals, tam-tam, triangle, tambourine, whip, ratchet, police whistle, flexotone, roto-toms, and metal plate. In addition to these, and to the standard orchestra, there are also a piano onstage and one offstage, harp, and mandolins. I suggest that you think of the offstage piano, and perhaps other instruments, as representing memory.

Make note of the ending of the symphony with its undulating brasses, the return of earlier melodies, and ultimately the slowly fading solo cello. What do you see, if anything? Waves? The disappearing faces and voices of loved ones who are gradually slipping away? Think for a moment of Strauss's *Tod und Verklärung* and ask yourself how that music addresses death in comparison to this music. The essential point again, and this is a vivid example: the word *death* in language is what it is. But *death* in music can have so many meanings, and we can find our way to understanding them if we listen openly and with care. And, of course, if I were to substitute other words—love, joy, honor, frailty, magic, sleep, etc.—this observation would be the same.

· ᗣ ·

Górecki: Symphony no. 3; London Sinfonietta; David Zinman, conductor; Dawn Upshaw, soprano; Elektra Nonesuch 9 79282-2

This recording of Henryk Górecki's Third Symphony was released in the early 1990s and became a runaway bestseller, and not only on the classical music charts. It was and remains a hugely popular work in Europe and has gained many followers elsewhere, too. The symphony, which includes extensive vocal passages sung with beauty and mystery by Dawn Upshaw, brings to mind some of the music of Ralph Vaughan

Williams. Some critical ears might consider the sound rather "New Age," but this work is interesting primarily because it indicates that with composers such as Corigliano, Glass, Henze, Górecki, and others, the symphonic tradition is alive and vital.

. ⟨⟩ .

Glass: Symphony no. 2, etc.; Vienna Radio Symphony Orchestra, etc.; Dennis Russell Davies, conductor; Nonesuch 79496-2

Philip Glass is an exponent of a different sort of music than Corigliano's and is one of the most popular and controversial composers at work today. For some his music is annoyingly repetitive, though for many it is deeply involving, even transfixing. Sometimes his music is described as rhythm based on a progression of small musical units. Sometimes one hears the word "minimalism" applied to his works, but it could also be argued that these smaller elements, by themselves, are only of passing interest but that in the aggregate they constitute an artist's expression that is of considerable significance.

Glass's use of polytonality—the simultaneous use of more than one key in different contrapuntal strands—may recall for you some of the sounds in Holst's *The Planets*.

Glass has written, "I am more interested in the ambiguous qualities that can result from polytonality—how what you hear depends on how you focus your ear, how a listener's perception of tonality can vary in the fashion of an optical illusion. We're not talking about inventing a new language, but rather inventing new perceptions of existing languages."

Keep his words in mind as you listen to his Second Symphony (1994). Ask yourself which composers of the past, if any, might embrace this music. We always talk about composers and audiences embracing or rejecting music of the past, but it would be intriguing to think what would happen if Bach or Berlioz or Mahler or Strauss or Prokofiev could hear the music of today. I think these five would all be intrigued with Philip Glass and would take a great interest in the future of music.

IN HIS OWN WORDS:
LEIF SEGERSTAM ON
MUSIC-MAKING

A conversation with Leif Segerstam (1944–   ) is more like standing under a Finnish waterfall in which ideas, insights, and digressions cascade in amazing abundance. Segerstam is one of the foremost musicians in Finland, and his prodigious energy and an all-encompassing embrace of everything within his sphere make him something a phenomenon even in this hypermusical nation.

Segerstam is one of the nation's foremost conductors, the music director of the Helsinki Philharmonic, and a frequent guest at the Savonlinna Opera Festival. He conducts regularly in Sweden (and reminded me that seventy percent of Scandinavian orchestras are headed by Finns). He also appears frequently all over Europe with major orchestras and opera companies. He studied conducting and composition at the Sibelius Academy in Helsinki and the Juilliard School in New York.

Such is his energy that in February 1999 he conducted all nine Beethoven symphonies in one day. In his view, "The conductor is the ambassador of the composer and the representative of the listener. He must be authoritative on the style and intention of any composer he intends to play." Segerstam is also the head of the conducting division of the Sibelius Academy, and has been essential in the development of new generations of Finnish conductors. "In my tradition," he said, "if you are given something, you have to give it back. So it is my pleasure to teach."

Most remarkable of all, Segerstam is a composer of astonishing fertility and inspiration. When I met him in

January 2002, the ink was drying on his sixty-second symphony and he was preparing for the sixty-third. He also writes chamber music, song cycles, and many other compositions. When I asked whether this output was perhaps too prodigious, he said "I don't mind being thought of as another Vivaldi!" Segerstam wrote twenty-five symphonies just in the year 2000, despite a full schedule of rehearsing, conducting, recording, and teaching. At the time we met, he was planning to record the seven symphonies of Jean Sibelius with the Helsinki Philharmonic.

The typical Segerstam symphony is eight pages long and lasts 25 minutes. He refers to most of his symphonic output as "symphonies without conductors." He said, "My works cannot be conducted. In my music, the instruments do not play together. It is like nature, with swarms of birds, and the sounds of other animals and natural effects, coming when they come." He is very specific about the influence of nature in his music: "You are not listening to nature, where one note can have harmony. There is an infinity of sounds in nature, and you must go beyond them."

Like many Finns, Segerstam lives close to nature and derives some of his inspiration from listening to the sounds of nature. He says that the sounds of his music are not random: "Composing is a creative deed. My works are exactly notated, with no options at all. It is formal notation, but with no bar lines [to separate measures]. There are letters in my scores that indicate the tempos. The realization of these tempos comes from cues that are telegraphed from one instrumentalist to another. Like in chamber music, I tell my individual instruments, 'Let's meet at the *fermata* [an important universal pause in a composition].'"

In effect, the orchestra musicians in a Segerstam symphony must play as if they were a large chamber music
ensemble. "The way I arrived at this style was a matter of
fate. In 1993 a colleague of mine, the Estonian conductor
Peeter Lilje, was supposed to conduct a performance in
Tallinn, but suddenly died." Segerstam agreed to conduct
the concert and, a few days before he left, he had a dream. "I
dreamt that forty-three members of the orchestra brought
forty-three sunflowers in memory of Lilje, who died at the
age of forty-three. I wrote a symphony in Peeter's memory
that I called *Flower Bouquette 3E*. The idea of this symphony being conductorless was that this music would be
played by an orchestra that had lost its conductor.

"I decided that the forty-third note should be an E,
which stands for *Ewigkeit* [eternity]. All of the instruments
would come to a halt at the fermata on the forty-third
note, with the stop suggesting that Peeter had died after
forty-three years. As it happened, I had made a mistake: I
did the parts in such a hurry (because I wanted to play this
symphony at the concert in his memory) that all the
instruments came to a stop after the forty-third note,
except for the harp. It seems that I had written one extra
note for that instrument. But like a Persian carpet, there
should be an imperfection—I am not God." Segerstam
contends, "When you do pioneering things you are snow-
blind, you don't see where you are." So the harp part kept
its forty-four notes, and the movement ends at the same
moment for all the other instruments. The symphony
proved quite successful, and the conductorless model
inspired him to write more compositions in this style.

And Segerstam continued to write his symphonies as
well as study and prepare other music to be done in the
future for concerts and recordings. "When I write, I don't

write quickly. I wrote 'enough slowly' to be in resonance with the speed of the writing hand."

On the flight from Tallinn to Finland, Segerstam met his future wife, Minna, the harpist who played the extra note. "Since then, she made three children and I made twenty-three symphonies."

ATTENDING A LIVE PERFORMANCE

A good concert is a little bit of hope that something better will come.
—*Arthur Rubinstein*

I am certain that by now you have begun to have a serious hankering to hear a live musical performance. This is, after all, the way music was meant to be heard, and the experience is unbeatable, despite the wonders of radio and recordings. There is nothing to compare with the excitement of a *live* performance of music, and all of the drama that entails. Audiences are full of eager anticipation, as are the musicians. The latter might also be rather nervous, which is understandable. They are about to play before a large room full of knowledgeable people who have paid good money not simply to hear music but, they hope, to have a transporting experience. The great pianist Arthur Rubinstein understood this, and so do most artists.

Think of a concert as a singular experience that cannot be repeated. There you are with perhaps two thousand other audience members who will never again gather as a group. You will hear a selected bunch of musicians, whom you may know well or who are new to you, playing music that you may have heard before or not. These variables will never all be the same again, nor will the weather outside, the news of the day, your mood, and the moods of everyone else in the room with you. And all of this comes before the musicians start to play!

Even if you are hearing an artist play the Mendelssohn Violin Concerto whom you have heard before, this time will be different because you know the piece better, and the musician has had more experience with it and may bring insights that he or she did not have before. We audience members live and grow with many pieces of music across the years, but musicians do it to a much greater degree than we do. So we are always in for some surprises. This is why we go again to hear great artists perform music that we know, as well as hearing other artists play the same music for the first time.

The hall in which we hear music also makes a great deal of difference. The Mendelssohn concerto, even when played by the same musicians, will sound different if you hear it in a large space or a small one. If you live in a town with one major concert hall, chances are that is where you hear most of your performances. You become used to the acoustics of that hall, and things sound a certain way to you. You are familiar with the design of the hall, its visual aspects, its rhythms, and you know the faces of many of the people who work there or attend performances.

Let us say that the Royal Concertgebouw Orchestra and their music director, Riccardo Chailly, come to your town and do a performance of music by Brahms and Mahler. You may be thrilled by the music and by their superb playing. Then let us say that you travel to Amsterdam and hear these same musicians perform the same program in their home theater, the Concertgebouw. Chances are the experience will be very different. First, the musicians are playing at home before an audience that knows them. When they were in your city they were on tour, so they might have been less rested, but more eager to do well because they were playing in a place where they were less known and more likely to be judged critically. Second, because the environment and acoustics in your hall are different from those in the Concertgebouw, the musicians might have had to adjust their playing to sound the best they could in your hall. At home they know their theater intimately and know how to play so they sound great in it. Third, the audience where you live will be different from the one in Amsterdam (unless you are a Dutch reader of this book), because audiences differ from place to place. And, inevitably, the thrill and anticipation in the presence of this great orchestra will create a palpable sense of excitement wherever they perform. It is a rare event in your city; the lucky Amsterdamers have this ensemble most of the time.

One of the great joys for a music lover is attending performances while traveling. It is not uncommon for people to plan their trips to Vienna, Berlin, London, or New York so they can hear specific concerts. If I know that I am scheduled to travel somewhere, I immediately check what concerts, operas, and theater works will be on while I am in that place. Then I purchase my tickets by phone, fax, or via the Internet so that I am assured of a place in the hall when I arrive. Traveling enables me to hear great artists who may not come to New York (my hometown) as often as I would wish, even though New York is almost unrivaled in its breadth of cultural offerings. And hearing performers in *their* hometowns, in front of their home audiences, is special indeed.

Cities such as New York, Paris, Berlin, Munich, Vienna, and, especially, London, have several orchestras appearing most every night of the year, and almost all of the performances are sold out. These are cities that take immense pride and interest in culture, and people flock to them to hear the best artists. While these artists appear in many places, they tend to have an extra urge to excel in these cultural centers, and performances there will be memorable.

Many European cities have great musical traditions, including Vienna, Salzburg, Graz, Zurich, Prague, Munich, Cologne, Berlin, Leipzig, Dresden, Brussels, Amsterdam, Paris, London, Birmingham, Edinburgh, Bergen, Helsinki, St. Petersburg, Moscow, Warsaw, Budapest, Milan, Venice, Bologna, Naples, and Barcelona, to name only a few. Every European nation is full of marvelous musicians.

Russia, for reasons of a grand tradition, superb musical education, and a temperament that prizes great artistry, has turned out brilliant artists for many decades. Since the end of the Soviet Union, many outstanding Russian musicians have moved abroad, particularly to Israel and New York City, enhancing the music-making in both of those places.

In the Americas, Buenos Aires has a storied musical history, and Argentina has produced many fine musicians. Santiago, Rio de Janeiro,

São Paulo, Caracas, and Mexico City are all important centers. Excellent music-making has always existed across Canada, particularly in Montreal.

Almost every nation in the world that enjoys Western classical music has a national orchestra and many additional musical groups. Japan, China, and, especially, South Korea have become a fertile source for a new generation of great musicians. Australians, New Zealanders, Indians, Turks, and artists from many countries have risen to worldwide fame. For such a tiny nation, Israel has given the world an uncommonly large and gifted group of musicians in the past fifty years, including Itzhak Perlman, Pinchas Zukerman, and Gil Shaham. Many of the world's top artists, most notably Leonard Bernstein, Zubin Mehta, Isaac Stern, and Daniel Barenboim (an Argentine who became an Israeli citizen) have spent a lot of time there.

In the United States, New York is certainly the city with the richest tradition, and its leading orchestra, the New York Philharmonic, is one of the world's oldest, having been founded the same year as the Vienna Philharmonic (1842). James Levine's Metropolitan Opera Orchestra, though primarily devoted to opera, has now risen to rank among the nation's finest orchestras, one that plays a great variety of standard repertory in concerts in Carnegie Hall and on tour. There are smaller orchestras in the city, too, including the American Composers Orchestra, American Symphony Orchestra, Brooklyn Philharmonic, the Jupiter Symphony Orchestra, the Little Orchestra Society of New York, the New York String Orchestra, the Orchestra of St. Luke's, the Orpheus, the Y Chamber Symphony, the Eos, and still others.

The New York Philharmonic is considered one of the "Big Five" American orchestras, along with the wonderful world-class ensembles of Boston, Chicago, Cleveland, and Philadelphia. These five all have grand traditions, and critics and music lovers have discussions that last for decades as to which one is the best. When Georg Solti was in Chicago from the 1970s to the early 1990s, many people thought it was the best orchestra in the world.

Every orchestra (not just the Big Five) has its trademark sound and playing style, forged by the artistic directors who work with them, but also by the taste and habits of the musicians who are its members and by the cities where they live. For many years, Chicago had a bright, brassy sound while Philadelphia had a deep, sonorous sound that came from glorious string playing and the particular acoustics of the hall the orchestra performed in. Cleveland was known for its sheer responsiveness to conductors and virtuosity in many styles. Boston forged close, enduring relationships with conductors and played as if in one unified voice. In contrast, New York's musicians were sometimes unruly and rather opinionated, and aware that they were inheritors of a grand tradition. On their best days, and when inspired by a great conductor and music, the instrumentalists of the New York Philharmonic were able to give performances of staggering excitement and brilliance.

I spoke of the reputations of the Big Five in the past tense only because this is the received wisdom you will encounter when you talk to music lovers about American orchestras. At this writing, all of these orchestras are in transition, though all can still claim to be among the five finest organizations in the United States.

But other outstanding orchestras can be found in Atlanta, Baltimore, Cincinnati, Dallas, Detroit, Houston, Indianapolis, Kansas City, Los Angeles, Milwaukee, Minneapolis, Newark, Pittsburgh, Saint Louis, Saint Paul, San Francisco, Seattle, and Washington, D.C. Many smaller cities and towns also have laudable musical organizations, even if they perform more infrequently. The creation of a symphony orchestra is considered a sign of civility and a key step forward for a city that seeks to establish itself as an important center. So it is not surprising that Las Vegas, the city with the nation's fastest population growth in the 1990s, now has its own Philharmonic, one that is getting better all the time.

In addition to a world full of orchestras, there are trios, quartets, and small groups who play chamber music. Choirs perform with instrumentalists, or on their own. Then there are all the solo artists—singers, pianists, violinists, cellists, and so on—who perform in venues large and small. Any place that has a university will likely have a series of concert programs, and churches everywhere have many musical events, both sacred and secular.

Beyond this there is a world full of music festivals in all seasons and with an almost endless variety of repertory. Probably the most famous are the Easter and Summer Festivals in Salzburg (Austria), but there is also the Maggio Musicale in Florence, the Aldeburgh Festival in Britain, the Bergen Festival in Norway, White Nights in St. Petersburg, Prague Spring in the Czech Republic, and the Tanglewood Festival in Massachusetts. New York City has the incredibly popular Mostly Mozart Festival every August at Avery Fisher Hall. Then there are the Lincoln Center Festival, the Next Wave Festival at the Brooklyn Academy of Music, and the Caramoor Festival just north of New York. Small cities and towns throughout the United States have lovely music festivals, particularly in the summer. Almost every world city that is the birthplace of a major composer will have an annual festival of his works.

· ◇· ·

All of this is to say that if you live in or near a medium-sized or large city, or in a community of any size, and can't find live performances of classical music, then you just are not looking hard enough. Listen to announcements on the local classical music stations, if you have one, or on public radio. Check listings in newspapers, magazines, and publications from universities and religious institutions.

If you have musical organizations in your town, call and ask to be put on their mailing lists. This will give you early notification of when performances will take place, and you can plan accordingly. If you don't have a hometown orchestra, there might be something like a civic arts society that presents touring musicians. There is a particularly rich tradition of this in the United States. I have heard the London Symphony Orchestra in Daytona Beach, Florida; the Vienna Boychoir in Madison, Wisconsin; and Vladimir Horowitz in Ann Arbor, Michigan.

Once you know where performances near you might take place, then comes the question of selecting what to hear. Each spring in most

American cities, the music organizations announce their upcoming season's programs and seek renewals from subscribers as well as purchases from new audiences. The seasons typically begin in the autumn and extend to late spring or early summer of the next calendar year. Major orchestras will do new programs every week of the season and will often give up to four performances of each program.

Smaller orchestras do more limited seasons, but this does not imply inferior quality. There are some cases in which a smaller orchestra will do multiple performances of the same program in different cities. For example, the Florida Philharmonic appears regularly in Miami, Fort Lauderdale, and West Palm Beach. The regional orchestra of Emilia-Romagna, in Italy, tours the same program to Bologna, Modena, Reggio Emilia, and Parma.

Some of the most important orchestras have their own concert halls, but others appear in multiuse performing arts centers. Given that any night when the hall is dark represents lost revenue, all of these theaters tend to present other artists aside from the local orchestra. Contact these halls and arts centers directly to find out what is being presented.

I can tell you that real music lovers are people who plan ahead. If they receive their new season brochure in March and notice that a great musician is coming the following January, or that the local orchestra is doing a superb program in February, they will hold the dates and purchase tickets as soon as they go on sale.

Music lovers who have subscriptions to one series often have first crack at single tickets to other performances. For example, I have subscriptions to vocal recitals and to orchestral concerts at Carnegie Hall. But if I see that there is another type of concert that appeals to me on the future schedule (let's say the Emerson String Quartet, or pianist Alfred Brendel, or violinist Joshua Bell), I will purchase a ticket and look forward to that event with great pleasure.

If you live in a city with several arts organizations, they often share their mailing lists, so you will learn of performances that you did not know existed. I would recommend that you apportion about 75 percent of your ticket budget to exciting things that appeal to you, and then devote the other 25 percent to music or performers you have never heard of. You may not like everything you ultimately hear, but in the act of going you gain experience and hone your tastes. And you may luck into an early performance by one of the great stars of tomorrow.

Many arts organizations will ask you to make charitable contributions (which, in the United States, are often tax-deductible) as well as purchasing tickets. This may seem odd, but the truth is that ticket prices typically cover only between 30 percent and 70 percent of the total costs of presenting performances. Why don't they charge more? Most arts organizations endeavor to have a wide range of ticket prices so that students and people with limited incomes are not excluded. If you are able to make a contribution, do so. This will not only give you the satisfaction of striking a blow for culture but will likely put you on a priority list when you attempt to purchase tickets for future performances or get the seat locations improved on your subscriptions.

Where you sit when you attend performances is based on three factors. The first is what is available when you try to purchase a ticket. The second is how much money you are able to spend. The third, which is very important, concerns your acoustical and visual preferences, or special needs. If you love to see the flaring nostrils of the violinist or the sweat on the conductor's brow, you have to sit close. If you want to see the hands of the pianist, you must sit on the left side of the auditorium, perhaps in an upper tier. If you believe that you may have to exit during the concert, be sure to purchase an aisle seat. If you require access to particular locations for reasons of disability, you must state that as you purchase your tickets. American theaters built since 1990 must have seats for blind patrons, and accommodations for those who use a wheelchair or special equipment for getting about. Some theaters even have seats for audience members with hearing impairments. Older theaters have been retrofitted to make these accommodations where possible.

The biggest consideration when you select your seat, I believe, is sound. Every hall has its own acoustics, and there is an almost unceasing debate as to what good acoustics are. This is something that can be measured numerically—the angle that sound waves travel, how long they linger before disappearing, etc.—but numbers cannot describe the physical and emotional sensation that comes when one feels that sound is being heard at its most opulent.

Words can also describe acoustical concepts, but they too fall short of the emotional sensation. For example, there is a difference between resonance, in which a pleasant reverberation of sound lasts for a few seconds, and echoes, which can be nightmarish. Softness and inaudibility are not the same, though not everyone makes the distinction. Similarly, bracing loudness and musical distortion are quite different.

People I meet around the world love to brag that the hall where they hear music has "perfect acoustics." This is a relative concept and an elusive one as well. Some people love warm rich sound in which all the notes blend into a gorgeous whole. Others prefers cooler, more clinical sound, similar to many modern recordings in which individual notes and orchestral voices can be picked out. Many new halls are built to imitate this cooler sound, which means that we may come to think that this is how all sound should be.

I think there are a great deal of variety and preferences to be embraced. For example, I might like to hear works by Brahms and Dvořák, with all their rich sonorities, in warmer acoustical environments. By contrast, listening to solo piano works by Chopin or Satie in a cooler acoustical space might be interesting to hear individual notes but may not always favor appreciating the resonance in the piano.

So there is no such thing as perfect acoustics, but rather environments that please *you* when you hear particular pieces of music.

There are some older halls which, by almost common acclaim, are considered excellent acoustically. These include Vienna's Musikverein, Amsterdam's Concertgebouw, London's Wigmore Hall, Naples's Teatro San Carlo, Buenos Aires's Teatro Colón, Boston's Symphony Hall, and New York's Carnegie Hall. Most older halls in regular use have decent acoustics.

It seems that the art of acoustical design ran into rough times at some point in the mid–twentieth century. In Europe, where concert halls were destroyed by war, the forward-looking new buildings that replaced them often favored the eye more than the ear. In the United States, the idea of performing arts centers with multiuse auditoriums began in the 1960s with New York's Lincoln Center. A couple of its halls were acoustical disasters when they opened, and millions of dollars and much prestige were spent to make them better. Around North America some new halls fare better than others and, for all the facts and figures and expertise that acousticians have at their disposal, things do not always work out and changes are needed. Among the modern halls that are usually considered acoustical successes are Meyerson Hall in Dallas, Bass Hall in Fort Worth, Benaroya Hall in Seattle, as well as the new halls in Lahti and Helsinki, Finland.

Regular concertgoers for whom sound is the utmost priority tend to find out where the best sound is in the halls they frequent. In most cases, it will be in the highest tiers of the hall and in areas where there is no overhanging balcony. The seats all the way upstairs tend to be the least expensive, and in many halls you find a big gathering of the most knowledgeable music lovers in the upper reaches of an auditorium. This is a good place to meet people who can deepen your musical insights, as long as you bear in mind that opinion and truth are not always the same thing.

Even the most ardent music lovers must acknowledge that, while concertgoing is primarily an aural experience, for many the visual components count as well. If you want to watch the musicians, a partial-view or no-view seat is probably not for you. Almost every theater has a seating chart and, given that you are spending good money for these tickets, you should endeavor to find out as much as you can over the telephone or at the box office window about the seat you are being offered. But also keep in mind that every hall has only a set amount of seats, that regular subscribers have access to the best ones first, and that purchasers of single tickets must then choose among what is left. And wouldn't it be better to at least *hear* a great artist or orchestra even if you cannot fully see them?

It must be stated, although it seems obvious to music lovers, that any hall that is intended for the performance of classical music does not use microphones or other forms of amplification. We go to hear *natural* sound, and any electronic intervention—no matter how sophisticated—alters the quality of the sound. When you hear the sound of a bow against a single string of a violin, even when you are seated high up and far from the stage, there is a sensation of intimacy and immediacy that microphones would kill. Similarly, the sound of a hundred instruments of an orchestra in full cry has a way of getting under the skin that amplification would distort.

There are some new halls that have electronic devices that are referred to (rather deviously, I think) as "sound enhancement" systems. These might be added because the natural acoustics of the hall turned out to be a failure. Or the hall might be built as multipurpose, so that a classical performance will happen on one day, a rock concert on the second, and then a road company of *Cats* on the third. Sadly, these halls seldom gratify the lover of unamplified sound. Finally, because much in modern life is so loud, certain cynical hall designers and arts presenters think that younger audiences will only be drawn to an event if it has microphones attached. All of this is a negative trend, and music lovers should do all they can to fight it. Once you learn to appreciate the purity of natural sound, nothing can top it.

You might ask, then, why when entering many major concert halls you see microphones hanging above the stage and in various parts of the auditorium. They have been installed for two purposes. The first is for recording, either for archival reasons or for possible release as a compact disc. Think of how many recordings there are of performers "Live at Carnegie Hall." The second reason for the hanging microphones is that many concerts are broadcast live on the radio, and this is how the sound is picked up.

• ∾ •

Once you have your ticket in hand, write the date, seat location (including section), starting time, and name of the orchestra or musician you are hearing into your datebook. If you lose your ticket, this will be the best reference to try to get a replacement. Most arts organizations keep records of subscription, mail order, and phone order purchases, but will not know the seat location of a ticket you purchased at the box office window.

Then the day of concertgoing arrives. What you need to do is quite simple really, and most of the prevailing rules are based on common sense. Yet it is amazing to me how many people seem unaware of these basics, although I know that you, dear reader, are not one of them. Nonetheless, I will now go over these concepts and recount a couple of true stories that will help make concertgoing better for you and those around you.

On concert day, you have placed the tickets in your wallet or purse. You have recorded your seat location and are carrying it separately.

Should you listen to a recording of the music you will hear before the concert? This is entirely up to you. In *Opera 101*, I strongly urged readers to do preparatory listening and study, but in opera there is the crucial element of storytelling that is almost always absent in the context of a classical music concert.

If you listen ahead before you go to a concert, you will have a better idea of the sound and style of the music, and then can pay attention to smaller musical details in the concert. Or you can let the music wash over you in performance because you already have some idea of what it might sound like. But you might prefer not to listen ahead of time, so that the concert itself can provide you with a sense of initiation to a piece in an exciting context—sharing the enjoyment of music with two thousand people is almost always more thrilling than hearing it at home alone.

As a new classical music lover, you would probably benefit from some advance preparation before hearing unfamiliar music, so it is probably worth it to listen to a recording of a piece before hearing it live. As an experienced concertgoer, I tend not to listen ahead of time to works by the most popular composers, from Bach to Gershwin, because I already have a sense of the styles and contexts. But if I am to hear music by a less familiar composer, past or present, I believe some advance study is in order.

Two of the questions I am most often asked by prospective concertgoers regard how to dress and when to applaud. I will address the
latter issue below. Nowadays, the operative words about dressing would
be comfortable and attractive. In the past people got very dressed up,
with the result that they were often hot and uncomfortable in bulky and
restrictive clothing. This sometimes prevented them from focusing on
the music and enjoying it. For concerts in fall, winter, and spring,
women should wear dresses, suits, or blouses with skirts. Men should
wear either suits or jackets and slacks. A tie is preferable, although the
collar and knot should be loose enough that they are not restrictive. In
smaller cities and towns, men sometimes wear open collars. You should
look around you and see what the prevailing style is, and then do what
you feel comfortable with.

If you wear an outer coat and have not stored it in your car (if
that is how you arrived), then consider checking it in the cloakroom.
There may be a small charge, but it is worth it. If you sit with your coat
surrounding you or fold it on your lap, it has the effect of a blanket and
will make you doze off.

These sartorial recommendations would be suitable for most of
the world, though people in Italy, Spain, Austria, Germany, Argentina,
and Japan tend to be dressier than those elsewhere. The British and
French tend to be well dressed, but emphasize comfort and panache
over the strictures of elegance. In North America, New Yorkers, Bostoni-
ans, Montrealers, Chicagoans, Washingtonians, and San Franciscans
tend to dress up more, although this practice is not universal.

If you attend galas or other events that involve a special invita-
tion, it is likely that there will be special wardrobe requirements, and
you should follow them carefully.

In the summertime, rules of dress are a bit different. At some
European festivals, it is required that people dress elegantly, which
might even mean formal wear. This is mostly the case in Germany and
Austria. Elsewhere, the impact of weather is taken into consideration.
Many older theaters do not have air conditioning, so people wear cooler
cotton or linen clothes. Ties on men tend to be on at the start of the per-

formance and then are discreetly loosened—though not removed—if necessary.

Summertime in North America is a different phenomenon. Theaters tend to be heavily air conditioned, often much too much. At Avery Fisher Hall, home of the Mostly Mozart Festival, older people often bring sweaters and shawls to guard against air conditioning that blasts at levels that would make a polar bear shiver. Part of the attraction when these festivals were created was a means to cool off on a hot summer night, but things have gotten out of hand.

The style of dressing for concerts in the American summer also has gone too far. In the recent past it was casual, which is to say pants or skirts and blouses for women and slacks or pressed jeans and a nice shirt for men. But in many aspects of American life the line has blurred between casualness on the one hand and sloppiness and indifference on the other. Now people arrive in tennis clothes, beachwear, or looking as if they had just run a marathon. I am not fussy or snobby, but do believe that there is a sense of occasion about a concert, and if the performers are making an effort, then I should too.

Of course, the rules are different for casual outdoor concerts. Here, the most essential item to wear is bug spray.

If you think back to the kind of setting I asked you to create to listen to your recordings (see page 7), you will have a sense of what to do in a concert hall. Just as you removed distracting smells, you should wear little or no fragrance when you go to a concert. Even if you like it, there is sure to be an allergic or asthmatic person nearby whose evening will be ruined. And if they start sneezing, then you will be disturbed, too.

No one should wear more than one bracelet per arm. If they move during the concert, they will collide and make noise.

• ⟨◇⟩ •

What to eat before a concert? This varies from one person to the next. I tend to eat quite lightly and do not consume alcohol. It is not a good idea to have a large meal before going to hear music. A full stomach will draw blood from elsewhere in the body, including the brain, and you will become drowsy. People with particular medical conditions who must eat at scheduled times should try to coordinate their eating with the concert times and bring a small amount of food to consume at the intermission, if necessary. I might have a coffee or juice at the intermission and a light bite after the concert.

I always visit the toilet just before a concert and at intermission, just in case. There are few more unpleasant things than being distracted and uncomfortable when you are in a quiet hall trying to listen to gorgeous music.

When to arrive? I try to be in my seat about fifteen minutes before the start of the concert. This way thoughts of the outside world fade away and I can focus on the music I am about to hear. While in the seat I will unwrap any lozenges I might anticipate needing. In many American concert halls you can get free cough drops in the lobby. These are often provided by Halls, the manufacturer, which wisely wraps the drops in wax paper to minimize that horrible sound of plastic or cellophane that encloses many candies. Another brand of drops I recommend for coughs or sore throat is Ricola, available in North America and Europe. These too are wrapped in quiet paper, and are not as strong as Hall's.

Ladies should take out lozenges, tissues, eyeglasses, and other needed items from purses, which should be closed before the conductor or solo musician enters the stage. Rustling in a handbag creates more noise than some women realize, and is quite disturbing to neighbors. If men have anything they need in briefcases, they should be taken out early on, the bags should be snapped shut and placed flat on the floor.

Why do I mention lozenges? There is a peculiar phenomenon of coughing during concerts. Sometimes a series of coughs from one or two persons is inevitable and cannot be suppressed. But many people have never learned that they do not need to put a voice and language (Uh-huhh, UH-HUHH) behind a cough. There are people who do not seem to realize that—how shall I say it?—in their need to liberate matter from their lungs and nostrils they audibly cough and blow until said material has been expectorated into a handkerchief. Barring an emergency, a concert hall is not the setting to address these needs loudly. It is possible to contain a runny nose by quietly applying a handkerchief or tissue to the nose, without blowing. As to sneezes, which are seldom anticipated or controllable, one does not need to verbalize and say AH-CHOO out loud. No words are necessary to sneeze.

You may notice that during performances of symphonies and concertos, most audience members dutifully suppress coughs, but then, between movements, there is an explosion of coughs that brings to mind the pulmonary ward of a hospital. This seems quite unnecessary, if you think about it. An audience can sit almost silently for a one-hour act of a play, a ninety-minute act of an opera, or a two-hour film. Yet in concerts they seem to need to cough uncontrollably every eight minutes. I can offer no explanation for this, and can only suggest that if you don't need to cough, then resist the temptation to break the musical mood in the middle of a symphony or concerto.

• ⟳ •

At many concert venues, particularly in North America, the printed program contains one or more articles or series of notes by expert musicologists who provide wonderful background on the music and the composer. Some of the finest are by Michael Steinberg, James Keller, Paul Schiavo, and the late Herbert Kupferberg, to name but a few. I have written some as well that might pop up in your local program.

Typically these notes begin with comments about the composer and the context in which certain pieces of music were written. Some notes then go into very detailed technical explanations of the music. These program notes are quite valuable, but I have some ambivalence about them. Certainly the background material is significant and will help the listener enjoy the music more. But in giving such explicit technical information to an audience member before the music is heard, the listener is perhaps more inclined to pay attention to and look for the technical components in the piece rather than allow the totality of the music to be absorbed. This is another example of something I have addressed elsewhere in these pages: understanding does not come merely in the recognition of facts, but in the unrestrained willingness to perceive without resorting to instant analysis.

Perhaps the best thing for you to do is to read the background material about the composer and the context of the piece but not the analytical breakdown that follows. If you then enjoy hearing the music live, you might purchase a recording and use these program notes at home for further exploration of the piece. Also read only the notes for the first piece on the program, and then listen to the music. Then read the notes for the second during the pause after the first piece, and so on.

I am often amazed and disappointed when I observe audience members who are deeply engrossed in reading their programs while music is being played. Clearly they are not paying attention to the music, which is their loss. It becomes background sound for their reading.

There is only one exception to this rule: when you attend a vocal recital in which the texts of the songs are printed in the program in the original language and in English translation, it is customary to closely read along as you listen. The reason is that music and text are of almost equal importance in art songs, and part of your appreciation of what you are hearing comes in knowing and understanding the subtleties in the words. It is customary during the vocal recitals for the lights in the auditorium to be slightly brighter to permit you to read the words.

The most important thing to look at before the performance begins is the main program page, which typically lists the name of the orchestra or performing artist you will hear. You will also find, when applicable, the name of the conductor and the names of any soloists. Then you will find the music listed in order of performance, and when the intermission occurs. A hypothetical program page might look like this:

CARNEGIE HALL

Tuesday Evening November 20, 2003, at 8:00
Isaac Stern Auditorium

CARNEGIE HALL Presents

Los Angeles Philharmonic

Esa-Pekka Salonen, *Music Director*

Esa-Pekka Salonen, *Conductor*
Leif Ove Andsnes, *Piano*
Deborah Voigt, *Soprano*

LUDWIG VAN BEETHOVEN **(1770–1827)**	Piano Concerto No. 1 in C Major, Op. 15
	Allegro con brio Largo Rondo: Allegro
	LEIF OVE ANDSNES, *Piano*
RICHARD STRAUSS **(1864–1949)**	Vier Letzte Lieder (Four Last Songs)
	Frühling September Beim Schlafengehen Im Abendrot
	DEBORAH VOIGT, *Soprano*

INTERMISSION

JEAN SIBELUS **(1865–1957)**	Symphony No. 2 in D Major, Op. 43
	Allegretto Tempo andante, ma rubato
	Vivacissimo Finale. Allegro moderato

Before the concert begins, please switch off
cell phones and other electronic devices.

The program page tells you much of what you need to know. The performance is scheduled to begin at 8 P.M., and therefore you should be in your seat before that time. In most concert halls, latecomers are not admitted until the first piece of music on the program has been completed. In the case of the Beethoven piano concerto, that means that all three movements must be played before a latecomer can go to his seat. This may seem severe, but the overwhelming majority of audience members arrive on time, and seating of latecomers would be a noisy disruption.

• ᧞ •

Let us use the hypothetical program shown above to imagine your concertgoing experience. Ticket takers appear outside the auditorium of the concert hall, typically thirty minutes before the scheduled start of the performance. Audience members enter, get a copy of the program, check coats, visit the toilet, and then go to their seats. They will turn off cell phones and pagers, unwrap cough drops, and settle into their seats. They will then review the program page.

While the audience members prepare, orchestra musicians will enter the stage and take their seats in a configuration created by the conductor to achieve the best balance of sound. You will hear the musicians randomly tune their instruments or play snatches of the music they are about to perform. In the middle of that stage will be a grand piano (for the Beethoven concerto), with the keyboard on your left side as you face the stage. Just behind it will be the conductor's podium.

By eight o'clock, all the orchestra members will be in their seats. Lights in the auditorium will dim, and the lights onstage may brighten slightly. Then, just past the hour, the concertmaster (principal violinist) will enter the stage and take a solo bow. He or she will then tune the orchestra in the note of A. There is some variation in orchestra tuning. Sometimes it is led by the concertmaster; at other times the note is played by the principal oboist. On occasions when a piano is onstage, the pianist may play the note before settling in to play.

Once tuning has occurred, it is the moment for the conductor to enter the stage. In this case, Maestro Salonen will enter from stage right (audience left), shake the hand of the concertmaster, and then might ask all of the orchestra members to rise for a bow. Sometimes, when there is a solo musician, he might enter with the conductor and they will bow together. On other occasions, the soloist might enter after the conductor has seated the orchestra. All of these entrances and bows are greeted by audience applause.

Note that the entrances I describe from stage right apply to most concert halls, but not all. For example, at the Concertgebouw in Amsterdam the conductor and soloists make an entrance down a long series of steps in full view of the audience, which is quite dramatic. In a few halls and concert venues, the conductor and soloists might enter the stage from another direction.

By the time the conductor is at the podium with baton in hand and the soloist (pianist Leif Ove Andsnes) is ready to perform, no latecomers are admitted. The conductor will face the orchestra, with his back to the audience. Over his left shoulder will be the pianist at the keyboard. The maestro's left hand will be visible to the pianist as a means of communication, and during the performance they will make frequent eye contact.

In our hypothetical concert, orchestra and soloist will perform the First Piano Concerto by Beethoven. You will have seen in your program that there are three movements in this work. There will be no seating of latecomers during the very brief pauses between movements, and under no circumstance should you applaud. Once the piece has ended, the audience will erupt into applause. American audiences are often quite eager to applaud, and they do not necessarily allow the last strains of the piece to fade away before they start pounding their hands together. I would encourage you to pause for a few seconds to drink in the last drops of glorious sound and then applaud as enthusiastically as you wish.

The pianist will take one or more solo bows, or in tandem with the conductor. If there are notable orchestral passages in the concerto featuring one or two musicians, the conductor might ask them to rise for solo bows. You might notice that members of the orchestra often applaud the soloist, with players of string instruments tapping their bows on their music stands.

You will also notice in concerts that it is customary for the conductor and solo musicians to go offstage after taking their first bows. They will return to the stage for more bows, and then go off again. This will go on for as long as it seems the audience is eager to applaud. The sound of applause will die down slightly as they walk offstage and will swell again as they re-enter the stage. If the conductor or soloist feels he or she has taken enough bows, they will inform the stage management offstage, and lights onstage will be raised somewhat to give a visual cue that the performance will now proceed.

Once the applause has concluded, the pianist and conductor will already be offstage. The orchestral musicians might go offstage but, more likely, will remain onstage. In this moment, while latecomers are being shown to their seats, stage personnel will appear and quickly remove the grand piano from the stage and then reconfigure the conductor's podium, chairs, and music stands, so that it will be ideal for the next piece of music. Because every piece of music has a different instrumentation, there will probably be a change in the number of musicians and where they will sit as we progress from the Beethoven to the Strauss in our hypothetical program. Once chairs and music stands are in place, the orchestra musicians will take their seats. The conductor's podium will be closer to the audience now that the piano is gone, and there will be a vacant space to the left of his podium, near the concertmaster's chair.

When everyone has settled in (including audience members), the soprano soloist, Deborah Voigt, will enter from stage right (the audience's left), threading her way through the orchestra to the vacant spot next to the podium. She will greet the concertmaster, perhaps bow to the orchestra, greet the conductor, and then turn and bow to the audience. Because you have seen on the program page that there are four songs, you will by now have turned to the pages in the booklet that contain the

German text and the English translation of Strauss's gorgeous *Four Last Songs*. You will read along as Voigt sings, but you will also want to keep an eye on her as well.

Maestro Salonen will conduct these songs. There will be brief pauses between each song, but you should not applaud, even if you desperately want to. Once Voigt has finished the text of the last song, this does not mean it has ended. Listen carefully to the achingly beautiful last instrumental music, and let it completely evaporate in the air before even lifting your hands to applaud. Let the music sink in. Chances are you were transported to a wonderful place, and you are not required to snap back to reality before you are ready.

There will surely be a thunderous ovation for singer, conductor, and orchestra, with many bows. Once this has ended, Voigt and Salonen will remain offstage, the lights will be made brighter in the hall, and the musicians will file off.

It is now intermission, which for most concerts in America is about twenty minutes. In Europe it may last longer, because restaurants and bars in the theaters do a fair amount of business. Intermission (called the interval in nations that use British English; *entr'acte* in French; *intervallo* in Italian; *Pause* in German; *entre acto* in Spanish) is the time to stretch your legs, have a refreshment, visit the gift shop or toilet, and chat with other audience members. You should also glance at the program notes about the symphony you are soon to hear, and read some of them. When the performance is about to resume, there will be bells, buzzers, or recorded sounds to indicate that it is time to go back into the hall. Remember, if you are not in your seat when the second half starts, you will be stuck outside.

As you re-enter the auditorium, you will notice that the seats and music stands onstage have been reconfigured again to serve the needs of the Sibelius symphony. There will be no gap next to the conductor's podium. Maestro Salonen will enter from stage right, shake hands with the concertmaster, ask the orchestra to rise, and all will take a bow. The hall will calm down, lights will dim, and the conductor will take the podium, raise his baton, and the symphony will begin. You know from the program that there are four movements in this work, so you will not applaud until they have all concluded. This will now be the end of the performance, and conductor and orchestra will take several bows.

At this point, the concert as indicated in the program has concluded. If the Los Angeles Philharmonic were performing at its home theater, this would be it. But sometimes touring orchestras offer encores (additional short pieces that are audience-pleasers), especially if they are appearing in major music capitals. It is possible that, with a Finnish music director, the L.A. Philharmonic might perform a generous 9½-minute encore of Sibelius's *Finlandia* in our hypothetical Carnegie Hall concert. The conductor might or might not announce from the podium what the encore would be prior to turning to lead the work.

Then the concert would truly be over. After additional applause, audience members would file out, basking in the glow of an excellent performance. If there are some dissenters, they will probably get into an animated debate with anyone who will join in.

• ⟨⟩ •

Concerts given by chamber music groups or solo instrumentalists and singers follow a similar pattern to what I described above, but on a smaller scale. It is much less likely that the stage will require reconfiguration during a performance, even if a piano is involved. At most, the piano might be pushed upstage (away from the audience) and seats and music stands for other artists moved downstage.

Performers will take bows and go offstage at the end of sections of a program. For example, if they play a string quartet by Mendelssohn to open a performance, they will go offstage before returning to play a quartet by, let us say, Borodin or Debussy. A singer may do a group of songs by Handel and then go offstage before returning to do a group by Schubert. Then she would go offstage again before returning for a group of songs by Hugo Wolf.

In concerts by solo artists you are more likely to hear encores. Think of them as bon-bons served after a sumptuous meal. They are usually small, vivid, often emotionally touching, and occasionally humorous. Encores are moments when an artist can slightly relax, having gotten through the pressures of giving a demanding recital program.

A performer is not required to give encores, but it is more or less customary for a soloist to play up to three encores at the end of a program. This assumes, of course, that the performer feels the concert went well, that he or she still has enough stamina and concentration, and that the majority of the audience is not rushing to the exits once the scheduled program has concluded. Typically a performer—a pianist, let us say—will conclude the program, take bows, walk offstage, and then, as the applause continues, return to the stage. You will notice a surge in applause when the pianist reappears, this being encouragement from the audience for an encore. The pianist may immediately return to the keyboard, or go back in the wings again before returning.

If the pianist chooses to do an encore, he or she may turn and tell the audience what will be played, or simply plunge into the music. Bear in mind that the sound of the performer's speaking voice breaks some kind of invisible wall. This may be pleasing and intimate, but it can also be occasionally jarring. We are transported from the language of music to the language of words.

At the conclusion of the encore, there will be more applause. The ritual of applause and bows, including trips offstage, will continue. You will detect the implicit give-and-take between enthusiastic audience and a performer giving a visual indication of gratitude through bowing or perhaps placing a hand over the heart. While some of this may seem artificial and insincere if you do not know this convention, it is actually comforting and familiar for many involved. Remember too that many performers do not speak the language of the audience they are performing for, so that music and gesture from the stage and applause and cheers from the auditorium serve as the principal means of communication.

If the typical three encores are given, then it becomes a rather delicate calculation as to whether there will be another. As long as there is a strong nucleus of audience members clamoring for more, the soloist is likely to oblige, assuming that he or she has additional material to perform. Otherwise, they might adhere to the true meaning of *encore* ("again," in French), and play a piece a second time. But if the auditorium really seems to be emptying, the performer will likely take a last bow, wave good-bye, and then disappear offstage. This is part of the old, infallible performer's wisdom: "Leave them cheering." Incidentally, it is tacitly known that critics do not review encores, and often they do not even acknowledge them in their articles. They have come to cover the announced program only. They might mention a particular encore only if it gave scintillating pleasure.

There are some circumstances in which encores will not be given. Sometimes a concert hall needs to be emptied to be prepared for another performance. This does not happen often in major concert halls, but in certain smaller venues it is typical. For example, I have a subscription to a Sunday-afternoon recital series at wonderful Alice Tully Hall at Lincoln Center. Performances usually start at 2 P.M. and the artist must leave the stage by 4 P.M. so that the stage and auditorium can be readied for an evening performance by some other artist or group.

Encores might often be skipped if an artist is truly tired or has performed an important, singular piece (such as Schubert's song cycle *Die Winterreise*) so that anything that might follow would detract from its impact and seem extraneous.

Then there are those rare occasions in which the artist is so dissatisfied with his own performance that he no longer wishes to play. I was fortunate to hear the brilliant Vladimir Horowitz on numerous occasions, and his performances were thrilling. Once, however, he was clearly off and played poorly. At the end of the scheduled program, he rose from the piano bench, bowed curtly, closed the keyboard cover, and left the stage. No amount of applause could have brought him back. It was clear to the audience that he was unhappy, and they applauded just long enough for him to hear them as he returned to his dressing room. Immediately following the performance, and for months after, there was a great deal of buzz among music lovers (this was before Internet chat rooms) that the great Horowitz was finished. About eighteen months later I heard him again. He played with brilliance, power, and clarity, and he and the audience knew that the previous concert was just a one-time fiasco. This time Horowitz, by then in his eighties, played seven encores.

• ◇ •

Up to this point we have largely discussed what happens in a concert from the musicians' point of view. Audience members are expected to be quiet and attentive while the music is being played. Most of them are, but there are always a few selfish people who have the potential of ruining the evening for others. Here are some war stories from the front, told by someone who has attended more than one thousand concerts.

I have it on good authority that there is a special ring of hell set aside specifically for people who do not shut off their cellular phones, beeping wrist watches, pagers, and other noisy devices that are certain to annoy performers and your fellow concertgoers. I was once in a hall in which a watch began to beep at three minutes before nine and others chimed in for the next seven minutes as each thought it was striking the hour. Similarly, all beepers and personal pagers must be silenced. The reason is obvious. If you are a doctor or some other person who might be paged during a performance, wear a pager that you are certain will vibrate but not make a sound. Be sure to purchase an aisle seat so you can exit without disturbing anyone. If your pager makes any noise, leave it with the house manager or chief usher and ask that you be fetched from your aisle seat in case there is a call.

The cellular phone has absolutely no place in a concert hall. It is useful if you have a flat tire on the highway, but what purpose could it possible serve when you are listening to music? Although an admonition to shut off the phone and its ringer might be indicated in the printed program or on signs posted outside auditoriums, and even projected on the rear wall of the stage (as is done at Carnegie Hall before performances), some people forget or simply do not care. When their phones ring during a concert, they fumble and make noise to shut them off, breaking the concentration of everyone in the hall, including the musicians! Have you noticed the irony in the fact that many of these cell phones don't have normal rings, but use passages from Bach, Mozart, or Beethoven to announce that a call is coming through?

It is bad enough when cell phones ring during performances, but I have twice seen audience members *place* a call during a concert. Once, during a gorgeous recital by soprano Renée Fleming at Carnegie Hall, a man took out his phone, dialed a number, and held the phone up so that the person at the end of the line could hear the music. A generous act of love, you might say, except that the recipient of the call kept yelling, "Hello! Hello! Who's calling?" loud enough for audience members to hear.

Worse still, I once attended a performance of Brahms's Second Symphony at Avery Fisher Hall given by the New York Philharmonic under Maestro Kurt Masur. During the first movement, a man in my row took out his phone, placed a call, and began a banal and annoying conversation. As the orchestra got louder, the man shouted to be heard. Audience members were too stunned to do anything, but I quietly climbed over seats and snatched the phone from the man. At the end of the symphony he lunged at me, but was stopped by two elderly women who clubbed him with their handbags. Security guards removed the man and his phone, and the ladies and I took a bow.

Before you say "Only in New York . . ." you should know that the first caller was from Pittsburgh and the second was from San Antonio, Texas.

Need I mention that there is absolutely no reason to speak to anyone next to you during a performance—not even a word—barring the most dire emergency in which immediate assistance is required? If you have a comment, save it for after the music has ended. When Franz Liszt was asked, during a performance, by the Emperor of all of the Russias why he stopped playing, the pianist boldly replied, "When Your Majesty speaks, all should remain silent." This ironic but telling remark says much about the impact of bad audience behavior on a performer.

• ∾ •

After you have attended the concert, it is pleasant to think about what you have heard, see if you can recall passages of music that touched you deeply, and talk about the concert with others. At this point you can shift to an actively analytical mode and explore your feelings about the music you have absorbed.

There is at least one person in the auditorium who was more likely to be in an analytical mode from the very beginning: the music critic. The very word *critic* sets us off on bad footing with this person, because we think that the title implies that he or she will be *negatively* critical. I tend to think of the best critics as expert chroniclers of an event, which they will then record for historical documentation. This is a lofty and important responsibility, and one that should be taken seriously by people who continue to freshen and renew their interest in music.

The role of the music critic is distinct from other critics in a key way. Someone who reviews films, plays, operas, and many dance performances writes not only to present impressions of what he or she has seen, but there is the implicit question that the reader asks of the critic: Should I buy a ticket to see this? In effect, the critic is giving an endorsement or discourages the reader from seeing the work in question. The same applies for the visual arts, because works tend to be installed for a period of time.

In most cases, a concert is a one-time thing (like a sports event) and the critic is telling you about what you did not see or hear, and why it was meaningful. There is one important exception to this: the orchestral subscription concert. For example, the New York Philharmonic often performs the same program on a Thursday, Friday, Saturday, and Tuesday. The review of a concert the critic has heard on Thursday will typically appear in Saturday's paper, so a positive review may incite the reader to purchase tickets for the Saturday or Tuesday concert, if any remain.

The music critic faces several daunting tasks, and most fulfill them responsibly. The critic must have an excellent background in musical history and performance, with a strong knowledge of the ideas, strengths, and weaknesses of all of the important composers. Chances are that a music critic will have heard almost all of what is called the standard repertory, either live or on recordings. This takes a long time and a lot of work, and is usually born of a genuine love of music.

Inevitably, in the act of learning, the critic develops preferences which, if applied in the wrong way, turn into prejudices. One critic might think that Schubert's songs are so sublime that nothing else compares. So if he hears an all-Schubert program, he might be pleased, but will perhaps feel a letdown if a program has not only a group of Schubert songs but also works by Wolf, Strauss, and Berg. I have observed some critics become restless when even a great artist performs music they might not like.

Similarly, our critic may hear an all-Schubert program and decide that the artist in question cannot possibly compare with one of the great singers of the past. This may well be true, but it is important that a critic evaluate the artistry of the person on the stage that night, and not be nostalgic for a singer from decades ago who might have seemed wonderful at the time but in retrospect may appear mannered or vocally insecure.

There is also the question of staleness. If a critic hears Dvořák's *New World* Symphony twice a year for twenty-five years, that is fifty performances. This is very possible—orchestras love to perform it, and it is often played on radio, too. No matter how wonderful this music is, even the most trained and admiring ear will not always give familiar music the consideration it deserves. So critics must require of themselves that they listen to every performance of well-known pieces with all of their faculties at full blast and with the desire to be pleased and surprised and moved.

Most music directors of major orchestras go out of their way to occasionally program pieces that are being heard for the first time in a city. Some big orchestras allocate money to commission world premieres, often from composers who are not well-known. The evening's conductor will invest prestige and extra time to launch this work, often in front of audiences who are resistant to the new and would be perfectly content with an evening of favorites by Mozart, Beethoven, and

Brahms. Often, when new works are presented, the composer will be present at rehearsals and attend the premiere.

In this situation it is the role of the critic to find the words to describe what the music sounded like and give some sense of his or her response to the music and—perhaps—indicate how the audience responded. In this case, the critic is not necessarily answering the "money question" for readers about whether to buy tickets, but will be giving an opinion about whether attention should be paid in the future to this composer and whether the music merits being performed elsewhere. It is a heavy responsibility.

The critic's judgment may not prevail in the long run, but may have significant impact at the time. Not everybody who encountered Beethoven's Seventh Symphony liked it on first hearing. Some found it brilliant, revolutionary, and groundbreaking. Others found it wild, anarchical, and undisciplined. I have read collected reviews of critics from around the year 1900, long after Beethoven's death, that said the the Seventh Symphony had cheap effects and none of the grace of the Sixth.

Tastes evolve and change. Composers and pieces of music go in and out of fashion. Gustav Mahler's music was largely ignored until Leonard Bernstein championed it in the 1960s, and now Mahler's symphonies and songs are performed all the time. One hopes that the tastes of critics—like those of other music lovers—also evolve and change with experience. Music that said nothing to me two decades ago may now be very close to my heart, while a piece I used to adore may now seem tired or simplistic.

Just as a critic can have great impact on our impressions of a piece of music (whether or not we have heard it ourselves), so too can he or she play a key role in the opinions we form about musicians. One of the critic's jobs is to cover the local debut of a highly touted artist who may be making a name for herself elsewhere. This is a thorny issue and must be handled with great care. I have read critics who are absolutely smitten with the performance of an eighteen-year-old pianist or violinist and proceed to give the kind of glowing review that will be hard for the young musician to live up to. Then the performer will return as a twenty-five-year-old and the critic may say that the musician has not lived up to her initial promise. If you did not hear the first or second concert but read the reviews, you would feel you missed out on something special initially but then saved your money the second time around.

It may well be that the critic was absolutely correct about the technical and interpretive abilities of the artist. It might also be that the musician (who is human, after all) simply had a bad night at the later concert. Similarly, the critic (equally human) may be having a bad night. If critics take the stance that you and I do—that a relationship with music lasts a lifetime—they can be more understanding about peaks and valleys and changes of taste.

Over the days I wrote these words, it happens that I attended three piano performances on consecutive nights. One was by eighteen-year-old Lang Lang; another by fifty-two-year-old Emanuel Ax; the third by seventy-eight-year-old Alicia de Larrocha. Each one is a magnificent artist, but for different reasons. All trained in different times and places, and were subject to different influences and experiences. The first is Chinese and brimming with youthful energy and technical prowess. The second is American, fully in his prime and at a moment when he can combine technique, elegance, and insight. The third is Spanish and has been playing in front of audiences for more than seventy years. She is a living legend who might seem above criticism. Yes, she did hit a couple of wrong notes, but also played with such intimacy, authority, and undimmed love of the music that one was entranced. There was also the palpable sense of being in the presence of a great figure, and a sense of gratitude to be able to hear her play.

If the same critic went to all three performances, it would be necessary to review them with a similar approach but a sense of the occasions being distinct. Lang Lang played Grieg; Ax and de Larrocha played Mozart. What would be important to describe are the ideas and talents that each pianist brought to the music at hand. It might help to recount what makes these performers special. Lang might be precocious talent; Ax might be the happy convergence of all of a pianist's requirements at their best; and de Larrocha could be the dazzling aura of greatness combined with pianism that may have lost just a little perfection but still possesses a heap of intangibles found only in this one artist.

The impact of reviews would differ from one artist to the next. Lang Lang is launching a major career and each new performance and recording will be listened to with heightened expectation. With Ax it would be a report that a wonderful career is progressing and the artistry continues to deepen. And the review for de Larrocha, fairly or not, would be written with history in mind.

The best critics can take on the role of advocate and educator. They might speak in public or conduct interviews with artists in front of an audience. They can write program notes for publication in other venues (but not where they review). If they see that an unusual piece of music will be performed in a city, they can write an article in advance of the concert to explain why the piece or the composer is notable. This will likely stimulate ticket sales and the critic will have done a service. It is a circumstance in which having favorites can be put to positive effect.

Even in reviews of familiar artists playing familiar repertory, the good critic can use the occasion to teach the reader. If the critic chides the artist, it helps to explain what the expectation was and what was missing. For example, if a cellist played a familiar concerto in a detached, automatic way, the critic can explain what impact this playing has on the music and the audience. Or if the cellist was brilliant but the conductor focused only on the orchestral parts and not on interacting with the soloist, what result did this produce?

There are some critics who become famous (and occasionally reviled) for the power of their prose and the ferocity of their opinions. George Bernard Shaw wrote criticism that is wonderful to read because it is amusing and penetrating, but often at the merciless expense of the musicians and composers he describes. In the latter half of the twentieth century, Claudia Cassidy wielded great power in Chicago. Her reviews had great impact on the fortunes of artists, the financial health of musical organizations, and public opinion. Some might say that she had too much power, while others feel that her seriousness and dedication were vital in helping Chicago become a world-class musical center.

A contemporary example of a controversial critic is the Pulitzer Prize–winning Martin Bernheimer. For many years he lived in Los Angeles and covered the music scene there. His reviews were informed, exacting and—some people said—unforgiving. Some musicians I know in Southern California felt that during Bernheimer's tenure he stifled local interest and enthusiasm for classical music with the severity of his opinions and prevented the art form from getting the local support it needed to grow and improve. But Bernheimer also had many supporters who said that because Los Angeles was a huge city with a diverse population, vast financial resources, and international ambitions, the city deserved world-class musical artistry and that this critic was the one to set the very high standard that Los Angeles merited. Bernheimer has since moved to New York and covers music and opera internationally, as well as playing an important educational role through radio and public appearances. (I should add, in full disclosure, that I have come to know him socially but feel I have fairly presented the divergent opinions about his work.)

Both Cassidy and Bernheimer (and Shaw, for that matter) worked in important international cities where one would expect to hear the best in musical performance. But what standards should a critic apply in a city of fifty thousand people with a community orchestra and a local choir? It might be that this critic once lived or studied in a major city, or has the occasion to travel often to important music capitals, enabling him to know what top-notch music-making is like. Should world-class standards be used to assess local performances? Should the critic be soft and turn a "blind ear" to miscues or weaknesses to help nudge along a small, struggling organization trying to establish roots and bring music to a community that does not have much of it? There is no easy answer to this situation, but you can now better understand the dilemma involved.

Critics nowadays face an additional challenge. They work for editors and publications who often think that classical music is marginal and does not merit the same space in the papers that movies, television, and pop music might receive. This is unfortunate because newspapers should provide leadership, and critics can play a role in this. And the particular nature of most classical music reviews (that they describe a past event rather than offering ticket purchasing advice for the future) means that editors are less motivated to run articles of any length.

The main newspapers and magazines in the cities that are home to the Big Five American orchestras (Boston, Chicago, Cleveland, New York, and Philadelphia) all have major critics and thoughtful coverage. Newspapers such as the *Washington Post* and the *Los Angeles Times* also give importance to music criticism. Beyond that, there is a vast range in the quality and extent of critical presence in American publications.

New York, with its incredible concentration of performances, presents a unique problem. The *New York Times*, which considers itself the newspaper of record, has five full-time critics (and some part-timers) who are out most nights covering performances at Carnegie Hall, Lincoln Center, and many other halls around town. Even at that, much does not wind up in the paper, or will appear in very short articles, simply because there is so much to cover. Young artists making debuts might get cursory coverage, if at all, and I have been to splendid performances by artists in mid-career that got no coverage at all. To fully cover all that New York offers in all the arts, the *Times* would have to run many pages of daily reviews. The *Times* does more extensive criticism than any other American paper, but even it cannot cover all that the city presents. This means that artists and their managements must compete and hope for that all-important *Times* review.

Other publications in New York cover classical music with greater or lesser seriousness. The *Wall Street Journal*, *The New Yorker*, and *New York* magazine have long records of dedicated music criticism, and their writers are quite influential. For many years, the *Village Voice* benefited from the perceptive, erudite, and fair criticism by Leighton Kerner, who had the advantage of being able to write at great length. Sadly, the *Voice* no longer seems to think that classical music merits much coverage.

Newspapers and all media can and should play important roles in the cultural affairs and well-being of the cities they serve and earn money from. Many publications, locally and nationally, will mention classical music only if there is some *People* magazine–type interest in a performer. If a very young, photogenic musician makes a splash and then agrees to pose in a sexy picture, that might get a mention in the mass media. Failing that, meaningful articles about classical music tend to be confined to newspapers in certain cities and in intellectual journals with small circulations. As you become a classical music lover, write to your local publications and encourage them to improve their coverage if you consider it inadequate.

Newspapers in the major music cities in Europe devote much more coverage than do the typical American publications. In part this is because of a broader interest even among readers who do not regularly attend musical performances. Classical music is part of the history and heritage of many of these nations, and world-famous artists from smaller countries are a source of great pride.

Critics in Germany, Austria, Italy, and France not only cover performances but the politics and polemics of the arts world. This is due in part to local interest, but also because many arts organizations in these countries receive public funding. It is an odd but true fact to realize that the instrumentalists of the Vienna Philharmonic are public servants. As such, government expenditure for the arts may appear in various sections of an Austrian newspaper: arts, economics, local politics, national politics, and gossip.

In England, where most newspapers are centered in London, coverage of the vast musical scene in the capital is wide-ranging and generally of high quality. You might find it quite informative to read reviews on the Internet from the *Financial Times*, the *Guardian*, the *Times* of London, the *Daily Telegraph*, and other British dailies. Also read *Grammophone* and other British musical publications.

How might you use local reviews to enhance your knowledge? In the days after attending a performance, read whatever coverage you can about it. Compare your feelings and impressions with those in the reviews. You may find over time that you usually tend to agree with critic A and disagree with critic B. In general terms you can read the reviews by critic A of performances you did not hear and have a sense of what you might enjoy. But always read critic B with great care, because he or she will challenge your opinions, make you think anew about ideas that you feel you have completely considered, and often be more valuable to you than critic A.

You probably never thought that such a lengthy chapter could be written about attending musical performances. In fact, whole books can be done on this topic. What it comes down to is preparedness and open-mindedness, and the belief, in the words of Arthur Rubinstein, that inherent in a fine musical performance is the promise of better things to come.

THE PIANO

After playing Chopin, I feel as if I had been weeping over sins that I had never committed, and mourning over tragedies that were not my own. Music always seems to me to produce that effect. It creates for one a past of which one has been ignorant and fills one with a sense of sorrows that have been hidden from one's tears.

—Oscar Wilde

P art of what Oscar Wilde spoke of in the passage above is music's supreme ability to reach the deepest part of the soul and to lay bare for us our feelings. We can exult in great triumphal music, find humor in passages that tickle us, develop insights into the human condition in song literature, or understand the chiaroscuro of emotions that are seldom as straightforward as the words we use to describe them.

For many people who care about music, no instrument can match the piano's capacity for touching a listener so deeply. Part of the reason for this, I believe, is that we come face to face and ear to ear with two elements: a singularly versatile musical instrument and the one person who is playing it. Part of the appeal in the piano repertoire is the cult of personality. You might say that the same could apply to singers, and this is true to a certain extent, but with one key difference. When singers do opera, they are playing characters and their own personalities merge with those of the roles they are playing. When the singer does a vocal recital, a great deal of her personality may be imprinted on the songs she sings, but the presence of words in these songs makes us listen differently. We hear music, words, *and* the temperament of the singer. Also, a singer looks at *us* as she performs.

A pianist will enter the stage silently, bow to the audience, and then sit at the keyboard and play. In so doing, she or he enters an almost trancelike state of concentration and the music begins. The pianist has direct physical contact with the instrument (with fingers on the keyboard and feet on the pedals) and the piano becomes almost a physical extension of the person, a conduit through which sound and feelings are transmitted from the pianist's body and soul to anyone who happens to be within hearing range. We become a witness to something incredibly intimate and personal and, when the music and performer capture us, we are powerfully moved.

You might say that a similar phenomenon can happen when a soloist plays the violin, cello, flute, clarinet, trumpet, or any other instrument. The difference, I think, is that these other instruments can be incredibly expressive, but they are surrogates for a single voice. Keyboard instruments, uniquely, have an almost infinite capacity to speak in many voices. Yes, great violinists and cellists often can bring great diversity to the voices of what they play, but you will surely agree that the sound of the piano is an experience apart. Before continuing in this chapter you might wish to reread the section about keyboard instruments (starting on page 79) to refresh your memory about the genesis of the piano.

The piano and the people who play it stand apart in the world of classical music because they embody, more than any other type of performance (except singing), the notion of *virtuosity*. This does not suggest being virtuous in any moral sense, but rather a person who possesses *virtù*, from the Italian, meaning extraordinary talents in certain areas. A politician can have them, so can a chef or a fisherman, but in describing a *virtuoso*—a person endowed with one or more *virtù*—it is almost always in reference to a performing artist and, most especially, to a musician.

The word *virtuoso* can be overused, as the word *diva* is. Diva means goddess, and it implies someone with extraordinary skills who can deeply touch and move us with her artistry and communicative ability. The notion of a diva being tempestuous and demanding is mistaken—that is a *prima donna*. (We say to someone, "Don't be such a prima donna!" not "Don't be such a diva.") In America the word *diva* has come to be used to describe almost any twenty-year-old pop singer with a new dance hit and an edgy look. The word needs to be reclaimed because it is too good to ruin.

So far, *virtuoso* has largely escaped the fate of *diva*. It still suggests someone of unusual talents and accomplishments, and is quite laudatory. In a pianist, the ability to handle the many technical demands of the instrument while making it express the way the performer understands the music makes him a virtuoso. As often as not, the piano virtuoso is not only a brilliant technician but one with an immense personality that is expressed in the playing.

When keyboard music was often part of a larger whole, in the eighteenth century, the performer played an important role but fit into the ensemble. Often, the keyboard player might conduct the ensemble while playing, especially if he was the composer. With the advent of the piano concerto in the latter part of the eighteenth century, and its growth thereafter as piano parts became more difficult to play, the focus of listeners shifted from the ensemble to the soloist. Pianists would often be "guests" of the orchestra, invited for that one performance rather than being a permanent member. As pianists gained fame in their solo careers, the cult of personality grew, and so did the adulation for the virtuoso properties of piano playing.

To create for you only the shortest list of the chronology of how this phenomenon evolved, let us recall that Bach and Handel were star keyboard players (organ, harpsichord, clavichord) in the years from about 1710 to 1750. In the 1760s and 1770s the young Mozart performed on the piano all over Europe to great acclaim. In the 1780s Mozart's piano rival was Muzio Clementi, and audiences would argue as to who was better. With rival groups of fans, this elevated the sense of comparison that listeners often make about musicians.

Mozart and Muzio Clementi were considered the greatest pianists of their time, at least in the musical world of Vienna. There was a performance contest between the two of them, before Emperor Franz Josef, which was declared a draw. The emperor asked the composer Karl

Ditters von Dittersdorf what he thought of the two pianists. "Excellency," replied the composer, "Clementi's playing is art alone. Mozart's playing is art and taste." It probably did not hurt Mozart's cause that Ditters von Dittersdorf was his friend, but there is an important point in his remark. Taste is a subjective concept, of course, and implicit in this is that we are speaking of *good* taste. But there is a virtue to playing with taste, whatever a musician interprets taste to mean. It could suggest restraint rather than gaudy showmanship, or perhaps a faithfulness to the written music, rather than looking for ways to "personalize" the piece so that it becomes unmistakably the performance of a particular artist.

But here we enter a difficult area. The written music is a constant, except in those cases in which there is more than one version of a piece. So the moment in which a musician comes into contact with the printed music is also the moment that issues of taste and personality enter. Each performer has his or her own response to the music, and the ability to play it is based on physical and technical abilities, combined with temperament, emotion, nerves, and the degree to which the musician has studied, analyzed, and felt the music. And somewhere in this process, taste makes its entrance. Can we describe it? Probably in only the most clumsy and approximative way, and using too many words. But I think you will agree that we know taste when we are in its presence.

• ❦ •

Mozart and Clementi were composers, of course, and many of the great pianists who followed in the nineteenth century were also composers. For the most part, they performed their own compositions, which were designed to show off their strengths. Modern pianists can understand a lot about a composer's playing because the music itself shows them various elements: Over how many keys could a pianist stretch his hands? How fast could he play?

In the nineteenth century, the Romantic movement in art helped elevate the cult of the individual pianist. It also heightened the interest in personality as an element of virtuoso playing by superstars such as Liszt and Chopin. Edvard Grieg would tour Europe for much of the winter, returning to his beloved Norway in the warm seasons to bask in the midnight sun and draw inspiration for composing new works.

Robert Schumann enjoyed a brief career that was curtailed by a hand injury and illness. His music was played by his wife, Clara, one of the first great female virtuosos. Louis Moreau Gottschalk (1829–1869) was the leading American composer of the mid–nineteenth century and also ranked among the great piano virtuosi. Brahms, Saint-Saëns, Rachmaninoff, Scriabin (1872–1915), who wrote more than 250 works for piano, and Gershwin were all great composer-pianists. One of the very finest, Ignace Paderewski (1860–1941), is now largely forgotten.

Paderewski was viewed as the natural heir to Chopin in that his music and style were highly romantic and he seemed to speak simultaneously in two voices: his own and that of Poland. From 1887 until the outbreak of World War I, he was considered the world's foremost pianist. Paderewski's most famous piece was his Minuet in G. So popular was this piece by the man who arguably was the greatest pianist of his day that other pianists recorded and played it, including Rachmaninoff.

After the war Paderewski became the first prime minister of Poland, and later held other offices. Despite his greatness as a performer, his foray into politics did not please everyone and there were two assassination attempts. By the early 1930s he returned, somewhat shakily, to performing, and the recordings we have of him from that period show great virtuosity but no longer the assurance he had at his peak. He died in 1941, while in New York, seeking financial and military assistance for Poland. Paderewski was buried in Arlington National Cemetery at the insistence of Franklin Delano Roosevelt. Paderewski asked that he remain there only until Poland was free. His body was returned to St. John's Cathedral in Warsaw on June 27, 1992, but his heart remains in the United States—literally. It is inside a bronze monument at the Our Lady of Czestochowa shrine in Doylestown, Pennsylvania. In this he emulated his countryman Chopin, whose mortal remains are in Paris but whose heart was returned to Poland. Some may feel a bit squeamish at these thoughts, but they bespeak two very important aspects of the piano repertory: Romanticism and Nationalism. Great pianists since then who were born in Poland include Arthur Rubinstein (1887–1982), Eduard Steuermann (1892–1964), who was also a composer, and Emanuel Ax, whom you will soon meet.

The rigors of war and politics seem to be a thread throughout the history of the piano. Beethoven was deeply affected by the political currents of his time and often played concerts to benefit Austrian soldiers. Paderewski's exploits are well known. During the Second World War, Dame Myra Hess performed noontime concerts during the London blitz to give courage to local people, who would then return to their bunkers. Musicians from the Soviet bloc would often make famous escapes to the West, and then triumphant or traumatic returns to their homelands. In 1958, an American pianist—Van Cliburn—made headlines around the world by winning the Tchaikovsky Competition in the Soviet Union, which led to the first tentative exchanges of dialogue and artists between the USSR and the United States. Leonard Bernstein often played the piano at events for political causes he held dear.

THREE GRAND PIANISTS

Although there are almost too many great pianists to name, and we have a wonderful recorded archive of performances from the last hundred years (make note of the excellent Great Pianists of the Twentieth Century series on Philips), three names will often be cited when the subject is virtuosity and temperament. The careers of Arthur Rubinstein and Vladimir Horowitz overlapped, and many music lovers consider Evgeny Kissin their natural heir.

Arthur Rubinstein (1887–1982) blazed a notable path throughout his career. Unlike many pianists, who communicate an air of suffering for the sake of their art, Rubinstein approached the piano and his life with great relish and vigor. His memoirs, *My Early Years* and *My Many Years*, read like picaresque novels of passion and derring-do, but those who knew him reported that the books were quite accurate.

He once remarked, "It is said of me that when I was young I divided my time impartially among wine, women, and song. I deny this categorically. Ninety percent of my interests were women." His bon vivant nature is often audible in his music-making, but never did it compromise or make superficial the passages that required sensitivity, introspection, or pathos. His playing and public personality combined Romanticism and intellectualism. After a youth filled with audacious playing and a fair amount of carelessness, his marriage in 1932 seemed to point him toward more seriousness in his approach, although he lost none of his verve. He also realized that with the advent of recording, less-than-superb performances on disk would become documents that would trail him.

As a very young musician—he began playing publicly at age four—he was championed by Joseph Joachim, the violinist who was a friend of Brahms. His early instruction came from Karl Heinrich Barth, a pupil of Liszt, who had been trained by Carl Czerny, who had studied with Beethoven. Rubinstein knew Paderewski, Eugene Ysaÿe, César Franck, Camille Saint-Saëns, and Claude Debussy.

"I don't feel that making art should be called work. Work is something disagreeable that you have to do." Although he practiced and perfected his playing for many hours, he rejected the notion of practicing more than he considered necessary. "It is not so good, in a musical way, to overpractice. When you do, the music seems to come out of your pocket. If you play with the feeling of 'Oh, I know this,' you play without that little drop of fresh blood that is necessary—and the audience feels it.

"At every concert I leave a lot to the moment. I must have the unexpected, the unforeseen. I want to risk, to dare. I want to be surprised by what comes out. I want to enjoy it more than the audience. That way the music can bloom anew. It's like making love. The act is always the same, but each time it's different."

With the death of Vladimir Horowitz (1904–1989), Isaac Stern asked, "How many musicians can say that they created a standard against which others will be judged? It was not only the personality that was extraordinary, but his pianistic and musical accomplishments, against which piano playing in the future will be measured . . . His concert performances were extraordinary. One I recall in particular was his return to Carnegie Hall [after a long period of not performing]. In the Chopin *Black Key* Etude, the way he threw his hands at the octave passages at the end drew a giant gasp from the audience, which was filled with musicians. And when you saw him playing up close, it was as if each of his ten fingers had a separate intelligence. Each moved in its direction at the right time and with the right weight, and he sat apart, observing it and controlling it from a central organism, without great effort. He will be regarded as part of the pantheon of musicians who influenced their times, and who left a special legacy that will be remembered and thought about by anyone who cares about performance."

Stern was impeccably accurate in his description and remarkably prescient. Horowitz, through his recordings and through the collective memories of thousands of people who saw him perform, retains a mythic status.

Due to the frailty of his nerves, he retired from performing four times, and canceled frequently. His returns were announced with great fanfare, as if a royal personage were deigning to be seen again by his subjects.

I heard Horowitz perform more than a dozen times and had the good fortune to watch him rehearse on several occasions. He was famously eccentric (for example, he almost always ate the same meal of sole, asparagus, and a baked apple), and could spend a half hour of precious rehearsal time in a concert hall asking stagehands to move his piano back and forth a fraction of an inch until he decided that the piano was exactly where he wanted it. He would then tinkle on the keys for a few minutes and then go home, not bothering to play through any piece that he had programmed for the following Sunday at 4 P.M. (the hour he insisted on late in his career). Whenever possible, he sought payment in gold rather than cash.

Yet all of these eccentricities added to his aura, and those fortunate enough to acquire tickets to his concerts were treated to thrilling showmanship and, almost always, riveting playing.

Emanuel Ax, upon hearing of Horowitz's death, said, "I knew people who worshiped Horowitz, as I did, and I knew people who hated him. But no one was indifferent. He brought the idea of excitement in piano playing to a higher pitch than anyone I've ever heard. For me the fascinating thing was a sense of complete control, and on the other hand, the feeling that everything was just on the verge of going haywire. It never did go over that line, but there was the sense of an unbelievable energy being harnessed, and the feeling that if he ever let it go, it would burn up the hall."

There are so many truly outstanding pianists before the public that you could quickly use all the fingers on both hands and many toes as well to count them. Some are revered, others admired, still others have seen their stocks rise and fall and rise again in the public estimation. Yet

only Evgeny Kissin (1971–   ) and perhaps Martha Argerich (1941–   ) are able to incite a stampede for tickets
and create an immense air of expectation before even
walking on the stage. Argerich has battled cancer and is
notoriously mercurial, canceling as often as Horowitz. Yet
her performances, when she does appear, are usually legendary events not only for her artistry but for the simple
fact that she appeared to play. Her virtuosity is characterized by color, atmosphere, broad sense of sweep across the
keyboard, plus immense fire and intensity.

Kissin plays with power, delicacy, and preternatural abilities. He tends to walk onto the stage, sit down at the piano
bench, and dive into the keyboard with little acknowledgment of the presence of an audience. Yet his remoteness and
air of fragility (whether justified or not) only add to his
appeal. Given his young age and splendid abilities and
insights, he has become the mythical pianist of our time.
This should not deter you from listening to many other
pianists, but bear in mind that every time you hear a Kissin
recording or performance, you should listen for the pure
beauty of music and not encumber your thoughts with the
sketchy details of his biography. Allow him to remain mysterious, and let the music pour forth generously. Whether or
not you enjoy his playing, you will hear in it music-making
at a level that leaves audiences awestruck and delirious.

• ◇ •

To me one of the most mind-boggling aspects of the career of a musician is memory for music. Almost every singer you see on a stage in an
opera or recital must remember endless words in many languages, plus
all the music that was written for these texts. Conductors lead whole
symphonies and operas from memory, sometimes playing the piano as

they lead an orchestra. Solo recitalists in piano, violin, cello, and other instruments are similarly able to recall hours and hours of music and immediately play them without reading a printed score.

There is the famous story about the great pianists Josef Hofmann and Leopold Godowsky at a party. An admirer noticed that the men's hands were rather small. "How can you great artists play the piano so magnificently with such small hands?" the woman asked. Godowsky replied, "Where in the world did you get the idea that we play the piano with our hands?" Of course, incredible dexterity is required to play the piano and most other musical instruments, but the real work comes from the brain (to which I would add that what gives the performance character comes from the heart).

The greatest feat of memory I have witnessed was when Daniel Barenboim conducted all nine Beethoven symphonies and conducted and played all five of the piano concerti without a score when he and the Staatskapelle Orchestra of Berlin visited Carnegie Hall in December 2000. This is what virtuosity is about.

In performance, most pianists tend to work without music, a precedent thought to have been set by Franz Liszt. This requires not only note memory but muscle and nerve memory which, with an immense amount of study, practice, and concentration, can become incorporated into the wiring of a musician. But even when all of this information is instilled, there is also the importance of spontaneity and attention to what happens in a live performance. If a musician "goes on automatic," that can be risky if he stops listening to the musicians around him. Even if all is going well, a musician on automatic can be quite dull.

The only exceptions to the general rule about pianists working without a printed score are in some chamber music performances and in vocal recitals. In the latter, you will sometimes see a page turner, a person seated to the left of the pianist who will rise periodically to turn the page in the music at the prompting of the pianist.

Liszt was a charismatic and flamboyant pianist and composer, and the rock star of his time. Adoring fans, especially women, were delirious at the sight of him. His dazzling fingerwork astonished listeners who could not find words to describe his virtuosity. He is also thought to be the first solo pianist to lift the lid of the piano's sound box, so the music became more sonorous and penetrated every corner of a room, tingling eardrums as no pianist had done before. Unlike most pianists one could think of, he often spoke to audience members between pieces, which drew them closer to the music and enhanced his aura. Because Liszt played in the era before recording technology, our only notions of his prowess come from accounts of the day. Yet the prevailing opinion of Liszt nowadays is less favorable than in his time. This is due in part to Ernest Newman, Wagner's English biographer, who was profoundly against Liszt (who was Wagner's father-in-law). Newman's influential writings shaped a point of view about Liszt in the early part of the twentieth century that persists to this day. He is thought of by some as a superficial showman, yet pianists are fascinated by his music not only for its possibilities in performance but as a means to understand the daunting challenges he might have mastered as a performer.

• ⟨⟩ •

A pianist, or any soloist, must endeavor to bring stylistic authority and expressive spontaneity to whatever music is being played. Another way of saying this is that while the musician must be faithful to the music as written and what is known of the composer's intentions, the performer must also attempt to bring personal insight and experience and technique to the work. So we might speak of Evgeny Kissin's Rachmaninoff or Vladimir Horowitz's Scarlatti or Glenn Gould's Bach or Alicia de Larrocha's Mozart. Or we could consider one composer and compare various interpretations. Would I want to choose among performances of Chopin by Martha Argerich, Emanuel Ax, Garrick Ohlsson, Maurizio Pollini, and Arthur Rubinstein? No, I would not; nor do I have to. I think each of these artists does wondrous things with Chopin, and recordings enable me to hear all of them. And because all but Rubinstein are still alive and very much part of the contemporary concert scene I can attend performances as well. We will discuss comparative interpretations later on, but I want you to bear in mind from the start that a performance by a solo musician is a bridge between deep knowledge of the music plus the freshness and personal input that the musician brings to the piece.

There are many fine pianists before the public today, and one of them is likely at some point or other to play in a hall near you. In addition, you can choose from thousands of recordings of piano music, not only from artists of our time, but from many of the greatest of the past. Here are names to look for:

From the past: Claudio Arrau, Gina Bachauer, Jorge Bolet, Shura Cherkassky, Aldo Ciccolini, Clifford Curzon, Walter Gieseking, Emil Gilels, Clara Haskil, Vladimir Horowitz, Wilhelm Kempff, Lili Krauss, Dinu Lipatti, Arturo Benedetti Michelangeli, Ignace Paderewski, Sviatoslav Richter, Arthur Rubinstein, Artur Schnabel, Rudolf Serkin, Vladimir Sofronitzky, Rosalyn Tureck, Carlo Zecchi

Great pianists of today: Pierre-Laurent Aimard, Piotr Anderszewski, Leif Ove Andsnes, Martha Argerich, Vladimir Ashkenazy, Emanuel Ax, Paul Badura-Skoda, Daniel Barenboim, Lazar Berman, Alfred Brendel, Yefim Bronfman, John Browning, Rudolf Buchbinder, Gianluca Cascioli, Frederic Chiu, Van Cliburn, Paul Crossley, Alicia de Larrocha, Misha Dichter, Barry Douglas, Philippe Entremont, Till Fellner, Vladimir Feltsman, Leon Fleisher, Claude Frank, Nelson Freire, Alexander Ghindin, Richard Goode, Gary Graffman, Hélène Grimaud, Horacio Gutierrez, Andreas Haefliger, Stephen Hough, Helen Huang, Byron Janis, Joseph Kalichstein, Lillian Kallir, Evgeny Kissin, Zoltan Kocsis, Lang Lang, Ruth Laredo, Elisabeth Leonskaja, Cecile Licad, Radu Lupu, Alexander Markovich, Ivan Moravec, Olli Mustonen, Soheil Nosseri, Garrick Ohlsson, Murray Perahia, Maria João Pires, Mikhail Pletnev, Ivo Pogorelich, Maurizio Pollini,

Viktoria Postnikova, Awadagin Pratt, Fazil Say, András
Schiff, André-Michel Schub, Peter Serkin, Jeffrey Siegel,
Alex Slobodyanik, Melvyn Tan, Christopher Taylor, Jean-
Yves Thibaudet, Maria Tipo, Alexander Toradze, Mitsuko
Uchida, Anatol Ugorski, Arcadi Volodos, Andre Watts,
Alexis Weissenberg, Earl Wild, Christian Zacharias, Krystian
Zimerman

Let us begin our study of the piano by taking a step backward
into the symphonic repertoire.

• ◌ •

*Beethoven: Symphony no. 6; the Royal Concertgebouw/Sawallisch recording
or Philadelphia Orchestra; Eugene Ormandy*

By now you have such formidable skills for listening to a symphony that
you require little guidance from me. Suffice it to say that Beethoven's
Sixth Symphony, known as the *Pastoral,* draws its inspiration from
nature and is surely the most pictorial of all of the composer's works.
You can hear the sounds of babbling brooks, singing birds, thunder-
storms, the gathering of country folk, and many more details. Sit back,
close your eyes, and allow yourself to be transported to an idyllic pastoral setting.

As soon as you have heard this symphony, turn immediately to
the next recording.

• ◌ •

*Beethoven and Liszt: Piano Transcriptions: Symphony no. 6; Glenn Gould,
piano; Sony SMK 52 637*

As you now know, Franz Liszt was one of the most inspired and charismatic pianists of all time, and among his talents as a composer was his
ability to take music from other sources and transcribe it for the piano.

He knew good music when he heard it, and used it as a means to show off his flamboyant keyboard skills.

You might ask whether a symphony, with its numerous orchestral voices and textures, could be translated into a score for piano that is meaningful. Or, to put it more bluntly, has the music been *reduced*? In musical terms, *piano reduction* is actually a way that a large score—typically an opera—is scaled down to be played on a piano to accompany a singer or other solo instrumentalist. This is done mostly for rehearsal purposes, or when a large orchestra is simply unavailable. A piano reduction on its own would not make for inspired listening.

A *piano transcription* has another aim. In it a composer—most famously Liszt—takes music for many instruments and creates a performing version for piano that is not supposed to represent the orchestral music in the strictest sense, but draws from it to make a composition that is exciting on the piano. A transcription aims to bring forth as many colors and textures as possible, all the while showcasing the pianist's virtuosity. It must have been dazzling to hear Liszt play his own transcriptions, with the music seemingly coming right out of his brain the moment it was played.

Canadian Glenn Gould (1932–1982) was a pianist whose technical brilliance and singular interpretive style (which some might call eccentricity) enabled him to put his own stamp on these Liszt piano transcriptions. It is probably not the way Liszt sounded, but you need to ask yourself whether that is the point.

KEY CONCEPT: *Is the goal of a musician to re-create what the music may have sounded like when it was originally performed, or should we embrace the evolution of performing styles, the instruments that musicians play, and the tastes of audiences?*

(I believe that there is no definitive answer to this question, but it is something we should periodically consider when we think about musical performance.)

As you listen to the piano transcription of Beethoven's symphony, try to keep the many orchestral voices as fresh as possible in your ears. You are listening comparatively, and relying on memory as much as on spontaneous response to music that you know in one way and are now discovering in another.

Your primary goal now is to discover the ability of the piano—and the pianist—to convey a remarkable range of expressiveness. The more piano music you listen to, and the more performances you hear of each piece you learn, the more you will realize that their communicative potential is extraordinary. Whether you are hearing delicate, hushed tones, lightning-fast finger work, or window-rattling power, a great pianist will draw you close. In some ways, this is a different kind of listening than an all-encompassing orchestral sound.

The solo piano does not necessarily wash over you in the same tidal way that an orchestra can, so you will often find yourself listening more closely and attentively. This is an important skill that you will acquire, and I encourage you to take this attentiveness and apply it to orchestral listening as well. It will deepen your appreciation of big orchestral playing, and make it more meaningful. For example, if you can pick out a cello or a clarinet in Beethoven's *Pastoral* Symphony and think of what it is expressing, then you will hear the music more profoundly. This is the same as hearing one or two fingers in the pianist's right hand picking out notes on the keyboard that say something special while the fingers of the left hand are developing a larger theme.

• ∽ •

J. S. Bach: Goldberg Variations; Glenn Gould, piano; Sony/CBS SMK 37779

It has been often remarked about the playing of the highly idiosyncratic Glenn Gould that he sounded as if he were making the music up as he went along. This was not necessarily a criticism, but rather attempted to explain the remarkable inventiveness and particular pacing he deployed in playing music. His performances of many standard keyboard works were considerably slower than other artists', but their very drawn-out nature was part of what made them intriguing and, to many listeners, valid and compelling. So slow, ruminative, and deliberate are certain passages that it is as if he is pausing to decide what to play next. Yet his understanding of the music enabled him to sustain it over longer arching periods than most other pianists could get away with. He knew how to surprise and challenge the listener. At his peak, in the 1960s, a new approach to traditional classical pieces was considered an important blast of fresh air.

Gould had a particular affinity for Bach's Goldberg Variations, imbuing them with clarity, elegance, mystery, and, yes, variety. You can think of a theme and variations as if you have learned a path from Point A to Point B, and then you discover other paths to travel the same route. In taking these different routes, you see—and in musical terms, hear—different things along the way. Bach received a commission for these works, from Baron von Keyserling, Russian ambassador to the Dresden court, and for a funny reason. The baron was an insomniac, and he wanted music his harpsichordist (named Goldberg) could play for him to while away sleepless hours. One cannot say for sure if the goal was to make the baron sleepy. One does have to listen closely and carefully as the music progresses, and I encourage you to stay awake. The change in moods throughout, from somber to giddy, is quite wonderful. Make a point throughout of keeping one ear attuned to the basic thematic material that serves as the springboard for the thirty variations.

If you ever hear a slight humming or singing sound on some of his recordings, that is Gould himself. It is a peculiar affectation that you will get used to, and is considered part of the uniqueness of this landmark recording.

· ∽ ·

J. S. Bach: Goldberg Variations, etc.; Wanda Landowska, harpsichord; EMI 7243 5 67200 2 2

To get closer to what the Goldberg Variations might have sounded like in the time of Bach, it is necessary to listen to the harpsichord. This is a valuable exercise because, after hearing the fullness of the piano sound, which is often enhanced and occasionally blurred by the use of the pedals, hearing the crisp attacks of fingers on keys and the quick dying off of notes that is typical of the harpsichord is quite startling. I point this out also because you will probably come to discover that Gould played the Goldberg Variations in a way that drew from harpsichord playing as much as possible. The attacks are very quick, the pedaling almost nonexistent, and there is a lightness of touch that clearly draws its inspiration from Bach's harpsichord. If you wish to compare styles, listen to the Goldberg Variations as played by András Schiff or Murray Perahia, which are more "pianistic." In effect, the Goldberg Variations for piano is a "transcription," though it really is a transition from one keyboard instrument to another.

Wanda Landowska, who was born in Poland and lived much of her life in the United States, was the most famous harpsichordist of the twentieth century. She single-handedly (well, perhaps, two-handedly) restored the solo harpsichord to its position as a virtuoso instrument rather than being sort of a funny spinning sound in the background in larger works or operas. She cut quite a figure on the stage, with a long face, long hair, and long fingers, which all seemed to pour into the keyboard as she played. Her technique was superb, but so too was the interpretive stamp she put on the music she played. If you develop an interest in the harpsichord sound, many Landowska recordings will give you great pleasure. Among today's harpsichord players, Anthony Newman and Trevor Pinnock are perhaps the most noteworthy and Igor Kipnis (1930–2002) was a seminal figure.

• ∾ •

Grieg: Peer Gynt *Incidental Music, Piano Concerto in A Minor; London Philharmonic Orchestra; Øivin Fjeldstad, conductor; Clifford Curzon, piano; London/Decca 448 599-2 is the recommended recording. Alternatives include those by Murray Perahia, appearing with the Symphonie Orchester des Bayerischen Rundfunks, conducted by Sir Colin Davis, Sony SK 44899, and by Dinu Lipatti on the Great Pianists of the 20th Century series, Philips/EMI 456 892-2.*

In listening to the Liszt transcription of the Beethoven symphony, we examined how to develop your listening skills by taking the attentiveness and concentration required when hearing a larger orchestra and applying these to listening to a solo piano. This is your first chance to do that, as we consider the famous Piano Concerto in A Minor by Edvard Grieg. In it, you will hear solo piano music, lush orchestral music, and many passages in which piano and orchestra are playing at the same time. Sometimes the music seems to be of a piece (that is, integrated to communicate common ideas) and at other times there are distinct contrasts. This is an important transitional moment in your study, as it will help your listening skills become even more sophisticated.

What *is* a concerto? The general definition is a piece of music that features one instrument (or sometimes more) played in front of an orchestra. At times the orchestra plays alone, at times the solo instrument plays alone, and at many points in a concerto all play together, though the solo instrument may be playing different music than the orchestra. In most cases, a concerto is made up of three movements; Vivaldi is generally given credit for creating this structure. In the Baroque era, the violin was the major solo instrument, but some composers created concertos for wind instruments: flute (Hasse, Quantz); oboe (Albinoni, Vivaldi, Handel); and bassoon (Vivaldi). Since Mozart's time, most concertos feature piano, violin, or cello, and there are a few nice ones for clarinet.

The Grieg Piano Concerto is considered a warhorse that some critics feel they can belittle, but there is no denying its visceral appeal and beauty. Every pianist seems to want to play it, and it is one of the most recorded of all works. One can hear performances dating back to the 1930s and 1940s (including a famous one by Arthur Rubinstein) as well as recent ones by Jean-Yves Thibaudet and by the Norwegian Leif Ove Andsnes, who is from Grieg's hometown of Bergen. As this book was being written, eighteen-year-old Chinese pianist Lang Lang made a huge smash with this concerto in his Carnegie Hall debut.

Grieg himself used it as a calling card in appearances all over Europe. He was a brilliant pianist who combined the lyricism of Chopin with the drama of Liszt. He is considered, along with Sibelius, the leading exponent of music from the Nordic countries, and his music has an infectious appeal because of its beautiful melodies. One thing to notice in this piano concerto is how Grieg overflows with ideas. They tumble upon one another as we hear the music, and in repeated hearings (preferably by different pianists) you will hear new things. This may be a warhorse, but that is because the piece's allure never seems to flag.

The concerto starts with a powerful, unmistakable statement from the piano that immediately grabs your attention and carries you with it. Soon, you hear fingers delicately dancing on the keyboard and that booming beginning is now but a memory. Then comes sensuous bowing on the strings (notice the different textures in the cellos and the violins), and then we hear the clarion sounds of brass. This leads to a hammering sound in the orchestra joined by similarly compelling hammering on the piano. Then, immediately, we hear rapturous solo piano passages with fluttering keys and silences. Do you see, in this vivid example, how silence is not the absence of music but another kind of music?

Make note of all these quicksilver changes in dynamics throughout, going from booming fortissimos to hushed murmurs to heart-racing crescendos. As the movement revs up for its end, there is a *reprise* (a return to) the opening notes of the work. Also, notice how many instruments in the orchestra become solo protagonists for a few moments. Particularly, you might want to think about the flute as the delicate contrast (perhaps antidote?) to the large orchestral and pianistic sections that surround it.

Do you hear any sort of structure in this piece, or does it seem like a stream of one gorgeous melody after another?

Once the piece has ended, see how many of the melodies you can hum or sing. It is interesting how fast some of Grieg's music can penetrate your brain. When you hear the melodies a second or third time, you will have learned them for life.

♪ Putting Feelings into Words ♪

Finding words to express the sound or feeling of music itself is as challenging and approximate as finding words to describe the smell, taste, and sensation of a wine. Yet many classical music critics find fascinating ways to describe the *playing* of pianists. When the music itself is more or less a constant (based on the printed composition), the distinctions and nuances that make each hearing unique appear in performance. I have culled the following adjectives from reviews that have appeared about piano performances given in New York, Chicago, London, and Vienna. As you read each adjective, consider what it might connote in pianistic terms:

> bejewelled, perfumed, shivering, shimmering, tremulous, febrile, lyrical, virile, atmospheric, instinctive, colorful, sensuous, strident, arresting, imperious, vivid, elegant, aristocratic, earthy, ardent, naive, guarded, heroic, tragic, poetic, mighty, invigorating, curving, stable, gregarious, steel, iron, sweet, amorous, intimate, noble, cool-headed, gracious, exuberant

Can you think of other adjectives that would suit piano performances you have already heard? In "El Puerto" from the wonderful *Iberia* suite by Albéniz, the composer asks the pianist to play "brusquely, joyously, and languorously." Think how these three temperaments merge and what kind of playing they might elicit. Then listen to recordings by pianists such as Claudio Arrau and Alicia de Larrocha of this music and decide whether they achieve these effects.

Now listen to the Grieg Piano Concerto again with a pad and pen at hand. As you listen, write down adjectives that come to mind about the *playing*, not about what the music itself sounds like or makes you feel. For example, parts of the performance of the second movement are what I might call tender and introspective. This is an important exercise because, until this point in your studies, we have focused more on the written music and less on the performers and interpretation. Keep in mind the words of Arrau, the legendary Chilean pianist, who remarked that every performance is 50 percent the work of the composer and 50 percent the work of the performer. You may or may not agree with him, but it is worth pondering.

From this point forward in your listening to music, I want you to give thought not only to music but to the way it is being played. We will explore this more fully with the Mendelssohn Violin Concerto.

• ∾ •

W. A. Mozart: Piano Concertos nos. 19 and 23; English Chamber Orchestra; Murray Perahia, conductor and piano; CBS/Sony SMK 39064

Emanuel Ax has remarked that he thinks of Mozart piano concertos in terms of the composer's operas. They have so many instrumental voices and there are internal dialogues among them and with the piano. For example, toward the end of the third movement of Piano Concerto no. 22, there is a beautiful echoing between piano and flute that seems to ignore the conductor and orchestra entirely. It is a wonderful moment. It is in part because Mozart wrote so well for voices. Here is music that is deceptively simple and agreeable, but actually quite complex and profound.

Many musicians contend that Mozart's music is "transparent," which is an interesting term worth exploring. The music of Mozart has an amazing naturalness, almost an inevitability, to it. Every note seems so right, even those that catch us by surprise. In other composers, an unexpected note may be jarring, confusing, upsetting, or challenging. These qualities are, in my opinion, all virtues in the right hands. But with Mozart, the unexpected note provides us with insights and fills us with wonder. Our response is a combination of "But of course!" and "How did he do that?" The transparency in this music comes from the pleasing and logical pattern that most of it follows, presenting us with comfortable inevitability and many surprises. In this context, every note counts, and each must be played or sung with just the right emphasis and texture. Also, because Mozart often worked with smaller orchestras than later composers, more responsibility rests on each instrumentalist. Any gaffe or exaggeration leaves a musician exposed.

It is interesting that, in music education curricula, Mozart's works are often taught at the start of the semester because it is believed that the music is so unfailingly appealing that it will draw the students in. Then, as the students progress to other composers (perhaps moving chronologically), Mozart is left behind and the impression of charm and facility remains, while works by Beethoven, Brahms, Mahler, Stravinsky, and others are considered more "serious." This is a terrible misapprehension; one must always remember that Mozart provided inspiration and astonishment for so many composers who followed him, including Mendelssohn, Tchaikovsky, and Richard Strauss.

His operas are similarly complex, daunting, and thrilling for musicians and audiences. In creating the sequence of study for *Opera 101*, I first taught works by Verdi, Puccini, Donizetti, and Rossini before I felt that the reader was ready for Mozart. In this book you met many composers before Mozart came your way. As part of your life's journey as a music lover you should return to him often. You will find among his more than six hundred compositions more treasures than is conceivable that one man could create. And only as you really come to love music will you appreciate how exquisite they are.

The pianist on this recording, Murray Perahia, is an acclaimed Mozart interpreter (as pianist and conductor). In the 1970s he recorded all twenty-seven piano concertos, and has since recorded some of them

again. He has observed that "music is an art. In an art you have to understand the principles of the art before you can get to the emotions."
Think of him, then, as an advocate of intense research, thought, and
preparation. His Mozart playing is certainly not lacking in emotion, yet
his approach has been to plumb the bottomless depths of this composer's genius and—it would appear—then allow emotions to enter as a
consequence of his immersion in everything Mozartian. Because
Mozart is not overtly emotional in the style of, say, Liszt or Mahler, Perahia's approach is very effective and persuasive.

I would like you to focus your attention on the Piano Concerto
no. 23. There are concertos that are more famous (such as nos. 21 and
26), but this one has a character all its own.

My first contact with it was in a French film whose name I have
long forgotten. In a particularly tender scene involving parents and
children, a portion of this concerto's second movement appeared in
the soundtrack. It was of such unsurpassed beauty and pathos, and so
right for the scene in the film, that I burst into tears upon hearing it.
The music so dominated my thought that I could barely focus on the
rest of the movie and waited to carefully read what this music might
be. I ran (literally) to a nearby record shop and bought it immediately.
There are two lessons here. One is that anyone doing film scoring has
to make sure that the music is not more compelling than the movie.

The other, more important, lesson is that there exists for all of us
one or more works of music that can immediately and completely penetrate our fiber and provide us with powerful emotional sensations. It is
not a given that you will feel about this second movement as I did (and
do), but you will one day find a piece of music that absolutely takes you
over. I hope it will be one of the many works you discover in *Classical
Music 101*.

In listening to this concerto, ask yourself about the juxtaposition
of the three movements thematically and temperamentally. Do you find
connections, or do the brighter spirits of the first and last movements
clash with the pathos of the second?

• ❧ •

W. A. Mozart: Three Piano Sonatas, K. 279, 457, 576; Fantasia, K. 475; Mitsuko Uchida, piano; Philips 412 617-2

The Japanese pianist Mitsuko Uchida has made such a specialty of Mozart that people often have trouble associating her with any other composer. Her playing is ethereal and translucent, and its delicacy suits Mozart beautifully. She captures so many emotions and reveals them without hitting you over the head with them. She brings these traits to other composers, too, and her interpretations are always worth serious consideration. The works on this recording suit her well, and may possibly give you an idea what Mozart the piano soloist may have sounded like.

• ❧ •

IN HIS OWN WORDS: ALFRED BRENDEL

In addition to being one of the world's great pianists, Alfred Brendel is an insightful observer of the art of making music as well as the ideas of composers. He has written extensively on musical ideas in books such as *Music Sounded Out* and *Musical Thoughts and Afterthoughts,* and an engaging book of humor called *One Finger Too Many.* Among the interesting things about Brendel is his ability to find humor in music where other artists might not see it. Here are some comments from a conversation with him held before an audience at Carnegie Hall in 2001:

"When I look at a piece of music, I try to receive a message from it, and the composer. I don't try to communicate a message to it." Brendel tries to approach a piece and return to it "with naïveté rather than a fully formed outlook."

"I have a reluctance to connect the life and the incidents of a composer with his works. He may be like most us in most ways. But there is, in composers, a remarkable ability to achieve the expression of an infinite range of emotion and ideas. Musicians go to look at the autograph [the original score in the composer's hand or, at times, the performing edition approved by the composer] to try to glean ideas.

"Classical music is often called 'serious music,' which is as sure a way as any to put some people off. There is humor in music by Haydn, Mozart, Rossini, Ravel, Satie, and many other composers. Late Beethoven has the full range of human feeling from the sublime to the profane. He was already deaf at this point, but his inner hearing was marvelous. . . . Sometimes musicians and listeners have such an overwhelming reverence toward certain music that we do not permit ourselves to respond to humor, pro-fanity, or simplicity. Not every piece of music is a sublime, mystical experience. For example, Beethoven wrote the Diabelli Variations, which I think are very humorous."

The Diabelli Variations are named for Anton Diabelli, a composer and publisher who commissioned fifty variations on one of his themes. Beethoven ultimately wrote thirty-three in all. First he wrote twenty-three, and years later he wrote ten more. According to Brendel, Beethoven was so fixated on doing these that at one point he interrupted work on the Ninth Symphony. "The theme itself is humor-ous, so these works can be viewed as a satire on this theme."

Like many musicians, Brendel has returned to certain pieces of music throughout his career, not only for the pleasure of playing them but also to plumb them for new ideas as he becomes more experienced in performing and in life. For example, he recorded the five piano concertos of Beethoven four times. The first time was with various conductors, including Zubin Mehta. The second cycle was with Bernard Haitink, the third with James Levine, and the fourth with Simon Rattle. The Levine cycle was recorded live in performance. "Returning to masterpieces can regenerate an energy that had flagged. When you approach great music again, there is the excitement of rediscovery, there are always new insights, and there is awe."

Having acquired some skills for listening to concertos and solo variations, listen on your own to Brendel's wonderful performances of these great Beethoven piano works:

Beethoven: *The Piano Concertos*; Chicago Symphony Orchestra; James Levine, conductor; Alfred Brendel, piano; Philips 456-045-2

Liszt said about the second movement of Beethoven's Fourth Piano Concerto that he "could hear Orpheus taming the beasts."

Beethoven, *Diabelli Variations*, etc., in *Alfred Brendel Plays Beethoven*; VoxBox CDX 5112

• ∽ •

Beethoven: Piano Sonatas nos. 8, 14, 21, 23; Wilhelm Kempff, piano; DG 447 404-2

Artur Schnabel was the first to record all thirty-two Beethoven piano sonatas, in the 1930s. His technical skills wavered, but his spirit and passion are so palpable and engaging that we thrill to his playing. In an interview in the year 2000, while Maurizio Pollini was in the midst of work on the sonatas, he remarked, "You become aware of the truth of what Schnabel said—'There are no minor works.' There are major works—the last sonatas, the *Appassionata,* are more important than the others. But every sonata, even the shortest, requires total immersion in order to achieve a satisfactory performance, because the experience with one doesn't help the understanding of another. It seems Beethoven wanted to work on pieces of extraordinarily different character at the same time, according to his mood. Put these sonatas in the same program, and the element of variety comes through."

If you become a devotee of the Beethoven sonatas, as I am, you may wish to find the CD transfers of the old Schnabel recordings, or perhaps performances by Brendel, Barenboim, or others. One of the most outstanding Beethoven interpreters was Wilhelm Kempff (1895–1991), who was also a brilliant teacher. Among his disciples is Alfred Brendel. He recorded the thirty-two sonatas, and this CD contains four of the most famous.

No. 8 (the *Pathétique*) is often called the work in which the Classical era ended and the Romantic era began. This process continues with no. 14 (the *Moonlight*). No. 21 (the *Waldstein*) seems to narrate the passage through dark and light, going from dusk to dawn. And the *Appassionata* (Impassioned) is exactly as it is described. Is Beethoven a Classical composer, a Romantic composer, or does he bestride both styles and eras?

• ∾ •

Dvořák: Piano Concerto; Schubert: Wanderer *Fantasy; Orchester des Bayerischen Rundfunks; Carlos Kleiber, conductor; Sviatoslav Richter, piano; EMI 7243 5 66947 2 9*

For now, listen to the Schubert and picture him as part of the transition from the Classical to the Romantic Style. Save the Dvořák for later.

• ∾ •

*Panorama: Schubert, listen to the second CD (*Trout *Quintet,* Moments Musicaux, *Military March for Piano Duet).*

There is a wonderful part of classical music called chamber music. The term comes from the Italian *musica da camera*, or music played in an intimate setting by a few musicians. Just about every musician I have ever spoken with, including many famous soloists, professes to adore playing chamber music. At the heart of the thrill is the fact that they are making music together without a conductor, which requires them to really listen to each other as the piece is played. James Levine, who often plays piano in chamber music performances, observed in a conversation that ensemble playing is "not just playing together, but *thinking* about the music together, breathing together. As a group you develop inner awareness and interaction" as you rehearse and perform the music. Levine also remarked that these qualities can be applied to orchestral performance, citing his mentor George Szell as a great exponent of this practice in his work with the Cleveland Orchestra. (A recommended recording for hearing this dynamic at work is Szell and the Cleveland playing Mozart's Piano Concerto no. 26, *Coronation*, K. 537, with Robert Casadesus as soloist.)

Chamber music encompasses many styles and centuries, and several instruments. A violin is almost always present, and there may be a cello, viola, piano, flute, clarinet, or other instruments. A typical string quartet has a first violin, a second violin, a viola, and a cello. Although chamber music is played without a conductor, the first among equals is usually the violinist. He or she would give the cue for beginning, and often will breath at key moments when other musicians might breathe as well. You might think that breathing is not an issue for string players, but in chamber music all the performers develop a degree of synchronicity, of oneness, that often results in their breathing together as they play through a score. Composers write in these moments, envisioning their pieces in terms of performance practice.

A fair amount of chamber music features piano, including Schubert's famous *Trout* Quintet. You will also encounter the trout theme when we study the song literature, but for now listen to this music and picture the piano as providing the flowing sound of a stream. The whole quintet is a sheer delight, and you should listen to it with abandon, avoiding any wish to analyze it. Picture yourself in a small salon in someone's home, with five musicians performing for the guests who are seated around them.

• ◌ •

A CONVERSATION WITH EMANUEL AX

Emanuel Ax is one of the most respected and versatile pianists now before the public. In addition to performances with orchestras, Ax performs a great deal of chamber music, often with artists such as violinist Itzhak Perlman and cellist Yo-Yo Ma. He also performs duo work with pianists such as Yefim Bronfman and, of course, is an outstanding soloist. Ask different music lovers what Ax's specialty is and you are likely to hear responses ranging across a broad spectrum of repertory and styles. Yet he is almost universally admired for his fluent and gripping performances of the music of Chopin.

In the following conversation, Ax talks about the life of a pianist and, specifically, about the music of Chopin and Liszt. He will be referring to two or three of his essential recordings:

Chopin: Piano Concertos nos. 1 and 2; Philadelphia Orchestra; Eugene Ormandy, conductor; Emanuel Ax, piano; RCA Victor 09026-68023-2 For comparison, listen to: Chopin: Piano Concerto no. 1, etc.; Orchestra of the Age of Enlightenment; Sir Charles Mackerras, conductor; Emanuel Ax, piano; Sony SK 60771.

Arnold Schoenberg: Concerto for Piano and Orchestra; Franz Liszt: Concertos for Piano and Orchestra nos. 1 and 2; The Philharmonia; Esa-Pekka Salonen, conductor; Emanuel Ax, piano; Sony SK 53 289

Question: We are talking about two concertos that happen to be the second by Chopin and Liszt, even though the Chopin concerto is called number one. When you approach these, or any piece of music, what is the approach? How do you start—with the notes? With biographies?

EMANUEL AX: *Well, usually a piece like the Chopin E Minor Concerto or the Liszt A Major Concerto are pieces that I already would have heard, either in recordings or in concerts. So there is a certain level of familiarity before I even open the music. And then I sort of dive right* *in and learn how my hands will get from one place to another, playing notes.*

Q.   Is it first a very technical approach with the notes and with the music? At what points do your ideas start entering?

A.   *My feeling is that you already have ideas before you begin to learn. You have thoughts about how the music should sound, how it should go. So I don't think it is possible to separate out something that is, say, a physical difficulty from deciding how it should sound, because obviously one will inform the other. Ideally, the way you want it to sound will tell your hands what to do rather than believing you have to do something [that is] telling you what it should sound like. That is not the good way. Because that is your own limitations. What you want to do is expand your limitations, you want to get your hands to do what your brain tells you is the right thing to do. And what your ear tells you is the right thing to do.*

Q.   Does an instrumentalist automatically have a point of view? And if he does, where does that come from?

A.   *You know, I feel that we are just like other people, we have a point of view on everything. So if you feel strongly about something, like I do about a piece of music, of course I will have a point of view. I may not be able to articulate it, I might not be able to describe it to you in words, but I will start out by having feelings about the music. No matter how neutral I think I'm being I will certainly have that.*

Q.   If you have your—what shall we call it?—your point of view, your feeling for a piece of music that is not a solo piece, and therefore you arrive at a rehearsal where a conductor also probably has his strong point of view, and perhaps certain members of the orchestra do too, how are these merged in rehearsal?

A.   *Usually it just happens. It is sort of like having a conversation, which goes very easily provided that you have another person you feel sympathy for, that you like that other person. That you feel you can talk to them. Now obviously, the two of you are distinct people, so that there is no way you could think exactly alike about everything. Even if you both love chicken, you can't love it in exactly the same way. But you can easily* *agree. And even if one hates chicken and one likes chicken, you decide, "OK, we'll go to a restaurant that serves veal." That's what happens, in essence, in a rehearsal. You feel very quickly what the other person is doing. And unless you really want to be someone who makes difficulties, it is pretty easy to adjust.*

Q. How much of this comprehension, this merging, happens with words, with language, and how much happens with music?

A. *I think not that much. I think it is pretty quick, particularly if you are a good listener, to reach that kind of compromise. Some people are better listeners than others. The best listener I know is Yo-Yo Ma. When I am onstage with him—now, we have played together for a very long time—what has always been true about playing with Yo-Yo is that whatever you do he will somehow react to. He might not do exactly what you do, but he will in some way acknowledge that he has heard what happened. You won't feel like, "Well, he's on his own there, and I'm not connected." In a situation in which you are playing with other people, the most important thing is to communicate, one way or another. Sometimes you tug away from each other, sometimes you are almost at war— musically at war—but you have to react, and then everything is fine.*

Q. Let us say that one of these pieces—it doesn't matter which—is one you have played many, many times, with many different orchestras. And you arrive in a new situation with an orchestra you have never played with, and a conductor you have never worked with. He or she may be older or younger, it does not matter. But you have much more experience with a piece, and knowledge, and this group is rather new at it. Do you try to guide them? Do you let the conductor try to find his way through?

A. *Sometimes, if it is a wonderful conductor who is really strong-minded and has a real feel for music, and has never done the piece but really wants to do certain things, then it's really easy to go along with that, especially because I have had a lot of experience. The more I know the piece, the more points of view I can legitimately feel. I find that you can have your strongest kind of single-mindedness when you know a piece least. Because all this music is so great, it is so exciting, so many-sided,* *that there is no way for any one performance to take in everything about the piece. See, you're getting to used to things changing all the time—in your own mind, in the minds of others. The more you know a piece, the more in a way flexible you are. So in that situation, I will be happy to adjust. But in a situation where the conductor will say, "We'd love to work with you, and do what you'd like," I will take the lead and say, "Let's do this," or "Let's do that." With me, it's all very amicable usually.*

Q.   Is it that way with other artists?

A.   *Not always. It depends. It depends on the person.*

Q.   To what degree do you bring your ongoing study of a composer and his ideas to your approach to the work of that composer?

A.   *I get excited when I read about what a composer did with his music. I think it's incredibly exciting to read, for example, the reports that were made on [listeners'] having heard Beethoven play certain pieces, because it is such an intimate connection. We get the feeling of "Wow, he played this music, I played this music, and he also played this music!" And he did certain things, so it is wonderful to read about that. I think the more you know about a composer, the period he lived in and the kind of things he was interested in, the more it informs your feeling about that composer. But this is by no means cut-and-dried.*

Q.   The two composers we have in front of us are in some ways very similar, but in many ways quite different. They were born a year apart—Chopin a year older, Liszt lived a much longer life. Both were famously great pianists and composed music that they performed. These two men, though they were so famous as pianists that it was a part of their image, were completely different. Do you, in playing their music, feel the character of both men, or does that not enter your thought?

A.   *Well, I think the character of the men appears in their music. For me, Chopin is absolutely at the top of the musical pyramid. Really as great as the greatest. The only limitations of Chopin are the limitations he put on himself. He was interested in music only. He wasn't interested in other things. It wasn't that he was not capable of doing other things, he* *wasn't interested. Liszt had a lot more interests and, perhaps because of that, developed things not as fully. Chopin—and you can tell this in the music, I think—was someone made of very disparate sides which combined somehow to make a perfect whole. On the one hand he was very romantic, very innovative. The most innovative, probably, in terms of writing for the piano, in history. Maybe only Liszt was next. Of course, Beethoven had a lot of pianistic ideas in terms of innovation. All the great pianists did. Mozart did as well. But for sheer leaps and bounds in the way pianists approached the instrument from the time of Schumann, to see what Chopin developed was incredible. It's unbelievable.*

Q.   What are some of those things?

A.   *Well, just the way the hand moved. The ability of the hand to do difficult things. To do things close together, to expand for big stretches, to do things in close proximity, to play thirds and octaves and sixths. All of this stuff is included in the Chopin etudes. It really does open the possibilities of the instrument. Chopin was [also] very concerned with neatness, good structure, above all a combination of neatness and balance. His favorite composers were Bach and Mozart. For him, Beethoven was talented, but much too rough and ready. He really had very little use for most of his contemporaries. Really, Bach and Mozart were his two. And what he admired about them was the combination of invention and proportion. He was so concerned with the right proportion. That is why all of his music sounds so fully satisfying. Liszt was a totally different personality as a composer. He was interested in what Wagner entitled "the Music of the Future." For example, the idea of developing short themes that would serve as themes for the whole piece in many different guises. He was interested in writing for huge [musical] forces as well as for the piano. He was interested in advancing the cause of composers who broke boundaries rather than ones who established them. Liszt did not develop any of his talents to the same level of perfection that Chopin developed his. So what you get is flashes of genius, and somehow slightly unfinished, maybe. This is not a value judgment; it's not that I feel he is in any way inferior. You know, Liszt was a great genius. I love his music and I play a lot of it. But it is more experimental than anything Chopin did.*

Q. Is it simplistic to say that there might be two major lines of musical development in history? There are many composers, such as Mendelssohn, Chopin, Tchaikovsky, and Richard Strauss, who speak of their love of Mozart and find that route. And maybe there are others— it is hard to group them—perhaps Beethoven, Berlioz, Liszt, and Bruckner . . .

A. *I don't know that this tells us much. There is certainly a conservative and liberal split, if you want to put it that way. The trouble with making any kind of generalization like that is that as soon as you make it, I am sure that both of us could come up with hundreds of examples of people and pieces who may be in the conservative camp—but then you say, "What about this?" It is impossible to really categorize neatly. Certainly in the nineteenth century there was a kind of music that Wagner pushed, "the Music of the Future," and the kind of line that Chopin and, perhaps by extension, Brahms were involved in, which was tradition, balance, harmony, and innovation—but definitely with an eye on the past.*

Q. And would those be the conservatives?

A. *You see, I hate to come down to that. That's the trouble. Because the rap on Brahms is that he was a conservative composer in the time of revolution. But Arnold Schoenberg, who was perhaps the most famous revolutionary of the early twentieth century, wrote a huge essay called "Brahms the Progressive," in which he very clearly—to my mind, anyway—demonstrates that Brahms, while being very concerned with structure and balance, was at least as innovative as Wagner; harmonically, in form, and in a lot of other ways. So it is difficult to say. That's what I meant by being pinned down. I would not care to answer that question in a categorical way. Certainly the Liszt A Major Concerto is perhaps a more progressive and forward-looking work than the Chopin E Minor Concerto, in the sense that you have the same theme in all four movements, which are played without pause. We note all these kinds of thing, which are a way of getting away from being the traditional three-movement structure of the concerto as performed by Beethoven, Mozart, and Haydn, and so forth and so forth. This does not necessarily mean that it is better or worse. It says nothing about value, it says nothing* *about enjoyment, it says nothing about real innovation in other areas. But that side of it is certainly easy to see.*

Q.   Arthur Rubinstein said that he could play a Liszt sonata or a big virtuoso piece without any effort, but "every note of Chopin needs the utmost concentration." What did he mean?

A.   *I would like to think that he meant that Chopin's virtuoso writing is very connected to Mozart in the sense that all the fast stuff, if you play it slowly, it still sounds good. And the reason it sounds good is that most of it is melodic writing. Most of it is in tune even when it is very, very fast. There is still a kind of a melodic intent. Whereas in Liszt very often the really fast writing can be to some degree formulaic. It's snippets of certain stuff that is done over and over again. Doesn't mean it's easy. It can be very, very hard.*

Q.   We have just studied the Grieg Piano Concerto. It came later, of course, but where do we place that in the line? It has beautiful melody, to be sure. It has virtuoso playing. Does it fit in the line, or is it completely on its own as a category?

A.   *It is a fabulous concerto. I think certainly it is traditional in the sense of the movements. You play a big cadenza at the end of the first movement. Grieg in a way was a special case. There is something very refreshing—maybe "Scandinavian" is a fair word to use. His tunes are very simple, the structures are very simple, often very repetitive, but the music is so heartfelt, so beautiful. It's the frankness and generosity that comes through, and not the repetitiveness. It's not complicated music the way Liszt can be, the way Chopin is all the time, the way Tchaikovsky is. But it is so inspired. I find that the quality of melodies is so wonderful that that's enough.*

Q.   These three composers (Chopin, Liszt, Grieg) are all men from small countries who traveled to make their livings. Other composers stayed still more. Many in Vienna; Haydn in Austria-Hungary and, only late in life, in London. Many in Italy. Many in England and France, too. Is there something about being a traveling person and gathering sounds and snippets and impressions? Or are their voices internal, and their music entirely their own?

A. *Even before Chopin started traveling a lot, he had already written a lot of revolutionary music. I'm sure that he learned a lot from hearing other people's music, particularly after he arrived in Paris. But he arrived having written already most of the two piano concertos, most of the etudes, probably the G Minor Ballade and the B Minor Scherzo. It's hard to conceive that travel broadened him that much. When you arrive with the F Minor Concerto in your backpack, it's easy to see that the inspiration came from somewhere else. But I am sure people are changed by travel. Liszt wrote a whole series of pieces on travels. But my opinion is that the internal life of a composer is probably more responsible for what his music is.*

Q. I know that Grieg often referred to "the wine cup of Italy" as an inspiration, by which he meant the sun, and what we think of as Italian character.

A. *There seems to be something about Italy that must have done something for a lot of northern composers. They all produced something special and different when they traveled to Italy. Brahms liked it, and some of his most gemütlich music came out of his journeys there. Tchaikovsky produced a truly great string sextet, called* Souvenir de Florence, *from his travels. There must be something very special—Strauss in his* Aus Italien, *Elgar in his* In the South—*about arriving at this place by the water, with the sun. Italians live well in the most basic sense. There is a kind of sybaritic feeling (in the best sense) about the place. The country is so beautiful. If I had to pick a city purely to live in, I would pick Paris. But I think most people would pick someplace in Italy, probably Florence or Rome.*

Q. I was in Paris in 1999 on the day that happened to be the hundred and fiftieth anniversary of the funeral of Chopin, which took place in Paris in the Church of the Madeleine. They played all the music that was played at the funeral in 1849. Everything but the coffin was there. They had Polish singers and musicians. How much can a city become an artist—and I don't only mean a composer but a performer—when an artist chooses to live elsewhere? Whether it is Beethoven in Vienna, Alfred Brendel in London, there are many people who are not from a place but go there and make a life there.

A.   *Well, Paris of course, was in a way Chopin's home. Don't forget that Chopin was only half-Polish, and the French side of him is extremely important in every way. His French nature is what I think of when I think of order, of balance. I think of the correctness of the gardens of Versailles. That's not Poland. And in Chopin there is a lot of that. I think that's what gives his music that character, that two-sidedness which is so wonderful. To take mazurkas, which are such a Polish thing—there is nothing more Polish than a polonaise or a mazurka— and to make that not only universal but to make these pieces real concert pieces that are meaningful for the whole world—that takes more than just being Polish. So maybe Paris was the perfect place for him. You notice how much he always complained about how much he missed Poland. He never went back, although he could have.*

Q.   Do you know for a fact—I hear this all the time—that when he was buried, his heart was buried in Poland?

A.   *Yes, yes. That is true. His body is in France, his heart is in Poland. I think it's good that he is two places. . . . With these great geniuses, is it really more scary to play Beethoven in Vienna than in Kalamazoo? I don't think so. Or it shouldn't be in any real sense. If Beethoven is around to hear us, he hears us just as well in Kalamazoo.*

Q.   This leads to something else. You, who play all over the world, must know characteristic differences within audiences, whether it is familiarity with music, or behavior in the theater.

A.   *There used to be more people who played instruments in European audiences than in America. I think that is changing, and not for the better. I am very much of the opinion that the people who will come to concerts in the future are the people who play instruments. I think the best thing we can do in terms of education is to give people instruments to play. It is more important than learning anything about music as arcana, because as much studying as you can do, you are better off practicing the violin thirty minutes a day. In that sense, I think that Europe is more in touch with the kind of stuff I do. But I think it is turning around. I am an optimist, I think things are turning around. I think people like*

Yo-Yo Ma especially have really had an influence on young people in America. That's wonderful.

Q: What happens when you practice? What is the procedure for looking at a piece of music or then, once learned mentally, practicing that piece of music?

A. *A lot of it is repetition to get things grooved, and a lot of it is experimentation—what sounds better, what feels better, which finger works better. And once you have decided, then you have to move all of those things.*

Q. Last week I went to hear Martha Argerich play. I had not seen her for a very long time. I noticed that she paid great attention to the bench, to its relationship to the piano, to her physical place in between the two. What is that about?

A. *I think some people are very particular; they like things a certain way. I am someone who likes to move around. Sometimes I sit lower, sometimes I sit higher. I don't want to be locked in very much. I would rather have a little bit of freedom there. But, of course, the relationship with the piano is crucial. I like to be friends with it. It should be a friendly relationship.*

Q. You encounter many different pianos in your travels. I know that Vladimir Horowitz brought his piano wherever he played. Some pianists have a preferred brand, make, year, or style—

A. *Yes, I use Steinway.*

Q. What makes a particular piano, in your case Steinway, preferable to another?

A. *I don't know, to be honest. I think they sound the best for me, but that is just my take on it. It's very personal.*

Q. Do pianos feel different?

A. *Sure.*

Q. What feels different?

A. *Sometimes the pressure on the key is different. You need more pressure or less pressure. Sometimes the response is quicker, sometimes slower. The depth of the key—all these things, which are probably infinitesimal, make a big difference to me. And sometimes a hall is just as important. It makes a huge difference as well. What you get back in response to your ear is going to affect a lot the way you play, and it is something you need a lot of time to learn—whether in a hall you need to force or don't need to force.*

Q. Because I have been fortunate to grow up in Manhattan, I have been fortunate to go to concerts here and elsewhere for forty-plus years. So to think about acoustics and sound in a fresh way for this book, I had to go to a hall I had never heard before. I went to the magnificent Concertgebouw in Amsterdam. I spent a week there going to concerts. I was taken aback by the things I heard in music I knew. What was happening there?

A. *It is a lot smaller than something like Carnegie Hall. It is a very immediate response, very echo-ey. It has a kind of sheen and not so much precision as other halls.*

Q. This raises something I have noticed in music performance: warmth used to have more of a value than precision.

A. *I think that's true. It is another development that I personally do not feel good about. I think it is inescapable. I think we spend a lot of time now in concerts trying to sound the way recordings sound. Instead of the other way around. There are still people who are taking chances. Maybe as I and my generation grow older we will be able to throw caution to the wind a little more and not worry about it.*

Q. You have recorded the Chopin concerto twice. On the second time, what instrument did you play, and how was it different from your first recording?

A. *I played an 1850 piano that Chopin almost could have played. I think it is a very pretty sound—not as loud as the modern Steinway, but more differentiated in terms of sound. In some ways more brilliant, if* *you can get close enough to it. The concerto on this piano was just as hard to play, I thought it might be easier. You need a lot of power to produce something on that piano. To play loud on it, you need a lot of strength, so it wasn't easy.*

Q.   Were the instruments in the orchestra period instruments as well?

A.   *Yes. This was an orchestra called the Orchestra of the Age of Enlightenment. They play instruments the way they would have been set up in the nineteenth century.*

Q.   And what did you and the conductor, Charles Mackerras, set out to do? Maybe you decided verbally, and perhaps not?

A.   *I had not met him before. So we took everything fresh and at face value. He would look at the music and say, "Why do you slow down there?" And I would say "Well, I always did, and maybe it is traditional." He would say, "Why don't you try not to?" So I think some things changed because of that. And I think the sounds of the instruments made for something different. The sound was more lively, a little more up-tempo and maybe dramatic in a way.*

Q.   What does the pedal do, and what is its role in a performance?

A.   *There are three pedals on a Steinway. The only ones that I need to be concerned about with Chopin and Liszt are the outer two. The right-hand pedal basically sustains whatever notes you press down, so that you are able to hit a bass note and keep it held while you are playing other notes at the same time. But, of course, it tends to blur, so you have to know when to change. The left pedal moves the whole mechanism of the piano over, so that instead of having three strings for each note in the middle of the piano, moving the mechanism over so that the hammer hits only one string makes everything softer. It is called the* una corda *pedal because it hits only one string instead of all three.*

Q.   Is it written in the music what you do with the pedal, or do you decide as a musician what to do?

A.   *A little of both. There are indications in the music, and I try to follow what Chopin would have wanted, but I also know that I have to* *make an adjustment for the given instrument and for the hall. If you are playing at the Concertgebouw, you don't pedal as much as you would at Avery Fisher Hall [at New York's Lincoln Center], for instance. The Concertgebouw gives its own pedal in a way; there is some blurring already.*

Q. Similarly, the composer will have written whole notes, half notes, quarter notes, eighth notes, sixteenths—these are time values that we may understand and have studied and see on a page and play them in relation to one another, but is a whole note always a whole note and a half a half, or do you find fractions of seconds of difference?

A. *Sure. You will say, "That note should really be held out to full value, and this note should be a little shorter." Sometimes composers acknowledge that by writing the word* tenuto *[held] over a particular note, which would indicate that maybe all notes were not necessarily held out to their full value, and if a composer really wants a note held out, he writes* tenuto. *It depends which composer. You will hear in a lot of recordings of [conductor] Roger Norrington of Beethoven—as opposed to Herbert von Karajan—that, aside from the tempos, a lot of notes are released sooner; there will be less pressure. And other notes, in fact, will be much longer. Notes with dots and a slur over them are held much longer than they were held thirty years ago. So it is a matter of what you think a composer would have wanted to hear or would have heard. It depends. Everything is open to question, unless the composer is there to tell you. And even if he is there—I have worked with a lot of living composers—you can get them to change their minds. You can say, "I really think this sounds better," and a lot of the time they will agree with you.*

Emanuel Ax has given you a great deal to think about. The life of a pianist—and all musicians, for that matter—is not simply acquiring and maintaining the mastery of an instrument. It is also about building countless relationships: with colleagues, with audiences, with instruments, with concert halls, and, most mysteriously and personally, with composers and their music.

A musician who reads music on a printed page not only sees notes and markings, but also must read between the lines of the musical staff to find thought. We know some of what composers thought because they wrote letters to others or jottings to themselves. But much of what they thought has to be intuited by a talented and sensitive musician. Part of the musician's job, when he or she looks at a score, is to find the composer's thoughts and bring them forth. To these, the musician brings a great deal of him- or herself, and this is what makes every performance singular.

Remember what Arthur Rubinstein, one of the greatest of all Chopin pianists, said: "I can play a Liszt sonata or a big virtuoso piece without any effort, but every note of Chopin needs the utmost concentration."

The reason for this, according to another outstanding pianist, Maurizio Pollini, "is because of the depth of the music. What happens in Chopin is what happens in practically every great composer: he invented his personal, but very natural, way of playing, and it is the responsibility of the interpreter to try to understand it."

With these thoughts, and the many insights of Emanuel Ax in mind, listen to Ax's performance of Chopin's Piano Concerto no. 1 in E Minor (which was actually the second concerto he wrote). The first time you listen, pay attention primarily to the movement of the music. Imagine that it is Chopin you are listening to, picturing his hands moving up and down the keyboard. Make your primary focus the flow of the melody, and note the *dynamics* of the performance: how fast or slow, how loud or soft, how gentle or firm, how joyous or how pensive. This is music that requires not only impeccable technique but incredible empathy and humanity to play.

Put this recording aside and let the music resound in your head. See how much actual music you recall and, more important, notice how this music has made you feel. After an hour or so, pick up the Liszt Concerto no. 1 and play it. The Chopin is 41 minutes, the Liszt is but 18. How is the impact of Liszt's music different for you? When it is over, sit back and think how you feel after listening to it.

Go do something else for a few hours, and then come back and listen to the Chopin concerto again. This time, imagine that it is Emanuel

Ax playing, rather than Chopin. Can you hear the musician connecting to the music? Do you hear passages in which Ax is expressing himself through Chopin's music? This is what the great pianists are able to do, if and when they choose to do so.

This time, also listen to the dialogue and interplay between piano and orchestra. Picture Maestro Eugene Ormandy on the podium and young Emanuel Ax at the piano, down behind the conductor's left shoulder. Try to see the give and take between them, imagining how moments of this performance were decided upon and whether the venerable conductor or the pianist took the lead. Or could it be that neither is really leading, and the two men and the orchestra are achieving that rare and elusive goal: making music?

If you wish to compare further, listen to Ax's later recording with Sir Charles Mackerras on period instruments, and see whether you feel closer to, or more distant from, Chopin as a result. For further comparative listening, try Brahms's sumptuous Piano Concerto no. 2, and compare it to the Chopin, Grieg, Mozart, and Liszt you have heard.

Then return to the Liszt, and listen to the dynamics in that piece. Think about how it sounds different from the first hearing.

Then think whether either the Liszt or the Chopin sounded revolutionary to you. And if neither one does, then play the Schoenberg concerto, which will help you open wide the door to music that is truly revolutionary.

• ⌀ •

Panorama: Frédéric Chopin, Andante Spianato, etc.; various artists; DG 289 469 127-2

Chopin's music is regal, rational, spiritual. Listen for these and many others as you go through the shorter works on this CD set.

Think about some of the important influences on Chopin, such as the keyboard music of Bach with its clean and fluid *attacks*, that is, the action of the fingers on keys and then of the strings being sounded in a way that made every note clear. Something to bear in mind is that the keyboard Bach played on had significantly fewer keys than Chopin's, so the flow and expressive variety for Chopin was greater and, in many cases, so was the difficulty. Chopin was also affected by the ability of Mozart to evince deep, often aching, feelings in a fleeting manner. This could often be done with an ingenious combination of just a few notes. Chopin also loved music for the human voice, and the things he cared about in Mozart's instrumental music also applied to his vocal writing.

Chopin loved opera and attended often. As an interesting exercise, listen to a recording of the aria "Casta diva" from Vincenzo Bellini's sublime opera *Norma* (1831). If at all possible, try to hear it sung by Montserrat Caballé, although versions by Maria Callas and Joan Sutherland are also acceptable. This is the epitome of *bel canto* (beautiful singing) and this aria was everywhere in the musical air when Chopin was in his early twenties. You can hear the beautiful vocal line, the sustained phrases uninterrupted by breaths, and the expressiveness and pathos. All of these characteristics found their way into Chopin's solo piano music, as if this instrument were the surrogate for his own voice.

French writer André Gide was madly devoted to Chopin's music, which he played feverishly, though his mother tried to dissuade him, because she felt this music prevented him from thinking pure thoughts. I say this because it is quite possible to hear Chopin as a flowing and burbling series of pleasant notes without detecting the heat in his music. If you listen with that in mind, however, even the most ethereal of his music can make you tingle and throb.

• ༺༚༻ •

Chopin: Nocturnes; Claudio Arrau, piano; Philips 416 440-2

Arrau was a master at playing much of Chopin, but I think his peak came in this recording of the nocturnes. If you sit in an almost darkened room and let the music flow through you, you will begin to see constellations of stars on your ceiling. Only on the next day should you read the program notes in the CD booklet.

• ◇ •

Panorama: Robert Schumann, Kinderszenen, Fantasia, *Arabeske, and Piano Concerto*

Schumann, in a letter to his wife, Clara, wrote that "history will say that our two hearts beat as one." When his injury and illness prevented him from performing in public, Clara—one of the century's great pianists—appeared in his stead and played. The idea of a muse performing the art she inspired is a compelling and romantic one that has happened to other composers as well. Grieg wrote his songs for soprano so that his wife, Nina, could sing them. Strauss created many songs for his soprano wife, Pauline. While theirs was a complicated relationship, it created great songs. Nowadays, the excellent mezzo-soprano Lorraine Hunt Lieberson sings music composed by her husband, Peter. I am particularly fond of his songs based on texts by Rilke.

Schumann's piano music is gorgeous and deeply emotional. *Kinderszenen* (Scenes of Childhood) came about when Clara said to Robert that he occasionally seemed like a child to her. This music takes an adult view, and a very beautiful one. I have played this for children in their playpens, and notice that they are more entranced by it than by most pieces. To me it is an idealized world of childhood contentment, one that can provoke nostalgia as much as Chopin's music did for Oscar Wilde. Listen to all the piano music on this recording, including the concerto. You might be startled, after hearing the concertos of Beethoven and Grieg, at how this one is devoid of showmanship. It is an eloquent piece nonetheless, and if you listen to it after hearing the Beethoven Fourth Concerto you might find some interesting parallels.

• ∿ •

Brahms: Piano Concerto no. 2; Boston Symphony Orchestra; Bernard Haitink, conductor; Emanuel Ax, piano; also contains Brahms Cello Sonata, performed by Yo-Yo Ma; Sony SK 63229

The second concerto for piano by Brahms is one of his masterpieces and an important touchstone in the progress of music for that instrument. The concerto has a classical structure that recalls Beethoven but also has so much tender and feeling music that it seems to be a summation of Beethoven, Chopin, Schumann, and just about every other composer who readily revealed his heart. What is also important to think about as you listen is that there are two other instruments—the horn and the cello—that have important and prominent roles in this work. The horn is present throughout to present contrasting themes and many of its own musical ideas. Indeed, this piano concerto is one of the greatest works of the horn repertory. The cello has a remarkable extended solo as it carries the main theme in the Andante (third movement) that basically makes it the center of attention. At approximately 50 minutes, this is one of the longest piano concertos in the repertory. If you think that the whole work is contemplative and mellow Brahms, you are in for a pleasant surprise, especially in the second movement.

• ∿ •

Tchaikovsky: Piano Concerto no. 1, Symphony no. 6; Los Angeles Philharmonic Orchestra; Erich Leinsdorf, conductor; Leonard Pennario, piano; Seraphim 7243 5 69034 2 5

For a piece that is now a warhorse in the standard repertory, Tchaikovsky's piano concerto received quite a rocky reception when it was new. It seemed to abandon many of the conventions of the form while not quite replacing them with something discernable and accessible. Yet it does not appear that the composer was attempting something radical. Rather, he wanted to create a showpiece with big melodies and exciting moments that challenge the pianist and become a test of his or her virtuosity. One might ask whether the pianist is given the chance to say much with this music, but it is now considered a key part of the repertory. And it is tough to play! The big introductory music may remind you of Grieg, and then Tchaikovsky introduces several gorgeous melodies, some of his own creation and a few from Ukrainian folk music. You have the skills by now to listen to this piece without much guidance from me. This version is less famous than those by Martha Argerich, Van Cliburn, and Vladimir Horowitz, which are held up as the classics. I feel that, wonderful though they are, these performances sound more like Argerich, Cliburn, and Horowitz, and one has to find Tchaikovsky underneath. It is as if these pianists brought their trademark bravura to bear on this music as a means of addressing its challenges. Their accounts are exciting, but they can be overwhelming.

• ❧ •

Dvořák: Piano Concerto; Schubert: Wanderer *Fantasy; Orchester des Bayerischen Rundfunks; Carlos Kleiber, conductor; Sviatoslav Richter, piano; EMI 7243 5 66947 2 9*

Now listen to the Dvořák Piano Concerto, thinking of it part of the late-nineteenth-century piano tradition of central Europe.

• ❧ •

Saint-Saëns: Concerto for Piano and Orchestra no. 4, Symphony no. 3, "Organ"; New York Philharmonic; Leonard Bernstein, conductor; Robert Casadesus, piano; Leonard Raver, organ; Sony SMK 47 608

Save the organ symphony for later. Now listen to the piano concerto, which the composer himself played at the premiere in 1875. You can sense the virtuosity required here to shift among many moods, from introspective to exuberant. The range of sonorities, tempos, and colorations are part of the appeal of this work to the listener, and a challenge masterfully met by French pianist Robert Casadesus.

• ∽ •

Ravel: Piano Concerto in G; Rachmaninov: Piano Concerto no. 4; Philharmonia Orchestra; Ettore Gracis, conductor; Arturo Benedetti Michelangeli, piano; EMI 7243 5 67258 2 9

An important historical document by a great pianist in two daunting piano works. The Ravel is special and wonderful, and it points the way to much twentieth-century piano music. There will be juxtapositions in sound and temperament that will take you by surprise, but who ever said that predictability is preferable to surprise? As you listen to this music, think of some of the jazz-inflected music of Gershwin, who greatly admired the older Ravel.

The Fourth Piano Concerto of Rachmaninoff is his least appreciated, but still important to the repertory. I suggest you listen to it before the Second or Third so that you can appreciate it on its own terms before dealing with the grand scope of the others.

• ∽ •

Rachmaninov: Piano Concertos nos. 1, 2, 3, 4; London Symphony Orchestra; André Previn, conductor; Vladimir Ashkenazy, piano; London/Decca 444 839-2

Rachmaninoff (depending on whom you ask, his name ends in either *v* or *ff*) was one of the greatest pianists of all, with huge hands that were strong and nimble. He had considerable personality and flair and knew how to put these in service of his art rather than having them be the dominant aspect of his persona. He wrote a lot of music for himself: etudes, preludes, sonatas, concertos, and transcriptions. The pianist Earl Wild, who estimated that he heard Rachmaninoff play forty to fifty times, observed that "he never overplayed, the tone was always very beautiful, and the balance between the hands—he was a master at that."

Unlike Grieg and Liszt, the Rachmaninoff legacy is largely recorded. This is a great benefit, of course, but represents a problem for subsequent pianists because they could be accused of copying him. However, given the fierce technical challenges inherent in that sort of imitation, it might not be a bad thing to find a pianist who could do that. "Rachmaninoff is definitely as hard as it sounds," pianist Misha Dichter has said.

Start with the First Concerto and listen to them in numerical sequence over a couple of days. Sit in a hard chair and think of yourself as being in a concert hall with a powerful pianist and a big orchestra. Play this music at a volume somewhat louder than you might for Mozart or Chopin, but not so loud that your ears ring. In listening to the four concertos, think of them as pieces that a pianist wrote for himself, realizing his technical strengths (his weaknesses were negligible). Ask yourself why, after the absolutely awesome character of the Second and the Third, that Rachmaninoff might have taken a different direction with the Fourth? Was he trying to say something new? Did he feel his skills were diminishing? Give it some consideration.

• ∾ •

Prokofiev: Piano Concertos nos. 1 and 3; Bartók: Piano Concerto no. 3; Orchestre Symphonique de Montréal; Charles Dutoit, conductor; Martha Argerich, piano; EMI Classics 7243 5 56654-2 3

This recording is a document of a great pianist giving thrilling performances of early-twentieth-century music that was not entirely understood in its time and is still more at the periphery of the repertoire than it should be. Argerich and conductor Charles Dutoit work together often because they seem to have considerable mutual comprehension and maintain a very interesting dialogue. Think of Argerich not only as a pianist—let your mind wander and think of her music as vocal music. Take the music of the orchestra (led by Dutoit) and think of him as a pianist who accompanies Argerich's "voice." This is indeed a fantasy, but an important one, to understand a relationship that can exist between instrumental soloist and conductor. While I am not necessarily suggesting a romantic link between these two artists (or whether such a relationship ever existed) there is nonetheless such intimacy and oneness in their performances that it is dazzling.

Focusing on this dynamic will be your way into appreciating the music on this recording. A note about the Prokofiev no. 3: listen to the prominent and interesting roles assigned to flute, clarinet, and bassoon. Prokofiev composed this concerto to play on his 1921 tour of the United States. It met with success at the time, but has since required champions to keep it in the ears of the public. The Bartók may surprise you with how conventional it sounds for a piece written (and not quite completed) as recently as the 1940s. It is an interesting valedictory for a composer who never got the esteem he deserved and was a refugee in New York after war drove him out of Europe. He died in 1945 as this concerto was being composed.

• ⟨∾⟩ •

Satie: Gymnopédies, *etc.; Aldo Ciccolini, piano; EMI 7243 5 67260 2 4*

If you wondered where many of the sounds of the twentieth-century piano you heard came from, listen to Erik Satie. His was a singular voice, one who looked back to the ruminative sound of solo Bach keyboard and Chopin solo music, yet was unquestionably pointing to the future in the juxtaposition of keys and chords. Much of his music, such as the *Gymnopédies* and the *Gnossiennes,* predates Debussy, and you can hear source material in Satie for Ravel, Prokofiev, and others. Now that their music is in your ears, listen to Satie and see how you connect his works to others. Some of this music may already be familiar to you, so you should try to listen to it with fresh ears.

• ⟨∾⟩ •

Poulenc: Organ Concerto, etc.; various artists; London/Decca 448-270-2

Save the organ concerto for later and focus on the music for two pianos, especially the concerto. How does the presence of two pianos change your feelings about the instrument, its sound, and, above all, the role you have given it as a solo voice? In this highly original, somewhat cheeky music, you can hear echoes of Mozart, Satie, and Ravel, and Poulenc plays as much as he possibly can with the possibilities of rhythmic juxtapositions. Remind yourself that modern (or recently modern) music can indeed be gratifying. If you had trouble with Prokofiev or Lutoslawski, remember that repeated exposure and a wide range of listening to all music will give you insights when you return to the most challenging music.

• ◌ •

Panorama: Gershwin, listen to Rhapsody in Blue, *Piano Concerto in F, Variations on "I Got Rhythm," Rhapsody no. 2*

While you know this music well, listen to it now with ears that have heard Satie, Ravel, and Poulenc. These musicians all seem part of a larger whole now and should not be confined to categories as generic as "American" or "French."

• ◌ •

Lutoslawski: Fanfare for the Los Angeles Philharmonic, *Concerto for Piano and Orchestra;* Chantefleurs et Chantefables; *Symphony no. 2; Los Angeles Philharmonic; Esa-Pekka Salonen, conductor; Paul Crossley, piano; Dawn Upshaw, soprano; Sony 67189*

Witold Lutoslawski (1913–1994) wrote music that was challenging to the musician and the listener, yet often thought-provoking. You may grapple with this music at first, but do return to it as you become a more experienced listener. You will be glad you did as you start to make connections with other, older forms of composition.

• ⟨∘⟩ •

John Adams: Century Rolls *(Concerto for Piano), etc.; Cleveland Orchestra; Christoph von Dohnányi, conductor, Emanuel Ax, piano; Nonesuch 79607-2*

It is often said, and I believe in error, that John Adams (1947–   ) is one of the foremost American composers active today. That description is too limiting for someone who is one of the foremost composers anywhere. His operas, *Nixon in China* (1987) and *The Death of Klinghoffer* (1990), made strong impressions on their debuts and have grown in stature ever since. He wrote an engaging and highly unusual violin concerto (1993) that is notable also for its clever deployment of percussion. To understand how the piano concerto can still be a valid form today, some 225 years after Mozart began writing his, listen to the piece that Adams created for Emanuel Ax and the Cleveland Orchestra. Read Adams's interesting program essay that comes with the CD, and then give a listen. Notice that Adams used the word *energy* prominently in has essay. See how you think it is applied in this music.

• ⟨∘⟩ •

Für Elise: Romantic Piano Pieces; *various artists; DG 289 469 632-2*

After listening to so much big music, let us go back to the small pieces of beauty and character that help feed the imaginations of composers, pianists, and audiences. Many of these appear on concert programs as encores. This is an interesting collection of miniatures played by several wonderful pianists. The common denominator of these pieces is that they communicate Romanticism (capital *R*) and, I believe, romance with a small *R*. Think of these as quick pen-and-ink drawings by master artists. Their brevity in no way detracts from their profundity but, rather, makes them all the more remarkable. You surely have heard Beethoven's *Für Elise* at some point in your travels, along with Schumann's dreamy *Träumerei* and Liszt's *Liebestraum* no. 3. Notice, if you can, the undulating sound, like a gondola on water, of Liszt's *Gondoliera* or the sense of moonlight in Debussy's *Clair de Lune* as compared with the adagio from Beethoven's *Moonlight* Sonata. Does Grieg's eponymous "Homesickness" convey that to you? Would you have felt that sensation if you did not know the name of the piece, or would you have felt something else?

• ∾ •

Horowitz in Moscow: Vladimir Horowitz, piano; DG 419 499-2
Yevgeny Kissin in Tokyo: Yevgeny Kissin, piano; Sony SK 45931

Here are two dazzling and thrilling examples of the excitement that a great pianist can generate in a live performance.

• ∾ •

♭ The Organ ♭

Read the discussion about the organ on page 88 before listening to the music that follows.

• ∾ •

J. S. Bach: **Great Organ Favorites;** *E. Power Biggs, organ; CBS MK 42644*

A classic recording that presents a powerhouse organist playing the music by perhaps the most famous composer for the instrument. E. Power Biggs is the most accurate name I have ever encountered in terms of effectively describing what the name's owner is all about. Biggs had a strong personality and a considerable amount of self-assurance, and could communicate these very well indeed, both at the organ and in life. Read his interesting notes that come with the CD. You will most likely recognize the famous Toccata and Fugue in D Minor, and will find the rest of Biggs's approach to Bach easily listenable. This recording is your best way into the world of discovering the organ.

• ❧ •

Handel: Organ Concertos op. 4 and op. 7; Amsterdam Baroque Orchestra; Ton Koopman, organ; Erato 4509 91932-2

Handel, superstar composer and man of the theater, was also an outstanding keyboard player and organist. Part of his appeal was his peerless improvisational ability that led to fascinating musical juxtapositions. He invested this in his compositions for organ, two of which are well performed here. Notice the dialogue between the organ and the other instruments.

• ❧ •

Saint-Saëns: Symphony no. 3 ("Organ"), Concerto for Piano and Orchestra no. 4; New York Philharmonic; Leonard Bernstein, conductor; Leonard Raver, organ; Robert Casadesus, piano; Sony SMK 47 608 (Or Symphony no. 3; Philadelphia Orchestra; Eugene Ormandy, conductor; Virgil Fox, organ; RCA Victrola 7737-2 RV)

The premiere of this popular and thrilling composition was conducted by Saint-Saëns in London in 1886. It is famous above all for the organ music (which you might recognize from the movie *Babe*), but the first part of the symphony merits attention for some passages of real beauty. Too many listeners tend to shut off their careful listening mechanisms until the organ cranks up, and that is a shame. When the organ does begin to speak, you might be intrigued at the delicacy and clarity of its voice. It is as if it is a solo instrument, more like a piano or even a violin than something capable of blowing the roof off the auditorium. This is an important musical gesture by Saint-Saëns, and I hope you notice it. Throughout the organ's music, pay close attention to how it is scored to dialogue with the orchestra. Ultimately, when the stops are pulled and the organ gets to really sing out, you will find it more exciting than if it had been at full blast from the start.

• ❧ •

Other organ listening is Poulenc, Organ Concerto, etc.; various artists; London/Decca 448-270-2, and the Organ Symphony of Aaron Copland merits your attention. Virgil Thomson, composer, critic, and colleague of Copland's, wept when he heard it because, he said, he was sorry he had not written this piece.

• ❧ •

A final observation: having now heard piano and organ, see if you can find a performance of the piano version of Mussorgsky's *Pictures at an Exhibition* by either Vladimir Horowitz or Evgeny Kissin. You will notice that they achieve a remarkable organ-like sonority through strong keyboard playing combined with carefully calculated pedaling. Think of the sound of an organ, think of your received sense of the sound of a piano, and then marvel at this effect. There is also a thrilling recording of this music by Byron Janis, one that may actually exceed the Horowitz and Kissin in many respects, but does not go to the daring extremes of the other pianists. For sake of comparison, after listening to the piano version that Mussorgsky knew, go back and see how Ravel developed it in his sumptuous orchestral arrangement.

THE VIOLIN

Jack Benny played Mendelssohn last night. Mendelssohn lost.
—*Anonymous*

Jack Benny was a better comedian than he was a violinist, although he was not as bad a musician as his comedy routines would suggest. He knew many of the great violinists of his day and actually enhanced their fame among audiences who would never otherwise come in contact with them. But for Benny, the best music was always laughter.

The great Isaac Stern once observed that there is a symbiotic relationship between the violin player and the violin, referring to it as "another arm, another appendage of the body." He said that to select a violin "you have to court it, have an affair with it, and then make the final gesture when you know that you and the instrument can live together." I have heard other musicians speak about the violin and other string instruments this way. There is a deeply emotional, almost erotic attachment that develops between player and instrument. Look at how a violinist or violist gently rests a cheek against the instrument and embraces the rest of it. Even more vivid is the way a player embraces a cello, as if it were a lover.

If the piano is an extension of the musician, one in which the hands and feet transmit the music in many voices through eighty-eight keys and out of a large sound box, the violin is held close to the heart, the ear, and the mind, and usually sings in but one voice, an extremely personal one.

The violin also requires great virtuosity and temperament, although these are being channeled into a much smaller instrument. If a finger is placed just slightly wrong on a string on the fingerboard (the black neck below the instrument's scroll), the note sounded will be incorrect. If bowing is too soft or too aggressive, this changes the volume and alters the violin's tone. The violinist must decide when the sound must be sweet and singing, and when some of the tonal beauty most be sacrificed for drama and expressiveness. A bow can glide slowly across a string to create the sort of lush sound we might hear in Brahms, or there can be the pleasantly agitated fast bowing in Mendelssohn.

· ◇ ·

Throughout the history of the violin there have indeed been virtuosos every bit as charismatic and musically involved as their piano counterparts. What Liszt was to the piano, Niccolò Paganini (1782–1840) was to the violin. His gift included outstanding technique, fiery temperament, and a certain diabolical glamour. In fact, he was often rumored to be in league with Satan, or perhaps to be the Devil himself. This only added to his attractiveness. Because there was not much dazzling solo music for the violin, Paganini wrote it himself. Nowadays we notice the showmanship more than the depth in his music and modern violinists usually save his pieces for showy encores.

More or less contemporary to Paganini was Ludwig Spohr (1784–1859), a composer who wrote thirty-six string quartets in his lifetime. He was one of Europe's original violin virtuosos, known for his playing as much as his composing. Ole Bull (1810–1880), from Norway, was a composer and violinist who was one of the most charismatic stars on the music scene. His music is seldom heard today, but his legend remains prominent, especially in his native land. Henri Vieuxtemps (1820–1881) was a Belgian child prodigy whose career included extensive performances along with the composition of six concertos.

Later in the nineteenth century and into the early twentieth, five prominent violinists were Joseph Joachim (1831–1907), Pablo de

Sarasate (1844–1908), Leopold Auer (1845–1930), Eugène Ysaÿe (1858–1931), and Fritz Kreisler (1875–1962). Joachim was a friend of Schumann and Brahms and other composers who created concertos and other works specifically for him. Tchaikovsky created his concerto specifically for Auer. Ysaÿe played premieres of works by César Franck and others. The first four violinists were influential teachers and, to this day, many young violinists speak of being of the "school" of Auer, Joachim, Sarasate, or Ysaÿe. Kreisler was a glamorous virtuoso who composed showpieces that best displayed his flashy talents.

Leading twentieth-century violinists whose recordings you want to hear as you come to love the violin include Mischa Elman, Zino Francescatti, Arthur Grumiaux, Jascha Heifetz, Leonid Kogan, Yehudi Menuhin, Nathan Milstein, Igor Oistrakh, Alexander Schneider, Isaac Stern, Joseph Szigeti, and Henryk Szeryng. Heifetz (1901–1987) is often spoken of as the titan of this group because of his absolute technical assurance, but all of them are outstanding in repertory that suited their temperaments and taste. As important as technique is emotion and communicativeness, and each of these artists had a lot to offer.

Nowadays, Itzhak Perlman (1945–   ) is often held up as the paragon of a violin virtuoso. He has an unmistakably sweet and warm tone. His work is impeccable and, despite many years of performing, always fresh and original. Just about any recording of his that you listen to will provide great pleasure. Yet Perlman is hardly the only great violinist before the public. Others include Salvatore Accardo, Joshua Bell (whom you will soon meet), Sarah Chang, Midori, Anne-Sophie Mutter, Gil Shaham, Maxim Vengerov, and Pinchas Zukerman. All have recorded extensively.

In addition, all of these active violinists are excellent:

Caroline Balding, Elisabeth Batiashvili, Dmitri Berlinsky, Sandra Cameron, Giuliano Carmignola, Kyung-Wha Chung, Pamela Frank, Tatyana Gridenko, Ilya Gringolts, Hilary Hahn, Oleg Kagan, Leonidas Kavakos, Nigel Kennedy, Patricia Kopatchinskaja, Gidon Kremer, Joan

Kwuon, Jaime Laredo, Cho-Liang Lin, Andrew Manze, Silvia Marcovici, Shlomo Mintz, Viktoria Mullova, Vadim Repin, Nadja Salerno-Sonnenberg, Dmitry Sitkovetsky, Kyoko Takezawa, Christian Tetzlaff, Uto Ughi, Elina Vähälä, Thomas Zehetmair, and Nikolai Znaider

Let us start our study of the violin by returning to Antonio Vivaldi's *Le Quattro Stagioni* (*The Four Seasons*). Last time you heard it, our focus was on colors and pictures, and on the very elaborate narrative of this work. This time you should put the story and visual images out of your head as much as possible, and revert to listening to it in as abstract a musical way as possible. Pay close attention to the sound of the solo violin and its dialogue with the other strings. Many pieces of music, from string quartets to massive symphonies, often have "first violin" and "second violin." These are either soloists or sections that play different music in the same composition, thus providing dialogue and contrast. When you listen to musical performances, especially live, it is fascinating to disentangle the sounds of the first and second violin sections. If you are able to pick out one and then the other, you find that the imagination of the composer meant for them to be parts of a whole.

There is also, in most pieces of any size, the concertmaster. He or she is, in effect, the heir to the solo violinist that you hear in *The Four Seasons*. In an orchestra, the concertmaster is the unofficial leader, second only to the conductor. He or she has a significantly higher pay scale than the rest of the musicians. When the orchestra is seated before a performance, you will see that the first chair to the left of the conductor's podium is empty. Just before the performance begins, the concertmaster will enter and take a solo bow. Sometimes the concertmaster will tune the orchestra in the note A, though this is often done by the oboe or, if present, on a piano. Once the concertmaster sits down, then it is time for the conductor to appear onstage.

Some performances of *The Four Seasons* are led by a conductor, while others are guided by the concertmaster or solo violinist from the first chair.

• ⌇• •

Haydn: Three Favorite Concertos; *Yo-Yo Ma, Wynton Marsalis, Cho-Liang Lin; CBS MK 39310*

The violin concerto on this recording is a good example of the evolution of violin playing with orchestra or ensemble. If you compare the solo violin in *The Four Seasons*, which was sort of a first among equals, to this one, in which the soloist is more freestanding, and with music that stands in more contrast to the group, you can detect the beginnings of what would become the virtuoso violin concerto of the nineteenth century.

• ⌇• •

Mozart: Violin Concertos nos. 1, 2, 3; St. Paul Chamber Orchestra; Pinchas Zukerman, conductor and violin; Sony SBK 46539

Read the excellent notes in the CD booklet before listening to this music. The St. Paul Chamber Orchestra is one of the world's finest and most versatile. Its longtime conductor and principal violinist Pinchas Zukerman leads the musicians in such a way that this is a collection of many stringed voices, with one more to the foreground. These are early Mozart compositions that give a sense of the work he did in his late teens. Make note in Concerto no. 3 that the second movement, the Adagio, is much slower than Mozart typically permitted. It is an adagio in the true sense of the word and, because it is unusual for Mozart, makes us sit up and wonder why he did this. Give it some thought.

• ⌇• •

Mozart: Sinfonia Concertante in E-flat Major for Violin and Viola, K. 364: Stern, Zukerman, Barenboim; Sony MK 36692

Isaac Stern observed that "you can hear more about the human condition in this work (and in all of Mozart) than you can read about in three different books. Mozart says things simply but profoundly. He says things you can think of but don't dare speak." As you listen to this piece, think about what Stern meant. How can notes and sounds address and describe who we are? Do you, in fact, agree with Stern?

You might be interested to know that the great choreographer George Balanchine created one of his most beloved ballets using this music. While Mozart did not envision this as dance music, Balanchine found it remarkably congenial, which was part of *his* genius. Do you hear the potential for dance in this music? What other pieces of music have you learned that might be suitable to choreography (not counting, of course, music written for dance)? Another piece that Balanchine used brilliantly was Georges Bizet's Symphony in C.

Mozart's Sinfonia Concertante is an unusual work because it draws from the forms of symphony and concerto. We have an orchestra with strings, horns, and oboe, and solo passages for violin and viola. These two instruments dialogue with the orchestra and with each other. If you think of these dialogues as an ongoing intimate conversation, you can understand some of what Stern was referring to. Notice the quicksilver changes in mood as the music progresses.

• ⟨◇⟩ •

Beethoven: Concerto for Violin and Orchestra; Triple Concerto; Berlin Philharmonic; Herbert von Karajan, conductor; Anne-Sophie Mutter, violin; Mark Zeltser, piano; Yo-Yo Ma, cello; DG 289 457 861-2

Written in 1806, the violin concerto was first played by Franz Clement, who was the concertmaster of the orchestra of Vienna's Theater an der Wien. Beethoven conducted. Although Clement received favorable notices, Beethoven did not. The *Wiener Theaterzeitung*'s critic wrote that "if Beethoven continues in this way, both he and the public will be the worse off. . . . [Any listener] not completely conversant with the rules and difficulty with the art would find virtually nothing to enjoy," because the concerto has "an excess of unconnected ideas and a continual uproar by certain instruments" which cause listeners to leave the concert "with nothing other than an unpleasant sensation of exhaustion." Rather than just dismiss the critic's opinions out of hand, when you listen to this concerto, ask yourself what he could possibly have been referring to.

This is usually considered the first violin concerto of the Romantic era, one in which the soloist steps considerably forward and establishes a voice that is quite distinct from the rest of the musicians. There are long lyrical solo passages, an important beautiful theme that you will quickly absorb and remember, and an exciting finale. Make note of the use of timpani in this music—they set a rhythm that will pervade the whole concerto.

The concerto only really found favor in 1853, when the young Joseph Joachim played it in Düsseldorf to great acclaim.

The Triple Concerto is a work of amazing brilliance. In effect, it is a chamber music trio set into an orchestra like a jewel in a glorious setting. Here is music for piano, violin, and cello, played in solo and collective passages, along with wonderful orchestration. It needs to be heard to fully appreciate how these pieces merge so effortlessly.

• ❧ •

Beethoven: Kreutzer Sonata; Franck: Violin Sonata in A Major; Itzhak Perlman, violin; Martha Argerich, piano; EMI 7243 5 56815 2 2

Beethoven's sonata writing is interesting for many reasons, but one is the more prominent role he gave to the piano. If something is called a violin sonata, one thinks of that instrument as the protagonist. Although the *Kreutzer* Sonata is named for the violinist for whom it was intended, you will quickly realize that one instrument is in no way subservient to the other. Both parts require immense virtuosity, and with Perlman and Argerich in peak form, you can hear how chamber music at its best is a vivid dialogue between musicians of equal stature. Save the Franck sonata for later.

• ❧ •

A CONVERSATION WITH JOSHUA BELL

While still a teenager, Joshua Bell's talent announced him as one of the foremost violinists of our time. Rather than simply rely on those gifts to forge a major career, Bell has continuously worked at honing his craft, investigating new repertory and revisiting works he had already gained fame with in order to deepen his understanding and relationship with them. In the conversation from 2001 you are about to read, Joshua Bell (then thirty-four) described how a musician's career and interests evolve.

In focusing on Mendelssohn's Violin Concerto no. 1, Bell gives you a lesson in comparative listening. Until this point I have emphasized other aspects of your education about classical music. This section represents a major turning point in *your* development: it is now time for you to listen to more than one performance of the same piece of music and decide how they differ and what each says to you.

Before the conversation, Bell and I listened to the opening movement of the Mendelssohn Violin Concerto, as played by three violinists whom I did not identify: Jascha Heifetz (whom I called A), Nathan Milstein (B), and David Oistrakh (C).

You should listen to these as you read this interview, and should also get the recording with Bell's own interpretation to listen to afterward so you understand how he applies his vision of this concerto to his performance.

Question. Thank you for listening to three performances of the first movement of the Mendelssohn Violin Concerto by violinists A, B, and C, all of whom are from the mid-twentieth century. When you heard A, within a minute you said to me, "That must be Jascha Heifetz." Why?

JOSHUA BELL. *Well, within two seconds I thought it was Heifetz. He probably has the most distinctive sound of any violinist. He's got this intensity that, when you hear it, you know it sounds like Heifetz.*

Also, he was notorious for taking the first movement very fast. I knew it was Heifetz even though I had not heard the recording for many years.

This piece is so interesting. The Mendelssohn concerto is unlike any other concerto in that it just thrusts you right into the piece right from the very beginning, without an introduction, without any kind of formality. It is kind of like a movie in that you are suddenly thrust right into the action where something has already been happening and you are taken there. It's amazing that Mendelssohn was able to do that. Actually, Schubert did that better than anyone, where within seconds you are drawn into this world. With some composers you feel like it takes a while to get you there because there is some form of introduction. Schubert does that [immediate thrust], and Mendelssohn does that with this piece.

And that is what is interesting—the choices that you as an artist can and have to make. And your choice at the beginning of this concerto is how and what you want this world to be because it is so unusual to have a violinist playing right off the bat with no introduction. It is a beautiful melody, so you have a choice of playing very beautifully and you can just take it as a gorgeous melody. I think, though, that when most people hear it they realize it is more than just that. There is something unsettled about the opening of the Mendelssohn. A lot of it has to do with the orchestra—what's going on underneath is an unsettled thing. It is not a comfortable accompaniment. So when you are unsettled, you have to decide what that means—"lost" unsettled or "agitated" unsettled, et cetera—and so Heifetz takes the energetic "agitated" approach, and I think his hallmark is this incredible amount of energy that comes out, so he takes this very quick, agitated view of the piece right off the bat. Not only are his tempos fast but, when you hear Heifetz play this piece, it feels like the whole movement goes by in a flash. The reason is that it is not only tempo that makes a performance seem endless or makes you think, "Wow, that went by fast"—a lot of it has to do with whether Heifetz chooses to smell the roses along the way.

In a way, I like that he sees the piece in broad chunks. He really leads you from the whole exposition all the way to the second theme as if it were one big chunk. [He approaches it] in a very organic way. He avoids being sentimental; perhaps he overdoes it—again, this is my view. He could have taken some time in some places. There are so many beautiful chord changes, and beautiful little things that, as an artist, you constantly have to face, especially in beautiful pieces by Mendelssohn and Schubert where every few bars there is some amazing thing and, if you *want to dwell on it and draw the audience's attention in some obvious way and overlook the large picture, [you must decide do you do that] or do you move on? That's always the choice. Heifetz seems to plow through.*

Q.   Does he sound like he has to catch a train?

A.   *A little bit. He rushed through it a lot and made the orchestra rush after him. There are a lot of clues to tempos. One of them is basically the way it is written. Mendelssohn double-dotted some of the wind parts (to indicate a faster tempo) and I think Heifetz pushes it. He might have been in a bad mood or in a hurry, but I think he is really trying to avoid being sentimental about the piece. He doesn't want to be corny or indulgent with the piece. For my taste, he goes to the extreme. I think also that with the second theme—this piece goes between incredible tenderness and intensity—I feel that Heifetz also pushes his way through that, not only with speed but also with dynamics. None of the three performances I have just heard took Mendelssohn's own dynamic in the second theme, which is* pianissimo, *not even* piano, *which is soft. He takes care to write* pianissimo, *which is really soft. None of the three took it to where you feel it is inside their hands, or really feel like they are taking you inside, but I feel like the second performer (B) did it the most.*

Q.   I want to ask you about the second violinist. Within four minutes of hearing him play, you said to me, "I prefer this guy." What was it you preferred?

A.   *Yeah. Well, right off the bat it felt that the sound was more beautiful. That might have been partially the recording sound, but it was a bit of a relief after hearing the first one that the tempo wasn't driving the orchestra crazy trying to keep up with him. I thought the second one achieved the best—I felt like he was telling a story more. When you play a piece of music you are telling a story, and I felt like he balanced what I was talking about regarding smelling the roses, and yet it felt very organic the way he did his transition into the second theme. It was so beautiful.*

For me, Mendelssohn wrote a masterpiece where he really laid it out so well for you as a player that the music almost plays itself. The way he goes into the transition from the exposition [the first section, containing the statement of the first theme] into the second theme you can almost play it the way it was written, without adding lots of ritard [gradual slowing of speed], without adding stuff with tempo. Mendelssohn takes you there in a natural way.

Anyway, the second violinist was much more beautiful and much more tender. Everything felt natural and right. It felt like he was writing the music when he was playing it, and not doing things to the music, which is very important, to feel like you are inside the music and not outside of it, doing stuff and saying, "Oh this will get them [the audience] here," and doing a little slide here or there. It is a very subtle thing. It is kind of like actors—with some actors you are aware that they are acting, doing stuff to their character rather than being that character. It is a matter of honesty.

All three performances were honest. It was interesting to hear these three older players because I find that their playing tends to be more honest than with a lot of today's performers. I think people are so worried about the fact that the piece has been played thousands of times so they attempt to do something to the music in an attempt to separate themselves. I felt like each one of these performances was honest playing. People talk about the older generation being very free, but in a way I feel today's generation is even more free, though not in a good way. They are more free, but there is something that the older players knew about being free, about keeping the rhythm going and being free within that. I think today there is much more of a tendency to distort the tempos and trying to be different.

Q. This modern distortion you are talking about, is that instigated by violinists or by conductors?

A. *I think that in the case of a violin concerto that it would most often be the violinist who is interpreting the piece. But you will find the same thing with conductors conducting pieces. With some of the older conductors, such as Bruno Walter or Toscanini, you never felt like they were messing with the music or doing stuff to it. It is a basic philosophy toward the music that is just an insecurity today, in wanting to be different and interesting—trying to be interesting—instead of just separating themselves. What an artist should do is let the music speak for itself, because that is where the greatness is, and we are there to bring that out.*

Q.   You were talking about the heart of performing this concerto or any piece is telling a story. Is it Mendelssohn's story in this case, which he has written and you are the teller, or is it Mendelssohn's story and Joshua Bell's experience and some of Joshua Bell's story? Or Jascha Heifetz's story, or whoever's?

A.   *I view it as definitely being Mendelssohn's story. He is the one who came up with it out of nothing, and it really is his story. But of course the interpreter brings a lot of things to the table. It is like in Shakespeare. It is Shakespeare's story, but every actor is going to see it in a different way based on his own experience. Even more than in Shakespeare—music is more abstract, so there is a lot more room. Every composer gives different cues. I think that a performer should approach it as a story and look to see what the composer wrote. It is amazing that, in all three of these recordings, how many markings that Mendelssohn took care to mark were ignored. Everybody does it. I am guilty of that too, particularly when I've learned a piece when I was younger and I haven't taken up the music [to read] in a while, you forget those things.*

Of course, if you make an intelligent decision that you really don't like it that way [as written], and it doesn't fit into your scheme of things, then I would say go with that, because in the end I think the composer would want that. The idea of music is that the story has to make sense within itself. A lot of this [disregarding of markings] is laziness, because ninety-nine out of a hundred times the composer's markings tell the story in the best way, because nobody knows the story better than the composer himself. But even following all of the markings of the composer, there is still so much room for how to do it. If he starts off the piece marked piano, *it could be a* piano agitato, *or a dreamy kind of* piano *or a beautiful kind of* piano. *The way you approach these completely changes the way one hears this piece. You are constantly making these choices and bringing your own self to it.*

I want the audience to come backstage after the performance and say, "My God, what an incredible piece that was!" Of course, I want them to like what I have done, but that makes me feel good about myself. [If they like the piece] it means that I have done my job right, that I have sold the piece and the story. They love the piece and were taken by it, rather than "Oh, look what you did to the piece!"

Q. If this is the same story that violinists A, B, C, and Joshua Bell, and other violinists are telling, why is it that violinist A took 10 minutes and 52 seconds, violinist B took 11 minutes and 9 seconds, and violinist C took 12 minutes and 44 seconds to play the same first movement? The story was 1 minute and 52 seconds longer between A and C. How does that happen?

A. *There is enough freedom within a piece that can allow for that. Violinist A thought of the piece in big terms and kind of pushed through. He didn't dwell on the details, at least not with tempo. Violinist C, for my taste, had a less intelligent approach than B. I found that certain things in the performance did not make sense. He put on the brakes at certain points where the music did not call for it, but it seems as if almost for technical reasons or being musically lazy. But he suddenly jarred me out of the story a couple of times. On the other hand, there were some incredibly beautiful moments, in taking the time to caress certain things. But there was a less of a thought-out architecture to the performance, though it had interesting moments. I think because he took a lot more time at certain places, it added seconds to the performance.*

Q. I happened to mention that all these musicians were men, but can you listen to a performance and say that is a man or that is a woman playing?

A. *I do guess sometimes, but I am not always right.*

Q. What might tell that it is one or the other?

A. *If it is aggressive and masculine-sounding, that means it is a young female playing [laughter]. No—I think it is impossible to tell. What makes one thing masculine or feminine is physical differences. So I guess with a man being usually stronger than a woman [you would think that would be a difference]. But if you play with a proper technique, you don't have to be incredibly strong to get a really big and powerful sound. With me it is really a difference in schooling [rather] than whether you are a male or a female. The second player here was probably the most elegant of the three, and in some ways one might call that a more feminine characteristic, more sensitive. In the Russian school, the* *old Russian players tended to be more outgoing and in your face, every-thing out rather than in. In my schooling, I came from [Josef] Gingold, who studied with [Eugène] Ysaÿe, which is more of the French-Belgian school, probably a more feminine approach to playing the instrument, more inward. The ideals that were stressed for me were of beauty over power. As I have gotten older, I have wanted to learn from everybody.*

And of course there is kind of a clichéd New York approach. When Europeans talk about a New York and American way of playing, it is way too generalized because there are a lot of people coming out of New York who don't play that way. But the stereotype is aggressive and testosterone-driven whether it is a female or a man. It is a stereotype.

Q.   So what if I were to tell you that these three men are all Russian? What is it that says they are all Russian and not out of the French-Belgian tradition?

A.   *The way they approach the instrument is in a very projective kind of way. They are projecting out. In a recording you actually have the lux-ury of not having to do that so much. These are older recordings, and I sort of felt that they played the way they played and it was recorded. Pro-jecting is not a bad thing, but you want listeners to be drawn in.*

Q.   A bit like stage actors?

A.   *There is always a difference when you play versus record, and you always have to be aware of that in a concert hall, you are forced to have project. I think the trick is to try to project. I feel that stage actors some-times overproject. They don't need to be doing as much as they think they need to be doing all the time. They are taught that everything has to be done ten times what you do in a movie. But if you are sitting in the back row and you feel it, then they are obviously doing too much, and that is the same with music.*

Q.   You recorded this concerto first when you were nineteen, and you rerecorded it when you were thirty-three. Many people only get to do a recording once in their lives, and certain people get to record it at various points. At thirty-three, now thirty-four, you are still quite young in the scope of a long career. What did you find to say differently, or what did you discover in returning to the concerto at thirty-three that you did not know at nineteen?

A.   *My approach to the piece has changed quite a lot. I was very eager to rerecord it because I was very young and the piece was still in a way kind of new to me. The way I thought about music then was quite different. I played by instinct and I think that as I have gotten older I have thought more about the architecture of the piece and what makes it flow. I understand more of the nature of what I am doing, and it helps me have a more cohesive performance. A lot of the details [have changed]. What I took at face value the first time I looked at it when was younger, I now see deeper meanings in certain parts. I have expanded my tonal palette and colors.*

Q.   What does that mean?

A.   *Meaning I have learned how to play the instrument better. I have learned how to change my sound. As you get more experience, you are painting with more colors. It allows you to do more; it lets you do subtleties. I own the piece. You have to own the piece in order to play it and to sell it. What is unusual is that I have written my own cadenza. I will probably get criticism for it, but this is one of the few concertos where the composer included the cadenza, but in fact, in the Mendelssohn concerto, it is thought that Ferdinand David [the violinist for whom it was written] really wrote most of the cadenza. For me, the ending of the cadenza itself is actually genius and I am sure that part Mendelssohn wrote. But I never thought of the cadenza itself as being the most interesting. I wrote one as an experiment and then I thought, "Why not include it?" That is a way to be different from the other recordings.*

Q.   What is a cadenza?

A.   *A cadenza is kind of involved. It started out as the end of the cadence or stanza or section where there would be an ornament that is improvised, not so different from jazz, or certain other music where one can improvise. Originally it started around one chord, and it was quite easy to improvise like that. As time passed, and the cadenza started taking on a larger role in the piece, in violin concertos, or any concertos, it became, by Mozart's time, quite an elaborate thing. I think in Mozart's time it was still possible that they would improvise on the spot, but I think it started to be more of a practice that they would think it out beforehand.*

Q. Like opera singers who would go off in their own direction with a musical improvisation—sort of a riff—and then they would come back at a certain point and look at the conductor, who would then cue the orchestra to play the next music that the composer had actually written?

A. *Right. It was very traditional that the cadenza would revolve around a certain chord, such as the 1-6-4 chord, which is one that feels like it needs to be resolved. So the idea of the cadenza is a big, elaborate way to getting back to the tonic, the place where you can say "Ah" when the orchestra comes in, because there has been resolution. In a way, this is what music is all about—conflict and resolution.*

Q. Let us switch to Johannes Brahms's concerto for a moment. The cadenza by Joseph Joachim, for whom Brahms wrote the concerto, was widely acclaimed, and he played it more than two hundred times. The estimable musicologist Michael Steinberg wrote that, in addition to the Joachim cadenza, he also admires others, including those of Ferruccio Busoni, Fritz Kreisler, Nathan Milstein, and Joshua Bell.

A. *Really? That's nice. I didn't know that.*

Q. Do you feel any particular affinity to Busoni, Kreisler, or Milstein?

A. *I feel a connection to these players because of my teacher, Gingold, who was of their generation. Gingold was a student of Ysaÿe, one of the great violinist-composers. He and a lot of his fellow students would write their own cadenzas, which was part of the educational process. Ysaÿe wrote many famous cadenzas. I was introduced by Gingold to a lot of these players, such as Milstein and Kreisler, whose recordings were played for me as examples at lessons. I feel a connection to that time, and*

I feel that this is a tradition that is sadly lost, that of the player-composer. It seems very natural that that is what you would do. As a classical artist today, when someone asks if you write your own music, most classical artists will laugh, as if that were a dumb question. But the reason why someone who may not know about classical music would ask that is it seems like the most natural thing in the world. In so many other areas of music they still have that.

I think that the fissure that [can exist] between the player and the composer may have resulted in unplayable music. When I say "unplayable," [I mean that] one can put part of the blame for why so much [newer] music is unlistenable on the fact that the composer got so abstract within the realm of theory and composing that it has gotten separated from the person who has to get up there and play it. It must have been a great time when you could go hear the music of Chopin and others who played their own works and cadenzas.

Q. A critic at the time of Brahms said that his concerto was not written for the violin, but against it. Pablo de Sarasate said that he would not play a piece where the main melody of the second movement was for the oboe. There may have been—please tell me what you think—at all times a tension between the performer and the composer in terms of outlook.

A. *I think in that case there was also a difference in philosophy about music. Joachim, who was possibly the greatest violinist of his day, was of a whole different school than Sarasate. The idea of what Brahms did was very similar to what Beethoven did. Beethoven took little bits of material and developed them rather than just laying out big tunes. It was a different way of appreciating music. Schubert was more about tunes, and Tchaikovsky was about huge beautiful tunes. Although he respected Brahms, Tchaikovsky could not understand why Brahms didn't just write about a big tune. For Brahms it was a way of understating that he had. There were different schools, even at that time.*

Q. Bach, Mozart, Beethoven did not work with a violinist when writing music for the instrument—

A. *Bach and Mozart played the violin.*

Q. Mendelssohn worked with David; Joachim with Bruch, Brahms, and Dvořák; Tchaikovsky had Yosif Kotuk; Elgar had W. H. Reed; Stravinsky had Samuel Dushkin; Bartók had Zoltán Székely; Shostakovich had David Oistrakh; John Adams had Gidon Kremer; and Nicholas Maw had Joshua Bell. This tradition of violinists and composers evolving a work together—how did that happen in your case, and what can you say about how it happened?

A. *If a composer did not play a particular instrument all that well, it probably is a good idea to consult someone who knew how to do it. First of all, there would be a better chance of that violinist taking it up if he feels he could play it. One of my favorite pieces is the Schumann concerto, which hardly anyone plays because there are parts of it that just don't fit. They just don't feel right. Apparently he asked Joachim, who felt the piece wasn't worthy. I don't agree with him, but there are parts that needed some tweaking. If somebody had taken that role, it could have been something playable.*

Look at the Brahms. I assume that all of that red ink was by Joachim. Almost all of the corrections made it better, even though Joachim was not one-tenth of the composer Brahms was. My dream is to be a composer someday. It is very possible that I don't have it in me, but I could be like Joachim, helping great composers make their pieces better, and writing my own cadenzas.

When Nicholas Maw decided to write this concerto . . . he does not play the violin or any string instrument. There were a lot of things I had to tell him didn't work. Some things were not playable at all. Some harmonics were not possible. Those are natural consultations.

Q. You worked on playing the soundtrack for the film *The Red Violin*, with music by John Corigliano.

A. *Corigliano's father was a violinist and he knows the instrument very well. Even among the older composers, some of them seem to write for the instrument. In the case of Mendelssohn, it seems that everything he wrote for any instrument was perfect; it was so beautifully laid out. Schumann, on the other hand, was less player-friendly. With Corigliano's music, my contributions were decorative, and in some cases were able to take it to the next level of virtuosity, in places where that is what he wanted. And I could bring it to that level because I knew what was possible.*

Q. Do you play chamber music with colleagues?

A. *Quite a lot.*

Q. Do you play publicly?

A. *I do. I have my own series at Wigmore Hall in London. I have done several recordings. I play more chamber music in Europe, in places such as Salzburg and Edinburgh, than I do in America.*

Q. Why is that so many great musicians say that chamber music is their favorite form of music-making?

A. *In chamber music you get a small group of very high-level musicians who really, really care what they are doing, and you end up playing off of each other and getting a greater result. You can talk about the music, you can perfect it in rehearsal, you have enough time to get to the highest level. When you play a concerto, there is never really enough time to rehearse. There are so many people involved and not all of them have the attitude about making music or the same level of commitment— even though most of them do—that you can find in a small group of chamber music players. Chamber music played with a small group is the best musical experience.*

Q. Isaac Stern, at a certain point, for technical reasons and—I believe—for emotional reasons, largely left solo playing and devoted himself to chamber music. Have you found that same sense of collaboration and listening that he did in this repertory?

A. *I really can't speak for him. A lot of composers reserved their greatest stuff for chamber music. The string quartet has always been a kind of holy grail for many musicians. The best music of Schubert and Beethoven are the quartets. Chamber music is technically less demanding than a concerto. As you get older, you may have less technique, but you have more understanding. That does not go away as one gets older. And there are even financial issues. You cannot make as much money doing chamber music in a small hall as you can as a soloist in a large one. You are splitting your fee, if you are making any money at all. When you get older, you can do that.*

Q. Final question: do you want to guess who B and C were?

A. *Yes, I'll take a guess. I thought B was—they're all Russian?*

Q: Yes.

A. *Was it Milstein?*

Q. Yes. That is why I asked you earlier if you felt any special affinity for Milstein. What did you like ultimately about Milstein's performance?

A. *I thought it was refined, classy, elegant, beautiful. Heifetz has always been my favorite on a certain level. He had the ability to make your hair stand up more than any other violinist, including Milstein. But for this piece, the Mendelssohn, if I had to go to a desert island, I would rather have the Milstein.*

Q. And violinist C?

A. *Hmmm.*

Q. What if I told you it was Oistrakh?

A. *It was beautiful playing, very open, a little turgid at times, at the beginning it was a little slow, the transition too. Parts were a little bit plodding. Sometimes in the Russian school—such as the second theme in the third movement of the Tchaikovsky Violin Concerto—something marked* poco meno mosso *[a little bit slower] becomes twice as slow. It might be a kind of a Russian School thing to take things slower. It is a different school.*

Q. This has been fascinating. Thank you very much.

A. *You are welcome.*

The following are the recordings mentioned in the conversation with Joshua Bell:

• ∾ •

Beethoven: Violin Concerto; Mendelssohn; Violin Concerto in E Minor, op. 64; Camerata Academica of Salzburg; Roger Norrington, conductor; Joshua Bell, violin; Sony SK89505

This was recorded in 2001 when Bell was thirty-three.

• ∾ •

Mendelssohn: Violin Concerto no. 1: Three Legendary Recordings; *Jascha Heifetz, Nathan Milstein, David Oistrakh, violin; Arkadia 78576*

This outstanding and moderately priced recording is not always available in record shops, but has been found by contacting Tower Records (800-275-8693; fax 800-538-6938; fax from outside the U.S. 1-916-373-2930; or visit www.tower.com) or Web sites such as www.amazon.com and www.bn.com (Barnes and Noble). If you cannot find this recording, there are easily located reissues of the Mendelssohn concerto by Heifetz, Milstein, and Oistrakh.

For comparison, you might wish to listen to Bell's first recording, at age nineteen in 1988, of the Mendelssohn concerto, comparing the cadenzas and the interpretation:

Bruch: Violin Concerto no. 1 in G Minor, op. 26; Mendelssohn: Violin Concerto in E Minor, op. 64; Orchestra of Academy of St. Martin-in-the-Fields; Neville Marriner, conductor; Joshua Bell, violin; London/Decca 421-145-2

Also:

Maw: Concerto for Violin and Orchestra; London Philharmonic Orchestra; Roger Norrington, conductor, Joshua Bell, violin; Sony SK 62856

Brahms: Violin Concerto in D Major, op. 77, cadenza by Joshua Bell; Schumann: Violin Concerto in D Minor; Cleveland Orchestra; Christoph von Dohnanyi, conductor. Joshua Bell, violin; London/Decca 444-811-2

• ∾ •

Before we leave the Mendelssohn concerto, there is one more step to take. Now that you have learned from Joshua Bell about comparative listening, you are on your own. Listen to a performance by either Bell, Heifetz, Milstein, or Oistrakh. Then listen to the version by Anne-Sophie Mutter on the compendium Panorama/DG recording of Mendelssohn. Come to your own conclusions and write comments that express what you have perceived. How are the two performances different? Come up with at least five examples and you will find that you have absorbed the tenets of comparative listening, which will prove useful to you in all forms of music from now on.

• ◦◦ •

Brahms and Tchaikovsky: Violin Concertos; Jascha Heifetz, violin, Fritz Reiner, conductor, RCA Victor 09026-61495; or Nathan Milstein, violin; William Steinberg and Anatole Fistoulari, conductors; Seraphim CDE 7243 5 69035 2 4.

Both of these recordings are outstanding documents that merit ownership. The Heifetz benefits from something rare nowadays—superb program notes by the great critic Claudia Cassidy and by Charles O'Connell. There are also biographical essays of conductor Fritz Reiner and of Heifetz, who made these recordings in the mid-1950s, when technology was improving though not at the levels of today. Yet the sound fidelity, the assured playing by the soloist, and the wonderful playing of Reiner and the Chicago Symphony make this something of a landmark. Milstein, with his inimitable tone, makes an appealing alternative.

The Brahms and Tchaikovsky rank among the most popular of all violin concertos. The Brahms was written for Joseph Joachim, who had quite a virtuoso pedigree. At thirteen he performed the London premiere of the Beethoven concerto, restoring that work to the repertory and making himself a star. While still a teenager he was the concertmaster in Weimar under Franz Liszt. Despite Joachim's talents, and Brahms's, too, the concerto had only a middling success during their lifetimes. It was not until Fritz Kreisler made the first recording of the work (1926) that the concerto was widely heard, and in a wonderful performance. This is but one example of how the recording industry not only changed the course of classical music but also restored works to the repertory that had been neglected.

One often hears of Brahms's warm sound, and here is a good place to think about how that comes about. The concerto starts with violas, cellos, and bassoons, and are soon joined by French horns, and then oboe. These are middle to low voices. They make for a very unusual mixture, but the result, I think you will agree, has a distinct warmth to it. This is a result of Brahms's sensitivity to the voices of instruments. By using these voices to create the temperature of the piece, the entry of the violin has a context that is quite defined. Think of other music for violin you have listened to, and compare the context in which the instrument's solo voice makes its entry.

As you listen to the first movement, note the cadenza played here, composed by Joachim. You can compare it to Joshua Bell's own cadenza, if you have acquired his fine recording. In the second movement (the Adagio), you will be startled by the long oboe solo. Pablo de Sarasate refused to play the Brahms concerto because he felt that the oboe got the better music. What do you think? Pay close attention to how the oboe introduces beautiful music, but then the violin takes it to another place. I think you will agree that Brahms knew exactly what he was doing.

Throughout the concerto we hear one beautiful melody after the next. See how many you can count, and then think about how they all interplay in the development of the whole piece.

Comparative listening:

Brahms: Violin Concerto; Chicago Symphony Orchestra; Carlo Maria Giulini, conductor; Itzhak Perlman, violin; EMI 7243 5 66992 2 9

If you wish to listen to a modern version after hearing Bell's distinctive performance with his own cadenza, listen to Perlman's and decide if he seems to be more in the style of Heifetz or Milstein (or neither one).

Tchaikovsky's violin concerto, like Brahms's and Beethoven's, got off to a rough start. The composer tried to interest one violinist and then another in the music, and they hesitated. It was taken up by Adolf Brodsky, and reports of the premiere were disastrous. Later it went to Leopold Auer, whom Tchaikovsky had tried to interest earlier on. Auer became a persuasive advocate and authoritative player of the music, and taught it to many outstanding violinists of the next generation, including Milstein and Heifetz. You have the skills to listen to this work on your own. One thing to bear in mind is that with Beethoven, Mendelssohn, and Brahms, the violin is a distinct voice in front of the orchestra. It is with Tchaikovsky, too, but it plays both in a concerto voice and that of the folk tradition of violin playing that Tchaikovsky knew well.

• ∾ •

Brahms: Violin Sonatas nos. 1–3; Itzhak Perlman, violin; Vladimir Ashkenazy, piano; EMI 7243 5 66945 2 1

More Brahms, this time beautiful chamber music. Pay close attention to what is, in effect, a prolonged and detailed conversation between violin and piano. Notice how one picks up subject matter from the other and proposes it in a slightly different way.

• ∾ •

Panorama: Berlioz, "Rêverie et caprice," Arthur Grumiaux, violin

This music is on the Berlioz recording you own. It is rapturously performed by Grumiaux and gives you a view into a more intimate side of the composer's work.

• ⟨◦⟩ •

Lalo: Symphonie Espagnole; *Vieuxtemps: Violin Concerto no. 5; Royal Concertgebouw Orchestra/ Philharmonia Orchestra; Charles Dutoit, conductor; Sarah Chang, violin; EMI 7243 5 55292 2 0*

Two exciting and colorful nineteenth-century classics from the French and Belgian traditions. Lalo wrote his piece for Pablo de Sarasate, the fiery Spanish violinist, who spent a good deal of time in France. This is one of the early examples of the cross-pollination of Spanish and French culture, of which the most famous work is Bizet's opera *Carmen* (1875), whose music Sarasate adapted for a brilliant solo. The *Symphonie Espagnole* is a virtuoso showpiece that Sarah Chang executes with dazzling assurance. Vieuxtemps is largely forgotten today but was a great virtuoso in his time. The Fifth is his most enduring violin concerto.

• ⟨◦⟩ •

Dvořák, Violin Concerto; New York Philharmonic; Zubin Mehta, conductor; Midori, violin; Sony SK 44 923

We will be studying the Dvořák Cello Concerto in considerable detail in the next chapter. If you are a fan of this composer's sumptuous lyricism (as I am), you should look into the Violin Concerto as well. It was dedicated to Joseph Joachim, but the premiere was given by František Ondříček in 1883. This recording also contains the beautiful Romance for Violin and Orchestra, one of the composer's first pieces, and the popular *Carnival* Overture.

• ⟨◦⟩ •

Listen to the Franck Sonata on Beethoven: Kreutzer Sonata; Franck: Violin Sonata in A Major; Itzhak Perlman, violin; Martha Argerich, piano; EMI 7243 5 56815 2 2; or Franck: Sonata for Violin and Piano; Brahms: Horn Trio; Itzhak Perlman, violin; Vladimir Ashkenazy, piano; Barry Tuckwell, horn; London/Decca 452 887-2

Much of César Franck's music was religious in flavor, but this sonata from the last years of his life was imbued with romance. The composer had developed a sentimental friendship with the beautiful composer Augusta Holmès, and this music is an outgrowth of his intense amorous feelings, which were not returned in kind. If you have read *Swann's Way* by Proust, the author talks of how a particular violin sonata his protagonist hears provokes intense feelings. The book is, in part, a meditation on how thoughts and emotions can grow from the sound of music. It is generally thought that the sonata that inspired Proust was this one by Franck. The sonata was written for the talents of violinist Eugène Ysaÿe. This is an extraordinary composition that requires violin and piano playing that is both intense and sensuous. Notice, by the way, how one instrument often imitates the sound of the other. Given what you know of the background of this piece, what do you think this imitation (or, if you prefer, echoing) could mean?

· ❧ ·

Panorama: Prokofiev, Violin Concerto no. 1; Shlomo Mintz, violin

Following in the seeming tradition of other great composers, the premiere of Prokofiev's First Violin Concerto, in Paris in 1923, was a failure. Yet several violinists, particularly Joseph Szigeti, understood the music's value and took up its cause. It has gradually found its place among the great concertos for violin. The first performance of this concerto in the Soviet Union, also in 1923, had nineteen-year-old Nathan Milstein as the violin soloist and, in place of the orchestra, Vladimir Horowitz—also nineteen—on the piano. As you listen, ask yourself whether Prokofiev was correct in feeling that he was misunderstood: he believed the violin line to be quite lyrical, but critics said otherwise. Another way to think about this is to ask yourself whether lyricism can only mean the graceful flow one hears in Brahms and Dvořák, or whether a lyrical voice can be found in a more modern context.

• ◦⟡◦ •

Stravinsky and Rochberg: Violin Concertos; Igor Stravinsky and André Previn,
conductors; Isaac Stern, violin; Sony SMK 64 505

An important document in that Stravinsky conducts his own concerto,
with Isaac Stern, in his prime, as soloist. It is paired with a violin concerto by George Rochberg, written in 1974, with Stern as soloist. The
program notes in the CD provide a valuable introduction to these
important modern works and will help you find your way. Before listening to the Stravinsky, return to the Beethoven concerto and listen to it
again. I am not suggesting that Beethoven influenced Stravinsky
(though he may well have—he influenced everyone else), but want you
to actively address the fact that both composers were considered radical
in their times. Listen to Beethoven this time for his radicalism rather
than the comforting classicism that we have become accustomed to.
Then, when you listen to Stravinsky, think of him not only as a radical
but as an heir to a tradition from which he often chose to depart.

• ◦⟡◦ •

Panorama: Gershwin, listen to Three Preludes; Gil Shaham, violin

Until now, you have listened to George Gershwin's music primarily in an
orchestral and piano context. How do his particular rhythms and
cadences sound to you on the violin? Picture the bowing that Shaham
must do, and compare it with the movement of fingers across a keyboard.

• ◦⟡◦ •

Berg: Violin Concerto; Chicago Symphony Orchestra; James Levine, conductor;
Anne-Sophie Mutter, violin; Deutsche Grammophon 437 093-2

A work of great beauty, intense emotion, and awesome technical
demands. You will notice at one point that Berg asks the violinist to bow

on one strung and pluck on another at the same time. I will resist telling you the various passionate events of Berg's life as this work evolved. Some were romantic, some tempestuous, some tragic. The reason I am not recounting this background is that you will look for specific musical cues to represent certain events, and in so doing you will miss some of the riveting intensity of this concerto in purely musical terms.

• ◆ •

Panorama: Jean Sibelius, listen to Violin Concerto; Christian Ferras, violin; Berlin Philharmonic; Herbert von Karajan, conductor
Alternate recording: Beethoven and Sibelius, Violin Concertos; Bruno Walter, Eugene Ormandy, conductors; Zino Francescatti and David Oistrakh, violin; Sony SBK 47659

Jean Sibelius, Finland's leading composer, created an extensive body of important music and influenced generations of young Finns to do the same. The national music academy in Helsinki, named for Sibelius, is one of the three or four most important in all of Europe. Sibelius was himself a violinist, and wrote an early version of this concerto that was a showpiece for the violin soloist but did not have much to offer the rest of the orchestra. It is interesting to listen to for comparative purposes, but the revised version heard here is much more accomplished. It still tends to showcase the soloist more than most concertos do, but not to the degree found in the Tchaikovsky and Bruch concertos. The opening of the Sibelius concerto is one of the most beautiful in all of classical music.

• ◆ •

Walton: Violin Concerto, Cello Concerto, Symphonies, Overtures; Bournemouth Symphony Orchestra etc; Paavo Berglund, Bernard Haitink, André Previn, conductors; Ida Haendel, violin; Paul Tortelier, cello; EMI Classics 7243 5 73371 2 0

Listen to the violin concerto, written specifically for the tone and musical voice of Jascha Heifetz. This concerto from 1939 is not performed as often as it deserves to be. William Walton (1902–1983) went through many phases in his career in terms of influences: neoclassical, neo-Baroque (especially Handel), Stravinsky, and the flavor of melodies of his native England. A characteristic throughout his music is beauty of tone.

• ◇ •

Looking toward the future, a violin concerto was composed by Marc André Dalbavie (1961–   ) in 1997 that merits your attention if it is recorded.

• ◇ •

More violin listening:

My Favourite Kreisler; *Itzhak Perlman, violin; Samuel Sanders, piano*

Fritz Kreisler had a knack for writing showstopping violin music of technical brilliance and, if he didn't write it, he knew how to select the music of others to show off his talent. Perlman plays these with all the dazzling technique that is required, but also with considerable warmth.

Favourite Violin Encores; *Arthur Grumiaux, violin; István Hajdu, piano; Philips 446 560-2*

As the name of this recording indicates, this is the music that might follow the big pieces on a program. These works reveal the extroverted side of a violinist and are big crowd pleasers. Here are works by thirty different composers. Some—Kreisler, Paganini—are closely associated with the violin. One of the most famous violin encores is from an opera: the "Meditation" from *Thaïs* by Jules Massenet. Be sure to compare the "Ave Maria" by Schubert with the one by Gounod. Which one did you know already? This is vocal music adapted for the violin. Similarly, the

Träumerei from Schumann's *Kinderszenen* is adapted from piano music. Do you think this kind of music belongs only to the instrument (or voice) for which the composer envisioned it, or can it work on the violin, too?

Let us now move on to the other members of the string family.

STRINGING ALONG
Music for Viola, Cello, and Double Bass

The violin is such a famous and charismatic instrument that its larger siblings in the string family often are ignored in comparison. Only the cello has managed to acquire any meaningful status, largely because the soulfulness of its sound has appealed to so many composers. The double bass provides deep resonance in orchestras and chamber music ensembles, and has established a separate identity as a protagonist in jazz. The viola is the sad child of this family. For the most part it is ignored, and has had few opportunities to speak on its own. In orchestral music it usually provides slightly deeper contrast to what the violin is saying. In some chamber music it gains a prominent role, but for the most part it really is "second fiddle." Viola players are often the butt of jokes in the music world, where they are stereotyped as lacking the brilliance of the violin or the heart of the cello.

I believe the viola has been sadly slandered. To me it is the voice of a more experienced woman who has lived and sometimes suffered, in contrast to the younger voice of the violin. When the viola has the chance to speak on its own, as in the pieces we will discover below, it can be eloquent indeed. In addition to the violists you will hear, you should also look for performances by Yuri Bashmet, Jaime Laredo, Paul Neubauer, and Pinchas Zukerman.

♭ The Viola ♭

Berlioz: Harold in Italy; *London Symphony Orchestra; Colin Davis, conductor; Nobuko Imai, viola; Philips 416 431-2*

Inspired by Byron's *Childe Harold's Pilgrimage*, but especially by a request for a concerto for viola from the great Paganini, Berlioz wrote this early form of symphonic poem with an excellent part for solo viola. Ultimately Paganini rejected the work because it was not the showy concerto he had hoped for. Yet the work met with deserved great acclaim. Note that the basic musical motive (Berlioz's *idée fixe*) appears in each of the five movements but, unlike in the *Symphonie Fantastique*, serves not merely as a reminder of an idea but rather as a fount for musical development. This motive, played on viola, represents Harold. The conductor on this recording, Sir Colin Davis, is one of Berlioz's greatest interpreters and advocates. He is an example of a musician who develops a great affinity for the art of one composer and gains renown for his interpretations. One thinks of Arthur Rubinstein and Chopin, Murray Perahia and Mozart, singer Marilyn Horne and Rossini, cellist Jacqueline Du Pré and Elgar, and conductor Charles Mackerras and Leoš Janáček.

Telemann: Viola Concerto, etc.; *Academy of St. Martin in-the-Fields; Neville Marriner, conductor; Stephen Shingles, viola; London/Decca 430 265-2*

During his lifetime, Georg Philipp Telemann (1681–1767) was considered the great German composer, a remarkable fact when you realize that Bach and Handel were his contemporaries. Part of this acclaim was due to the fact that Telemann was very savvy about music publishing, realizing that the more his works circulated, the more fame and better commissions he would receive. He is probably most famous for the *Tafelmusik* (Table Music), which, in effect, is good music to dine by. It is excellent music indeed, and was widely performed in his lifetime. It remains today a very popular feature in the chamber music repertoire.

He also wrote a pleasing concerto for viola at a time when most composers wrote almost exclusively for solo violin. In so doing, he created a piece that would give work to violists for years to come.

• ∽ •

Panorama: Mendelssohn, listen to Octet for Strings; Academy of St. Martin-in-the-Fields Chamber Ensemble

The Octet for Strings is often described as the greatest work ever written by a very young composer. Advocates of Mozart and Rossini may dispute this assertion, but this is undeniably a very sophisticated piece of chamber music by the sixteen-year-old Mendelssohn. By turns full of tenderness and exuberance, it is also remarkable for the dialogue among the instruments. As you listen to it, picture yourself seated among the musicians rather than in an auditorium with them on the stage. Notice how they seem to breathe together, as often happens in great chamber music performances. Notice how at times the instrumental voices concur, and at other times contrast or diverge. You will notice too how beautiful and vital the music is for viola and you will acquire a deeper appreciation for this instrument.

• ∽ •

Bruch: Works for Clarinet and Viola; Orchestre de l'Opera de Lyon; Kent Nagano, conductor; Paul Meyer, clarinet; Gérard Causse, viola; François-René Duchable, piano; Erato 2292-45483-2

Listen to this recording, paying special attention to the viola.

• ∽ •

Walton: Concertos for Violin and Viola; Royal Philharmonic Orchestra; André Previn, conductor; Nigel Kennedy, violin and viola; EMI CDC7 49628-2

William Walton's introspective Viola Concerto shows off well many of the tonal properties of the instrument, which is rapturously played here by Kennedy.

♩ The Cello ♩

In our own times the foremost cellist, and one of the most beloved of all classical musicians, is Yo-Yo Ma. He combines remarkable musicianship with gorgeous tone and an openness to all kinds of repertory. New composers clamor to create works for him, such as the remarkable concerto for cello and orchestra by nonagenarian Elliott Carter which had its premiere in 2001. As we study the cello in this chapter, many of the recordings will feature other artists so you can contrast their styles and skills. Ma has recorded all of this music and you may wish to get his recordings to compare his performances with those you will be hearing, especially in the case of the Bach Cello Suites and the Dvořák Concerto.

The other titan of the cello in our time is Mstislav Rostropovich, though now he spends less time as a cellist and more as a conductor. Other great cellists past and present include Anner Bylsma, Gautier Capuçon, Pablo Casals, David Cohen, Jacqueline Du Pré, Pierre Fournier, Maurice Gendron, Natalia Gutman, Matt Haimovitz, Ofra Harnoy, Lynn Harrell, Gary Hoffman, Steven Isserlis, Ralph Kirshbaum, Julian Lloyd Webber, Mischa Maisky, Dimitry Markevitch, Truls Mørk, Gregor Piatigorski, Sharon Robinson, Leonard Rose, Heinrich Schiff, Denis Shapovalov, Janos Starker, Marta Sudraba, Paul Tortelier, Frances-Marie Uitti, and Pieter Wispelwey.

In listening to recordings of Yo-Yo Ma, Rostropovich, Casals, Du Pré, and all of the other artists you will hear, one of the things to focus on is tone. Depending on the music being played, the cello can be soulful, sensuous, or quite exposed and vulnerable. While the violin often has a singing sound that can have many of the same attributes as the cello and other string instruments, there is something particular about the cello that reaches a certain part of our being that no other instrument can achieve.

Another appealing aspect of the cello is the undeniable sensuality in its physical appearance and sound. Seeing Ma or another cellist embrace the instrument like a loved one as they make music together is a beautiful sight indeed. The cello is able to speak in so many voices, occupying a range of high, middle, and low that is more akin to the human voice than most other instruments. It is reassuring and direct, and few things are more affecting than sitting quietly in a small room listening to a recording or, better still, a live performance of Bach's Cello Suites.

J. S. Bach: Cello Suites; Heinrich Schiff, cello; EMI 7243 5 74179 2 1

Before listening to these suites, read the interesting essay in the booklet that comes with the CD. Some of the ideas may strike you as too Freudian, but they will provoke your thinking about the cello in interesting ways.

In case you did not notice, these six suites last more than two hours, making this one of the very longest solo works in all of classical music. The stamina, concentration, and involvement required of an artist is Herculean. Many of the same qualities are required of audience members who would choose to listen to a performance. Yet there is also a wondrous sense of a journey made together when one attends a performance of the suites, and you will be awed by a cellist who plays all this music from memory, not merely executing all of the notes perfectly, but filling this cycle with expressiveness and unique insights.

You might wish to listen initially to the first suite only, and devote yourself to careful appreciation. Then, after listening to and learning about the possibilities one has with the cello in music by other composers, come back to the Bach Cello Suites, take two wonderful hours' leave from the world, and sail away with some of the most singularly communicative music there is. In listening to Suite no. 1, notice how the cello seems to speak in many voices at once: the individual notes that are sounded at the same time become the vivid harmonic canvas that we hear.

· ✧ ·

Panorama: Haydn, listen to Cello Concertos nos. 1 and 2, Pierre Fournier, violin; Rudolf Baumgartner, conductor

These vivacious works in the classical style reveal Haydn's versatility yet again. Aside from 104 symphonies, fifty-two keyboard sonatas, plus operas, sacred music, and splendid instrumental music, he wrote concertos for many instruments, including violin, cello, flute, oboe, trumpet, horn, keyboard and organ. The first concerto calls for the sort of virtuoso display by solo instrument that one does not usually find in most of Haydn. Listen to both concertos and see if you can describe in words the many ways you think they differ.

• ◇ •

Panorama: Schumann, listen to the Cello Concerto; Leningrad Philharmonic Orchestra; Gennadi Rozhdestvensky, conductor; Mstislav Rostropovich, cello

This was probably the first important cello concerto of the nineteenth century, written late in Schumann's career (1849) when his hand injury had brought an end to his piano playing. He found the cello as a surrogate instrument and expressive voice. Its plangent sound in this concerto, in which the cello sings with the orchestra rather than apart from it, is notable indeed and pointed the way to works by Saint-Saëns, Dvořák, and Elgar.

• ◇ •

Dvořák: Cello Concerto; Tchaikovsky: Rococo Variations; Berliner Philharmoniker; Herbert von Karajan, conductor; Mstislav Rostropovich, cello; DG 447 413-2. For comparison, listen to the live recording by the New York Philharmonic, conducted by Kurt Masur and played by Yo-Yo Ma. This recording also has the rarely heard Cello Concerto by Victor Herbert (Sony SK 67 173).

What is referred to as Dvořák's Cello Concerto is actually his Cello Concerto no. 2. So incredibly popular is this work that it all but obliterated the first. In fairness, the first was left in sketch form at Dvořák's death and was orchestrated by the German composer Günther Raphael and performed posthumously.

Dvořák heard Victor Herbert, whom we think of primarily as a composer of operettas, play the premiere of his own concerto in Brooklyn in 1894, and was inspired to then write the work we are about to listen to. The Cello Concerto (as we shall now call it) was written in New York during 1894 and 1895, although Dvořák changed the ending upon his return to Bohemia and the death of his beloved sister-in-law. The concerto was written for his friend Hanus Wihan, who provided considerable technical advice as the concerto was being written.

Many cellists and music lovers will tell you that this is the most beautiful of all concertos for the instrument. Indeed, it is awash with gorgeous melodies, but also has intensity, expressiveness, and a remarkable balance between the solo cello voice and the many voices of the orchestra. Listen to this concerto as if it were a warm bath and you will best appreciate its unique appeal.

Brahms: Cello Sonatas; Yo-Yo Ma, cello; Emanuel Ax, piano; RCA 09026 63267-2; or Brahms: Piano Concerto no. 2; Boston Symphony Orchestra; Bernard Haitink, conductor; Emanuel Ax, piano; recording also contains Brahms D Major Cello Sonata, performed by Yo-Yo Ma; Sony SK 63229

Discover another facet of Brahms's art in his sonatas for piano and cello. One appears on Ax's piano concerto recording, while the other recording is devoted entirely to the sonatas. The emotionalism of Brahms find a soulmate in the sound of Ma's cello.

Elgar: Cello Concerto, Sea Pictures; London Symphony Orchestra; Sir John Barbirolli, conductor; Jacqueline Du Pré, cello; Dame Janet Baker, mezzo-soprano; EMI 7243 5 56219 2 4. For comparison, listen to the recording of the Elgar concerto along with the one by William Walton. Again, it is the London Symphony Orchestra; André Previn, conductor; Yo-Yo Ma, cello; CBS/Sony MK 39541. Or listen to Paul Tortelier's performance on the Walton on EMI Classics 7243 5 73371 2 0.

Before reading the notes below or the notes that accompany the CD, listen to Du Pré's performance of the Elgar Cello Concerto in a slightly darkened room, alone, and focus completely on the music. Only after listening to the music and thinking about it for a while should you read the following comments.

· ᴏ᷈ · ·

To be in physical pain, though horrible and shattering—or, at the very least, annoying—is nonetheless comprehensible because we can usually find words, such as *throbbing*, *burning*, or *stabbing*, to describe it. But in certain works of music we can find a nonverbal expression of pain that can bring us to the very essence of what pain means in a way that adjectives cannot. Such music, I believe, can be found in the Cello Concerto by Edward Elgar.

This is music that depicts pain and grief in a way that we can understand on a purely emotional and physical level, yet any words we might find would not do it justice. Here the cello tone is jagged, spiky, and raw, but no less beautiful than what we hear in Bach or Dvořák. It simply addresses another part of the human psyche in the unique way that a cello can.

Edward Elgar (1857–1934) is too often thought of as the musical embodiment of the British Empire because of his popular *Pomp and Circumstance* marches and works such as the *Imperial* March written on the occasion of Queen Victoria's Diamond Jubilee. He also wrote songs, two fine symphonies, oratorios, and a violin concerto. However, nothing would compare with the Cello Concerto (1919). It is usually called his response to the senseless devastation and the collapse of the old order that was the result of the First World War.

Yet there is so much more to find in this concerto. It is the work of a composer trying to write in a style different from what he was known for. He is taking an instrument that is known for its mellifluous tone and asking it to do something new. When, in the first movement, you hear the solo instrument being plucked while the orchestra cellos are being played with bows, it is a powerful metaphor for a whole range of ideas: the isolation of an individual who is different; the difficulty of being pained when others appear not to be; the unheard cry of plaintive melancholy; and many more ideas that I know you will discover on your own. As the concerto progresses the mood darkens and changes, though this is not a depiction of a progression into a personal hell. Rather, it is an exploration of the many facets and moods of grief. You might wonder what is happening when the music later takes on a cheery tone, but this could be thought of as a kind of elation that often comes hand-in-hand with despair. I will leave it up to you to decide what, if anything, the ending means.

The reason I asked you to listen to the music before reading my comments is that your take on this music may be entirely different from mine. It is important with all music, but especially with iconic works such as this one, to come to your own conclusions without initially being influenced by the prevailing point of view.

What you also may not have known is that this is a legendary recording, and Jacqueline Du Pré (1945–1987) would have achieved immortality with this performance even if she had done nothing else. She was twenty years old when this recording was made, yet she imbues her performance with such overwhelming pathos and life experience that one is agog in its presence. Because within a decade after this was played she would become ill and slowly lose her ability to perform, we look back through the sad story of her life and find prescience in the grief and pain she expresses when she was near the peak of her powers.

Now that you have explored the cello to some extent, return to the Bach Cello Suites. You will marvel that this is the same instrument that Elgar made sound so wrenching. Yet I think you will find the emotionalism and passion in Bach's cello as palpable as it is in Dvořák, Brahms, or Elgar.

• ∽ •

Other cello music worth listening to:

Lalo and Saint-Saëns: Cello Concertos; Orchestre National de France; Lorin Maazel, conductor; Yo-Yo Ma, cello; CBS/Sony MK 35848

Kodály: Sonata for Unaccompanied Cello; Britten: Suite no. 3; Henze; Capriccio; Berio: Les Mots sont allés; Matt Haimovitz, cello; Deutsche Grammophon 445 834-2

The highlight of this recording is the cello tour de force by Zoltán Kodály (pronounced Coh-die-ee; 1882–1967), a thrilling and audacious work. The recording also contains important cello music by leading twentieth-century composers Benjamin Britten (1913–1976), Hans Werner Henze (1926–), and Luciano Berio (1925–). All are expertly played by the talented Matt Haimovitz and will give you a sense of how the cello's voice could find expression in recent times in music written after the Elgar Cello Concerto (except for Kodály's 1915 composition).

Tavener: The Protecting Veil; Britten: Cello Suite no. 3; London Symphony Orchestra; Gennadi Rozhdestvensky, conductor; Steven Isserlis, cello; Virgin 7243 5 61849 23

Jonathan Harvey: Imaginings; Frances-Marie Uitti, cello; Harvey, conductor; Chill Out CHILLCD 007

At the time this book was published, there was not yet a recording of Elliott Carter's Cello Concerto, written for Yo-Yo Ma; its 2001 premiere, performed by Ma and the Chicago Symphony, was considered by many the year's most important musical event. Some listeners were impressed by the fact that a ninety-three-year-old composer could summon his muse yet again to write this bracing and challenging work, but the lasting impact will not be Carter's age when he wrote it, but that it will stand the test of repeated hearings and continue to enthrall the listener. Let us hope this concerto receives the recording it merits.

♭ **The Double Bass** ♭

The double bass provides its characteristic ballast to string ensembles and many orchestral works. You have heard it in many pieces of music. Return to these three recordings you own and listen to the music I suggest with special regard to the double bass. What role does this instrument fulfill in these works? Imagine how the music would sound if the double bass were not there.

- Panorama: Schubert, listen to the *Trout* Quintet.

- Panorama: Prokofiev, listen to the *Romeo and Juliet*.

- Janáček: Suite for String Orchestra, from Sinfonietta and Other Works; various artists; (London/Decca 448 255-2). Listen to the title suite.

Here are recordings for exploring other string instruments on your own:

- Harp: *The Art of Lily Laskine* (works by Handel, Boieldieu, Bochsa; Pierné); Lily Laskine, harp; RCA Victor 60023-2-RG

- Mandolin: Vivaldi, Concerti per Mandolini, I Solisti Veneti; Claudio Scimone, conductor; Ugo Orlandi, Dorina Frati, mandolins; Erato ECD 88042

THE WOODWINDS

A ccording to Luis Baptista, an ornithologist at the California Academy of Sciences, and an expert on such things, most forms of human music have an ornithological analogue: "Some birds sing like a flute, some like an oboe. There's even a Costa Rican bird that sings the first four notes of a Mozart concerto on a bassoon." Needless to say, humans and birds have listened to each other for good song melodies for as long as there has been music. For a moment, think back to the bird in *Peter and the Wolf*.

In an orchestral setting, the wind instruments provide the most immediate contrast to the sweeping sounds of the stringed instruments. Although, with only some variation, the violin, viola, cello, and double bass are all played in the same way, each wind instrument has different demands and presents a very distinct aural personality. Flutes are piping, bird-like, and often optimistic or wistful. Oboes are subdued, pensive, and somewhat exotic. For many listeners, the clarinet is the instrument of love, and one often finds it in music that suggests romance. In the same vein, the clarinet can be sensuous and sexy, whether in Mozart, jazz, or klezmer. The bassoon has a darker tone that can sound wise or weary.

When played alone or in combination, the woodwinds contribute a considerable degree to the composer's palette. Let us begin.

The flute, whose roots date back to the earliest of instruments, has one of the most recognizable and beguiling tones of all the instruments. In Mozart's opera *Die Zauberflöte* (The Magic Flute), the instrument protects the hero from harm every time he plays it. Tamino's flute-playing also has properties that make him very attractive to women. Many flautists also play the piccolo, a smaller and more piping version of the flute. Some of the most famous performers, past and present, include James Galway, Jean Pierre Rampal, Paula Robison, Ransom Wilson, Carol Wincenc, and Eugenia Zukerman. Galway in particular has a famous solo career, and Rampal was the grand master who opened the repertory for all who followed.

•   ᴐ   •

Beethoven: Symphony no. 5; Royal Concertgebouw; Sawallisch; conductor recording or the Philadelphia Orchestra; Eugene Ormandy, conductor (alternate)

Yes, you have heard this famous symphony more times than you can count even before I asked you to listen to it earlier on. But now you will hear it in a new way. While listening, pay attention primarily to the wind instruments, especially the flute. Pretend you are sitting right on stage, in the middle of this huge orchestra, and that you are the flute player. Notice every time the flute comes in. See how well your mind works at anticipating these entrances. You will be startled at how much you remember from the one previous hearing of the symphony since you began reading this book, not to mention all the previous times you have heard this music. In listening to this symphony with a bias toward the winds, ask yourself what it would be like if the winds were not there. Could the final movement, in which the flute engages in a musical parrying with the rest of the orchestra, have been the thriller it is?

•   ᴐ   •

Mozart: The Flute Quartets; Jean-Pierre Rampal, flute; Isaac Stern, violin; Salvatore Accardo, viola; Mstislav Rostropovich, cello; CBS/Sony MK 42320

Here is an example of chamber music performed by an all-star four-some. In the later stages of his career, Isaac Stern slowed down his solo performing and increased his devotion to chamber music. Only he could have summoned these leading exponents of the flute, viola, and cello to collaborate in this four-hander in which the flute has some justification in thinking of itself as a first among equals.

Although these men were all major stars at the time of this recording, make note of the egalitarian spirit that prevails here. This is the essence of chamber music performance.

• ⌒ •

Other flute music worth listening to:

Mercadante: Three Concertos for Flute; English Chamber Orchestra/I Solisti Veneti; Claudio Scimone, conductor; Jean-Pierre Rampal, flute; Erato ECD 55012

Though mostly considered a nineteenth-century opera composer, Mercadante wrote these charming concertos, performed here by Jean-Pierre Rampal, the great French flute virtuoso, who unearthed a great deal of treasurable music for flute so that he would have more things to perform.

Haydn: Concertos for Flute, Oboe, and Trumpet; various artists; Sony SBK 62 649

Haydn wrote fifty-two piano sonatas and a total of fourteen hundred works. In his extreme old age, wracked with arthritis, he remarked, "What a shame, for only now have I begun to understand the woodwinds." This recording shows off Haydn's dexterous use of individual instruments in a concerto context. If you happen to listen to the three concertos together, note how the orchestral scoring in each is suited to complement the sound and personality of the solo instrument.

Rampal's Greatest Hits; *Jean-Pierre Rampal, flute; CBS/Sony MK 35176*

Something of a showpiece of virtuoso flute playing.

Music for Panpipe:

Vivaldi and Telemann: Concertos for Flute and Orchestra; I Solisti Veneti; Claudio Scimone, cond.; Simion Stanciu "Syrinx," panpipe; Erato ECD 88166

♭ **The Oboe** ♭

It is almost inevitable that you will hear the oboe by itself when you attend a concert. It comes before the music-making starts. Notice that after the cacophony of fiddling and blowing dies down, you might hear the sound of the oboe come forth, playing an A. This is the moment when the orchestra tunes itself. When the A is sounded, all the other instruments will then tune themselves to that pitch. Once done, all of the sound stops and the conductor can enter. You may find some orchestras in which the A is sounded by the concertmaster or, if a piano is onstage, on the keyboard, but the oboe is the traditional source of that famous A pitch.

You remember the sound of the oboe from *Peter and the Wolf*. It represents the duck, which is slightly funny, somewhat awkward, and rather sad. This is a very particular instrument in that it can connote nobility and pathos in the same instant. Its sound, though not forceful, is unusually penetrating, and when played in an orchestral setting, you almost always hear it no matter what else is going on. So composers use this sound judiciously, and often with great effect. It is also quite compelling as a solo voice. Heinz Holliger is unquestionably the foremost exponent of oboe playing, though in recent years he has devoted more time to conducting. His recordings are usually the ones to turn to, although Paul Goodwin's performances of baroque oboe music (central to this instrument's repertory) are brilliant, too.

Albinoni: Concertos for Oboe; Camerata Bern; Hans Elhorst, conductor; Heinz Holliger, oboe; Archiv 427 111-2; and/or Telemann: Concertos for Oboe; Academy of St. Martin-in-the-Fields; Iona Brown, conductor; Heinz Holliger, oboe; Philips 412 879-2

Albinoni's concertos represent the oboe at its most beautiful. Notice how the instrument weaves and insinuates through the music, with a sound that could charm a snake right out of its skin. If you listen to the Telemann as well, compare the orchestral texture and tonal quality of the oboe in these works by two Baroque composers of more or less equal stature. Because you have the same oboist in both recordings, it is interesting to ask whether Holliger always has the same tone or whether he adjusts it to each piece he plays.

· ∾ ·

Haydn: Concertos for Flute, Oboe, and Trumpet; various artists; Sony SBK 62 649

See description in the Flute section above (page 381).

· ∾ ·

Mozart: Oboe Concerto, Bassoon Concerto; R. Strauss: Oboe Concerto; Weber: Andante e Rondo Ungarese; Philadelphia Orchestra, Eugene Ormandy, conductor; English Chamber Orchestra, Daniel Barenboim, conductor; John de Lancie, oboe; Neil Black, oboe; Bernard Garfield, bassoon; Sony SBK 62 652

This is an older recording that showcases fine music for oboe and bassoon. Mozart created a silken solo line for his oboe and bassoons here and, because it is Mozart, the music is not simply beguiling but also creates a gentle tug at the heart. You might find a little less feeling in Weber, though his music is admirable for its structure and balance.

· ∾ ·

♪ The Clarinet ♪

If it makes sense to you that Prokofiev would assign the oboe to suggest a duck, do you see how the clarinet is the surrogate for a cat? Deliberate, self-assured, clever are some of the instrument's traits, plus a playful sexiness (call it "kittenish"). All of these characteristics are immediately palpable in Gershwin's *Rhapsody in Blue*. Before proceeding with this section, go back and listen to that wonderful piece again, focusing entirely on the clarinet as a voice, perhaps that of the composer.

The clarinet is one of those middle-voiced instruments like the viola and the cello, or the mezzo-soprano and the baritone, that have a particular allure and honest directness. We are drawn to it because it sounds like us.

Much of the most famous music for clarinet is by Mozart and Carl Maria von Weber (1786–1826). Mozart wrote his music for a friend, Anton Stadler, and Weber wrote with the talents of one musician, Heinrich Bärmann, in mind. Brahms, for that matter, wrote clarinet music for his friend Richard Mühlfeld, and Aaron Copland had Benny Goodman. We who love music should be grateful for the many instrumentalists and singers throughout history who inspired composers to create music they might otherwise not have written.

On page 67 is a list of other composers who wrote for the clarinet, and we shall listen to some of these. Pay particular attention to the Poulenc Sonata for Two Clarinets (there is a recording by Sabine Meyer and Wolfgang Meyer). In addition, a little-known but very fine clarinet concerto is by Theodor von Schacht (1748–1823), who deserves to be rediscovered. When you learn Schubert's wonderful song "The Shepherd on the Rock," listen to the important role given to the clarinet. An important new clarinet concerto by Finnish composer Magnus Lindberg received its premiere in 2002.

• ❧ •

Mozart: Clarinet Concerto in A, K. 622, Clarinet Quintet in A; Boston Symphony Orchestra; Charles Munch, conductor; Budapest String Quartet; Benny Goodman, clarinet; RCA RCD1-5275. For contrast, listen to the concerto played on the bass clarinet by Charles Neidich with the Orpheus Chamber Orchestra (DG 423 377-2).

Although he was most famous as a jazz and big band performer, Benny Goodman could play classical clarinet pieces with the best of them, and his old recording of the Mozart Clarinet Concerto is still a touchstone. Most other fine clarinetists—including Emma Johnson, Reginald Kell, Thea King, Paul Meyer, Sabine Meyer, Charles Neidich, Antony Pay, David Shifrin, Richard Stoltzman, Frederick Thurston, and Lar Wouters van den Oudenweijer—have made works by Mozart and Weber central to their repertory.

For all the praise that has been heaped on the genius and wonder of Mozart, I think it is still fair to say that his music for clarinet is not given its due. He managed to make this instrument both sensuous and exhilarating. You can hear this in the concerto and the quintet, but I would also direct you to his most undervalued opera, *La Clemenza di Tito* (1791). In it, two showstopping arias, Sesto's "Parto, parto" and Vitellia's "Non più di fiori" are practically duets for voice and clarinet.

The concerto was written in 1791, Mozart's last year, in which his output was furious, prodigious, and brilliant. There has been considerable debate among musical historians as to how much of the concerto Mozart actually wrote. A manuscript exists with 199 bars in the composer's hand, but otherwise there might be other composers involved. Or not. As you listen to the concerto, see if you think it is pure Mozart, or if it has a diluted or mixed flavor. If you come to no definitive conclusion you are not alone. I think that at least the clarinet part bespeaks pure Mozart.

The quintet, composed in 1789, is richly enjoyable and deeply moving in the Mozartian way. By turns buoyant, romantic (especially the second movement), or deeply searching (in the last movement), there is a remarkable range of color and richness of melody. This is a brilliant and accessible way in to chamber music if you have not yet developed a feeling for it.

• ❧ •

Weber: Clarinet Concertos nos. 1 and 2, Concertino, op. 26, Grand Duo Concertant; English Chamber Orchestra; Paul Tortelier, Gerard Schwarz, conductors; Emma Johnson, clarinet; Gordon Back, piano; ASV DCA 747. For contrast, listen to Antony Pay and the Orchestra of the Age of Enlightenment, who perform an "original instrument" version of some of this music (Virgin VC 7 59002-2).

Carl Maria von Weber is often called the trailblazing composer of the Romantic movement, one whose musical and aesthetic ideas influenced Berlioz, Wagner, and many others. This approach is epitomized in the grand sweep and devotion to nature that are part of his opera *Der Freischütz*. The expression of Romanticism in the rest of his music is more subtle. In the clarinet pieces, which are among his best, there is a virtuosic solo line that relies on the personality and temperament of the clarinetist to a greater extent than one might see in Mozart, whose more Classical outlook incorporated the clarinet music into the texture created by the other instruments.

• ❧ •

Bruch: Works for Clarinet and Viola; Orchestre de l'Opéra de Lyon; Kent Nagano, conductor; Paul Meyer, clarinet; Gérard Causse, viola; François-René Duchable, piano; Erato 2292-45483-2

If you heard this piece before, you were probably listening to it from the point of view of the viola. This time, listen from the clarinet's side. Isn't it interesting how one can selectively parse the listening mechanism, as if you were an editor or a conductor? This is an important lesson, because you may have thought that hearing music can only be done in its totality, yet you have found that you can adjust your listening to the things you most wish to hear.

• ❧ •

More clarinet listening:

Brahms: Quintet for Clarinet and Strings, Horn Trio, Busch Quartet; Reginald Kell, clarinet; Testament SBT 101

This wonderful work is notable particularly for the vast range of expression that Brahms has created for the clarinet.

Copland: Clarinet Concerto (plus Stravinsky: Ebony Concerto; Bartók: Contrasts; Bernstein: Preludes, Fugues, and Riffs); Columbia Symphony Orchestra; Leonard Bernstein, conductor; Benny Goodman, clarinet; Sony SK 43337

Copland wrote a wonderful concerto geared specifically to the talents of Benny Goodman. This recording includes other pieces created for the great clarinetist, all of which show the clarinet's suitability in the modern classical idiom.

♪ The Saxophone ♪

Although the saxophone is of relatively recent origin and entered the orchestra gradually in the nineteenth and twentieth centuries, it has added a certain blue color (if I were to select a color) to the orchestral sound. I do not mean "the blues," but if the flute might be yellow or white, the trumpet a blazing reddish orange, and the tuba a rich brown, then I would describe the saxophone sound as bluish purple. You may have an entirely different vision of color for these instruments, and you should use the ones that make sense to you.

• ∾ •

Philip Glass: Concerto for Saxophone Quartet and Orchestra; Rascher Saxophone Quartet and the Stuttgart Chamber Orchestra; Dennis Russell Davies, conductor [on the recording of the Glass Symphony no. 2]; Nonesuch 79496-2

You might find this work challenging at first, but you should use it as a tonal exercise to refine your listening skills. Glass has used four different saxophones, each with its own character and tonal quality: soprano, alto, tenor, and baritone. If you think of these as human voices, each with its own way of saying things, this will be a way into your finding the merits of this worthy if somewhat difficult piece. Can you distinguish among the saxophone voices as you hear them and perhaps chart the variation directions the instruments take during the course of this four-movement concerto?

♩ The Bassoon ♩

The last work by the eclectic Camille Saint-Saëns was a bassoon sonata with piano. It is rarely played, but you can enjoy it for the rather dry and ironic tone the instrument takes. It is an interesting use of the bassoon's voice, and different from the somewhat retiring and grandfatherly feeling it often projects.

Vivaldi: Six Bassoon Concertos; I Musici; Klaus Thunemann, bassoon; Philips 416 355-2

The prolific Vivaldi proved particularly adept at finding subtlety and variety in the voices the bassoon could possess. While you might find that six bassoon concertos more than fills your quota, these works are interesting as an exploration of Vivaldi's art and for the way a less prominent instrument can assert its eloquence.

• ∽ •

Mozart: Oboe Concerto, Bassoon Concerto; R. Strauss: Oboe Concerto; Weber: Andante e Rondo Ungarese; Philadelphia Orchestra; Eugene Ormandy, conductor; English Chamber Orchestra; Daniel Barenboim, conductor; John de Lancie, oboe; Neil Black, oboe; Bernard Garfield, bassoon; Sony SBK 62 652

This recording is described above in the oboe section. If you have listened to the Vivaldi works beforehand, you will see again the mastery with which Mozart can give deep expressiveness to most any instrument he turns his attention to.

♪ The Recorder ♪

Music for the recorder lies somewhat at the periphery of the classical music repertoire, though it was more prominent in early and baroque music. If you are interested in listening to music for recorder, you will do very well to select recordings of performances by Michala Petri, its foremost interpreter.

THE BRASS FAMILY

A s you discovered in chapter 4, which was devoted to the voices of the orchestra, the brass family, led by the trumpet, provides attention-grabbing volume, radiance, and—need one say it?— brassiness to the palette of orchestral colors. But it would be crude and unfair to leave the description at that. The brass can have a blazingly sunny sound (think of Stravinsky's *Firebird*), bespeak nobility in the horns, have a sinister sound (such as the trombones in Gluck's opera *Orfeo ed Euridice*), or offer a stolidly reassuring oom-pah in innumerable passages for tuba.

Yet when brass instruments are allowed to speak on their own rather than providing texture or color to an orchestral ensemble, they can be as eloquent as the strings or the woodwinds. Think of Handel's trumpets in music you have already heard (*Water Music* and *Music for the Royal Fireworks*) to understand how grand and bracing the sound of these instruments can be. Let us explore other pieces in which brass has been used.

• ◇ •

♪ The Trumpet ♪

Just as jazz musician Benny Goodman excelled in the clarinet repertory (and Keith Jarrett has distinguished himself on classical piano), Wynton Marsalis has carved a career as a musician that covers all the great repertory for trumpet from Baroque to Louis Armstrong to Marsalis's own compositions. You should also find many outstanding performances by Maurice André, as well as Håkan Hardenberger, Adolph Herseth, Crispian Steele-Perkins, Edward Tarr, and Pierre-Jacques Thibaud.

Baroque Music for Trumpets *(various composers); English Chamber Orchestra; Raymond Leppard, conductor; Wynton Marsalis, trumpet; CBS/Sony MK 42478*

It may be a bit of a stretch, but not too much, to draw parallels between the Bach suites for solo cello and Baroque music for trumpets. Each is entirely evocative of the same era, and is distinct because the sound is so very personal and relies on the temperament and focus of the instrumentalist. He or she must make many decisions in learning the music, such as whether or not some beauty of tone can or should occasionally be sacrificed for emotional or dramatic emphasis. You might think that music so far removed from our own time is more austere, more circumscribed in performance style, and less emotive. This process of categorizing music and ascribing it a "style" is interesting academically, but these are first and foremost musical compositions that live and breathe *in performance*, not on the page. You might say that a jazz musician might bring a different—and perhaps corrupting—point of view to this music, and I would respond that a musician of any kind who is insensitive to what the music says would treat it with comparable lack of care. Marsalis brings care and freshness to the music, and makes it special because of his superior technique as a trumpeter combined with his attentiveness to the shape of phrases and the places where he can or should breathe. Needless to say, when a wind or brass instrumentalist takes a breath, this breaks up an arching musical phrase. Composers write music so that breaths can be taken, but some musicians do not have the breath control or the stamina to fulfill the requirements as written. Others, such as Marsalis and André, generally have the gifts and breath control to easily play the music as written. And when wind and brass players have supreme talents, they can often shape phrases securely and create additional musical pleasures for the listener. On this recording, pay attention not only to the beauty and expressiveness of the music but to Marsalis's breath control and the stylistic choices he makes. Then you will realize why great trumpet playing can be a source of great pleasure.

Further listening:

Trumpet Voluntary *(various composers); Wurttembergisches Kammerorchester Heilbromm; Jörg Faerber, conductor; Academy of St. Martin-in-the-Fields; Neville Marriner, conductor; Maurice André, trumpet; Erato ECD 55015*

• ᢍ •

Panorama: Haydn, listen to the Trumpet Concerto, played by Adolph Herseth, trumpet; Chicago Symphony Orchestra; Claudio Abbado, conductor; for comparison, listen to Wynton Marsalis on Haydn; Three Favorite Concertos; CBS MK 39310

As I have observed elsewhere in this book, music is inextricably linked to memory. It becomes part of what we know, who we are, and different pieces invariably evoke memories of events and emotions from our past. It may be as simple as the song that a couple picks for their wedding, or music that was played at an important moment. When we hear the music, we think of the event. Yet music can often summon moods that can come forth when we hear the music again (see my description of Mozart's Piano Concerto no. 23, page 304 to understand this better).

Haydn's Trumpet Concerto has a special place for me, as it does for many people. If I were to sift back through decades of musical and personal memory, I believe that this was the first piece of music I loved. I could not have been more than four years old, and I had already had the good fortune to be surrounded by all kinds of music. But this was the first piece of music that grabbed me, making me literally sit up and listen when it was played. I think because my father recognized this he played it often, so this concerto is tied up not only in my love of music but in my memories of him.

I think this is also the first piece of music of any length that penetrated my memory. As I write this I can easily summon the work and sing it aloud. This is no special gift of mine, but an example of how the mind of a young child is nimble enough (and empty enough!) that if you fill it with good music you are giving the child a lifetime gift. If you have a small child at home, start playing many of the pieces you are learning in this book (not too loud!) and you will give your child pleasure and help develop his or her mind and listening skills.

Listen to this piece as an exponent of the concerto form born in the Classical era with Haydn. Imagine other instruments in place of the trumpet, and then decide if the music that surrounds the trumpet could exist in a concerto for any other instrument, or whether Haydn created an orchestral texture (with its notable brightness) that is uniquely suited for trumpet. Written in 1796, five years after the death of Mozart and in the earliest stages of Beethoven's career, the piece stands as a bridge between past and future. Classical in style, it nonetheless contains the sort of virtuoso music for soloist that would characterize concertos in the two centuries to follow.

This concerto is also a famous example of how changes in musical instruments lead to changes in compositions. Anton Weidinger had only recently invented a new kind of trumpet, one with keys, that permitted more modulation of notes and sounds. As it happens, the keyed trumpet would be superseded in 1813 by the valve trumpet, which is still in use today.

♭ The French Horn ♭

Mozart: Horn Concertos; Philharmonia Orchestra; Herbert von Karajan, conductor; Dennis Brain, horn; EMI CDH 7610132

Mozart wrote these concertos with the talents of his friend Joseph Leutgeb in mind. At the time, the horn did not have valves, making the playing much more difficult than it is today. The result, you may find, is music that is beautiful and serene, but not as virtuosic as horn music written in later centuries. Here and there you will hear hunting motifs, but they are more for accent than as a dominant thought. Listen throughout for signs of musical humor. Mozart put numerous funny and irreverent moments throughout these works.

Brahms: Horn trio; Franck: Sonata for Violin and Piano; Itzhak Perlman, violin; Vladimir Ashkenazy, piano; Barry Tuckwell, horn; London/Decca 452 887-2

The unusual combination of violin, piano, and French horn makes for an unusual sound, but the results are beautiful because the voices of these three instruments stand in such high contrast. The second movement is especially effective.

Panorama: Richard Strauss, listen to the Horn Concerto no. 2, played by Norbert Hauptmann horn with Berliner Philharmoniker; Herbert von Karajan, conductor

Franz Joseph Strauss, father of the composer, was the principal horn player in the Munich Court Orchestra for forty-nine years, and among the earliest sounds that baby Richard must have heard are those of his father playing. The instrument figures prominently throughout his compositions, from an early horn concerto (1883) written while his father was still performing, through works such as *Till Eulenspiegel* and *Der*

Rosenkavalier, to the Second Concerto, composed when Strauss was seventy-eight. You will also hear the horn figure prominently when you study his *Four Last Songs*. For the horn player, the Second Concerto is much more difficult to play than the first. If you have listened to the Mozart concertos, then you will be agog at the virtuosic requirements of the Strauss. But you will find that this piece is not empty showmanship, but a fully fleshed and heartfelt musical expression of all kinds of moods and colors. That the horn is the principal voice rather than, say, the violin or the clarinet, is because of Strauss's particular affection for, and complete understanding of the technical capabilities of, the French horn.

• ✧ •

Janáček, Sinfonietta and other works; various artists; London/Decca 448 255-2

In *Mládí* (Youth), a sextet written in 1924 when he was seventy, Janáček uses the horn for wistful expression in a chamber music context. You will hear a facet of this instrument's coloration that is less evident in the rollicking music of Mozart, Strauss, and others.

• ✧ •

Other listening: the Horn Concerto by Oliver Knussen (1952–   ), written in 1994 for Barry Tuckwell, merits a hearing if you can find it in performance or on a recording.

♭ The Trombone ♭

Although the trombone has managed to make itself heard in important music through the centuries (see page 74), it does not often get a prolonged moment in the sun. In part because it is fiendishly difficult to play in a sustained way, and in part because its voice is rather unusual when listened to at length on its own. But it can be played with great suaveness, and I for one love to hear it.

Albrechtsberger, Wagenseil, L. Mozart, M. Haydn: Trombone Concertos; Northern Sinfonia; Alain Trudel, trombone and director; Naxos 8.553831

This recording is a real showcase for trombone virtuosity. Listen to it to understand the great variety of expression and flavor that this instrument can achieve as the solo protagonist in eighteenth-century works by several composers, including Mozart's father and Haydn's brother.

• ∾ •

Copland: Fanfare for the Common Man, and other works; various artists; London/Decca 448 261-2

Aaron Copland was an adept musical portraitist, whether of Abraham Lincoln, Billy the Kid, or the Common Man. It is a special skill that few composers master, and his music is full of knowing and sensitive vignettes that enable you to really envision the subject at hand. As you listen to these works, try to pay special attention for the sound of the trombone that lurks in and out in key places. This is the instrument's usual function, but Copland has made particularly effective and telling use of the trombone here.

♭ The Tuba ♭

Vaughan Williams: Symphony no. 5, Three Portraits from "The England of Elizabeth"; Concerto for Bass Tuba and Orchestra; London Symphony Orchestra; André Previn, conductor; John Fletcher, bass tuba; RCA Victor 60586-2-RG

Ralph Vaughan Williams carved a particular path through music, at times writing works that were overtly connected to English pastoral traditions and literary heritage, at other times creating beautiful and original music that had no discernible source of inspiration. The highly engaging Concerto for Bass Tuba takes this lonely and taken-for-granted instrument and lets it finally give voice to a much broader range of expression than one might ever imagine.

For more enjoyable listening to the music of Vaughan Williams, start with the collection called *Serenade to Music* (EMI CDM 7 64022) conducted by Sir Adrian Boult. Most of the recordings by this conductor of Vaughan Williams set a very high standard.

• ᴏᴗ •

Additional brass listening:

Canadian Brass: Any recording you hear by this popular ensemble will have works specifically composed for brass, along with compositions for other instruments that have been intriguingly adapted for brass ensemble.

Lutoslawski: Fanfare for the Los Angeles Philharmonic, *Concerto for Piano and Orchestra, Chantefleurs et Chantefables, Symphony no. 2; Los Angeles Philharmonic; Esa-Pekka Salonen, conductor; Paul Crossley, piano; Dawn Upshaw, soprano; Sony 67189*

The unusual piece *Fanfare for the Los Angeles Philharmonic,* for brass and percussion, is modern and compelling.

THE PERCUSSION
Bells, Whistles, Thunder, and a Beating Heart

I n your traversal of the classical music repertoire to this point, many if not most of the pieces you have heard use percussion instruments as part of the palette of orchestral colors. While pieces by Handel, Haydn, Gluck, and Mozart may have been limited to judicious use of drums and perhaps a couple of wood blocks and bells, and Beethoven may have added a few more drums for dramatic impact, subsequent composers found a great deal of expressive range in the sounds of the numerous instruments that you read about on page 76.

In the nineteenth century and especially the twentieth, cultural and commercial exchanges increased between Europe and other continents, bringing with them unusual-sounding instruments that composers began to work into their compositions. Then composers in the Americas embraced native and imported percussive instruments, and these too began to appear in more compositions. Many composers traveled widely and were influenced by the sounds of the places they went to; for example, think of pieces you have heard by Saint-Saëns, Ravel, Debussy, and Prokofiev.

Because you have subconsciously been exposed to so much percussion already, we will use this chapter to focus on works by two great twentieth-century masters, George Gershwin and Dmitri Shostakovich, to develop skills that you can then use in all of your listening. With

Gershwin we will discover how percussion can add unexpected atmospheric richness to music, and with Shostakovich we will see how these instruments can become fully participating voices in a major work rather than being peripheral and lightly applied color.

Panorama: Gershwin, An American in Paris, Cuban Overture, Porgy and Bess Suite

Paris, Cuba, and the rural South Carolina of *Porgy and Bess,* Gershwin's exquisite opera, are all distinctive places with particular aural connotations. Perhaps Cuba is the place for which you might be able to imagine a series of percussion sounds. Paris could be more of a challenge, because there is not, per se, a Parisian sound as there might be a Cuban one. *Porgy and Bess* is an opera from which this suite is derived. Its music is deeply rooted not only in atmosphere but in the characters' stories and emotions.

Start by listening to these three pieces, without thinking too much of their geographical and cultural associations. Listen to the music in an attentive and straightforward way, paying special attention to any appearances by percussion instruments. For now, don't think about what they may be trying to say, but simply focus on what they sound like.

Then go back to *An American in Paris* (1928). Because Gershwin wrote in both classical and popular idioms, his classical compositions are often undervalued by listeners who do not think of him as "serious." One of the miracles of his music is its great complexity and sophistication for performers, yet it is irresistibly fresh and immediate each time it is heard. Some of these works are among the first I learned more than forty years ago as a small child, yet I never tire of them. Repeated hearings do not evoke nostalgia, but rather inspire awe at how brilliantly they hold up.

You may have realized—and have been surprised—that of the three pieces you listened to, the one set in Paris has the most varied range of percussion sounds. This makes sense, if you think about it. Paris is a big city with an infinite selection of sounds and sensations. In this symphonic poem, Gershwin evokes Parisian sound brilliantly. Listen a second time and then try to envision the cityscape, asking yourself how, from the very first note, Gershwin uses percussion to create his portrait. There are bells, snare drums, timpani, xylophones, a wind machine, wood blocks, cymbals, and one other element: the *claxon*. This is French for the horn used on Parisian taxis. The composer purchased four of them while in Paris, and incorporated them into the music. Notice also that throughout the piece additional splashes of percussive sound appear and vanish in seconds, like little apparitions that sideswipe you on busy Parisian streets. Also note how often there is an undercurrent of drums, even when the brass, winds, or strings are playing the dominant music.

After pausing for a few minutes, listen to the piece again (this is no hardship, I assure you). This time, look at the whole title of the work: *An American in Paris*. It is fair to say that this piece has at least two subjects—the person and the city.

Gershwin was a cosmopolitan man who easily fell into the swirl of life wherever he was. It is probable that the American in the title is the composer himself. Ask yourself whether this sophisticate is agog at the Parisian scene, or more admiring and in the moment. My feeling, which you may or may not concur with, it that this American in Paris delights in the excitement but also has a touch of homesickness (in Gershwin's case, for New York). If you wish, listen again to *Rhapsody in Blue* to get a sense of his New York before listening to the piece about Paris.

As you listen, think about the emotions you hear in the percussion instruments. Is it possible that these sounds can evoke feelings in addition to actual things? Let your imagination run with the xylophone, the wind machine, and the wood blocks.

Now go to the *Cuban* Overture. What is arresting here is that Gershwin did not do the predictable thing by having a huge percussive presence, but rather uses the strings and horns to create a portrait of this place. For most of the piece we hear glimmerings of percussion, confirming what we would expect but then mysteriously disappearing. Only at 7 minutes and 40 seconds, within two minutes of the end of the piece, does a percussion section really kick in. Yet even here the percussion is more like seasoning in a savory dish than the dominant flavor.

Then go to *Porgy and Bess*. This music is so beautiful, emotional, and pictorial that even if you do not know the opera, you will overflow with feelings and emotions. Across a canvas of thirty minutes of music pay attention to the subtle ways that all sorts of percussion weave in and out. Notice that these are largely accents, and ask yourself whether any other instrument (a flute? a saxophone? a cello?) could communicate similar feelings. To understand what I mean, when you hear a xylophone, try in your head to replace it with a flute playing the same music. This will give you an insight into how composers decide which instruments to deploy for particular passages of music.

One parting thought: when you return to listen to any of these pieces again, especially *An American in Paris*, pick out the percussion instruments as individual voices that speak directly to you. This will contrast in meaningful ways with the manner in which percussion instruments are used in the Shostakovich symphony you are about to learn.

• ‹◊› •

Shostakovich: Symphony no. 5; Leningrad Philharmonic Orchestra; Evgeny Mravinsky; Erato 2292-45752-2

There is a truism, which I believe to be only somewhat true, that a composer (particularly a modern one) will only be fully appreciated and respected a hundred years after his death. By that standard, Gustav Mahler (1860–1911) is only now coming into his own and Dmitri Shostakovich (1906–1975) has a very long way to go. Mahler has finally seemed to have entered the pantheon of great composers, but I don't think Shostakovich will have to wait so long.

As a composer of fifteen symphonies, Shostakovich might have merited discussion in the earlier chapter on the symphony, yet there he probably would have disappeared into the mix, and he deserves better. His creative life neatly overlaps with the time frame of the existence of the Soviet Union and he, like Prokofiev, is thought of not so much as a

Russian composer but as a Soviet one. This is unfortunate because it superimposes a political system on him in a way that few other composers must endure. This is a Cold War and Western point of view.

Indeed, some of Shostakovich's music is political or, at least, expresses a reaction to the events of his times. The towering Seventh Symphony is called the *Leningrad* because it was largely inspired by the travails and heroism of the people of that city during a nine-hundred-day siege in the Second World War. When it premiered in 1942 it galvanized world attention to the bravery and sacrifices of millions in the USSR and elsewhere. Carl Sandburg called it music "written with the heart's blood," and Shostakovich was featured on the cover of *Time* magazine.

The Fifth Symphony, which we shall listen to, was premiered in 1937 on the twentieth anniversary of the birth of the Soviet Union. One can argue at great length as to whether Shostakovich identified himself as a Soviet composer rather than being a composer who lived in the Soviet Union. There is a difference. It is worth noting that he was, at various points in his life, honored and reviled by Stalin and other political leaders. His opera, *Lady Macbeth of Mtsensk*, was a stinging portrayal of values and mores in the Soviet Union, and Stalin was quite disapproving. Yet works such as the Seventh Symphony made him a hero. Later in his life, Shostakovich was often forced to make public pronouncements on behalf of the Soviet state that were so clearly not his own sentiments.

It is important to acknowledge the presence of this overwhelming political and social entity that was the Soviet Union when we think of Shostakovich, but we should not use it to define him. He was hardly the only composer for whom politics were important. Others include Mozart, Beethoven, Wagner, Verdi, Britten, and Bernstein. When we listen to the music of these composers, there are some explicit political references, yet almost all of it stands on its own terms as pure music. This is how you should listen to all of the music of Shostakovich and then, on repeated hearings, explore it for possible political implications.

Let us look at the Fifth Symphony. It was first performed on November 21, 1937, by Evgeny Mravinsky and the Leningrad Philharmonic. The recording I suggest you listen to features the same forces, but documents a live performance given on given on April 4, 1984. Shostakovich had been dead for nine years, and Mravinsky was an old man. He had lived with this work and much of the Shostakovich repertoire for decades (he conducted the premieres of symphonies nos. 4, 5, 8, 9, 10, and 11). The orchestra had the composer as part of its tradition, and his musical style and language were second nature to most of these musicians. This does not mean that they were bored and inattentive. Rather, Shostakovich was part of this orchestra's DNA the way Brahms and Mahler are for the Vienna Philharmonic and Copland and Bernstein are for the New York Philharmonic.

The symphony begins quizzically, mysteriously, as if posing a conundrum that will require significant working through to achieve some sort of epiphany. You will notice in this movement a dazzling variety of sounds, rhythms, and musical thoughts, as if all these random ideas are being tossed into the light in an effort to find some rational structure. Yet this music does have structure and balance if you listen carefully. The brass play an important role in this movement, along with a rich string section.

After fifteen minutes of this unusual and compelling music (this movement has remarkable originality and is unlike anything else you have listened to), the music ends with what sounds like a question mark. Then we come to a very short second movement. Shostakovich almost taunts us with its brevity, making us ask whether he left anything out, or whether this short, somewhat grotesque statement is complete unto itself. What do those squawking horns say to you?

The third movement then comes as a surprise with its lush strings, harps, and celesta. Notice that there is no brass whatsoever. Are we going in a more ethereal direction here? That is hard to say, because the sound of the instruments may tell us one thing, but the sound of the music tells us something rather different. There is great anguish and soul searching here, some of which may echo the feelings you experienced while listening to the Elgar Cello concerto. You will hear percussion here and there in the first three movements, but nothing prepares you for what is to come.

The transcendent final movement of this great symphony is justifiably famous. The brass reasserts itself, and the strings and woodwinds
join in to this throbbing dialogue among many instrumental voices that
culminates in one of the most thrilling climaxes in all of symphonic
music. Shostakovich carefully calibrated the tempos of this movement,
speeding things up and then slowing them down, and then, when we
have caught our breath, suddenly things accelerate again in a crescendo
that gets both louder and faster.

Although brass and other instruments are the protagonists for
much of the symphony, the final movement would be but a shadow of
itself if Shostakovich did not deploy an amazing array of percussion.
You will hear timpani that are the heartbeat of the whole enterprise,
along with snare drum, bass drum, triangle, cymbals, tam-tam, bells,
xylophone, harps, plus piano and celesta. Here we should think of the
piano as a truly percussive instrument rather than the means for the
soulful expression of one musician.

While listening to this movement, think of each percussion
instrument as an important voice that is part of this gathering of voices,
this grand traversal from the chaotic, random, and unformed through
the spiky adolescent flavor of the second movement, and on to the brilliant alignment of the musical stars into an extraordinary denouement.
In other words, if Gershwin used percussion instruments in the works
we studied as a means of atmospheric color, Shostakovich does not
make these instruments stand apart, but brings them right to the heart
of the action.

Listen to the symphony attentively before reading any further.
Remember, if the percussion represents anything particular, it is likely to
be ideas and temperaments rather than car horns and footsteps.

• ∽ •

Now that you are probably rattling from the great finale, there is more to
think about. I had told you that the Fifth Symphony was performed on
the twentieth anniversary of the birth of the Soviet Union. You probably

thought that the work was a specific homage to the young, exciting, and struggling nation. It may have sounded to you like so much patriotic chest-pounding.

You should know that Shostakovich had a different, and very specific thought, for this work. "The theme of my symphony is the making of a man," he said. "I saw man with all his experiences as the center of the composition. . . . In the finale, the tragically tense impulses of the earlier movements are resolved in optimism and the joy of living." So perhaps now you might think of this piece less as Soviet propaganda and more as an heir to some of the humanistic pronouncements of Beethoven, or the outsized expressions in Richard Strauss's tone poem *Ein Heldenleben*.

You might ask, could all of this sound, this tectonic shifting that seems to speak for a whole nation and ideology, really be about one man? When you discover that the answer is yes, you will then find the key to this work, that it is about the potential for human greatness in each of us. Then you will understand what Shostakovich was trying to say. If you listen to the final two movements again, and notice the central role of the percussion instruments in the making of a man—the engineering and hardwiring that is taking place in musical terms, then you will understand why this work is considered so great.

Additional Listening

Bartók: Concerto for Orchestra; Music for Strings, Percussion and Celesta; RIAS-Symphonie-Orchester Berlin; Ferenc Fricsay, conductor; Deutsche Grammophon 447 443-2

Bartók: Sonata for Two Pianos and Percussion, etc.; Martha Argerich and Nelson Freire, piano; Deutsche Grammophon 439 867-2

The time has probably not yet arrived for the music of Béla Bartók (1881–1945) to receive the acclaim it deserves. The same could probably be said for his fellow Hungarian, Zoltán Kodály. Their music is quite accessible and immensely gratifying, but has had few advocates aside from Hungarian conductors such as Georg Solti, Ferenc Fricsay, and Antal Dorati. Thus, these works have been stuck in the category of musical nationalism rather than being appreciated on their own terms.

These two recordings contain compositions in which Bartók makes inventive use of percussion. The Music for Strings, Percussion, and Celesta presents complex rhythms using an unusual lineup of instruments: side drum, snares, bass drum, kettle drum, tam-tam, xylophone, piano, harp, cymbals, and celesta. The finale is fabulous.

In addition, you should listen to his Concerto for Orchestra, a great work that is finally appearing with some regularity on concert programs.

As this book was going to press, a new work by Philip Glass, the *Concerto Fantasy for Two Timpanists and Orchestra*, received rapturous reviews in its London premiere and seems destined for further performances.

EARLY MUSIC
From These Roots

Almost every composer we have explored together was born around the late seventeenth century (Bach, Handel, Vivaldi, Telemann) or later. The musical eras we have studied extend from the high Baroque (1700–1750), the Classical era (1750–1825), and Romanticism and Nationalism (most of the 1800s) to music of the twentieth century, including everything from the Second Viennese School (Schoenberg, Berg, Webern) to all the various movements from the Second World War to the current day.

You might question why I did not start you at the very beginning of musical history and bring you to today. Part of my thinking is that this is not primarily a history book, and moving you along a timeline would not give you the skills you need to really listen to and absorb the centuries of music that is referred to as "classical." Making you listen to ninth-century music before eighteenth-century works would probably deter you from listening further. This is not because early music, as it is called, it not likable, but because you probably had no exposure to it before opening this book. Even if you did not grow up in a musical environment or study it in school, through osmosis you have heard works by Bach, Handel, Haydn, Mozart, Beethoven, Tchaikovsky, Dvořák, Ravel, Gershwin, Copland, and Bernstein. You would be more receptive to learning these first rather than pieces by Hildegard von Bingen, Gesualdo, or Monteverdi.

> KEY CONCEPT: *Terms such as "early music," "sacred music," "secular music," "classical music," and others were not products of their times, but subsequent attempts by historians and musicologists to define and categorize the past. In most cases, composers and musicians made "music," and little further definition was required. Only as musical history became longer, and composers reacted to the past, was additional terminology employed.*

Early music is, in fact, most of musical history. From prehistory until about 400 A.D. music probably occupied the two principal areas it would continue to hold until practically the year 1800. Some music was for popular entertainment, for the diversion and enjoyment of the listener, whether he be a king or a peasant. We call this secular music. Then there is music that is referred to as sacred music, which is usually connected to religious ritual. I like to think of a third type of music, ceremonial music, which can draw from sacred and secular music and has the specific purpose of being for a grand occasion, usually royal. It is probable that opera rose from the ceremonial form of music, although sacred and secular music made their significant contributions as well.

Our knowledge of ancient music (up to the time of the Romans) is based more on what people of that era wrote about it than what we actually can hear of it. Music was an oral tradition passed from one person to another, and its tradition and evolution were due to this human contact. Music-making on one's own could be pleasurable, but making music for and with others was an exciting communal event. It still is.

Do not think that with the arrival of musical notation as we now know it (devised by Guido d'Arezzo, who died in 1050) that all music was then written down. In fact most of the world's music until quite recently was passed down orally and through shared performance.

Again, just because one form is called Western Classical Music does not mean that it was all music. There is magnificent music from all the world's cultures dating back thousands of years. Even much of early jazz was not written down.

The most prolific composer in history goes by the name Anonymous. We hear his or her music all the time throughout the world. Think of architecture. There are many famous buildings whose designers and builders we can name. A few of them have a style we quickly recognize, such as Palladio or Wright or Gehry. But for almost every building in the world, we have no idea who designed it and what he was aiming to achieve. The same goes for music. What we are studying in this book are the famous musical structures, the ones with a pedigree and a great creative artist behind them.

Ideas about music go back to ancient times. Pythagoras wrote about structure of musical forms. St. Augustine (354–430) wrote about music, especially its ability to drive a listener toward good or evil. Boethius (480–524) was a Roman philosopher who wrote *De institutione musica*, a treatise in which he attempted to describe the musical ideas of the Greeks.

Ambrosian Chant: *In Dulci Jubilo; Alberto Turco, director; Manuela Schenale, soloist; Naxos 8.553502*
In Passione ed Morte Domini (*Gregorian Chant for Good Friday); Nova Schola Greogriana; Alberto Turco, director; Naxos 8.550952*
Jerusalem: *Discantus Ensemble; Brigitte Lesne, director; Opus 111 OPS 30-29*

From the fall of the Roman Empire until the early twelfth century most of the "classical" music we still know of came from the Catholic Church. Jewish liturgy, with its chanting, influenced Christian observances. It appears that in Syria, where Christian and Jewish faiths coexisted, antiphonal chanting (in which two choirs alternated singing) began.

Soon after, as Latin replaced Greek as the language of the church in the Mediterranean, music was adapted to that language's sounds (remember that Latin was the forerunner of Italian, which still remains the fundamental language of music). Milan was a major center of Christianity because of the presence of a native son, St. Ambrose. He was bishop of Milan and is said to have introduced antiphonal music to the Catholic Church in Europe. To this day, something ambrosial is honeyed and flowing, as his voice was said to be. In Rome, St. Cecilia is the patron saint of music, but in Milan it is St. Ambrose. The city's opera house, Teatro alla Scala, has its opening night every December 7, this being the day that all of Milan celebrates the saint's birth.

In Rome, Gregorian chant, named for Pope Gregory I (born 540, ruled 590–604), saw the widening of the types of chant to be used in the Catholic liturgical service. It was under his leadership that melodies began to be codified, and he created the first *schola cantorum* to teach singing. We don't know too much about it because the music that we today call Gregorian chant dates from the year 800 and is really an amalgam of chant traditions from Italy, France, and Spain. This chant, whatever we call it, differed from antiphony because the music-making was composed of one chorus, all of whom sang the same music in unison.

Whether Gregorian or Ambrosian, the *chant* (which means singing in unison rather than a mere pronouncing of words) was the dominant musical form. The word root is the French *chanter*, to sing. Chanticleer, whose name has the same origins, is an excellent San Francisco–based group whose specialty is early music. Another way of saying *unison* is monophony, meaning that everyone is singing the same thing at the same time. But they do not all sound the same even if the notes and words are the same. When, earlier in the book, you learned about instruments as being voices in the orchestra, the idea came from a gathering of human voices of various colors, pitches, and characters into a chorus.

Plainchant (or plainsong), as this music was known, was passed down by oral tradition. There were early attempts at notation of music, but the great advance did not come until the innovations of Guido d'Arezzo.

This era also saw the early development of polyphony—music in which two or more melodies are heard at the same time. These were first described as the *vox principalis* (the original melody) and the *vox organalis* (a second voice heard at the same time as the main one). Pérotin (1160–1225), an early composer in the School of Notre Dame in Paris, revolutionized polyphony by expanding it to three and then four voices. Through the centuries, polyphony would wax and wane as a preferred style, but it would always influence the way composers considered the possibilities they had at their disposal.

The motet, from the French *mot*, meaning "word," was also born in the School of Notre Dame in the thirteenth century. This was polyphony in three voices, with the different musical lines sometimes sung at different speeds, and with different words. This gradual evolution of variety in musical expression would help enlarge the compositional tools composers could use.

· ◇ ·

Hildegard of Bingen: A Feather on the Breath of God; *Gothic Voices; Christopher Page, director; Emma Kirkby, soprano; Hyperion CDA66039*

The German abbess Hildegard von Bingen (1098–1179), along with Pérotin, is among the earliest known composers and has in only recent years achieved a fame that make her the most famous early composer. A daughter of nobility, she was sent to live in seclusion in a walled-up cell, which gave her a lot of time to reflect and give free rein to her fantasy. Among the things she did was to create her own language, which she referred to as *lingua ignota* (unknown language). This was used to record her prophetic visions, both in poetry and music. Many of these were gathered in her *Symphonia harmonie celestium revelationum*, which includes more than seventy lyrical poems with their music. She later left the convent with other nuns and formed a community near Bingen, where she continued to write poems and music. As you listen, try to hear the ecstasy that was central to Hildegard's visions. Although the music is relatively narrow in scope, it is still highly communicative and expressive.

• ❧ •

Music of the Troubadors: *Ensemble Unicorn, et al.; Naxos 8.554257*

Almost all of the early music we have explored to this point has been of religious inspiration. Some of the earliest secular music was of the troubadors, poet-musicians who sang of courtly love in twelfth-century France. They did not sing in Latin, but in *langue d'oc*, which has given its name to a region of southwestern France. In northern France, there were comparable musicians called *trouvères*. This recording has excellent program notes and well-translated texts so you can follow along as you listen. The title character in Verdi's popular opera *Il Trovatore* is, in fact, a troubadour. The music of the troubadors could be both monophonic and polyphonic.

• ❧ •

Close Encounters in Early Music; *various composers and artists; Opus 111 OPS 3000*

Listen to this recording if you wish to get a more varied sense of the sounds of sacred and secular early music around Europe.

• ❧ •

The Glory of Early Music; *various composers and artists; Naxos 8.554064*

Music would take a great leap forward in the first half of the fourteenth century with the development of the *Ars Nova* (New Art) movement in France. Lest you think that movements are only a phenomenon of the past three centuries, here we discover otherwise. The term *Ars Nova* was first used by a composer and musical theorist named Philippe de Vitry (1291–1361) as the title of a document he wrote around 1320 to expound on his new views. The most important break with the past is that music could be written in numerous rhythmic patterns. In addition, secular texts were more readily accepted for music by "serious" composers such as Guillaume de Machaut (1300–1377). Gradually, the wall between sacred and profane broke down and secular themes of love and exaltation of nature were acceptable. So too were religious allegories that were not specifically related to music for worship.

Most important, in the years between 1350 and 1500, polyphony spread everywhere and became an esteemed musical form. Among the leading composers in this era were Guillaume Dufay (ca. 1400–1474), who was instrumental in the development of the mass and other religious works, and Heinrich Isaac (1450–1517), who wrote more than one hundred polyphonic mass settings but also wrote secular songs in French, German, and Italian. Also important were Francesco Landini (1325–1397), who brought the *Ars Nova* style to Italy, and John Dunstable (1390–1453) who expanded polyphonic writing into England.

• ∽ •

Music of the Spanish Renaissance; *Shirley Rumsey, lute; Naxos 8.550614*

So much of Renaissance music was polyphonic and this led to the melodic music of the Baroque era. Some of the most vivid came from the courts of Spanish royalty. It was often polyphonic, but also had influences of the troubadors from the north and Moorish flavor from the south. Instruments such as the lute, *vihuela,* and guitar became indispensable, and led to the Spanish tradition of a singer harmonizing with the instrument being played. As you listen to this recording, make note of the particular sounds of the instruments and ask yourself how they flavor the sound—and the mood—of this music. Notice too how the voice of a singer interacts and draws inspiration from the instruments.

· ∽ ·

Gesualdo: **Prince of Madrigalists;** *Marilyn Horne and other artists; Sony SBK 60313*

The madrigal was one of the leading musical innovations in Italy, and one of the first examples of a nation establishing a distinct musical style. The origins of the word are unclear. It may come from *mandriale*, suggesting the pastoral subjects found in the first madrigals, or *matricale*, "in the mother tongue."

There were actually two flowerings of madrigal singing in Italy. The first was in the fourteenth century; the songs in two or three voices that exalted nature and pastoral love. This was one of the first examples of secular polyphony. By "voices" we can also mean a high singing voice (usually tenor) accompanied by two lower-voiced musical instruments.

The second form of madrigals came in the sixteenth century and could be music with five or six voices (again, "voices" here would suggest both the human voice and musical instruments). Carlo Gesualdo (1560–1613) was one of the leading madrigal composers. He wrote about 110 pieces for five voices. His sophisticated arrangements of these voices included unusual chords and juxtapositions of sounds. Gesualdo's madrigals are among the best and, as you listen to them, you will be able to pick out trends and styles that began with Gesualdo but seemed to be the work of much later composers. He was famous for word-painting, in which there were particularly felicitous connections between what the word meant and how it sounded when sung. These are the beginnings of expressive art songs and, later on, opera.

In England, the madrigal was more lighthearted, even risqué. All sorts of outstanding music was written in England during the Renaissance, which is thought to have been the last golden age in British music until the twentieth century. Among the great composers were Thomas

Morely (1557–1602), John Wilbey (1574–1638), Thomas Tomkins (1572–1656), Orlando Gibbons (1583–1625), Thomas Weekles (1576–1623), and John Dowland (1563–1626). In a class by himself was William Byrd (1543–1623), who wrote more than two hundred religious and secular compositions based on English texts, eighty motets, one hundred keyboard pieces, and important religious music in Latin. Along with Thomas Tallis (1505–1585), who may have been his teacher, Byrd obtained monopoly rights from Queen Elizabeth I for music publishing in Britain.

• ∽ •

Monteverdi: Vespro della Beata Vergine 1610; *Taverner Consort, Choir and Players; Andrew Parrot, conductor; Virgin Veritas 7243 5 61662 2 6*

Claudio Monteverdi (1567–1643) one of the great radicals in music, was the first important opera composer. He began as a madrigalist and also devised a way to divide the orchestra into sections, enabling them to listen to one another as they played. This division, and the increased thought about instrumentation it implied, meant that composers changed the way they thought about their work. It also produced a more dramatic sound for the listener.

Monteverdi learned about the importance and technique of combining words and music so that each would become more expressive when paired with the other than when they stand alone. Each holds a part of what the other needs for a sense of completion; when merged, they create something that is more interesting. The sound, volume, and direction of the music is determined in part by sound and meaning of the words. This talent, developed for opera, also influenced secular and sacred music, as you can hear in this valuable recording of one of Monteverdi's major religious works.

• ∽ •

Other important composers worth finding out about who come at the end of early music and lead to Baroque:

- Emilio de' Cavalieri (1550–1602) claimed to write the first oratorio, but it was more of a spectacle than a somber oratorio allows. It had actors, costumes, and ballet, making it more like an opera.

- Giovanni Carissimi (1605–1674) played it straight and can probably be credited with writing the oratorio as we know and love it today. His most famous is *Jeptha*, which has three main characters and a narrator. In addition the chorus is fully integrated into the action—indeed, it is a character—and so is the orchestra. Here are the roots of opera.

- Heinrich Schütz (1585–1672) was probably the foremost innovator in Germany in this era, creating the more sober German form of oratorio that Bach, Handel, and Haydn would build on and do great things with.

- Jean-Baptiste Lully (1632–1687) wrote operas and grand spectacles. He was one of the first conductors, which led to his demise. He used to bang out rhythm with a pole. Once he impaled his foot with it and soon died of gangrene.

- Henry Purcell (1659–1695) led a short, productive life, but was England's greatest composer before the twentieth century. Whether in songs, operas (especially *Dido and Aeneas*), or instrumental music, he distinguished himself for the easy beauty and expressiveness of his music.

• ◌ •

You have already listened to music by Johann Sebastian Bach. Listen to the following recording to hear how Bach drew from early music and pointed toward the future:

J. S. Bach: Cantatas 51, 93, 129: Münchener Bach-Chor und Orchester; Karl Richter, conductor; Edith Mathis, Anna Reynolds, Peter Schreier, Dietrich Fischer-Dieskau, singers; Archiv 427 115-2

The style and sound of the cantata can seem to be a direct outgrowth of some early music. Listen to this recording now without actively studying it, just to have a sense of the musical progression from early music into Baroque and then to the Classical era. We will be listening to Bach cantatas soon.

• ⟨∿⟩ •

Several modern composers have adapted or been influenced by early music. Two prime examples are Ottorino Respighi (*Ancient Airs and Dances*) and Ralph Vaughan Williams (*Fantasia on a Theme by Thomas Tallis*). These are good places to start and then work your way into the sounds of early music.

THE SINGER'S ART
Lieder and Vocal Music

The song literature takes us deeper into understanding the human condition than anything else I can think of.
—Phyllis Curtin

For many singers in classical music, standing alone on a stage without a costume or much makeup, no scenery except a grand piano, is the most daunting but thrilling expression of their art. In opera they get to play a character, to interact with other singers *in front* of an audience without directly relating to it. A large orchestra pit separates the singer from listeners who, for a singer, are in a distant darkness.

In a vocal recital, the exciting trappings of opera are stripped away, and replaced by the splendid pleasure of intimate and direct communication between singer and audience, and collaboration between singer and pianist. Here, every word has meaning, every gesture must be telling, and if the singer assumes the character of the person in a song, it is for an intense few minutes rather than three hours. Acting, when it happens, is more epigrammatic than histrionic, so the singer's voice, face, and body must all be fine-tuned and synchronized to become one expressive instrument. In fact, in a recital context a big operatic voice must almost always be scaled down to the intimacy that is inherent in so many songs.

To find all the meanings in the words and the music, the singer must study and reflect constantly. And the singer has to have lived! So many of the experiences described in these songs are about the human condition, but someone who has not experienced the many vicissitudes that life can throw our way is less likely to bring emotional heft and insight to a song. Phyllis Curtin, who in her great thirty-eight-year career as a singer of recitals and opera, became a leading exponent of superb recital artistry, then took all of her experience to become a superb teacher of young singers. One of her specialties is American song literature, and she has been a leading interpreter of and advocate for this wonderful and underappreciated branch of classical music. Her interpretations of Copland songs, available on CD, are legendary. Even when you listen to these old recordings by the singer in her youth, you realize that she studied, thought, and lived.

Enrico Caruso, arguably the most famous tenor in opera history, once said that to sing one needs a great voice, a great technique, a fantastic memory, and to have suffered a great deal. Perhaps it is asking too much of a singer that he or she must also have suffered, but we should at least ask that the singer has lived fully and developed enough human understanding and empathy that he or she is able find the emotional honesty to express what words and music mean.

Then, very important, when it comes time to perform, the singer must be able to detach just enough so that she is in complete control of her vocal resources and abilities. The study of a song (or an operatic role) and the evolution of its performance must come through long periods of reading the words, reflecting on their meaning, and finding connections to one's own experience. As the song grows within the singer, it takes on a life of its own. The singer must communicate all of this, combining skill and insight. In musical performance, but especially in art songs (as much of the classical repertoire is called), craft plus soul equal art.

Artifice shows, and few singers can get by on artifice for very long. If the singer cannot feel and communicate the song, we audience members perceive that and are seldom engaged by the performance.

This dictum is not the exclusive province of classical singing. The honesty and insight we hear in the performance of great gospel singers—Mahalia Jackson, Marion Williams, Shirley Caesar, to name three—combine with their brilliant singing skills to make for great

music. In folk music, Joan Baez, Judy Collins, and others have this quality. So does Emmylou Harris in country music. In the prime of his
career, Frank Sinatra had it, and late in his career Tony Bennett has fully
blossomed with it even if his vocal resources are no longer what they
were. It does not matter, because the humanity, the simplicity, and the
honesty are there, and listening to Tony Bennett is an immensely gratifying experience.

The pop singer George Michael has a gorgeous voice, a splendid
technique, considerable intelligence, and has probably has done his
share of living and suffering. At his best he ranks with the greats, but
very often does not integrate his attributes to make for definitive performances. But he has the potential to do so. Most other current pop
stars do not have the makings for this kind of total performance.

Ella Fitzgerald had such a dazzling technique that it was often
overlooked how entirely she got under the skin of a song and made it
unmistakably her own. Few singers in any category can compare with
her. Billie Holiday, at many stages of her career, could not control her
technique, but imbued her singing with so much feeling—she really did
suffer—that listening to her becomes hard because we sense that we are
eavesdropping on something so very intimate. Yet her artistry was never
less than compelling, and she is remembered as a great artist. The same
thing could be said about both Janis Joplin and Judy Garland.

Aretha Franklin is in a category unto herself. She brings together
every necessary attribute for great singing and can traverse so many
styles so well that when she ever so occasionally shows a weakness we
need to remind ourselves that she is indeed human. I am not sure she
could handle a group of art songs by Schubert or Mahler, but one never
knows, and I would be glad to be proven wrong.

In the realm of classical art songs, which may be sung with piano
or full orchestra, the singer must summon very different skills than
those required to sing opera. In opera a singer plays a character, is in
costume and makeup, and is part of an ensemble that stands amid grand
scenery. A story is told in the arc of hours.

In a recital setting there is only one singer on the stage, the interaction is not with other singers but with the audience. The singer wears a gown, a suit, or evening clothes, and communicates stories and quick-changing emotions in minutes. We focus more closely on her or his face and eyes. A hand gesture has more meaning because, in the strictest sense, the singer is not acting. Yet if the song is, say, about a young man in love, a singer might try to suggest that not only with his voice and diction, but also with his physical presence. Exaggeration does not work—it is artifice. But underplaying can be dull too, so a singer must find a middle ground that communicates music, words, and ideas effectively.

The creation of a recital—a series of songs performed by a singer, almost always with a pianist as a musical partner—involves many decisions. First, the singer must select songs that are congenial to his or her voice. While composers may have written particular songs with a particular voice in mind (such as Schubert's *Winterreise* for baritone), sometimes a talented singer can transpose this music to suit another type of voice. The next decision is whether the singer feels wholly comfortable in the languages the songs are written in. Memorization of words is a poor substitute for the intimate knowledge of words' nuances and sounds, which are essential for a singer to really get into the meaning of a song.

Then the singer must decide whether the subject matter of the songs is meaningful and compelling. If the songs do not first touch the singer in some way, he will probably have a hard time making them matter for his listeners. Songs often come in groups, and singers will usually sing the group because collectively the songs have more weight then individually. There are also many song cycles that are meant to be sung together, and in order, because they chart different and important psychological and musical journey.

A singer doing several song groups on a program may seek to have a thematic or musical thread that links them. For example, I once heard a wonderful recital on Mother's Day given by Elisabeth Söderstrom in which she sang twenty-four songs by twenty-two composers that communicated the world of motherhood. It was brilliant because the artist had clearly given it so much thought and then sang rapturously, with James Levine partnering her wonderfully at the piano. Yet it is also possible for a singer to do unrelated song groups with no connective thread, so that moods can change and audience members can hear versatility in languages and ability to communicate many different states and ideas.

To begin to understand how a singer needs to plumb a song, we will focus on just one song, "Das irdische Leben," from Gustav Mahler's settings of twenty-one songs drawn from texts of *Des Knaben Wunderhorn* (The Young Man's Magic Horn). This is an anthology of poems gathered from centuries of German-language folk tradition that was printed in the early nineteenth century to foster a sense of German nationalism. The title of the book, and of Mahler's settings, is named for the first poem in the first volume of the anthology. Mahler composed these songs for two voices and orchestra, but many singers select to perform them in recital with piano. Mahler was deeply influenced by these poems for their depiction of nature as well as scenes from daily life. He would use some of this music later on in his Second, Third, and Fourth symphonies.

Mahler: **Des Knaben Wunderhorn;** *The London Philharmonic; Sir Charles Mackerras, conductor; Ann Murray, soprano; Thomas Allen, baritone; Virgin UV 7243 5 61202 2 0; or Royal Concertgebouw Orchestra; Leonard Bernstein, conductor; Lucia Popp, soprano; Andreas Schmidt, Baritone; DG 427 302-2*

At the core of the vocal tradition is *Lieder,* which are songs in the German language by composers such as Schubert, Schumann, Hugo Wolf, Gustav Mahler, and Richard Strauss, but also Beethoven, Mendelssohn, Liszt, Wagner, Berg, and others. A *Liederabend* (an evening of songs) is one of the most central and rewarding events of musical life in German-speaking lands. Ideally these are held in intimate settings rather than big halls so that there is immediate contact between singer and listener. In Schubert's time they were often held in homes and, when they involved his music, were called Schubertiades.

While most lieder are performed with piano, certain songs in the tradition have been performed with either piano or orchestra. The latter, of course, requires a larger setting and changes the nature of the performance. In this chapter, we will be exploring vocal music that is paired with piano or with orchestra.

Although lieder has gained preeminence because so many great composers have written songs in the German language, you should not undervalue the great song literature in other languages, including French, Italian, Spanish, Norwegian, Swedish, Finnish, Czech, and Russian. Too many English-speakers hold the song literature written in England, Ireland, Wales, Scotland, and North America in low regard, for no other reason than the accessibility of the language somehow makes these songs less estimable. In fact, the opposite is true, and many great singers (Leontyne Price, Marilyn Horne, Phyllis Curtin, Dawn Upshaw, Ian Bostridge, Bryn Terfel, and Thomas Hampson, to name but a few) have been great advocates for this music.

The skills you learn studying German lieder will serve you when you listen to any songs, so let us begin.

First, without consulting the texts, listen to one song: "Das irdische Leben." Although you probably do not understand the German, try to develop a narrative that expresses what you think is happening in this song. I would be very surprised if you got what is happening in this brief and searing song replete with enough psychological issues to be fleshed out on a psychiatrist's couch for years. But that is not the point of this exercise. It is to try to use music and the communicative skills of a singer to make your own connections to it. This is a valid musical experience, and you should always remember that even if you are sitting in a concert hall in some faraway place where you do not know the language and no translations are available, you still have the capacity to derive satisfaction from music you hear.

Once you have listened to the song, read a translation of the text in the left-hand column below. *Do not go to the right column until I ask you to.* Pay close attention to the punctuation as you work your way through the text.

Life on Earth	**Earthly Life**
"Mother, mother, I am hungry.	"Mother, oh mother, I'm hungry.
Give me bread, or I shall die!"	Give me some bread or I'll die!"
"Wait, just wait, my darling child!	"Just wait, my dear child,
Tomorrow we shall quickly	tomorrow we'll hurry and go
reap the corn!"	harvesting."
And when the corn was reaped,	And when the corn was harvested,
the child still kept on crying:	the child went on crying:
"Mother, mother, I am hungry.	"Mother, oh mother, I'm hungry.
Give me bread, or I shall die!"	Give me some bread or I'll die."
"Wait, just wait, my darling child!	"Just wait, my dear child,
Tomorrow we shall quickly	tomorrow we'll be quick and
thresh the corn!"	thresh it."
And when the corn was threshed,	And when the corn was threshed,
the child still kept crying:	the child went on crying:
"Mother, mother, I am hungry.	"Mother, oh mother, I'm hungry.
Give me bread or I shall die!"	Give me some bread or I'll die."
"Wait, just wait, my darling child!	"Just wait my dear child,
Tomorrow we shall quickly bake	tomorrow we'll be quick and
the bread!"	bake it."
And when the bread was baked,	And when the bread was baked,
the child was laid out on the bier!	the child lay on the funeral bier.
—by an uncredited translator in	—William Mann, translator, for
the Virgin Classics recording	the Bernstein DG recording

There are, in effect, three people in this song. There is a child, a mother, and a narrator. When a singer thinks about how to approach the text and the music, many decisions need to be made. Will the singer enact three different characters, or only two and take the role of the narrator? Assuming that the singer is a woman, will the narrator be a man or a woman? For that matter, is the child a girl or a boy? And how old is the child? Once the singer has made these decisions, they will dictate certain interpretive choices, including vocal coloring to delineate the three people in the text.

> KEY CONCEPT: *What makes interpretive choice fascinating and one of the many allures of the art of the song recital is that as we come to know the great works of song literature, we realize that each singer can make a significant personal imprint on these works.*

Go back to the text in the left-hand column and slowly read it aloud. Decide who is speaking when. Make your own decision about the variables I have just posited about a singer's choices.

Now play the recording again, reading the text in the libretto booklet closely (with your eye flitting to the German original to have a sense of where you are). Could you envision what was happening and, more to the point, could you picture a singer performing it? Is she moving her hands? Does she change the position of her head? What about her facial expressions? Picture her on a stage—is she looking at the audience or is she drawn in and focused on the song?

After thinking this through, you will listen to the song yet again. This time, closely read the German text and listen to its sound as the singer performs it. Mahler created music that would shape—and be shaped by—the meaning and the sounds of the German words. Do you hear these two components wedded in this song? Notice how the singer emphasizes certain consonants for dramatic effect while lightly glossing over others. Her choices are evident here and, in another performance, you might hear very different choices.

Now you might need a slight rest from this song, but please return to it before studying anything else. There is a lot more to consider. First, this is a powerful text with frightening implications. Is the mother starving the child intentionally? Is there no food available and is she trying to placate the child because there is no hope? Is she highly irresponsible and does not notice the problem at hand? The way you, or a singer, answer these questions would affect the way the song is perceived and performed.

This is where someone with mastery of another language has a clear advantage and is why singers must be proficient in speaking a language before they should dare sing in it. You, as a listener who probably does not speak German, need to rely on translated texts, and here the role of the translator is essential. Go back to the texts above (page 427), and compare them line by line in the two translations. I think you will be astonished at the differences. Had you used the second translation instead of the first, would your concept of this song be different? Which title seems more appropriate: "Life on Earth" or "Earthly Life"?

Let us look at the first four lines of the German text. Even if you do not speak German, you will see what Mahler drew from and you may come to certain conclusions about the translations:

> "Mutter, ach mutter, es hungert mich.
> Gib mir Brot, sonst sterbe ich!"
> "Warte nur, warte nur, mein liebes Kind!
> Morgen wollen wir emten geschwind!"

Here are a few key words: *Mutter* (mother); *ach* (oh); *hungert* (I'm hungry); *gib* (give); *Brot* (bread); *sterbe* (die); *warte* (wait); *Kind* (child); *Morgen* (tomorrow).

I do not intend to give you my opinion about which is the preferable translation (or if there is good and bad in both) because it is more important that you come to your own conclusions. But you can see the role of translation in making a song meaningful to singers and listeners. You have also just gone through the process that a good singer must do in approaching any song, classical or otherwise.

Before leaving "Das irdische Leben," I want you to reflect on something else. Just because a singer has learned a song does not mean that she will perform it that way for the rest of her career. As a young singer she might identify more with the needs of the child. As she gets older (and perhaps becomes a parent) her view may shift to that of the

mother. At one point, she may choose to stand back from these characters and try to find a degree of detachment as the narrator. This evolution does not apply only to this song (though it makes a great example),
but can have almost universal application. Do you think Aretha Franklin
has sung "Respect" the same way her whole life? Surely the words have
grown and changed in meaning for her as her life has progressed.

Remember, in studying song texts, to leave yourself open to multiple meanings. Take the word *you*. The *you* in question might be you the
listener. But this is seldom the case. It could be God. It could be a loved
one who is present or one who is gone. And it could be many other
things. *Approaching texts with openness rather than literalness, and using
music to answer questions that may seem unclear, is the way to think about
the texts.*

Now hone your skills by studying and listening to the other songs
on this recording of selections from *Des Knaben Wunderhorn*. In listening to these performances and all others to come, bear in mind the
words of baritone Thomas Hampson, who refers to the eternal triangle
of singing. There is the *spiritual*, in which one strives to achieve the
essence of the music. There is the *physical*, which is the correct use of
the apparatus (brain, ears, mouth, vocal chords, lungs, diaphragm, and
the whole body). And then there is the *emotional*, in which the singer
finds a specific context for each word, phrase, and song being performed. As you think of a singer studying and rehearsing vocal music,
see what meaning Hampson's triangle has for you.

• ◇ •

How does a composer create a song? Typically the inspiration comes
from words or a literary source. The composer will consider the sound
and the meaning of words and then create music that expresses what the
composer has drawn from those words. To cite an example you know,
think of the song "Summertime," by George and Ira Gershwin from
their opera *Porgy and Bess*. Certainly, the words are very evocative:

"Summertime, and the living is easy. Fish are jumpin', and the cotton is high. . . ." The music draws from the words to create a wonderfully rich and languid portrait of what summer feels like. The key thing, though, and part of the song's greatness, is that if someone told you that there was a piece of music called *Summertime,* and you heard only the music, chances are you would still experience feelings of summer. Whether the song is sung by Kathleen Battle, Ella Fitzgerald, or Janis Joplin, it has great communicative power because of its simple but haunting words and its equally simple but brilliant six-note melody. Yet if you hear only the music, without words, as part of the suite from *Porgy and Bess* on the Gershwin Panorama album (page 400) or as a violin solo (Jascha Heifetz recorded a wonderful one), you can *hear* summer.

· ∾ ·

R. Strauss: Don Juan; Vier Letzte Lieder; Tod und Verklärung; *New York Philharmonic; Kurt Masur, conductor; Deborah Voigt, soprano; Teldec 3984-25990-2*

These beloved songs by Strauss are correctly cited in translation as "Four Last Songs" rather than "The Four Last Songs," as one often reads. There is a world of difference in the omission of the article. These were written near the very end of Strauss's long life (1864–1949) and it once was generally thought that they were his last songs and his last artistic statement. In fact, he wrote another song afterward, called "Malven," and perhaps he worked on other music as well.

Because of when they were written, listeners immediately equate the songs with mortality. This is indeed an element, but I think you would agree that they are at least as much about life as about death. When, in the last song, the singer asks, "Ist dies etwa der Tod?" (Is this perchance death?), it is as if death simply has crept in like a not unwelcome visitor. And when you listen to the music that follows these words, death sounds pretty nice.

Listen to the four songs knowing only what I have told you. Sit back, close your eyes, and let the music surround you. Notice how exquisite and atmospheric the orchestral scoring is. Then pause and let the music sink in, singing to yourself parts that you remember. Then listen again, reading along with the texts.

For comparative listening, you own the Gundula Janowitz performance on the Strauss Panorama recording. Compare the approach of the two singers and the qualities of their voices. Nowadays, most sopranos who are asked to sing this music tend to have more of a Janowitz-type lyric voice, following in the footsteps of the famous recordings by Elisabeth Schwarzkopf. So it is important to remember that the first singer to do these songs was the Norwegian dramatic soprano Kirsten Flagstad, whose interpretation was probably more majestic. Voigt, I believe, captures the best of both types of soprano voices in this music, and that is why her performance is so treasurable.

Alternate performances to consider are numerous, including those by Elisabeth Schwarzkopf, Lisa della Casa, Kiri Te Kanawa, Jessye Norman, Renée Fleming, Barbara Bonney (performed with piano), and Karita Mattila.

Here are other performances to listen to as you discover how solo voice marries with orchestra or with numerous instruments:

Villa-Lobos: Bachianas Brasileiras nos. 1, 2, 5, 9; Orchestre National de la Radiodiffusion Française; Heitor Villa-Lobos, conductor; Victoria de los Angeles, soprano; EMI CDH 7610152

Listen to no. 5 (tracks 1 and 2) and notice how Villa-Lobos evokes the flavor of Bach in combination with the sounds of his native Brazil. Think about how the wondrous voice of Victoria de los Angeles, whom the composer selected to sing this, serves as an instrument as much as a human voice.

Brahms: Alto Rhapsody; Atlanta Symphony Orchestra and Chorus; Robert Shaw, conductor; Marilyn Horne, mezzo-soprano; Telarc CD-80176

Read the notes about Brahms that come with the CD, and then listen to the Alto Rhapsody without reading the text. After absorbing the music and reflecting upon it, then return to it, this time with text in hand.

Lamenti (various composers): Musica Antiqua Köln; Richard Goebel, conductor; Anne Sofie von Otter, mezzo-soprano; Archiv 289 457 617-2

Many singers like to start recital programs with early music, either song literature or opera arias (called *arie antiche*) that have survived when the operas were lost. Singers claim this is most congenial for the voice and helps warm it up for the music to come. But please do not think of this gorgeous music as vocal exercises. It is remarkably expressive and, when you listen to the instruments that accompany it, you get a wonderful sense of being in an entirely other time and place. What unites all of the songs on this particular recording is that they are laments. Think of this as you might think of a recital program built around one them.

Vivaldi: Il Giardino Armonico; Giovanni Antonini, conductor; Cecilia Bartoli, mezzo-soprano; London/Decca 466 569-2

The music on this splendid recording was impeccably researched by Cecilia Bartoli, who went to libraries and archives to find great music by Vivaldi to bring before a modern audience. Listen to Bartoli's accurate yet compelling use of Italian, and her ability to link the meaning and sound of words to the music. In the hands of a less-prepared interpreter, much of this music could sound alike and rather quickly become wearing. After listening to this recording, you may wish to pull out your recording of *The Four Seasons* and do some comparative listening—do you think the voice can be considered a surrogate for the violin in Vivaldi's music, or are these compositions very different? After thinking in these terms, ask yourself whether Bartoli's interpretation makes her sound like the way a woodwind instrument might be played. In reflecting on this, one concept to keep in mind is, how and when does Bartoli breathe? Would this be like a wind instrument?

Sor: Seguidillias; Martin y Soler: Arias and Songs; Teresa Berganza, mezzo-soprano; José Miguel Moreno, guitar; Philips 411 030-2

This music, written not long after Vivaldi, will give you the sense of the sound and style of composers working in Spanish. It is interesting that Spain has produced a seemingly endless line of marvelous musicians, but one is hard-put to name its major composers. You have encountered some in this book, including Albeniz and Granados, and Sor and Martin y Soler are others. The wonderful Teresa Berganza, entirely at home in her own language and idiom, makes these songs meaningful.

♪ Lieder ♪

Schubert: Die schöne Müllerin; Three Lieder; Fritz Wunderlich, tenor; Hubert Giesen, piano; DG 447 452-2

Gian Carlo Menotti said that in his work he sought to emulate the "divine simplicity" of the music of Schubert. While other composers (including Mozart, Grieg, Wolf, Fauré, Mahler, Richard Strauss, Samuel Barber, Ned Rorem, and Lee Hoiby) have left us many wonderful songs, it is probably fair to say that Schubert is the grand master to whom all others are compared. He wrote more than six hundred lieder, most of amazing quality. To realize, when admiring the depth and psychological insight of Schubert songs, that he did not live to celebrate his thirty-second birthday, one must be amazed at the sophistication and human insight of his works. Certainly the words in most Schubert songs are beautiful and appealing, but it seems that the music perfectly captures the essence of what the words and ideas are all about in a way that perhaps no composer can match.

Up until Schubert's time, the piano's part in music-making was not as prominent. In a song he wrote at the age of seventeen, *Gretchen am Spinnrade* (Gretchen at the Spinning Wheel), set to a Goethe poem, all of this changed. One can hear the spinning wheel in the piano, along with many more musical ideas. His songs evoke all the moods and feelings of life, indeed all of the events of life. As you listen to them, and to all songs, notice the interplay between the musical line for voice and that for piano.

This presence of the piano is palpable in *Die Schöne Mullerin* (The Pretty Maid of the Mill), written in 1823, when the composer was a mere twenty-six years old. This is a *song cycle*, something you have not encountered yet. Unlike *Des Knaben Wunderhorn*, which is a collection of songs based on texts from many sources (then gathered in an anthology) that a singer can select from, a song cycle is a collection of songs, many of brief duration, that are always performed in sequence and, in their totality, create a narrative that individual songs cannot achieve. (You might claim that Strauss's "Four Last Songs" are a cycle, and with some justification, but I see them more as a marvelous category of one with aims that are different from a song cycle.)

If you carefully read the poems by Wilhelm Müller that Schubert used, you will find that this is much more than a story of a young man's love for the pretty girl at the mill. In the texts the young man is referred to as the wanderer. This fellow's sunny outlook changes as he finds that she does not feel for him as he does for her. With the arrival of a hunter (*Der Jäger*), who represents a rival for the girl's affections, things change more. Then, in two songs, *Die liebe Farbe* and *Die böse Farbe* ("The Favorite Color" and "The Hateful Color"), note how the color green comes to represent everything the wanderer feels. By the last song, his innocence is quashed; his view of love and the world have changed.

Schubert captures these brilliantly in musical terms. As you read the poems before listening to the music, come up with mental imagery for music. Then notice, as you listen to the cycle, what images appear. There is the unmistakable presence of water here (the mill is powered by a stream), especially in the first six songs. But this flowing stream exists throughout the cycle as a metaphor for whatever you imagine it to be—constancy, change, flow, impermanence. As a musical element it is quite compelling.

Fritz Wunderlich was a splendid tenor who died tragically young, much like Schubert, and he brings youthful ardor and immediacy to this music, and is ably abetted by the pianist Hubert Giesen.

· ❦ ·

Schubert: Winterreise; *Dietrich Fischer-Dieskau, baritone; Alfred Brendel, piano; Philips 289 464 739-2. Among many alternate recordings are those by Wolfgang Holzmair, baritone, with Imogen Cooper, piano (Philips 446 407-2) and a devastatingly powerful version with Christa Ludwig, mezzo-soprano, with James Levine, piano (DG 423 366-2, difficult to find).*

For more than a few music lovers, *Winterreise* (Winter Journey) is the absolute pinnacle of the lieder tradition. The story is deceptively simple, yet stunning when performed by a great artist. We have a young man who has been rejected as a lover, and he has begun to walk a lonely road in winter. He moves farther and farther away, into an entirely other physical and emotional landscape. As the notes by Karl Schumann in the Fischer-Dieskau recording tell us, "The wanderer incorporates a large measure of autobiography and self-portraiture, reflecting Schubert's loneliness as he worked without public support, his conviction that his end was near, his early disappointments in love, and his awareness of being an outsider in . . . society."

Having learned how to create musical images in your mind that are inspired by texts, apply this again here and in all the songs you learn from now on. Do you hear snow, wind, bleakness, footsteps? Do you see this as purely a geographical journey, or also an inward emotional journey? Take special note of the last song, *Der Leiermann* (The Organ Grinder). There are so many images here: "outside," "organ-grinder," "numb fingers," "barefoot on the ice," "no one looks at him," "dogs snarl," "he lets it all go by," "strange old man, should I go with you?" "Will you turn your organ to my songs?" These images cascade fast and furiously, and the music, powerful yet simple, communicates everything the words say, and so much more. Do you think the final question is answered? What picture comes to your mind as the song ends? Is this resolution? Drift? Despair?

Listen not only to the remarkable singing and phrasing, but also to the incredible piano playing of Alfred Brendel. Notice how singer and pianist seem to breathe together. Christa Ludwig, in discussing the great baritone Dietrich Fischer-Dieskau, observed that he chose to work with "pianists (such as Pollini, Brendel, and Barenboim), not accompanists." Her comment may sound a bit harsh, but the point is worth exploring. Until perhaps the mid-1970s the person who played piano at a vocal recital was usually called the "accompanist" which has a servile connotation. When Emanuel Ax and Yo-Yo Ma play the Brahms cello sonata, it is not that Ax "accompanies" Ma. These are two collaborative artists making music together.

Similarly, a singer and a pianist collaborate in recital. Nowadays the preferred term for the pianist is usually "collaborator" or "partner," and at a recital the program will say something like "Deborah Voigt, soprano, and Brian Zeger, piano." There are many fine pianists today who devote much of their performing to vocal recitals because they enjoy it and have meaningful things to say interpretively. No longer is there the tinge that existed that implied that the pianist accompanied because he was not good enough to be a soloist. Some of the leading collaborators today are Martin Katz, Warren Jones, Zeger, Steven Blier, Malcolm Martineau, and Roger Vignoles.

In the past, some "accompanists" achieved fame on their own because of their talents. The most notable is probably Gerald Moore, whose work you can hear on innumerable recordings from the 1950s and 1960s. While Fischer-Dieskau and Moore had fruitful collaborations, he also worked with pianists who are known primarily as soloists. Simply put, this is another form of chamber music, in which one of the instruments is a voice.

Modern examples of singers and solo pianists (and conductors) who join up today because they find that they achieve exciting artistic results are Cecilia Bartoli/Daniel Barenboim; Renée Fleming/Jean-Yves Thibaudet; Ewa Podlés/Garrick Ohlsson. James Levine has been an inspired partner with countless great recitalists and is a close and frequent collaborator with Jessye Norman.

Although Schubert wrote many of his songs for male voice, great female singers have been able to make them their own. If you can locate the recording of *Winterreise* with Christa Ludwig and James Levine, you will be richly rewarded and find many areas for interesting comparisons.

• ◇ •

More Schubert listening:

Schubert: 12 Lieder, 6 Moments Musicaux; Elisabeth Schwarzkopf, soprano; Edwin Fischer, piano; EMI 7243 5 67494 2 9

A classic old recording with a regal yet intimate Schwarzkopf and a sensitive Fischer will give you a sense of traditional lieder singing in the middle of the twentieth century.

Schubert: Lieder; Barbara Bonney, soprano; Geoffrey Parsons, piano; Teldec 4509 90873-2

A fluid and carefully considered interpretive account of Schubert songs by Barbara Bonney, an American who proves that lieder need not be the exclusive province of native German speakers. This is good example of modern singing, and you can compare her work with artists from the past. Enjoy "The Shepherd on the Rock" and its clarinet music as well as an excellent rendering of "Gretchen am Spinnrade."

Schubert: Schwangesang; Bryn Terfel, bass-baritone; Malcolm Martineau, piano; Sain SCDC 4035)

A music publisher put together fourteen of Schubert's songs after his death and called them *Schwangesang* (Swan Song). Though the composer did not intend them to be a song cycle, they are usually performed as such.

• ✐ •

R. Schumann: Frauenliebe und -leben; *5 Lieder, op. 40, 15 Lieder; Anne Sofie von Otter, mezzo-soprano; Bengt Forsberg, piano; DG 445 881-2*

Robert Schumann wrote many wonderful songs, and two great cycles: *Dichterliebe* (The Poet's Loves), usually sung by a man, and the wonderful *Frauenliebe und -leben* (A Woman's Love and Life). Before reading the texts or listening to the songs, read the fine essay by Susan Youens that accompanies the CD. I wonder whether men and women who read these texts find different meanings in them? Admittedly one could quarrel with the idea that a woman can only realize herself as the companion to a man. But it is important to remember that this cycle was feverishly written in 1840 as Schumann sought to marry his beloved Clara.

What is fascinating, and what the musicians on this recording evoke so well, is the progression of a woman's life. While the previous cycles you have studied have headed to bleak conclusions, this one goes in more directions, chronicling things gained as well as things lost. Read the texts thoroughly, creating musical images in your head that may be less tangible and more emotional than in the Schubert.

Clara Schumann: Lieder; Lan Rao, soprano; Micaela Gelius, piano; Arte Nova 74321 43308 2

Unfortunately, there are no translated texts in this recording, but you may wish to listen to it to understand what Clara Schumann was thinking and doing while her husband was writing music that was full of his love for her. Pay special attention to "Liebst du um Schönheit," with a text by Friedrich Rückert that would later be set by Mahler.

• ∽ •

Brahms and Liszt: Lieder; Thomas Quasthoff, baritone; Justus Zeyen, piano; DG 289 463 183-2
Wolf: 22 Lieder; Elisabeth Schwarzkopf, soprano; Wilhelm Furtwängler, piano; EMI 7243 5 67570 2 8

You now have the skills to study these songs on your own. The Brahms and Liszt are sung by Thomas Quasthoff, one of the great singers now before the public, and a memorable collection of songs by Hugo Wolf is sung by Schwarzkopf in her prime, with a great conductor, Furtwängler, at the keyboard. Think of these songs as beautiful miniatures—tiny portraits and fleeting emotional moments.

• ∽ •

IN HER OWN WORDS: CHRISTA LUDWIG

Christa Ludwig (1928–   ) was born just at the right time and place, at least in terms of fashioning one of the great careers in music. Anyone who ever heard her will not forget this complete artist. Raised in Berlin by musical parents, she lived at a time when she could hear artists who were trained in the nineteenth century, often by great interpreters or composers. A girlhood in a turbulent era in European history provided contact with the realities of life that she could invest in her approach to songs and opera characters.

She was born seventeen years after the death of Mahler and twenty-one years before the death of Richard Strauss. These masters, and a remarkable number of great conductors and singers, carried on an immense musical tradition and, in many ways, deepened it. Ludwig began her career just after the Second World War as theaters were reopening and people sought the solace and excitement of music as they rebuilt their lives. The beginnings of her career also coincided with the development of the long-playing record (LP), and all of the important labels clamored for artists of her generation (Elisabeth Schwarzkopf, Victoria de los Angeles, Leontyne Price, Dietrich Fischer-Dieskau, Hermann Prey, Fritz Wunderlich, and Marilyn Horne, among many) to document much of the standard song repertory. We are the more fortunate because of this incomparable documented legacy of a great artistic outpouring. The recordings are touchstones for anyone who wishes to study the singer's art. However, we should not undervalue many of the great recitalists of today, many of whose performances are recommended in this chapter.

Because of the time frame of Christa Ludwig's life, and her talent and versatility, she has been able to pass on to younger artists much of her accumulated wisdom about singing. The following observations by Christa Ludwig are culled from an interview and two master classes I had the good fortune to attend.

"The recital tradition in Germany and Austria is very much alive because it is part of the local language and culture. When I sang German songs in America or France I sometimes overdid it to make myself understandable. I had to tone it down again when I returned to sing in Germany and Austria."

Programming is very important—one must think of who the listeners will be. "You must sing one-third for the audience, one-third for the critics, and one-third for your-self. Only in New York, Vienna, Berlin, and perhaps Munich and London can a singer select the repertory [based entirely on what] she wants to do." It is important to do modern music that is outside the most traditional repertory, but "you must put the modern composer after the intermission or the audience will leave." The setting for a recital is impor-tant, because it is such an intimate art form: "Most concert halls are too big. In Carnegie and Avery Fisher Halls (in New York) the people in the back cannot see a singer's face. A recital is for a room, like Schubert playing at home."

Ludwig has also given a considerable amount of thought to aspects of the recital that other singers seldom discuss. "In a recital you must have the right dress. People will look at you for one and one-half hours and the dress must relate to what you sing. So white would be wrong if you are singing Hugo Wolf—too plain, too pure.

"I don't want a female accompanist—only one of us can look good! I once had a female page turner in a miniskirt and I didn't let her stay. There is, in some music, a certain erotic dialogue between singer and pianist, and I don't achieve that with a woman."

Ludwig's comments are interesting because they reflect a viewpoint on music-making that clearly comes from her own ideas and approach. I have heard recitals with a male singer and pianist, or a female singer and pianist, in which an erotic dialogue did not occur in music that was very much about love and lust. Does this necessarily mean that it was less involving? Let us say that a heterosexual female singer is performing with a gay male pianist—is there an erotic dialogue? There very well might be, as there could be with two musicians of the same gender, whatever their sexual preference.

Part of the eroticism between singer and pianist that can develop stems from fantasy, often unspoken, which enters into the creation of a performance. When singer and pianist collaborate to take music and words in hand to forge a joint idea of a song or recital program, each brings many things to the equation, much of which is spoken, and some of which remains part of a mystery that many great artists keep within them.

What is compelling in Ludwig's comments is that she has devoted great thought and introspection to deciding what works for *her* to make her performance indelible. This is one of the lessons for each singer and creative person to take away.

According to Ludwig, "Nothing is lost that you have experienced, loved, or suffered." This, she says, is the message of Mahler's song "Urlicht" (from *Des Knaben Wunderhorn* and used in his Second Symphony). It is also the necessary philosophy for a singer who hopes to sing recitals.

For Ludwig (and all great recitalists), lieder singing requires different skills than those used in opera. "There are singers who sing lieder, and there are lieder singers . . . A beautiful voice can get you far, but not make you an artist." One must learn breathing and vocal technique, be at home in a language, and be able to dig into the meanings of words and how they are expressed in music. "Singers live not in the present, but in the past . . . with poets and composers.

"With lieder you must show yourself. You have no costume, no wigs, no special makeup. We have to undress our heart and our soul, and do this in front of people." But she cautions against doing so much investigation into the ideas of a song or composer that the singer is robbed of her own essence: "It is a problem when analysis of a text and score is so overbearing that the mystery is gone."

Her approach to language and to the styles of composers is treasurable: "In pronouncing words, find meaning in their meanings *and* in the sound of the words. *K* or *T* or *M* are all formed with a different shape of the mouth, and so produce a different sound and a different musical sound. The *K* cuts, the *T* separates what comes before and after, and the *M* creates a hum that can be mischevious or meditative.

"In performing works by different composers, each asks different things from us. When we do Beethoven and Schubert, who are linked to the Classical era, we should bring reflected emotion [rather than a more direct kind]. With Brahms and Mahler you can give emotions more readily. In Wolf there are tiny spoken things in the music [that make for intimacy] while the feelings in Strauss, even in a small song, 'can be more operatic in presentation' even if one scales the volume back to a level suitable for the room."

But the most important tool is the ability to breathe correctly. Many people are unaware of their breathing (though they do it constantly) and singers often inhibit their breathing when it is called to their attention rather than letting it happen naturally. "It is the most normal thing to breathe. To discover this, lie down and breathe normally. This is how breathing happens when we don't pay attention to it. Look at a dog or a cat lying down and watch how they breathe."

Ludwig, like Marilyn Horne and certain other senior artists, has devoted much time and thought to teaching. "To be frank and honest is the first thing a teacher should be to a young singer. If the teacher thinks there is not a career here, she must say so."

Bruckner: Symphony no. 6; Wagner: Wesendonck Lieder; New Philharmonia Orchestra; Otto Klemperer, conductor; Christa Ludwig, mezzo-soprano; EMI 7243 5 67037 28

The Wesendonck Songs, by Richard Wagner, have been performed in versions for orchestra and soloist, or for piano and soloist. They were written to texts by Mathilde Wesendonck, wife of Otto, a wealthy merchant in Zurich, where Wagner was living in exile from the politically turbulent German states of the mid-nineteenth century. Wagner lived with the Wesendoncks and benefited from their generosity. They, in turn, were enthralled by this charismatic genius and it is quite probable that he and Mathilde had a romantic relationship. These richly ripe poems have considerable eroticism and, in this performance, Christa Ludwig finds just the right amount of erotic interplay with the whole orchestra! This is not a mild joke, but an observation that this fine artist was indeed able to scale her performances to the size and character of her musical partners. Study the texts carefully and give them thought. Try to picture what sounds may accompany these words, especially in the last song, *Träume* (Dreams). Then listen to the music and judge how your images compare with those of Wagner. It is interesting to note that these are among the very few songs written by Wagner in a nonoperatic setting. Do they sound "operatic," whatever that word means to you? Some of his ideas for his then-germinating opera, *Tristan und Isolde*, can be found in this music, especially in *Träume* and *Im Treibhaus* (In the Greenhouse).

Also to ponder: Based on the sound of this music, do you think Wagner was in love with Mathilde Wesendonck? Based on the texts of the poetry, do you think Mathilde was in love with Wagner?

• ❧ •

Mahler: Lieder eines fahrenden Gesellen, etc.; various conductors; EMI 7243 5 67557 2 7

Although you have already begun to explore Mahler's music, here are more classic songs that merit study. For an interesting contrast, listen to these performances and then contrast them with those by Christa Ludwig (EMI CDM 7 69499 2).

Unfortunately, this CD does not include texts.

• ‹◇› •

Mahler: Rückert Lieder (plus works by Handel, Lieberson, and Brahms); Lorraine Hunt Lieberson, mezzo-soprano; Roger Vignoles, piano; BBCW 1002-2

Having listened until this point to mostly native German speakers singing lieder, it is interesting to hear an American, in this case the excellent Lorraine Hunt Lieberson, make a foray into Mahler and Brahms. I wonder if you would sense any differences in diction, style, commitment, and impact if I had not told you the nationality of the singer? It is important to understand that all great art songs (to use a word that covers lieder and repertory in other languages) belong to the world, and every serious artist can make an important statement with them whether or not she is a native speaker.

This recording is of a live performance given in London's Wigmore Hall on November 30, 1998. Musicians famously rise to the occasion, giving all they have, when they perform in great halls such as the Wigmore, the Musikverein in Vienna, the Concertgebouw in Amsterdam, and Carnegie Hall in New York. The Wigmore is one of the world's most perfect settings for a vocal recital. Not only is the room ideal, but the audience is always knowledgeable and involved. I think you can detect Lieberson's interpretive sensitivity by her breathing and beautiful phrasing of the texts. She is a superb artist, but is also mindful that she is singing in a place where listeners are discerning and appreciative. Read the texts as she sings, just as you would do in a real recital.

In this performance, she has programmed five of the wonderful and engrossing songs by Mahler set to texts by Friedrich Rückert. One of my favorite songs in the entire recital literature is *Ich bin der Welt abhan-*

den gekommen (Lost Am I to the World). After you have listened to the whole recital, return as a music lover to this one song and parse it as you learned to do with "Das irdische Leben."

Some singers, though fewer all the time, put opera arias in their recital programs. Here we find two by Handel, one in Italian and one in English. Hunt was surely mindful that in London there is a long Handel tradition and he was an adopted "native" son. *Theodora*, from which "As the rosy steps the morn" derives, was written for London audiences. More unusual is that the Handel works do not lead off the program to "warm" the voice and the audience. Instead, Hunt plunged into some of the most demanding music first, setting the tone for the evening. I think that the Handel actually sounds better after the Mahler, but this was an unorthodox choice on the singer's part.

Then come songs, wonderful ones, by her husband, composer Peter Lieberson. They follow in the tradition of Grieg, Strauss, and others in which the wife is the muse for the husband's muse. Then comes a wonderful performance of "Deep River," here called an "American spiritual" rather than the older designation "Negro spiritual." For the most part, this repertory has been sung by African-American recitalists, and it is a valuable sign of the recognition of the glory of this music that it is being embraced by other singers as well. Great music belongs to the world.

The concert ends with a beautiful Brahms song.

♭ Songs in French ♭

Berlioz: Les Nuits d'Été, *etc.; Berliner Philharmoniker; Anne Sofie von Otter, mezzo-soprano; James Levine, conductor; Cord Garben, piano; DG 445-823-2*

Hector Berlioz was a great and original artist who lived passionately and channeled his feelings into his art. He took the orchestral mantle from Beethoven and found ways to make the symphony more titanic and expressive. He also pioneered the tone poem, which Liszt, Strauss, and others would build on. You can read about his *Symphonie Fantastique* (page 213) and *Harold in Italy* (page 368) to refresh your memory of him.

We must also credit Berlioz with being the composer who first paired a song cycle with orchestra. He wrote *Les Nuits d'Été* (Summer Nights) in 1841 to six poems by Théophile Gautier, at first for either mezzo-soprano or tenor with piano. In that form they are beautiful miniatures that contrast with the grandeur of many of his other compositions.

He later tried his hand at orchestrating one of the songs, then another, and by 1856 they all had gorgeous orchestrations to give color and texture to the words and vocal line. They are now sung by sopranos too, because they are so desirable that these singers felt left out. What I want you to think about, as you listen to them sung first by a mezzo (von Otter) and then a soprano (Régine Crespin) is how the sound differs. You might find, as I do, that some songs work better for one voice and some for the other. This is not because one artist is better than the other, but just that some songs lie higher or lower than others.

Pay attention also to the sound of French. After listening almost entirely to German-language songs to this point, it is a revelation how different music can seem when the words have a different sound. Notice how French vowels differ from German ones. Some are more open, many sound more closed. Certain letters, such as *N* or *R*, have a completely different flavor in French than German. This requires the singer to think and understand these variations, and create idiomatic and meaningful interpretations. As you will see, the songs are about love, but also in the context of absence and separation, which gives love a bittersweet tinge. How does love sound different here from other songs you have listened to?

After listening to von Otter's wonderful performance, compare it with Régine Crespin's performance on the Berlioz Panorama recording (using the texts from the von Otter). Crespin was one of the great interpreters of song in her native French, as well as being a thrilling opera singer who drove audiences wild with her glorious voice, considerable glamour, subtle acting, and exciting singing. As you listen to Crespin's performance, keep in mind something she said and think about whether you agree: "The voice is carried on the vowels, not on the consonants."

• ∾ •

Canteloube: Chants d'Auvergne; *Royal Philharmonic Orchestra; Antonio de Almeida, conductor; Frederica von Stade, mezzo-soprano; Sony 63063*

A certain category of song literature features music drawn from national traditions of language and literature. You know *Des Knaben Wunderhorn* and *Bachianas Brasileiras,* and you can also find folk-inspired melodies in Czech (by Dvořák), Hungarian (Bařtók), English (Vaughan Williams), Russian (Mussorgsky), as well as the wonderful American songs gathered and orchestrated by Aaron Copland.

Joseph Canteloube (1879–1957) was probably the leading advocate for finding provincial French music, much of which is sung in local languages and dialects. The most famous are the four volumes he published between 1923 and 1930 that are songs from the Auvergne, a mountainous region in southwestern France. The language is Auvergnat, an almost indecipherable patois that seems to draw bits and pieces from all the Romance languages. Many of these songs are pastoral in flavor, and feature the voices of shepherds and shepherdesses. Listen to the orchestration's lush and perfumed evocation of this idyll. I can give you no sense of whether Frederica von Stade is handling the language well, but if anyone can I am sure she does. Other lovely interpretations of these songs are by Victoria de los Angeles, Kiri Te Kanawa, and Dawn Upshaw.

• ∾ •

More French listening:

Soirée Française (various French composers); Elly Ameling, soprano; Rudolf Jansen, piano; Philips 412 628-2

Elly Ameling, from the Netherlands, was a special type of singer who devoted herself entirely to songs in many languages and did not sing opera. She was a master of the art form and, when the day came that she decided she could not sing up to the level she expected of herself, she simply stopped. She had a lovely stage personality, endearing without being sugary, serious when necessary though not morose, and despite her choice not to expand to overly dramatic extremes, she managed more than most singers to make every song distinct, varied, meaningful, and unforgettable. Listening to her sing was like going through an art gallery full of wonderful detailed miniatures that each merited prolonged inspection and reflection, and gave great pleasure. Perhaps her only rival in this category is the late and much-missed American singer, Jan de Gaetani.

Perhaps because she is Dutch, Ameling has an extraordinary facility with languages, seeming entirely at home in French, German, and English, and many other tongues. This is a very appealing evening of French *chansons* (including one of the Auvergne songs) by fourteen composers covering more than a century of styles.

• ⟨⟩ •

Lutoslawski: Chantefleurs et Chantefables *(on* Fanfare for the Los Angeles Philharmonic*) etc.; Los Angeles Philharmonic; Esa-Pekka Salonen, conductor; Paul Crossley, piano; Dawn Upshaw, soprano; Sony 67189*

Composers have often written music to verse in languages other than their own. This was certainly the case with Korngold, Weill, and other refugees from Nazi Germany who wrote music to English-language texts when they moved to America. In this case, the Polish Lutoslawski was drawn to surreal poems by Robert Desnos that are full of wordplay and unusual images from the plant and animal worlds. As the program notes inform us, Lutoslawski felt a bond with Desnos. While the composer survived detention during the Second World War, the poet was killed at the concentration camp at Terezin. As you read the texts and listen to the music, listen for evocation of the surreal and the ironic, asking yourself if what seems childlike may have additional meaning.

• ✧ •

♪ Songs from the British Isles ♪

The Vagabond, songs by Vaughan Williams, Finzi, Butterworth, Ireland; Bryn Terfel, baritone; Malcolm Martineau, piano; DG 445 946-2

Bryn Terfel, the Welsh baritone (and often called bass-baritone for the lower extension of his voice) is a consummate artist. Whatever language he sings in, his fidelity to the sound and ideas of each word and phrase is remarkable. His beautiful voice and charismatic temperament always seem to wed singer, voice, music, and words into one perfect whole.

English was actually Terfel's second language, having grown up speaking Welsh, but he makes every word and sound here count. In these songs one can smell the brine of the sea, see mists in the Lake District, and have other views of the English landscape, both spiritual and physical. This is a persuasive case for English song, and asks that we not have reduced expectations of it because we think we understand every word. We may recognize every word when a singer's diction is as crystalline as Terfel's. But in songs we understand the words when we hear what musical notes and effects to which they are sung.

• ✧ •

Elgar: Cello Concerto, Sea Pictures; London Symphony Orchestra; Sir John Barbirolli, conductor; Jacqueline Du Pré, cello; Dame Janet Baker, mezzo-soprano; EMI 7243 5 56219 24

Dame Janet Baker was a revered artist in Britain and elsewhere. She lived for her music and made great sacrifices for it, such as choosing not to have children because she felt she could not effectively be a mother and an international singer. When she quietly retired, her departure from the scene was mourned and lamented by many music lovers. Baker brings quiet grace and respect to these orchestra-accompanied *Sea Pictures* songs that evoke images of coastal Britain. Unfortunately texts were not included with this recording, but you will understand most everything.

More listening from the British Isles:

The English Songbook; *Ian Bostridge, tenor; Julius Drake, piano; EMI 7243 5 56830 2 1*
Britten: Serenade for Tenor, Horn and Strings, etc.; Ian Bostridge, tenor; various artists; EMI 7243 5 56871 28

The fine English tenor, Ian Bostridge, is one of the foremost recitalists before the public today. Although he does an excellent job in all the music he sings, he has made important contributions to the revival and recording of repertory from England which is too frequently overlooked.

• ◇ •

A CONVERSATION WITH MARILYN HORNE

Throughout her long and brilliant career, the great American singer Marilyn Horne has been showered with encomiums, honors, and praise. All of these were deserved, and more. She had extraordinary success in her performances of many of the great mezzo-soprano roles in opera, blazing a trail in the rediscovery of works by Rossini, Handel, Vivaldi, and others that had long been forgotten. Throughout her operatic career, she had a parallel life as an esteemed and very busy recitalist.

Much of her work now, as a self-described "senior artist," is devoted to passing on what she has learned to a new generation of singers, especially in the field of lieder and art songs of all type. She created the Marilyn Horne Foundation in 1994 to preserve and foster this kind of singing and, thanks to the foundation's efforts, many outstanding young singers have taken flight on wings of song. You can read more about the foundation on page 566. Horne also teaches at the Music Academy of the West in Santa Barbara, California. She has been an enlightened mentor to many young people in the arts (not only singers) and an outspoken defender of the importance of the arts in our society.

Although Horne is strongly identified with roles in Italian and French opera, and as an interpreter of the great lieder repertory and songs from many European nations, she is also one of the most admired and talented singers of the vast and wonderful treasure trove of American songs. She kindly sat down to talk about singing, interpretation, lieder, and American music, and you can read and learn from her opinions and knowledge.

Question.   For a singer who can pick and choose among many forms of performance, what is the appeal of doing a vocal recital?

MARILYN HORNE: *I would say that the appeal first has to be the music and the poetry. You have to want to perform that and live that before the public. But you know, this is the kind of music you can also enjoy in your living room, as they did in the old days when they didn't have television, and they didn't have radio, and they didn't have phonograph records or CDs. We forget that if they wanted to hear something twice, they had to go hear it again in public. So these songs that we deal with, on into the more modern ones that obviously have been around in the electronic age, are still things that can be of entertainment in someone's home, if they choose not to watch their TVs with everybody in a different room. But, bringing these songs out onto the stage, I'm not exactly sure when that happened. [At first] it was really more salon music, if we go back to Schubert. These things were done in salons and parlors and things like that. The singer has to want to explore this literature and has to want to do it in front of the public.*

Also, I would say that the singer, and her accompanist, of course, like performing in these circumstances in which the onus rises and falls on what they do that night. Early on, before I gave any thought to anything when I was young, I just did it because I liked it. I had been doing this kind of thing my entire life. I also loved very much that I could be different characters in one evening, and sing in many languages. If a song is just a single song, and not a cycle, then I can tell a little story in that song. And that is basically what song singing is.

Q. You were talking about being many characters in one evening. People may know you as an opera singer before they might know you as a vocal artist. How do you go from being a character for three or four hours—say, as Carmen—to being a character for perhaps three and one-half minutes? What do you have to do to make that happen?

A. *I, with the pianist, we have to make it all happen. Whereas in doing Carmen, we have a lot of help. We've got the sets, lights, chorus, orchestra, other characters to be playing against all evening. So you get a lot of help that way. In doing a recital, all we've got is the singer, the pianist, the music, and the poet, and it all rises and falls on what we do.*

Q. Let us say that in one song you are a young girl in love, in the next song you are a war widow, and in the next song you are an older woman looking back on life. This may happen in certain song cycles. Do the shifts that you make happen in your head? Do they happen before an audience in a way that an audience would see?

A. *I think both. First of all, you've got to know in your head what you want to do with it, and hopefully you and your pianist have heavily explored this song. So it has to be in your head that you switch characters. Let's face it—that has to be the actress (in a singer) who can do that.*

I want the audience to see the change on my face. I want them to see it in a body position, with a subtle change in my hands. Take, for instance, Mahler's "Das irdische Leben," I felt—especially for audiences that may not know this music at all—that if I just keep my hands just slightly open and supplicating, that I can be the child. Obviously my voice takes on different colors, I hope, too. But then when I want to sing as the mother, I turn my hands over as the mother is trying to say, "Wait, wait." You would say "wait, wait" with your hands up, and you would say it with your hands down, saying "patience, patience." And then the coloration comes in, too.

I learned a great, great saying from Lotte Lehmann, who was my song teacher and who really showed me what a song can be. . . . Once when I was preparing a couple of roles I said, "For this role I am going to color my voice very sweetly, and for that role I will doing something else." And she said to me, "If you know what the character is all about, and you feel the character, then it is going to happen automatically." And that is the same thing with songs, I feel. If you really understand that character, and you really understand what those words are about, you are going to automatically get the color you want.

Q. I brought along three songs. I have all your recordings.

A. *You might have more than I do!*

Q. Three that I selected [all from the recording, *I Will Breathe a Mountain*] are "The Daisies" and "The Secrets of the Old" by Samuel Barber, and "The Bustle in the House" by William Bolcom. Part of what I was interested in with these three songs is that they are of such different moods, and I suspected that you had devoted an incredible amount of time and thought to taking them apart.

A. *Oh sure. But I have to tell you honestly that "The Daisies" is a song that I learned when I was probably seventeen or eighteen. When I did it then I gave it some thought, but I gave it a lot more thought later. But that is quite a simple song, and it is almost like a folk song, it's that simple. For me, it just makes a lovely statement.*

Q. Given that you recorded this album relatively late in your career—

A. *Shall we say "late in life"?*

Q. OK. The song itself in this recording has such amazing freshness and youth, that I felt you decided that this is an element of the song.

A. *Again, it comes from the text. Sure, you could say this could be an older person having memories, but it is also the way that Barber set it makes it simple—what is this, his opus 2?—so he was still getting going. But in a way this is like Schubert. Some of his earliest songs are still some* *of the best. I also think that the whole setting really dictates to me the color that I want. I don't think that with "The Daisies" I labored too much over what it would be about.*

Q. "The Secrets of the Old" is by Barber, with a text by Yeats. The opening line really sets the tone: "I have old women's secrets now that had those of the young."

A. *Well, obviously this song was also chosen—I don't know how many years ago I began to sing it, but it was chosen by the fact that it was definitely mature, and I think that a lot of the fact that can maybe lend success to singing that song is the audience knows that I am also a mature woman now. It is not something that I would have chosen to sing when I was young.*

Q. Now that we are on the topic of the age of a woman: Schumann's *Frauenliebe und -leben*. At what point can a woman sing that and get it?

A. *I think you can get it. First of all, I feel that with all of these very difficult cycles, such as that one, and* Die Schöne Müllerin *and* Winterreise, *the younger you start singing these things, the better you are going to be singing them thirty years later. And I think that—we're talking about someone with talent who is going to be doing these things, right?— obviously it is going to be very, very different twenty-five years later, but I think that what the young person has to say is valid. So when one of my kids whom I am teaching at the Music Academy in Santa Barbara says, "I am working on* Die Schöne Müllerin" *and this person is twenty years old, I think that is great. We are not talking about something that is going to tax the voice. It is something that is going to tax the* mind.

Q. But do you think that if a young singer forms a habit or an acquaintance with a song and doesn't learn to bring her life experience to certain words when she revisits the text after becoming a mother, after becoming a grandmother . . .

A. *It's got to be different. I can tell you that in my own experience I sang my first* Frauenliebe und -leben *when I was about twenty-six and did not have my child until I was thirty-one. I remember that I sang it in* *public about ten times and then I wanted to take it to Lehmann. I had the possibility to sing that cycle for her and get an opinion! With my great teacher and accompanist, Gwendolyn Koldofsky, I drove up to Santa Barbara and I sang the cycle for Lehmann. She said to me, "I have nothing to say. It is absolutely wonderful." And then she said, "The only thing I would say to you is that when the postlude comes and you are standing there and that long postlude is playing on the piano, you might slowly, slowly, slowly let your hands drop to your sides." Now she was talking about a bit of an effect.*

I thought, "Why not? That's a really good idea." I was singing at Carnegie Hall not too long after that and a very good friend of mine named Trude Rittman was at the recital. The next day, we talked. She said, "It was the most wonderful recital, but one thing did not ring true. When you dropped your hands to your side at the end of the cycle . . ."

So you see, what was there was that the teacher had given something that did not become organic to me. Sometimes these things don't work.

Q.   Did you ever do that again in future performances?

A.   *I did not.*

Q.   Do you think it was just not destined to be organic?

A.   *Yes. I just decided that's not for me. There is something about it I am not comfortable with. That is a long postlude, as you know, but there are other ways to feel it. Sure, we do things at the ends of songs to put a finality on them, like dropping the head. Lord knows I have closed my eyes many times at the ends of songs.*

Q.   How do you set about deciding what becomes a recital program?

A.   *There are so many things. I was so fortunate to have had so many good teachers, Gwen Koldofsky especially. She was the first woman—the first person—to found an accompanying department in a school that gave a degree. This was at the University of Southern California. That was a bachelor's degree, and then there was a master's, and then they gave the first doctorate in accompanying. I was so fortunate to have her* *guiding me on how to build a program. In building a program, you have got to take into consideration where you are singing. If you are singing for a much more erudite public than you would be somewhere else, then I think you can program your music accordingly and put a little bit tougher, more esoteric stuff on it.*

It was a long time, frankly, before I felt comfortable enough with my name selling tickets that I could take an aria out of my recitals on the road. I did not feel that I could necessarily do that outside of New York, and yet I never did it in Europe—isn't that interesting? I should never say "never" because it has been so long. The closest thing that I did to an aria in Europe was that big long cantata by Rossini, Giovanna d'Arco, which is like singing ten arias! But it still wasn't called an opera aria, so I felt I could put it on recital programs.

In my case, I have always felt that I have the ability to be very versatile. So therefore I programmed music according to that. Whether one agrees with me or not, I felt as comfortable singing Schubert or Hugo Wolf as I did singing Samuel Barber or Bill Bolcom or John Jacob Niles folk songs.

Q. Do audiences in America, Europe, Japan, or elsewhere distinguish among songs and say that one is profoundly classical, such as Schubert, while another may be more folklike and therefore they will have another opinion about that song when you open your mouth or they see it in the program? Or is it all music?

A. *I am not sure, to tell you the truth. I think maybe yes and I think maybe no. Take Brahms, for example, and his series of folk songs that he arranged. Nothing can be more beautiful than some of those songs, such as Da unten im Thale, and that is a folk song. But I don't have people say, "Well, that's a folk song." I think it is all the same. It makes a tremendous impression on an audience, and I have never had anything less than great success with it—the simplicity of it! So that's the other thing that I was able to do, whether people agreed with me or not. I felt that I was able to do complicated things, and very simple things, and put them on a program.*

I think this comes from my background. I think this comes from the fact that I was singing from the time I was a kid. I recently found some conversation that somebody had with one of my aunts. All my life I was saying that I sang for the first time in public just before I was four. But one of these notes I found said that my first public appearance was when I was eight days before being two! So you see how long I have been at this.

Q.   You are an American, and you sing in English, Spanish, French, German, Italian, Russian . . .

A.   *Just a bit in Russian. I loved singing in Russian and I am sure if I were a young singer now, I would be singing in Russian and Czech. All the young singers do now. But all the things of that type that I did, I sang in English.*

Q.   But as an American, at least when you began your career, your song literature in your language was not necessarily given the reception it is now—

A.   *You bet!*

Q.   You had to sing in other people's languages, in their countries, in front of people in Vienna and Berlin with very discerning ears and long memories.

A.   *Oh please! Yes, and rightly so. They, of course, were thinking they really knew.*

Q.   What did you, and what do singers from an English-language background, have to do to master that?

A.   *First, learn the language. I started out by learning them phonetically. I didn't speak the languages when I was very young, but you really do have to learn them. You really need a great ear to learn a language, but you really need a great ear to be a singer anyway. And, the joy of being able to do it in another language. I love speaking another language. It has given me lots of pleasure.*

Q.   Let us take one word in German, one that every singer, native speaker or not, seems to pronounce in a slightly different way: *Sehnsucht* [nostalgic longing].

A.   Sehnsucht? *How do they pronounce it differently?*

Q. Some buzz the first *S*. Some hiss the second *S*. Some accent the *CH*. Some nail the *T*. Some take the *U* and make it an oooh instead of an uhh [rhymes with the vowels in "book"]. I have heard that word pronounced every different way.

A. *I don't think it's an oooh. I could be wrong. ZAIN-ZOOCHT. ZAIN-ZUHHCHT. It's not quite an oooh, it's somewhere in between, it's a little bit of an uhh sound for me. And both of those S's are Z sounds. And a pretty tight E vowel on the sehn. That's a pretty closed vowel for me, if I were teaching that, that's the way I would teach it. And I always put a big T on it because that's German. And I am always saying to my pupils, "Exaggerate the German. You must exaggerate the consonants." I just refer them to Fischer-Dieskau recordings and I say, "Listen how he does those consonants."*

Q. The reason I asked this is because if a singer looks at a single song in German, there are so many obstacles there linguistically, even if she understands every word's meaning. These obstacles come in terms of emphasis, in terms of choices that can be made—and not only in German, of course. We have it in English, and I think in every language. How would you take, or how would you teach a singer to take, one song and literally analyze it without killing it, but to make sure that every thought and feeling that singer has is put into that song?

A. *But you have just said it. I would take it and analyze it right from the very beginning. One of my favorite quotes about me in the newspaper was a few years ago when one of the critics of the New York Times came. He obviously had been to several master classes and he said, "If you want a line-by-line editor, Marilyn Horne is the one." That is what I do. I take it line by line. I hopefully keep the big picture in mind, but I really think that you can take it like an editor.*

Q. What comes first—the sound of a word or the meaning of a word?

A. *The meaning. You have got to dig into that first.*

Q. And so you would express the meaning in terms of the music that is written for that word rather than the sound of the word?

A. *I don't know if you can divorce one from the other. We are assuming that the person knows how to pronounce the word, right? So I think that when you go for the meaning, then you also go for the way the composer set it. What kind of a chord is on it? Is it a minor chord? Is it a major chord? That can really change enormously what you feel about it. But I would go for the words first, and then see what the composer did with it.*

Q. In your recording of Aaron Copland's *Simple Gifts*—which is a song you have sung many times, and many of us have sung many times—aside from the beauty of the singing, what struck me was your enunciation and pronunciation of the word "gift." Each time, you use the word as an accent, but without being overbearing with it. So, it is as if you constructed the song: "'Tis a gift, to be simple; 'Tis a gift, to be free," with the slightest pause after the word "gift." I mention this now after talking about German because I think an American, or an English-speaker, would not understand that the same effort you applied in German has to be applied in English as well.

A. *Probably with a little less effort, perhaps, in English. I think it happens more naturally. I think that in that case I was doing two things. I was trying to make the word understood, and you've got two T's there. You've got the "gift to." You don't really want to sing, "'Tis a gif T To"— but you have got to lay on those T's. So, "'Tis a gift [very quick pause] to be . . ." I probably did it unknowingly, in the beginning.*

But I think that everyone, bar none, sings better in his native tongue. There is no question about it. When I audition people, I want to hear them sing in their native tongue. I remember once, with Jimmy Levine, I took a tenor to him to hear. The tenor is Icelandic, so Jimmy wanted to hear something in Icelandic. There is a freedom that comes with that. I see it with my kids every summer [at the Music Academy of the West]. We have an eight-week term, and at the end we really sort of let our hair down and do a cabaret concert. So we are dealing with musical comedy, operetta, stuff like that. Suddenly, all those damned vowels that I couldn't get, that I worked so hard to get in other languages, came automatically in English. Their voices go into the right place, and they don't struggle. It's amazing.

Q. You have become a very famous teacher.

A.   *Frankly, I am amazed. I never thought about teaching. I was too damned busy keeping it all together for myself. But I discovered, first of all, that I like it. I really like it. And I guess that somehow, over the years, my thoughts were strong enough, and I can really dig into those and impart them in a course. As with every teacher, I have learned much much more as I have taught. I have found things within myself to teach that I did not think of for myself.*

Q.   Your goal in establishing the Marilyn Horne Foundation is to safeguard, to promote and preserve the art of the vocal recital.

A.   *Right.*

Q.   You have done a famously, conspicuously wonderful job in the educational aspect of this for singers. You have produced recordings that are sent to libraries and radio stations for archival and educational purposes. How do you educate an audience to listen to a vocal recital?

A.   *Well, first of all, you've got to get them there. I just think you have to educate them in a couple of ways. We have begun to experiment with supertitles, which I think are here to stay. Audience response in surveys has been overwhelmingly positive. We know we have to tweak them, and we know that there are still some technical limitations, but they are here to stay.*

You have to prepare really good translations. I have to tell you that has always been one of my great frustrations, because I have always gone to great pains to make sure that the translations in the program book were really good, really readable. I wanted the print to be large in the program book. But it doesn't always happen. If you are going to sing in, say, let's pick a city—Kalamazoo—great name—maybe they didn't print them the way you wanted them. Maybe people can't see them. You walk out on stage and you thought you were going to have the lights strong enough to read, and they are not. We go through all of this, but you just have to roll with it. And so if I feel people can't see their notes, I will say, "Excuse me a second, I think we need a little more light," and I will go off and ask the stage manager if I could have the lights up a little bit. Again, that also relaxes an audience.

I find that a New York audience really knows what to expect at a recital. There are degrees to which an audience knows what is going on at a recital. In other places, I do feel that in this day and age it is not unheard of that the singer should speak to the audience a little bit. I think that really relaxes an audience. I have tried that myself, and I can tell you that there were times when I felt a distance between myself and the audience and I did not think it was the way we were performing. I could be wrong—maybe we weren't reaching them. But I can recall turning to my accompanist (more than likely Marty Katz, but it could have been Warren Jones or Brian Zeger) and saying, "I think I've got to speak to them a little bit." It would just be telling them about the song I was going to perform. I really think it relaxes the audience and helps them feel that it not such a formal thing to be at a recital, and we can just relax about it.

You know, when we think of recitals in the old days, they were kind of a formal situation and people dressed up to go to performances, which they don't anymore. There is a big difference, and I think that our relationship to the public has to try to bridge that a little bit, too. I mean, a woman singer sometimes does not even wear a gown. Sometimes she wears a pants outfit, and I think that plays into it. But getting an audience's attention, I think the first song has to be something that will grab them. It is a simple song, if it's a Handel aria—Handel or Vivaldi or Purcell seem to go well, even if they are from operas, and let's face it, they warm up your voice.

I really stuck to that concept for most of my career. And the experiences I have had—and I have told this to my students, too—that when I have started a recital with a group of songs that called for major finesse of dynamics, like pianissimos here or there floating high, I never felt I really got my voice open for the night. But when I have sung the Baroque music that really gets my voice going out there, then I have had the finesse I wanted later on in the evening. I still recommend this to singers. Now you really have got to have your "chops" together to sing Handel. As you know, the Handel revival has happened, so we have a lot of singers out there singing Handel.

Q.   Last question . . .

A.   *Oh, it's the last question already?*

Q.   All right, not last question. Let's go to the Bolcom. This cycle, *I Will Breathe a Mountain*, was created specifically for you to sing at the hundredth anniversary of Carnegie Hall. Was it you who requested that all the texts in this cycle be by women?

A.   *You bet. And all Americans.*

Q.   What was your reason?

A.   *I think it is still part of the neglect of women writers, poets, painters, the whole thing. I was still feeling that, and that there are such good women poets out there and we should give them their due.*

Q.   And William Bolcom responded to the challenge?

A.   *Absolutely. He started sending me poems to look at. Obviously things that he wanted to set, which I felt was more important in a way. The one thing I wanted to tell you about with "The Bustle in the House" set to a poem by Emily Dickinson: when my brother was killed in a terrible plane accident that killed a hundred and fifty people, I spoke at his memorial. They played a recording of mine of* Bist du bei mir, *by Bach. I wanted something special to say about him at the end of the eulogy about him. A friend of mine who is a writer suggested "A Bustle in the House" and I read it and said oh yes, that's perfect. That Emily Dickinson, she really could speak to us, couldn't she? And I told Bill Bolcom that I really wanted to set that and he gave it a fantastic setting. In fact, it's got so many beautiful Americana chords in it. But I have sung it at another funeral without any piano. Frankly, I didn't know I was going to sing it. It was for one of my dearest friends.*

And another song in this cycle, "Never More Will the Wind" speaks really at a sad time. In fact, I sang it at Henry's funeral [conductor Henry Lewis was Horne's former husband].

Q.   I did not know this story of your special relationship to "A Bustle in the House." Yet when I listened to the cycle again this morning, though I loved everything, this was the song that jumped out at me.

A.   *Interesting.*

Q.   Though I loved everything, I just stopped because this song really grabbed me.

A. *Bill is a great songwriter. He's a great composer, no question, but his songs—so many of them are standard repertory now because singers bring them in to study them. Last summer, I had a girl bring "The Fish" to me, which is the last song in the cycle and impossibly hard. But she knew it cold, and I thought, OK, this cycle is really catching on now.*

Q. Do you think that the fact that "A Bustle in the House" jumped out at me, even though I loved all the songs, was that based on my characteristics as any given listener, or is it perhaps based on something added that you brought in the singing of that song, given your history with the poem?

A. *I don't think I can answer that. To be honest, I just think it is a great poem and it so speaks to what goes on after a death, especially what goes on in the end:*

> The Sweeping up the Heart
> And putting love away
> We shall not want to use again
> Until Eternity.

That just says it all. And what is going on after a death—you've got a bustle in the house. There are all these preparations that have to be made. And in the old days, of course, the body was probably laid out in the parlor. We don't do that so much anymore. That is my first memory of seeing someone in a casket, when my grandfather died—I was probably about four or five—and there he was at the end of the parlor. Now we are talking about a very small parlor, but in the head of this little child that parlor seemed enormous. I remember my dad asking my older sister and me if we wanted to go over and see him up close. My sister said, "Oh, yes," and I said, "Oh, no."

But I do think that the poem and the way Bill set it is just kind of perfection, isn't it?

Q.   When a singer has life experience, such as the example you just gave about your grandfather, is it a good idea to summon those experiences and invest them in a song?

A. *No question about it, and in opera, too. I suppose it is a little bit about Method acting. People always had to do that, whether it is called the Method, or Stanislavsky or whomever. You always had to tap into your own emotions. Or, let's face it, there is another way to do it. Hopefully one is an actor, too, so you can conjure these emotions up because you can imagine what those feelings are. That works, too.*

Let me give you an example. I have sung many male roles [in my operatic repertory]. Hey—I have had to figure that out in my head. I always felt that I got on the boots and the armor and the helmet and the sword, that helped to make me feel more butch. But I certainly had to imagine what it is like. You have to call on everything. A singer has to call on all of the emotions that one has felt. It is a huge, huge gamut.

Q. There are singers, and also pianists and violinists and other musicians, who have—at least externally—a placid and even proper demeanor. And their playing seems very correct, very appropriate, very polite.

A. *Well, look at Heifetz. He certainly was a very formal, sort of stiff presence, shall we say. But look what came out of that fiddle! Everything that anybody would ever want. Singers are a little different. We are looking them in the eye.*

Q. Does a singer need to show her temperament?

A. *Yeah, I think it has to come through. I don't think you have to waltz around the stage, but it has to come through in the inflection of the words or whatever. Sure. Certain songs call for much, much more.*

You started to ask me one question and I skipped over it and I want to return to that. You asked me did my approach to anything change over the years. With the Frauenliebe und -leben, *I cannot tell you how much—I don't know if I sang it better or made it clearer to the audience. But with the song after the baby is born [*"An mienem Herzen, an miener Brust"*], it says "Only a mother can know what this is all about." Well, I just felt that entirely differently after my own daughter was born. Before, it was acting. Afterward, it was feeling. Because I knew what it is like to say "Mother love, no one can ever feel this but a mother."*

Q. Therefore, perhaps, a singer who has not experienced certain things before in her life—or his life—for example, *Winterreise*, if sung by a man, maybe he has not experienced certain of these things . . .

A. *But he will! So I would say, get started.*

Q. If a song has a lyric that might be considered kind of silly, such as Copland's "I bought me a cat," how do you take a lyric like that, which is meant to please or beguile the listener, but is also about something, simplistic though it may be.

A. *But it also is basically a children's song, so you've got to really relate that it is a children's song, and making all those animal noises you really get into that. As long as you can get that playfulness into it, and remember the words. I always have to go over in my mind who says what, and in what order. This song is not so very easy, because at a certain point you have to go backwards.*

Q. Musicians have to have amazing memories, and . . .

A. *Oh please! Singers above all, because of the words. Marty Katz has always said that he has never seen a singer go onstage before a recital and say, "I'm worried about my voice." They say, "I'm worried about the words." And sometimes, when I am learning a song that is extremely complicated, I have counted the words just to tell myself that I really am learning a hard song.*

Q. Rarely now, but still occasionally, one sees a singer in a recital with a music stand onstage, turning pages as she sings.

A. *We know that a lot of great singers have done that, but I have opted not to because I know that it creates barriers between me and the audience. In the old days, and nobody seems to be doing it nowadays, singers had these lovely booklets to refer to. So I have worked to commit music to memory.*

Q. How does a musician commit music to memory?

A. *Every singer is different. I write the words out as a way of seeing that I have learned them.*

Q. Breathing is something fundamental to your art, but may be something that the reader of this book may take into consideration only secondarily.

A. *About twenty years ago [1981] Joan Sutherland, Luciano Pavarotti, and I did a concert in Avery Fisher Hall. We did a panel together at the intermission. The man interviewing us, Robert Jacobson, asked us to talk about breath support. Each of us chimed in, more or less at once, "Breathing is everything." But that part of the interview was cut out, which was a shame because if young singers could hear the three of us say it at once, they might have understood that we meant it.*

Q. How do you support breath?

A. *With your whole body. The diaphragm is like the bellows along with the lungs. But you cannot support it with your lungs. You have to use muscles. So there are these tremendous muscles that one uses in parts of the body. In the buttocks, legs, stomach, down to the feet. That's why I am tired physically after a recital, not much more than in the throat apparatus. Singing is a very physical activity. I am talking about real singing: half artist, half athlete. That's got to be it.*

Q. How can readers of this book become involved with the Marilyn Horne Foundation?

A. *I would like the readers to support the foundation in any way they can, but mostly with money and attendance. We need money— there is the old saying that the church has to stay in the town. So we need every bit of financial support we can get. We are basically a small foundation, but we have had such wonderful support from the press that people might think we are bigger than we are.*

And attendance is major. When a recital is presented by us and funded by us, we need bodies in those seats.

Q. In just a very few years, many of the young people you have worked with—let's call them the Horne Scholars—have gone on to strong careers in opera and recital. When you see this, how does it make you feel? What does it feel like to see that these seeds you have planted and watered have borne fruit?

A. *I can tell you, because when you say this it brings me to tears. I am so thrilled for these kids. My joy is so deep because I know how hard it is to have a life in music. If they are coming along and being accepted, that is just fabulous.*

I Will Breathe a Mountain: Songs of Barber, Bernstein, Bolcom; *Marilyn Horne, mezzo-soprano; Martin Katz, piano; Tokyo String Quartet; RCA Victor 09026-68771-2*

Beautiful Dreamer: The Great American Songbook; *Marilyn Horne, mezzo-soprano; Carl Davis, conductor; English Chamber Orchestra; London/Decca 417 242-2. The five Copland songs also appear on the Copland "Double-Decker" compendium you own (London/Decca 448-261-2).*

♪ American Songs ♪

The United States has created a remarkable body of song literature that is only beginning to gain the acceptance and admiration it deserves. Some of it comes under the category of "American Popular Song." The American popular songbook covers a range of songs composed from about 1910 to 1960. It forms an important segment of song literature that many classical artists—including Dawn Upshaw, Renee Fleming, Marilyn Horne, Anne Sofie von Otter, Bryn Terfel, and Thomas Hampson—are now including in their recital programs. To the credit of these singers, American popular songs often appear in their concerts and recordings in renditions that are idiomatic and in no way grandiose or operatic. We see again what great works of art they are, and one always has to insist that the term "crossover" not be appended to these performances—it is demeaning to the music and the singers.

The best of these songs blend clever or poetic lyrics with gorgeous melodies in a seamless way. Like all great art songs, they create a mood and a world in just a few minutes. These songs were not originally intended for the concert hall, having often been written for films or Broadway musicals. But they stand apart for their quality, and are performed in concerts and on recordings.

Jerome Kern (1885–1945), Irving Berlin (1888–1989), Cole Porter (1891–1934), George Gershwin (1898–1937), Duke Ellington (1899–1974), Richard Rodgers (1902–1977), and Harold Arlen (1905–1986) are the unmatched geniuses of American popular song. There were many other fine practitioners, including Richard Whiting (1891–1938), Harry Warren (1893–1981), Hoagy Carmichael (1899–1981), Arthur Schwartz (1900–1984), Vernon Duke (1903–1969), Dorothy Fields (1905–1974), Jule Styne (1905–1994), Johnny Mercer (1909–1976), Burton Lane (1912–1997), and Jimmy Van Heusen (1913–1990).

All of these composers wrote splendid songs, the best of which rank with great art songs of the classical tradition. Some preferred to write their own lyrics, such as Porter, but many collaborated with lyricists such as Sammy Cahn, Ira Gershwin, Oscar Hammerstein, Yip Harburg, Lorenz Hart, and Mercer.

It is important to note that Gershwin and Elllington stand apart from the other composers in this group, because the scope of their genius embraced so many musical forms, all of which they mastered. In addition to his marvelous songs and theater music, Gershwin wrote a wonderful opera, *Porgy and Bess*, orchestral pieces, and lots of brilliant piano music. Ellington drew a lot from the New Orleans jazz style, including polyphonic writing, which he then took in his own direction. He wrote secular and sacred music, songs, suites, instrumental works, and more. Whether we choose to include him as part of a classical or popular tradition, he was certainly a great composer.

Gershwin and Ellington followed in the tradition of great European composers by depicting in their music the world that surrounded them. The sounds, the things (their evocation of subway trains and great railway trains), the people (we can picture Ellington's "Sophisticated Lady"), and the sensations are very much of their time and place.

• ◇ •

Apart from American popular song, there is—and has long been—a tradition of American songs for the concert stage, some of which come from older popular and folk traditions, such as those by Stephen Foster, or were avowedly "classical" from the start. In addition, there are the musical traditions of many American ethnic groups, most especially African-Americans, whose contributions have been formidable. Spirituals, which were born in churches and cotton fields, are a gorgeous and sincere expression of character and belief that have found their way to concert halls and are, in every way, art songs even if they were never created with that in mind.

But in most cases, American composers of recital songs forged a new idiom that speaks both of national character and personal expression. American recital singers have had to battle to include a lot of American music on their programs, especially in Europe, because critics there (and sometimes in the United States) have been dismissive of this repertory.

Some songs and compositions by Copland, and a song group such as *Knoxville: Summer of 1915* by Samuel Barber, are about many things, of course, but one of them is American simplicity and directness (in the best sense of these words). These songs may recount things as mundane as sitting on a porch and watching the world go by, but they are also about the quiet satisfaction and pleasure these provide. While some European art songs gush in their effusive expression of sentiments, many of these American songs derive their eloquence from their simplicity.

There are so many American song composers to discover. Here are but a few: Charles Ives, Stephen Foster, Aaron Copland, Leonard Bernstein, Lee Hoiby, Ned Rorem, William Bolcom, Samuel Barber, Virgil Thomson, and Ricky Ian Gordon.

To the Soul: Songs to the Poetry of Walt Whitman; *Thomas Hampson, baritone; Craig Rutenberg, piano; EMI 7243 5 55028 2 7*

Start your study by reading the wonderful essay in the CD program booklet by Thomas Hampson and Carla Maria Verdino-Süllwold, a virtual primer about Walt Whitman as a voice of America and Americans. All of the songs on this recording are set to his texts, and most of the music is by Americans, although there are interesting contributions by Charles Villiers Stanford, Kurt Weill, Ralph Vaughan Williams, and Paul Hindemith.

Hampson's pronunciation and phrasing (music *and* words) is literate without being overbearing, and he clearly loves both the texts and the melodies that go with them. Listen to this recording without reading along. You will be able to make out almost everything on first hearing, and will experience the thrill of direct communication between singer and listener. Later, on your own and for pleasure, read the texts without the music and see how much melody returns to your ears from the songs. Do you think that because you comprehend English that you absorbed words more than melody? If so, go back to the recording again and listen to the *music*, letting the words go slightly muddy as you focus on the sound.

Barber: Hermit Songs, Knoxville Summer of 1915; *Leontyne Price, soprano; Samuel Barber, piano; New Philharmonia Orchestra; Thomas Schippers, conductor; RCA 09026-61983-2*

The *Hermit Songs* were written specifically for the beautiful voice and exquisite talents of American soprano Leontyne Price, and her mastery of them is such that it was a long time before other singers included it in their repertory. Price had a particular affinity for the music of Barber and her performance of the *Knoxville: Summer of 1915* cycle is also outstanding. This is a landmark recording, but you should also listen—for sake of comparison—to the more recent version of *Knoxville* by Dawn Upshaw. Her voice is less sumptuous than Price's but also has a particular clarity that often brings the words into more focus. It is a case of an intelligent, knowledgeable, and highly communicative artist, which

Upshaw is, recognizing what her strengths are and using them to great effect. Compare this to the Price interpretation, which is ravishing, and you can understand how music that might seem to be "owned" by one artist can actually be very meaningful when essayed by others. If you can locate the recording of *Knoxville* by Eleanor Steber from the 1950s, that will be further evidence of how this music can be sublime when sung by different artists.

Take the same listening approach that you did with the Walt Whitman songs, making sure that you hear the music as much as the words.

♪ Russian Songs ♪

Sviridov: Russia Cast Adrift; *Rachmaninoff: 9 Songs; Dmitri Hvorostovsky, baritone; Mikhail Arkadiev, piano; Philips 446 666-2*

One could devote whole chapters to Russian songs, and I would encourage you to make your own explorations into those of Tchaikovsky, Mussorgsky, Rimsky-Korsakov, and Rachmaninoff. Artists past and present who give persuasive accounts of Russian music include Jennie Tourel, Feodor Chaliapin, Galina Vishnevskaya, Boris Christoff, Nikolai Ghiaurov, Nicolai Gedda, Martti Talvela, Dmitri Hvorostovsky, Olga Borodina, Galina Gorchakova, and Ewa Podlés.

Hvorostovsky, a Siberian baritone, has been blessed with a beautiful voice and a singer's ear, but in some ways has been burdened with his famous good looks. To some extent he is promoted as a matinee idol but, to his credit, he endeavors to do song recitals of serious and challenging music that will expand the repertory for singers. His most successful effort was a song cycle, *Russia Cast Adrift* (1977) by Georgii Sviridov.

First, read the texts for the lovely Rachmaninoff songs, creating as many mental and emotional pictures as you can in preparation for listening. Then listen to the songs—both vocal line and piano—and do your best to follow along, connecting your ideas to the sounds you hear.

As you approach the Sviridov cycle, read the essay by Harlow Robinson in the CD booklet. Then carefully read the texts (starting on page 10), bearing in mind that this is a song cycle in the Schubert mode, with poems to be read in sequence whose totality means much more than each individual poem.

Because you cannot cross-reference to the Russian, learning this cycle will be more of a challenge than with German or French texts unless you are able to read the Cyrillic alphabet. But as you listen, pay close attention to the piano accompaniment for aural cues about the ideas and feelings in the songs. Hvorostovsky and his pianist, Mikhail Arkadiev, do a beautiful job of making us feel this music.

♩ Recitals ♩

You have heard a live recital by Lorraine Hunt Lieberson. Here is another one for you to consider as you develop a love for the recital form and for the world of song literature.

Salzburg Recital; *Kathleen Battle, soprano; James Levine, piano; DG 415 361-2*

This recording is a fine document of an actual recital given before a very discerning audience in Salzburg during the famous annual festival. Battle was at her best here, and Levine was an ideal partner on the piano. The programming is typical of the type of recital a versatile artist might give. Beginning with early music (in English, Battle's native language, and one that is foreign to many even in the international audience that

Salzburg attracts). What follow are beautiful songs by Mendelssohn, Strauss, Mozart, and Fauré that readily show off Battle's beautiful voice and her facility with German, Italian, and French. Ask yourself whether you think she is stronger or more effective in one of these languages, or do the performances all seem to be of the same quality?

The performance concludes with spirituals. Many artists, in recital, like to conclude programs with music that either bespeaks a tradition they are a part of or feel close to. So Karita Mattila might sing in Finnish, Renée Fleming might sing Ellington, Bryn Terfel might sing in Welsh, and Kiri Te Kanawa in Maori. Battle, who grew up in the African-American church tradition, presents these spirituals in a genuine and heartfelt way, making them very much at home on this varied evening of music.

Another recital recording to explore:

Schubert, Brahms, and Schumann: Lieder; Vesselina Kasarova, mezzo-soprano; Friedrich Haider, piano; BMG 09026-68763-2

• ⌒ •

Other fine song collections in various genres:

Eighteenth-Century Bel Canto; *Gewandhausorchester Leipzig; Kurt Masur, conductor; Elly Ameling, soprano; Philips 412 233-2*

Ameling gives a lyrical and word-sensitive cast to music that is often more known for pyrotechnics. In arias and concert arias (music written expressly for the recital stage, but with a dramatic intention), she essays music by Giordani, Vivaldi, Paisiello, Heinichen, Handel, Gluck, Pergolesi, Mozart, and the achingly beautiful "When I am laid to rest" from Purcell's *Dido and Aeneas.*

Love's Twilight *(Berg, Korngold, R. Strauss); Anne Sofie von Otter, mezzo-soprano; Bengt Forsberg, piano; DG 437 515-2*

Lovely twentieth-century lieder, expertly sung.

Sentimental Me; *Elly Ameling, soprano; Louis van Dijk, piano; John Clayton, double bass; Philips 412-433-2*

The great Dutch soprano sings music from the American popular songbook.

LIFT EVERY VOICE
Music with Chorus

U ntil this point, when I have spoken of the blending of voices to produce music, these were instrumental voices. Yet polyphony first came about in the blending of human voices, and this is at the heart of choral singing. When you listen to a chorus, there are times when every member is singing the same music in unison. At other times, different voices or groupings in a chorus sing different music in a way that contrasts beautifully and often dramatically.

The power of a hundred voices filling a church or concert hall is an overwhelming musical experience. Composers have recognized this effect and have used it often in religious and secular music. Of course, the chorus is an essential component in opera, but look at *Opera 101* for more information on that.

Choral music can be sung *a capella*. This term, meaning "in the chapel," suggests that there is no instrumental accompaniment. Many choral works also feature vocal soloists, and most have musical instruments as well.

Two of the most popular musical forms that use a chorus are the *oratorio* and the *mass*. Both almost always have religious affiliations, with an important difference. The oratorio is often the recounting of a story, typically from the Bible. These were, in effect, music dramas, though performed in churches and concert halls without scenery or specific costumes. Contrast this with opera, which is also storytelling, but in which costumes, scenery, lighting, and stage direction play an important role.

The oratorio is thought to have originated in Rome in the late sixteenth century as a sort of religious play with music. It is generally said that the first true oratorio (named for a part of a church known in English as an oratory) was Emilio De' Cavalieri's *La rappresentazione di anima e di corpo* (The Representation of the Soul and of the Body), presented in Rome's Oratorio della Vallicella in 1600 (just a year or so after the first operas were staged in Florence). Originally, opera tended to draw its subject matter from mythology, thus providing sharp contrast with the biblical stories told in oratorios.

An oratorio typically has a narrator (sometimes called a *historicus*), characters portrayed by solo singers and speakers, performing text that is spoken and/or sung. Then there is a chorus representing "the people." You should understand that "the people" not only refers to the biblical masses but can be thought of as surrogates for those who are listening to the performance. Think too that this was not only a musical event but often a form of religious instruction. If you think of the visual arts in that era, religious paintings by artists such as Rubens were admirable not only for their technique but for their ability to tell an often cautionary religious story to people who could not read. The same applies to the oratorio.

The oratorio spread to other Italian cities, with the strongest traditions being in Bologna, Modena, Florence, and Venice. The earliest oratorios were sung in Latin, and later in Italian. The form spread to other nations. Vienna, in particular, became a popular location for oratorios, where they were presented on a regular basis in the royal court, which decreed that in the period of Lent, oratorios should be performed instead of opera. Most of these were written by Italians.

In France, local composers wrote oratorios, most of which were performed in Latin. Marc-Antoine Charpentier (1634?–1704) is usually credited with bringing the oratorio to France, where composers such as

François-André Philidor (1726–1795), François-Joseph Gossec (1734–1892), and Jean-François Lesueur (1760–1837) continued the tradition.

Certainly the most famous composer of oratorios (with due respect to J. S. Bach) was George Frideric Handel (1685–1759), a remarkably versatile and cosmopolitan man who was born in Germany, traveled widely in Italy absorbing many ideas and enjoying some of his earlier triumphs, and then moving to England and becoming so established (loved by many, but also reviled by other composers) that he is often thought of as a British composer. His music covered a wide range of styles and subject matter, including forty-two operas (most based on mythology or classical literature), twenty-two oratorios (mostly religious subjects, except for *Semele* and *Hercules*), plus all sorts of music for instruments and solo voice. Among the great Handel oratorios, many set to English-language texts, are *Saul, Samson, Israel in Egypt*, and the *Messiah*.

In Handel oratorios, the chorus takes on a much bigger role than in his operas. They play an important part in the storytelling. In addition, the solo voices—the protagonists in the story—are vividly portrayed characters of almost operatic dimension.

In German-speaking lands, the oratorio was a vehicle for storytelling not only in Catholic churches but also in Lutheran ones. An oratorio might tell the story of Christmas or other events in the Christian year, but there was a related form, the passion, that was specifically used on Good Friday and throughout Holy Week. The passion had its roots in the form of evangelical narration of stories by Gregorian chant. As the passion came into being, it was typical to have three solo narrative voices. The lowest belonged to the singer portraying Christ; the middle voice was that of the Evangelist; and the highest voice was used for other characters and for the people. Probably the most famous passions are both by Bach—one according to St. John; the other according to St. Matthew. The latter had been lost until it was rediscovered and presented by Mendelssohn in 1829. It seems that Bach wrote five passions, but only these two survive. Mention should also be made of *The Cre-*

ation (1798) by Haydn, a beautiful work that is not performed as often as it should be.

By the nineteenth century, oratorios and passions were less in demand, although music in this genre continued to issue from the pens of composers who found relevant ways to tell stories. These include Mendelssohn (who wrote *Paulus* and *Elijah*), Berlioz (*L'Enfance du Christ* and the quite original *La Damnation de Faust*, whose nonreligious subject leads some to call it an opera), Liszt (*Christus* and *Die Legende von Heiligen Elisabeth*), Massenet (*Marie-Magdeleine*), and César Franck (*La Rédemption* and *Les Béatitudes*). In Italy, Lorenzo Perosi (1872–1956) devoted much of his work to creating religious music, and formed something of a bridge between older and newer styles.

The twentieth century saw the creation of important oratorios and religious works more themed to the issues of the times. But these works maintained the meditative and philosophical components that characterized oratorios of earlier centuries. Arthur Honegger is known for his *Le Roi David* and, especially, *Jeanne d'Arc au Bûcher*, a dramatic telling of the story of Joan of Arc at the stake. Other important oratorios include Schoenberg's *Jacob's Ladder*, Hindemith's *Das Unaufhörliche*, Frank Martin's *Le Vin Herbé*, Schnittke's *Nagasaki*, and Henze's *Raft of the Medusa*. In a category of one is Stravinsky's *Oedipus Rex* (1927), which he called an opera-oratorio. He meant for it to be presented on an opera stage, but with the spare and static "staging" of an oratorio.

• ∾ •

The mass became the principal liturgical form of the Roman Catholic Church for most of its history, and in its present form since about the year 1000. The subject matter changed according to the time of the year and the subject at hand. Five sections (based on Latin texts) were almost always included in masses—*Kyrie, Gloria, Credo, Sanctus, Agnus Dei*—while others came and went according to the celebration (these included *Introitus, Graduale, Alleluia, Offertorium*, and *Communio*).

Masses and other music for religious services were written by most composers until nearly 1800. Masses in the nineteenth century took a new direction for two reasons. The first is that in the Europe following the American and French Revolutions, the relationship between peoples, national governments, and the Church began to change. Many creative artists, including Beethoven, Verdi, and Wagner, were drawn to the possibilities of a new kind of enlightened government in which religion, though important, remained separate from civic life. Secondly, as the orchestra began to expand and diversify under Beethoven and others, many masses and religious music took on a more symphonic tone in which the orchestra played a role as important as chorus and soloists.

Notable works include Beethoven's *Missa Solemnis*, a work of intense religiosity that was not necessarily intended for religious observances. Other important nineteenth-century works in this vein were produced by Schubert, Rossini, Berlioz, Liszt, Bruckner, Gounod, and Perosi. In the twentieth century, composers took the mass in interesting new directions. Notable works were produced by Satie, Poulenc, Pizzetti, Malipiero, and Casella. Stravinsky wrote an unusual mass for voices and ten wind instruments in 1948. Janáček's *Glagolitic Mass* is a wonderful fusing of modern musical idiom and ancient Slavic liturgy.

It is often and mistakenly assumed that a mass is related to death. This is not necessarily true. Masses were religious celebrations, with masses for the dead, known as *missa pro defunctis or requiem*, a separate category. These requiem masses (now often simply called requiems) had the *Kyrie, Sanctus*, and *Agnus Dei* sections, leaving out the *Gloria* and the *Credo*, and added the *Dies Irae*. The most traditional requiems have nine sections.

In the late eighteenth century, Mozart and others found the vein for great expressive and emotional power in requiems, and soon many composers sought the chance to write one. Among the most famous are those by Cherubini, Berlioz, Verdi, Dvořák, Duruflé, and Fauré. Brahms's German Requiem, in his native language, stands apart in that the texts are in his own language and are not organized in the traditional sections as other requiems are.

The twentieth century has several notable requiems, most famously the War Requiem by Benjamin Britten (1961). Earlier, Kurt Weill wrote his Berliner Requiem based on texts by Bertolt Brecht. Also worthy of mention are a requiem by Gyorgy Ligeti (1965), *Requiem für einen junger Dichter*, by Bernd Alois Zimmerman (1969), and a requiem written in 1993 by Henze.

You might wonder whether a requiem heard years after its composition can offer the solace that it provided at the moment of its first performance. I think that requiems are deeply moving experiences that connect us to feelings for loved ones no longer alive. Most of them are intended, in part, not only to give a dignified burial to the dead but also to console the living. A famous exception is Verdi's splendid *Messa da Requiem*, which is full of anger and fury as it rages against death before coming to terms with it. But I also pass along the words of my friend Nimet Habachy: "A requiem does not suffice. It cannot pretend to. At best, it recognizes death or a calamity." She said this on the radio on March 6, 2001, before playing Duruflé's Requiem in memory of students killed by gunfire by a classmate in a school near San Diego. And she has a point.

Another important musical form that sprang from religious observance is the is the Stabat Mater which, since the thirteenth century, was part of the Good Friday observance. It tells the story of the suffering of the Virgin Mary before the cross. The text is attributed to Jacopone da Todi, and some of the most famous Stabat Maters were composed by Desprès, Palestrina, Alessandro Scarlatti, Pergolesi, Rossini, Verdi, and Dvořák. They include solo singers and chorus.

Then there is the cantata, which is closely linked to Bach, though it long predates him. Originally it was an outgrowth of medieval madrigals and referred to most any piece that was sung (*cantare* means "to sing" in Italian). This word contrasts with the all-purpose word *sonata*, which was a work that was played (*suonare* means "to play" in Italian).

The cantata did not originally have a religious connotation. Giacomo Carissimi (1605–1674) is thought to have been the first composer to create the distinct form of the cantata, which came in two forms. The *stile recitativo* paid more attention to the recitation of the words, with music as a supporting feature. The *stile arioso* focused more on a memorable melody.

Many Italian composers in the late seventeenth to early eighteenth centuries produced seemingly endless cantatas, most of which were for one or two voices, with accompaniment by a few instruments that would typically "dialogue" with the voices. Cantatas were often intimate and amorous in tone, and very beguiling. At some point, the cantata added a small chorus in Italy, and it was enlarged in other countries, especially France. Soon many cantatas contained orchestra, chorus, and soloists.

At this point, there was the development of what Italians called the *cantata sacra protestante*. This was the form used by Dietrich Buxtehude (1637–1707), Georg Philipp Telemann (1681–1767), and especially Johann Sebastian Bach. Their cantatas were quickly composed for use at weekly church services and, in the case of Bach's, proved to be of lasting musical value. These cantatas used texts from the Bible or were commentaries written in verse on the biblical texts that were being studied. Bach wrote about three hundred sacred cantatas and about fifty profane ones. These latter are not rude and irreligious. Rather, they are based on secular themes and draw inspiration from the style and content of the Italian cantatas. One of my favorites is the "Coffee Cantata."

The use of a chorus was not part of the original design of the symphony, but it came to be incorporated in certain symphonies to great effect. You will discover two of the greatest of these, Mahler's Second and Beethoven's Ninth, later on.

Let's begin:

Bach: Cantatas: Jauchzet Gott in allen Landen, BWV 51; Wer nur den lieben Gott läßt walten, BWV 93; Gelobet sei der Herr, mein Gott, BWV 120;

Münchener Bach-Chor, Münchener Bach-Orchester; Karl Richter, conductor; Archiv Galleria 427 115-2

Bach: Cantatas: Coffee Cantata, Peasant Cantata; Kammerorchester Berlin; Peter Schreier, conductor; Archiv Galleria 427 116-2

Note that works by Bach are number by "BWV" just as Mozart's music is preceded K.

There is a treasure trove of Bach cantatas to be found in the moderately priced Archiv Galleria line. These two recordings are representative of some of the best. The first one contains religious cantatas, written for churchgoers who speak German. Imagine yourself in a church in Germany three hundred years ago on a Sunday morning.

Open the libretto booklet to page 14–15 and listen to the first cantata ("Jauchzet Gott") while reading along in the *German* (the middle column). It does not matter if you do not understand the language. Your goal this time is to hear what music Bach wrote to accompany the *sounds* of these words. Pay special attention when you reach words such as *Gott* (God), *Himmel* (heaven), *Kreuz* (cross), *Leben* (life), *Kinder* (children), *Sohn* (son), and *Amen*. What is the music doing in these places to support the sound and the meaning of these words?

Now listen to the cantata again, this time reading the English translation. You will have a more complete understanding of the meaning of the words, but I wonder if you think something is lost in translation? That is, the sound of the original language. Can *God*, with its soft *D* at the end, compare with the more imperative sound of *Gott*? How does *Kreuz* (pronounced "croyts") sound different from the softer, more hissing *cross*? Does *Himmel* sound more or less heavenly than *heaven*?

KEY CONCEPT: *Words have meaning not only in their definition but in their sound. A writer or composer may be drawn to a particular word or name because its very sound makes a statement about its meaning. This applies when working in the same language or when a word is being translated.*

Think too about the syllables in a word or name. Taking the subject at hand, if the name Jesus is used instead of Christ, one reason might be because the first name has two syllables and the second has one. Or the opposite may be the case, with Christ being preferred because it is shorter. If you think of a passage of music in terms of its beats, then you can think of these as syllables. Composers who set existing texts, such as poems, have to work to make the music accommodate the words in a pleasing and meaningful way. But if the text is being created for the music, then there can be some give and take between the person writing the words and the one creating the music.

With syllables we again find the challenge of translation: if a word has two syllables in English and German (such as "heaven" and "*Himmel*"), it is easy as long as the accents are the same. But the same word in French (*paradis*) has three syllables, and Italian it has four (*paradiso*). This makes things difficult, unless other words in a sentence are shorter to make up the total. But it is not mere translation of language that is required, but a fidelity to the rhythm and melody of the original. This is why most classical music that is sung is performed in the original language. And it is better that way.

From now on, when you approach any piece of music that has words, ask yourself how the composer was inspired by the sound and the meaning of the words. And how did he or she attempt to give additional sense and texture to the meaning and sound of the words with the music attached to the words?

Before leaving this cantata, think how the chorus sounds. Is it in unison or in several voices? Does its impact on you musically, and in terms of the message of the words, come differently from those of solo voices?

If you wish, put aside the booklet and listen to the piece a third time in purely musical terms. Now that you have some idea of what it is talking about, do those feelings come across in the sound of Bach's music?

Take the skills you have just acquired and then listen to the next two cantatas in the same way. Notice that these cantatas begin with chorus rather than solo voice.

After listening to these three sacred cantatas, then turn to the delightful "profane" ones. I particularly love the opening words of both cantatas, which really set the tone for what will follow. Take the "Coffee Cantata," for example. The narrator admonishes us to "Keep quiet and no talking, and listen to what now happens: here we have Herr Schlendrian together with his daughter Liesgen. He is going on like a grizzly bear: listen to what she has done to upset him!" Needless to say, these secular cantatas were meant for performance outside religious settings.

As it happens, these two cantatas do not contain chorus—many do not. But I presented them to you so you can understand the contrast between the sacred and profane styles of cantatas, and the remarkable versatility of Bach.

• ❧ •

Bach: St. Matthew Passion; Chicago Symphony Orchestra and Chorus; Georg Solti, conductor; Te Kanawa, von Otter, Rolfe Johnson, Krause, Blochwitz, Bär, London/Decca 421 177-2

This is one of many fine recordings of the St. Matthew Passion. Another is conducted by John Eliot Gardiner, and the soloists include Rolfe Johnson, Schmidt, Bonney, von Otter, Chance, and Bär (Archiv 427 648-2). Be sure that the recording you select has the text enclosed.

This work, a passion, was intended for performance on Good Friday. It was first performed in Leipzig in 1727. I think that you will notice in its sorrowful tone that it is really a recounting of the death of Christ. In musical terms there are no hints of the resurrection that will come. It is as if worshipers were expected to go through the story of Christ and, as of Friday at least, the news is not good. Here again is the didactic form that much religious music took in the years before many churchgoers could read.

The St. Matthew Passion (sometimes called "The Passion According to St. Matthew") is drawn from chapters 26 and 27 of his gospel. If you listen attentively, you will find this work a riveting drama that is almost operatic in nature. Indeed, it has received several theatrical stagings in recent years, but in purely musical terms the drama is all there. I think the death of Christ you might picture in your head is more riveting than anything that can be put on a stage.

Before listening to the recording (if you are using the Solti), read the interesting essay in the libretto on pages 20–25. It will provide a valuable context for listening to this massive, cosmic work in which Bach takes an important moment in religious history—and yes, in human history—and turns it into a throbbing drama full of compassion. I think it creates a setting in which death, whether of Jesus or anyone we love, can be understood and accepted, no matter how awful and with so much sadness. The absence of the promise of redemption is part of the power of this work.

Listen to the work while reading the libretto. Skip back and forth between the German and English, endeavoring to understand the progression of the story while being mindful of the sound of the words in the original language. And please remember: this is music, so your principal mental activity should be *listening*—closely, carefully, completely—to the music, with your eyes abetting the listening as you read the words.

Here are two more things to think about. There are actually two choirs in this work—the full adult choir and the boys' choir. What do you think about the sound and impact of this distinction? What, for you, does the sound of the boys' choir represent? Why did Bach use this device?

Then, think about the fact that this is very beautiful music that is used to tell a terrible, brutal story. Do you think Bach created beautiful music here because he did not know how to write any other kind? Or is this beauty meant to convey something else in addition to the story—

solace? compassion? Use your thoughts on this topic to explore in other choral and vocal music the effect of beauty or lack of it on the way the words and story are perceived.

• ◌· •

Handel: Messiah; *Collegium Musicum 90; Richard Hickox, conductor; Joan Rodgers, Della Jones, Christopher Robson, Philip Langridge, Bryn Terfel; Chandos 0522/3*

At several points in this book I have mentioned how we grow with certain pieces of music and they change in meaning for us as our life changes. An example of this is Handel's *Messiah*, parts of which are so familiar to even the non–music lover that we tend to take for granted how splendid and varied this work is. We all know the "Hallelujah Chorus" that comes toward the end of the work. This chorus is one of the few pieces where people all stand when it is sung. (Americans also have their national anthem, which is always sung standing up, and "Take Me Out to the Ball Game" for the seventh-inning stretch at the ballpark.)

Messiah captures us with its beauty, drama, simplicity of storytelling, and the rich variety of choruses and arias that were the secret to Handel's greatness. For many music lovers, it is the greatest oratorio of all. As so often happens, when a work becomes so overwhelmingly beloved, it tends to cast others in the shadow. This is the case with Handel, whose many other marvelous oratorios do not get the regular performances they deserve because *Messiah* is the one choirs and conductors so often return to. Each Christmas season there are numerous performances of this work (and Bach's *Christmas Oratorio*) in every major city in North America and much of Europe. The work has become popular in part because it is a component of the Christmas tradition for many people, and they return to it as if it is part of the completion of an annual cycle. While many performances are heartfelt and well-prepared, in many cases the presentation of this work is done in a routine way by people who have performed it too many times. This can happen when music is so familiar that we no longer recognize its exquisite force. George Bernard Shaw wrote that "we have all had our Handelian training in church; thus we get broken into the custom of singing Handel as if he means nothing."

Messiah has always been part of my tradition. I return to it not for reasons of religious faith, but because it is indisputably a great work that offers rewards with each hearing. I attend one or two performances per year, and occasionally like to go to those in which the audience is encouraged to sing along in all the choruses. By now the work is part of who I am.

But a performance I heard on December 16, 2001, will always stand out from the dozens of others in my experience. Occasionally I have attended performances of *Messiah* at Trinity Church in lower Manhattan. The oratorio has been given there each holiday season since 1770, only twenty-eight years after the piece was composed. In fact, this was the location of the first performance of *Messiah* in the American colonies. The tradition at this church is to perform it with the instruments that were featured in Handel's original score.

Trinity Church is only about 600 feet (less than 200 meters) from the place where the World Trade Center stood. Miraculously and inexplicably, the old church remained virtually intact when just about everything around it was pulverized. The ash and smoke from the disaster had seeped through the church, lining the ninety organ pipes, and leaving that unmistakably acrid odor of death and devastation that had become all too familiar to New Yorkers. Although the organ had not been repaired, the rest of the church was lovingly cleaned.

On December 16, a little more than three months after the attack on New York, there were still fires at Ground Zero that had not yet been extinguished but finally would be in the next few days. The odor, though unmistakably present, was not as intense as it had been a month or two earlier.

Despite considerable obstacles, and as part of New Yorkers' collective defiance of the brutality that had been visited upon them, *Messiah* received its 231st annual performance. I was fortunate to be there, and asked myself how the singers could breathe and musicians could play when the air from outside shortened their breath and stung their eyes. But the spirit of the moment and the glory of the music each worked their power, and soon we were swept up in the narrative of what is really a story of adversity, suffering, the hope for salvation and ecstasy of rebirth. The lessons of brotherhood, solidarity, and tolerance were lost on no one. And then the visceral release of the "Hallelujah Chorus" produced a collective explosion of tears drawn from wells of sadness and joy. The work continued, as lines such as "Oh death, where is thy sting? Where is thy victory?" were uttered, and proceeded to a conclusion that was—in the purest sense of the word—satisfying. When it concluded, one felt whole again, at least for a time.

Will I ever be able to hear *Messiah* without returning to the feelings of this performance? Can I ever hear the work on its own terms without bringing these additional associations to it? Can I hear the bass soloist sing of "they that dwell in the land of the shadow of death" without making an immediate association with this one performance? It remains to be seen, but for now I have no desire to separate from those feelings. This is a very personal example of music as part of life experience. Although I would never wish for anyone to have to endure what so many Americans and others went through in the autumn of 2001, I share this example with you to explain that music we have always considered meaningful can acquire unexpected depth and resonance, and it can give us insight and strength when we most need it. And to show you how personal some works of music can become for each one of us—sometimes for purely aesthetic reasons, other times because of emotion or circumstance.

• ◇ •

In the case of most works of music we have examined in this book, I have asked you to listen to recordings, either with or without prior reading or preparation. In the case of *Messiah*, I would rather that you first experience it in performance. This is not only music, but storytelling, and the effect is different when you hear this story live, told with the enthusiasm and involvement that live performance requires. Then you may want to get a recording of the oratorio so that you can explore it further on your own.

Listen to how the music moves from the gravely serious to the ecstatically celebratory. Pay attention to the way singers phrase and pronounce the words in the English-language text—this is how a story is told, whether in narration or singing. Be aware of the variety and tone of the arias, from those of imposing grandeur to the simple but gorgeous "How Beautiful Are the Feet." Notice the sensitivity of the conductor in shaping musical phrases to support the words being sung. And pay close attention to the many wonderful choruses Handel wrote. The German-born composer, well-traveled in Italy before arriving in England in 1712 when he was twenty-seven, drew on the English choral tradition to change the nature of the oratorio by expanding the role of the chorus.

Unlike in continental Europe, oratorios in England were entertainments that were presented in theaters and concert halls. They were commercial ventures. The fact that many told religious stories did not matter. It was only later, in Europe, America, and Britain, that *Messiah* and some other Handel oratorios could be found in churches, although to this day many of these works are more ubiquitous in concert halls.

When Handel wrote this work, at the age of fifty-six, he was highly esteemed, though battle-scarred from years in the rough-and-tumble musical world of London, where musical performances were expected to make profits for presenters, and composers vied for the attention of audiences. Handel was contemplating retirement when he received a handsome commission in the summer of 1741 from the Lord Lieutenant of Dublin to write a sacred oratorio. This would be used in a charity concert to benefit prisoners in various jails, as well as Mercer's Hospital and a Charitable Infirmary.

With Charles Jennens, an evangelical clergyman, Handel created a text that told the story of Christ as the world's savior. It is drawn from the Old and New Testaments and, interestingly, does not really name characters. What is intriguing, if you look closely at the words, is that they were meant to inspire contemplation. Read them apart from the music and they may seem rather didactic.

In his music, Handel infused the story with drama and real outbursts of joy. This music is one of history's most famous examples of fevered inspiration of the type that Mozart experienced in long stretches, most especially in the last months of his life in 1791. There are isolated cases throughout music history in which towering, large-scale works were created in brief spans of time, but few match *Messiah* and some of what Mozart achieved.

Various accounts I have read report that Handel wrote this work anywhere from fifteen to twenty-five days. He toiled day and night, and food was slipped under his door to give him sustenance. The charity concert was set for April 13, 1742. There was a wild demand to attend the premiere of a work by one of the greatest living composers. The concert organizers issued an announcement that at the performance ladies could not wear hoop skirts and gentlemen could not carry swords. This way, there would be more room, and more tickets could be sold.

Following its ecstatic reception in Dublin, *Messiah* was performed in London on March 23, 1743, in the presence of King George II. A few notes into the "Hallelujah Chorus," the king rose to his feet, reportedly swept up by the music. And that is how the tradition began to stand up when this music is played.

It is believed that Handel conducted the work thirty-six times in his life. You may have noticed that these performances were given in springtime, rather than at Christmas. This is because the custom of the time was that opera could not be performed during the forty days of Lent, so this is when oratorios came to the fore. The work's Christmas associations only came later, when presenters and churchmen thought that performing an oratorio about Jesus around the time of his birthday might not be a bad idea.

After learning *Messiah*, I encourage you to devote yourself to discovering other Handel oratorios. They are wonderful. Start with *Israel in Egypt*.

. ∿ .

Mozart: Mass in C minor, K. 427; New Philharmonia Orchestra; John Alldis Choir; Raymond Leppard, conductor; Kiri Te Kanawa, Ileana Cotrubas, soloists; EMI CDC 7 47385 2

This work, composed 1782–83, is usually referred to as *The Great Mass*, as opposed to *The Coronation Mass* (K. 317), also written in the key of C minor. It is a mass written for a church service and is in no way a requiem. Mozart had vowed to write a mass upon his marriage to his wife, Costanze, to be played in Salzburg when he presented his new wife to his suspicious father. Musically and structurally the mass looks backward to Bach and Handel, but is unmistakably Mozartean in sound and in its particular transparency. As with all Mozart, it sounds easy to execute because the music seems so natural. In fact, this kind of music is among the most difficult to perform, and this is a wonderful rendition.

. ∿ .

Mozart: Requiem, KV. 626: Wiener Philharmoniker; Wiener Singverein; Herbert von Karajan, conductor; Tomowa-Sintow, Molinari, Cole, Burchuladze, soloists; DG 419 610-2. (This is one of many fine recordings. Be sure that the one you select has the texts enclosed. An excellent second recording, though regrettably without texts, is EMI 0777 7 62892 2 9, which combines the Mozart Requiem conducted by Daniel Barenboim with the Verdi Requiem conducted by Sir John Barbirolli.)

Here is one of the most famous of all requiems, and not only for its extreme beauty and power. Mozart received the commission in July

1791 from an anonymous donor. It is well-documented that Mozart, as his health was failing, was furiously at work attempting to finish this mass. He died on December 5 of that year. This work was done as he was completing two operas: *La Clemenza di Tito* and *Die Zauberflöte*, and other pieces. It is listed as Mozart's last work, which would be notable even if it were not a requiem. Whether he wrote it with the notion that it would be his own requiem will forever remain a mystery. Read the program essay on pages 7–9 in the CD booklet before you start.

Although Mozart was using the traditional texts for a requiem, the music is extraordinary in its power and variety. I suggest that you listen to this work the first time without reading along with the texts. The message comes through eloquently. See what pictures and images come to your mind as you listen. Here are some things to ponder:

- Do you hear, in the opening section, a funeral procession?

- What do you see during the choral passages of the Dies Irae (Day of Wrath)?

- Pay attention to the trombone solo that introduces the solo vocal music. Do you find the trombone an unusual and inspired choice as a single instrumental voice? Or is it unsettling?

- Make note how the soprano voice weaves throughout the work, often in contrast to some of the most powerful and fear-inducing music. Why do you think Mozart used the soprano this way and what does it represent?

- What is happening in the Confutatis (track 7)? You do not need to know what is happening according to the text, but what is happening in your *head*? What do you make of the sound of the tenors and basses compared to the sound of the sopranos? What could it mean?

- Mozart only completed the first eight measures of the Lacrimosa (track 8), supposedly singing it tearfully in the hours before he died. Does your awareness that these were the last notes he wrote change your feelings about them, or can you listen to them principally as part of a larger work?

- The rest of the Requiem was written by Franz Süssmayer from Mozart's sketches. Can you tell the difference? Does it matter to you?

Now listen to Mozart's Requiem again, reading the words in English (unless you know Latin). Try not to analyze as you read, but simply gather the words and their meanings, all the while listening with great care to the divine music.

• ✺ •

Beethoven: Missa Solemnis, Choral Fantasia; *New Philharmonia Orchestra; John Alldis Choir; Otto Klemperer, conductor; Barenboim, piano; Söderström, Höffgen, Kmentt, Talvela, soloists; EMI 7 69538 2. (This recording includes both works and texts; a later issue, EMI 7243 5 67547 2 0, does not include the Choral Fantasia or texts.)*

The *Missa Solemnis* is a work you can study on your own, drawing on skills you have already acquired. Read the valuable essay in the program booklet (pages 4–9) and then listen. One notion to bear in mind is whether Beethoven constructed this like a mass of the types you have already heard, or whether this piece is closer to a symphony in five movements (he was leading up to the composition of his Ninth Symphony by now). Note too Beethoven's use of organ as an intriguing musical protagonist in this work, the degree to which the singers are real soloists, and the remarkable power and character of the choral writing.

The *Choral Fantasia* is a piece of pure listening pleasure. It has sometimes been described as awkward, ungainly, imperfect. These perceptions, I believe, owe in part to the fact that the work was not successful at its premiere. Since then the work has unjustifiably carried this taint. I love the contrast of piano with chorus and orchestra. It is as if these are three equal components, with the piano providing giddy joy and the chorus an unbridled ecstasy. To understand how joy and ecstasy differ yet can be sublimely matched, listen to this work. Make note also how the music expresses the feelings of the words, and remember that this is a secular work whose elation derives from humane ideals.

• ⌒ •

Rossini: Petite Messe Solennelle; *Coro Polifonico del Teatro alla Scala; Romano Gandolfi, conductor; Freni, Pavarotti, etc., soloists;* Stabat Mater; *London Symphony Orchestra and Chorus; István Kertész, conductor; Lorengar, Minton, Pavarotti, Sotin, soloists; London/Decca 455 023-2*

Most people who think of Rossini recall his brilliant operatic comedies (especially *The Barber of Seville*), and some people know that he wrote magnificent serious operas with great sweep and grandeur, with a seemingly endless supply of glorious melodies. Even in his serious works the music often sounds joyous, with the result that many serious music lovers think of Rossini as a lightweight. He was extraordinarily able in music and in social life, first in Italy and later in Paris, and he had the talent to charm most anyone he encountered. He also was quite sybaritic, enjoying food, wine, and sex unabashedly.

All of these attributes would seem to make Rossini a poor candidate to write solemn religious music. Yet he was also someone who battled illness and nervous exhaustion for most of his years, and was prone to depression. His social success was so complete that few people witnessed, or could envisage, a more sober side to the composer. The Stabat Mater was completed in 1841, twelve years after Rossini had written his last opera (*William Tell*). He was forty-nine years old and had already been ill for several years. One can hear a certain foreboding in this work, which is also characterized by beauty and moments of great joy.

Rossini's *Petite Messe Solennelle* is notable because it was written in 1863 and orchestrated in 1867, a year before his death. Though he lived into his seventies and maintained an active life, he had numerous medical afflictions. His "Little Solemn Mass" is not a requiem—it is a mistake to think of it thus—but reflects a summation of the composer's life. He was quite nostalgic for the past, not at ease adjusting to the present (his famous wit often expressed the ironic musings of a person who felt out of sorts), and he was pessimistic about the future. Listen for all of these qualities in the music of his mass, and think about one more thing: is this music backward-looking or forward-looking, or both? I find an evident nostalgic vein, but also some indications of moving past Romanticism to some of the modernity that would characterize the music of the early twentieth century.

* ✧ *

Verdi: Messa da Requiem; *Atlanta Symphony Orchestra and Chorus; Robert Shaw, conductor; Dunn, Curry, Hadley, Plishka, soloists; Telarc CD-80152. (Alternates for further exploration: Philharmonia Orchestra and Chorus; Carlo Maria Giulini, conductor; Schwarzkopf, Ludwig, Gedda, Ghiaurov, soloists; EMI Classics ZDCB 56250; and Vienna Philharmonic Orchestra and Vienna State Opera Chorus; Sir Georg Solti, conductor; Sutherland, Horne, Pavarotti, Talvela, soloists; London/Decca 411944-2.)*

It is often asserted—too often, say I—that the *Messa da Requiem* is Giuseppe Verdi's greatest opera. Cute, and in some ways insightful, but not accurate. So accomplished was Verdi as an opera composer that critics and some audiences were unable to accept that he could write something as brilliant as this work. Yet they fail to acknowledge that composers such as Handel, Haydn, Mozart, and Berlioz could write splendid operas and also be highly accomplished in other areas. This attitude derives in part, I believe, from an ingrained prejudice against Italian composers in the past two hundred years that held that they were great masters of opera but not much else.

    I want you to keep in your ears all of the requiems you have already listened to, and all of the masses for that matter, and then approach Verdi's piece on its own terms. It is well-known (and the notes in the CD booklet explain further) that Verdi was first moved to write commemorative music following the death of Rossini in 1868. Verdi was also an immense admirer of Alessandro Manzoni, author of *I Promessi Sposi* (The Betrothed), which is considered the great Italian novel. Manzoni died on May 22, 1873, and Verdi set to work on a requiem to be performed on the first anniversary of the writer's death.

People who hear and analyze this work talk of its intense drama, its raging against death, and the passions that seem perhaps out of keeping with the consoling aspects of a requiem mass. But think back to Mozart's requiem, with its throbbing *Dies Irae,* and you will see that this sort of depiction is not new with Verdi. It is just more raw and emotionally exposed, which is why we in modern times can accept it in a way that was probably difficult in 1874.

What is not discussed, but which you should think about, is the degree to which Verdi was depicting his idea of Manzoni, whom he admired but had only little personal contact with. Is Verdi writing of his view of death in this work, or of Manzoni? Both, I believe. Some of the titanic aspects of this music might describe the author, who was an outsized national hero.

Another thing to bear in mind is that there was a gradual secularization of life in Europe, certainly in cosmopolitan circles of cities such as Milan and Paris (where Verdi composed much of this music). So the requiems of Verdi and Brahms (1868) reflect the outlooks of men who were not particularly religious (or at least not attached to organized religion) but who nonetheless found the means in music to address the issues of death and loss. Remember: one might write a requiem as a mass for the dead, but the intended audience is all living.

One might question my selection of the Robert Shaw/Atlanta Symphony recording I have recommended. The work is practically part of the DNA of the musical forces of Milan's La Scala, and there are two fine recordings led by Riccardo Muti with excellent singers. The two alternate recordings I mention above also have great singers, marvelous conductors, and fine orchestras. If you develop a passion for the Verdi Requiem, you will want to explore these versions, too.

But the recommended version has Robert Shaw as conductor and chorus master. There have been finer conductors, to be sure, but Shaw was arguably the greatest choral conductor of the twentieth century. Any chorus that was put in his charge achieved results far beyond their wildest dreams, and the Atlanta Symphony Orchestra and Chorus were his home company for much of his career. The colors and dynamics you will hear in this chorus on this recording will take your breath away.

The CD was made in 1987, when all of the soloists were in good vocal estate and the recording technology was advanced enough to capture nuances that the older versions do not. I think the fact that the soloists are not stars of the magnitude found on some other recordings is in some way advantageous. We focus on their music more than their celebrity, and they come to occupy equal standing with the orchestra, chorus, and conductor.

Given that you now have a good general sense of the requiem text, listen to this recording without it (at somewhat high volume, if possible) in a way that you are completely surrounded by the music. You will soon realize what a radical departure this piece is, no more so than in the hair-raising *Dies Irae*, in which chorus and percussion create a frightening vision of the Last Judgment.

Equally memorable are the tenor's *Ingemisco* (track 2.8) and the ethereal *Libera Me* sung by soprano and chorus as the requiem comes to an end.

· ◈ ·

Brahms: **Ein Deutsches Requiem;** *Chicago Symphony Orchestra & Chorus; Georg Solti, conductor; Te Kanawa, Weikl, soloists; London/Decca 414 627-2*

Why would Brahms start thinking about composing a requiem at the age of twenty-eight (in 1861)? Most composers were considerably older when they began their requiems and perhaps had more contact with the emotions of death and loss. Mozart and Berlioz wrote requiems in their mid-thirties, but each had a lucrative commission. Brahms had nothing of the sort. He was a rather morose and pensive man, in many ways older than his years. Joseph Hellmesberger, the concertmaster of the Vienna Philharmonic, said of the composer, "When Brahms is in extra good spirits, he sings 'The grave is my joy.' "

Yet I don't think we can categorize Brahms as a depressive in the ways that composers such as Handel, Berlioz, Rossini, and Tchaikovsky were said to be. I think that Brahms was deeply sensitive and very connected to human feelings and emotions, whether joyous or sorrowful. His music is rich with emotion, and he used it as a means to explore the issues of life. Mortality and death would be part of this exploration, even at a young age.

In addition, the twenty-three-year-old Brahms observed up close the illness and painful death of his mentor, Robert Schumann, and remained close to his widow, Clara. This no doubt was an impetus for thoughts of mortality and the meaning of life. Brahms began to gradually draft the requiem in 1861, but the work took on more depth and urgency with the sudden death of his mother in February 1865. The seven-movement work was completed in its present form in 1868.

It is in many ways a radical work. Brahms discarded the traditional Latin text of the Roman Mass for the Dead and replaced it with German language translations of biblical texts he selected. He called the work *Ein deutsches Requiem* (A German Requiem), implying that this was indeed a requiem in German but was not meant to be the definitive way to honor the dead. He wrote in a letter in 1867, "I would happily omit *German* and simply say *Human*." Above all, Brahms—sensitive man that he was—was keenly aware of the feelings of the listener. He begins the requiem with the words "Blessed are they that mourn" and concludes it with "Blessed are the dead." Listen to the work with the idea that Brahms sought to provide consolation and warmth.

On first hearing, read the text carefully, looking at the German to understand the pairing of the sounds of words with the music. At the same time, look at the translations, because Brahms cared deeply about the ideas here. On second hearing, put aside the libretto and bathe in the rich and powerful feelings in the music.

• ◇ •

Fauré: Requiem; Orchestre de la Société des Concerts du Conservatoire; Choeurs Elisabeth Brasseur; André Cluytens, conductor; Victoria de los Angeles, Dietrich Fischer-Dieskau, soloists; EMI 7243 5 66946 2 0

Gabriel Fauré (1845–1924) was an essentially gentle, unassuming, and restrained man, and these adjectives could also be ascribed to his music. This is not a negative judgment, but rather an acknowledgment that we must listen with care and openness to find our way to what this composer is saying. He wrote to his son, "The work of the imagination consists in attempting to formulate all that one wants that is best, everything that goes beyond reality. . . . To my mind art, and above all music, consists in lifting us as far as possible above what is." Call him a utopian idealist or perhaps a dreamer, but you can sense the way Fauré approached his work.

After the emotions of the requiems you have listened to, you will be struck by how this one (first version 1887, current version 1900) explores the mystery of death, loss, and remembrance in gentle, grace-ful, and often hushed music that draws you in with its ethereal beauty. Note that he omitted the *Dies Irae* section, preferring to leave the day of wrath to other composers.

This recording is a classic, featuring the splendid conductor André Cluytens in a moment of real inspiration, and two of the greatest singers of the twentieth century, Victoria de los Angeles and Dietrich Fischer-Dieskau, plus outstanding choral work.

Listen to the music without the texts so that you will completely immerse in Fauré's sound world. On a second hearing, draw the words close and read them as you listen.

• ◇ •

Janáček: Glagolitic Mass; Wiener Philharmoniker; Riccardo Chailly, conductor; London/Decca 289 460 213-2

There is only one amendment I would make to *Opera 101*—in it I described Puccini and Richard Strauss as the greatest opera composers of the first part of the twentieth century. I have come to consider Leoš Janáček their equal. Alban Berg (1885–1935) wrote one complete opera, *Wozzeck*, and left his *Lulu* unfinished. These are works of genius, but Berg simply did not have enough operatic output to be ranked with Puccini, Strauss, and Janáček.

I am not alone in considering Janáček one of the most under-rated of all composers. Though he has long been admired in his native Czech Republic, his work has gained wider appreciation only in recent years. Part of the reason is that more Czech artists have championed their national music abroad and have the language skills to perform it.

Much of the credit for the Janáček revival is due to conductor Sir Charles Mackerras, who has been the leading advocate for this composer. Although this recording is led by the talented Riccardo Chailly, you can be sure that any Janáček recording led by Mackerras will be of high quality.

This piece is sometimes called the *Slavonic Mass* because its text uses the early Slavonic alphabet. This 1926 work is also an outgrowth of the composer's enthusiasm for the independent Czech nation following the First World War and reflects his desire to imbue it with a national flavor that extends far beyond Brahms's choice to use the German language in his requiem.

Before listening to the recording, read the notes in the program (pages 4–6), including the comments about composers Alexander Zemlinsky (1871–1942) and Erich Wolfgang Korngold (1897–1957).

Listen to the work the first time without texts to get a feeling for the flavor of the music. Note the role of the chorus as the voice of the people. When you return to it, use the texts, trying hard to get a sense of the sound of the Czech language that was so dear to the composer.

• ◇ •

Poulenc: Gloria; *Orchestra and Chorus of la Suisse Romande; Jesús Lopez-Cobos, conductor; Sylvia Greenberg, soloist; London/Decca 448 270-2*

This is one of the first pieces of music I ever learned (in first grade!), way back in the 1960s when classical music was a necessary part of instruction in New York City public schools. Every classroom had a piano, and the teacher was expected to sit down and play music that she would teach. Although we did not know what we were singing about, I recall that we were taught the Latin text in a way that we could absorb it. For example, "*Gloria in excelsis deo*" became "Gloria in egg-shell cease day-oh." The words became the vehicles for the music and, with our tender, unclogged minds, we learned dutifully and completely. The words and music of Poulenc's *Gloria* have never left my head.

What stuns me now is that when I learned this music it was not yet five years old. They were not only teaching ancient musical classics in elementary school but a modern and eclectic piece that is nominally religious. I wonder if any public school in America teaches this work now?

I have added *Gloria* to this chapter because it is indeed a modern classic, one of the few pieces in recent years that has joined the standard repertory. This is a joyous work that brings to mind the spirit of Bach's secular cantatas and seems to presage the Second Vatican Council in the mid-1960s that sought to reform masses and religious observances in a way that would make them more relevant and appealing to younger people.

Yet Poulenc's *Gloria* is much more than relevant. Its treatment of liturgical texts is refreshing, genuine, and loving, and infuses a naive but persuasive spirituality in these words.

Listen to this music without texts (which are not provided with this recording anyway). Do the unexpected scale leaps and jaunty rhythms please you, or do you think they are inappropriate for religious music?

Play the secular Bach cantatas again, and then return to the Poulenc. Do you see the same boundless feeling of joy and exuberance?

• ⌖ •

Britten: War Requiem; Melos Ensemble/London Symphony Orchestra; Benjamin Britten, conductor; Vishnevskaya, Pears, Fischer-Dieskau, soloists; London/Decca 414 383-2

Why is it that when a brilliant opera composer such as Verdi writes a requiem he becomes a target of criticism from many quarters before the work ultimately gains wide acceptance, while another brilliant opera composer, Benjamin Britten, can write his requiem and find great acclaim right away? The difference, I believe, is the times. Opera was not as central to civic and political life in the 1960s as it was in the 1870s, but those who loved music could immediately see the genius in Britten's War Requiem. This work is admired by cognoscenti, but still does not occupy the central place in the repertory that it deserves.

As it happens, Britten wrote a *Sinfonia da Requiem* (op. 20) in 1940 that was his response to the horrors of World War II. This early statement, though powerful, is only a hint of what would come with the composition of the War Requiem in 1961. This was the year that the wall was erected in Berlin, and it was a period of great tensions between East and West.

As you will discover in reading the excellent program essay (pages 7–13), Britten was an ardent pacifist who was outraged at the willingness of nations to wage wars to address their conflicts. Drawing from the works of poet Wilfred Owen and from Latin texts, Britten created a libretto that reflected his point of view. He borrowed from Owen to write on the title page of the score: "My subject is war, and the pity of war. The Poetry is in the pity. All a Poet can do today is warn."

This requiem was first performed in the ruins of Coventry Cathedral in 1962, an event loaded with obvious symbolism. This recording was done a year later. You should note that the soloists are a Russian soprano (Galina Vishnevskaya), a British tenor (Peter Pears, Britten's companion), and a German baritone (Dietrich Fischer-Dieskau). This casting was fraught with symbolism as Britten made a very clear statement about music superseding all borders and ideologies. With three choirs, one of them a boys' chorus—think back to the *St. Matthew Passion*—a chamber ensemble, and a full orchestra, this is a work of vast scope.

It is also a rare chance to hear a conductor lead his own masterwork in its definitive performance. There is an excellent recording led by Simon Rattle that brings with it a great conductor's perspective on a fellow countryman's work, but the recommended recording is an extraordinary document of inspired music-making. It also contains some rare sounds: Benjamin Britten in rehearsal. On tracks 5 to 15 of the second CD you will have the highly unusual chance to listen to some of the sounds of how a rehearsal works. Note the exactness with which Britten tries to bring home certain concepts. Can you also sense the tension in the air that is part of some rehearsals? This is fascinating lost-and-found sound, and you should carefully listen to it after your first hearing of the Requiem.

The first time out, listen to this work while reading the texts. The poetry is extraordinary, and you will want to see how Britten interwove it with the traditional Latin texts. After hearing this powerful work wait a day or so before returning to it for a second hearing without the libretto.

I think that you will agree that there is much beauty in this music, but that its aims go far beyond those of other requiems we have heard. This is not simply a consolation, but a warning, and this is where its power resides.

FEELING MUSIC
Gustav Mahler's Symphony no. 2

What is best in music is not to be found in the notes.
—*Gustav Mahler*

Mahler: Symphony no. 2; New York Philharmonic; The Westminster Choir; Leonard Bernstein, conductor; Barbara Hendricks, soprano; Christa Ludwig, mezzo-soprano; DG 423 395-2

Up to this point, you have played a very active role in developing your knowledge of and love for classical music. You have devoted yourself to careful study, attentive listening, and thought about all sorts of details and concepts you probably never knew existed. And I hope that it has been gratifying and enriching. (I suspect it was, or you would not have reached this point in the book!)

But there is one more step—important and profound—that you must take. Having learned how to listen to music by paying active attention to it, you must now learn how to *feel* music. This action is probably counterintuitive to all that you have done to this point, not only with classical music but with many areas of your life. Ours is a culture that encourages analysis and explanation, one that devalues mystery.

I believe that mystery plays a fundamental role in experiencing the great things in life. If you can determine the chemical components in a food or wine, does that help you understand why you like how they taste? Do you think that being able to list all the reasons you love a person enables you to love that person more or better or differently? Can you define "love" in words? If something is unsurpassingly beautiful to you, can you really explain why in a meaningful way?

There are many sensations and feelings that we know we can experience but not fully define. Once we give up the belief that definition of these emotions is necessary or possible, we can actually experience them more completely because we have lifted the analytical filter we use to find definitions.

This behavior is possible in music, and will make you love it all the more. Having learned how to listen, you have now integrated this behavior into your being, and you no longer need to focus on it.

I want you to approach the Second Symphony of Mahler a bit differently from how you have listened to other pieces. Of course, create a quiet environment in your listening space that will not be disturbed. But instead of sitting back in a chair, spread out on your back on a bed, extending your arms and legs. If you do not have a bed in the room where you listen, then place a sheet or very large towel on the floor and spread out there. Shut your eyes, but listen intently, taking care not to fall asleep.

Play this recording somewhat louder than you have some of the others. Do not make it too loud, or there will be slight distortion in the sound and you will hurt your ears. But the idea is that you should receive the music through all of your pores. This is a 2-CD set, so if you are able to program your CD player to have one disk immediately follow the other, that would be ideal.

Before your first hearing, do not read any notes or lyrics that come with the CD. Do not read my comments beyond the point I tell you. Simply let the music suffuse your body. Do not analyze—just focus entirely on hearing the music and letting it pass through you.

Once the music has ended, continue to lie where you are, with your eyes shut. You will continue to hear and feel the music for quite a while. This is a remarkable and incredibly sensual feeling, and you should experience it to the fullest. Even when you think you have fully absorbed this music, continue to stay where you are, with eyes shut. You may feel twitching in your synapses, and distant echoes in your ears. Pictures may continue to sail through your mind's eye, or you may "see" abstract images and colors. I suspect that even several minutes after the music has stopped, your body will still be processing sensations that you would miss out on if you sat up abruptly and opened your eyes.

Then, when you feel you have experienced—have felt—this music thoroughly, you can, ever so gradually, open your eyes and let the sounds of the room enter your mind (there are sounds even if you think it is perfectly silent). Gently sit up, breathe in and out, and then pick up this book again.

Stop here and listen to Mahler's Second Symphony.

• ⟨◇⟩ •

Now, after your first hearing, keep reading:

According to Gustav Mahler, "The symphony is the world! The symphony must embrace everything."

The world of Gustav Mahler was one full of conflict and contradiction. He was born a Jew in Bohemia in 1860 and died a Christian in Vienna in 1911. He lived in the years of decline of the Austro-Hungarian Empire, a period when all the presumptions and suppositions of *Austria Felix* (Happy Austria) were disintegrating and being severely questioned. One of the most influential and revolutionary thinkers of Mahler's time was another Viennese Jew, Sigmund Freud, whose theories about human nature and behavior swept away most of the ways that people—especially creative artists—looked at how we live.

As it happens, Mahler sought the services of Dr. Freud, not in his famous studio in Vienna, but during a long walk on a Dutch beach in 1910. While we do not know all that doctor and patient discussed, we do know that part of the conversation was about Mahler's concerns that his wife, Alma, was romantically interested in other men. Mahler was by then seriously ill with a heart ailment (a mitral valve defect) that silently plagued him for years, and he would die in less than a year. Interestingly, the beach was in the town of Leiden, whose name in German means "suffering."

Mahler was as brilliant a conductor as he was a composer. Other musical figures, including Mendelssohn, Brahms, Strauss, Rachmaninoff, and Leonard Bernstein could make such a claim, but it seems that Mahler and Bernstein faced the greatest challenges in integrating the two aspects of their art. Both were so much in demand to lead orchestras that they often felt that they neglected their composing. It should not surprise you that Bernstein became Mahler's greatest champion and found affinity with the composer's life and music on countless levels.

Mahler moved gradually up through the ranks of opera houses in the Empire and in Germany, acquiring extensive experience and fame as one of Europe's greatest conductors. In 1892 Tchaikovsky went to Hamburg to conduct the German premiere of his opera *Eugene Onegin*. So impressed was he with Mahler's talents that he passed the baton to the young conductor and implored him to lead the production. Tchaikovsky later wrote that Mahler was "a man of genius."

Unlike Bernstein, who was proud of his Jewish heritage and wrote some beautiful pieces that draw upon it (especially *Kaddish* in 1963), Mahler experienced great conflict in his faith. True, the Austro-Hungarian Empire (and much of Europe) was rife with anti-Semitism. But Mahler's conversion to Roman Catholicism in 1897 has always been a lightning rod for debate. Did he do it to advance his career? For his safety and that of his family? For genuine religious convictions? This open question is one of the many mysteries of Gustav Mahler.

We do know that in the same year he was offered the most prestigious job of his career, as artistic director of the Vienna Court Opera, and that in anti-Semitic fin de siècle Vienna he would encounter a great deal of hostility if he remained a Jew. We also know that to many people, his conversion did not—in their eyes—strip him of his Jewishness. This was a source of considerable anxiety for Mahler. If you listen to his music, it is often possible to discern vivid strains of anxiety in a way that had seldom been depicted before.

In his early years, full of energy and zeal, Mahler was able to conduct and compose at the same time, but soon he found the challenge of working on a grand scale with unflagging devotion to be too much.

Because his conducting occupied so much of his time—and he needed to do this work to pay his bills—for most of his life his composing was confined to summer vacations. As was the custom in Austria, summer holidays were meant to be spent in nature. Mahler had three favored retreats: one was at Steinbach, near Salzburg; another was at Maiernegg, on the south shore of Wörthersee (Lake Wörth) in Carinthia; and the third in Toblach, a town that is now called Dobbiaco in northeastern Italy. I have visited these three retreats (as have many of the composer's admirers) to see the settings in which he worked and to try to understand some of the sources of his inspiration.

What these places have in common, even today, is a degree of silence that permits one to hear the sounds of nature that would otherwise be lost if there were the din of traffic or "civilization" nearby. You can hear wind, the scurrying of animals, the crackling of twigs and branches, birdsong, the tapping of woodpecker beaks against bark, and much more. Above all, you can hear silence. This may sound like a contradiction, but pure silence is one of the most gratifying aural sensations of all. You think that you hear nothing and then, suddenly, sound rushes into your head. But it is sound coming from your own brain and your own being. This must be part of the miracle of composition.

I was once happily trapped alone in Mahler's composing hut in Maiernegg during a torrential rainstorm. This was nature at full force, both cataclysmic and beautiful. I thought to myself that Mahler must have had the same experience in this very place. Did he feel, as I did, both the power and grandeur of nature, as well as the smallness and fragility of being human in this spot? I did not experience fear at that moment, but came to discover that this enforced and splendid isolation, while pleasing to me for a limited time period, could provoke unease or alarm in certain persons.

As the storm abated, the local sounds in the immediate environs of the hut sprang to life. I could again hear brooks babble, birds sing, and leaves rustle in the waning wind.

While certain composers (among them Vivaldi, Beethoven, Rossini, and Wagner) can suggest sounds of nature with effective use of instrumental voices in the orchestra, once you hear certain passages in Mahler, you realize that most other composers only approximate what he could achieve. Part of the reason for this, I believe, is that while other composers sought to represent sounds of nature, Mahler had the unique gift to infuse these sounds with the mystery and power of nature. In other words, rushing water or crackling leaves are a sound, but these sounds when placed in a larger natural context can be thought of as the music of nature.

You can hear this in many of his symphonies, in the accompaniment to song cycles such as *Lieder eines fahrenden Gesellen* (Songs of a Wayfarer), *Des Knaben Wunderhorn* (The Boy's Magic Horn), *Rückert Lieder* (based on poems by Friedrich Rückert), and especially *Das Lied von der Erde* (The Song of the Earth), which is really a six-part symphony that includes songs for mezzo-soprano (or baritone) and tenor.

Deeper, darker, tragic nature can be heard in *Kindertotenlieder* (Songs of Dead Children), a five-song cycle written between 1901 and 1904, a musical setting of poems by Rückert. This topic can certainly seem morbid and gruesome, but was familiar to anyone who lived in Europe in the era before vaccines. More than seventy years earlier, Schubert dealt powerfully with the subject of a dead child in his song, *Das irdische Leben*.

Mahler was one of fourteen children, five of whom died in infancy, another at age thirteen, and another as a suicide at age twenty-five. Although Vienna was one of the world's great centers of medicine, this was still an era when diseases could sweep through the city at epidemic proportions. So the death of children, and the many-leveled implications that attend it, was something known to most people and that a supreme and emotional artist such as Mahler could find a way to depict and explore.

Mahler married the beautiful and charismatic Alma Schindler, with whom he had two daughters. One of them, Maria Anna, died of scarlet fever in 1907. The superstitious Mahler believed that the cause of her death were the *Kindertotenlieder* songs that he had published three years earlier.

The death of his daughter made the composer think even more about his own death. Although the seriousness of his heart condition had not yet been diagnosed, Mahler became obsessed with death. On the one hand, he almost seemed to have a death wish. On the other, this sense of imminent demise made him compose more fervently and, in a few short years, he turned out several splendid and gargantuan symphonies.

His profound superstition made him resist composing nine symphonies, thinking that Beethoven had forever lay claim to that number. He noticed that Schubert died after composing his Ninth, and Bruckner only completed three movements of his. After completing his mammoth Symphony no. 8 (usually called *Symphony of a Thousand* because of the huge musical forces required to perform it), Mahler would not call his *Das Lied von der Erde* his Ninth Symphony. He did ultimately write a gorgeous Ninth Symphony (completed in 1910) and set to work on a tenth, of which we have fragments. He died before completing it.

Mahler's music was admired by many composers and conductors, but was savagely attacked by critics, who often had no problem describing it as sick, sordid Jewish music. So virulent was the anti-Semitism that the music could be roundly dismissed with little outcry. He had many great achievements at the Vienna Court Opera, but left it in 1907 when he received an offer to conduct in New York at the Metropolitan Opera and the New York Philharmonic. By all accounts these performances were brilliant, and galvanized the music world in New York. His Philharmonic debut came in the autumn and his Met debut, with Wagner's *Tristan und Isolde*, came on New Year's Day 1908. Only a few years before, New Yorkers heard both Tchaikovsky and Dvořák conduct in Carnegie Hall, and now Mahler and later the great Arturo Toscanini would do the same.

He had a few glorious years in New York, but overwork and his bad heart led to his collapse in that city. He sailed to Paris for treatment, and was then transferred to Vienna so that he could die in the city about which he was so ambivalent.

Mahler seemed to be the last exponent of Romanticism, though much of his music pointed toward the radical changes that music would undergo with composers such as Schoenberg, Debussy, Berg, Stravinsky, and others.

One particularly intriguing element in Mahler's music is that it is so often the case that each instrumental voice seems apart and independent. This is very modern and very much how we live now. As you listen to music by Mahler, you will notice that, despite remarkable surges in sound that come from the collective cry of a mass of instruments, there are many occasions in which each instrument makes itself heard even if many are being played at once.

The massive and universal character of his music was drawn in part from Bruckner's approach to symphonic composition, but also as a tribute to the colossal Ninth Symphony of Beethoven and *Tristan und Isolde*. As a brilliant conductor, Mahler had a special insight into the Olympian stature of these works.

As a composer, he sought to emulate the grandeur and sweep of his models and to infuse his music with heartfelt humanity. Sometimes one feels that Mahler's great symphonies are enormous vessels of emotion that threaten to explode and inevitably do. These explosions, thought by some to be overwrought solutions to musical problems he could not solve, are seen by others as apotheosis, transfiguration, or resurrection.

More than a few people I know consider Mahler the absolute summit of classical music. In our times, Mahler is a mainstream composer, thanks largely to the advocacy of Leonard Bernstein and other conductors and the abilities of orchestras—especially the Vienna Philharmonic, the Royal Concertgebouw in Amsterdam, and the New York Philharmonic—to give extraordinary accounts of his music.

You could spend several lifetimes trying to pick Mahler's music apart musicologically. One conductor, Gilbert Kaplan, has devoted almost all of his work and thought to only one composition in all of classical music: the Mahler Second Symphony.

This is a large-scale work from early in his career (1894), and Mahler would go on to write several symphonies that are much bigger. Mahler conducted a performance of the first three movements with the

Berlin Philharmonic on March 4, 1895, and led the first performance of the entire symphony with the same orchestra on December 13 of the same year, along with chorus and two female soloists. He would make revisions to the score for much of his life, as late as 1909.

In a letter to his wife, Mahler said that the Second Symphony is "so much all of a piece that it can no more be explained than the world itself."

The genesis of the work began in 1888 when Mahler had visions of himself dead. He wrote a large portion of what is now the first movement of the symphony, referring to it as *Todtenfeier* (Funeral Rites). This music was not initially intended to be part of a symphony, but came to be useful when Mahler began to construct the Second Symphony.

I have avoided telling you until this point that this work has acquired the name *Resurrection Symphony*. Mahler never gave it that name, but it has gained common currency because of the text of the song in the last movement. One wonders what a Jew, even one who converted to Catholicism, would make of his music being given that name.

The words used in the fifth movement are the text of *Auferstehung* (Resurrection Ode) by the poet Friedrich Gottlieb Klopstock (1724–1803). Klopstock was a religious Protestant, but the source of his faith was based more in emotion than theology. The notion of resurrection is useful in thinking about this music, but you should not make it the keyhole through which all of your thoughts pass. The feelings of release and gratification you personally experience are highly unlikely to be ones of resurrection, but whatever they are, they are yours. And they are meaningful because this music—in pure terms—helped provoke them.

So I encourage you, as you listen to this symphony for the second or third time, not to think of it—even in Mahler's terms—as being only of resurrection. That is only a narrow segment of the implications of this symphony which, as Mahler had hoped, can be seen as a depiction of all the world.

The first movement, which some say depicts the death of a hero, is, at 24 minutes and 53 seconds, longer than many symphonies. The chilly first notes, with the stabbing sound of cellos and basses, gives way to a strangely unsettling melody played by the winds and the horns. After 2½ minutes we have the sense that this could be a funeral march, though if we allow our minds to float freely it could be many other things—or nothing that we can really identify. Within another minute, the violins present a delicate and serene melody. Then, around 4½ minutes into the work, the stabbing lower strings return, and then comes a gripping melody on the brass. By 5½ minutes it all sounds unwieldy with emotion, but completely right. The endless shifts, the pieces of sound coming from all directions that gradually form a massive sonic tapestry, are what characterize this symphony and much of Mahler's music.

Mahler's is not a world of comfortable structure, as in Bach, Haydn, Mozart, or Brahms. His music reflects his interior life as well as the disintegrating civilization that surrounded him. Think of listening to his music as the traversal of a vast earthly expanse, as a life journey full of joy and tragedy, stability and unpredictablilty.

The second movement, at 12 minutes, is much gentler, with the cello setting the tone. The third movement (11 minutes and 24 seconds) is a scherzo that provides some comic relief from the weighty matters at hand. It is drawn from the humorous song about St. Anthony preaching to the fishes that appears in *Des Knaben Wunderhorn*. Notice how this movement ends in a sort of abrupt silence.

The fourth movement is a peaceful song, *Urlicht* (Primal Light), that is also drawn from *Des Knaben Wunderhorn*. It is sung by a mezzo-soprano or contralto. On this recording we have the divine Christa Ludwig, who so completely understood Mahler and had a long-term musical collaboration with Leonard Bernstein that was magical. The music sounds so pleasant and benign, but read the words! (page 23 in the libretto) ". . . Man lies in direst need! Man lies in deepest pain! I would rather be in heaven . . ." Here again is Mahler's fascination with death.

Remember that in the cultural climate of nineteenth-century Europe, especially as shaped by Wagner, death was a step on the road to redemption. I doubt this appealed to the Jewish Mahler, but it may have held some sort of attraction for the Christian Mahler.

I do believe that insight into, and experience of, death gives one a more intense appreciation and fervent gratitude for life. That is one of the means by which I make my way into this symphony.

The fourth movement moves us silently and inexorably toward the symphony's concluding music. The final movement starts with an amazing crash, followed by wispy strains of many melodies, many of which will return in meaningful ways in the music to come.

The fifth movement is an amazing 47-minute journey through uncharted musical terrain. Even if one can point to similarities with works such as Beethoven's Ninth Symphony, this is a work unto itself. You will hear birdcalls, distant fanfares, and then the chorus, as if from nothing, appears surreptitiously and magically. The music of the chorus in this movement is heart-stoppingly exciting and is matched by the wonderful singing of soprano Barbara Hendricks and Christa Ludwig. The orchestra, clearly inspired by Bernstein, soars to incredible heights in this live performance that was recorded at New York's Avery Fisher Hall in 1987.

To me the concluding passages of the symphony (track 15 on disk 2) are not unlike the feeling of scaling the last and most precarious inches of a craggy and treacherous mountain and then beholding the view that suddenly appears. What do you see? Is it the "other side," to use a euphemism? Or is it the rest of our world, of a piece with what we already know, and waiting to be discovered? You may experience something entirely different.

On your second hearing, read the text as you listen to the fourth and fifth movement, and then put it away with the CD box. This is the kind of hair-raising music that asks you to focus entirely on the sound, rather than reading while it is played.

In case you have not noticed, you now have unleashed your capacity to be touched by great music, to feel it. The experience of music is a journey—we start from one place and pass many more before coming to the journey's end. When we sit in a concert hall with others, we make a collective journey, although the experience of it is different for each one of us. When we listen to the same music again, even if it is the same recording, each journey is different.

The way to feeling music, now that your head is full of ideas of what music is, comes when you can turn off all of your analytical faculties and let the music suffuse your every fiber as you did on your first hearing of Mahler's Second Symphony, and I suspect, as you will do many times again.

• ᔕ •

You might want to contrast this listening of Mahler's Second Symphony, with a recording you already own:

Mahler: Symphonies nos. 1 and 2; London Philharmonic Orchestra; Klaus Tennstedt, conductor; EMI Classics 7243 5 74182 5

MOUNT OLYMPUS AND ELYSIAN FIELDS
Beethoven's Ninth Symphony

The music of Beethoven opens the realm of the colossal and the immeasurable for us.

—*E. T. A. Hoffmann*

Beethoven: Symphony no. 9, "Choral"; Chorus and Orchestra of the Bayreuther Festspiele, Wilhelm Furtwängler, conductor; Elisabeth Schwarzkopf, Soprano Elisabeth Höngen, contralto; Hans Hopf, tenor; Otto Edelman, bass; EMI 7243 5 66953 2 0

At the beginning of this book I described classical music as a vast terrain full of many structures, each with many doors leading to fascinating and unusual places. My goal was to give you the tools to embark on a journey of discovery. You now have reached sacred and much-trampled ground: Beethoven's Ninth Symphony.

This work is often called Olympian because of its grand scope. This is a reference to Mount Olympus, where the gods of antiquity lived (though they fought so much that it could hardly have been a Utopian setting). In the text by Schiller that Beethoven inserted at the end of the symphony, there is mention of the Elysian Fields. Homer said this terrain was open only to heroes. I think of this land as the terrain of the glories of music. Elysian is a better metaphor for this work than Olympian.

The Ninth Symphony is probably the most famous piece of classical music, one that nearly everyone on the planet has heard all or part of. It is quite possible that, as you have come to love classical music while reading this book, you could not wait to listen to Beethoven's Ninth Symphony. This is more probable if you already invested in a boxed set of the nine symphonies to listen to the Fifth, Sixth, and Seventh symphonies. Although you have most likely heard this symphony before, at least the famous choral section. But you did not ever hear it with all the knowledge, insights, and skills you now bring to it.

Beethoven's music was popular in his lifetime and he enjoyed a great deal of renown, despite his often ornery personality. His funeral in Vienna in 1827 was attended by more than twenty thousand mourners. The city's schools were closed in his honor. There probably would have been this outpouring even if Beethoven had never composed the Ninth Symphony, but this is the work that has pushed his reputation into the stratosphere, even if its success was not unqualified during his lifetime.

I do not wish to imply that this is the *best* piece of classical music—there is no such thing. Yet it is singular for so many reasons that it has achieved cult status.

Beethoven wrote his Eighth Symphony in 1812, so there was a considerable gap before the Ninth would first be played on May 7, 1824. In the intervening time, the political and social map of Europe changed radically. The ideals of the French Revolution had faded or been corrupted. Napoleon was vanquished and the map of Europe was redrawn at the Congress of Vienna (1815). For many, including Beethoven, idealism was tarnished by the harsh realities of the world: war, illness, deception, greed, and so on.

In addition to the sufferings of the world, Beethoven had had plenty of his own: deafness, other illnesses, unrequited love, problems with relatives, and intense anger and frustration. By 1812 he was totally deaf, and in a deep depression. Even before this time, he famously struggled to create his art, and part of our received image of him when we hear much of his music is of the battle to create. When, after years of silence, Beethoven roused himself to compose again, he literally had to look inward for the music because there were no longer sounds he could hear. In addition to this symphony, his works in his last years included the sublimely beautiful late string quartets (op. 127, 130, 131, 132, 135), the searching *Missa Solemnis*, and some of the *Diabelli Variations* with their cheeky and ironic touches of humor. I find that the humorous pages of his music can be as inspiring as the tragic and noble ones, for the simple reason that he was able to summon humor despite so much adversity.

In writing this music, whose ideas had germinated in one form or another since he read Schiller's *Ode to Joy* as a twenty-two-year-old (1792), Beethoven sought to reassert his belief in man's better nature. Although he had thought of setting the Schiller text to music since he first read it, not until 1823 did it occur to him to insert it in a symphony. Beethoven found that what he had to say here could not be expressed by instruments alone. With music sung by vocal soloists and the addition of a huge chorus, Beethoven created a new kind of symphony that would push the boundaries of the form in terms of expression. Now, a large orchestra, chorus and singers would take music from its beautiful abstraction and inject it with specific ideas. This would influence how Wagner would later write his operas and how other composers—especially Mahler—would believe what a symphony could be.

The mystique of the Ninth was such that some later composers were eager to write nine symphonies but were superstitious about exceeding that number. This was particularly the case with Bruckner and Mahler, who did not call certain big works symphonies so that they would not exceed the magic number. By contrast, Shostakovich boldly moved forward and wrote fifteen symphonies, and by the time Hans Werner Henze's wonderful ninth symphony had its premiere in the late 1990s, he was deep into work on his tenth.

It was Beethoven's desire that this symphony be an affirmation of the loftiest humanitarian principles. It has often been played at the Olympics; Leonard Bernstein conducted a performance as the Berlin Wall fell in 1989. It has been used at the World Cup of soccer; for promotion of the European Union; and to ring in the millennium. Although its subject is joy, this symphony has also served on somber occasions to assert the resolve that the sinister elements of the human soul shall be vanquished by our better nature. Thus, it was chosen to be performed by the New York Philharmonic on September 11, 2002, the first anniversary of the terrorist attacks on the United States.

The recommended recording of this symphony came about in similarly charged circumstances. It was made at the reopening of the Bayreuth Festival in 1951. Bayreuth was the site of the annual summer performances of many of the operas of Richard Wagner (1813–1883), one of the most influential and controversial of all composers. His works are brilliant, but his legacy was a mixed one, in that he was openly anti-Semitic. The Nazis used his music for propaganda and, when they took power fifty years after Wagner's death, Bayreuth became something of a shrine for their ideology. Some of Wagner's heirs, especially his daughter-in-law, were enthusiastic collaborators with the Nazis, and Bayreuth went from being a shrine of great art to one that was deeply tarnished.

It was decided, when the festival resumed activity after World War II, to begin not with Wagner but with Beethoven. This composer represented the sort of ideals that postwar Germany hoped to embrace. Beethoven's art was loved by Wagner, who claimed that the Ninth Symphony was a source of immense inspiration in terms of what music could achieve. Wagner was a great advocate of this symphony and conducted it often. This performance on this recording served as a metaphor for a return to the roots of Wagner's art, and would open the way for a return to the staging of his great operas in a way that could speak to new generations.

Still, it was audacious to try to help Bayreuth reclaim its place in the community of world music with Beethoven's symphony, in a performance that included certain artists who had been accused of collaborating with the Nazi regime during the Third Reich. Foremost among these was conductor Wilhelm Furtwängler. His involvement with the Nazi party is a topic of considerable debate and was even the subject of a play. He claimed that as a musician it was his job and duty to continue performing the music he knew and loved, and that music would speak for him and his ideals. He said that, as a German, he should remain in his own country, while German artists conspicuously joined the Nazi Party, including Richard Strauss (who nonetheless professed that he had little enthusiasm for it), Furtwängler never gave it a public endorsement.

Furtwängler remained active in musical life and performed when and where he could in his nation, in front of audiences that were often full of Nazis. Yet music was his doctrine and beliefs, if we are to accept his repeated assertions. It should also be said that many outstanding German musicians left their country before or during the war and publicly denounced Nazism and Fascism. Thus Furtwängler's silence on the subject raised considerable doubts and suspicions about his true feelings.

· ◇ ·

I would not have selected this performance for you simply because of the story behind it. This recording is a grand account of this symphony and is often held up as the definitive version. I would never make such a pronouncement, in part because I want you to explore other performances and come to your conclusions. There is no single best performance, and at least fifty recordings of this symphony have been made since this 1951 account.

If I had not told you all of this, you would still likely be impressed with the passion and fire of this performance. And you still should be. It is worth noting that, at about 75 minutes, this is a rather long performance of the symphony. Furtwängler took the music at a leisurely pace, finding all of the drama and feeling he could from the music and musicians without, I believe, ever letting the tension snap.

Recent theories by scholars of period performances assert that the tempos were much faster in Beethoven's time, and that the composer himself, when he conducted the premiere, probably laid down his baton much sooner. In our times, the speed record probably belongs to Sir John Eliot Gardiner, whose 1992 recording takes about an hour.

You could probably devote a great deal of study to the many approaches given to this one symphony. Among the conductors I recommend are Arturo Toscanini, Bruno Walter, Leonard Bernstein (from the 1960s with the New York Philharmonic and again in a radically different interpretation in front of the Berlin Wall in 1989), Herbert von Karajan, Georg Solti, Kurt Masur, and Gardiner.

• ✦ •

Let us begin to listen. You might wish to use my notes below as a reference, or you can write down your own description of what is happening, in musical terms, in this symphony. Because this is an old recording in monaural sound of a live performance, you will notice some imperfections. For example, at about 2 minutes and 45 seconds into the first movement there is the sound of coughing. In compensation, there is the extra excitement of a live event. If you bear in mind that this superlative performance did not benefit from any technological adjustment (and no chance to do something again if it did not come out right the first time), you will marvel at the quality of music-making and not mind the less-than-perfect recording conditions.

Notice throughout the symphony the sound of the kettledrums, which seem to serve as a heartbeat, bringing to mind the more modern assertion that "where there is life there is hope."

Also realize that this symphony breaks new ground in another way. Until then, the traditional classical symphony was about a contrast of tempos and moods among the movements. In this case, the first three movements are statements of one kind or another, introducing ideas that may or may not be returned to. The final movement is a summing up, drawing on many of the ideas of the earlier movements, and then drawing them into a greater whole before moving into a thrilling climax. In a way, this structure is much more operatic or, if you prefer, narrative. Beethoven is telling us things in the one language that was left to him—music.

The first movement starts with mysterious rustling of strings, with voices of various instruments coming forth, as if positing questions or ideas, mostly in the notes of E and A. Soon there is a sense that all of this sound will develop into something monumental in size and import. Suspense gives way to temporary calm, which in turn gives way to thunderous orchestral eruptions.

The second movement starts with the introduction of a joyous melody that combines with a soothing, consoling other theme. This whirling, dance-inflected music that always seems to be on the brink of collapse is reminiscent of the feeling we find in the Seventh Symphony.

Hector Berlioz said of the third movement, "As for the beauties of these melodies, the infinite grace of the ornaments that envelop them . . . the tenderness, and dreamy religious feeling they express—if my prose could but give an approximate idea of them, music would have found a rival in written speech." This is Berlioz's description of that most remarkable aspect of music, which is to eloquently say things that words cannot. Its pathos is almost too much to bear.

Think for a moment of the sharply different moods and statements of the first three movements before everything is shattered by the music that follows.

The fourth movement has a clamorous beginning that leads to small musical reminders from the previous three movements. What is happening here is that Beethoven entices us with music we have heard (and, again, playing with our abilities to incorporate music into memory) and then, curiously, he rejects all of that music and introduces a new theme that is called the "Ode to Joy."

It is introduced delicately by violas and cellos, as if it is an idea or an impulse that must first be stated tentatively. Then the violins join in as if they too concur with the idea, Following their lead, the rest of the orchestra joins in, and we listeners are swept up with it.

After all of this heats up, there is what sounds like a chaotic crash. Orchestral music has said all it can, for the moment, and now it is time for human sounds. The baritone steps up to sing, "O friends, not these tones! Let us take up a more joyous strain." He then sings a melody all of us know. It is unfortunate that this, and so many recordings of the Ninth, do not include the text in German and in translations. I have seen the text translated in radically different ways that seem to suit the purpose of the people who would sing it. Some of the most literal translations include Schiller's key words that joy, to which his verse is dedicated, is a "daughter of Elysium." Here is a translation from the 1920s that will give you some of the flavor of the German original:

> Joy by fairest gods inspired
> Maiden from Elysium
> We with new ambition fired
> To thy sacred shrine have come.
>
> Thro' thy spell in bonds supernal
> Free and joyful once again
> All mankind unites, fraternal
> Where thy gentle wings remain.

When I was a schoolboy in the 1960s, we sang the "Ode to Joy" in an English translation that began as follows:

> Joy, the gift of God immortal,
> given to us from heaven above.
> From the fires of war extinguished,
> comes the joy of peace and love.
>
> If there is a single person
> who has a heart and soul his own,
> and denies all men are equal,
> may he live and die alone.

You can imagine the powerful effect such words can have on a child's formation. Although the teacher did not discuss the meaning of the text, it was imprinted so naturally that, thirty-seven years after I learned it, I was able to type it without having to check any notes.

Back to the music: a brief hush heralds the distant arrival of what sounds like a marching contingent. The tenor, mezzo-soprano, and soprano also sing parts of the "Ode," and soon they join in a quartet of individual voices before the chorus—the voices of humanity—join in. All the singers and instrumentalists reach what seems like a climax when there is another pause. When it seems all have come as far as they can, Beethoven ratchets things up further, sending all of the musicians to a soaring and euphoric finale that sums up, in words and music, everything he intended to say.

Had I presented this symphony to you at the beginning of your studies, you would only be reminded of the things you already knew. Now you are able to hear this work in all of its complex majesty and really understand what it is all about.

This music, and text, became part of a life view of mine that perhaps you might embrace. You may receive all kinds of messages from the Ninth Symphony, and you should explore them deeply and candidly. Here is part of what it tells me: the communal aspect of music-making, in which you as an audience member are an important part of the process, is a metaphor for the best aspects of the human condition. We have an awareness of being part of a larger world, one in which my humanity is bound up in your humanity (and vice versa) and in which a shared sense of well-being is more vital than a self-oriented focus.

And yet for all of the importance of brotherhood (and, of course, sisterhood), there is a dignity and nobility in each individual that is just as treasurable. If it was Schiller who could express these ideas in words, then it was Beethoven who took these words and turned them into action. It is his music, and all music—the mysterious, nonverbal side of our consciousness that speaks to us in deep and eloquent ways—that makes us understand what these ideas really mean.

• ❧ •

At the premiere of Beethoven's Ninth Symphony, the composer stood at the podium to conduct. As you might expect, his deafness prevented him from really leading the orchestra, chorus, and soloists as a conductor must. Another conductor stood discreetly to one side and behind him, doing much of the actual leadership. When the performance ended, the Viennese audience rose to give the music a roaring ovation. Beethoven stood there, his back to the audience, unaware of the reception until Karoline Unger, the mezzo-soprano soloist, gently stepped forward to turn Beethoven around to see the reaction to his most famous creation.

CODA
Some Final Notes

So long as the human spirit thrives on this planet, music in some living form will accompany and sustain it and give it expressive meaning.
—*Aaron Copland, 1954*

We have now been to all the edifices on the vast musical terrain we will visit in *Classical Music 101*. You have acquired a firm foundation to learn and love all the classical music—and, for that matter, most any music—you will encounter. You did this by reading, and by taking cues from me, but primarily by listening, listening, and listening again. You brought your character and intelligence to this effort, but also another very important trait—openness.

It is time for you to explore on your own.

Where to now? A wonderful, lifelong adventure awaits you, with an almost infinite amount of great music to discover. Along the line, you will encounter a few prophets of musical doom. It has become a commonplace to say that classical music is in crisis. Critics bemoan the traditionalism in programming of many musical institutions. In response, these companies say that they have to create the programs they do because audiences will only be drawn to "bread-and-butter" works, those wonderful but overplayed pieces from the standard repertory. Sometimes one finds a program in a concert hall that might contain a new piece as the second work of three to be played, with, say, a Mozart before and a Brahms after. It is as if the new work were a bitter pill that must be sugar-coated to go down more easily. Also, by placing it in the middle of the program, there is the cynical thought that you have to sit through it to get to another familiar work. That is no way to inspire curiosity and openness when the implicit assumption is, "Sit still and listen, it's good for you."

It is also true—primarily with orchestras that give only a limited number of concerts per season—that many lesser-known works of the past, even by the greatest composers, do not get performed as often as they ought to be. The main reason is that these pieces simply have not entered the golden circle of what are thought of as the greatest hits. We so often hear the later symphonies of Schubert and Dvořák, but how frequently do we get to listen to the early ones?

It is important to realize that if we limit the repertory to old chestnuts even the most traditional audience can get restless. Fortunately, much of the wider repertory of classical music exists on recordings, primarily from the past when such works were routinely recorded by important artists. As you deepen your interest in particular composers or repertory, there is an immense catalogue of recordings you can turn to.

What can be done to bring wider repertory to audiences today? And how can audiences be motivated to step outside the most familiar works to try something new? Much can be solved, I contend, if we reflect on the way most people think of classical music.

Part of the problem is that a marketing mentality has infected many perceptions about an art form that requires less marketing and more education. It is as if culture must be sold to be appreciated. When that happens, the "consumer" tends to evaluate the experience based on whether he got his money's worth. Marketing may get someone to buy a ticket to a concert, but education is what will make him come back. Nowadays, most people approach the art form without the serious preparation that you have undertaken, so their point of view on hearing one or two pieces of music is more "Is it worth it?" rather than "What does this music say to me?" That is why I wrote this book.

It is not surprising that these new listeners are unprepared. Most educational systems worldwide no longer embrace music as part of a curriculum, despite all the evidence that young minds nurtured with music tend to grow to be more nimble and creative. Some fortunate people have exposure to classical music at home, where they are imbued with a love and respect for the art form. But for most people contact with classical music comes in haphazard ways. Think, for example, how much music you have heard in snatches on the radio, in advertising, as the score of cartoons, as background music in restaurants, and on the telephone during those interminable waits for customer service. It penetrates our minds in one way or another, even if we really don't listen. Yet that music is not associated with pleasure or emotional transport.

An important consequence of this passive listening is that when we hear these pieces again while actually paying attention to them, much of what we are taken with is their familiarity. When we have already heard in some form the cardinal pieces of Pachelbel (1653–1706), Bach, Vivaldi, Mozart, Beethoven, Schubert, Mendelssohn, Chopin, Tchaikovsky, Grieg, Debussy, Ravel, Gershwin, Strauss, and others, we tend to embrace them again because we have subconscious recognition of them. The first response is, "I know this!" One hopes that the next exclamation will be, "I like this!" This does not happen with works by these composers that we have not heard, and certainly does not occur with less famous but significant ones such as Monteverdi, Galuppi, Couperin, Weber, Salieri, Dittersdorf, Spohr, Borodin, Fauré, Wolf, Smetana, Ives, Nielsen, Scriabin, Janáček, Berg, Sibelius, Poulenc, and so forth. Yet one might still display some openness to these composers because they seem to be part of the classical tradition.

Most composers of the past seventy-five years don't enjoy the same luck. Somewhere around the time radio and recordings became available, people could choose between the music of the present and the music of the past. With Debussy, Schoenberg, Stravinsky, and others blazing new tonal and harmonic paths, some music lovers pulled away from those experimental developments and sought refuge in the familiar. Since then, a segment of the audience seemed to develop an allergy to new works. This is a learned behavior and can be unlearned by those who are willing to be open.

Nazism and the Second World War added further disruptions to the progress of new and unfamiliar music. Many European musicians who were Jews or anti-Fascists came to America and, though they were steeped in a tradition that encouraged new as well as older music at home, in the United States they found more receptivity for the older style. Bartok, Rachmaninoff, Stravinsky, Britten, Weill, and Schoenberg enjoyed varying degrees of success in the United States. They also became teachers and mentors, and planted the seeds for a great deal of musical innovation. Music lovers in North America have a vast range of newer works to choose from, if they are open to that.

The great conductors of the postwar era, whether in Europe or America, devoted most of their focus on returning to the past, in part because the terrible rupturing schism that the previous two decades created made many crave a return to the older, more familiar things that had survived. Some conductors used the occasion to search the past for works that were ignored but might offer new meaning. The most famous example is Leonard Bernstein's return to the entire symphonic repertory of Mahler.

In the 1950s and 1960s, much new music in Europe, North America, and parts of Asia and Latin America was highly academic and required a great degree of musicological knowledge and patience to embrace. No matter how valuable this music was, most of it was roundly disdained. As in the art of all eras, some of it will eventually be rediscovered and appreciated, and may receive wider audiences. By the 1960s, though, the impression that new music was unsavory or weird had become so ingrained that subsequent composers have had to battle just to be heard.

The music of so many living composers is exciting and challenging. To name John Adams, Thomas Adès, William Bolcom, John Corigliano, Deborah Drattell, John Eaton, Philip Glass, Osvaldo Golijov, John Harbison, Heinz Werner Henze, Aaron Jay Kernis, Oliver Knussen, Libby Larsen, Steven Mackey, Krysztof Penderecki, Tobias Picker, Steve Reich, Bright Sheng, John Tavener, and an untold number of Finns is to show you only a small segment of a very large and promising group. Artists such as Yo-Yo Ma, Anne-Sophie Mutter, Joshua Bell,

Thomas Hampson, Daniel Barenboim, and others have the clout and devotion to commission new works and see them performed and recorded. One hopes that, as James Levine assumes the podium at the Boston Symphony in 2004, he will use it as a bully pulpit for contemporary music.

New music does require an investment and a commitment above and beyond that required for performing older works. Often, a grant or sponsorship must be procured to help the composer survive while the piece is being written. The cost of copying musical parts for all the instruments is quite expensive, and this might be part of the funds used to commission the work. New works often require longer rehearsal periods than standard repertory because musicians are approaching them for the first time and need to investigate the thoughts and the sound world of unfamiliar composers. And then there is the potential of smaller revenue at the box office because a segment of the audience resists new music like the plague.

Whether unfamiliar music was written today or centuries ago, it deserves to be played and heard.

• ⟨⟩ •

As an open-minded lover of classical music (in its broader and imperfect sense of being "serious" music as opposed to pop or folk), you can play a role in assuring that it is not viewed entirely as an irrelevant thing of the past, with our concert halls serving only as museums full of relics. Doing this is a matter of understanding how some people perceive classical music and helping them adjust their approach to it.

If we go to an art museum, we can admire works from three thousand or more years ago and see the continuum of expression in the visual arts. Knowledgeable museumgoers know that new art may be different, sometimes less accessible and often more confrontational, but no less meaningful. They try to understand and connect with these works and, if all is not immediately clear and comprehensible, they return often to regard them anew. In so doing, they approach these works with openness and bring their own preferences and critical faculties to them. This can be done with music.

Every era has created great literature, including our own. Certainly it is pleasant to take an extended refuge in the past. In works by Cervantes or Dickens or Wharton one can find many time-tested truths as well as incisive portraits of the eras and societies in which the authors lived. Yet this is no less so among the finest authors of today. What they depict may not always be pleasing, and the writing may be tougher and more astringent, but the best of these works are compelling and necessary. We read new literature in part because it is a mirror of who we are, a sort of report from the front lines. So is new music.

In dance, many audiences seem to hunger for exciting new works to put alongside the wonderful story ballets of the classical repertory. As in all art forms, it is not that every new dance piece will find a lasting place in the repertory, but at least choreographers are appreciated for trying to understand the modern world and put it in a context of movement and gesture. New composers deserve the same sort of interest and expectation.

Opera, which is an amalgamation of great music, theater, dance, and the visual arts, is the most vibrant of all the art forms and, despite articles you may read about its being in crisis, is actually growing and appealing to new audiences who find it exciting and relevant. Attendance in Europe remains level to slightly higher; Japan and Korea have very devoted operagoers; in Australia, Canada, and especially in the United States, there is an explosive growth and enthusiasm for opera. If you have not yet been bitten by the opera bug, pick up a copy of *Opera 101: A Complete Guide to Learning and Loving Opera.*

Modern theater is in something of a limbo. Contemporary playwrights struggle to find audiences and producers who will mount their works. In America, nonprofit theater companies tend to shoulder most of this burden and, if a work is deemed financially viable, then producers may invest to give the work a commercial run. In the United Kingdom and France there are more outlets for playwrights, although they must struggle in most other countries. But the crisis in theater, if there is one, is that of finding what to say, a way to say it, and a place to say it. Theater audiences do not turn their backs on a play because it is new if they perceive it to be exciting. If anything, theater faces the opposite problem of classical music in that it is harder to get audiences to attend classics by Euripides, Molière, Sheridan, Ibsen, Strindberg, Chekhov, Shaw, O'Neill, and even Shakespeare than to see the latest hit play. The theatrical past has been marginalized in a way that older classical music is not.

Film is probably the art form of our times, with popular music (rock hip-hop techno, grunge, rap, jazz, soul, rhythm and blues, gospel, popular song, Latin, and everything that falls under the rubric of "world music") probably the second most important. With movies we all seem to have the imperative to attend, and there is a vast selection to choose from. Yet movies have also experienced the split between "cinema" (those films that aspire to some kind of artistic expression that is pure and not directed at a target audience), popular films (those that are well crafted by talented people and aim to tell a story in a way that will attract wide audiences), and mass-market commercial films (whose goal is to draw huge crowds and make hundreds of millions of dollars without much regard to art). Of course, there is some degree of overlap in these categories in that those who make art films and popular films are not averse to making money, but their artistic goals occupy a much greater part of their decisions than happens with mass-market filmmakers.

The key thing about films of all types is that we as audiences tend to investigate in some way what they are about and then make decisions about what to see. If we like a particular director or actor (for classical music, think "composer" or "performer"), we might see his or her film without any further deliberation. If, in finding out about a film, we are drawn to the subject matter or genre, we might see it for that reason. We learn of films through advertising, of course, but we also find about them through articles and coverage in print and broadcast media. The most commercial of news media tend to cover only the most mainstream movies (don't forget: in many countries some media companies also have movie production divisions), but many filmgoers seek a wider range of media to learn about that small, intriguing movie playing on only one screen in town. This spirit of inquiry and investigation, which is second nature to film audiences, can be applied to classical music.

The same sense of segmentation of movies into art, popular expression, and unbridled commercialism characterizes most of the works of so-called popular music. (I have always despised the term "popular" music because it suggests that other music is unpopular or not of the people.) Although our subject here is classical music, I passionately love many types of popular music and find in them an artistry, immediacy, and visceral pleasure I would never want to abandon.

It is a mistake to assume that all popular music comes to us readily on radio and in music videos. In fact, most popular music has to be sought out to be heard. There are few radio stations for jazz, popular standards (Sinatra, Bennett, Clooney, and dozens of other great artists), gospel, "world music," and even most rap songs. Only rock, hip-hop, and country get wide exposure on radio. But lovers of one or another kind of music tend to want to share it with their friends by playing them recordings or taking them to live performances. You can do the same with classical music.

As to videos, these are a different medium that "deliver" music in visual terms. They were intended as a sort of marketing tool for pop music, and the best videos certainly have important artistic merit. They are valid, of course, but are about so many things aside from the music. And they have had one significant negative consequence: the ears and attention span of the video generation are not readily accepting of the kind of focus that classical music asks for. I like the best music videos for what they are, but they tend to detract from the pure appreciation of music.

Videos have also driven longer-format music of most types off regularly scheduled television programming. In the not-too-distant past (the mid-1980s), it was still possible to see orchestras and solo classical artists on a somewhat regular basis on public broadcasting networks. But the twin factors of music videos and the belief that marketing an art form is more essential than providing regular access to it signaled the decline of classical music on TV. It was thought that there is not enough to look at in a classical performance, though I enjoy focusing on musicians as they play. Nowadays, only a sexy violinist or a handsome singer doing light repertory seem to appear on television in America and, increasingly, elsewhere. This is a sad acknowledgment of the fragmentation of attention and thought (and lack of reflection) that characterizes business, politics, and interpersonal relations in our frenetic time. Classical music is so valuable now because it can give back to our minds a way to function as they were intended to.

• ✧ •

How do you find and select music you might like? In the past there was a tradition, now all but extinct in the United States and some other nations, of having a listening room in record stores. Staff in the stores would typically be passionate about the music in the section they worked in, and listened to recordings to keep up to date. They were able to direct record buyers to the type of music and performers they would ask for, and perhaps to other works of interest as well. The vehicle for this was the listening room, where a client could listen to a recording and then decide whether to purchase it. This hand-selling of music helped create a relationship between seller and buyer much like that of the neighborhood bookshop, but this practice has become increasingly rare.

Some record chains, such as Tower, have headphones on the racks that enable you to listen to a few dozen of the latest releases. This is certainly a good thing, but it means that you can only hear those works. With modern technology, there must be a way (perhaps via computer) that a record shop can access a disk for a customer to listen to, and I believe this would help stimulate sales. In the meantime, you should seek out the knowledgeable and passionate salespeople in your local record shop, buy a disk or two when you can based on their recommendation, and then go back and talk to them about what you have heard. You may not have enjoyed or understood everything you listened to but, in the act of exploring why, you will learn something valuable. When book shopping, I take this same approach with owners and salespeople at independent bookstores and with dedicated employees at chain bookstores. The lesson here is of dialogue in the marketplace, rather than permitting yourself to be a tiny element in a huge corporate framework, one wooed by the blandishments of marketing rather than the delights of discovery. Art is personal; mass commerce is impersonal.

Another good way to learn about a wide range of repertory is by reading many articles in good newspapers plus magazines devoted to classical music. Do not be deterred by the fact that mainstream American media such as *Time* and *Newsweek* give scant coverage to all of the arts (unlike in the past), and classical performers might only get a mention if they are good-looking and have the services of a high-powered publicist. A magazine such as *Entertainment Weekly* does not seem to consider classical music, opera, and dance to be entertaining. Corresponding publications in Britain, France, Italy, Spain, Germany, Austria, Russia, and Japan all include the "serious" arts as part of their regular coverage.

In much of American society cultural things are considered newsworthy principally if they are money-making. Most magazines and broadcast media have abandoned their position as opinion leaders and respond instead to popular trends driven by mass-market commercial art. (I am not saying that commercial art is not valid or important, but that it is only a small part of the overall cultural landscape.)

As you know, classical music performances face a particular challenge in that reviews in newspapers tend to be documentation of what has transpired as opposed to what there is to see. You can use these for musical education at least as much as for deciding whether to buy tickets. Even if a particular program will have multiple performances, by the time you read the review there will likely be only one or two performances left and tickets may not be available. You can go on-line to read provocative and thoughtful reviews in publications such as the *New York Times* (www.nytimes.com), the *Washington Post* (www.washingtonpost.

com), the *Chicago Tribune* (www.chicagotribune), the *Los Angeles Times* (www.latimes.com), the *Boston Globe* (www.boston.com/globe), the *Wall Street Journal* (www.wsj.com), the *Financial Times* (www.timeoff. ft.com/goingout)), the *Guardian* (www.guardian.co.uk), and foreign publications in languages you might understand.

Gramophone, founded in 1923, is probably the most important magazine devoted to classical music. As you seek to deepen your knowledge, consider becoming a regular reader. *Stereo Review* is another fine publication. The BBC in England also publishes a magazine for music lovers. On the Internet go to www.andante.com/magazine for interesting interviews and coverage. This site can connect you to many valuable resources for becoming more knowledgeable.

A service that classical music critics can provide (and many do) is to write ahead of time about an important upcoming concert and encourage readers to attend it. And this is where you and all classical music lovers come in. Your openness to new compositions and to the rediscovery of older music asks you to be an enthusiastic and supportive audience member. Yes, this does represent an outlay of funds, and few people have unlimited resources. I know I don't. But by researching when new works will be presented in theaters in my hometown or in the places where I travel, I can endeavor to support these efforts and test my perceptive faculties all at once. If you cannot routinely afford performances at the local concert hall, find performances in churches, universities, and smaller groups that will be within your budget. Many of these, in fact, are free.

And bring someone with you, taking care to explain to your guest the context and some of the ideas in the work you are to hear. I have come to know numerous readers of *Opera 101* who have become Pied Pipers of opera, sharing their enthusiasms with friends and creating new opera lovers. Author Ann Patchett was so taken with opera after reading the book that she wrote *Bel Canto* (2001), a wonderful novel with an operatic setting.

• ᠂ᢙ᠂ •

There is but one more thing for you to think about as you embark on your own musical journey: your relationship with time. If you can give wholly of your precious time when you listen to music, you will be rewarded handsomely.

Our twenty-first-century lifestyle puts a premium on multitasking, the ability to do many things at once. This attitude has penetrated our thinking and behavior on many levels and, I believe, it is profoundly unhealthy. We are a people who skim or bump superficially over most of our experiences, seldom stopping to look deeply, to think and reflect, or just to breathe. Music, if you give it your full attention, can enable you to breathe, to refresh, *to feel something*, to reach for emotions where words neither suffice nor matter.

If you tend to feel like a pinball that ricochets without direction or meaning, then just stop, at least for a while. Reduce your multitasking so that you focus on one single thing: a glorious piece of music. Over time, let music change your life so that it is not one concerned with arriving at touchstones and thresholds. Don't think of life (or music) as an exam to be completed. The contentment you will find is inexplicably blissful and will affect other aspects of your existence and sense of meaning.

A life in music can truly be called a state of grace. For you this is the start of a grand, life-changing experience that will grow and deepen in time. Music—including classical music—will become an important part of the sum of your life. James Levine once observed to me that "as you get older and use your life experience more, everything means more than it did before. The hundred percent that is your life is greater than it was earlier."

This is what is meant by a life in music, and it is yours to begin.

• ◇ •

Now close your eyes. Open your ears. Relax your mind and let the clutter of thoughts float away. Release your preconceptions and prejudices, and replace them with openness. And let the music—all that music that is now in your head and is part of you—play.

DISCOGRAPHY FOR
CLASSICAL MUSIC 101

What follows is a list of recordings used in this book to help you develop your love and knowledge of classical music. These are not in every case the recordings that offer the definitive version of a particular piece. "Definitive" is a term that is both subjective and elusive. If we devote too much care to whether something is the absolute best, we will miss out on the great pleasure to be found in simply listening. The list below provides more than fifty years of recorded performances of wonderful music by outstanding artists. Wherever possible a moderately priced recording full of great music was selected, with additional attention given to letting you discover the widest range of orchestras, conductors, and soloists so that you will be exposed to many styles and interpretations.

The recordings indicated in **boldface print** are essential for studying the repertoire in this book. Those in normal print are recommended for additional listening if you wish to go more deeply into a particular subject. In many cases, you will find duplicate listings for recordings that are used in more than one chapter.

Chapter 1: First Hearing

Beethoven: Symphonies nos. 4, 5, 6, 7; Royal Concertgebouw Orchestra; Wolfgang Sawallisch, cond.; EMI Classics 7243 5 73326 2 0. Alternate: Beethoven: Symphonies 5, 6, 7, 8; Philadelphia Orchestra; Eugene

Ormandy, cond.; Sony SB2K 63266. If you are a more ambitious collector of recordings, or have some extra money to spend, you might consider investing in a boxed set of the nine symphonies of Beethoven, all of which will give you great pleasure. There are many sets to choose from, all identified by their conductor. Three famous ones are by Leonard Bernstein, Herbert von Karajan, and Georg Solti. More recent ones by Claudio Abbado and Daniel Barenboim are worthy, too, and a great historical document is the set from the late 1940s by Arturo Toscanini. What they lack in recording sophistication is more than compensated for by absolutely thrilling performances.

Chapter 4: Voices of the Orchestra

Children's Classics; *New York Philharmonic; Leonard Bernstein, cond.;* Sony SMK 60175. (*Prokofiev:* Peter and the Wolf; *Saint-Saëns:* Carnival of the Animals; *Britten:* The Young Person's Guide to the Orchestra)

Chapter 5: Colors and Pictures

Ravel: Bolero; *Debussy:* La Mer; *Mussorgsky:* Pictures at an Exhibition; *Berlin Philharmonic; Herbert von Karajan, cond.; DG 447 426-2*

Stravinsky: The Firebird; *Scriabin:* Prometheus; *Kirov Orchestra; Valery Gergiev, cond.; Alexander Toradze, piano; Philips 289 446 715-2*

Panorama: George Gershwin Rhapsody in Blue, *etc.; various artists; DG 289 469 139-2*

Handel: The Music for the Royal Fireworks; Amaryllis Suite; Suite from the Water Music; *Royal Philharmonic Orchestra; Yehudi Menuhin, cond.; RPO records/MCA Classics MCAD 6186.* (This is an outstanding recording, but most any recording you have of the Fireworks and Water Music will do.)

De Falla: Nights in the Gardens of Spain; *Albéniz: Rapsodia Española; Turina: Rapsodia Sinfónica: London Philharmonic Orchestra; Rafael Frühbeck de Burgos, cond.; Alicia de Larrocha, piano; London/Decca 410 289-2*

Rimsky-Korsakov: Scheherazade, *etc.; L'Orchestre de la Suisse Romande; Ernest Ansermet, cond.; London/Decca 443 464-2*

J. Strauss: Waltzes: The Blue Danube; *Wiener Philharmoniker; Willi Boskovsky, cond.; London/Decca 443 473-2.* If one disk of this music suffices, the same forces may be heard on London/Decca 289 467 413-2. For an enjoyable live performance, try the 1992 New Year's Concert with the same orchestra led by Carlos Kleiber (Sony SK 48376).

Smetana: Moldau; Má vlast; *Wiener Philharmoniker; James Levine, cond.; DG 427 340-2*

Panorama: Richard Strauss, Also sprach Zarathustra, *etc.; various artists; DG 289 469 208-2*

Vivaldi: The Four Seasons; *I Musici; Roberto Michelucci, violin; Philips 289 468 111-2.* (This is an outstanding recording, but most any recording you have of the Four Seasons will do.)

Holst: The Planets; *Orchestre Symphonique de Montréal; Charles Dutoit, cond.; London/Decca 417 553-2.* (Note: this has been reissued in later editions. Just be sure that you get one version or another of this performance, recorded in 1987.)

J. S. Bach: Brandenburg Concertos *Nos. 1–6; Bath Festival Orchestra; Yehudi Menuhin, cond.; EMI 7243 5 68516 2 7.* (This is an outstanding recording, but most any recording you have of the Brandenburg Concertos will do.)

Chapter 8: The Symphony

W. A. Mozart: Symphonies 40 and 41; *Wiener Philharmoniker; James Levine, cond.; DG 429 731-2*

Panorama: Joseph Haydn, Symphony no. 94, *etc.; various artists; DG 289 469 148-2*

Beethoven: Symphony no. 5; *Royal Concertgebouw/Sawallisch.* Or the Philadelphia/Ormandy alternate.

Panorama: Franz Schubert, Symphony 8, etc.; various artists; DG 289 469 196-2

Panorama: Felix Mendelssohn, The Hebrides Overture, *etc.; various artists;* DG 289 469 157-2

Panorama: Hector Berlioz, Symphonie Fantastique, *etc.; various artists;* DG 289 469 118-2. Also see the Berlioz disc issued by Seraphim/Virgin CDE 7243 5 69020 2 2.

Panorama: Robert Schumann, Symphony no. 1, etc.; various artists; DG 289 469 199-2. If you wish to purchase a good collection of Schumann's four symphonies, consider the recording by the Bamberger Symphoniker conducted by Christoph Eschenbach; Virgin Classics 7243 5 61884 2 6.

Brahms: Symphony no. 4; Wiener Philharmoniker; Carlos Kleiber, cond.; DG 289 457 706-2. If you wish to purchase a good collection of Brahms's four symphonies, consider the recording by the Berliner Philharmoniker conducted by Herbert von Karajan; DG 289 453 097-2.

Tchaikovsky: Piano Concerto no. 1; Symphony no. 6; Los Angeles Philharmonic Orchestra; Erich Leinsdorf, cond.; Leonard Pennario, piano; Seraphim 7243 5 69034 25. For a wonderful rendering of Tchaikovsky's last three symphonies, Symphonies nos. 4, 5, 6: Leningrad Philharmonic Orchestra; Evgeny Mravinsky, cond.; DG 419 745-2.

Dvořák: Symphonies nos. 7, 8, 9; The Cleveland Orchestra; Christoph von Dohnányi, cond.; London/Decca 421 082-2

Bruckner: Symphony no. 6; Wagner: Wesendonck Lieder; New Philharmonia Orchestra; Otto Klemperer, cond.; Christa Ludwig, mezzo-soprano; EMI 7243 5 67037 2 8

Bruckner: Symphony no. 4, "Romantic"; The Philadelphia Orchestra; Eugene Ormandy, cond.; Sony SBK 47653

Mahler: Symphonies nos. 1, 2; London Philharmonic Orchestra; Klaus Tennstedt, cond.; EMI Classics 7243 5 74182 5

Mahler: Symphony no. 7; Chicago Symphony Orchestra; Claudio Abbado, cond.; DG 445 523-2

Panorama: Richard Strauss: Don Juan, Till Eulenspiegels Lustige Streiche, *and* Ein Heldenleben; *DG 289 469 208-2*

R. Strauss: Don Juan, Vier Letzte Lieder; Tod und Verklarung; *New York Philharmonic; Kurt Masur, cond.; Deborah Voigt, soprano; Teldec 3984-25990-2*

Panorama: Serge Prokofiev, Classical *Symphony, etc.; various artists;* DG 289 469 172-2

Vaughan Williams: Symphony no. 5; Three Portraits from "The England of Elizabeth"; Concerto for Bass Tuba and Orchestra; London Symphony Orchestra; André Previn, cond.; John Fletcher, bass tuba; RCA Victor 60586-2-RG

Elgar: Symphonies nos. 1 and 2, etc.; BBC Symphony Orchestra; Andrew Davis, cond.; Teldec 0630-18951-2

Panorama: Jean Sibelius, Karelia Suite, *etc; various artists;* DG 289 469 202-2

Corigliano: Symphony no. 1; Chicago Symphony Orchestra; Daniel Barenboim, cond.; Erato 2292-45601-2

Gorécki: Symphony no. 3; London Sinfonietta; David Zinman, cond.; Dawn Upshaw, soprano; Elektra Nonesuch 9 79282

Glass: Symphony no. 2, etc.; Vienna Radio Symphony Orchestra, etc.; Dennis Russell Davies, cond.; Nonesuch 79496-2

Chapter 10: The Piano

Beethoven and Liszt: Piano Transcriptions: Symphony no. 6; Glenn Gould, piano; Sony SMK 52 637

J. S. Bach: Goldberg Variations; *Glenn Gould, piano; Sony/CBS SMK 37779*

J. S. Bach: **Goldberg Variations,** *etc.; Wanda Landowska, harpsichord;* **EMI 7243 5 67200 2 2**

Grieg: **Peer Gynt** *Incidental Music;* **Piano Concerto;** *London Phil-harmonic Orchestra; Øivin Fjeldstad, cond.; Clifford Curzon, piano; London/Decca 448 599-2.* This is the recommended recording. Alternatives include those by Murray Perahia, appearing with the Symphonie Orchester des Bayerischen Rundfunks conducted by Sir Colin Davis, Sony SK 44899, and the performance by Dinu Lipatti on the Great Pianists of the 20th Century series, Philips/EMI 456 892-2.

W. A. Mozart: **Piano Concertos nos. 19 and 23;** *English Chamber Orchestra; Murray Perahia, cond. and piano; CBS/Sony SMK 39064*

W. A. Mozart: Three Piano Sonatas, K. 279, 457, 576; Fantasia, K. 475; Mitsuko Uchida, piano; Philips 412 617-2

Beethoven: The Piano Concertos; *Chicago Symphony Orchestra; James Levine, cond.; Alfred Brendel, piano; Philips 456-045-2*

Beethoven: Diabelli Variations, *etc., from* Alfred Brendel Plays Beethoven; *VoxBox CDX 5112*

Beethoven: **Piano Sonatas nos. 8, 14, 21, 23;** *Wilhelm Kempff, piano; DG* **447 404-2**

Dvořák: Piano Concerto; *Schubert:* Wanderer *Fantasy; Orchester des Bayerischen Rundfunks; Carlos Kleiber, cond.; Sviatoslav Richter, piano; EMI 7243 5 66947 2 9*

Panorama: Schubert, "Trout" Quintet; Moments Musicaux; Military March for Piano Duet

Chopin: Piano Concertos nos. 1 and 2; Philadelphia Orchestra; Eugene Ormandy, cond.; Emanuel Ax, piano; RCA Victor 09026-68023-2

Arnold Schoenberg: Concerto for Piano and Orchestra; Franz Liszt: Concertos for Piano and Orchestra nos. 1 and 2; The Philharmonia; Esa-Pekka Salonen, cond.; Emanuel Ax, piano; Sony SK 53 289

Chopin: *Piano Concerto no. 1, etc.; Orchestra of the Age of Enlightenment; Sir Charles Mackerras, cond.; Emanuel Ax, piano; Sony SK 60771*

Panorama: Frédéric Chopin: "Andante Spianato," etc; various artists; DG 289 469 127-2

Chopin: *Nocturnes; Claudio Arrau, piano; Philips 416 440-2*

Panorama: Robert Schumann, Kinderszenen, Fantasia, Arabeske, and Piano Concerto

Brahms: Piano Concerto no. 2; Boston Symphony Orchestra; Bernard Haitink, cond.; Emanuel Ax, piano; Sony SK 63229. Recording also contains Brahms cello sonata, performed by Yo-Yo Ma.; Sony SK 63229.

Tchaikovsky: Piano Concerto no. 1; Symphony no. 6; Los Angeles Philharmonic Orchestra; Erich Leinsdorf, cond.; Leonard Pennario, piano; Seraphim 7243 5 69034 2 5

Dvořák: *Piano Concerto; Schubert "Wanderer" Fantasy; Orchester des Bayerischen Rundfunks; Carlos Kleiber, cond.; Sviastoslav Richter, piano; EMI 7243 5 66947 2 9*

Saint-Saëns: Concerto for Piano and Orchestra no. 4; Symphony no. 3, "Organ"; New York Philharmonic; Leonard Bernstein, cond.; Robert Casadesus, piano; Leonard Raver, organ; Sony SMK 47 608

Ravel: *Piano Concerto in G; Rachmaninov: Piano Concerto no. 4; Philharmonia Orchestra; Ettore Gracis, cond.; Arturo Benedetti Michelangeli, piano; EMI 7243 5 67258 2 9*

Rachmaninov: Piano Concertos nos. 1–4; London Symphony Orchestra; André Previn, cond.; Vladimir Ashkenazy, piano; London/Decca 444 839-2

Prokofiev: *Piano Concertos nos. 1 and 3; Bartók: Piano Concerto no. 3; Orchestre Symphonique de Montréal; Charles Dutoit, cond.; Martha Argerich, piano; EMI Classics 7243 5 56654-2 3*

Satie: Gymnopédies, etc.; Aldo Ciccolini, piano; EMI 7243 5 67260 2 4

Poulenc: Organ Concerto, etc.; various artists; London/Decca 448-270-2

Panorama: Gershwin, Rhapsody in Blue, *Piano Concerto in F, Variations on "I Got Rhythm," Rhapsody no. 2*

Lutoslawski: Fanfare for the Los Angeles Philharmonic; *Concerto for Piano and Orchestra; Chantefleurs et Chantefables; Symphony no. 2; Los Angeles Philharmonic; Esa-Pekka Salonen, cond.; Paul Crossley, piano; Dawn Upshaw, soprano; Sony 67189*

Adams: Century Rolls, *Concerto for Piano, etc.; Cleveland Orchestra; Christoph von Dohnányi, cond., Emanuel Ax, piano; Nonesuch 79607-2*

Für Elise: Romantic Piano Pieces; *various artists; DG 289 469 632-2*

Horowitz in Moscow: *Vladimir Horowitx, piano; DG 419 499-2*

Yevgeny Kissin in Tokyo: *Yevgeny Kissin, piano; Sony SK 45931*

J. S. Bach: Great Organ Favorites; *E. Power Biggs, Organ; CBS MK 42644*

Handel: Organ Concertos, opp. 4 and 7; Amsterdam Baroque Orchestra; Ton Koopman, organ; Erato 4509 91932-2

Saint-Saëns: Symphony no. 3, "Organ"; Concerto for Piano and Orchestra no. 4; New York Philharmonic; Leonard Bernstein, cond.; Leonard Raver, organ; Robert Casadesus, piano; Sony SMK 47 608. Alternative recording: Symphony no. 3; The Philadelphia Orchestra; Eugene Ormandy, cond.; Virgil Fox, organ; RCA Victrola 7737-2 RV

Chapter 11: The Violin

Haydn: Three Favorite Concertos; *Yo-Yo Ma; Wynton Marsalis; Cho-Liang Lin; CBS MK 39310*

Mozart: Violin Concertos nos. 1, 2, 3; St. Paul Chamber Orchestra; Pinchas Zukerman, cond. and violin; Sony SBK 46539

Mozart: Sinfonia Concertante in E-flat Major for Violin and Viola, K. 364: Stern, Zukerman, Barenboim; Sony MK 36692

Beethoven: Concerto for the Violin and Orchestra; "Triple Concerto"; Berlin Philharmonic; Herbert von Karajan, cond; Anne-Sophie Mutter, violin; DG 289 457 861-2

Beethoven: Kreutzer Sonata; Franck: Violin Sonata in A Major; Itzhak Perlman, violin; Martha Argerich; EMI 7243 5 56815 2 2

Beethoven: Violin Concerto; Mendelssohn: Violin Concerto in E Minor, op. 64; Camerata Academica of Salzburg; Roger Norrington, cond.; Joshua Bell, violin; Sony SK89505

Mendelssohn: Violin Concerto no. 1: Three Legendary Recordings; Jascha Heifetz; Nathan Milstein; David Oistrakh, violin; Arkadia 78576. (This outstanding and moderately priced recording is not always available in record shops, but has been found by contacting Tower Records [800/ASK-TOWER or 800/275-8693; fax 800/538-6938; fax from outside the USA +1-916/373-2930; or visit www.tower.com] or sites such as www.amazon.com and www.bn.com [Barnes and Noble]. If you cannot find it, there are easily located reissues of recordings of the Mendelssohn concerto by Heifetz, Milstein, and Oistrakh.)

Bruch: Violin Concerto no. 1 in G minor, op. 26; Mendelssohn: Violin Concerto in E Minor, op. 64; Orchestra of Academy of St. Martin-in-the-Fields; Neville Marriner, cond.; Joshua Bell, violin; London/Decca 421-145-2

Maw: Concerto for Violin and Orchestra; London Philharmonic Orchestra; Roger Norrington, cond., Joshua Bell, violin; Sony SK 62856

Brahms: Violin Concerto in D Major, op. 77 (cadenza by Joshua Bell); Schumann: Violin Concerto in D Minor; Cleveland Orchestra; Christoph von Dohnanyi, cond.; Joshua Bell, violin; London/Decca 444-811-2

Brahms and Tchaikovsky: Violin Concertos; Jascha Heifetz, violin, Fritz Reiner, cond.; RCA Victor 09026-61495; or Nathan Milstein, violin; William Steinberg and Anatole Fistoulari, conds.; Seraphim CDE 7243 5 69035 2 4

Brahms: Violin Concerto; Chicago Symphony Orchestra; Carlo Maria Giulini, cond.; Itzhak Perlman, violin; EMI 7243 5 66992 2 9

Brahms: Violin Sonatas nos. 1–3; Itzhak Perlman, violin; Vladimir Ashkenazy, piano; EMI 7243 5 66945 2 1

Panorama: Berlioz, "Rêverie et Caprice," Arthur Grumiaux, violin

Lalo: Symphonie Espagnole; *Vieuxtemps: Violin Concerto no. 5; Royal Concertgebouw Orchestra; Philharmonia Orchestra; Charles Dutoit, cond.; Sarah Chang, violin; EMI 7243 5 55292 2 0*

Dvořák: Violin Concerto; New York Philharmonic; Zubin Mehta, cond.; Midori, violin; Sony SK 44 923

Franck: Sonata for Violin and Piano; Brahms: Horn Trio; Itzhak Perlman, violin; Vladimir Ashkenazy, piano; Barry Tuckwell, horn; London/Decca 452 887-2

Panorama: Prokofiev, Violin Concerto no. 1; Shlomo Mintz, violin

Stravinsky and Rochberg: Violin Concertos; Igor Stravinsky and André Previn, conds.; Isaac Stern, violin; Sony SMK 64 505

Panorama: Gershwin, Three Preludes; Gil Shaham, violin

Berg: Violin Concerto; Chicago Symphony Orchestra; James Levine, cond.; Anne-Sophie Mutter; Deutsche Grammophon 437 093-2

Panorama: Jean Sibelius, Violin Concerto; Christian Ferras, violin; with Berlin Philharmonic; Herbert von Karajan, cond.

Beethoven and Sibelius: Violin Concertos; Bruno Walter and Eugene Ormandy, conds.; Zino Francescatti and David Oistrakh, violin; Sony SBK 47659

Walton: Violin Concerto; Cello Concerto; Symphonies; Overtures; Bournemouth Symphony Orchestra, et. al; Paavo Berglund, Bernard Haitink, André Previn, conds.; Ida Haendel, violin; Paul Tortelier, cello; EMI Classics 7243 5 73371 2 0

My Favorite Kreisler; *Itzhak Perlman, violin; Samuel Sanders, piano*

Favorite Violin Encores; *Arthur Grumiaux, violin; István Hajdu, piano; Philips 446 560-2*

Chapter 12: Music for Viola, Cello, and Double Bass

Berlioz: Harold in Italy; *London Symphony Orchestra; Colin Davis, cond.; Nobuko Imai, viola; Philips 416 431-2*

Telemann: *Viola Concerto, etc.; Academy of St. Martin-in-the-Fields; Neville Marriner, cond.; Stephen Shingles, viola; London/Decca 430 265-2*

Panorama: *Mendelssohn, Octet for Strings; Academy of St. Martin-in-the-Fields Chamber Ensemble*

Bruch: *Works for Clarinet and Viola; Orchestre de l'Opera de Lyon; Kent Nagano, cond.; Paul Meyer, clarinet; Gérard Causse, viola; François-René Duchable, piano; Erato 2292-45483-2*

Walton; Concertos for Violin and Viola; Royal Philharmonic Orchestra; André Previn, cond.; Nigel Kennedy, violin and viola; EMI CDC7 49628-2

J. S. Bach: Cello Suites; Heinrich Schiff, cello EMI 7243 5 74179 2 1

Panorama: *Haydn, Cello Concertos nos. 1 and 2; Pierre Fournier, cello; Rudolf Baumgartner, cond.*

Panorama: *Schumann, Cello Concerto; Mstislav Rostropovich, cello; Leningrad Philharmonic Orchestra; Gennadi Rozhdestvensky, cond.*

Dvořák: *Cello Concerto; Tchaikovsky: Rococo Variations; Berliner Philharmoniker; Herbert von Karajan, cond.; Mstislav Rostropovich, cello; DG 447 413-2.* For comparison, listen to the live recording by the New York Philharmonic, Kurt Masur, cond.; Yo-Yo Ma, cello; Sony SK 67 173. This recording also has the rarely heard cello concerto by Victor Herbert.

Brahms: Cello Sonatas; Yo-Yo Ma, cello; Emanuel Ax, piano; RCA 09026 63267-2

Elgar: *Cello Concerto; Sea Pictures; London Symphony Orchestra; Sir John Barbirolli, cond.; Jacqueline Du Pré, cello; Dame Janet Baker, mezzo-soprano; EMI 7243 5 56219 2 4.* For comparison, listen to the recording of the Elgar concerto along with the one by William Walton. Again, it is the London Symphony Orchestra; André Previn, cond.; Yo-Yo Ma, cello; CBS/Sony MK 39541.

Lalo and Saint-Saëns: Cello Concertos; Orchestre National de France; Lorin Maazel, cond.; Yo-Yo Ma, cello; CBS/Sony MK 35848

Kodály: Sonata for Unaccompanied Cello; Britten: Suite no. 3; Henze: Capriccio; Berio: Les Mots Sont Allés; Matt Haimovitz, cello; Deutsche Grammophon 445 834-2

Tavener: The Protecting Veil; *Britten: Cello Suite no. 3; London Symphony Orchestra; Gennadi Rozhdestvensky, cond.; Steven Isserlis, cello; Virgin 7243 5 61849 23*

Jonathan Harvey: Imaginings; *Frances-Marie Uitti, cello; Harvey, cond.; Chill Out CHILLCD 007*

Panorama: Schubert, "Trout" Quintet

Janáček: Suite for String Orchestra, from Sinfonietta and other works; various artists; London/Decca 448 255-2

The Art of Lily Laskine, *works by Handel, Boieldieu, Bochsa; Pierné; Lily Laskine, harp; RCA Victor 60023-2-RG*

Vivaldi: Concerti per Mandolini; I Solisti Veneti; Claudio Scimone, cond.; Ugo Orlandi, Dorina Frati, mandolins; Erato ECD 88042

Chapter 13: The Woodwinds

Beethoven: Symphony no. 5; Royal Concertgebouw; Sawallisch cond.; recording (or the Philadelphia/Ormandy alternate)

Mozart: The Flute Quartets; Jean-Pierre Rampal, flute; Isaac Stern, violin; Salvatore Accardo, viola; Mstislav Rostropovich, cello; CBS/Sony MK 42320

Mercadante: Three Concertos for Flute; English Chamber Orchestra/I Solisti Veneti; Claudio Scimone, cond.; Jean-Pierre Rampal, flute; Erato ECD 55012

J. Haydn: Concertos for Flute, Oboe, and Trumpet; various artists; Sony SBK 62 649

Rampal's Greatest Hits; *Jean-Pierre Rampal, flute; CBS/Sony MK 35176*

Vivaldi and Telemann: Concertos for Flute and Orchestra; I Solisti Veneti; Claudio Scimone, cond.; Simion Stanciu "Syrinx," panpipe; Erato ECD 88166

Albinoni: Concerti per oboe; Camerata Bern; Hans Elhorst, cond.; Heinz Holliger, oboe; Archiv 427 111-2

Telemann: Concerti per oboe; Academy of St. Martin-in-the-Fields; Iona Brown, cond.; Heinz Holliger, oboe; Philips 412 879-2

Mozart: Oboe Concerto, Bassoon Concerto; R. Strauss: Oboe Concerto; Weber: Andante e Rondo Ungarese; Philadelphia Orchestra; Eugene Ormandy, cond.; English Chamber Orchestra; Daniel Barenboim, cond.; John de Lancie, oboe; Neil Black, oboe; Bernard Garfield, bassoon; Sony SBK 62 652

Mozart: Clarinet Concerto in A, K. 622; Clarinet Quintet in A; Boston Symphony Orchestra; Charles Munch, cond.; Budapest String Quartet; Benny Goodman, clarinet; RCA RCD1-5275. For contrast, listen to the Clarinet Concerto in A; Charles Neidich, bass clarinet; with the Orpheus Chamber Orchestra; 423 377-2.

Weber: Clarinet Concertos nos. 1 and 2; Concertino, op. 26; Grand Duo Concertant; English Chamber Orchestra; Paul Tortelier, Gerard Schwarz, conds.; Emma Johnson, clarinet; Gordon Back, piano; ASV DCA 747. Antony Pay and the Orchestra of the Age of Enlightenment perform an "original instrument" version of some of this music on Virgin VC 7 59002-2.

Bruch: Works for Clarinet and Viola; Orchestre de l'Opera de Lyon; Kent Nagano, cond.; Paul Meyer, clarinet; Gérard Causse, viola; François-René Duchable, piano; Erato 2292-45483-2

Brahms: Quintet for Clarinet and Strings; Horn Trio; Busch Quartet; Reginald Kell, clarinet; Testament SBT 101

Copland: Clarinet Concerto; Stravinsky: Ebony Concerto; Bartók: Contrasts; Bernstein: Preludes, Fugues, and Riffs; Columbia Symphony Orchestra; Leonard Bernstein, cond.; Benny Goodman, clarinet; Sony SK 43337

Philip Glass: Concerto for Saxophone Quartet and Orchestra; Raschèr Saxophone Quartet and the Stuttgart Chamber Orchestra; Dennis Russell Davies, conductor; [on the recording of the Glass Symphony no. 2]; Nonesuch 79496-2

Vivaldi: Six Bassoon Concertos; I Musici; Klaus Thuneman, bassoon; Philips 416 355-2

Mozart: Oboe Concerto; Bassoon Concerto; R. Strauss: Oboe Concerto; Weber: Andante e Rondo Ungarese; Philadelphia Orchestra; Eugene Ormandy, cond.; English Chamber Orchestra; Daniel Barenboim, cond.; John de Lancie, oboe; Neil Black, oboe; Bernard Garfield, bassoon; Sony SBK 62 652

Chapter 14: The Brass Family

Baroque Music for Trumpets (various composers); English Chamber Orchestra; Raymond Leppard, cond.; Wynton Marsalis, trumpet; CBS/Sony MK 42478

Trumpet Voluntary *(various composers); Wurttembergisches Kammerorchester Heilbromm; Jörg Faerber, cond.; Academy of St. Martin-in-the-Fields; Neville Marriner, cond.; Maurice André, trumpet; Erato ECD 55015*

Panorama: Haydn, Trumpet Concerto; Adolph Herseth, trumpet Chicago Symphony Orchestra; Claudio Abbado, cond.; listen to Wynton Marsalis on Haydn: *Three Favorite Concertos;* Yo-Yo Ma; Wynton Marsalis; Cho-Liang Lin; CBS MK 39310.

Mozart: Horn Concertos; Philharmonia Orchestra; Herbert von Karajan, cond.; Dennis Brain, horn; EMI CDH 7610132

Brahms: Horn Trio; Franck: Sonata for Violin and Piano; Itzhak Perlman, violin; Vladimir Ashkenazy, piano; Barry Tuckwell, horn; London/Decca 452 887-2

Panorama: R. Strauss, Horn Concerto no. 2; Norbert Hauptmann, Berliner Philharmoniker; Herbert von Karajan, cond.

Janáček: Mládi, from Sinfonietta and other works; various artists; London/Decca 448 255-2

Albrechtsberger; Wagenseil; L. Mozart; M. Haydn: Trombone Concertos; Northern Sinfonia; Alain Trudel, trombone and director; Naxos 8.553831

Copland: Fanfare for the Common Man, etc.; various artists; London/Decca 448 261-2

Vaughan Williams: Symphony no. 5; Three Portraits from "The England of Elizabeth"; Concerto for Bass Tuba and Orchestra; London Symphony Orchestra; André Previn, cond.; John Fletcher, bass tuba; RCA Victor 60586-2-RG

Chapter 15: The Percussion

Panorama: Gershwin, An American in Paris; Cuban Overture; Porgy and Bess Suite

Shostakovich: Symphony no. 5; Leningrad Philharmonic Orchestra; Evgeny Mravinsky; Erato 2292-45752-2

Bartók: Concerto for Orchestra; Music for Strings, Percussion, and Celesta; RIAS-Symphonie-Orchester Berlin; Ferenc Fricsay, cond.; Deutsche Grammophon 447 443-2

Bartók: Sonata for Two Pianos and Percussion, etc.; Martha Argerich and Nelson Freire, piano; Deutsche Grammophon 439 867-2

Chapter 16: Early Music

Ambrosian Chant; *In Dulci Jubilo; Alberto Turco, dir.; Manuela Schenale, soloist; Naxos 8.553502*

In Passione ed Morte Domini (*Gregorian Chant for Good Friday); Nova Schola Gregoriana; Alberto Turco, dir.; Naxos 8.550952*

Jerusalem: Discantus Ensemble; *Brigitte Lesne, director; Opus 111 OPS 30-29*

Hildegard of Bingen: A Feather on the Breath of God; *Gothic Voices; Christopher Page, dir.; Emma Kirkby, soprano; Hyperion CDA66039*

Music of the Troubadors: *Ensemble Unicorn, etc. et al.; Naxos 8.554257*

Close Encounters in Early Music *(various composers and artists), Opus 111 OPS 3000*

The Glory of Early Music *(various composers and artists); Naxos 8.554064*

Music of the Spanish Renaissance; *Shirley Rumsey, lute; Naxos 8.550614*

Gesualdo: Prince of Madrigalists; *Marilyn Horne and other artists; Sony SBK 60313*

Monteverdi: Vespro della Beata Vergine 1610; *Taverner Consort, Choir and Players; Andrew Parrot, cond.; Virgin Veritas 7243 5 61662 2 6*

J. S. Bach: Cantatas 51, 93, 129; *Münchener Bach-Chor und Orchester; Karl Richter, cond.; Edith Mathis, Anna Reynolds, Peter Schreier, Dietrich Fischer-Dieskau, singers; Archiv 427 115-2*

Chapter 17: Lieder and Vocal Music

Mahler: Des Knaben Wunderhorn; *London Philharmonic; Sir Charles Mackerras, cond.; Ann Murray, soprano; Thomas Allen, baritone; Virgin UV 7243 5 61202 2 0. Or: Royal Concertgebouw Orchestra; Leonard Bernstein, cond.; Lucia Popp, soprano; Andreas Schmidt, Baritone; DG 427 302-2*

R. Strauss: Don Juan, Vier Letzte Lieder; Tod und Verklarung; *New York Philharmonic; Kurt Masur, cond.; Deborah Voigt, soprano; Teldec 3984-25990-2.* Then listen to the version by Gundula Janowitz on the Panorama Strauss recording.

Villa-Lobos: Bachianas Brasileiras *nos. 1, 2, 5, 9; Orchestre National de la Radiodiffusion Française; Heitor Villa-Lobos, cond.; Victoria de los Angeles, soprano; EMI CDH 7610152*

Brahms: Alto Rhapsody; Atlanta Symphony Orchestra and Chorus; Robert Shaw, cond.; Marilyn Horne, mezzo-soprano; Telarc CD-80176

Lamenti (various composers); Musica Antiqua Köln; Richard Goebel, cond.; Anne Sofie von Otter, mezzo-soprano; Archiv 289 457 617-2

Vivaldi: Album; Il Giardino Armonico; Giovanni Antonini, cond.; Cecilia Bartoli, mezzo-soprano; London/Decca 466 596-2

Sor: Seguidillias, etc.; Teresa Berganza, mezzo-soprano; José Miguel Moreno, guitar; Philips 411 030-2

Schubert: Die Schöne Müllerin/3 Lieder; Fritz Wunderlich, tenor; Hubert Giesen, piano; DG 447 452-2

Schubert: Winterreise; Dietrich Fischer-Dieskau, baritone; Alfred Brendel, piano; Philips 289 464 739-2. Or Wolfgang Holzmair, baritone; Imogen Cooper, piano (Philips 446 407-2); Christa Ludwig, mezzo-soprano; James Levine, piano (DG 423 366-2).

Schubert: 12 Lieder; 6 Moments Musicaux; Elisabeth Schwarzkopf, soprano; Edwin Fischer, piano; EMI 7243 5 67494 2 9

Schubert: Lieder; Barbara Bonney, soprano; Geoffrey Parsons, piano; Teldec 4509 90873-2

Schubert: Schwangesang; Bryn Terfel, bass-baritone; Malcolm Martineau, piano; Sain SCDC 4035)

R. Schumann: Frauenliebe und- leben; 5 Lieder, op. 40; 15 Lieder; Anne Sofie von Otter, mezzo-soprano; Bengt Forsberg, piano; DG 445 881-2

Clara Schumann: Lieder: Lan Rao, soprano; Micaela Gelius, piano; Arte Nova 74321 43308 2

Brahms and Liszt: Lieder; Thomas Quasthoff, baritone; Justus Zeyen, piano; DG 289 463 183-2

Wolf: 22 Lieder; Elisabeth Schwarzkopf, soprano; Wilhelm Furtwängler, piano; EMI 7243 5 67570 2 8

Bruckner: Symphony no. 6; Wagner: Wesendonck Lieder; New Philharmonia Orchestra; Otto Klemperer, cond.; Christa Ludwig, mezzo-soprano, EMI 7243 5 67037 2 8

Mahler: Lieder eines fahrenden Gesellen, etc.; various conductors; EMI 7243 5 67557 2 7, with Christa Ludwig, mezzo-soprano; various conductors; EMI CDM 7 69499 2.

Mahler: Rückert Lieder (plus works by Handel, Lieberson, Brahms); Lorraine Hunt Lieberson, mezzo-soprano; Roger Vignoles, piano; BBCW 1002-2

Berlioz: Les Nuits d'Été, *etc.; Berliner Philharmoniker, Anne Sofie von Otter, mezzo-soprano; James Levine, cond.; Cord Garben, piano; DG 445-823-2*

Canteloube: Chants d'Auvergne; *Royal Philharmonic Orchestra; Antonio de Almeida, cond.; Frederica von Stade, mezzo-soprano; Sony 63063*

Soirée Française *(various French composers); Elly Ameling, soprano; Rudolf Jansen, piano; Philips 412 628-2*

Lutoslawski: Fanfare for the Los Angeles Philharmonic; *Concerto for Piano and Orchestra; Chantefleurs et Chantefables; Symphony no. 2;* Los Angeles Philharmonic; *Esa-Pekka Salonen, cond.; Paul Crossley, piano; Dawn Upshaw, soprano; Sony 67189*

The Vagabond: Songs by Vaughan Williams, *Finzi, Butterworth, Ireland; Bryn Terfel, baritone; Malcolm Martineau, piano;* DG 445 946-2

Elgar: Cello Concerto; Sea Pictures; *London Symphony Orchestra; Sir John Barbirolli, cond.; Jacqueline Du Pré, cello; Dame Janet Baker, mezzo-soprano;* EMI 7243 5 56219 2 4

The English Songbook; *Ian Bostridge, tenor; Julius Drake, piano;* EMI 7243 5 56830 2 1

Britten: Serenade for Tenor, Horn, and Strings, etc.; Ian Bostridge, tenor; various artists; EMI 7243 5 568712 8

I Will Breathe a Mountain: Songs of Barber, Bernstein, Bolcom; *Marilyn Horne, mezzo-soprano; Martin Katz, piano; Tokyo String Quartet; RCA Victor 09026-68771-2*

Beautiful Dreamer: The Great American Songbook; *Marilyn Horne, mezzo-soprano; Carl Davis, cond.; English Chamber Orchestra; London/ Decca 417 242-2.* (The five Copland songs also appear on the Copland "Double-Decker" compendium you own, London/Decca 448-261-2.)

To the Soul: Songs to the Poetry of Walt Whitman; *Thomas Hampson, baritone; Craig Rutenberg, piano; EMI 7243 5 55028 2*

Barber: *Hermit Songs;* Knoxville Summer of 1915; *Leontyne Price, soprano; Samuel Barber, piano; New Philharmonia Orchestra; Thomas Schippers, cond.; RCA 09026-61983-2*

Sviridov: Russia Cast Adrift; *Rachmaninoff: 9 Songs; Dmitri Hvorostovsky, baritone; Mikhail Arkadiev, piano; Philips 446 666-2*

Salzburg Recital: *Kathleen Battle, soprano; James Levine, piano; DG 415 361-2*

Schubert, Brahms, Schumann: Lieder; *Vesselina Kasarova, mezzo-soprano; Friedrich Haider, piano; BMG 09026-68763-2*

Eighteenth-Century Bel Canto: *Gewandhausorchester Leipzing; Kurt Masur, cond.; Elly Ameling, soprano; Philips 412 233-2*

Love's Twilight *(Berg, Korngold, R. Strauss): Anne Sofie von Otter, mezzo-soprano; Bengt Forsberg, piano; DG 437 515-2*

Sentimental Me *(collected songs): Elly Ameling, soprano; Louis van Dijk, piano; John Clayton, double bass; Philips 412-433-2*

Chapter 18: Music with Chorus

Bach: *Cantatas; Jauchzet Gott in allen Landen, BWV 51; Wer nur den lieben Gott läßst walten BMV 93; Gelobet sei der Herr, mein Gott BWV 129; Münchener Bach-Chor, Münchener Bach-Orchester; Karl Richter, cond.; Archiv Galleria 427 115-2*

Bach: Cantatas; Coffee Cantata; Peasant Cantata; Kammerorchester Berlin; Peter Schreier, cond.; Archiv Galleria 427 116-2

Bach: St. Matthew Passion: Chicago Symphony Orchestra and Chorus; Georg Solti, cond.; Te Kanawa, von Otter, Rolfe Johnson; Krause, Blochwitz, Bär; London/Decca 421 177-2. (This is one of many fine recordings. Another is conducted by John Eliot Gardiner, and the soloists include Rolfe Johnson, Schmidt, Bonney, von Otter, Chance, and Bär; Archiv 427 648-2. Be sure the recording you select has the texts enclosed.)

Handel: Messiah. Collegium Musicum 90; Richard Hickox, cond.; Joan Rodgers, Della Jones, Christopher Robson, Philip Langridge, Bryn Terfel. Chandos 0522/3

Mozart: Mass in C Minor, KV. 427; New Philharmonia Orchestra; John Alldis Choir; Raymond Leppard, cond.; Kiri Te Kanawa, Ileana Cotrubas, soloists; EMI CDC 7 47385 2

Mozart: Requiem, KV. 626: Wiener Philharmoniker; Wiener Singverein; Herbert von Karajan, cond.; Tomowa-Sintow, Molinari, Cole, Burchuladze, soloists; DG 419 610-2. (This is one of many fine recordings. Be sure that the one you select has the texts enclosed. An excellent second recording, though regrettably without texts, is EMI 0777 7 62892 2 9, which combines the Mozart Requiem conducted by Daniel Barenboim with the Verdi Requiem conducted by Sir John Barbirolli.)

Beethoven: Missa Solemnis; Choral Fantasia; *New Philharmonia Orchestra; John Alldis Choir; Otto Klemperer, cond.; Daniel Barenboim, piano; Söderström, Höffgen, Kmentt, Talvela, soloists; EMI 7 69538 2. Includes both works and texts; a later issue, EMI 7243 5 67547 2 0, does not include the Choral Fantasia or texts.*

Rossini: Petite Messe Solennelle; *Coro Polifonico del Teatro alla Scala; Romano Gandolfi, cond.; Freni, Pavarotti, etc., soloists; Stabat Mater, London Symphony Orchestra and Chorus; István Kertész, cond.; Lorengar, Minton, Pavarotti, Sotin, soloists); London/Decca 455 023-2*

Verdi: Messa da Requiem; Atlanta Symphony Orchestra and Chorus; Robert Shaw, cond.; Dunn, Curry, Hadley, Plishka, soloists; Telarc CD-

80152. For further exploration: Philharmonia Orchestra and Chorus; Carlo Maria Giulini, cond.; Schwarzkopf, Ludwig, Gedda, Ghiaurov; EMI Classics ZDCB 56250; Vienna Philharmonic Orchestra and Vienna State Opera Chorus; Sir Georg Solti; Sutherland, Horne, Pavarotti, Talvela; London/Decca 411944-2

Brahms: **Ein deutsches Requiem;** *Chicago Symphony Orchestra and Chorus; Georg Solti, cond.; Te Kanawa, Weikl, soloists; London/Decca 414 627-2*

Fauré: Requiem; Orchestre de la Société des Concerts du Conservatoire; Choeurs Elisabeth Brasseur; André Cluytens, cond.; Victoria de los Angeles, Dietrich Fischer-Dieskau, soloists; EMI 7243 5 66946 2 0

Janáček: Glagolitic Mass; *Wiener Philharmoniker; Riccardo Chailly, cond.; London/Decca 289 460 213-2*

Poulenc: **Gloria;** *Orchestra and Chorus of la Suisse Romande; Jesús Lopez-Cobos, cond.; Sylvia Greenberg, soloist; London/Decca 448 270-2*

Britten: **War Requiem;** *Melos Ensemble/London Symphony Orchestra; Benjamin Britten, cond.; Vishnevskaya, Pears, Fischer-Dieskau, soloists; London/Decca 414 383-2*

Chapter 19: Mahler's Symphony no. 2

Mahler: **Symphony no. 2;** *New York Philharmonic; The Westminster Choir; Leonard Bernstein, cond.; Barbara Hendricks, soprano; Christa Ludwig, mezzo-soprano; DG 423 395-2*

Mahler: **Symphonies nos. 1 and 2;** *London Philharmonic Orchestra; Klaus Tennstedt, cond.; EMI Classics 7243 5 74182 5*

Chapter 20: Beethoven's Ninth Symphomy

Beethoven: **Symphony no. 9, "Choral";** *Chorus and Orchestra of the Bayreuther Festspiele; Wilhelm Furtwängler, cond.; Elisabeth Schwarzkopf, Soprano; Elisabeth Höngen, contralto; Hans Hopf, tenor; Otto Edelman, bass; EMI 7243 5 66953 2 0.* (This is the 1997 digital remastering rather than the one done in 1984.)

Resources for the
⊷ Classical Music Lover ⊶

I am sure that in the course of reading this book and learning the music it covers, you often thought to yourself that you wanted to know more about a particular composer, performer, or type of music. Just as this book sought to give you the tools to learn and love classical music, the listings below should help you find more information in your areas of interest. In addition, addresses are listed that I consider useful or important.

To find radio stations that broadcast classical music, turn to the travel section and look under the city where you are. This list is comprehensive but by no means exhaustive.

There are thousands of books on classical music. You might wish at some point to read one on the whole history of classical music. Some books can teach it as if on a timeline. But these must be massive books and, even at that, they cannot cover every detail. You might choose to concentrate on particular periods in music that interest you.

Biographies exist of almost every major composer, though some are full of inaccuracies. Remember that a biographer must be an impeccable researcher who has the ability to synthesize facts with conflicting ideas and accounts to describe a life. And describing a creative life is more difficult, I contend, because the wellspring of genius is nearly impossible to discover, especially in someone who has been dead for two hundred years.

I enjoy reading contemporary accounts of the lives of composers because they capture details in behavior and appearance that modern biographers can only speculate about. Yet someone writing a book today has access to much more scholarship and research materials. Aside from biographies, there are countless books that dissect and illuminate the musical works themselves. These may come in large authoritative accounts of whole forms, such as the symphony or the concerto, or in short insightful essays on a single work, such as Beethoven's *Diabelli Variations.*

You can learn a lot by reading composers' letters, especially when they write to each other. Famous correspondences include Haydn-Mozart, Liszt-Wagner, and Verdi-Boito. In recent times, composers have done teaching that has been documented on video- and audiotapes, and their lectures have been printed in books. The most famous are probably by Leonard Bernstein, but there is also much to read by Aaron Copland, Virgil Thomson, and others. There is a vast collection of writings by musicians through the centuries that give us their insights on music and composers. My favorite books by a contemporary performer are by the pianist Alfred Brendel.

There are wonderful reference materials of many kinds. The most monumental is the twenty-volume, $2,300 *New Grove Dictionary of Music and Musicians,* which you can also subscribe to online (www.grovemusic.com) for much less than the price of the books. It is also possible to see some of the *Grove* by going to the Web site of New York's leading classical music station, WQXR (www.wqxr.com), which has a link to the dictionary. There are smaller Grove dictionaries that focus on particular topics, such as women composers, and there is the *New Norton-Grove Concise Dictionary of Music.*

The presses of universities such as Oxford, Cambridge, and Harvard also produce excellent reference volumes that are in many ways more accessible than the *Grove* and are quite authoritative. Books issue forth all the time from major publishing houses that can help expand your knowledge about composers, performers, and musical forms of all types. Smaller publishers such as Da Capo, Dover, and Amadeus have a rich selection of music titles.

Certain magazines give careful coverage to classical music, most notably *Gramophone,* which is something of a bible for this field. There are also *Classic FM, Fanfare, BBC Music, The Strad* (for string players and those who love them), and *Stereo Review.* Many publications about recordings also devote sections to classical music; Tower Records has a monthly free magazine in its stores about music, with a section devoted to classical.

A wonderful new Web site, www.andante.com, combines a magazine with musical news and means of access to outstanding recorded and live performances. You will find yourself visiting it often. There is an excellent page of links at www.macmillan-reference.co.uk/grovemusic/links.htm that will take you to all sorts of other musical topics you might be wondering about or have never heard of.

Also visit www.classical.net, which has many well-researched listings and provides names of many good books that you might wish to read. Then visit the WWW Virtual Library of Classical Music (www.gprep.pvt.K12.md.us/classical), which has impressive listings if you want to introduce classical music to young people, as well as impressive links for adults who are eager to learn. Also, ClassicalUsa.com has outstanding links and easy access to many news stories about classical music.

Some of these sites provide links to record companies and Web pages of individual artists. Certain performers, such as violinists Hilary Hahn (www.HilaryHahn.com) and Joshua Bell (www.JoshuaBell.com), routinely post their comments and musings on different musical topics. An excellent source for finding artists' Web pages and many other professional sites is the Classical Music Search Engine (www.classicalsearch.com/welcome.htm). This is a page you should bookmark for frequent reference.

For more interesting reading with excellent content, go to www.artsandlettersdaily.com. Part of this erudite site is devoted to music (scroll down and look in the left column for music listings and links).

Most major orchestras around the world maintain Web sites that provide information about schedules, ticket availability, and sometimes offer concertgoers the chance to read program notes in advance. One of the best sites of this type is operated by the New York Philharmonic (www.newyorkphilharmonic.org), which has excellent information and navigability for anyone interested in classical music, whether or not you will be in the New York area.

In the ever-expanding offerings that one can find on the Internet, you must now add the possibility of seeing and hearing performances of classical music from around the world. Among the artists I have heard are singer Anne-Sofie von Otter, cellists Lynn Harrell and Yo-Yo Ma, and conductor Valery Gergiev, all of whom regularly reach out to audiences who do not normally attend live classical music concerts. On the 'Net you can travel to the world's concert venues without ever leaving your desktop. Needless to say, the sound quality and the experience cannot equal your actually being in the hall, but this technological advance certainly has its virtues.

Global Music Network (www.gmn.com) offers outstanding sound quality and Online Classics (www.onlineclassics.net) has more options for customizing the "performance" you see. Both have a wide selection of fine music and musicians to choose from. Other sites worth investigating are www.webconcerthall.com and www.centerseat.com. And don't forget www.andante.com, mentioned above.

There are several excellent sources for purchasing recordings on-line or by telephone. My first pick is Tower Records: www.towerrecords.com; tel. 800-ASK-Tower, because the people you deal with there are often quite knowledgeable about the music you are ordering. Another address is www.amazon.com, a fine source for books as well. So is Barnes and Noble (www.bn.com).

ORGANIZATIONS FOR THE CLASSICAL MUSIC LOVER

Here are other important addresses as you develop your life in music:

The Marilyn Horne Foundation
250 West 57th Street, Suite 603
New York, NY 10019
tel 212-582-2000; fax 212-582-6934
mhornefdn@aol.com; www.marilynhornefdn.org

Founded by the great singer Marilyn Horne in 1993 with the mission to "encourage, support, and preserve the art of the vocal recital through the presentation of vocal recitals and related educational activities in communities across the United States," the foundation has succeeded remarkably in its mission by nurturing a new generation of young singers and providing them with instruction from artists such as Phyllis Curtin, Christa Ludwig, Shirley Verrett, Luciano Pavarotti, Joan Sutherland, James Levine, Martin Katz, and Horne herself. In addition, the foundation organizes concerts for these singers in large cities and tiny towns across the nation, and then tapes these performances for radio broadcast. Recently a 13-CD set with 213 titles by sixty-seven composers, performed by artists supported by the foundation, was produced. It will be used for radio, but has also gone to two hundred university libraries to be used for educational purposes. This is a worthy foundation whose work merits your support.

Classical Action
165 West 46th Street, Suite 1310
New York, NY 10036
tel 212-997-7717; fax 212-997-7897
classicalaction@bcefa.org; www.classicalaction.org

  Classical Action is an important nonprofit organization that devotes itself to providing financial and medical support for persons with AIDS, some though not all of whom might be classical musicians. The monies raised by Classical Action benefits AIDS services across the United States. Many of the world's greatest musicians donate their talents to Classical Action by performing at fund-raising events. These musicians include Cecilia Bartoli, Joshua Bell, the Emerson String Quartet, Renée Fleming, Stephen Hough, Lang Lang, Yo-Yo Ma, and Jean-Yves Thibaudet.

The Classical Music Lovers' Exchange
9941 64th Avenue, Suite A15
Rego Park, NY 11374
www.cmle.com

  This is where single people looking to meet others who love classical music can go. While your ideal partner (what Beethoven would call "Immortal Beloved") probably needs to have more attributes than a love of classical music, it is a good beginning.

TRAVELING TO HEAR CLASSICAL MUSIC
Concert Halls and Theaters
Around the World

One of the pleasures you can have while traveling is hearing music in many different theaters and performance spaces. You can often hear music and musicians you might never encounter at home, and you will be fascinated by audience behavior and traditions from one place to another.

Before I embark on a trip, I use the Internet to conduct some research about what might be playing while I am in a place. Using a search engine and then entering the name of the place I will visit is always a good start. This usually leads to links to tourist offices, chambers of commerce, local newspapers and, occasionally, directly to arts organizations.

You can also do an advanced search. Let us say you plan to visit Houston, Texas. Typing "Classical Music + Houston" may lead to interesting listings. With most cities, using either the word *symphony* or *orchestra* plus the name of the city will give good results. So trying "Houston+Symphony" would get your desired result there. Other good resources include:

http://www.culturefinder.com; http://www.classicalhub.com; and http://www.music.indiana.edu/music_resources/orchestr.html.

For information on orchestras in North America, go to http://www.artsinfo.com/orchlist/docs/by_alpha.html

For information on festivals in Europe, visit www.euro-festival.net or see listings for individual countries. Whatsonwhen.com has good listings for daily musical highlights the world over.

• ❧ •

You will also find a few listings below for radio stations that play classical music. There are many fine stations around the world. Some of the best, such as New York's WQXR, also stream on the World Wide Web, so that you can listen anywhere if you have a computer equipped for this. In the USA, many stations on National Public Radio (NPR) include classical music as part of their programming. Among the most important shows on NPR are "Performance Today," "Symphonycast," "Soundcheck," and "Music from St. Paul." Two good Internet sources to find an NPR station are http://www.classical.net/music/links/musradio.html and http://www.npr.org/programs/pt/ptstations/index.html. The latter will tell you where "Performance Today" is broadcast, and thus is a likely source for classical music on the radio in that city.

In the United States, almost all classical radio programming apart from NPR is local, so that one has to find the station in the city you are in. Not too long ago one could easily listen to shows by formidable musicologists such as Karl Haas, George Jellinek, and Robert Sherman, but these are now harder to find outside certain major markets.

Most other countries have state or national networks that broadcast classical music, such as the BBC in Britain, Raitre in Italy, and so forth. These are easy to find as you spin the radio dial. Many European countries have orchestras known as radio symphonies that perform in a concert hall and have some or all of their performances broadcast nationally. For example, hundreds of thousands of Finnish listeners hear every performance of the Finnish Radio Symphony. Germany has many outstanding radio orchestras, all of which do live performances, recordings, and radio broadcasts. For good general information about radio broadcasting on the Internet, go to http://classicalwebcast.com

The list here below is a mere selection of many important festivals, venues, and musical organizations that merit your attention. A whole book could be made with listings from around the world.

ARGENTINA (country code +54)

BUENOS AIRES

Without a doubt, the Teatro Colón is one of the world's great theaters. It is beautiful, rich in tradition, and has a very discerning audience.
Teatro Colón
Dirección Postal Cerrito 618
1010 Ciudad de Buenos Aires
tel 011/4378-7110; fax 011/4384-5200
www.teatrocolon.org.ar; info@teatrocolon.org.ar

AUSTRALIA (country code +61)

For information about arts-related tourism in Australia, contact:
Australian Tourist Commission
PO Box 2721, Level 4
80 William Street
Woolloomooloo, Sydney, NSW 2011, Australia
tel 02/9360 1111; fax 02/9331 2538

A good source on-line for classical music events in Australia is www.netspace.net.au/~laflutist/EVENTS/html. For recordings, visit www.buywell.com.

ADELAIDE

Adelaide Festival of the Arts
www.adelaidefestival.org.au

One of Australia's premier cultural events, the Adelaide Festival is held for three weeks each March in even-numbered years. The best means to contact them is on their Web site.

CANBERRA

The Canberra International Chamber Music Festival is held annually in late April and early May. The venue is:
Old Parliament House
King George Terrace
Parkes, Canberra, Australian Capital Territory 2600
tel 02/6270 8222; fax 02/6270 8111; oph.info@dcita.gov.au

MELBOURNE
Melbourne Symphony
120-130 Southbank Boulevard
Southbank, VIC
tel 03/9626 1111; fax 03/9626 1101
mso@mso.com.au; www.mso.com.au

SYDNEY
Australian Chamber Orchestra
Opera Quays
2 East Circular Quay
Sydney NSW 2000
tel 02/8274 3800; fax 02/8274 3801
www.aco.com.au; headoffice@aco.com.au

Australian International Music Festival
    Beginning on the fourth Monday in June each year since 1990 contact:
World Projects Australia
288–306 Wattle Street, Suite 104
Ultimo, NSW 2007
tel 02/9571 1188; fax 02/9571 1126

City Recital Hall
Angel Place, off Pitt Street
Sydney NSW 2001
tel 02/8256 2222; fax 02. 9233 6652; tickets@cityrecitalhall.com

Sydney Festival
www.sydneyfestival.org.au

Sydney Opera House
tel 2/9250-7777; www.soh.nsw.gov.au
    There are two auditoriums at the Sydney Opera House. Curiously, the
smaller one is used for opera and the larger one is used for orchestral and
other classical concerts.

Sydney Symphony Orchestra
Level 5, 52 William Street, East Sydney
tel 02/ 9334 4600; fax 02/9334 4660; symphony@sso.com.au

AUSTRIA (country code +43)

Austria overflows with splendid classical music performances and festivals throughout the year. You can plan an entire vacation there devoted to performances and visiting composers' homes. For complete information from the Austrian National Tourist Office, go to www.anto.com.

GRAZ

Styrian Summer Festival
Sackstrasse 8010 Graz tel 0316/825 000; fax 0316/8773836; www.styriarte.com

SALZBURG

Salzburg, though a small city, is one of the world's great musical capitals. This is due to the fact that Salzburg had the rare luck to be the birthplace of Mozart, and has been benefiting from this ever since. Given the local love and care devoted to music, it is likely that Salzburg would have been important even without Mozart, but his presence, musical and otherwise, has made the city a magnet for people who love him. The Salzburg Festival, which includes orchestra performances, chamber music, solo recitals, theater, and opera, has taken place every summer since 1920. While Mozart is always a presence in the Festival, you can hear music from many centuries, countries, and composers. The city is full of performance spaces, including auditoriums built for the Festival, but also churches and academies. You can hear classical music performances in the Mozarteum, the Grosses Festspielhaus, the Kleines Festspielhaus, the Felsenreitschule, and St. Peter's church. People from all over the world clamor for tickets, and planning is essential. Tickets for the summer festival usually go on sale in early January. If you plan to attend several performances, it is possible to purchase a subscription that will represent, usually, a 10% discount on ticket prices. These are available a few days before single tickets.

Ticket Office of the Salzburg Festival
A-5010 Salzburg, Austria Postfach 140
tel 0662/8045-579; fax 0662/8045-760; info@salzburgfestival.at
http://www.salzburgfestival.com

Music lovers who become *Förderer* (patrons) of the Festival have access to tickets and other benefits before subscribers and the general public. Friendship comes at a cost: at this writing US $1000; UK £500; or 900 Euros

For information, contact:
Freunde der Salzburger Festspiele
Mönchberg 1; A-5020 Salzburg, Austria
office@festspielfreunde.at; http://www.festspielfreunde.at
tel 0662/8045-222; fax 0662/8045-474

The Salzburg Festival, in the year 2000, instituted a reduced price program for young people up to the age of twenty-six. You must write directly to the administration at the address below, giving your name, address, date of birth, and occupation. These tickets tend to go on sale in late February, but you should inquire well in advance.
Direktion der Salzburger Festspiele
att. Ulrich Hauschild
Hofstallgasse 1
A-5020 Salzburg, Austria

Because Salzburg is a small city, the demand for hotel rooms far outstrips supply. Remember, not only do concertgoers need beds, but so do the hundreds of musicians who come to the city to perform. You should immediately book a room once you have your concert dates. Either contact hotels directly or seek help from the local tourist office:
Tourismus Salzburg GmbH
Auerspergstrasse 7
A-5020 Salzburg, Austria
tourist@salzburginfo.at
http://www.salzburginfo.at
tel 0662/88987-314 to 317; fax 0662/88987-32

VIENNA
Musikverein
Bösendorferstraβe 12
1010 Wien
tel 01-5058-8190; fax 01/505-8190-94; www.musikverein.at
One of the world's great concert halls, home to the inimitable Vienna Philharmonic, as well as site of many music festivals and appearances by the world's finest musicians. No visit to Vienna is complete without hearing music at the Musikverein. Its Web site is very useful.

The Vienna Philharmonic may be reached at the Musikverein contact information, or go to www.wienerphilharmoniker.at; philoffice@wienerphil harmoniker.at.

BELGIUM (country code +32)

Belgium, though small, is a nation rich in music of many types. Churches often have concerts of early music and fine performances of sacred works. Churches with important organs often have great concerts with that instrument. Belgium is also a leader in contemporary music, and you will find many exciting events that you should investigate. While in the country, be sure to devote time to its excellent cuisine. For general information, go to www. visitbelgium.com.

The country also has two major festivals. The Flanders Festival is a major arts events that includes performances in Antwerp, Bruges, Brussels, Ghent, Kortijk, Limburg, Mechelen, and eighty other cities. For complete information, go to www.festival-van-vlaanderen.be/index_english.html, write to info@festival.be, or call 09/243-9494. In the French-speaking part of the country is the Festival de Wallonie (www.festivaldewallonie.com), held in Namur, Stavelot, Saint-Hubert, Liège, and Hainaut.

ANTWERP
The Flemish Opera (De Vlaamse Opera); Frankrijklei 3; tel 03/233-6808; fax 03/232-2661; infor@vlaamseopera.be; www.vlaamseopera.be. Antwerp's opera house is also the site for concerts and vocal recitals.

DeSingel; 25 Desguinlei; tel 03/248-2828; fax 03/248-2800; tickets@ desingel.be; www.desingel.de. The principal concert hall of Antwerp.

De Kolveniershof. Kolveniersstraat 20; tel 03/658-6886; fax 03/618-0374. Another important hall for classical music.

Stadsschouwburg, Theaterplein 1, tel 070/344-111.

BRUGES
The Concertgebouw is a beautiful new concert hall that opened on February 20, 2002, during the year the Bruges was the European Capital

of Culture. It contains a large concert hall and a more intimate chamber music hall. Concertgebouw Brugge; 't Zand 34, B-8000 Brugge; tel 050/476999; fax 050/476979; info@concertgebouwbrugge.be; www.concert-gebouw-brugge.be

Musica Antiqua is a leading early music organization based in Bruges: www.musicaantiqua.com

BRUSSELS

Tickets for many musical events in Brussels and elsewhere in Belgium may be purchased in the bookstore of the FNAC store at the City 2 shopping center, rue Neuve, Lower Town, tel 02/209-2239.

Bruocsella Symphony Orchestra, www.come.to/bruocsella. Mailing list: bso.orchestra@hotmail.com

Cathédrale des Sts. Michel et Gudule, place St. Gudule, Upper Town, tel 02/217-8345; fax 02/343-7040. The city's largest cathedral, and a frequent venue for music.

Chapelle Royale, Eglise Protestante, 5 Coudenberg, Upper Town, tel 02/673-0581. A favorite of many musicians.

Conservatoire Royal de Musique, 30 rue de la Régence, Upper Town, tel 02/511-0427; fax 02/512-6979. A smaller hall, with great acoustics.

La Monnaie/De Munt

Although this is primarily a theater for opera and ballet, it is a place of such extraordinary importance and influence that you should not miss it when you go to Belgium. A riot at a performance in the early 1830s led to the formation of the Belgian nation. So many activities here are cutting edge and the next big thing, and it is a point of reference for much of Europe. Not to miss. There is also an outstanding book and recording shop just to the left as you look at the façade of the building. The theater occupies the Place de la Monnaie (with an attractive food market in front by day). The box office is on Leopoldstraat 4; 1000 Brussels; tel 070/233-939. You can order tickets by e-mail: reservering@demunt.be; www.demut.be or reservation@lamonnaie.be; www. lamonnaie.be.

L'Eglise des St. Jean et St. Etienne aux Minimes, 62 rue des Minimes, Lower Town, tel 02/511-9384. Many fine performances are given in this church, particularly of the music of Bach.

Palais des Beaux Arts, 23 rue Ravenstein, Upper Town; tel 02/507-8200; fax 02/511-0589; pbapskbl@skynet.be; this is the home of the National Orchestra and many major arts events, including the International Queen Elisabeth Music Competition.

Theater St. Michel, 2 rue Pere Devroye, Etterbeek, tel 02/734-1665

GHENT

Concertzaal De Bijloke, Bijlokekaai 7; tel 09/233-6878; fax 09/255-6582; info@debijloke.be; www.debijloke.be

The Flanders Festival's head office is in Ghent: Kasteel Borluut, Kleine Gentsraat 46, 9051 Ghent; tel 09/243-9494; fax 09/243-9490; info@festival-van-vlaanderen.be

The Flemish Opera (De Vlaamse Opera); Schouwburgstraat 3; tel 09/223-0681; fax 09/223-8726; info@vlaamseopera.be; www.vlaamseopera.be; Ghent's opera house is also the site for concerts and vocal recitals.

BRAZIL

RIO DE JANEIRO
Theatro Municipal
Praça Maresciao Floriano
　　Opened in 1909, this gorgeous building in downtown Rio is the home for opera, ballet, and symphonic programs. It is favored by excellent acoustics.

Museu Villa-Lobos
Rua Sorocaba, 200-Botafogo
Rio de Janeiro RJ
www.ibase.org.br/~mvillalobos
　　Opened in 1986, this museum is dedicated to the life and work of Heitor Villa-Lobos (1887–1959), Brazil's most famous classical composer. Though small, it conveys much of his love for music and his homeland (he said, "In my

music I let the singing seas and rivers of this huge country be heard"), as well as featuring a fine collection of programs, recordings, and other artifacts of his life, including his cello and his coffee cup. He wrote more than eight hundred pieces, and observed that "My musical work is a consequence of predestination. It is so plentiful because it is the fruit of a vast, warm land." Researchers can also apply to work in the archive. Each year, festivals of music by Villa-Lobos are held in Rio starting on November 17, the anniversary of his death.

SÃO PAULO
Theatro Municipal

Opened in 1911, in a period of theater construction in the major cities of South America, this auditorium has many of the same performers who appear in Rio. Classical artists from abroad are engaged for tours that might include the two major Brazilian cities, as well as Montevideo (Uruguay), Santiago de Chile, and Buenos Aires. Opera productions done in Rio are not often seen here, because each theater has pursued an independent course and there remains an intense rivalry between the two cities.

BULGARIA

For general information on musical events in Bulgaria, contact apolonia@technolink.com, which is the address for the Bulgarian Festivals Association. For radio, go to Classic FM Bulgarian Radio (www.classicfm.ttm.bg/#Classic%20FM). The site has a good English-language link. This station began broadcasting on December 19, 1994. They can be reached at contacts@classical-fm-radio.com.

CANADA (country code 1)
CALGARY

Calgary Philharmonic Orchestra; 205 8th Avenue SE, Calgary, Alberta T2G 0K9; tel 403/571-0849; fax 403/294-7424; info@cpo-live.com

EDMONTON

Edmonton Symphony Orchestra; Winspear Centre; #4 Sir Winston Churchill Square (Corner of 99th Street and 102 Avenue) Edmonton, AB; tel 780/428-1414 or 800/563-5081; fax 780/425-1913; www.edmonton-symphony.com

MONTRÉAL

Notre Dame Basilica is the site for many wonderful concerts, especially of religious music and works that use the organ.

116 Notre Dame Street West; Montréal, QC H2Y 1T2; tel 514/842-2925

Orchestre Symphonique de Montréal/Montréal Symphony Orchestra; tel 514/842-9951; fax 514/842-0728; general@osm.ca; www.osm.ca/en

Place des Arts is the city's principal performing arts center. Its halls include Salle Wilfred-Pelletier and Théatre Maisonneuve.
175 St. Catherine Street West
Montréal, QC H2X 1Z8
tel 514/842-2112

OTTAWA

National Arts Centre, PO Box 1534, Stn B, Ottawa, ON K1P 5W1 (street address: 53 Elgin Street, at Confederation Square); tel 613/947-7000 (box office ext. 280); 866/850-ARTS; info@nac-cna.ca; www.nac-cna.ca/en

Home of the National Arts Centre Orchestra and many important musical events by visiting artists.

TORONTO

National Youth Orchestra of Canada, 1032 Bathurst St., Toronto, Ontario M5R 3G7; tel 888/532-4470; www.nyoc.org

An excellent organization devoted to the discovery and training of young Canadian musicians.

Roy Thomson Hall, 60 Simcoe Street; Toronto, Ontario M5J 2H5; tel 416/593-7769; box office: 416/872-4255; fax 416/593-9918; www.roythomson.com.

This is the main hall in Toronto for classical and other important performing arts events, and the home of the Toronto Symphony Orchestra (www.tso.on.ca). A smaller venue at the same location is Massey Hall (www.masseyhall.com). Also visit the excellent Music Store for recordings.

VANCOUVER

Vancouver Symphony Orchestra, www.vancouversymphony.ca

WINNIPEG

Winnipeg Symphony Orchestra; Centennial Concert Hall; 555 Main Street; Winnipeg, Manitoba R3B 1C3; tel 204/949-3999; boxoffice@wso.mb.ca; www.wso.mb.ca

CHINA

HONG KONG

Hong Kong Cultural Center 85-2-2734-2009 (home of the Hong Kong Philharmonic)

CZECH REPUBLIC (country code +420)

There was an expression in the eighteenth century, "Scratch a Czech and you will find a musician." This is still true today almost anywhere you go in Bohemia and Moravia. In Prague it seems that every church and theater has some sort of musical performance almost every night. For information on the whole country, a good Web site is www.czechmusic.com. Some leading music festivals outside of Prague include the Smetana Litomysl (www.smetanovalitomysl.cz), the Hluboká Musical Summer (tel 038/965041; fax 038/965436; www.volny.cz/ajghluboka); the South Bohemia Music Festival (held in thirteen towns; tel and fax 02/24910079; e-mail: pavel.janda#ecn.cz); the Cesky Krumlov International Music Festival (every August; www.czech-musicfestival.com/en_cmhf.html); and the Moravian Autumn in Brno (www.mhfb.cz/en/festival).

For radio listening, go to vlatava radio (www-ext.rozhlas.cz/vltava/portal).

BRNO

Brno International Music Festival
Ars Koncert
Úvoz 39
602 00 Brno
tel 05/43233116; fax 05/43233358; www.arskoncert.cz

Monument to Leoš Janáček (an exhibit on his life)
Smetanova 14
602 00 Brno
tel 05/41212811; ww/mzm.cz

HUKVALDY

Here is the hometown of Leoš Janáček.
Hukvaldy International Music Festival (June and July)
tel 0658/699323

Monument to Leoš Janáček (an exhibit on his life)
tel 0658/699252

PRAGUE

National Museum—Museum of Czech Music (an excellent archive and source).
Velkoprevorské námesti 4
118 00 Prague 1
tel 02/573200 or 573259; www.nm.cz

The National Theater
Narodni 2
110 00 Praha 1
tel 02/24901-448; www.narodni-divadlo.cz

Prague Spring Festival (one of the most famous in Europe)
Hellichova 18
118 00 Praha 1
tel 02/530293; fax 02/536040; www.festival.cz

The Rudolfinum (including Dvořák Hall and Suk Hall) is the home of the Czech Philharmonic.
Alsovo nábrezí 12
110 00 Praha 1
tel 02/24893352; www.czechphilharmonic.cz

Smetana Hall (Municipal House) is the home of the Prague Symphony Orchestra.
Namesti Republiky 5
110 00 Praha 1
tel 02/22002100

Museums:
Antonin Dvořák Museum

Ke Karlovu 20
120 00 Praha 2
tel/fax 02/298214; www.nm.cz

The Bedřich Smetana Museum
Novotného lávka 1
110 00 Praha 1
tel 02/24226488; www.nm.cz

DENMARK

Danish tourism Web sites are www.visitdenmark.com and www.visit-copenhagan.dk.

COPENHAGEN
Royal Theater
tel +45-33 69 69 69; fax +45-33 69 69 30; www.kgl-teater.dk

Tivoli Gardens
tel +45 33 15 10 01; fax +45 33 75 03 81; www.Tivoli.dk; www.Tivoligardens.com

ODENSE
Annual Organ Festival is held from June to August at the churches of Sct. Canute and Sct. Hans.
Odense Tourist Bureau
tel +45 12 75 20; www.odenseturist.dk

ENGLAND (country code 44; drop first zero when calling from abroad)

A general Web site for music festivals throughout the UK is www.artsfestivals.co.uk. Another useful site is www.theartspages.com/links/Exhibitions/musiclinksfestivals.htm. For radio throughout the UK, listen to BBC3 (www.bbc.co.uk/radio3) and ClassicFM (www.classicfm.co.uk).

ALDEBURGH
Aldeburgh is inextricably linked with Benjamin Britten, who founded a festival there in 1948 with Peter Pears and Eric Crozier. It is one of the most important music festivals in Europe. Snape Maltings Concert Hall, Snape, Saxmundham, Suffolk, 1P17 1SP, tel 01728/687100; fax 01728/687120; www.aldeburgh.co.uk

BIRMINGHAM

City of Birmingham Symphony, Paradise Place, Birmingham B3 3RP tel 0121/634-4281; fax 0121/634-4110; www.cbso.co.uk

This is a cleverly designed Web site offering valuable information and links about classical music. (Also use this contact information for the Birmingham Contemporary Music Group.) Concerts at Symphony Hall: tel 0121/780-3333.

BOURNEMOUTH

Bournemouth Symphony Orchestra, 2 Seldown Lane, Poole, Dorset, BH15 1UF; tel 01202/670611; fax 01202/687235; www.orchestranet.co.uk/bournsym

Founded in 1893, this is yet another excellent orchestra in a nation full of them.

CAMBRIDGE

The King's Consort was founded in 1980 by conductor Robert King and is now one of the foremost period instrument ensembles. It performs in Cambridge and tours frequently: www.the-kings-consort.org.uk.

CHELTENHAM

The Cheltenham International Festival of Music is usually held in the first two weeks of July and features prominent musicians. Some performances are given in Gloucester Cathedral: tel 01242-227979. While in Cheltenham, visit the Holst House, a museum dedicated to the composer.

DERBY

East of England Orchestra, Derby College, Wilmorton, Pentagon Centre, Beaufort Street, Derby DE21 6AX: tel 01332/207570; fax 01332/207569; www.orchestranet.co.uk/eeorch

LEEDS

The English Northern Sinfonia began as the resident orchestra for Opera North, and now also gives symphonic concerts. Opera North, Grand Theatre, Leeds LS1 6NU; tel 0113/243-9999; fax 0113/244-0418; www.orchestranet.co.uk/engnophi

LIVERPOOL

Royal Liverpool Philharmonic Orchestra, Philharmonic Hall, Hope Street, Liverpool L1 9BP; tel 0151/709-3789; info@liverpoolphil.com; www.liverpoolphil.com

The original hall was built in 1849 and, following a fire, was rebuilt in 1939. It is one of the most important concert halls in the UK.

LONDON

London is a city with one of the richest and most varied musical traditions in the world. New York and Berlin are the only cities that equal it on a daily basis, though Vienna, Paris, Munich, Tokyo, and Chicago can often match them for quality and interest. London is where Handel enjoyed his greatest success, and where Haydn crowned his career. Composers and instrumentalists have always sought to perform here because the English capital has audiences that are both knowledgeable and appreciative. London probably has the most varied and incisive music press of any city in the world, with many magazines and newspaper columnists providing extensive coverage. There is a substantial early music scene here, a taste for contemporary music, and a love of chamber music and vocal recitals. There are many orchestras in the city, including the BBC Symphony Orchestra, the London Concert Orchestra, the London Philharmonic (which usually performs at Royal Festival Hall at South Bank), the London Sinfonietta (www.londonsinfonietta.org.uk), the London Symphony Orchestra (usually appearing at the Barbican Centre; www.lso.co.uk), the excellent Orchestra of the Age of Enlightenment (www.oae.co.uk), specializing in eighteenth-century repertory; the Philharmonia Orchestra (often found at the Royal Festival Hall at South Bank; www.philharmonia.co.uk), and the Royal Philharmonic Orchestra. Not to miss are the Proms (see below), one of the most enjoyable of all music festivals.

Academy of St. Martin-in-the-Fields

One of England's most famous parish churches has one of the richest music programs of any church in the world, and a bevy of splendid recordings. A real treat for anyone visiting London or living there.

Trafalgar Square; tel 020/7839-8362; fax 020/7839-5163; boxoffice@smitf. co.uk; www.stmartin-in-the-fields.org

Barbican Centre, Silk Street; tel 020/7638-8891; tickets@barbican.org; info@ barbican.org.uk; www.barbican.org.uk

This is the largest multi-arts complex in Europe. The London Symphony Orchestra plays here, and there is a large selection of concerts and festivals throughout the year. This is also the London home of the Royal Shakespeare Company.

Purcell Room is the setting for performances of music from the past and present. See Royal Festival Hall, below.
tel 020/7928-8800

Queen Elizabeth Hall. See Royal Festival Hall, below.
tel 020/7960-4242

Royal Albert Hall
Kensington Gore
www.royalalberthall.com

Built by Queen Victoria in 1871 in memory of her consort, this beautiful and unusual-looking space is the site of performances for much of the year. One of the most popular and enjoyable are the Proms concerts held every summer since 1941, which are full of great artists and responsive audiences. Tickets for the seats at the Proms are very hard to come by if you don't plan ahead, although many people line up to stand. About a thousand standing places are sold the day of the performance for a very cheap price. This practice gives the "Proms" their name. Promming is the act of standing in the promenade area. If you purchase a season ticket, you will enjoy several advantages in securing good seats. The last night, which is always extraordinary, has its own ticketing requirements. All performances are broadcast on BBC Radio 3.
tel (0)207-589-8212; www.bbc.co.uk/proms

Royal Festival Hall is found at the South Bank Centre, another large arts complex in central London. This is the home of two orchestras: the Philharmonia and the London Philharmonic. Outstanding musicians perform regularly at the Royal Festival Hall, Queen Elizabeth Hall, and the Purcell Room, all of which are in the South Bank Centre. tel 020/7960-4242; www.sbc.org.uk

St. John's, Smith Square

Built in 1728 and restored following the Second World War, this church has wonderful acoustics and is a major concert venue. This is the home of the esteemed Academy of Ancient Music, an outstanding period instrument orchestra (www.aam.co.uk). Information on all music at the church can be found at www.sjss.org.uk.

Somerset House Courtyard is the splendid setting for concerts by ensembles such as the Orchestra of the Age of Enlightenment. tel (0)207-960-4242

Wigmore Hall
36 Wigmore Street
London W1H 9DF
tel 020/7935-2141; www.wigmorehall.org.uk

Wigmore Hall is one of the world's most beloved small halls for recitals and chamber music. Its staff is very devoted to the place and to those who attend, and audience members tend to hold this place close to their hearts.

You might enjoy visiting the house where George Frideric Handel lived from 1723 to 1759. It is located at 25 Brook Street, in Mayfair. Had he lived in the twentieth century, Handel's next-door neighbor (at no. 23) would have been Jimi Hendrix, who lived there in the 1960s. This is the only museum in London dedicated to a composer.

MANCHESTER

The BBC Symphony (Gianandrea Noseda, principal conductor) and the Hallé Orchestra (Mark Elder, conductor) regularly appear at Bridgewater Hall, one of the most outstanding places to hear music in all of Great Britain. Bridgewater Hall, Lower Mosley Street, Manchester M2 3WS; tel 0161-907-9000; fax 0161/907-9001; box@bridgewater-hall.co-uk; www.bridgewater-hall.co.uk

Manchester Camerata: www.manchestercamerata.org.uk

NOTTINGHAM

The Nottingham Philharmonic Orchestra (npo@nottinghamphilharmonic.co.uk; www.nottinghamphilharmonic.co.uk) performs in Albert

Hall (tel 0115/941-9419), the Royal Concert Hall (tel 0115/989-5555), and Southwell Minster in Southwell (tel 01636/812291).

OLDHAM

The hometown of Sir William Walton (1902–1983), Oldham holds a festival of his music each October. Look for information at www.oldham.gov. uk/leisure.

WORCESTERSHIRE

Visit the Elgar Birthplace, dedicated to composer Edward Elgar.

FINLAND (country code +358; drop the zero on city codes when calling from outside Finland)

There is no country in the world that has, per capita, a more intensive commitment to classical music. Finland has 5.2 million citizens, all of whom seem to love classical music, opera, dance, jazz, theater, and the visual arts. In 2001 the Finnish government spent 300 million Euros (US$270 million) on funding for the arts. This is about $59 per citizen each year, which is astonishing when you compare it with the most recent expenditure for the arts by the American government: 64 cents per citizen! France, also a very culturally committed nation, spends about half per capita on the arts what the Finns spend.

The Finnish expenditure on the arts does not include arts education, which is remarkably widespread. The Sibelius Academy is the third-largest university-level music institution in Europe, but it is only the top of this musical iceberg. There are eleven more conservatories around Finland, and 150 music institutes. The country produces many fine composers and conductors (70 percent of Scandinavian orchestras have a Finnish conductor). Finland itself has thirty-four orchestras and had the same number of classical music festivals in 2002.

An ideal vacation for a music lover is to spend a week or two in Finland breathing in fresh air, discovering the pleasures of sauna, admiring the considerable tradition of visual arts and architecture, and doing a total immersion in music.

For general information about culture and festivals in Finland, here is a valuable Web address: www.kulttuuri.net

Or contact: Finland Festivals

Uudenmaankatu 36 D 21

00120 Helsinki, Finland

tel +358-9 6126760 or 612 67 611

www.festivals.fi; info@festivals.fi

Below is only a very selective list of the many musical treasures to be found in Finland:

HELSINKI

(a Web link to all cultural activities in Helsinki is www.hel.fi)

Alexander Theater

Bulevardi 23–27

tel 09/17331331

This small old theater is a gem. It was built when Russia still dominated Finland, and this was the place where Russian plays and music were performed. When the Finns regained their city, the Alexander Theater became the home of the Finnish National Opera until it moved to its big new home. Now many kinds of cultural events happen at the Alexander Theater, including classical music performances.

Finlandia Hall

Finlandia-Talo

Karamzininkatu 4

tel 09/409611

Designed by Alvar Aalto and built in 1971, this is a famous and versatile concert hall that is home to the Helsinki Philharmonic Orchestra (founded in 1882; www.hel.fi/filharmonia; helsinki.philharmonic@hel.fi) and the Finnish Radio Symphony Orchestra. Many other concerts are also held here too.

The Helsinki Festival is the nation's largest and most important arts festival, and includes an important musical componenet. It is held in late August through early September.

Helsinki Festival, Lasipalatsi
Mannerheimintie 22–24, FIN-00100 Helsinki
tel 09/612-65100; fax 09/612-65161; info@helsinkifestival.fi; www.helsinki
festival.fi

Kultuuritalo
Sturenkatu 4
Another important hall for concerts, including those by the Finnish
Radio Symphony.

Musica Nova Helsinki, Lasipalatsi
Mannerheimintie 22–24, FIN-00100 Helsinki
tel 09/612-65100; fax 09/612-65161; musicanova@lasipalatsi.fi; www.
musicanova.lasipalatsi.fi
Held in March, this is an important festival for new music, especially
chamber music.

The Sibelius Academy
Founded in 1882 as the Helsinki Music Institute, this is now one of the
top music academies in the world, and the place where Finland's great
young musicians get their training. Sibelius studied here from 1885 to 1889,
and it was named for him in 1939. Attending a student performance will
give you first hearing of some of the great artists of the future.
Töölönkatu 28
PO Box 86, FIN-00251 Helsinki
tel for concert inquiries: 09/405-4685; tel 09/405441; fax 09/4054600;
info@siba.fi; www.siba.fi

JÄRVENPÄÄ
Held in October, the Järvenpää Sibelius Festival honors Finland's most
famous composer, who lived in 'the local town of Ainola for more than fifty
years.
PO Box 41, FIN-04401 Järvenpää
tel 09/271-92201; fax 09/271-92727; juhani.airas@jarvenpaa.fi; www.
jarvenpaa.fi/tapahtumat

KORSHOLM
Korsholm Music Festival
Keskustie 4, FIN-65610 Mustasaari

tel 06/322-2390; fax 06/322-2393; music.festival@korsholm.fi; www.korsh-olm.fi/music

KUHMO
Kuhmo Chamber Music Festival
Torikatu 39, FIN-8899900 Kuhmo
tel 08/652-0936; fax 08/652-1961;kuhmo.festival@kuhmofestival.fi; www.kuhmofestival.fi

LAHTI
Lahti Organ Festival
Kirkkikatu 5, FIN-15110 Lahti
tel 03/782-3184, fax 03/783-2190; lof@pp.phnet.fi; www.lathiogran.net

.   The Lahti Symphony Orchestra is an outstanding orchestra for such a small town, and it has a rich recorded legacy under its Music Director Osmo Vänskä. It performs at the beautiful new Sibelius Hall, set in a great location right on a lake. The hall is stunning to see, and has excellent acoustics.
Ankkurikatu 7
tel 03/814-2800; fax 03/814-2820; www.lahti.fi/sibeliustalo

MÄNTTÄ
Mänttä Music Festival
Virkamiehenkatu 4, FIN-35800 Mänttä
tel 03/488-8612; fax 03/488-8645; info@mantanmusiikkijuhlat.fi; www.mantanmusiikkijuhlat.fi
    This is Finland's only regular summer piano festival.

MIKKELI
    The Mikkeli Music Festival, held in late June and early July, is one of the country's best, and is held in the beautiful lake district.
Vuorikatu 3A, FIN-50100 Mikkeli
tel 015/162 076; fax 020/516 6031; festival@mikkelimusic.net; www.mikkeli music.net

NAANTALI
    The Naantali Music Festival, held in June, is the first major event of the summer festival calendar. The offerings are typically quite rich.

PO Box 46, FIN-21101 Naantali, Finland
tel 02/434-5363; fax 02/434-5425; info@naantalinmusiikkijuhlaf.fi; www.
naantalimusic.com

SAVONLINNA

Although this book is devoted to classical music, if you are in Finland in
July you should not miss the Savonlinna Opera Festival, whose setting and
musical quality are unforgettable. In 2002, the 800-seat Savonlinna Hall
opened as a venue for concerts.
Savonlinna Opera Festival
Olavinkatu 27, FIN-57130 Savonlinna
tel 015/476-750; fax 015/476-7540; info@operafestival.fi; www.operafestival.fi

TURKU

Turku Music Festival
Uudenmaankatu 1, FIN-20500 Turku
tel 02/251-1162; fax 02/231-3316; info@turkumusicfestival.fi; www.turku-
musicfestival.fi

FRANCE (country code +33; drop first zero when calling from abroad)

France has a remarkably rich and diverse musical life, and most cities
of any size have at least one concert hall. There is also a rich tradition of
music in churches, especially works for the organ. An excellent source for
information on musical activities in France is www.francefestivals.com,
sponsored by the Fédération Française des Festivals Internationaux de
Musique.

AIX-EN-PROVENCE

Summer Festival, Boutique du Festival d'Aix-en-Provence, 11 rue Gaston de
Saporta, 13100 Aix-en-Provence; tel 04/42173434; fax 04/42631374; www.
festival-aix.com

COLMAR

Colmar International Festival, for tickets: Tourist Office, 8 rue Kleber, 68000
Colmar
tel 03/89206897; fax 03/89413413; festival-international@ot-colmar.fr

ORANGE

Chorégies d'Orange, Box 205, 84017 Orange; tel 04/90342424; fax 04/90110404; www.choregies.asso

A popular summer festival.

PARIS

Orchestre de Paris, 252 rue du Faubourg saint-Honoré, 75008 Paris; tel 01/45616560; fax 01/42892449; www.orchestredeparis.com

Paris is full of halls, churches, and auditoriums where excellent and varied performances are given. You should also consult *Pariscope* magazine for the latest listings. Here are some worth knowing:

Amphithéatre Richelieu de la Sorbonne, 17 rue de la Sorbonne, 75005 Paris; tel 01/42627171

L'Archipel, 17 bd de Strasbourg, 75010 Paris; tel 01/48000435

Basilique Sainte-Clotilde, 23 bis rue Las Cases, 75007 Paris; tel 01/42776565

Cathédrale Sainte-Croix des Arméniens, 13 rue du Perche, 75003 Paris

Centre culturel de Russie, 61 rue Boissière, 75016 Paris; tel 01/44347979

Cerise, 46 rue Montorgueil, 75002 Paris; tel 01/46345726

Cité de la Musique, 221 av. Jean Jaurès, 75019 Paris; tel 01/44844484

Conservatoire supérieur de Paris-CNR, 14 rue de Madrid, 75008 Paris; tel 01/44706411

Eglise Americain, 65 quai d'Orsay, 75007 Paris

Eglise de la Madeleine, place de la Madeleine. The church where Chopin's funeral was held is the site of many concerts.

Eglise de la Trinité, place d'Estienne d'Orves, 75009 Paris

Eglise Notre Dame du Perpetuel Secours, 55 bd du Ménilmontant, 75011 Paris

Eglise Saint-Julien-le-Pauvre, 23 quai de Montebello, 75005 Paris; tel 01/43871601

Eglise Saint-Medard, 141 rue Mouffetard, 75005 Paris

Eglise Saint-Roch, 296 rue saint-Honoré, 75001 Paris; tel 01/44706410

Eglise Saint-Severin, 2 rue St. Jacques, 75006 Paris

Maison de Radio France, salle Olivier Messiaen, 116 av. du President Kennedy, 75016 Paris; tel 01/56401516

Musée Carnavalet, 23 rue de Sévigné, 75003 Paris

Musée national du Moyen Age, 6 place Paul Painlevé, 75005; tel 01/53737816. This museum of the Middle Ages features music from that time, including music of the troubadours.

L'Olivier, 18 rue des Wallons, 75013 Paris; tel 01/43313604

Opéra Comique; tel 01/42444546. Although built for opera presentations, this hall frequently has chamber music as well as performances by the Orchestre National de France and other ensembles.

Oratoire du Louvre, 145 rue Saint-Honoré, 75001 Paris; tel 01/42509618

Salle Cortot, 78 rue Cardinet, 75017 Paris

Salle Gaveau, 45 rue de la Boétie, 75008 Paris; tel 01/42337289

Salle Pleyel, 252 rue du Faubourg saint-Honoré, 75008 Paris; tel 01/45616589

Théâtre des Champs Elysées, 14 av. Montaigne, 75008 Paris; tel 01/49525050

Théâtre de la Ville, 2 place du Châtelet; tel 01/42742277

Théâtre de l'Ile Saint-Louis, 39 quai d'Anjou, 75004 Paris; tel 01/46334865

Théâtre du Châtelet, place Châtelet; tel 01/40282840. A lovely theater right in the city center with innovative programming.

Théâtre du Tambour Royal, 94 rue du Faoubourg du Temple, 75011 Paris; tel 01/48067234

TOULOUSE
Orchestre National du Capitole de Toulouse, which performs in the Théatre du Capitole (place du Capitole) and the Halle aux Grains (Place Dupuy), is one France's great orchestras. tel 05/61631313; www.onct.mairie-toulouse.fr

GERMANY (country code +49; drop first zero when calling from abroad)

BADEN-BADEN
The Festspielhaus in Baden-Baden has a rich selection of cultural attractions year-round, including a major summer festival. Beim Alten Banhof; 76530 Baden-Baden; tel 07221/301-3101; fax 07221/301-3211; www.festspielhaus.de

BAD KISSINGEN

Kissinger Sommer Festival, Postfach 2260, 97672 Bad Kissingen, Germany; tel 0971/807110; fax 0971/807191; www.badkissingen.de/kissinger-sommer; kissingersommer@stadt.badkissingen.de

An important summer music festival, typically from mid-June to mid-July, in a beautiful setting.

BERLIN

The Berlin Philharmonic (Berliner Philharmoniker; www.berlin-philharmonic.com), one of the world's outstanding orchestras, plays in one of the most unconventional concert halls anywhere, the Philharmonie. Opened in 1963, it is widely admired for its acoustics, though its design elicits divided opinions. It has 2,440 seats, and a second hall (opened in 1987) has 1,180 seats, and is often used for chamber music. In both halls, the musicians sit in the middle and are surrounded by the audience. Guided tours are given most days at 1 P.M., and you should book ahead by writing to presse@philharmonic. sireco.de.

Tickets: box office 030/25488-132 or -301; general information 030/25488-0; advance orders for people outside of Berlin: Kartenburo des Berlin Philharmonic Orchestra, Herbert-von-Karajan-Straße 1, 10785 Berlin; tel 030/25488-126 or -194; fax 030/25488-323; kartenburo@berlin-philharmonic.com

Festivals: As one of Europe's great cultural capitals, Berlin has festivals throughout the year. You can find out about them by contacting Berliner Festspiele GmbH, Postfach 15 01 69, 10663 Berlin; tel 030/25489-0; fax 030/25489-111; info@berlinerfestspiele.de; www.berlinerfestspiele.de

Berlin Radio Symphony Orchestra (Rundfunk-Sinfonieorchester Berlin) Charlottenstrasse 56, D-10117 Berlin; tel 030/20298715; fax 030/20298729; info@rsb-online.de; www.rsb-online.de

COLOGNE

WDR Sinfonie-Orchester Köln; www.wdr.de/radio/orchester/sinfonieorchester

DRESDEN

Dresden Philharmonic; Kulturpalast am Altmark, PSF 120 424, 01005 Dresden; tel 0351/4866-306; fax 0351/4866-353; ticket@dresdnerphilharmonie.de; www.dresdnerphilharmonie.de/englisch

FRANKFURT
The Alte Oper is the site for many concerts.
tel 69-134-0400; www.alteoper.de

HAMBURG
North German Radio Symphony Orchestra (NDR Sinfonie Orchester)
Musikhalle Hamburg, Spitalerstraße 22, 20095 Hamburg; tel 01801/787980;
fax 01801/787981; ticketshop@ndr.de; www.ndr.de

KIEL
The Schleswig-Holstein Music Festival is held in many sites around
Northern Germany, especially in Kiel and Lubeck. Postfach 3840, 24038
Kiel; tel 800/7463-2002 (toll free); fax 0431/5704747; bestellung@shmf.de;
www.shmf.de

LEIPZIG
Leipzig Bach Festival, Bach-Archiv Leipzig, Postfach 101 349, 04013 Leipzig;
tel 341/964-4182; fax 0341/964-4195; www.bach-leipzig; de
    Held in May in honor of the most famous composer to live and work in
this city.

Leipzig Gewandhaus Orchestra, Augustus 8, 04109 Leipzig; tel 0341/1270280;
info@gewandhaus.de; www.gwandhaus.de
    One of the oldest and finest orchestras in the world.

Mitteldeutscher Rundfunk (The Middle German Radio Orchestra), PF 67,
04251 Leipzig; tel 0341/300-8705; fax 0341/300-8701

MUNICH
Munich Philharmonic (Münchner Philharmoniker), Kellerstraße 4/III,
81667 München; tel 089/48098-508; fax 089/48098-525; philharmoniker@
muenchen.de; www.muenchenerphilharmoniker.de

Prinzregententheatre, tel 089-2916-1414

SCHWETZINGEN
Schwetzinger Festival, Kartenservice, 1 Carl-Theodor-Strasse, 68723 Schwetzingen; tel 062/022-05520; 062/022-05530; www.markt-schwetzinger.de

WIESBADEN

A popular music festival is held in wine country in July and August. www.rheingaufestival.de

GREECE (country code +30)

ATHENS

Athens and Epidaurus Festival
tel 01/9282900; fax 01/9282933; pr@greekfestival.gr; www.hellenicfestival.gr

HOLLAND: See The Netherlands

HUNGARY

A good general Web site is www.artsfestivals.hu.

BUDAPEST

A highlight is the annual Budapest Spring Festival. Information can be found at www.festivalvaros.hu or by calling +36-1-302-3841. Throughout the year many musical performances are given at the Academy of Music (tel +36-1-341-4788) and at the Hungarian State Opera House, +36-1-353-0170 www.bpo.hu.

Radio: Bartók Radio (www.radio.hu/bartok/) is the classical channel of the Hungarian State Broadcasting Company.

ICELAND (country code +354)

REYKJAVIK

The Iceland Symphony Orchestra; Háskólabió v/Hagalorg; PO Box 7052; IS-127 Reykjavik; tel 562-2255; fax 562-4475

IRELAND

DUBLIN

Two of Ireland's principal orchestras are both under the aegis of the national radio, and their performances are frequently broadcast.
National Symphony Orchestra of Ireland; music@rte.ie; www.rte.ie/music/nso RTÉ Concert Orchestra; music@rte.ie; www.rte.ie/music/rteco

ISRAEL (country code +972)

Since 1961, the annual Israel Festival of the Performing Arts is held in spring and summer at various locations around the country, but especially Jerusalem. The Israel Philharmonic, the Jerusalem Symphony Orchestra, the Israel Symphony Orchestra-Rishon LeZion, the New Israeli Opera, plus the world's leading musicians, actors, and dancers take part. Address: P.O. Box 4409; 91044 Jerusalem. For general information: tel 2-561-1438; fax 2-566-9850; israel_f@internet-zahav.net; www.festival.co.il Ticket reservations can be made calling 2-624-0896. General information about musical events in Israel can be found at www.goisrael.com, and North Americans can call 1-888-77-ISRAEL. These information numbers can also inform you of arts events occuring in Israel during the rest of the year.

ITALY (country code 39; *don't* drop first zero when calling from abroad unless you are calling to a mobile phone)

A useful Internet site in Italian is http://members.tripod.it/classical. For listings of music festivals in Italy, go to www.italiafestival.it.

ASOLO
Festival Internazionale Incontri Asolani
Asolo Musica
Via Browning 141
31011 Asolo (TV)
tel 0423/950150; fax 0423/529890
Dedicated to chamber music, this festival is held each September in this attractive town not far from Venice.

BERGAMO
Teatro Donizetti, Piazza Cavour 15, tel 035/4160602

BOLOGNA
Teatro Comunale, Largo Respighi 1, tel 051/529999

BRESCIA
Teatro Grande, Corso Zanardelli, tel 030/2979333

CATANIA
Teatro Bellini, Piazza Teatro Bellini, tel 095/7150921

CITTÀ DI CASTELLO
Festival delle Nazioni
Pizza Fanti 1
06012 Città di Castello (PG)
tel 075/8552461; fax 075/8521450

A festival is held in late summer in this pleasing Umbrian town near the border with Tuscany. Each year since 1968, the festival organizers select a different nation to provide inspiration for the music to be performed.

FLORENCE
Teatro Comunale di Firenze
Corso Italia, 16
www.maggiofiorentino.com
ticket office tel 055/211158 or 213535; fax 055/2779410

This theater, home to the opera as well as concerts and ballets, is the site for most performances of the Maggio Musicale Fiorentino, one of the oldest and most important music festivals in Europe. While the festival itself is in May and June, there are outstanding concerts here throughout the year.
Teatro Goldoni, Via Santa Maria 15, tel 055/211158
Teatro della Pergola, Via della Pergola 18, tel 055/2479651

GENOA
Teatro Carlo Felice, Passo Eugenio Montale 4, tel 010/589329

MERANO
Settimane Musicali Meranesi
Corso Libertà 45
39012 Merano (BZ)
tel 0473/221447; fax 0473/221449

Held from late August through September in an attractive spa town, this festival attracts top international artists.

MILAN
Auditorium, Corso San Gottardo (at Via Torricelli)
Site for many concerts, especially by the Orchestra Sinfonica di Milano Giuseppe Verdi, tel 02/83389-201/-202/-203
Teatro alla Scala, Via Filodrammatici 2, tel 02/72003744

In addition to opera performances, this theater has concerts by the house orchestra, visiting ensembles, and many soloists.

NAPLES
Cortile della Reggia di Capodimonte, tel 081/5499688
Teatro di San Carlo, Via San Carlo, tel 081/797-2111; www.teatrosancarlo.it

PADUA
Chiesa di Santa Maria dei Servi, tel 049/666128

PALERMO
Teatro Massimo, Piazza Verdi, tel 091/6053249 or 6266654

RAVENNA
Ravenna Festival
Via Dante Aligheri 1
48100 Ravenna
tel 0544/213895; fax 0544/36303
box office: Via Mariani 2; tel 0544/32577; fax 0544/215840

Held in June and July, the Ravenna Festival has now joined the ranks of the important international music festivals, and includes opera, symphonic, chamber, and vocal music.

REGGIO EMILIA
Basilica Beata Vergine della Ghiara, tel 049/666128

RIMINI
Sagra Musicale Malatestiana
Assessorato alla Cultura del Comune di Rimini
Via Gambalunga 27
47037 Rimini
tel 0541/26239; fax 0541/24227

This is one of the lesser-known musical events in Italy, but it is of high quality. Regular visitors include the great orchestras of Amsterdam, Paris, St. Petersburg, Tel Aviv, and elsewhere. The season is a long one, with varied offerings.

ROME
Accademia di Santa Cecilia
Auditorio di Via dell Conciliazione;
tel 06/6880-1044; www.santacecilia.it

Saint Cecilia is the patron saint of music, and Rome's principal concert hall—close to the Vatican—is dedicated to her.

All Saints Church, Via del Babuino 153, tel 06/86800125

SPOLETO
The Festival dei Due Mondi
Via Cesare Beccaria 18
00196 Roma
tel 06/3210288; fax 06/3200747; toll-free box office number in Italy 167-011834

One of the most famous festivals in Italy runs from late June to mid-July in the beautiful Umbrian hill town of Spoleto. All of the arts are represented here, including classical music.

TRIESTE
Teatro Comunale Giuseppe Verdi
Via Libertà 11
34121 Trieste
tel 040/367816 or 6722149; fax 040/366300

The chief theater in this culturally vibrant city hosts a wide range of musical and cultural offerings.

TURIN
Associazione Lingotto Musica
Auditorium Giovanni Agnelli
Via Nizza 262
tel 011/6640452; www.a-torino.com/concerti/lingotto

Teatro Reale, Piazza Castello 215, tel 011/8815241

Conservatorio Giuseppe Verdi, Piazza Bodoni, tel 011/43606

VENICE
Scuola Grande di San Giovanni Evangelista, Campo San Giovanni Evange-lista; tel 041/786764

A church that is the site of frequent concerts.

VERONA
Arena di Verona, Piazza Bra, tel 045/595216

JAPAN (country code +81)

Japan has one of the most active classical music scenes in the world. It is said that in Tokyo alone there are twenty-five classical music performances each night. For general information on Japan, go to www.jpan.org, or the site of the Association of Japanese Symphony Orchestras, www.jpan.org/orches/index.html.

HIROSHIMA
Hiroshima Symphony Orchestra; 15-10, Hatchubori, Naka-ku, Hiroshima-shi, Hiroshima-ken, 730; tel 082/222-8448; fax 082/222-8447

KYOTO
Kyoto Symphony Orchestra; 103 Tatemoto-cho, Kita-ku, Kyoto-shi, Kyoto-fu, 603; tel 075/222-0331; fax 075/222-0332

NAGOYA
Nagoya Philharmonic Orchestra; Nagoya City Plaza, 1-4-10, Kanayama, Nagoya-shi, Aichi-ken, 460; tel 052/322-2774; fax 052/322-3066

OSAKA
Osaka Philharmonic Orchestra; 1-1-44 Kishinosato, Nishinari-ku, Osaka-fu, 557; tel 06/656-7711; fax 06/656-7714
Founded in 1947.

SAPPORO
Pacific Music Festival, founded in 1990 by Leonard Bernstein and held each July, is one of Japan's most important musical events. For information, go to www.pmf.jp/E or write to pmfoc@hi-ho.ne.jp.

Sapporo Symphony Orchestra; Sapporo Concert Hall, 1-15, Nakaji-makoen, Chuo-ku, Sapporo-shi, Hokkaido, 064; tel 011/520-1771; fax 011/520-1772

TOKYO
Important Concert Halls:
Bunkamara, tel 3-3477-9111

New National Theater, tel 3-5352-9999

Suntory Hall, tel 3-3584-9999; www.suntory.co.jp

These halls are the sites of frequent performances by the NHK Symphony Orchestra, the New Japan Philharmonic, the Tokyo City Symphony, and visiting ensembles.

Important Musical Organizations:

Japan Philharmonic Symphony Orchestra; 1-6-1 Umezato, Suginami-ku, Tokyo-to, 166; tel 03/5378-6311; fax 03/5378-6161; j-phil@vcom.or.jp

Japan Shinsei Symphony Orchestra; Mariushi BLD, 3-16-4, Nishi-ikebukuro, Toshima-ku, Tokyo-to, 171; tel 03/3985-4836; fax 03/3981-0510; www.st.rim.or.jp/~~bernon/

New Japan Philharmonic; Sumida Triphony Hall, 1-2-3, Kinshi, Sumida-ku, Tokyo-to, 130; tel 03/5610-3820; fax 03/3499-1646; www.njp.or.jp

NHK Symphony Orchestra; 2-16-19, Takanawa, Minato-ku, Tokyo-to, 108; tel 03/3443-0271; fax 03/3443-0278
     Founded in 1926.

Tokyo Metropolitan Symphony Orchestra; Tokyo Bunkakaikan, 5-45, Ueno-koen, Taito-ku, Tokyo-to, 110; tel 03/3322-0727; fax 03/3322-0729

Tokyo Philharmonic Orchestra; Tokyo Opera City Tower, 11F, 3-20-2, Nishishinjuku, Tokyo-to, 163-14; tel 03/5353-9521; fax 03/5353-9523
     Founded in 1911.

Tokyo Symphony Orchestra; 2-23-5, Hayakunin-cho, Shinjuku-ku, Tokyo-to, 169; tel 03/3362-6764; fax 03/3360-8249

Yomiuri Nippon Symphony Orchestra; Kiyosumi Riverside Bldg., 1-1-7, Kiyosumi, Tokyo-to, 135; tel 03/3820-5841; fax 03/3820-5846; www.yominet.or.jp/yomikyo/

LEBANON

BEIRUT

Al Bustan Festival-International Festival of Music and Arts
PO Box 11-3764, Riad El Solh-Beirut 1107, 2150 Beirut
     Although set in Lebanon, much of the organizational activity happens in London:
Festival Office London

Mail Box 343

56 Gloucester Road, London SW7 4 UB, England

fax +44-207-937-2633; festival@albustan.co.uk; festival@albustan-lb.com; www.albustanfestival.com

The festival usually takes place in late winter, and is often themed around a particular topic. In 2001, it was "From Venice to Amsterdam: A Musical Journey."

LUXEMBOURG (country code +352)

ECHTERNACH

Festival International Echternach; PO Box 30, 6401 Echternach; tel 728347; fax 727112; www.echternachfestival.lu

MALAYSIA (country code +60)

KUALA LAMPUR

Dewan Filharmonik Petronas Concert Hall

Level 2, Tower 2

Petronas Twin Towers

Kuala Lampur City Centre

500088 Kuala Lampur

tel 3/207-7007; fax 3/203-7077; dfp_boxoffice@petronas.com.my; www.dfpmpo.com

Opened in 1998 next to what is now the world's tallest building, this is the home of the Malaysian Philharmonic Orchestra.

MEXICO (country code +52)

ACAPULCO

Acapulco Philharmonic Orchestra

Av. Costera Miguel Alemán #4455 Local K

Int. Centro Internacional Acapulco

tel 484 66 26; fax 484 448 54; www.acapulco2000.com/filarmonica

MEXICO CITY

Palacio de Bellas Artes

Eje Central Lazero Cardenas y Avenida Juarez

tel 512-2593

THE NETHERLANDS (country code +31)

<u>AMSTERDAM</u>

The Concertgebouw is one of the world's top concert halls, famous not only for its marvelous acoustics but for its embracing atmosphere. Built in 1888, it is the site of about 650 performances a year. Its primary tenant is the Royal Concertgebouw Orchestra, a splendid ensemble that is one of the great orchestras of the world. Already in 1897, Richard Strauss described the orchestra as "truly wonderful, full of the freshness of youth and enthusiasm." The orchestra is particular famous for its performances of Mahler, who was a frequent guest conductor. The Mahler tradition has been lovingly handed down through the decades.

Any orchestra or musician touring Europe dreams to play at the Concertgebouw, and no visit to Amsterdam would be complete without your hearing music in the hall, which is close to several of the city's great museums.

Tickets typically go on sale three months prior to a performance. You may order tickets by e-mail at www.concertgebouw.nl; by mail to Het Concertgebouw, Antwoordnummer 17902, 1000 WR, Amsterdam, The Netherlands; by fax to +31-(0)20/573-0460; by phone to +31-(0)20/671-8345. A 24-hour information line gives you updates on last-minute availability of tickets (+31-(0)20/675-4411).

The Web site for the Royal Concertgebouw Orchestra is www.concertgebouworkest.nl.

Festival: The Holland Festival; Kleine-Gartmanplantseon 21, 1017 RP Amsterdam, Netherlands. Tel 020/5307110; fax 020/5307119; www.holndfstvl.nl; info@hollandfestival.nl

<u>EINDHOVEN</u>
Philips Hall
Heuvel Galerie 140 (near the Markt)
5611 EE Eindhoven
postal address: Postbus 930, 5600 AX Eindhoven
tel 040/2655600; fax 040/2464020; bespreekbureau@philipshall.nl; www.philipshall.nl

The principal concert venue of Eindhoven is the home of the Het Brabants Orkest (The Brabant Orchestra: tel 040/2655699; fax 040/2463459; www.brabantsorkest.nl).

ROTTERDAM

Founded in 1918, the Rotterdam Philharmonic Orchestra is an excellent ensemble that has benefited from a long relationship with superstar conductor Valery Gergiev.

RphO

t.a.v.Wil Slavenburg

Postbus 962

3000 AZ Rotterdam

tel 010/2171707; fax 010/4116215; www.rpho.nl

The main concert hall of Rotterdam also functions as a congress center. It is called deDoelen. Tel 010/2171700; box office tel 010/2171717; fax 010/2171772

UTRECHT

Vredenburg Concert Hall

tel 030/231-4544; info@vredenburg.nl; www.vredenburg.nl

The Old Music Festival is held in late summer, playing music from the Middle Ages until the early nineteenth century on original instruments. Throughout the year, there are approximately ninety concerts held in beautiful historic sites.

tel 030/230-3838; 030/230-3839; www.oudemuziek.nl

For information about concerts in the churches of Utrecht, go to www.utrecht-musiekstad.net.

Radio: A good central source for the country is De Concertzender; Postbus 275; 1200 AG; Hilversum, Holland. Tel 035/677-3102; fax 035/677-3104; Concertpost@concertzender.nl.

NEW ZEALAND (country code +64)

For general information on cultural events in New Zealand, visit www.artscalendar.co.nz, www.url.co.nz/arts/nzarts, and www.creativenz.govt.nz. For ticket sales for major venues, go to www.ticketek.co.nz.

AUCKLAND

Auckland Philharmonia; PO Box 56 024, Auckland, NZ 1030 (1 St. Albans Avenue, Mt. Eden); tel 09/630-9687; fax 09/638-7073; www.aucklandphil.co.nz

Town Hall is the principal concert venue; fax 09/309-2679.

CHRISTCHURCH

The Christchurch Arts Festival. For information: www.thoseguys.co.nz/arts

The Christchurch Symphony; PO Box 3260, Christchurch, NZ; tel 03/379-3886; fax 03/379-3861; info@chsymph.co.nz; www.chsymph.co.nz

Town Hall is the principal concert venue. It has a famous pipe organ and there is an important organ series each year; fax 03/366-1840; www.nzorgan.com.

WELLINGTON

The Michael Fowler Centre is the principal concert venue. It is in the Wellington Convention Centre. 111 Wakefield Street, PO Box 2199, Wellington, NZ; tel 04/801-4242; fax 04/801-4310; www.wfcc.wcc.govt.nz

The New Zealand Symphony Orchestra; 101 Wakefield Street (2nd level MOB Building), PO Box 6640, Wellington, NZ; tel 04/801-3890; fax 04/801-3851; info@nzso.co.nz, www.nzso.co.nz

The orchestra gives regular concert seasons in Wellington and Auckland, and also performs in Christchurch, Dunedin, Hamilton, Hawke's Bay, and Palmerston North.

The Wellington Sinfonia; PO Box 11-977, Manners Street, Wellington, NZ; tel 04/801-3882; fax 04/801-3888; www.wellingtonsinfonia.co.nz

NORTHERN IRELAND (country code +44)

BELFAST

Waterfront Hall is a beautiful venue for listening to classical music. Box office tel 028/9033-4400; box ofice@waterfront.co.uk; www.waterfront. co.uk

NORWAY (country code +47)

A good general site for information is www.norwayfestivals.com. If you love Edvard Grieg, as I do, a home page worth looking at is www.mnc.net/norway/EHG.

BERGEN

The Bergen Festival, PO Box 183, 5001 Bergen; tel 0552/10630; fax 0552/10640; info@fib.no; www.fib.no

A marvelous festival held each spring in Edvard Grieg's beautiful hometown.

OSLO
The Oslo Philharmonic Orchestra performs at the Oslo Konserthus. www.oslophil.com

TRONDHEIM
Trondheim Symphony Orchestra, Postadresse Pb 774, N-7408 Trondheim; tel 735398800 or 81533133; fax 73539801; post@tso.no; www.tso.nso

POLAND (country code +48)

WARSAW
Warsaw Autumn, 27 Rynek Starego Miasta, 00-272 Warsaw; tel 022/831-1634; fax 022/831-0607; www.warsaw-autumn.art.pl

WROCLAW
Wratislavia Cantans, 7 Rynek, 50-106 Wroclaw; tel 071/34207257; fax 071/343-0833; www.wratislava.multinet.pl

PORTUGAL

LISBON
Radio: Antena 2 is the second radio station of RDP, the Portuguese public broadcasting company.

RUSSIA

MOSCOW
Bolshoi Theater
Teatralnaya Ploshchad 1
tel 292-9986
Ensemble XXI Moscow
Information in English: www.paqo.demon.co.uk/ensintr1.html
Glinka Hall and Museum
Ulitsa Fadayeva 4
tel 972-3237

Tschaikovsky Conservatory
Bolshaya Nikitskaya Ulitsa 13
tel 229-8183

Maly Zal is the city's most important chamber music auditorium, and the Bolshoi Zal Konservatorii is the large hall for symphonic music.

Russian National Orchestra
Ulitsa Garibaldi 19
Moscow, Russia
tel +7095/120 7409 or 128-7811; fax +7095/ 120 7409; www.rno.ru; info@rno.ru US contact: Russian Arts Foundation; tel +1-925/943-2248; fax +1-925/943-1164; rwalk1@pacbell.net

Founded in 1990 and made up of fine musicians, the RNO tours extensively when not performing at home. Its genesis was to be the first Russian orchestra since 1917 to not be under government control.

Scriabin Museum
Bolshoi Nikolopeskovsky Pereulok 11
tel 241-1901

ST. PETERSBURG

Glinka Philharmonic Chamber Hall
Nevsky Prospekt 30
tel 312-4585

An important venue for solo and chamber performances.

Hermitage Theater
Dvortsovaya Naberezhnaya 34
tel 311-3465

A little jewel that is the former court theater of the Winter Palace.

Mariinsky Theater
www.mariinsky.spb.ru

This is the famous theater that is often called the Kirov, a legendary place for concerts, opera, and ballet, and currently the base of operations for concerts, opera, and ballet, and the indefatigable maestro Valery Gergiev. He might be here conducting if you visit, especially at the White Nights Festival in early June, but you are just as likely to hear him in New York, Washington, Los Angeles, London, Berlin, Salzburg, Milan, and many other cities.

Shostakovich Philharmonic Hall
Mikhailovsky Ulitsa 2
tel 311-7333
Home of the St. Petersburg Philharmonic Orchestra.

SCOTLAND (country code +44)

Also see general Web site listings under England.

EDINBURGH

The Edinburgh Festival, held every August, claims to be the world's largest arts festival. It certainly is one of the most diverse, covering everything from classical music to punk rock, and stand-up comedy to Wagner. tel 0131-473-3000; www.eif.uk

Usher Hall, Lothian Road, Edinburgh EH1 2Ea1; tel 0131/228-8616; fax 0131/228-8848; www.usherhall.co.uk
This is the city's premier concert hall, home to the Scottish National Orchestra and the Scottish Chamber Orchestra.

GLASGOW

The Glasgow Royal Concert Hall is the home of the BBC Scottish Symphony Orchestra and is the site for many important performances by visiting artists. 2 Sauchiehall Street, Glasgow G2 3NY; tel 0141/353-8000; www.grch.com

SOUTH AFRICA

PORT ELIZABETH

Eastern Cape Philharmonic Orchestra, PO Box 12148, Moffat Place 6002; tel 041/581-7747; info@ecpo.za.org

PRETORIA

Pretoria Bach Choir; www.ptbachchoir.org.za/history.htm

SPAIN

BARCELONA

L'Auditori tel +34-93-247-9300; www.auditori.com
Palau de la Musica

Festival: Summer Festival of Barcelona
Institut de Cultura-Ayuntament de Barcelona
La Rambla 99
08002 Barcelona
tel 93/3017775; fax 93/3016100; infoicub@mail.bcn.es

CAMPRODRON

Isaac Albéniz Festival. The town of the composer's birth, in the province
of Girona, holds a festival each summer in his honor.
www.festivales.com/albenizcamprodron or www.elripolles.com/isaacalbeniz

CANARY ISLANDS

Festival de Música de Canarias
www.festivaldecanarias.com; e-mail: festival@socaem.com
While most music festivals happen in summer or around holidays, this
one traditionally begin on January 7 and extends into early February. It is held
at various sites throughout these beautiful islands—especially in Las Palmas
and Santa Cruz de Tenerife—and has attracted many first-rank artists.

GRANADA

Granada Festival of Music and Dance, held in this beautiful city from
mid-June to early July. C/Cárcel Baja no. 19, 3°, Granada 18001; www.
granadafestival.org

LEÓN

Festival Internacional de Órgano, held in the Cathedral of León from
mid-September to late October. Gran Via de San Marcos, 5-5° A; 24001 León
www.fiocle.org

LLEIDA

Festival Enric Granados. Held in late October/early November and dedicated to the music of Granados. www.paeria.es/auditori; e-mail: auditori@
paeria.es

PALMA DE MALLORCA

Festival Mediterráneo de Música Clásica. A new festival, held from mid-
June to early July on this beautiful island. Set Cantons, 4-2° Dcha-Palma de
Mallorca.es.geocities.com/festivalmediterraneo

SAN SEBASTIÁN.

Quincena Musical de San Sebastián. Although a quincena is a fortnight, as the festival was when founded in 1939, it now lasts almost the entire month of August in this beautiful Basque city. Centro Kursaal, Avenida Zurriola, n°1; 20002 Donostia-Gipuzkoa

SEGOVIA

Musical Summer is held from late June to mid-September. The festival dates back to 1938, and offers a great range of classical music and other arts. Juan Bravo, 7, 1°, 40001 Segovia. www.fundac-juandeborbon.com

TARRAGONA

Pablo Casals International Music Festival. From mid-July to late August, held in the town where the celebrated cellist was born. Avenida Palfuriana 34 (Sant Salvador), 43700 El Vendrell (Tarragona). www.elvendrell.net

VALENCIA

ENSEMS, Festival of Contemporary Music. Held in late April/early May, since 1978. Barcas 2, Valencia. www.festivales.com/ensems

SWEDEN

A good general site for information is www.musicfestivaler.se Swedish Tourism Information www.gosweden.org

GÖTEBORG

National Orchestra of Sweden
tel 031/615300

LAKE SILJAN

Music on Lake Siljan is a music festival held each July. tel +46 248/10290; fax +46 248/51981

STOCKHOLM

For good information on Stockholm culture, go to www.stockholm-town.com. There are three principal concert venues in the Swedish capital, and additional performances occasionally are given at the Opera House. Berwaldhallen, Strandvägen 69; tel 08/784-1800; www.sr.se.berwaldhallen

Concert Hall, tel 08/102110; www.konserthuset.se

This hall opened in 1926 as the home of the Royal Stockholm Philharmonic Orchestra.

Music Academy, Nybrokajen 11; tel 08/407-1600; www.musakad.se

The Royal Opera, Gustaf Adolfs Torg., tel 08/248240; www.kunligaoperan.se

Music at the Royal Palace, Kungliga Slottet, SE-11130 Stockholm; tel 08/102247; fax 08/215911; concerts@royalfestivals.se

A delightful setting and one of Sweden's major music festivals. As the name suggests, wonderful musical performances, many of them classical, are given in Sweden's royal palace every August.

SWITZERLAND (country code +41)

GENEVA
Grand Orchestre de La Suisse Romande, Rue Bovy-Lysberg 2, 1204 Genève, Suisse; tel 022/807-0017; fax 022/807-0018; music@osr.ch; www.osr.ch. english

GSTAAD
Menuhin Festival Gstaad, PO Box 65, Haus des Gastes, 3780 Gstaad; tel 033/748-8338; fax 033/748-8339; www.menuhinfestivalgstaad.com

This is a popular festival held from late July through August.

LAUSANNE
Théâtre Municipal, tel 021-310-1600

LUCERNE
The Lucerne Festival is another worthy destination. There is a series of concerts at Easter, another in late summer, and a piano festival in November. Performances are held at various sites, including the Musikhochscule, the Matthäuskirche, Franziskanerkirche, Marianischer Saal, and the Luzerner Theater. tel 041/226-4480; www.lucernemusic.ch

MONTREUX
Montreum Voice and Music Festival, 5 rue du Théatre, Box 353, 1820 Montreux; tel 021/966-8025; fax 021/963-2506; www.montreux-festival.com

<u>VERBIER</u>
Verbier Festival and Academy
Case postale
1936 Verbier, Switzerland
tickets: tel 027/771-8282; fax 027/771-7057
administration: tel 021/925-9060; fax 021/925-9068
www.verbierfestival.com; info@verbierfestival.com

In just a few years the Verbier Festival has risen to be one of the world's most important music festivals. Central to its mission is education, and many fine young musicians have ready access to master musicians in the context of large-scale rehearsals and classes as well as one-to-one training. The UBS Verbier Festival Youth Orchestra is the ensemble that performs here, and they are led by world-class conductors. Members of the public spend two weeks (late July to early August) attending marvelous performances by these great musicians together with some of the pupils. For example, the amazing roster of artists in 2002 included Yuri Bashmet, Joshua Bell, Lynn Harrell, Paavo Järvi, Evgeny Kissin, Gidon Kremer, Steven Kovacevich, James Levine, Kurt Masur, Zubin Mehta, Heidi Grant Murphy, Michala Petri, Vadim Repin, Fazil Say, Kiri Te Kanawa, and Jean-Yves Thibaudet.

TURKEY (country code +90)

<u>ANKARA</u>
International Ankara Music Festival: tel 0312/427-0855; fax 0312/467-3159; sca@ankarafestival.com; www.ankarafestival.com

<u>ISTANBUL</u>
Istanbul International Music Festival, Istiklai Caddesi 146, Luvr Apt., 80070 Beyoglu-Istanbul; tel 212/293-3133; fax 212/249-5667; music.fest@istfest-tr.org; www.istfest.org

Various important cultural events take place throughout the year under the auspices of the Istanbul Festival, with the rich musical offerings usually happening in June.

• ◅◦▻ •

UNITED STATES OF AMERICA (country code 1)

<u>ALBUQUERQUE, NM</u>
New Mexico Symphony Orchestra
3301 Menaul Blvd NE
Albuquerque, NM 87190-0208
tel 505/881-9590; www.nmso.org

<u>ANCHORAGE, AK</u>
Anchorage Symphony Orchestra
400 D Street, Suite 230
Anchorage, AK 99501
tel 907/274-8668; fax 907/272-7916; www.anchoragesymphony.org; aso@corecom.net

<u>ANN ARBOR, MI</u>
University Musical Society, University of Michigan
Burton Memorial Tower
881 North University Avenue
Ann Arbor, MI 48109-1011
tel 734/764-2538 or 800/221-1229; fax 734/647-1171; www.ums.org

Although music schools such as Juilliard, Indiana, and Yale may be more famous, Michigan's is also outstanding. Its vocal faculty is particularly strong, with singers such as Shirley Verrett, and it has perhaps the best school for pianists who accompany singers, led by Martin Katz. In this climate, it is not surprising that one of the nation's top performing arts series would here too. Many of the world's top artists pass through Ann Arbor to play for receptive audiences. This place was a particular favorite of Vladimir Horowitz. Performances are held in seven different venues.

<u>ANNANDALE-ON-HUDSON, NY</u>
Bard Music Festival
tel 914/758-3226; www.bard.edu

A very fine music festival held each summer on the campus of Bard College.

• ∿ •

ASPEN, CO
Aspen Music Festival
2 Music School Road
Aspen, CO 81611
tel (school) 970/925-3254; fax 970/920-1643; school@aspenmusic.org
tel (festival) 970/925-9042; festival@aspenmusic.org; www.aspenmusicfestival.com

Founded in 1949, this is one of the world's most important festivals that has education as its focus.

It is worth the trip to hear music in this splendid setting each summer while watching the development of young artists. Many top stars perform here as well.

ATLANTA, GA
The Atlanta Symphony Orchestra, with a line of important conductors that includes Robert Shaw, Yoel Levi, and Robert Spano, is an important regional organization that gets better all the time. Most performances are at the Woodruff Arts Center. Box office: 404/733-5000. It is also possible to order tickets online at www.atlantasymphony.org.

AUSTIN, TX
A good general Internet site for culture in Austin is www.austinlinks.com/Arts/Listings include the Austin Symphony Orchestra

BALTIMORE, MD
Baltimore Symphony Orchestra
Meyerhoff Symphony Hall
1212 Cathedral Street
Baltimore, MD 21201
tel 410/783-8000; fax 410/783-8131; www.baltimoresymphony.org

The Peabody Conservatory of Music is part of Johns Hopkins University. This is one of America's top music schools, and there is a full calendar of concerts. Performances are mostly in the Friedberg Concert Hall, 609 North Charles Street; tel 410/659-8100, ext. 2; www.peabody.jhu.edu.

BARTLESVILLE, OK
OK Mozart Festival
tel 918/336-9800; www.webtek.com/okmozart

Held each June in the Community Center (designed by the Frank Lloyd Wright Foundation), Mozart meets the Oklahoma oil patch and everyone wins.

BERKELEY, CA

The Berkeley Symphony Orchestra is a rising company, thanks to good local support and the leadership, at this writing, of the excellent conductor Kent Nagano. They perform in both Zellerbach Hall and Hertz Hall. For information:

2322 Shattuck Avenue
Berkeley, CA 94704
tel 510/841-2800; fax 510/841-5422; mail@berkeleysymphony.org; www.berkeleysymphony.org

BLOOMINGTON, IN

Indiana University School of Music
Bloomington, IN 47405-2200
tel (tickets)812/855-9846; (school) 812/855-1583; www.music.indiana.edu

Unquestionably one of the world's great music schools, IU (as everyone in the music world calls it) has turned out too many brilliant musicians to name. If you are in Bloomington, attend whatever performance is on and you will likely hear one of the stars of tomorrow.

BOSTON, MA

Boston has an excellent musical life, with performances in many small and medium-sized halls balancing the presentations in some of the larger venues. The many colleges and universities also have active musical programming worth investigating. But even if this city only had the Boston Symphony Orchestra, it would be worth the journey to hear music at Symphony Hall. Berklee College of Music: tel 617/747-8890

The Boston Conservatory: tel 617/917-9240

Boston Symphony
Symphony Hall
301 Massachusetts Avenue
Boston, MA 02115
tel 617/266-1492

Symphony Hall opened on October 15, 1900, and is ranks on a very short list (including New York's Carnegie Hall, Leipzig's Gewandhaus, Amsterdam's Concertgebouw, and Vienna's Musikverein) of those places with incomparable acoustics.

Founded in 1881, the Boston Symphony has a laudable history that includes performing more than three hundred world premieres. It has enjoyed long relationships with outstanding conductors, including Serge Koussevitzky (1925–1949), Charles Munch (1949–1962), Erich Leinsdorf (1962–1969), William Steinberg (1969–1973), and Seiji Ozawa (1973–2002). With James Levine's arrival in 2004, this grand tradition continues.

The Boston Symphony also participates in one of the world's great summer music festivals, at Tanglewood in the Berkshire Mountains, where it has appeared annually since 1937. The symphony's Web site is www.bso.org, and it will also provide links for Tanglewood. Tel: subscriptions 617/266-7575 or 888/266-7575.

Handel & Haydn Society: tel 617/266-3605

Longy School of Music: tel 617/876-0956

New England Conservatory of Music: tel 617/585-1122
One of America's leading schools of music, the NEC has frequent performances by students, faculty, and famous artists who appear in Jordan Hall.

The Wang Theater: tel 617/482-9393;800/447-7400
Radio:
WCRB (102.5 FM) Classical music
WBUR (90.9 FM) NPR
WHRV (95.3 FM) Harvard University's radio station includes classical music and opera in its programming

BROOKVILLE, NY
Tilles Center for the Performing Arts
tel 516/299-3100; www.tillescenter.org
Many of the great arts organizations that visit New York City give an additional performance at the Tilles Center on the campus of C.W. Post College on Long Island.

BUFFALO, NY
Buffalo Philharmonic Orchestra
tel 716/885-5000 or 800/699-3168; www.bpo.org

BURLINGTON, VT
Flynn Center for the Performing Arts
tel 802/863-5966; www, flynntheatre.org

Vermont Mozart Festival
tel 802/862-7351 or 800/639-9097; www.vtmozart.com

Vermont Symphony Orchestra
tel 802/864-5741 or 800/876-9293; www.vso.org

CARMEL, CA
Carmel Bach Festival
tel 831/624-2046; www.bachfestival.org
   This venerable festival has been in business since 1937.

Monterey Symphony
PO Box 3965
Carmel, CA 93921
tel 831/624-8511; fax 831/624-3837; www.montereysymphony.org;
info@montereysymphony.org

CHARLESTON, SC
Spoleto Festival USA
tel 843/579-3100; www.spoletousa.org; receptionist@spoletousa.org
   Held in late May and early June, this is one of America's top arts festivals.
Originally connected to the eponymous festival in Italy, it now is on its own.

CHARLOTTE, NC
Charlotte Symphony Orchestra
201 S. College Street, Suite 110
Charlotte, NC 28244
tel 704/972-2000; www.charlottesymphony.org

CHICAGO, IL
Symphony Center
220 S. Michigan Avenue
Chicago, IL 60604
tel 312/294-3000; 800/223-7114; fax 312/294-3329
ticket hotline 888/294-3550

This hall is home to the fabulous Chicago Symphony Orchestra (www. cso.org) and is the venue for performances by the top visiting artists from around the world. The orchestra was incorporated in 1891 and quickly found its place in the cultural firmament of which Chicago is so justifiably proud. At its World's Columbian Exhibition appearances in 1892–93, guest performers included Paderewski and Dvořák, and since that time the orchestra has attracted just about every major artist. Without question it is one of the world's great orchestras.

Radio: WFMT

CINCINNATI, OH

The Cincinnati Symphony (www.cincinnatisymphony.org) is the fifth oldest orchestra in America. They perform in historic Music Hall throughout a full season, and as part of the city's famous May Festival. Established in 1873, this is the oldest choral music festival in the western hemisphere, and has long been under the artistic leadership of James Conlon.

Music Hall
1241 Elm Street
Cincinnati, OH 45210
tel 513/381-3300

CLEARWATER, FL
Ruth Eckerd Hall
1111 McMullen Booth Road
Clearwater, FL 33759
727/791-7400; www.RuthEckerdHall. Com

This is a very active hall that presents many fine musicians. There are excellent acoustics too.

CLEVELAND, OH
The Cleveland Orchestra
11001 Euclid Avenue
Cleveland, OH 44106
tel 216/231-1111; 800/686-1141; fax 216/231-5311; www.clevelandorch.com

Part of the "Top Five" American orchestras and one of the world's great ensembles, the Cleveland Orchestra merits your attention if you are anywhere near it or it is near you. They perform at historic Severance Hall, do a summer season at the Blossom Music Center, and tour often to great acclaim.

Radio: WKSU

COLUMBUS, OH
Columbus Symphony Orchestra
Ohio Theatre
55 East State Street
Columbus, OH
tickets: tel 614/228-8600; 614/224-7273; customerservice@columbus symphony.com
Radio: WOSU

COSTA MESA, CA
Orange County Performing Arts Center
tel 714/556-2787; www.ocpac.org
The Center's Segerstrom Hall is a major venue in Southern California for important cultural events of all kinds, including performances by the Orange County Philharmonic Society, the Pacific Chorale, touring orchestras, and an important chamber music series featuring top ensembles from all over.

DALLAS, TX
Dallas Symphony Orchestra
2301 Flora Street, Suite 300
Dallas, TX 75201-2497
tel 214/871-4000; www.dallassymphony.com
The Dallas Symphony performs at the Morton H. Meyerson Symphony Center, considered one of the finest acoustical performance spaces to be built in recent years.

DENVER, CO
Colorado Symphony Orchestra
Denver Place, North Tower
999 18th Street, Suite 2055
Denver, CO 80202
tel 303/292-5566; fax 303/293-2649; www.coloradosymphony.org; administration@coloradosymphony.org

Denver Center for the Performing Arts
14th & Curtis Street
Denver, CO 303/893-4100; www.denvercenter.org
   Home of the Colorado Symphony Orchestra and site of performances by
many fine musical organizations and soloists.
   Radio: KVOD 90.1

DETROIT, MI
Detroit Symphony Orchestra
Orchestra Hall
3711 Woodward Avenue
Detroit, MI 48201
Tel 313/576-5111; fax 313/576-5109; www.detroitsymphony.com; info@
detroit symphony.com
   Established in 1914, the Detroit Symphony is, at this writing, one of the
few orchestras that still enjoys nationally syndicated broadcasts of its per-
formances, giving the company a reach far behind its hometown.

EUGENE, OR
Eugene Symphony Orchestra
tel 541/682-5000; www.eugenesymphony.org

Oregon Bach Festival
tel 541/682-5000; www.bachfest.uoregon.edu
   Held in late June through mid-July.

Oregon Festival of American Music
The American Music Institute
PO Box 1497
Eugene, OR 97440-1497
tel 541/687-6526 or 800/248-1615; www.ofam2.org; info@ofam.net

FORT LAUDERDALE, FL
Broward Center for the Performing Arts
201 Southwest Fifth Avenue
Fort Lauderdale, FL
tel 954/462-0222; fax 954/468-3282

A multipurpose performing arts center that includes many fine classical music performances by touring groups as well as the Florida Philharmonic Orchestra and the Symphony of the Americas.

The Florida Philharmonic Orchestra
3401 NW 9th Avenue
Fort Lauderdale, FL 33309-5903
tel 654/938-6700; fax 954/561-1390; tickets 800/226-1812
   The Florida Philharmonic Orchestra performs in four different communities: Miami, Fort Lauderdale, Boca Raton, and West Palm Beach.

Symphony of the Americas
199 N. Ocean Boulevard, Suite 200
Pompano Beach, FL 33062
tel 954/545-0088; fax 954/545-9088; www.symphamer.com; symphamer.com@aol.com

FORT WORTH, TX
Nancy Lee and Perry R. Bass Performance Hall
230 East 4th Street
Fort Worth, TX 76102
Box Office: 525 Commerce Street
tel 817/212-4280; toll-free 877-212-4280; www.basshall.com
   Opened in 1998, Bass Hall is one of the most beautiful and acclaimed of all new theaters. It is the home of the Fort Worth Symphony (www.fwso.org) and many other arts organizations.

The Van Cliburn Foundation
2525 Ridgmar Boulevard, Suite 307
Fort Worth, TX 76116
tel 817/738-6536; fax 817/738-6534; www.cliburn.org; clistaff@cliburn.org
   Named for the famous pianist, the Van Cliburn competition is one of the world's most renowned piano awards. The foundation has done a great deal to foster the careers of many pianists.

• ✧ •

HARTFORD, CT
Hartford Symphony Orchestra
229 Farmington Avenue
Hartford, CT 06105-3596
tel 860/244-2999; www.hartfordsymphony.org

HONOLULU, HI
Good general listings can be found at http://calendar.gohawaii.com/performing arts. Also visit www.cliffsclassics.com.
Neal Blaisdell Concert Hall
777 Ward Avenue
Honolulu, HI
tel 808/526-4400
Home of the Honolulu Symphony and other arts organizations.

Honolulu Symphony
The Dole Cannery
650 Iwilei Road, #202
Honolulu, HI 96817
tel 808/792-2000
www.honolulusymphony.com

Oahu Choral Society
3215 Pali Highway
Honolulu, HI 96817-5202
tel 808/595-0327; toll-free (US only) 888/284-6742 (PIN 0940); fax 808/595-8616
Radio: KHPR 88.1 FM (Honolulu); KIPO 89.3 FM (Honolulu); KANO 91.1 FM (Hilo); KIFO 1380 AM (Pearl City); KKUA 90.7 FM (Wailuku)

HOUSTON, TX
Houston Symphony
615 Louisiana Street, Suite 102
Houston, TX 77002
Administrative office 713/224-4240; fax 713/222-7024
www.houstonsymphony.org

INDIANAPOLIS, IN

Indianapolis Symphony Orchestra
Hilbert Circle Theatre
45 Monument Circle
Indianapolis, IN 46204-2919
tel 317/639-4300 or 800/366-8457; www.indyorch.org

The outstanding British conductor Raymond Leppard took over the ISO in 1987 and has made it a fine musical organization.

International Violin Competition of Indianapolis
tel 317/637-4574; www.violin.org

Founded in 1982 under the great Josef Gingold and now run by Jaime Laredo, this festival should not be missed by lovers of the violin.

Radio: WFYI 90.1 carries performances of the Indiana Symphony Orchestra twice weekly and features other fine music as well.

JACKSONVILLE, FL

The Jacksonville Symphony
tel 904/354-5547 or 877/662-6731; www.jaxsymphony.org

Founded in 1949, this is Florida's oldest orchestra.

KANSAS CITY, KS

Kansas City Wind Symphony
Music Department of the Village Church
6641 Mission Road
Prairie Village, KS 66208
tel 913/671-2344; concert hotline 913/671-2315; fax 913/262-0304;
concerts@kcwindsymphony.org; www.kcwindsymphony.org

This is a fine organization devoted entirely to performing transcriptions of orchestral music on a gathering of wind instruments.

KANSAS CITY, MO

Kansas City Symphony
1020 Central, Suite 300
Kansas City, MO 64105-1672
tel 816/471-1100; tickets 816/471-0400; fax 816/471-097; www.kcsymphony.org

The Kansas City Symphony performs at the Music Hall in downtown Kansas City and at Yardley Hall in Overland Park, KS.

KATONAH, NY

Caramoor Center for Music and the Arts

tel 914/232-1252; www.caramoor.com

The late Walter and Lucie Rosen built a huge house and then had to decide what to do with it. In the 1960s they began to offer concerts there, and gradually added the Venetian Theater and another wing. In the years since it has become one of the most beguiling and musically valid summer festivals in the Northeast.

KNOXVILLE, TN

Knoxville Symphony Orchestra

tel 865/523-1178; www.ksoknox.org

LAS VEGAS, NV

The Las Vegas Philharmonic

1289 S. Torrey Pines Drive

Las Vegas, NV 89146

tickets: tel 702/895-2787

admin: tel 702/258-5438; fax 702/258-5646

lvphil@anv.net

www.lasvegasphilharmonic.com

LENOX, MA

Equidistant between New York and Boston, Tanglewood is the most popular summer music festival in the eastern United States. Read more in the listing for the Boston Symphony in Boston, above.

297 West Street

Lenox, MA 02140

tel 413/637-1600; www.bso.org

LOS ANGELES, CA

Disney Hall

www.waltdisneyconcerthall.org

With its opening in 2003, this Frank Gehry–designed building is the new home of the Los Angeles Philharmonic.

Hollywood Bowl
2301 N. Highland Avenue
Hollywood, CA 90078
tel 323/850-2000; www.hollywoodbowl.org
This is a popular outdoor venue for all kinds of music, including summer performances by the Los Angeles Philharmonic.

The Los Angeles Philharmonic
135 North Grand Avenue
Los Angeles, CA 90012-3042
tel 323/850-2000; fax 213/972-7560; www.laphil.org
One of the oldest arts organizations in Southern California, the Los Angeles Philharmonic was founded in 1919. It has had several important music directors, including Artur Rodzinski, Otto Klemperer, Alfred Wallenstein, Zubin Mehta, Carlo Maria Giulini, André Previn, and since 1992, Esa-Pekka Salonen.

Los Angeles County Music Center
135 North Grand Avenue
Los Angeles, CA 90012
(the box office is on the Hope Street side)
The main performing arts center of Los Angeles, including the Dorothy Chandler Pavilion, the Ahmanson Theatre, Mark Taper Forum, and the brand-new Disney Hall (see above).
Radio: KCRW 89.9 FM

MEMPHIS, TN
Memphis Symphony Orchestra
tel 901/324-3627; www.memphissymphony.org

MIAMI, FL
The Florida Philharmonic: see listing under Fort Lauderdale.
Miami Symphony Orchestra performs at the Gusman Concert Hall in Coral Gables, the Lincoln Theatre in Miami Beach, and the Dade County Auditorium. For information call 305/275-5666.

New World Symphony
Lincoln Theatre
541 Lincoln Road
Miami Beach, FL 33139
tel 305/673-3331 or 800/597-3331; fax 305/673-2302; www.nws.org; email
@nws.org

Established in 1987 under the artistic direction of Michael Tilson Thomas, this outstanding musical organization is made up of younger musicians who receive three years of intensive training in an academy and work with many of the world's top artists. They have toured to Europe, Asia, and throughout the Americas. They have also made several acclaimed recordings under Maestro Tilson Thomas.

MILWAUKEE, WI
Milwaukee Symphony
Uihlein Hall, Marcus Center for the Performing Arts
929 North Water Street
tel 414/291-7605 or 800-291-7605; www.milwaukeesymphony.org

MINNEAPOLIS–ST. PAUL, MN
Minnesota Orchestra
Orchestra Hall
1111 Nicollet Mall
Minneapolis, MN 55403
tel 612/371-5656 or 800/292-4141; 612/371-7191; www.mnorch.org

Since 1903 the Minnesota Orchestra has been a major force in the arts climate of the culturally rich Minneapolis–St. Paul area. One need only name some of its music directors to understand this orchestra's pedigree: Eugene Ormandy, Dimitri Mitropoulos, Antal Dorati, Stanislaw Skrowaczewski, Neville Marriner, Edo de Waart, Eiji Oue, and Osmo Vänskä. The orchestra also has a long tradition of commissioning works by major composers.

Ordway Center of the Performing Arts
345 Washington Street
St. Paul, MN 55102
tel 651/224-4222 or 800/292-4141; www.ordway.org

Home of the superb St. Paul Chamber Orchestra, the Minnesota Opera, and second home to the Minnesota Orchestra. It is also the home of the Schubert Club.

St. Paul Chamber Orchestra
Ticket Office: 438 St. Peter Street, Suite 500
St. Paul, MN 55102
tel 651/291-1144; www.thespco.org

When it is not on a world tour or making a recording, the St. Paul Chamber Orchestra performs at Ordway Hall. This is a musical organization of international stature, and yet another jewel in the Twin Cities' cultural crown.

Schubert Club
302 Landmark Center
75 West Fifth Street
St. Paul, MN
tel (gen) 651/292-3267, (tickets) 651/292-3268; fax 651/292-4317; www.schubert.org; schubert@schubert.org

Established in 1882, the Schubert Club presents outstanding recitals and other programs. Its 2001–2002 season, for example, included Leif Ove Andsnes, Daniel Barenboim, Grace Bumbry, Thomas Quasthoff, and Christian Tetzlaff.

For radio information in Minnesota, visit http://access.mpr.org/stations/. An independent classical station, based in Northfield, MN, is WCAL (89.3).

NASHVILLE, TN
Nashville Symphony
tel 615/252-4600; www.nashvillesymphony.org

Tennessee Performing Arts Center
tel 615/782-4000; www.tpac.org

NEWARK, NJ
New Jersey Center for the Performing Arts
One Center Street
Newark, NJ 07102
tel 888/466-5722; fax 973/642-5229; www.njpac.org

This excellent arts center, opened October 18, 1997, is the home of the New Jersey Symphony (whose Web site, www.njsymphony.org, is very useful). It also has outstanding programming that features many of the world's great artists, most of whom play appearances in New York and then add a date in Newark. The New Jersey Symphony performs in seven halls around the state: Englewood (John Harris Center); Morristown (Community Theater); Newark (NJPAC); New Brunswick (State Theater); Princeton (Richardson Audiotorium); Red Bank (Count Basie Theater); and Trenton (War Memorial).

Radio: See stations for New York, NY

NEW HAVEN, CT
New Haven Symphony
Woolsey Hall
70 Audubon Street
New Haven, CT 06510
tel 203/776-1444 or 800/292-6476; www.newhavensymphony.org

Yale School of Music
tel 203/432-4158; www.yale.edu/schmus
One of the nation's top music schools is the setting for frequent performances by students and faculty.

NEW YORK, NY
New York is the classical music capital of the United States, and has few rivals elsewhere—perhaps only Berlin and London—for the depth and variety of its offerings each night. Certain, though hardly all, significant events happen each night at Lincoln Center (www.lincolncenter.org), and you should look into what is being performed there on any given day. There are just too many musical organizations and venues to list here, but what follows is a significant sampling.

Alice Tully Hall: see Lincoln Center below.

American Composers Orchestra
Founded in 1977 to champion new works by American and international composers, the ACO has played works by five hundred composers, including more than one hundred world premieres. Its work in promoting new music is unmatched.

1775 Broadway, Suite 525
New York, NY 10019
tel 212/977-8495; fax 212/977-8995; www.americancomposers.org;
aco@americancomposers.org

American Symphony Orchestra
850 Seventh Avenue, Suite 503
New York, NY 10019
tel 212/581-1365; fax 212/489-7188; www.americansymphony.org

Under music director Leon Botstein, the ASO does some of the most original and provocative thematic programs anywhere. Often based in literary, cultural, or political contexts, these performances are invariably fascinating. A typical program is "Lord Byron in Music," which would feature the little-known *Parisina* by William Sterndale Bennett (1835), followed by Liszt's *Tasso* and Schumann's *Manfred*. Many ASO performances are at Lincoln Center's Avery Fisher Hall.

Avery Fisher Hall, Lincoln Center, tel 212-875-5030; www.lincolncenter.org; home of the New York Philharmonic, 212/721-6500; newyorkphilharmonic.org

Bargemusic

On a former coffee barge on the Brooklyn side of the East River, chamber music has been played four nights a week since the mid-1970s under the aegis of Olga Bloom, who realized her vision of a place where instrumentalists could gather to make music while floating on water in the presence of a divine vista. This is one of New York's hidden treasures.
tel 718/624-4061 or 718/624-2083; www.bargemusic.org

Brooklyn Academy of Music (BAM)

Founded in 1859, this is America's oldest arts center in continuous operation. Home to the excellent Brooklyn Philharmonic (www.brooklynphil.com) and the Next Wave Festival, one of the world's top cultural gatherings. Not to be missed by anyone who cares about culture.
tel 718/636-4100; www.bam.org

Caramoor: see Katonah, NY

Carnegie Hall
881 Seventh Avenue (57th Street)
tel + 1-212/247-7800 www.carnegiehall.org

This magnficent theater opened May 5, 1891, with a gala concert that featured Tchaikovsky among its performers. In 1893, Dvořák conducted the world premiere of his *New World Symphony* here. For musicians and music lovers, Carnegie Hall is one of the world's great destinations. Just about every important classical artist of the past century has played at Carnegie Hall, and the walls seemed to have absorbed and preserved the music. You can genuinely feel a sense of history here. The decor is old and gracious, the auditorium beautiful without being ostentatious. The acoustics are excellent, the programs thoughtfully written, and every employee treats you as if you are welcome in this special place. As you wander throughout the soberly elegant corridors you will see framed photographs, letters, and sheet music with autographs of legendary musicians and composers. Next to the main hall (2,804 seats; called the Isaac Stern Auditorium, honoring the late violinist who led the fight to save Carnegie Hall from the wrecking ball in 1960), you will find the exquisite little Weill Hall (268 seats), as perfect a venue as I can think of for vocal recitals, chamber music, and interviews with musicians that are part of Carnegie's educational mission. Zankel Hall (650 seats), on Seventh Avenue, offers a versatile third space for performances and educational activities. Carnegie Hall has an excellent exhibition space, the Rose Museum, with worthy shows on musical topics. There is a small but well-stocked gift shop. On your next visit to New York, be sure to attend a concert at Carnegie Hall. One-hour guided tours are given Monday through Friday at 11:30 A.M., 2 P.M., and 3 P.M. They begin in the main lobby. Tour tickets may be purchased from the box office on tour days. Tours are not given during the summer.

Chamber Music Society of Lincoln Center: see Lincoln Center below.

Colden Center for the Performing Arts at Queens College
tel 718/793-8080; www.coldencenter.org

After appearing at Carnegie Hall or Lincoln Center, many great musicians give an additional performance in Flushing, Queens, at the Colden Center. If you could not get into a performance in Manhattan, see if it is being given again here.

Aaron Davis Hall
tel 212/650-7148; www.ccny.cuny.edu
   An important venue at City College of New York in Harlem.

Great Performers: see Lincoln Center below.

The Juilliard School
60 Lincoln Center Plaza
New York, NY 10023-6588
tel 212/799-5000; www.Juilliard.edu
   Many consider Juilliard the top place in the world to train to be a musician, though the United States is full of splendid institutions, as is Europe. Juilliard enjoys a unique reputation for quality that is well-earned. Aspiring performers from around the country clamor to get in, and those who do receive a superb education. Juilliard also benefits from being part of Lincoln Center, with all of the cultural resources that institution brings. For most of the year, Juilliard's music students (and their colleagues in the theater and dance programs) give performances in various auditoriums in the building, including the Juilliard Theater and Paul Hall.
   If you live in New York or plan to spend time there, look into the evening program with its marvelous range of courses on musical topics that you can enroll in. If you are in a position to make donations to scholarship funds for artists in the future, I encourage you to do so. It is a worthy investment in the future listening pleasure for us all.

Sylvia and Danny Kaye Playhouse, Hunter College
68th Street and Lexington Avenue
tel 212/722-4448; fax 212/650-3661
   A major venue for a great variety of cultural events, including classical musicians visiting New York.

Lincoln Center
64th Street and Broadway
New York, NY 10023
tel 212/875-5000; ticket info 212/875-5050; www.lincolncenter.org
   Without question the most important performing arts center in the world. Here are Avery Fisher Hall (home of the New York Philharmonic and hundreds of guest artists each year) and Alice Tully Hall (a real gem that is the site

of marvelous vocal recitals and lots of chamber music concerts). Lincoln Center Inc. organizes the Great Performers series, the Mostly Mozart Festival, and the Lincoln Center Festival each summer. Other constituents in the center include the Metropolitan Opera, the New York City Opera, the New York City Ballet, the Film Society of Lincoln Center, Jazz at Lincoln Center, the Chamber Music Society of Lincoln Center, the Juilliard School, the Lincoln Center Theater, and the Library for the Performing Arts. Additional Lincoln Center performances are held in the Damrosch Park bandshell each summer and at nearby John Jay College Theater (212/237-8359) during the rest of the year.

If you are planning a visit to New York, go to the Lincoln Center Web site and use its links to its constituent organizations. You can purchase tickets for many Lincoln Center presentations by calling CenterCharge at 212/721-6500. Or, for Chamber Music Society of Lincoln Center, tel 212/875-5788; www.chambermusicsociety.org; New York Philharmonic: tel 212/875-5656; www/newyorkphilharmonic.org. This is a superb Web site for music lovers. Not only does it tell you all the news about the orchestra and how to purchase tickets, but also lets you look things up in the *Grove Encyclopedia*.

Little Orchestra Society
tel 212/971-9500

An important group geared to offering educational programs for children as well as specialized repertory for adults interested in lesser-known works extending from the Baroque era to the present.

Manhattan School of Music
120 Claremont Avenue
New York, NY 10027

Since 1918, this has been one of the foremost musical academies in America. Many musical performances can be heard here by talented students, by faculty, and visiting artists. Performances are in the Borden Auditorium or the Hubbard Recital Hall. Call 212/749-2802, ext 4528, for a recorded listing of the week's performances, updated every Monday; 212/749-2802, ext 4428, for ticket orders; www.msmnyc.edu

Mannes College of Music

Another excellent music conservatory in the city with a large number of appealing concerts.

tel 212/229-5488; 212/496-8524 (for a recording listing presentations); www.mannes.edu

Merkin Concert Hall
129 West 67th Street
tel 212/501-3330; www.elainekaufmancenter.org

In many cities, this would be the chief hall and principal presenting organization. But it New York it is but one of many excellent venues for hearing all sorts of music. It sits about three blocks north of Lincoln Center, yet manages to present a season that is as varied and valued as its huge neighbor.

New York Festival of Song
307 Seventh Avenue, Suite 1601
New York, NY 10001
tel 646/230-8380; fax 646/230-8381

This organization provides a valuable service by bringing talented singers together with outstanding pianists such as Steven Blier and Michael Barrett for concerts of song literature from many nations. Performances are given at the Kaye Playhouse, the Weill Recital Hall at Carnegie Hall, and other venues. The group has toured to Washington and other cities.

New York Philharmonic
Lincoln Center
New York, NY 10023
tel 212/875-5656; www.newyorkphilharmonic.org

One of the most legendary musical organizations, the New York Philharmonic was established in 1842, the same year as the Vienna Philharmonic, making it one of the world's oldest orchestras. Almost every great conductor and many composers have led it in performances. Its music directors in recent decades have included Dimitri Mitropoulos, Leonard Bernstein, Pierre Boulez, Zubin Mehta, Kurt Masur, and Lorin Maazel. From 1891 to 1961 its home was Carnegie Hall, and since that time it has resided at Avery Fisher (from 1962 to 1976 it was called Philharmonic Hall) at Lincoln Center. Fisher Hall has had a notoriously rough time improving its acoustics, but they are better now than in the past and its is quite possible to hear a splendid performance from most seats. The Philharmonic is one of the world's best-traveled ensembles, has a superb archive that documents its storied past and its vibrant present, and also has excellent educational and community outreach programs. The orchestra's legacy, like those of Boston, Chicago, Cleveland, and Philadelphia, is a treasure trove of great performances. Its Web site, www.newyorkphilharmonic.org, is one of the best around for anyone eager to learn about classical music, and I encourage you to visit it even if you do not have plans to be in New York to hear the orchestra live.

Orchestra of St. Luke's and St. Luke's Chamber Ensemble
320 West 42nd Street, 9th Floor
New York, NY 10036
tel 212/594-6100; www.orchestraofstlukes.org

Founded in 1979 at the Caramoor International Music Festival, the Orchestra of St. Luke's is a versatile chamber orchestra that has worked with important conductors such as Charles Mackerras, Roger Norrington, and Donald Runnicles, and many notable guest artists. The ensemble also records extensively and has important educational programs.

Orpheus Chamber Orchestra
tel 800/677-4387; www.orpheusnyc.com

The Orpheus is as famous for what it has (a tradition of great music-making) as for what it does not (a conductor). It was founded in 1972 by a group of musicians who sought to make music in a collaborative way. They rotate seat positions so that each one occasionally occupies the principal chair and provides leadership before ceding the post to a colleague. The musicians select their own repertory, are self-governing, and have evolved what is known as the Orpheus Process of collaborative efforts for mutually satistfying results. For each piece of music, a core group is established to provide leadership in the rehearsal period, and other members often listen from the side to offer opinions. The Orpheus Process has been widely studied in business schools as a model for the corporate world.

Grace Rainey Rogers Auditorium
Metropolitan Museum of Art
212-879-5500; www.metmuseum.org

An excellent music series, as good as any in town, is presented each year in the auditorium of New York's great art museum.

Kathryn Bache Miller Theater
Columbia University
tel 212/854-7799; www.columbia.edu/cu/arts/miller

This small theater presents excellent, innovative programming, including education and seminars. The Miller is a leader in contemporary music programming, giving an important boost to composers and performers who do not always get the attention they deserve. Figures such as Daniel Barenboim and Valéry Gergiev often appear here to play music and then discuss it brilliantly.

92nd Street Y
Tisch Center for the Arts
1395 Lexington Avenue
New York, NY 10128
tel 212/415-5500; www.92ndsty.org

Another of New York's treasures. In most cities this would be the leading arts center, but here it is one of many excellent centers. The Y, as every New Yorker calls it, has one of the richest cultural programs in town, with superb musical offerings by its own chamber orchestra, visiting ensembles and soloists, and many fascinating evenings of words and music, whether classical or other. The Y is also one of the leading poetry centers in the nation, and the vocal recital (blending poetry and music) is prominent here too.

Tillis Center: see Brookville, NY

Town Hall
123 West 43rd Street
tel 212/840-2824; www.the-townhall-nyc.org

Opened in 1921, this historic venue has been a home to many great musical performances, speeches by leading world figures, and is the New York base for National Public Radio's *A Prairie Home Companion*. It has fine acoustics and there is not a bad seat in the house.

Radio:
WQXR (96.3 FM) is the best classical music station in America. You can listen to it on the Internet at www.wqxr.com Classical music
WNYC (93.9 FM) www.wnyc.org (NPR)

WKCR (89.9 FM) Columbia University's radio station features classical music programming as part of a lively mix. Each year at Christmas time there is a Bach marathon.

WFUV (90.7 FM) Fordham University's excellent station includes classical music in its programming.

OAKLAND, CA
Oakland East Bay Symphony
400 29th Street, Suite 501
Oakland, CA 94609
tel 510/444-0801; fax 510/444-0863; www.oebs.org

The Paramount Theatre of the Arts
2025 Broadway
Oakland, CA
tel 510/465-6400; fax 510/893-5098

Site of performances by the Oakland East Bay Symphony and other musicians.

OKLAHOMA CITY, OK
Oklahoma City Philharmonic Orchestra
428 West California, Suite 210
Oklahoma City, OK 73101
tel (tickets) 405/842-5387, (admin) 405/232-7575; fax 405/232-4353; www.okcphilharmonic.org; info@okcphilharmonic.org
Radio: KCSC 90.1 FM

ORLANDO, FL
Orlando Philharmonic Orchestra
tel 407/896-6700; www.orlandophil.org
Radio: WFME 90.7

PHILADEPHIA, PA
Academy of Music
The august old home of the Philadelphia Orchestra is now used more for the Opera Company of Philadelphia and the Pennsylvania Ballet, though it is also a site for other classical music events.

The Curtis Institute of Music
1726 Locust Street
tel 215/893-5262; fax 215/893-7900; www.curtis.edu

Located on Rittenhouse Square, Curtis is one of the world's finest conservatories and site of frequent concerts.

Kimmel Center for the Performing Arts
260 South Broad Street on the Avenue of the Arts
tel 215/790-5800; tickets 215/893-1999; fax 215/790-5801; www.kimmel center.org.

Opened in 2001, this is the dazzling new home of the wonderful Philadelphia Orchestra (resident in Verizon Hall) and venue for many important classical music events. There is also the Perelman Theater, home of the Chamber Orchestra of Philadelphia (www.concertosoloists.org) and the Philadelphia Chamber Music Society (www.pcmsnet.org).

The Philadelphia Orchestra
260 South Broad Street, Suite 1600
Philadelphia, PA 19102
tel 215/893-1900; www.philorch.org

Almost since its founding in 1901, the Philadelphia Orchestra has been one of the truly great ensembles in the world. Its famous music directors have included Leopold Stokowski, Eugene Ormandy, Riccardo Muti, Wolfgang Sawallisch, and Christoph Eschenbach, all of whom have maintained the rich, burnished tonal character that is known as the Philadelphia Sound.

Radio: WHYY NPR

PHOENIX, AZ
Phoenix Symphony Orchestra
455 N. Third Street, Suite 390
Phoenix, AZ 85004-3942
box office tel 602/495-1999 or 800/776-9080; fax 602/253-1772; www. phoenixsymphony.org; info@phoenixsymphony.org

The Phoenix Symphony plays at the three halls listed below. These theaters also host a great range of performances by other arts organizations and soloists.

Symphony Hall
225 East Adams Street

Orpheum Theater
203 West Adams Street

Scottsdale Center for the Arts
7380 East Second Street
Scottsdale, AZ

PITTSBURGH, PA
Pittsburgh Symphony Orchestra
Heinz Hall
600 Penn Avenue
Pittsburgh, PA 15222-3259
tickets: tel 412/392-4200; Customer_Service@pittsburghsymphony.org; www.
pittsburghsymphony.org; PSO_Inquiries@pittsburghsymphony.org

An excellent orchestra founded in 1896 in a city that has a very strong and admirable tradition of support of the arts. Patrons such as Carnegie, Mellon, Heinz, Frick, and others led the way, but Pittsburgh is notable for its widespread belief in culture as a positive force and a city asset.

Radio: WQED-FM 89.3 (in Johnstown, 89.7)

PORTLAND, OR
Portland is a city rich in music. The first symphonic concert took place there on June 15, 1866. In 1896 the Portland Symphony Society (forerunner of the Oregon Symphony) was established. This was the first orchestra in the West and one of only seven established before 1900 that are still active. The Oregon Symphony is only the most famous organization, but there are many more worth investigating, including Cappella Romana; Chamber Music Northwest; Chamber Music Society of Oregon; Metropolitan Youth Symphony; Portland Baroque Orchestra; Portland Youth Philharmonic; and the Rose City Chamber Orchestra.
Oregon Symphony
tel 503/228-1353, 800/228-7343; www.orsymphony.org

PROVIDENCE, RI
Providence Performing Arts Center
tel 401/458-6000; www.providenceri.com

RALEIGH, NC
North Carolina Symphony
2 E. South Street
Raleigh, NC 27601
tel 919/733-2750; www.ncsymphony.org

RICHMOND, VA
Richmond Symphony
tel 804/788-1212; www.richmondsymphony.com

ROCHESTER, NY
Rochester is the home of the Eastman School of Music, one of the foremost conservatories in America. There are frequent performances given by students.

26 Gibbs Street
tel 585/274-1100; www.rochester.edu/Eastman

Rochester Philharmonic Orchestra
108 East Avenue
Rochester, NY 14604
tel 585/454-2100; www.rpo.org
    Radio: WXXI

SACRAMENTO, CA
Sacramento Performing Arts Center
tel 916/452-7722; www.lightsup.com
    A venue for many performing arts events.

Sacramento Philharmonic Orchestra
tel 916/264-5181

ST. LOUIS, MO
St. Louis Symphony Orchestra
Powell Symphony Hall
718 North Grand Boulevard
St. Louis, MO 63103
box office 314/534-1700; fax 314/286-4111; www.slso.org; tickets@.slso.org

The St. Louis Symphony is widely admired for the ever-increasing quality of its music-making, and has made notable recordings under Leonard Slatkin and Hans Vonk.

Radio: KFUO 99.1 FM

SALT LAKE CITY, UT
Utah Symphony
Abravanel Hall
123 West Temple
Salt Lake City, UT 84101-1496
tel 801/533-6683 (subscribers); 801/355-2787 (nonsubscribers);
www.utahsymphony.org

SAN DIEGO, CA
San Diego Symphony
Copley Symphony Hall
750 B Street
San Diego, CA 92101
tickets: 619/235-0804; administrative offices: 619/235-0800;
www.sandiegosymphony.com

SAN FRANCISCO, CA
San Francisco Symphony Orchestra
Louise M. Davies Symphony Hall
201 Van Ness Avenue
tel 415/864-6000; www.sfsymphony.org; marketing@sfsymphony.org,

Davies Hall is the home to the San Francisco Symphony and host to many visiting orchestras and solo artists. The Symphony was born in 1911, and has been central to the cultural life of this music-loving city ever since. Under the dynamic leadership of Michael Tilson Thomas, the SFSO has gained international prominence. One of its specialties are festivals that offer intensive exploration of particular musical topics or the works of certain composers.

Chanticleer
tel 415/392-4400 or 800/407-1400; www.chanticleer.org

This is a world-famous male vocal ensemble based in San Francisco that specializes in early music but has a wide repertory.

SAN LUIS OBISPO, CA

San Luis Obispo Mozart Festival
1160 Marsh Street
San Luis Obispo, CA
tel 805/756-2787; www.mozartfestival.com; staff@mozartfestival.com

Since 1971 the music of Mozart has been front and center at a festival each summer in this beautiful town.

SANTA BARBARA, CA

Music Academy of the West Summer Festival
tel 805/969-8787; www.musicacademy.org

One of the nation's foremost music schools has a festival from late June to mid-August.

SANTA FE, NM

In addition to its famous opera company, beautiful Santa Fe has had an excellent chamber music festival since 1972. Typically it takes place in the summer months. Many performances are at the Lensic Performing Arts Center.

Santa Fe Chamber Music Festival
PO Box 2227
Santa Fe, NM 87504-2227
tel 505/983-2075; fax 505/986-0251; www.santafechambermusic.org

SARASOTA, FL

Florida West Coast Symphony
709 N. Tamiami Trail
Sarasota, FL 34236
tel 941/953-4252; www.fwcs.org

Sarasota Music Festival
tel 941/953-3434

SARATOGA SPRINGS, NY

Saratoga Springs Performing Arts Center
tel 518/587-3330; www.spac.org

A rich program of offerings can be found here, highlighted by the summer seasons of the Philadelphia Orchestra and the New York City Ballet.

There is also the Saratoga Chamber Music Festival and several important contemporary music events.

SEATTLE, WA
Seattle Symphony
Benaroya Hall
200 University Street
Seattle, WA 98101
[Mail to: PO Box 21906, Seattle, WA 98111-3906]
box office tel 206/215-4747; fax 206/215-4748; www.seattlesymphony.org; info@seattlesymphony.org

   This talented company performs in one of the top new concert halls in the world.

   Radio: KING-FM 98.1 An excellent classical music station that broadcasts the Seattle Symphony, Opera, and many other events. You can listen on the Internet at www.king.org.

SYRACUSE, NY
Syracuse Symphony Orchestra
411 Montgomery Street, Suite 40
Syracuse, NY 13202
tel 315/424-8200; www.syracusesymphony.org

TAMPA–ST. PETERSBURG, FL
Tampa Bay Performing Arts Center
1010 N. W.C. MacInnes Place
Tampa, FL 33602
tickets: 813/229-7827 or 800/955-1045; fax 813/222-1080; www.tampa center.com

The Florida Orchestra
101 S. Hoover Blvd., #100
Tampa, FL 33609
tel 813/286-1170; www.floridaorchestra.com

   The Florida Orchestra performs at the Morsani Hall of the Tampa Bay Performing Arts Center.

TETON VILLAGE, WY
Grand Teton Music Festival
tel 307/733-1128; www.gtmf.org

Held 12 miles (20 km) from Jackson in the summer, here is a festival where the beauty of the setting rivals that of the music. There is also a winter concert series. Performances are broadcast throughout Wyoming on Wyoming Public Radio (www.uwadminweb.uwyp.edu/wpr/).

VAIL, CO
Vail Valley Music Festival
PO Box 2270
Vail, CO 81658
tel 970/827-5700, toll-free 866/827-5252; fax 970/827-5707; www.vailmusic festival.org; bravo@vail.net

WASHINGTON, DC
The John F. Kennedy Center for the Performing Arts
2700 F Street, NW
Washington, DC 20566
tel 800/444-1324 or 202/467-4600; www.kennedy-center.org

Built in memory of a president who understood the central role of the arts to a vibrant and creative society, the Kennedy Center probably is only exceeded by New York's Lincoln Center for the quality and diversity offered in its halls. As the arts center in the nation's capital, the Kennedy Center welcomes many visiting companies from abroad and serves as a venue for local and national arts organizations too. It is also the home of the National Symphony Orchestra (www.nationalsymphony.org), which was incorporated in 1931.

WEST PALM BEACH, FL
Kravis Center for the Performing Arts
701 Okeechobee Boulevard
West Palm Beach, FL 33401
tel 561/832-7469; www.kravis.org

Palm Beach County's leading performing arts center hosts local companies and the top international artists.

Radio: WXEL 90.7 FM NPR (serving Palm Beach and Broward Counties)

UZBEKISTAN

<u>TASHKENT</u>
Bakhor Concert Hall
5 Mustaqilik Square
tel 394004 or 335025

Tashkent State Conservatory
31 Pushkin Street
tel 335274 or 335568

Turkistan Concert Hall
2 Alisher Navoi Street
tel 91425 or 357100

Uzbek State Philharmonic Society
11 Uzbekistansky Street
tel 3334643 or 333769

WALES (country code +44)

Also see general Web site listings under England.

<u>SWANSEA</u>
National Chamber Orchestra of Wales
Griff Harries
40 Tudor Court
Murton, Swansea, SA3 3BB, Wales, UK
tel 01792/232387; fax 01792/234868; http://freespace.virgin.net/griff.harries; ncowales@hotmail.com

BBC National Orchestra and Chorus of Wales
www.bbc.co.uk/Wales

INDEX

Opera 101

A Complete Guide to Learning and Loving Opera

FRED PLOTKIN

A clear, friendly, and truly complete handbook to learning how to listen to opera. With an in-depth analysis of eleven key operas, from Verdi's thunderous masterpiece *Rigoletto* to the psychological complexities of Richard Strauss's *Elektra*.

Jazz 101

A Complete Guide to Learning and Loving Jazz

JOHN F. SZWED

Entertaining and enlightening, this book takes readers on a tour of the major types of jazz and the significant jazz musicians of the 20th century and offers insightful commentary on how jazz changed the way the world looked at music.

Ballet 101

A Complete Guide to Learning and Loving the Ballet

ROBERT GRESKOVIC

The first comprehensive handbook on how to watch and appreciate one of the most beautiful examples of the performing arts. With a complete analysis of sixteen ballets, from the classical *Swan Lake* to the modern efforts of Twyla Tharp in *Push Comes to Shove*.

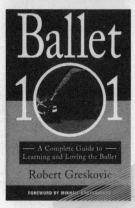

HyperionBooks.com